Between Two Worlds

ALSO BY MONIQUE RAPHEL HIGH

The Four Winds of Heaven

Encore

The Eleventh Year

The Keeper of the Walls

Thy Father's House

Between Two Worlds

Monique Raphel High

DONALD I. FINE, INC.
New York

Copyright © 1989 by Monique Raphel High
All rights reserved, including the right of reproduction in whole
or in part in any form. Published in the United States of America
by Donald I. Fine, Inc., and in Canada by General Publishing Company Limited.

Library of Congress Cataloging-in-Publication Data

High, Monique Raphel.
Between two worlds : a novel / by Monique Raphel High.
        p.   cm.
ISBN 1-55611-139-8 (alk. paper):   88-46164
I. Title.   II. Title: Between two worlds.
PS3558.I3633B48   1989
813′.54—dc19

Manufactured in the United States of America

10   9   8   7   6   5   4   3   2   1

DESIGNED BY IRVING PERKINS ASSOCIATES

For you, Ben, for making every dream come true and proving that miracles and perfect love do happen in real life; and because I prayed for you and you came to me, wrapped in humor and comeliness and gallantry.

This book is about love, romance, and going after one's dreams; and so it's also about us, and the fragile beauty of heartfelt perseverance.

Author's Note

*I*N any book about Russians, the awful business of Russian names is bound to come up, and sooner rather than later. The good news is that Russian names aren't really so awful, once you learn the simple rules. Here they are:

Russians don't call each other "Mr. Gorbachev" or "Miss Makarova." Instead, they use the full first name, followed by the *patronymic*, that is, the father's first name. Thus, Zeinab Poliakova is *Zeinab Lazarevna,* because her father's name is Lazar. Kyril Ostrov's father is Victor, so he is called *Kyril Victorevitch.* (The "evna" and "evitch" suffixes, as you've already guessed, mean "daughter of" and "son of.") Note that these forms are used only when talking to or about other people. Kyril and Zeinab call *themselves* Ostrov and Poliakova, and that's how their signatures read.

Russian nicknames appear complex because we aren't used to them, and because each name has several different diminutives. In fact, there are *degrees* of diminution. The equivalent in English would be if Richard were called "Rick," "Ricky" and "Ricky-Icky." Rather than explain how each nickname is formed, I'll just help you out by listing who goes with which nickname. Most of them will make sense—I hope:

Zeinab Lazarevna . . . Zica, Zicotchka
Yakov Lvovitch . . . Yasha, Yashka, Yashenka
Kyril Victorevitch . . . Kyriusha
Evgeny Lazarevitch . . . Zhenya
Elizaveta Borisovna . . . Lifa
Elena Yossifovna . . . Lena
Kyril Vadimovitch . . . Kyra
Victor Grigorievitch . . . Vitya

These are the main characters. Other nicknames include Aniuta (Anna), Natasha (Natalya), Senya (Semyon) and Vova (Vladimir). You'll be pleased to know that Russians *never* use the patronymic with the nickname in direct address. So you'll be certain to see at least one name you recognize, no matter who's being talked about.

Acknowledgments

MANY good people have shared in the making of his novel. First among them is my editor, Susan Schwartz, whose belief in the book and in the characters made this a work of love for us both. I also wish to thank my publishers, Don Fine and Mark Barty-King, for their support and enthusiasm.

My agent, Barbara Lowenstein, faced the difficult task of coming *in medias res* and pulling rabbits out of her hat. And Sherry Robb brought me to Susan in the first place.

My young friend, Kirill Kipnis, didn't mind going over the Russian to make sure I had gotten everything right. *Balshoya spasibo*!

Of course, this book would not have reached completion but for the continual help of my husband, Ben Pesta, a fine writer and editor who proofread, xeroxed, fax'd, and held my hand.

Only last month, my dear friend and mentor, Ruth Zagat Murphy Casselman, passed away at the age of ninety-one. She was a great lady, a patroness of the arts and a healer of mankind. Throughout my career, she gave me affection and encouragement, as she did to other, younger artists that crossed her path. I had meant to surprise her with this book, for I have based the character of Anna Voorhies mostly on her. But unfortunately, she has not lived to find herself in these pages. Dear Ruth, I thank you too, for the inspiration you have given me, in this book and in all the others.

M.R.H.
May, 1989

. . . All the world's a stage,
And all the men and women merely players.
They have their exits and their entrances,
And one man in his time plays many parts . . .

SHAKESPEARE
As You Like It, II, vii, 139

I hold the world but as the world, Graziano—
A stage where every man must play a part,
And mine a sad one.

SHAKESPEARE
The Merchant of Venice, I, i, 77

Book I:
Innocence

Chapter I

As was customary for the month of January, a pewter dusk was already falling over the city of Rostov-on-the-Don in Southwestern Russia. The boy kicked at the snow, his worn black boot punishing the embankment relentlessly. He was small for his nine years, and somewhat frail—his winter garments made this only more obvious, the wool cap pushed down low over his forehead, the mittens dwarfing his hands, and the red and white muffler all but eclipsing chin and mouth. His triangular face peeked out just enough to display beautiful green eyes, already mournful, and a small nose sculptured into a pronounced 'V,' its tip as sharp as a dot.

He was a handsome child, with high cheekbones and cheeks like raspberry cream. In the wide avenue, he was dwarfed by the tall, bare trees weighted down by pillows of snow. Abruptly, he stopped and shifted his pack of schoolbooks from his left to his right shoulder.

Suddenly, a group of larger children erupted into the avenue, jostling one another, laughing and shrieking. The young boy turned, his shoulders hunched. He stood glued in place, his green eyes wide and scared.

A heavy-set boy with green earmuffs and a long, yellow scarf approached him. His round face split into a wide grin. "Hey!" he screamed to his pals. "Look who isn't home yet! It's the plucked chicken from fourth grade, who lives on Pushkin Street!"

The other children ran up. *"Tsyplionok! Tsyplionok!"* they cried, swinging their schoolbooks in sharp semi-circles. "Little chicken! Little chicken!"

The young boy squared his shoulders. Now his jaw jutted out above his muffler. "I am not a chicken!" he shouted. "Leave me alone, Seryozha!"

The large boy threw his books to the ground. "Says who?" he taunted. "We don't listen to *Jews!* Dirty *Yid!*"

Echoing him, the others called out: *"Zhidok! Zhidok! Gryasnyi Zhid!"*

The young boy's voice broke as he shouted: "I am not a yid! My father is a native Russian! Leave me alone!"

Seryozha, the round-faced boy with the nasty grin, began to laugh. "Your mama's a Jewish whore, who's ashamed to go out of the house! Yids are yids because of their mothers—aren't they, Alyosha?"

"Damn right! Let's teach him a lesson!" The boy called Alyosha joined his friend, and they rolled up their sleeves. The young boy stood his ground, trembling, his lower lip caught between his teeth, his eyes filling with tears. It would not do to show them how frightened he was, to let them know how hard his heart was hammering inside. He would face up to them once and for all, face them and tell them off. "Go ahead!" he said. "See if I care!"

Alyosha kicked him, and he doubled over. Seryozha jumped on his back and began pounding on his head. His cap fell off. He could hear ringing in his ears. The metallic taste of blood choked him. Now other boys and girls had come up. A large circle had formed, with him and his two aggressors at the center. The others were throwing snowballs at him, pelting him over the shoulders and in the face. His cheeks stung and his left eye felt sore and swollen.

Then, as suddenly as it had begun, the beating ended. Alyosha and his companions ran off, chanting: "Yid! Yid! We thrashed the yid!"

He could not get off the ground. His knee was hurting. His head felt bruised. The new year had brought no changes to his life: *It had happened again,* just as it had so many afternoons of the previous year, and the one before that.

The year 1905 would be no different from 1904, except that this January his father was fighting in the war with Japan, under General Mishchenko, along with six thousand other Cossacks. At least *he's* not around to hurt me and Mama, the boy thought, rising with supreme effort and limping toward Pushkin Street.

"It's going to be all right," Elena said, pressing an ice cube to his swollen eye. "Don't cry, Kyriusha, even if it hurts. Don't ever cry. It does no good to let them know how much they've hurt you. You are *Kyril Victorevitch Ostrov*—and you will live to make this name meaningful. Those boys are nothing but hoodlums, doomed to spend their lives swimming in mediocrity."

He was silent, enduring the sharp, burning sensation. He could see her breasts from where he sat, her lovely round breasts beneath the woolen blouse directly in his line of vision. *They had called her a whore, a Jewish whore.*

"Mama," he said, "why are they always attacking *me?* And why do they call me a *'Zhidok'?"*

"Because I am a Jew, and the Jewish religion is handed down through the mother. Technically, you are a Jew, although I no longer go to temple." Her voice sounded sharp. "It doesn't seem to matter who your father is. It makes no difference that your father is a Cossack, fighting in Ying-Kow. All that matters in Russia is where *I* come from, and who *my* people are."

"But your people don't even speak to us," the boy protested. "They've never wanted to see me—not since I was born."

"Kyriusha, that is life. That is what it means to be a Jew in Russia. Your own parents throw you out for marrying a gentile, and the gentiles will not speak to you because you are a Jew. That's why I stay at home, and read my books. Books, my pet, cannot hurt you."

"They said you stay at home because you're ashamed."

Elena sighed. Stepping back, she sank into a chair. She was beautiful, her face much like her son's, triangular and exotic, with pronounced cheekbones, wide blue eyes, and a red mouth like a cupid's bow. Her chin, like his, had a delicate cleft. But her hair was jet black. Pulled back from her broad forehead, it formed a pompadour with a Psyche knot at the back of her head. "No," she said, her voice suddenly soft. "They were wrong, Kyriusha. I am merely tired of fighting, and resigned. Your father is ashamed of having a Jewish wife, but I am not ashamed. *This is who I am.* I merely stay at home because I have nowhere else to go. My parents have shut their door to me, and I have no friends in the city." She sighed, and her lips turned down at the corners into an expression of bitterness. "How appropriate our name is . . ." she remarked. "'*Ostrov*' . . . the Russian word for 'island.' Indeed, I have become a human island, apart from everyone."

The young boy touched her knee. "You have me, Mama," he told her. "And I shall never let you down."

Suddenly she smiled. "I know you won't, Kyril," she said. "Thank God for that."

* * *

Climbing on a stool, the girl propped her elbows on the sculptured windowsill, peering out. Heavy snow fell like flakes of chiselled white soap onto the elegant street below. From this high vantage point, she could see the serpentine Sadovoye Koltzó, the aristocratic quarter of Moscow, encircling the city center. She could distinguish the Moscow River and Red Square, leading to the Kremlin—an awe-inspiring citadel dating back to the twelfth century. Its thick, turreted red battlements sectioned off a mysterious assembly of domed palaces, churches, monasteries, armories, and bastions. She could even perceive the spiralling cupolas of the magnificent Cathedral of Vassili Blazhennyi, Byzantine and exotic, no more than a short distance.

So *romantic,* she thought wistfully. It must be fun to be Russian Orthodox and attend services where prelates in garments of woven gold brandished huge crosses encrusted with sapphires, diamonds, rubies, and emeralds... where the pungent scent of incense transported you to the birth of Jesus and the arrival of the Three Wise Men, predicting Christ's grandeur. Where sculpted icons smiled down from their golden perches and reassured you that the world was a good, safe place in which to dwell.

She sighed as she stepped down from her niche. At nine, her breasts were still flat, and she tugged at the short-waisted bodice of her red velveteen dress. Its skirt was full. A box pleat, fastened with three large jet buttons, neatly descended from the neck to the hem, allowing her calves and ankles to show. The cape collar was trimmed with sable; she ran her forefinger over its smooth, soft plushness, experiencing pleasure. How she loved to touch the luxurious black fur! It reminded her of the white rabbit she had owned a few years back, on the summer estate in Rigevka, in the south.

Today was a special occasion. Her Papa was turning fifty. Today, she would meet Count Witte, the famous President of the Committee of Ministers, who had come to Moscow to confer an honor upon her esteemed parent. Mama had cried: "Count Witte will come to a Jewish home!" and the servants had *oohed* and *ahhed.* Today was the day, the fateful day. If she didn't hurry down from the attic, she would miss the fanfare, the pomp and the festivities. Her black curls danced on the back of her cape as she rushed down the white staircase, ignoring the wrought-iron ramp. In the drawing room—furnished in the Empire style of Napoleon I—the giltwood and ormolu pieces had been moved aside, making way for dancers who would perform a ballet later that afternoon. Carpets had been rolled back. The girl edged forward, curious, her small black pumps squeaking against the parquet floors.

"Zica!"

She wheeled around, startled, as her mother appeared. Baroness Elizaveta Borisovna Poliakova had once been quite a beauty, but now, at the age of thirty-eight, her figure was round and full. Her moon-shaped face, alive with large black eyes, appeared somewhat doughy. But her gown was elegant. Turquoise blue, it had bishop sleeves that tightened at the wrists, a cinched waistline (how hard Masha must have tugged at Mama's corset to get it hooked up!), and a full-length skirt that flared from the Baroness's generous hips all the way to the floor.

"Zica." Her mother knitted her brow. "I've been looking for you everywhere! We're waiting for you to start the lunch. *You-Know-Who* is due to arrive in time for dessert, and we can't afford to fall behind schedule."

Zica sighed. "I know, Mama: *Count Witte*. Why is it such an unusual thing for a minister to come to the house of a Jewish man? Isn't Papa important in the city?"

"Sergius Witte happens to be a good minister, who has always spoken against anti-Semitism and the pogroms," her mother replied. "But still, sweetheart, members of the Imperial Court do not come to see a Jew in his house. Even a man such as your father, who is powerful and rich and titled."

"Is it a sin to be born Jewish?" Zica asked. "Why are we always apologizing for any privilege the gentiles come by naturally?"

"It is a sin to question the system too much," Elizaveta Borisovna declared. "You simply learn what is accepted behavior and make the best of it. At least, that's how I see things." She sighed audibly, and touched her pompadour. "Your father feels somewhat differently," she continued. "He thinks that the Tzar and his ministers can be changed—that anti-Semitism is a disease just like influenza or the pox, and that it can be cured, by patient example. He says the Tzar is frightened of the Jews because he does not know them—does not know how gentle a people we are, how bookish and quiet. And that this fear of the unknown has made Nicholas intolerant."

Zica chewed on the inside of her cheek, thoughtfully. She had her mother's huge black eyes, ringed with long lashes, and her mother's small, upturned nose and wide, generous mouth. Elizaveta Borisovna was a Georgian Jew from Tiflis, and her culture had been more ingrown than that of her husband. The Georgian Jews tended to marry within their own culture.

"Your father is a man of the world, Zica," Elizaveta Borisovna said. "And I, at heart, am still a woman of the provinces. He believes that habits and prejudices that have existed in this country for centuries can be transformed, almost overnight, by the power of reason and demonstration. I am more skeptical, however. . ."

The little girl shrugged. She was beginning to grow bored. She had been looking forward to the ceremony and a birthday, and, instead, she was being regaled with a lecture on civics and Jewish history. In fact, she was accustomed to this from her father. He felt an obligation to inform his children about the work that needed to be accomplished on behalf of the dispossessed Jews of Russia. The Poliakovs were called the First Jewish Family of Moscow. And Baron Lazar Solomonovitch was considered a *shtadlan,* a high-placed Jew who often acted as an intermediary between the government and his less-fortunate co-religionists.

Zica knew that her father relished the role—that it mattered more to him than his railroads all over the country, his sugar refineries in Kiev, his mines of semi-precious stones in the Urals, his windmills, his lands in Siberia, his shipping company on the Volga, and his tramway business in Odessa. Papa loved helping the poor, and above all, the poor Jews. They were, he liked to explain to her and her brother Evgeny, "the lowest of the low." Jews in Russia were not treated as citizens, he complained: they possessed few if any rights.

Zica had often been told about the Pale of Settlement in Southwest Russia, the line of demarcation which enclosed Jews within a prescribed area of the nation. Only wealth could earn them dispensation to travel and dwell beyond that line. Her paternal grandfather had made a fortune buying up taverns in the vicinity of Minsk. Then he had purchased other failing businesses that could be bought up for a song. He had become a rich *kupetz,* a merchant who had bribed officials in Moscow into granting him a permit of residence. It was rare, "oh so rare" (as Papa liked to stress), for any Jew to be granted residence in the cities of Moscow and St. Petersburg—the most elite cities in the vast nation that comprised "Mother Russia."

Around 1875 (Zica couldn't remember all the details of the story), the title of Baron had been bestowed upon her grandfather. Grandpa Sioma (Solomon Gavrilovitch Poliakov) had purchased huge plots of forests in Finland. He had furnished lumber for the Imperial Family, for their summer home in Tsarskoie Selo as well as the Winter Palace in St. Petersburg. The Tzar (Alexander II, grand-father of Nicholas II) had granted them the baronage because, as her Papa explained, it was less expensive than paying a competitive price for the lumber. People always laughed when he told this anec-dote, but their Jewish friends laughed with constrained faces. To them the joke wasn't as funny as it sounded to Zica: a Tzar, saving money to heat his home by trading a title for some logs!

The little girl liked hearing stories about her family. Her mother and father's love affair had always ranked as one of her favorites, with side twists as exotic as some of the tales of *The Arabian Nights*. Her mother's folk had been rich *kupetzi* in Tiflis, in the heart of Georgia (although not nearly so rich as her father's people in Mos-cow), and her mother (called "Lifa" by her family) had been reared in extreme seclusion. She was only allowed to mix with the members of her parents' intimate circle. Her father's people, the Barons Poliakov, were fluent in French, the language of the Russian aristocracy—but Lifa Palagashvili hadn't even spoken Russian. The Caucasian province of Georgia boasted a special dialect, and the young girl had understood nothing but Georgian and a smattering of Yiddish.

The Georgians were proud, courageous, and haughty, concealing a romantic tenderness beneath their upright demeanor. After the age of three, Lifa's brothers seemed to be constantly on horseback. They only descended from the saddle to take their meals and sleep. Tiflis, the capital of the province, was a pleasant city boasting its own university, theater, and factories. Grandpa Boris Palagashvili, Lifa's father, had owned lush vineyards on the southern slope of the province, and his sons had helped him to oversee the crops and manufacture delicious wines. As Jews, they had kept to their small, tight community. The beautiful Lifa, with her hourglass figure and large black eyes, had been shy and retiring. She had known nothing of the world outside Georgia.

The Caucasus boasted several springs of healing waters, most no-tably Narzan's, which was carbonated. People came there to "take the waters." It was during a summer holiday in 1885 that Baron Lazar first saw Lifa, when she was accompanying her mother for a cure. Lifa had been eighteen years old. Lazar had been twelve years her senior, a mature thirty—still unmarried and searching for the ideal woman. One look at Lifa, and he had made up his mind. He would marry no one but her. He had followed her to Tiflis, plead-ing with Boris Palagashvili for her hand in marriage.

In spite of Lazar's millions and of his reputation as a *shtadlan* and a scholar of Judaic lore, Boris Palagashvili had insisted on a two-year engagement. During that time, Lazar had made numerous visits to Tiflis. He had taught his fiancée both Russian and French. When they had finally married, in 1887, Lifa Palagashvili had been converted from a parochial girl of the Georgian provinces into a cosmopolitan Baroness, ready to move into the white, columned palace in the Sadovoye Koltzó district of Moscow.

Since those romantic days, eighteen years had passed. Zica's mother, Elizaveta Borisovna, had become a staid pillar of Muscovite society—although, on occasion, she would talk about her Georgian roots. Zica found it amusing and somewhat quaint . . . like her Georgian relatives.

"Come, Zica," her mother now said, taking Zica's small hand. "We must present your father with his gift. Your brother Evgeny is waiting for you, and so are our guests."

In the enormous dining room, with its glimmering chandeliers and recessed sconces, the table had been extended to seat thirty-six. The damask tablecloth was adorned with centerpieces of fruit and orchids in bowls of blood-red crystal. Servants bustled around, bringing the *zakuskis* for hors d'oeuvres.

Evgeny stood at attention, looking annoyed. He was tall and handsome, dark and slender for his thirteen years—almost ready for his bar mitzvah, which would take place that summer. Zhenya was going to become a man, like Papa; this, Zica ruminated ruefully, would put a distance between the two of them. She knew she would still be deemed a child, and treated as such. Zhenya would be allowed to go out at night with their parents to the theater, to the ballet, and to the symphony, while she would still be relegated to the *nyanya* who had nursed her, and to her governess, Fraulein Verlag. It didn't seem fair . . .

"The gift is ready, Zica," her brother announced sternly. "You disappeared, so Papa had to delay things and take people to the gallery to show them his new collection of Egyptian artifacts. What happened to you?"

She shrugged, embarrassed. Impatiently, Zhenya escorted her into the small parlor at the back of the dining room. The butler closed the partition door. Zica heard her mother's voice, ordering the butler to summon the guests back to the table. Against the wall stood the family's birthday gift for Baron Lazar: a bronze plaque, depicting the Baron seated in an armchair, his wife Elizaveta behind him, and their two children flanking them on either side. The plaque was of modest size, maybe a meter large and two-thirds long. A visiting Austrian sculptor had made all the portraits the previous summer. After making molds, he had returned two weeks ago to deliver the finished product. It was quite handsome, Zica thought—regal, fit for her Papa's fiftieth birthday. An honor to go with Count Witte's visit and the medal he would bestow on her proud parent.

The door opened, and the butler appeared. "It is time now, Evgeny Lazarevitch, Zeinab Lazarevna. Everyone is seated." The butler hoisted the heavy plaque on his shoulder, bending his frame so that both children could walk in holding an edge of the bas-relief. They carried it to the head of the table, where their father was seated like a prince. An expectant smile softened his razor-sharp features.

"Well now, my children . . . what have we here?" Baron Lazar Solomonovitch Poliakov was tall and thin, and never raised his voice. Though he was not handsome, his looks were distinguished. He had a small head, with soft, rather long and silky gray hair, the same shade of gray as his close-cropped mustache. His nose was long and straight, his mouth soft and thin and wide, with a straight jaw and a receding chin line. Papa, Zica thought, resembled nothing so much as a tall bird, with his vulture's scrawny neck and his raven's nose—but there was no one she adored more in the entire world. In Moscow, he was popular, as was apparent from the turnout for the birthday celebration. Jew or not, Baron Lazar was much admired in Muscovite society.

"Happy birthday, Papa," Zica chanted in unison with her brother. They stood back as the butler laid the bas-relief on a high-backed chair, displaying it to the assembly of august guests in their elegant finery. As the Baron opened his arms to the children, servants popped the corks of chilled champagne. Zica snuggled against her father's chest. How strange it is to be a grown-up, she thought. Birthdays are such formal events . . . Papa was old now, fifty already, sleek and silver-gray.

A servant gently extricated her from the Baron's arms. Zica was led to the far end of the table, where she was seated between her brother and a distant cousin with a goiter. She sipped her champagne silently, observing the laughing people. Who was a Jew? she wondered. And which of these people went to the big, onion-domed cathedral to worship golden icons and watch the Russian priests swing pots of incense?

The meal was wonderful, replete with pheasant and raspberry *kissel*. Dessert was a big brown chocolate cake with tiny candles glowing bright and fiery. As it was being wheeled in, the butler scurried to announce "Count Sergius Witte, President of the Committee of Ministers." A towering behemoth of a man strode in, his chest blazing with medals. His huge head was imposing, his step regal. The guests grew hushed.

"Count Witte," Zica's Papa said, greeting him with outstretched hands. "Welcome to our little gathering."

Sergius Witte inclined his massive head. As Elizaveta Borisovna came up to take him to the place of honor beside her, he kissed her plump, jewelled hand. The seat on her right that had been conspicuously empty all during the meal was now occupied by the great man. The other guests felt a wave of relief wash over the room: Witte's arrival had been a success, like the wonderful meal that had preceded his grand entrance.

Various guests raised flutes of Dom Perignon. It was a delicious champagne, imported from Paris. While they began making flowery toasts—Zica, her head spinning, sat mesmerized by the illustrious guests from St. Petersburg. This was the man who presided over the Tzar's Ministers!

The butler cut the cake while a half-dozen young stewards darted like small, quick ants, depositing slices in front of each guest.

Finally, Witte spoke. "It is a privilege to be here, my friends. And my mission is a worthy one indeed. I have come to Moscow to bestow the Order of Saint Anne upon Baron Lazar Solomonovitch Poliakov, on the occasion of his silver birthday." Zica watched, fascinated, as Witte presented her Papa with a long and very wide ribbon to wear across the chest. It was of deep red silk with a tiny gold border running along both sides. As he pinned the golden medal on the left side of Papa's chest, the guests applauded loudly.

Then the minister added, his voice resonant and mellifluous. "In addition, in the name of our Tzar, Nicholas II, it is with pleasure that I confer upon Baron Poliakov the title of Evident State Senator. Congratulations, Lazar Solomonovitch, from the Imperial Court."

Baron Lazar blinked in amazement. His usual composure seemed shattered by this sudden announcement. Across the table, Zica observed that her mother had turned pale with emotion. Elizaveta Borisovna, looking at her husband, shook her head and bit her lower lip in confusion and bewilderment.

"Papa didn't expect this at all," Evgeny whispered. "Do you realize that this is the most exalted title in the land, except for those given to the members of the Imperial Family?"

Zica shook her head. What an incredible bonus the Count had brought...! Ever since Witte's entrance, her father's party had taken on an aura of magic. Like a Fairy Godfather, he had transformed everyone in the room into exalted courtiers. She ran her forefinger over her sable cape again, and tried to capture the magical sensation. Good food, pretty lights, the bas-relief, her father's embrace... Zica Poliakova had never felt such ecstasy.

"Oh, Zhenya," she said to her brother. "How I wish I could freeze this moment and make it last forever—like Papa's bas-relief of the four of us, happy and perfect... "

In Southwest Russia, not far from the Rumanian border, stretched the province of Podolia with its fields of wheat and barley and sugar beets. In the summer, the wheat stalks shimmered in the sun. Wildflowers bloomed on the gentle slopes around the Bug River. Beyond, mysterious oak forests rose like medieval guards around the open country.

The village of Rigevka lay some thirty miles from the primitive city of Uman. At the start of the century, Uman had already begun to spread out, but the roads, though wide, were unpaved and without sidewalks. Only the main highways had sidewalks, consisting of elevated wooden planks along the foundations of the houses. The high sidewalks protected pedestrians from the messy slush of the spring and fall mud seasons.

Hatas, or peasant houses, were built of wood speckled with pebble-dash. The single-story dwellings with thatched rooftops were wide, separated from their nearest neighbors by vegetable gardens and orchards. Stables, cow sheds and chicken coops lay clustered around them. Three or four houses had roofs of light green corrugated iron. In town was a two-story hotel used by families waiting to take the train to Kiev, Odessa, or Khazatin. The Hôtel de l'Europe consisted of small suites, for entire households. Although some stores existed in Uman, and though it was shown as a city on every map, it was actually no more than a large, sprawling peasant village.

To reach Rigevka, one had to cross immense fields, following the rutted paths left by carriages and horses' hooves. In hot weather, clumps of dry earth slowed the horses; thick, gluey mud turned the fields to swamp in the spring and autumn.

Rigevka had some five thousand inhabitants. At the center was a pretty white church. Small, well tended *hatas* were surrounded by cherry orchards and trellised rose bushes. In Rigevka farmers sowed wheat, harvested it, and at the end of the summer beat it down with machines on the threshing-floors behind their gardens.

Wealthy landowners held thousands of acres in the villages and townships. The owners of Rigevka were Baron Lazar Poliakov and his wife Elizaveta. They had financed two sugar refineries on their property. When they visited each summer, Evgeny and Zica were thrilled by the innocent peasant ceremonies that reminded them of their father's popularity. After harvesting hundreds of acres of wheat and barley, the peasants would come to the owner's house to serenade the Poliakovs. They always offered the Baroness a wreath of wheat stalks, on which a freshly baked loaf of bread had been placed. The children, fascinated by these sentimental songs of the earth, sun and rain, leaned over the fence and listened with intent faces. At the end their Papa would come down the porch steps and hand the foreman a large gold coin, to be traded in at the head office for small change. The change would then be divided among the workers. (In this same office, he would also invite them to drink a glass of vodka—to the health of owners and peasants alike!) During the season, this scene was a daily ritual that occurred whenever a field was harvested.

Not fifteen miles from Rigevka was a small Jewish *shtetl* called Peredelkino. Each summer, Lazar Solomonovitch went there with purses full of gold coins, which he distributed among the inhabitants according to their needs. Evgeny sometimes went with him. Zhenya always returned with a sad, serious face, but he refused to tell his sister the details of what had taken place.

"Girls don't become *shtadlanim*," he once explained to her. "I'm going to have to take care of these people when Papa grows old, but you won't need to. You'll be married and living in your own country house, and the Jewish question won't have much bearing in your life." Zhenya always made a point to show her how grown-up he was. He used adult terms, like "the Jewish question," to remind her that she was only a girl, and still too young to comprehend worldly affairs. Inevitably, the distance between them only increased as he began to prepare for his bar mitzvah.

The denizens of Peredelkino existed for the visits of their benefactor, whom they regarded as their means of salvation. During three seasons of the year, they accumulated their requests and bided their time until the following summer, when they would deluge

Baron Poliakov with pleas for financial aid. They always had long lists of problems to be solved. To Evgeny's puzzlement, few if any of the younger generation thought to leave the hamlet. They easily could have changed their lives for the better. But his father explained to him, with a somber expression on his razor-thin features, that it wasn't so simple.

"Where could they go?" the Baron asked. "To another small village, as crowded and overpopulated as this one? Or to one of the 'thriving metropolises' of the Pale, such as Minsk or Odessa? A village Jew from Podolia would probably starve there: too many are already lining up for too few jobs, and besides, such big cities would confuse and frighten a rural person. Most of the inhabitants of Peredelkino are quite religious; to them, an Odessa or a Minsk would seem like a den of iniquities. They would feel displaced and lost without their rabbi and their cantor."

No thatched roofs over whitewashed cottages for the Jews of Peredelkino. Their homes were slats of wood with uneven windows, their streets dry ruts in the summer and puddles of mud in wintertime. A permanent atmosphere of hopelessness hung over the *shtetl*. Apart from the kindness of their landlord, the denizens of these villages lived an existence with no future.

That harsh January of 1905, the *reb* didn't feel like teaching long classes at the *shtetl* school. He was growing older. The cold penetrated his aching bones like slivers of ice. The walls of the one-room *yeshiva* were thin. What good did his teaching do? he reflected. The boys studied the Talmud and the Torah for a few brief years; then, when they reached the age of eleven or twelve, their harried parents removed them from class to insert them into the family business— carpentry, smithcraft, or other manual labor. In Peredelkino, learning was a luxury that no one could afford. Men grew old quickly, relegating their workload to their teen-age sons as soon as the young ones could bear the burden.

The *reb*, Meyer Aronovitch Zlotkin, wished things could be different. Now fifty-six years old, he had been teaching young boys for twenty years. He had been born in Peredelkino, and had never lived anywhere else. The parents and grandparents of the boys were his familiars; he knew everyone in the village by name—knew each ailment that had beset them throughout their lives. Some of the boys had once been gifted; under different circumstances, they might have become doctors, lawyers, or scholars. But no one ever got out of Peredelkino unless to be conscripted for twenty years into the Tzar's army—a fate far worse than life imprisonment within the *shtetl*.

The single exception—the single way out—was through the Poliakovs. If approached by the *reb,* the Baron could be inveigled into arranging for a particularly gifted child to go to a professional school . . . provided that the parents, in their frightened ignorance, didn't oppose Meyer Aronovitch and snatch their son away from his interference.

The *reb* had grown up with a boy called Lev Pokhis—"Lyovushka," the fellows called him. Now, in his mid-fifties, Lyovushka was stooped, with graying hair and jowls that hung in loose pockets like turkey wattles. Back when Lyovushka was small, young and wiry, he and Meyer had been childhood friends. But whereas Meyer's parents had allowed him to study with old Reb Feldman, Lyovushka's father had forced him to quit the *yeshiva* at the age of ten. Now Lyovushka was the town peddler, travelling to and from Uman in a circumference of a hundred miles. He mostly sold his wares to Jews, but sometimes even to the Russian peasants who were always on the look-out for a good bargain.

Upon quitting school, Lev had joined his father, peddling second-hand furniture and scraps of material, battered pots and pans and even jars of pickles made by the old women in the village. While Meyer had become the *shtetl reb,* Lev had inherited his father's broken-down cart and the old brown mare . . . and the boys' easy camaraderie had fallen by the wayside. A shame, Meyer Aronovitch had often thought, when childhood friendships unravelled like that. But it couldn't be helped: one simply had to proceed with one's own life.

But, Lev Pokhis had a son, Yakov—little Yasha, the violin player, who would one day go to the Moscow Conservatory, God willing. If Baron Lazar Solomonovitch Poliakov could only spend an hour listening to him play! He, Reb Meyer Zlotkin, would make it a point to help the boy, his old friend's son, in any way he could. Yasha's playing was like God's own music—manna from heaven—a feast for the ears!

This January afternoon, a thick snow was falling over the hamlet. Reb Meyer was tired, and looked across the room at the five boys sitting behind their wooden desks, notebooks in hand. Yasha Pokhis was certainly the smallest, if not the youngest. He resembled his father Lev at that age: he was wiry and nervous, with intelligent ebony eyes and black, curly hair. He had small features and high cheekbones. While he wasn't particularly good looking, there was something *alive* about him, something appealing and *different*. Often, the *reb* wondered what that something was, yet he hadn't quite succeeded in putting his finger on it.

The boys were bored. He couldn't really blame them. After all, what possible difference would it make in their own bleak destinies to discuss King David's responsibility in the death of Uriah? These boys would grow up in spite of David, Uriah, and Bathsheba— these Biblical figures were in no position to do them any practical favors. Nothing they studied here would provide them with un-hoped-for riches or get them an exit visa out of Peredelkino.

Today, the *reb* decided he would take pity on them and release them early. "Time to go home, boys," the *reb* announced, gathering his own materials together. He sighed. Year after year he faced these children. His sense of defeat was burdensome. Nothing ever mattered, because nothing ever changed.

The five boys were scurrying to twine their school books to-gether before going out into the snow. Suddenly Yasha tapped one of the older boys on the shoulder. When the boy turned around, Yasha took a hesitant step forward, tugging at his right earlobe.

"Mendelah, my son . . . I am heavy with the weight of my years. Would you not carry me home on your shoulders, that I might impart the wisdom of God to you?" Yasha croaked.

The other laughed.

"The stories I could tell you about this *shtetl* we live in . . ." Yasha continued in a sing-song tone. His voice had grown salacious and plaintive at the same time, inflected exactly like that of an old man. "About Yitzhak and his Olinka . . ."

Another boy wheeled around, grinning. "Olinka Merpert? The half-wit?"

Yasha touched an imaginary hump on his back and coughed, deeply. "Half-wit? *Half-wit . . . ?* Why, dear child, Olinka is even dafter than you think. After she married Yitzhak, she went to bed with a pillow under her *tukhas!* The poor thing thought her brain had shifted to the middle of her body. But now I am afraid for *Yitzhak's* brain: he praised her, and called her his smart lit-tle girl . . . !"

The Rabbi cleared his throat, one hand covering his mouth to hide his amusement. Yasha's imitation was perfect—and very funny. But it would not do to laugh in front of these children. The object of their amusement was someone they all knew, a girl in her twenties. Olinka had always been thought to be backward, perhaps even an idiot. But Yitzhak Polsky had married her, and now Olinka went about the streets with a lopsided grin on her slack features, and a strange glint in her rather unfocused blue eyes.

Yasha Pokhis had hit on something that was now causing wild eruptions of merriment among the five boys. The Rabbi said, loudly: "Yasha! Olinka is not a joking matter. She's a person, with feelings."

"I'm sorry, *Reb*," Yasha said. And his face was serious again, even somewhat penitent. "I only meant to make everyone laugh here in the *yeshiva*."

"Nevertheless . . . you never know which walls may have ears in Peredelkino. Go home now, and don't tarry."

The five boys in their woolen overcoats and caps, books tucked under their arms, pushed their way out of the school room. The Rabbi shook his head, smiling. Olinka Polskaya, and her blessed pillow . . . That little rascal, Yasha! He'd have to tell Lev to keep him at his violin, to prevent him from getting into mischief. That boy was always turning life into a joke. His hilarious tales often bore as little resemblance to the actual facts as borsch did to the beets you plucked out of the earth. But, just the same, they were tasty.

The *reb* went to the small closet to retrieve his coat. Lifting it from the hook, he paused, perplexed. A strange noise had begun to penetrate the room, dim and yet disturbing. The sound came from the street, far down the road. Slipping rapidly into his long black overcoat, Meyer Zlotkin swung open the door of the school room. A gust of strong, freezing wind almost knocked him down.

He could now hear the cries—the cries of the five that had exited only moments ago. Alarmed, he clamped his tall hat on his head and rushed outside, bracing himself against the wind. Up the street, he could see the boys—and some strange, dark figures on horseback.

Horror seized him. He ran back inside the *yeshiva*. Wild-eyed, he scanned the room. An old broom stood in the corner, where his wife had left it the last time she had swept up for him. Grabbing the broom, *Reb* Meyer ran out again, slamming the door behind him. In the street, a blizzard was building. The winds slapped him back against the wall of the *yeshiva*. Fighting the cross-currents of wind, he trudged on through the snow toward his boys.

Suddenly, his world turned sideways. *Reb* Meyer Aronovitch Zlotkin felt himself being knocked to the ground. His hip hit a snow-covered bank of ice, and cracked. He felt searing pain in the same instant that he saw a gray figure on a rearing black stallion. For an instant, he recognized the narrow astrakhan collar, saw a raised sword—and then, a shimmering curtain of blood fell over his eyes, and pungent vomit clogged his throat. Reb Meyer Zlotkin thought: "I'm sinking . . . I'm dead."

And then he passed into another consciousness, a leaden sleep that enveloped him like a cold, dark shroud.

When he awakened, the pain was so sharp that he could feel his heart rebelling, pounding erratically. Little red dots swam before his eyes. Yakov Pokhis, Lyovushka's boy, was standing over him, his wiry body bundled up into a thick red coat. "*Reb! Reb!*" Yasha was calling, as though from a great distance. "Tell me you're alive!"

"I'm alive, Yasha," Meyer whispered. The left side of his head was giving him jagged bursts of pain, like sharp thrusts. He gingerly brought one hand to the side of his face.

His fingers felt mush—sticky mush, like potatoes in gravy or baby food. Terrified, the Rabbi looked at his fingers and saw that they were red with blood. He turned his head with difficulty, and saw that he was lying in the snow, and that the snow was pink and red around his head. Then he saw the ear.

It was his own ear.

"It's all right, *Reb*," Yasha Pokhis was saying, his voice choked with tears. "They didn't kill you, after all. They killed old Babushka Starskaya, up the road, and tore down most of the houses in the *shtetl*. And they raped poor Olinka."

"How long have I been lying here?" the Rabbi asked.

"About two hours. We couldn't move you. The others went for help. Grishka went to get my father and the midwife. She'll know what to do. She lived through two pogroms in Hashchévato . . . But I didn't want to leave you here alone."

"Who did this?" Meyer demanded.

"It was the Cossacks, *Reb*. Nobody knows where they came from. They plowed through the village on horseback. They tried to get us here in the road, but we ran away from them—and then they saw you. They came rushing at you. They were shouting that the Yids killed Minister Plehve. They said we're all Social Revolutionaries—it's our fault the railway lines are striking and police are being murdered. What were they talking about?"

Meyer Aronovitch Zlotkin closed his eyes and murmured: "It doesn't matter, son . . . " He felt himself being sucked back into the black hole again, down, down . . . just as Yakov's small warm hand, in its red mitten, took hold of his own.

Chapter II

*A*T the dining room table, Victor Grigorievitch Ostrov was sitting back, eyes semi-closed after a large meal of his favorite beet soup, cutlets, and kasha pilaf. He was a large, beefy man with a florid complexion and dark eyes, a fleshy nose, and a head of vital light-brown hair that rose in a crest off his high forehead. Although not handsome, he exuded a sensual virility that commanded the attention of those around him—in this case, a small maid, his wife Elena, and his son Kyril.

Seated at his father's side, Kyril concentrated on the sketch he was drawing, making an effort to breathe as silently as possible. He tried not to make any noise with his pencils. *If I'm completely still, he won't remember I'm here,* the boy thought, passing a nervous tongue over his lips.

Kyril looked up again, this time at his mother, seated across from Victor, and exchanged one covert, worried glance with her. Elena had a beautiful face, but it seldom looked at peace. A constant furrow kneaded her brow. Anxiousness haunted her eyes. Her shoulders were slightly stooped as though she were ready to assume a new burden, or to receive yet a new blow from an unexpected source.

Only we know the source, the boy thought angrily. We both know *exactly* whom to fear, and why.

Victor Ostrov stirred and opened his eyes. Coming out of his stupor, he shook himself like a dog to clear his mind. "Lena," he announced, "I have a meeting tonight. You and the boy go to bed and don't bother waiting up for me."

His wife nodded silently. As Victor rose, his son observed him with awe. His full height was six feet, four inches—much of it muscle. In the war with Japan, he had served as a physician for a Cossack division. His rank was Captain. In civilian life, he practiced

28

medicine in Rostov and in the farmlands that stretched beyond it. But he had remained on friendly terms with his companions in the fabled *Division Sauvage,* composed of the fiercest warriors. They respected him as one of their own.

Victor himself came from a Cossack background. He had been reared in the belief that his people were a superior breed. In his youth, he had ridden wild stallions and learned to manipulate the sword. A portrait of him as a young man hung in the living room. In the portrait he wore a gray coat with a fur collar, tall black boots, and a fur hat—and he carried a whip. Next to him, his mother stood, regal and imperious in an embroidered caftan and soft, dark-leather boots. They were the elite of Russia, the proudest, and the noblest of the native Russian demes.

Rising, Elena asked hesitantly: "Is it the Black Hundred?"

For a split-second, Victor's features froze into a mask of pure hatred. Blood suffused his neck. He exploded. "Damnit, Lena! It's enough that I tell you not to wait up!"

Elena shrank back, rebuffed. "The Black Hundred are a rowdy lot," she said softly. "They are cruel and without scruples. I wish you'd leave them, Vitya." She glanced around the room to make sure the maid was in the kitchen before adding, a little breathless: "They are responsible for half the pogroms in the area. They *hate* the Jews!"

Victor shrugged. "Leave me alone, woman, with your Jewish fears. No one will hurt you. No one would *dare,*" he added, a sneer on his face. Striding to the costumer, he struggled into his deep gray astrakhan coat. "Where's my hat?" he demanded. His dark eyes fastened on his son.

For a moment, Kyril held his father's penetrating stare. Then, abashed, the child looked down. "I don't know where it is, Papa." His voice shook.

"I see . . ." Victor marched over to Kyril's place and picked up the sketch. Kyril had been drawing the outline of a doe and its young. The likeness was well-executed, but Victor tossed it to the ground with a disgusted snarl. "Men don't waste their time on such non-sense," he declared. "Now where's my hat?"

Kyril got up, knocking over the chair in his terrified haste to get out of the room. He stumbled against a low coffee table and tripped. Uttering a small cry, he fell to the floor. Instantly, Victor yanked him up by his shirt collar. "Get me my hat, you snivelling idiot!" he yelled, his voice booming. Shaking the boy by his lapels, he peered into his face. Suddenly he let Kyril go. "Get out of here, little girl!" he called derisively. "And you, Lena, get me my sable hat and stay out of the way!"

Elena, head bent, hastened from the room.

In the hallway she found her son cowering against the wall, tears bathing his face. She cupped his chin in her hand. The ten-year-old boy began to sob. "I hate him!" he cried. "I wish he'd die!"

"For God's sake, hush up, Kyriusha," his mother whispered, glancing over her shoulder. Taking him into her arms, she hugged him tightly. "We have each other," she murmured. "And as long as I have you, I can bear anything and anyone!"

Her voice began a sing-song. "Kyriusha will make things all right for Mama," she crooned. "Won't you, my little swallow . . . ?"

Unexpectedly, the boy broke free and pushed her away. He ran into his room, bolting the door behind him. Throwing himself onto the narrow bed, he held his hands over both ears and shut his eyes against the nightmare. In his mind's eye, he saw himself a toddler again, at his mother's side, being rebuked for a minor offense. "If you don't behave," Elena had remonstrated, "the Black Hundred will come after you!"

The Black Hundred, or *Chornaya Sotnya*, was a political group representing the extreme Right; its members were hooligans and ruffians, and many respectable homes refused to admit them. His father had always belonged to the *Chornaya Sotnya*. As far back as Kyril could recall, Victor and Elena had always argued over this issue.

Other children were afraid of bad fairies or of evil monsters. But Kyril Ostrov was terrified of a political group. His mother had given him fair warning: "If you stay with Mama, and don't leave her alone, you shall have a good, clean, happy life. But if you follow the evil precepts of your father, the Black Hundred will hurt you in ways you can't even imagine!"

The little boy sat up and hugged himself, rocking back and forth. He was already ten, and growing stronger. Soon, it would be time. He could count the years, months, weeks and days until he reached the age when he would be able to leave them both—his cruel Cossack father, and his plaintive, clinging, bookish Jewish mother. "I hate you both!" he burst out, suddenly kicking at a small stool beside his bed. "I want you both out of my life!"

But, as usual, he was careful to keep his voice to a bare murmur, so no one would overhear his cries of rage. He felt safe nowhere.

* * *

In the small cart, sitting next to Reb Meyer Zlotkin, Yakov kept his hands neatly folded in his lap. The *lineika*, in which they were travelling, was nothing more than a padded wooden slat on springs, set over four wheels. Above the wheels was wedged a two-by-four where they rested their feet. This was a comfortable arrangement; and besides, for Yakov, it represented his first trip away from home. He was breathless with excitement.

Up front, the driver from Peredelkino sat fully upright behind the two plodding horses. It was thirty miles from the Jewish hamlet to the larger town of Rigevka. The hot July sun beat down upon the travellers, and Reb Meyer kept adjusting his hat to cover the hideous red scar that marked the place where, six months before, his ear had been.

"This is Rigevka," the Rabbi announced, his hand making a large sweep of the village they had just entered.

With sweat pouring down his face, Yakov rolled up his sleeves and leaned forward. His eyes were wide with amazement. He had never seen anything so pretty as this village—so different from their own! The houses were cob-walled and whitewashed, all except for the north walls that had no windows and had been painted blue ("to scare the Devil away," the *reb* explained). Each house was crowned with a thatched roof and all were surrounded by small, well-tended gardens where cherry trees blossomed. Six-foot tall sunflowers and hollyhocks grew outside the doors. The church with its pointed steeple and a round cupola was topped by a green corrugated iron roof which the travellers had noticed from afar. On an elevation, beyond the largest yard Yakov had ever seen, was a mansion larger than any Yakov had ever dreamed of. "Is *this* where the Baron lives?" he asked, impressed.

"Indeed, it is."

The driver maneuvered the *lineika* through the main street and up into the hills. The horses crossed a large green yard—a grassy oval circled with bushes and shrubs, protected by a white picket fence. To the left stood a laundry-house, where the laundress and her children lived, and next to that a long, low building. They passed by a coach-house in which two landaus, a victoria, and an immense covered sleigh were neatly lined up; then came a fully equipped, pungent-smelling harness room, followed by the stable in which five saddle horses were whinnying nervously. Next to the saddle horses were the eight carriage horses. Finally came a long shed housing twenty cows, a bull, and some oxen, with an interior enclave for the calves.

At the end of the building, where the courtyard also abutted, the driver reined in his horses. Yakov and the *reb* climbed down from the cart, the boy holding his violin case and the man the music sheets, contained in a thin, pigskin briefcase.

As they walked toward the main house, they passed the chicken-coop, then the cellar and the ice house. The boy had never seen an ice house before. It took his breath away. Huge blocks of ice stood propped against the walls, lining the room.

Further along were the servants' quarters and an enormous kitchen filling one whole wing of the master's house. Then, at long last, the man and the boy reached a circular grassy area from which they could view the village below, its neat little houses undulating in the sunlight like a string of beads.

Two proud oaks rose up from this expanse of green. At the far end, a rose garden had been erected. A broad path encircled the lawn. Beyond, in the far distance, some small houses had been built for the two Poliakov coachmen and their large families.

At the end of the courtyard, between the main house and the path leading toward the lawn (on one side), and the end of the building with the sheds and stables (on the other), stood the estate manager's home. Here, too, were the offices from which the Baron conducted his affairs.

The child was awed by the spectacle of such grandeur. "How many people live on this property?" he asked.

Reb Meyer smiled. "Some fifty, I believe. The Baron takes good care of his people. The Baron, Yasha, takes good care of *every*one, and this you must never forget."

Yasha nodded, silently. Side by side, they surveyed the lawn. On one side stretched a long, thickly wooded clump of acacias, oaks, and sweetly scented lilacs. In the shade of this grove, the Baroness had ordered chairs set up for five o'clock tea.

The rest of the garden—some twelve sweeping acres—was dotted with fruit trees. Flower beds surrounded a long bench; below, Yakov noticed a large vegetable garden. Near the bench was a croquet set, a cross-beam for gymnastics, a swing, and two sand hills for little children. These appeared to have dried out from disuse.

"The Baron's children are growing up," the Rabbi explained, smiling as he caught Yakov's expression. "Evgeny Lazarevitch is now thirteen, and Zeinab Lazarevna, bless her, is already ten—like you."

Yakov could only nod. Everything to do with Baron Poliakov filled him with a conflict of emotion—fear and anticipation, awe, excitement . . . and also, envy. The Baron's children evidently lived like tzars.

"Come now, son." Reb Meyer gave Yakov a playful shove. They walked toward a covered terrace adorned with climbing vines. The ten steps leading to the main house were bordered by large and colorful flowerpots.

Reb Meyer knocked on the glass door. A servant answered.

"Baron Poliakov is expecting you. This way, please, Rabbi."

Following his mentor, Yakov passed into a large, pleasant drawing room with a piano and spacious lounge chairs. A tall, thin man with silvery hair, in his summer cottons, was sitting at an antique secretary. How distinguished and elegant he looked. Even his "simple" afternoon clothes had an appearance of resplendent opulence! Yasha had seen him before—when the exalted man had come to Peredelkino—but never had he stood so close to him!

Smiling, the Baron rose and shook Reb Meyer's hand.

"Rabbi, how nice to see you again." He scrutinized Yakov. "So this is the child prodigy you've been raving about," he commented. His expression was friendly. "Yasha . . . I would like to hear you at the violin. My manservant has set up a stand for you, and I should like you to play for me and my children."

Yakov felt his mouth go dry. His mother and the *reb* had made him practice hours at a time for this occasion, but now his hands felt clammy. In the cool, shaded living room, he could only stand at attention. He was speechless.

Fortunately, at that moment a tall, handsome, dark boy walked in, and nodded to Yakov. "This is my son, Evgeny," the Baron announced. "Zhenya, this is Yakov Pokhis from Peredelkino."

The older boy shook his hand, formally. Yasha remembered him from the previous summer, when he had come to the *shtetl* with his father. Zhenya Poliakov was a serious boy, already full of his own importance—or so Yasha interpreted his rather self-possessed expression. Looking at the finely tailored combed-cotton-and-linen clothes, Yakov thought: Here stands a real *gentleman*, as I shall never be . . . no matter how well I perform at the Conservatory. *He* knows it, and so do I . . .

The Rabbi motioned him toward the stand. Yakov set up his sheet music, opened his violin case and gently, with great care, took out his instrument. And then, just as he looked up toward the Baron and Zhenya, his breath was taken away. Someone else had come into the room, a creature as beautiful and otherworldly as a fairy. He had never seen such a girl—not in his whole life!

She was slightly taller than he. Budding breasts were pushing out at her white linen day dress. She had a rounded face and huge sloe-eyes ringed with the most perfect, long black lashes. Her nose was small and pert—hardly Jewish in appearance—and her long black hair, in unruly waves, cascaded out of its simple Psyche knot, tumbling down her back like the hair of a mermaid. Her coloring was pink and healthy, her chin little but firm—her heart-shaped lips were a warm, deep rose. She had the hands of an angel, delicate and white—hands his own mother had probably never possessed, even at that age.

Yet it was impossible to resent her. She was beautiful, so beautiful, healthy and round and strong, yet also feminine, with features as well-chiselled as a china doll's. Her eyes showed so much interest, such tenderness! She had moved close to her brother. Now shyly, she held out one of her small hands to him, Yasha Pokhis!

"I'm Zica," she said, in a clear, bell-like voice. "And you?"

"Yasha. Yakov Lvovitch Pokhis," he stammered, remembering his manners.

Her brother, in a formal voice, presented her. "My sister, Zeinab Lazarevna Poliakova."

Yakov thought: I shall have to ask the *Reb* why she has such a strange name: *Zeinab*... He had never heard it before. "Zenaïde," yes. The Zenaïdes he'd known had all been nicknamed "Zina." But she'd called herself "*Zica*." He liked the sound of that—almost foreign.

"What shall you play for us?" she asked him curiously. "Zhenya and I study the piano," she continued in a rush, lifting her chin toward the instrument in the corner of the room.

Yakov's throat had tightened. For an instant, he blanked out. He knew he was blushing intensely. "A piece from *The Four Seasons* adapted for solo violin," he finally managed, as he positioned himself behind the stand.

He waited, his eyes safely riveted on the Baron's face.

At the latter's signal, Yakov took a deep breath. He tried to blot out the people watching him. Only the instrument mattered—the instrument and his music. He cradled his violin in the crook of his shoulder and began. Immediately, he felt himself lifted up with the Vivaldi melody, carried by its flow. How was he performing...? He wasn't sure, had almost ceased to care, so consumed was he by the music. And then, shyly, he ventured once more to look at Zica Poliakova. She was)tting beside her father on a low settee, her ankles crossed demurely, her hands folded in her lap. Her face expressed rapt attention, the tip of her tongue protruding childlike, between parted lips.

When Yakov finished his piece, and bowed as *Reb* Meyer had taught him, he saw that she was smiling, her eyes dazzled as if she were under a spell.

"Yasha, you're very good," the Baron slapped Yakov on the shoulder enthusiastically. "I think you shall do very well in Moscow!"

But all Yakov could think of was the expression of wonder and bewitchment he had caught on Zica's face as he had been playing. Yes, he thought, I *was* good this time . . . and it was because *she* was here, the most beautiful girl in the world.

In the Troika Café, the attention of the men of the *Chornaya Sotnya* was focused on Victor Grigorievitch Ostrov. He rubbed his hands together and blew on them. Abruptly, he bellowed with laughter. Raising his large, leonine head, he looked from one to another of his attentive companions. His hooded lids narrowed over shrewd, calculating eyes. "Black ball in the corner pocket," he declared, the corners of his mouth turning up almost impishly.

Around him, the other men stood silent, tense. "It's impossible to beat him when he's on a winning streak," Sasha Tartov muttered to Pavlik Morosov. "He must've scored a hundred points in a row tonight! When Vitya's on a winning streak, nobody else gets the chance to play!"

The other nodded, eyes intent on Victor. In their black shirts and pants, the men of the *Chornaya Sotnya* resembled large tarantulas, predatory and ominous in the crowded confines of the small tavern. And with its flickering lights and dark corners, the Troika Café truly resembled a den reserved for thieves. Besides the infamous Hundred, it catered to pimps and rascals and other members of the nether world of Rostov-on-the-Don. Victor Ostrov and his friends—all members of the Black Hundred—were received there with open arms and free drinks. They came regularly to gamble and play pool, placing heavy bets. Sooner or later those bets resulted in a pay-off for the owner—a small, bent man known only as Edyk the Rat.

Victor liked to toss his hat in the corner and lose himself playing hour upon hour of billiards and cards—even when he lost. And he lost quite a bit, especially at poker and belotte. At pool he consistently won, but his winnings didn't quite make up for what he'd lost earlier in the evening.

Lately, his losses at the card table had begun to make him nervous. Hidden from his wife Elena were dozens of little pieces of paper scrawled with large sums representing the I.O.U.'s he signed away each night. These calculations he squirreled away in suit pockets or odd drawers. He'd been a gambler since his adolescence. In the *Division Sauvage*, he had made quite a reputation for himself, especially as a pool player. He found himself incapable of resisting a pool table. This game, he would tell the admiring Morosov, had nothing whatsoever to do with chance: it was a game of skill— pure, calculated skill, something which Victor Ostrov believed he had possessed in great measure all his life.

"Whatever I lose tonight at cards, I shall make up tomorrow at pool," he would boast to his friends. And sometimes he did.

These days, however, he often did not win it back. His concentration was not what it used to be. Sometimes, just when it seemed most crucial to plot the next move, he would find his mind wandering. He'd shake himself to alertness, finding that he had blanked out. Perhaps it had only been for a few seconds of the game—but a few essential seconds. And Pavlik Morosov would be staring at him, his green eyes probing, disapproving. Pavlik's basilisk eyes revealed what he knew—that Victor had had his mind on other matters, and not on the game at hand.

During those moments of inattention, Victor often thought about Maroussia. He fantasized about her light red hair, her large, pink breasts, and her blue eyes. Maroussia Klimova was twenty years old, plump and laughing. Spirited and loyal, she was like the passionate girls of his youth. But where the Cossack women tended to be dark and bony, this girl was round and voluptuous—a dream, well worth the money.

He knew she loved him. He also knew she was pregnant, and that it would cost him. Just as Tanya had cost him . . . and Varya. And Murka. Sometimes, he had paid for them to go away; sometimes he had performed the necessary operation, depending on the girl and on the situation.

But Maroussia was different: She was exactly the sort of girl he should have married. Simple, sweet, and docile. Not like Elena—a troublemaker, an intellectual. Elena was a Yid in the bargain—the worst kind of woman imaginable. She was afraid of him, which was her only saving grace. But she whined, she pouted, and she could be silent for days at a time, nursing her wounds. Her silence and her wounded eyes always accused him.

Once he had hit her across the mouth, and she had said nothing, uttered not a cry of protest. But afterwards, for three whole weeks, she had gathered her lithe, thin, agile body into a block of impenetrable steel, and she hadn't opened her mouth. She had sat in her room in the five-story house on Pushkin Street—the house he'd purchased with her dowry money—and had read Turgenev and Tolstoi. Silently, she had refused to submit to his sexual advances, refused to do more than set a plate of food before him and watch him eat. She would not even sit down beside him at the table.

A tough one, Lena . . . tough and dark, like the Cossack women, but also pitiful and broken, like all Jews. It was in their blood to whine, and she had whined. After three weeks he had found her crying, her face a mess. Then she had let loose, asking him why she had given everything up for him—her parents, her home, her riches, her suitors. "*Why?*" she had hurled at him, violating him with her anger. "*Why* did I do it? You are a worthless man, a *samocer*—a 'shit-eater' who creates his own doom, wastes his talents, ends up with nothing. You are a vulgar swine, a disgusting fool— and *I*, a greater fool for having loved you, for having believed you could be faithful and decent and hard-working, like my own father!"

Like her own father . . . Fine man *he* had turned out to be . . . ! The man had abandoned Elena—given her some gold coins in a lacquered coffer, then had the maid bring down her trunks packed full of fine clothes. She would have no occasion to wear her finery anymore, her father had reminded her. This man she was marrying, Victor Ostrov, was only a country doctor! So her fine, elegant father with the trim little Van Dyke beard and the thin, aquiline nose had turned his back on his daughter and her husband. Yossif, Yosska Byitch, the merchant with the education, had given her up without so much as a regretful glance in the mirror. And Victor knew that Elena often compared him, her husband, to this small, narrow, petty man who knew nothing of life, and that somehow it was he, Vitya, who came out the loser. Time had changed her perceptions, had in fact changed her, completely.

What good was a father-in-law like Yossif Byitch? He could only count his gold coins like the Yid he was, stingy and grasping. Yet he had the temerity to find *Victor* at fault and lacking—not good enough for his daughter.

Elena had been Victor's most costly mistake. Certainly, she had brought him the lacquered coffer full of rubles and loose diamonds. In that coffer he had found gold, silver, and pieces of paper that represented land deeds and bank accounts. She had brought him unhoped-for wealth... in the beginning. They had bought the house on Pushkin Street, and the boy had been born. But after that, Victor had gambled away a lot of her money, and the old man hadn't even wanted to see his own grandson. No further money had been forthcoming!

Then Tanya had entered his life, followed by Varya, the singer, and all the others after them. And they had cost him plenty of money—money to set them up, money to keep them quiet, money to clothe them and keep them beautiful. For all of them had wanted to be like his Jewish wife. All had hoped he would divorce her and marry them: all had wanted to live on Pushkin Street, instead of squirreled away in undersized, over-furnished apartments. None had taken well to the notion of being the "other woman."

"You should let us make mincemeat out of her," Pavlik Morosov had said to Victor one night, feeling murderous toward Elena. "Why not, Vitya? Just say the word, and we'll cut her throat. We wouldn't touch the lad, he isn't a Yid—but we'd finish *her* off for you. Then you would be free. Just think! All her money would be yours. You'd be free to bring Maroussia home. We'd leave the Troika Café forever—meet in Pushkin Street!"

But Victor's stomach turned. He didn't want to hear any more. He wanted to dump Morosov in the gutter and turn his back on all of them—on Lena, on Kyril, on his own friends. None of them understood. They thought him a fool. No matter how much he despised Lena, she was still his wife, and Cossacks didn't kill their wives unless they caught them in bed with another man. You punished your wife, you left her, maybe... but you didn't just cut her throat. "We've raped plenty of Jewish women," Sasha Tartov had added, laughing. "Remember the girl whose house we ransacked last May...?"

The Black Hundred was known for instigating pogroms, for terrorizing Jews and driving them out of town. Victor had gone with them, sword brandished. He had smashed glass windows and delicate crystals belonging to Jews. He'd slashed the fine evening clothes right off their backs. But none of these faceless Jews had been his wife, the mother of his son. Victor Grigorievitch Ostrov still had his honor, his honor as a Cossack and as a man. You could beat up your wife, but you didn't allow your cohorts to violate your home and family.

This morning, he had delivered twins to a farming couple on the outskirts of town. He was tired, bone tired. He should have gone to see Maroussia, instead of coming here with the boys. Maroussia would have brought him his bottle of vodka and his herring, and his borsch. He would have lain on her soft, pillowy breasts, and smelled her milky odor, so young and sweet and innocent. She was already getting fat because of the baby—it was too late to remove the child. But still—she appealed to him. Her innocence appealed to him, and so did her cow-like acquiescence to everything he said. "Yes, Vitya," she would say, in her breathless voice, "yes, my darling, I'll do anything for you, I would die for you if you asked me, I would jump from the window and slit my wrists and write you a love letter with my dying blood!" Victor would smile, and shake his head, and then laugh. Then he would tumble her down on the bed and enter her without preparation. He would hear her little cry of pain, muffling it with the palm of his hand, "Quiet now, woman! Quiet now, little girl, *maya devochka krasivaya, maya blyat*, my pretty little whore . . ."

He should have gone, but he hadn't; instead he was here and Pavlik Morosov was handing him the chalk and his cue, looking at him expectantly, wondering if he would score once again.

Would he win the bet?

Of course he would. He owed Edyk the Rat four thousand rubles. Tonight, he would win them back. He'd be damned if he'd sign away another goddamned I.O.U.—or worse yet, have to part with the money the farmer had paid him for delivering the twins. This time, he would win more than he had lost, and come home with his pockets full of cash.

He had to.

Edyk the Rat had been making threats recently—thinly veiled, but threats all the same. If Victor didn't pay soon . . .

And suddenly, from behind the counter, Edyk winked. The wink had meaning.

Victor's honor was at stake, as well as the safety of his family.

No—he could not lose again. Not tonight.

Once more, Victor bent over the table and aimed for the corner pocket.

Chapter III

"*B*UT I thought I was going to Moscow!" Yakov exclaimed, his face hurt and uncomprehending. As he looked at his father, Lev, sitting so calmly with hands folded in front of him, the boy felt himself rebel. Why had he let himself pour out so much of his soul to those rich folk in Rigevka? That tall, thin man had made empty promises, dangling Yasha's life like a marionette on a string. The Baron had never intended to sponsor him for the Conservatory of Music! He was too involved in his own life and in his own importance to care about a lowly Jewish boy from a village in the Pale. Yet Yakov had shown his purest feelings out through the music of his violin. He had looked into the heart and soul of the Baron's daughter, Zica Poliakova. And he felt *sure* she had heard what he had tried to express.

But, what had come of this? An offer to go to *Odessa!* In an instant, the dream of Moscow had been shattered.

"Why *Odessa?*" he demanded, clenching his small fist.

"The Baron explained it all to the *reb*." His father's voice was soft with years of resignation. "Your mother and I are to serve his sister, Madame Aschkenasy, in her household. We shall have good jobs, Yashka—good jobs, and in a big city where Jews are allowed to live and make money. Meanwhile, you shall study the violin with Mikhail Perlman. The Baron told Reb Meyer that Perlman is one of the foremost Jewish violinists in Russia. He will prepare you for the Conservatory."

"Why can't I go to Moscow immediately?" Yakov demanded.

"The *reb* says that first, you must go through an apprenticeship. The Baron cannot sponsor someone he has heard play only once. You must be recommended by a worthy music teacher, and you

40

need to prove yourself for a period of years. The entrance requirements for the Conservatory are quite strict. The Baron's word must be based on solid evidence. The audition with him is only one step along the way."

Yakov stood up, his small frame rigid with outrage. "So you and Mama will become house servants!" he cried. "To be ordered about by the Baron's sister! I think Lazar Solomonovitch Poliakov should be ashamed of himself, Papa! Turning you two into a maid and—*what*, Papa? What will *you* be doing for this Madame Aschkenasy?"

Lev took a deep breath and looked up into his son's face. His own eyes were cool and proud, and he answered, gently: "I shall be doing whatever is demanded of me, my son. Because Bella and I want what's best for *you*, and this means moving to Odessa." He sighed. "Yasha, Yasha... what am I doing *here*, do you think? I sell bric-a-brac, broken pieces of furniture, old pots and pans, and ragged clothing. I bring home a few *kopeks* a day, and consider myself a lucky man for doing so. In Odessa, your mother and I shall have respectable jobs in a rich Jewish home. We shall wear nice, clean clothing, and reside under a warm roof that doesn't leak when it rains or snows; we shall have a stove that works, and healthy food every day of the year. Whatever Madame Aschkenasy asks of me won't ever be enough. I shall bow to her in thanks, that she has made it possible for my son to study with Mikhail Perlman, the great violinist. And we shall have a better life, Yasha, a far more prosperous life, than we have here in Peredelkino. Don't forget it, either!"

The boy twisted his mouth into a jagged, thin line of resentment. "But here, you are your own man, Papa," he countered. "You're nobody's servant."

Lev shook his head and smiled his slow, mournful smile. "Here, Yashenka," he replied softly, "I am abused by those who buy from me, who hurl insults at me and call me a thief for making even one *kopek* of profit from my merchandise—and I am jeered by those who sell to me, who look upon me as the village bum. They think I am the human garbage dump, who has no choice but to accept their refuse and their hand-me-downs. My child, in this area, I am *everybody's* servant—the most despised citizen of Peredelkino, which itself is the most despised village in this district."

Yakov snorted, and turned his back on his father. Despair crowded his heart. Then Lev murmured, very gently: "Pride is a luxury, my darling. It is a luxury that Jews from the Pale can seldom afford, and Jews from Peredelkino, *never*. You must make your peace with this fact, for I fear you have no other choice."

The boy nodded, trying to fight back tears. Brushing his eyes with the back of his hand, he mumbled, "Yes, Papa. I understand." But his head was swimming with disappointment and rage, and, yes, *jealousy*. He was jealous of the Poliakovs, jealous of Evgeny and Zica in their palace in Rigevka. He had never known, until now, what it meant to be so jealous of other human beings that your very guts twisted inside you.

We are *all* human beings, he thought: why then do some of us live like tzars, while others must become their servants?

He recalled the pretty little girl, with her luminous black eyes and her beautiful pink face, her lips parted in ecstasy. Could he hate her for being rich? She had been born that way, that was all. She had not demanded any of the wealth that had been given to her.

And what of her beauty? Zeinab Lazarevna Poliakova was the loveliest girl-child in the city of Rigevka . . . probably in all Moscow as well. Yakov was sure of it. The memory of her was spellbinding. She had noticed him, too, had addressed him with greater deference than anyone in his whole life.

I cannot hate her, he decided. I cannot really hate anyone simply for being who they are. What I can do is become the most successful violinist in Russia—as famous as Nicolo Paganini, in Italy, sixty years ago. I can learn to compose, and I shall have my own chamber orchestra and perform all over the nation, like a real virtuoso . . .

Yet something leaden was pulling at his heart. With a rude start, he realized what it was: *he didn't really want to be a virtuoso*. He loved playing the violin, loved the sensuous contours of his instrument, the sounds that emerged from the soft, dark silence. But *he didn't really want to play for his living*. He didn't want to depend on playing the violin in order to become *somebody*. Paganini, he was certain, had risen each morning with a singleminded passion to wrest sound from his strings—whereas he, Yasha Pokhis, rose with quite another set of desires. But *what*, indeed, *were* these desires. . . ?

Could it be that I have no definite ambitions? the boy wondered. When I am with people, I love to make them laugh. But honestly, can one term this an *ambition?*

And yet, that was it: he loved making people laugh, whether it was the Rabbi or his pals at the *yeshiva*, his parents or the old shop woman who pickled herrings. When he made people laugh, something magical exploded within him.

But this was no ambition. It would provide no exit visa out of the Pale of Settlement, no commutation of sentence for a Jewish serf held back by centuries of repression in this land of Christian mysticism.

Because of some gift, a little touch of talent, he was well-liked in his *shtetl*—and if he wanted, one day, to have a wife like Zeinab Poliakova—then he would have to concentrate on the single skill that would raise him one notch above the other Jewish boys in the Pale. Making love to his violin had already rescued his family from Peredelkino; some day soon, it would get him to Moscow.

And he, Yakov Lvovitch Pokhis, intended to court his instrument day and night in order to make certain he would get there—even if this meant he would have no time to spare for making jokes. Jokes passed the time away, nothing more, while virtuosity awarded special privileges.

In her boudoir in the house on Pushkin Street, Elena Ostrova heard the strange, muffled cry from the attic. She sat up with a start. Odd—was anyone else in the house? The young maid, Alla, had gone to the market; the boy was in school. Only Elena was at home.

She put down her book and strolled restlessly around her boudoir. Anatole France was a particular favorite of hers. Reading in French, the language she had cultivated in her childhood, always reminded Lena of her childhood.

She had been the beloved daughter of *kupetz* Yossif Byitch. Until her marriage to Victor, Elena and her father had been extremely close. How she had admired him! Yossif Byitch had been a middle-class Jewish merchant, an upstanding member of the First Guild. He had lived in a beautiful brick house and had sold fine, antique furniture obtained from the richest estates. He had not grown up speaking French. Industriously, he had acquired the language, wishing to improve his circumstances with the wealth he was accruing. And so his only daughter, Elena, had benefited from private lessons and trips to the spas. She had sometimes traveled to Kiev, Odessa, and Moscow on special permits occasionally released to well-heeled members of the First Guild.

Elena fully realized that her boudoir was a retreat from the world she had stumbled into when she married Victor. She bandaged her wounded ego with her books... shelves and shelves of books, ranging from the poetry of Catullus to the biographies of the French kings. Somehow, it kept her father's spirit and ideals alive. And she had taught the boy, Kyril, to read French fluently... teaching him all the time his father was away carousing with his ill-famed friends of the Black Hundred. Always in secret—for Victor would have battered them both had he caught her instilling culture into their son. He called it "sissy black magic."

These days, Elena did not deny the truth: she wished she had never married Victor Ostrov. Vitya was loud, vulgar and cruel, a bad husband and a harsh, judgmental father—not like her own. But it was useless to bemoan the loss of her parents, Yossif and Olga. To her, they were as well as dead. Yossif Byitch would never forgive her for having eloped with the dashing Cossack who had seduced her with a roll of his dark eyes and the touch of his rough, demanding fingers.

Vitya had loved her once. He had braved rejection from his own family for marrying a Jewish girl. Now, she knew he despised her. She often felt that he wished she would slide away into oblivion. She had read the signs on his face. And so she had only the boy.

Almost miraculously—for he'd had no contract with his grandfather—Kyril had inherited the finesse of her father's distinction. But he was also a child of the Steppe, a golden child, with the blond hair of his paternal grandfather. Elena was proud of her son's fair handsomeness.

Now, in 1912, he was seventeen years old. No longer the "little chicken" as the neighborhood children had taunted him, he appeared a young man with good, strong muscles and the sensitive face of a poet. He had her face, only fair-skinned, the features the same but on a larger scale. He looked neither Jewish nor Cossack, but, strange to say, typically Russian.

This will stand him in good stead, Elena had caught herself thinking. He will be able to pass for being native Russian. Kyril, the jewel in this dreadful, ill-conceived marriage, would redeem both his parents and go on to become someone great—someone accepted by all. Neither Elena, a Jew, nor Victor, whose culture was lacking, could ever hope to reach the heights that Kyril would scale.

Abruptly, Lena's reflections ended. She again heard a sound. There *was* someone in the house. She thought she'd heard a man cry out.

If a prowler had entered her home... She rose, hurriedly, gathering her skirt up in one hand. Rushing from the room, she prayed:

Dear God, let it not be one of the *Chornaya Sotynya* come to attack me here, alone...

In the kitchen she stopped. Silently opening a drawer, she pulled out a long kitchen knife. If it *was* one of Vitya's's ill-reputed club-men, he would get a rude surprise from the little Jewish woman! She felt her arms and scalp go damp with apprehension and dread.

Walking on the balls of her feet, Elena mounted the stairs, hugging the wall of the staircase. The small door leading to the attic was ajar. Her breath coming in short gasps, Lena pushed it open.

And then she screamed.

Her husband, Victor, was dangling from the mansarded ceiling of the attic with his neck wrapped in a thick rope and his large head at an acute angle, lopping loosely to his shoulder. He stared at her with dull, unseeing eyes. His color was a sickly, suffused purple; his swollen tongue filled his gaping mouth like the smoked tongue of cattle that were displayed in butchers' windows: bloated, meaty, and crimson-brown.

Yanking at the rope with quivering hands, Elena called out: "Vitya! Vitya! Why have you done this?" The knot was too tight. She gave up, weeping.

Her eyes fell to the floor. A piece of scribbled paper had fallen from her husband's pocket. Picking it up with a trembling hand, she tried to decipher it. "Total owed to Edvard Palchik," Victor had written, "five thousand rubles." It bore yesterday's date.

She had never heard of this Palchik. But she knew, with chilling clarity, that, whoever he was, he would soon come to collect this debt.

Her head reeled. Bile rose in her throat. Elena Ostrova stumbled blindly down the staircase, clutching her husband's note in her trembling fingers.

The debt was staggering. If Victor had killed himself because of this debt, she could be sure that there were other debts as well, other pieces of crumpled paper stashed away, bearing the names of other creditors. Victor had, in all probability, gambled away all of their family savings... everything that was left of her dowry money, everything that was left of his mediocre earnings as a country doctor. Seeing this, Elena was terrified—of more than death, of more than widowhood.

She was now terrified of penury, of losing her house and her security... of starving alone with her son. And then, like a drowning person, she remembered Kyril. He would save her, she thought, grasping at the notion as though it were a single liferaft on a churning ocean of horrors: *Kyril would save them both.*

Zica Poliakova knew she was beautiful. She knew it from the stares she received whenever she and her mother went into the city and climbed down from their carriage. She saw the affirmation in men's eyes whenever she and her brother went to a high tea. Men stared at her and their eyes would widen with admiration. She wasn't particularly tall, but she had a perfect hour-glass figure. Her hands and feet were small and dainty. Her face had lost its childhood chubbiness. High cheekbones were now discernible, underscoring her large black eyes. Her hair was thick and lustrous, gathered tonight into a cluster of curls around a heavy pompadour with a small topknot, where she had wedged her jewelled comb.

Zica should have loved balls, but in fact they never failed to disappoint her. She was always hoping to find a Prince Charming who would awaken her, but he never came. Tonight, in particular, his absence was sorely noted.

She was wearing a ball gown made in Paris by Paul Poiret. It was fashioned of a deep coral silk, with a scooped neckline that revealed the tops of her voluptuous young breasts. Its sleeves were snug to the elbow, but a long ruffle of Belgian lace, dotted with tiny makeshift diamonds and opals, cascaded over her forearms. The tight bodice showed off her tiny, cinched waist; the skirt was a form-fitting hobble finished off by a train, which she could hold up with a loop while dancing. At her throat she displayed a river of diamonds, which her father had given her for her seventeenth birthday that summer.

Each prominent family of Moscow gave one or two balls a year during the winter season. This year, Zica had come out in society, and she had been attending balls all over the city. Tonight was her parents' second ball, a particularly glittering affair, and Zhenya had been most clever in helping to design the special features of the evening. Now, in his tuxedo, he made a resplendent Master of Ceremonies as he directed the dancing. Zica was very proud of him.

For one of the cotillion figures, he had prepared two cushions on which he had pinned cardboard tags bearing the names of famous couples throughout history: Paul and Virginie, Dante and Beatrice, Romeo and Juliet, Adam and Eve, Castor and Pollux, the Hare and the Tortoise, Faust and Marguerite. At the appointed time, after midnight supper, the servants would pass the cushions around, and everyone would be asked to pick out a card and find the person who had drawn the name of the "other half" of the couple. The "partners" would then have to dance together. Zica wondered which figure in history or literature would come to her. She was secretly hoping for Cleopatra, but there were no attractive candidates for Antony except her own brother—and it was hardly fun to have to dance with your own brother!

Her mother, Elizaveta Borisovna, had purchased fifty toy flutes and fifty children's trumpets. She and Zica had had fun sewing up a hundred caps of stiff muslin, decorated with white puffs of cotton on which they had pasted black cotton commas—to imitate sleek, furry ermine toques. Now, standing at the entrace to the dining room, Zica surveyed the dancing couples, and smiled a "No, thank you" to a young man in uniform. She felt a little heartsick, because, yet again, no one had captured her fancy.

I must be the most difficult woman to sweep off her feet, she decided, contemplating the intriguing uniforms floating through the room. There were the military officers—who weren't permitted to dress in civilian clothes anywhere—and the cadets. Then there were the gymnasium boys in their gala outfits, and the university "men," each school defined by its own uniform. Those who were seeking a degree in the arts and sciences were in navy blue with gold buttons, stiff high collars and gold-trimmed cuffs. The law students were in emerald green, with silver embroidery. The pages were in royal blue with collars and cuffs of deep crimson, trimmed with gold, with two large bands of gold embroidery down both sides of their tunics.

Zica noted fewer tuxedos than uniforms. She couldn't help but think of the tuxedoed men as black dots in the midst of colorful costumes and ball gowns. The cavalry officers sported tall black boots of the finest leather, and kept their spurs on for the mazurka, when they would click their heels together with suggestive bravado.

All at once, Zica's mother called a temporary stop to the dancing. It was past midnight. Fifty couples formed a line and filed into the dining room, which had been set up with many tiny tables.

Zica searched for her brother. She wanted to go in with him. But she saw that he had already given his arm to a Baroness de Gunzburg, who was here from St. Petersburg visiting her aunt. Zica sighed.

Her parents were standing by the door, jovially handing out fake ermine toques, with a toy flute or a trumpet, to the ladies and gentlemen as they filed in. There was a lot of laughter, and raucous tooting of the horns. Suddenly, she was startled by a hand on her arm.

"Zeinab Lazarevna, let me take you in to supper." The young man who spoke was tall and rather distinguished. He sported the uniform of a law student, green with silver trim. Zica couldn't remember who he was, but she quickly took note of his thick dark hair, his thin, long nose, and his dark eyes. *Another Jewish bird, though not bad looking*, she thought—but she also knew that Jewish birds, though reminiscent of her own father, were of no great appeal to her.

"My name is Misha Kira," the young man said, giving her his arm. "Mikhail Aronovitch Kira. We met at Madame Cahn's reception two weeks ago. I thought you were the loveliest woman there."

"Thank you," she answered as they took their place behind another couple. She wondered how she would keep herself amused at supper. Misha Kira was exactly the sort of man her parents wanted her to marry—a prosperous, respectful, nice-looking young Jewish boy. But he didn't interest her at all.

Glancing over her shoulder, she saw that the servants were airing out the ballroom behind her. Ten minutes of open windows would do the trick; for outside, the temperature was twelve degrees Fahrenheit. Zica allowed her escort to find her a place at the choicest table in the room—the one with the most beautiful young girls and men in the most dashing uniforms. With a smile, Zica started to chat with the girl across the table from her. When Misha Kira brought her food and champagne, she thanked him—and she pretended to listen politely to his prattle. Was she fated to marry a man like him? She would prefer to stay with her parents, she thought, than to get married to a man for whom she did not feel the slightest tug of attraction. Poor Misha Kira!

After supper, the guests flooded back into the ballroom. With the benefit of the airing, it was once again pleasant and cool. The time had come for the servants to pass around the little velvet cushion. Zica drew the name "Laura." But *who was Laura?* she asked herself. When she questioned her brother, he informed her—one eyebrow cocked in amusement—that Laura was the poet Petrarch's beloved. Zica felt the weight of her ignorance; once again, Zhenya had

proved to her that he was superior and that she was still an uneducated schoolgirl. She knew nothing about this Petrarch, who was
now about to claim her.

Still, he was a poet. Zica liked Lermontov and Pushkin. Those
were romantic poets she could understand. And, of course, she
liked the sonnets of William Shakespeare's, which she had read with
her English tutor. So she had drawn a poet, albeit an unknown one:
this was a good sign, she thought.

The cavalry officer who handed her his card, with the name "Petrarch" scrawled upon it in Zhenya's bold script, was tall, muscular,
and elegant. He swept her to the dance floor for the mazurka. For a
moment, her head spun. Then, charmingly, all the male dancers
placed one knee on the ground while the ladies held the tips of their
fingers and twirled around them. Suddenly, Zica realized that her
skirt was caught beneath Petrarch's boot. To her dismay, she heard
the silk tear. She kept on dancing—to have stopped in the middle of
this figure would have been a breach of manners. When she had
finished twirling and Petrarch rose to resume the dance, she saw,
through a haze of tears, that her train had completely unravelled.

"I'm so sorry, Zeinab Lazarevna," her partner said, leading her to
a small sofa in back of the room. "Will you ever forgive me for such
clumsiness?"

"There is nothing for which to forgive you," Zica replied politely. But now the embarrassed young man no longer seemed distinguished to her. Zica saw only that his nose was shining and there
were coarse spots of color on his cheekbones. "But you shall have
to excuse *me*."

Without so much as a backward glance, she slipped out of the
ballroom, holding the ruined piece of material in her hand. Though
sad that her dress was destroyed, she was nevertheless relieved that
she would not have to spend the rest of the night dancing with one
buffoon after another. She would have to beg her mother and father
not to give two balls the following winter: one would be quite
sufficient!

Outside, Zica paused for a moment, listening to the lively mazurka music; then she ran lightly up the stairs to her mother's reading room, closing the door carefully behind her. Near her secretary,
Elizaveta Borisovna had placed the magazines and tabloids that arrived every week from France: *Le Matin*, *Le Journal*, *Le Temps*.
Zica's favorite, *L'Illustration*, had charades and enigmas to be solved
—word games that Zica liked to play with her father, who always

resolved them because he was so clever. Glancing at the German *Woche* and all the Russian newspapers, she ignored them and, instead, walked resolutely to the bookcase. The case was filled with shelf upon shelf of "yellow novels," the kind that were sold in France for three francs fifty. Her mother had read them all. She ordered them by the crateful. Zica often liked to sneak in and read, losing herself in the trials and tribulations of the imaginary heroines.

Tonight, she would read about Maryse and her lover Paul. Seating herself in her mother's wing chair, Zica let her dancing slippers fall to the floor. She tucked her feet comfortably beneath her. In the distant ballroom below, music was playing and couples were dancing; but she had ceased to care. Maryse and Paul would keep her company for the rest of the night.

What did it matter that her father was always remonstrating with her? He wanted her to become interested in serious things. She didn't care if she never read another word of Dostoyevsky, or of Gogol. She didn't like George Sand. Her tastes, as Zhenya had been known to remark, were decidedly childish. She cared nothing for the serious music of which he was so fond—Bach, Purcell, Telemann. She liked the dramatic music of Mozart and the easy listening music of Beethoven. She liked to watch *The Nutcracker* at the ballet, and not Isadora, whose barefoot rebellion left her scratching her head in perplexity.

If I can't find Prince Charming, Zica thought, settling down with her book, let them leave me to my own devices. They can at least leave me in peace!

But she closed her eyes, and for one marvelous moment, imagined the man of her dreams. He would be blond, with wide light eyes—blue, green, hazel perhaps; he would have white teeth and a perfect nose, a small chin and broad shoulders. His height? It hardly seemed important. But he would have to be muscular and lean, and his voice would have to ring out melodically, trilling the Russian language like a sensuous song. His French, she decided, would be dry, humorous, somewhat mocking.

Somewhere in the world, this man existed. One day he would find her, claim her, and whisk her away. She just knew he would.

As Kyril looked up at the tall, narrow brick house, he swallowed hard. Raising his hand to the knocker, he waited with pounding heart. He patted his fine golden hair nervously. If I can be here, he thought, then it means that I have truly outgrown my days of being the little chicken. *Perhaps, after all, I am not a coward.*

More than anything in the world, the seventeen-year-old boy wanted this: *not to be a coward.* Contemplating the desolate landscape of his childhood, he began to reexperience, deep within his bones, his own pervasive fear—a fear that had existed within him as far back as he could recall. He'd been afraid of everything, of everyone —but most of all, fearful of the father who bullied and oppressed him. His classmates, too, had treated him unfairly, singling him out for punishment. Kyril had grown up believing that he had little power of his own—that other people could do what they pleased with him.

But lately, in his final year at the gymnasium, he had become aware that he was not so entirely powerless anymore. He had begun to catch a look in other people's eyes—especially women's. They all but blinked with amazement when they saw him. He observed that other boys—taller and stronger boys—were always jealous of the attention he got. Their faces became ugly as they smirked, "Little gentleman! Ladies' man!"

He received their taunts with mixed emotions. They knew that he was better looking and, therefore, *more powerful.* And as a result, they tried to be hurtful. For, Kyril realized, *power was everything.* It defined who you were, what you became, how much money you acquired. It meant being respected and revered. It meant the difference between being someone of value and being tossed aside and ground into the dirt. Power, which always seemed so mercurial, had to be pursued at whatever cost.

He had acquired some measure of power through his beauty, because he knew that he was unusually handsome. His body was compact, like that of a boxer. In fact, he had forced himself to study boxing in order to overcome accusations that he was a weakling— the "little chicken" of the neighborhood. He had shot up quickly, and now he was tall for his age. But his face, though handsome, held surprising qualities. The features were slightly asymmetrical, the large, sculptured, elegant nose somewhat twisted from a childhood wrestling match. But the effect of his appearance was striking. He seemed an exotic creature, half-man, half-girl, his skin so clear it was actually perfect, his eyes translucent, almond-shaped and hypnotic.

Sometimes the others teased him and called him *devochka*—little girl. His father too had called him that. And he honestly understood why. There was a female side to his good looks which made girls identify with him. They compared his eyelashes to theirs: his golden hair to their fine, blond curls. His tastes were also those of a girl: he preferred to stay indoors and paint, or read quietly. Yet it pained him that he was this way. He would have preferred to be a man's man, like his father—to play cards and drink vodka and have many mistresses. At seventeen, he had yet to have his first sexual experience. He was afraid—afraid the girl would find him disappointing and laugh at him.

"Why would you want to be like *your father?*" his mother had upbraided him.

It was the day after the funeral. Till then, Kyril had held back his grief—but suddenly he was sobbing. His father—the one who had caused such terror when alive—had left a gaping hole in Kyril's life. He felt as if something he'd never really owned had been torn away from him. That his father had killed himself—hanged himself with his own hand—was a source of infinite desolation.

"He's brought us to ruin!" Elena cried bitterly.

Yet Kyril had caught the flicker of anguish in his mother's voice. Even at this late date, she had not succeeded in extinguishing her love. And he had replied: "Father made people take notice of him."

She had given him a malevolent look, as if to say: Your words are a betrayal. How could you regret such a man? But, in fact, he had felt anything but regret. Once the tears were over—the loss recognized—Kyril had felt relief, waves and waves of relief washing over his soul, releasing him, letting his dignity emerge, allowing his humanity its space in the sun. And so he had finally said, hesitantly: "Mama, I'm glad he's gone. He was the worst person in the world —he hurt us both continually, and now we can both begin to live."

But he could not explain to her that he also felt *envy*—sheer, unadulterated envy—for Victor had been a vital, strong, compelling man.

But he couldn't have explained these feelings to his mother. Elena was too angry, too hurt, too frightened. She was self-involved, churning with bitterness because Victor had abandoned her. She was left to deal, God-knew-how, with the mess of his unaccountable debts. Victor had left her in disgrace and fear; he had also, quite simply, *left her.* He hadn't trusted her enough to confide in her and ask her for her help, nor loved her enough to consider staying alive to be with her. His mother felt rage, but also a sense of loss. Neither was mutually exclusive, Kyril realized. In fact, they were so tightly intertwined that he could only distinguish the shadows of mingled grief and rage.

His own feelings were simple, really: he had always wished for Victor's death. True, he had mourned the loss: he had felt the desolation. Yet his own life would be easier with his father dead. By hanging himself in the attic, Victor had freed his son's soul.

Kyril knew about his father's womanizing and it bothered him. The boy loved girls—their charm and their beauty—but he could not see himself chasing after them. Then again, he hadn't met many girls, only the prostitutes on street corners with their garlic breath, and the shopgirls with their vapid smiles and badly pressed clothes. He never went to parties and cotillions, because his parents had no friends. His father's only cohorts had been the men from the Black Hundred whom Elena refused to receive in her home. The Ostrovs were virtual pariahs, excluded from the circle of Elena's childhood friends. Kyril, unlike the other boys at his gymnasium, belonged neither to the Jews nor to Cossack society. He had never been invited anywhere, in spite of his good looks and pleasant manners.

He sometimes dreamed of courting a beautiful girl, of showing her off to his classmates. He imagined a perfect partner, with rounded hips, a slim waist, and full breasts. He never thought beyond, to what he would do if he were alone with her. *Wouldn't they laugh at him if he couldn't measure up to her expectations?* He wanted a girlfriend but he was afraid. In this domain at least, his father had bested him. Victor had been a winner in the sexual arena . . . where his son had never even sought to compete.

Now that he is gone, I can try whatever I want, the young man thought fiercely. *Now that he is gone, I can see whether the girls will go for me . . .*

But for now he stood on the threshold of the Byitch residence, his grandfather's elegant house.

A new life was about to begin—if his grandfather would have him. It was the ultimate test of courage, for if he failed, there were few alternatives for Kyril. Who would he find on the other side of the door, inside the brick house? Kyril could feel the lump of apprehension growing in his throat. He willed himself to be strong. He had come on a mission of courage, and he wasn't going to back down now.

The massive oak door swung open, revealing a bent old woman dressed in black, sporting a white apron and a ridiculous starched white cap. Her shrivelled face was like a ripened olive. Little raisin eyes squinted up at him. "Who are you? What do you want?" she demanded.

Kyril took a deep breath. "Good day, Madame. My name is Kyril Victorevitch Ostrov, and I have come to speak to my grandfather."

The old woman uttered a dry, crackling sound. "Your grandfather? And who might *that* be?" Her voice was rude. Yet Kyril was certain he had come to the right address.

"Is this the residence of Yossif and Olga Byitch?"

The old crone stepped back, motioning for him to enter. "Didn't know Yossif Adolfovitch *had* a grandson," she mumbled. The foyer was dark and smelled of mothballs. High walls were hung with antique tapestries depicting knights, castles, and maidens. "You wait here," she told him curtly, turning her back on him.

Left to himself, Kyril looked around. Glass cabinets, displaying porcelain dishes and figurines, took up the space between the tapestries. In the far corner stood a mahogany costumer with outstretched arms, loaded down with hats and umbrellas. He couldn't help shivering. Had he made the right decision, coming here? Probably not—but it was too late to retreat now. An elderly gentleman in a maroon velvet dinner jacket was entering the hall. His oval face was trimmed with a white beard and mustache. His fine brows were etched in a mask of bewilderment.

The old man was shorter than Kyril, and thin—frail, almost, with translucent skin like ancient parchment. His hair was thin and white, and a silk yarmulke sat atop his finely boned head. He had large blue eyes like Elena's, an aristocratic nose, and thin, bloodless lips. His face suggested refinement and vulnerability.

"Who are you, young man?" The old gentleman's voice quivered slightly. Its tone was courteous, though devoid of emotion.

Kyril gulped down his nervousness. "If you are Yossif Adolfovitch, then I am your grandson, Kyril Ostrov."

The old man stepped back a pace and stared levelly at the handsome young man.

After a moment he nodded. "You look like her," he murmured. "You don't have her coloring, but your face has the cast of her features."

"May I come in and speak with you?" Kyril asked.

The old man suddenly appeared confused. "Yes, yes, of course. Follow me. . . . " He showed the way into a drawing room as dark and gloomy as the foyer. Velvet drapery, dripping ornate tassels, hung at the shuttered windows. Kyril wondered how his mother could have lived in this mausoleum all the years of her youth. All at once he understood how she had come to fall in love with the lusty, joking Victor—the bawdy Cossack who, for certain, had made her laugh. Kyril's father had brought the fresh air of the Caucasian Steppe into Elena's entombed existence.

Seating himself on a brocade sofa, Kyril's grandfather made an elegant gesture, indicating that Kyril should take a seat opposite him in an upright Louis XVI chair. When Kyril was seated, the old man leaned forward and asked softly: "Why did you come, Kyril? Why have you chosen to intrude upon my life, Kyril Ostrov?"

"Because my mother and I need your help, Grandfather. My father—"

"—has hanged himself," Yossif finished curtly. "I had heard this, yes."

Kyril opened his mouth to protest, but could not reply. The watery pale eyes stared at him relentlessly. "But, if you knew," Kyril burst out, "how could you have stayed away? My mother needed you!"

"Once, long ago, my headstrong daughter made a decision," the old man sighed. "It was, of course, the wrong decision. Elena was proud, and she refused to listen. I knew at once that the man she had chosen would cause her nothing but grief and shame. And, as you know, I was correct in my prediction."

Horrified, Kyril stood up, upsetting a small crystal vase on the low table before him. "So you have sat here all these years, gloating about how right you were, while my father continued to abuse my mother—and me? I'm sorry I came. I thought you were our flesh and blood. I thought perhaps it had all been a misunderstanding! But it was nothing of the kind! You were simply too complacent to reach out to your own daughter. You're not human! How can you pretend to care for anyone?"

The old man smiled. But his smile was tired, not warm. "You are a firebrand, like your mother," was all he replied. He contemplated Kyril a moment. "Sit down, my young friend. You know nothing of life, and can comprehend *less* than nothing."

Kyril's mouth had tightened into an ugly line, but he did as he was told. "Explain it to me then, *Grandfather!*" His voice dripped sarcasm.

"Elena broke our hearts. To us, religion was important. She broke a tradition that had kept our family alive for generations. Her defiance was harsh and cruel. Had she married a fine, upstanding man, we would have forgiven her this act of impulsive ignorance. We would have come to her, and partaken of her existence. This, however, she failed to do. She chose an ignoramus, a wife-beater, and a gambler. She chose a flagrant anti-Semite, a member of the Black Hundred—an abomination of a human being if there ever was one. I could not bear to be witness to what would occur. I knew that he would betray her, and then, eventually, he would bring her to ruin. This was her choice—but it was my choice to close my eyes to so much waste. So much unnecessary agony and pain—she brought it on herself!"

"Why did you never make the effort to know me?" Kyril demanded. "I had nothing to do with what my parents did!"

"Had I met you even once, my boy, I would have loved you. And I could not afford to love the son of a man I so profoundly despised. Tell me, my wise young friend . . . what could I have done to protect you against Victor Ostrov? Given to choose between us, as she was once asked to do when she was eighteen, Elena would have sided against me as she did the first time. I would have remained a powerless bystander, a grandfather with his heart in his hand, rejected and sent away. You would have won nothing by my interference—and I would have come home with a heart more profoundly shattered than before."

Kyril shook his head, unable to think of a proper answer. His throat was so tight it hurt. He pressed his eyes shut, hoping no tears would come to embarrass him. For a full minute, he remained this way. Then he felt something soft and light, like a bird's silk wing, come to rest on his shoulder. "Cry, cry, my boy," the old man said, patting his shoulder. "We have all shed many tears in this household."

But Kyril knew that if he cried, he would be relinquishing his power. This would not do. He needed to hold onto it, didn't he? He needed to set things right. Rising, he met the old man's gaze, dry-eyed. His voice only barely shaking, he asked: "So you will come? You will mend relations with Mama, and forgive her? You will let us come home to you here?"

His grandfather abruptly turned away. "This I cannot do," he murmured. "This I cannot do . . ." He shook his head. "Your mother didn't think of what she was doing to us." His voice was barely a whisper. "She thought only of her pleasure, and of her lust for this young man. But you see, Kyril, we were more fragile. Your grandmother never survived the shock of Elena's elopement. She died, three months later, of a heart attack."

"Mama never told me," Kyril said, catching his breath. "I had no idea..."

"There are many things, I'm sure, that you were never told," the old man remarked, sarcastically. Then his tone became serious again: "I do not have the strength to begin a new life. I cannot involve myself with you and your mother. You will have to forgive me, Kyril. I am full of years, and full of sadness. My hope had always been to end my days with Olga at my side—but God and Elena contrived to thwart this wish. What I can promise is that I will provide for your education. You must pick a profession, my boy, and you must pick it soon, before I am dead and can no longer be of use to you. When you have decided, send me a note to let me know of your choice. I shall be glad to send you to university, or to medical school, or to law school—whatever you elect."

"But... you will not see me again?"

Yossif Adolfovitch Byitch took a long look at his young blond grandson, and shook his head. "If I take you into my life, you will bring back the past. You will stir up memories of Lena and Olga. I'm not strong enough to face these memories in my old age. I have made my peace with my loneliness, and this is how I wish to greet death when it comes to me. Some day, Kyril, you will understand."

The young man turned away, tears blurring his vision. "I shall never understand," he declared. "Never, so long as I live! And neither shall my mother."

"Ah, but she will, she will..." the old man countered. "Because she owes me such a final understanding." And with that, he walked out of the room, leaving Kyril with his grief.

He had come on a mission, and he had failed.

Yet he *had* come away with something, hadn't he? For now he had his chance at a profession. At least there was that hope to cling to.

Zica hadn't wanted to visit her Aunt Anna Aschkenasy, her father's younger sister. She didn't much like Odessa, where Aunt Aniuta lived. For that matter, she didn't like Aniuta. She had never met her cousins Sonia and Siegfried, but her mother's words had prepared her for the worst. Zica's mother had exhorted her to be kindhearted to these two poor children. Given the eccentric behavior of their grandfather, old Yitzhak Aschkenasy, it appeared they had their own crosses to bear.

The Aschkenasy mansion was large and beautiful. It was located on the very tip of the Boulevard, the long, straight thoroughfare which was Odessa's principal avenue. On one side of the avenue stood the city's most elegant homes; on the other, a sidewalk bordered by tall, stately trees, protected by a stone parapet. Below stretched a public park, devoid of trees, and then the sea. There was a port, but it could not be seen from the homes on the Boulevard.

The Aschkenasys had long been the most prominent Jewish family of Odessa. Aniuta's mansion was long and wide. Four stories high, its proportions were grand. Its impressive granite facade was decorated with cherubs, lutes and horns. On the first floor were the reception rooms. The old man, Yitzhak, Uncle Ossip's father, occupied the second floor. When Aniuta had married Ossip, the young couple had been given spacious apartments on the third. And their children lived above them, adjacent to the servants' quarters.

As a young bride, Aniuta, accustomed to the luxury of the Poliakovs, had been horrified. Soon after her arrival, she had discovered that old Yitzhak and his only son had been living in virtual penury, dining off cheap crockery. The simple Jewish fare was prepared by servants who knew nothing of culinary art. Obviously, no woman had exercised her influence over the household for many years. No gracious touches could be noted anywhere.

But the young wife had brought an extensive trousseau. She at once set about refurbishing the house, beginning with linens and housewares. Curtains went up on the bare windows. She fired the old Jewish servants and hired Europeans. She planned elaborate menus, ordered dishes from Sèvres in France. The best silversmith in town made a tea set for her guests. Her father-in-law was so appalled that he took to his bed. Hadn't life been pleasant enough till the arrival of this arrogant young Baroness from Moscow?

Aniuta was ashamed of him. Every day he would come down to the drawing room to see his children, dressed in a stained, tattered, fifteen-year-old suit—the only suit in his wardrobe. Behind his back, she ordered him a new suit. She paid twelve rubles and convinced him to wear it by telling him she had paid only three to a peddler. But, a month later, Yitzhak began to reappear in his original threadbare costume. When Aniuta asked why he was not wearing his new suit, the old man scratched his head and grinned, pleased with himself.

"I'm a good businessman, my little dove," he informed her, preening. "What did I need with *two* good suits? You paid three rubles for the other, and so I sold it for five to a clothing salesman last week. See what a clever deal I made?"

These stories had been bruited about the Poliakov household in Moscow for a good many years. Aunt Aniuta had two children— Sofia, whom they called "Sonia," and little Siegfried "Sigi," whom she had named after the Wagnerian hero of the *Niebelungen*. Both children were younger than Zhenya and Zica; they had never been taken to Moscow to meet their cousins.

Aunt Aniuta was a short woman with a small, upturned nose. Her foreshortened upper lip allowed her front teeth to show. Steel- blue eyes were sunk beneath heavy brows. But her blond hair and pink complexion, combined with her ability to dance and charm society, had made her one of Odessa's leading ladies. She was the founder and directress of several fund-raising organizations and benefits. In her home, her guests encountered opulence. Aniuta sur- rounded herself with the same style she had known during her Mos- cow youth, controlling her husband through intelligence and perseverance. Even the old man, Yitzhak Aschkenasy, had been forced to submit to the sheer strength of her will.

Zica, like her mother, found her aunt dry and head-strong, a stubborn woman who brooked no contradiction and even less criti- cism. The only realm in which she had surprised her relatives had been that of child-rearing.

"My son and daughter are intelligent," she had said to Lifa Polia- kova, her sister-in-law. "They will see for themselves how one must behave in society. We are rich, and therefore they must have whatever they desire. For I believe that by denying one's own flesh and blood, one causes them unnecessary pain."

And so, when Aniuta invited Zica to visit during the spring of 1913, the young girl felt a measure of apprehension. Sonia was six- teen years old, her brother Sigi thirteen. What would they be like . . . indulged in such unrestrained fashion since their earliest youth?

To make matters worse, Zica would have to travel alone to Odessa. She could no longer rely on Zhenya's company, for the latter was now a man of twenty-one, working at the family offices. He was already helping to run the business; furthermore, he had recently become engaged to that Gunzburg Baroness from Peters- burg, the one who had been visiting her aunt the previous winter. They had met at the Poliakov ball. Now Zhenya would be getting married, probably even moving to Petersburg. Zica felt as if she had lost him . . . and suddenly, life seemed peculiarly empty.

The young girl was put on the train in Moscow, with recommen- dations to be patient and kindhearted to her cousins. She had hidden some of her mother's French "yellow novels" in her travelling case, and read them as the train chugged its way southwest. All the time, she dreamed of the young blond prince who was going to sweep her off her feet and into his arms—perhaps in Odessa? Her Aunt Aniuta had promised to take good care of her—to introduce her to the choicest society.

But, after all, Zica reflected, she was a Muscovite, *accustomed* to meeting "the best." How, then, would a provincial city have anything better to offer her? My only hope is Petersburg, Zica thought —or, possibly, Paris, London, Rome...

Thoughts of Petersburg reminded her of Zhenya's fiancée. Vera Alexandrovna de Gunzburg was small, with white skin, blue eyes, and black hair. She came from a powerful Jewish family, likewise ennobled in the previous century by the Tzars and some foreign powers. Vera's father was a banker in Petersburg. Zhenya had been lucky: he'd found his ideal woman, and they had fallen in love. But the fact was, there were many more attractive Jewish girls than there were young men: Vera's brother Fedya, for example, had a beaked nose and hunched his shoulders when he walked. He looked like what he was—a prematurely wizened banker.

The conductor entered her compartment to announce "Odessa!" Zica slipped into her sable coat and stood by the window, peering out. With a screeching of the wheels, the train slowed. Zica waited for the attendants to bring out her baggage. She tipped them and stepped from the train to the cold pavement. Her eyes scanned the crowd for her Aunt Aniuta. But only strangers milled about the terminal, well-dressed matrons kissing men in fur coats, family members greeting one another, liveried porters loading and unloading luggage from the train onto little carts.

"Baroness Poliakova...?" It was a male voice. Zica was momentarily startled. Who would know her here? She turned, blinking. The person who had addressed her was a slight young man with black curly hair and a lively expression in his coal-black eyes. His features were small and sharp. He appeared to be about her age, eighteen or twenty. He twirled a cap in his hand, nervously fingering its band.

"And who are *you*?" she asked pleasantly. "Has my aunt sent you to pick me up?"

"Indeed she has, Baroness. The landau is outside, and the porter has already placed your suitcases in it. I wasn't sure I'd recognize you..."

Her eyebrows shot up, amused. "Oh? Had we ever met?"

"At your summer estate, in Rigevka, some years ago. Eight to be exact . . . We were children then, and our *reb* had brought me out for an audition with your father. I . . . I played the violin, and you listened with your brother. Do you by chance remember the occasion?"

Zica smiled. "I'm afraid not. Papa used to bring a lot of people home in those days. . . ." She hesitated, afraid she'd hurt his feelings. "I'm sorry if I can't recall the time you came. What's your name?" she asked.

The young man blushed. "Yakov. Yakov Lvovitch Pokhis. My parents"—and now he cast his eyes aside in embarrassment—"my parents work for your aunt and uncle."

"Well then, Yakov," the young woman said, shivering slightly and hugging herself in her fur coat: "Let us get to the carriage, shall we? Meanwhile, you can tell me more about your parents. Is your father Uncle Ossip's secretary, or maybe his librarian . . . ?"

The young man's hands were clenched on the cardboard visor of his cap. "My father is Ossip Yitzhakovitch's *factotum*." He spit out the last word. "Papa is his driver. He also supervises the gardeners, and he is Anna Solomonovna's *maître d' hôtel*. On occasion, he grooms the horses as well, though he's had no training for this at all, coming as he does from a Jewish *shtetl* hardly renowned for its equestrian stables."

Zica couldn't help but flinch at the underlying bitterness of Yakov Pokhis's words. They left the terminal in silence. Yakov led the way, clearing a passage for her among the porters and passengers milling about the entryways. Deferentially, he opened the door of the landau and gave his hand to help her in.

As Zica sat down, rearranging her skirt over her boots, she looked down at him. For a moment their eyes met—hers serious, enquiring, friendly—his angry and ashamed. She hesitated, then lightly squeezed his hand in sympathy. Immediately she felt embarrassed at her own gesture.

He was the servant boy, she the niece of the lady of the house. Averting his eyes, Yakov quickly closed the door of the landau and hopped onto the driver's seat. His face was crimson.

She is even more beautiful than I had remembered, he was thinking. More beautiful—and wholly out of reach for someone like me. To her, I don't even exist. To her, I am like the carriage and the horses. She simply expects me to be there for service. I am the driver, that's all, and that's as it should be.

Still, it would be hard to pretend she was just another guest. Zeinab Lazarevna was still the little girl who had heard him play in Rigevka, her face rapt with attention. It would be difficult to forget the expression she had worn that day, eight years before. But clearly, she didn't even recall the episode!

He couldn't blame her. She was a baroness, after all, and he was the son of the *shtetl* peddler who happened to be a rich man's house servant on the Boulevard. Yakov's soul filled with loathing. Suddenly he hated himself and his father, loathed Ossip Aschkenasy and his bossy wife, Anna Solomonovna . . . loathed the two brats, Sofia Ossipovna and her brother Siegfried. But somehow, he could not hate the beautiful young woman in the back seat of the landau. She lay beyond the pale of his dismay, beyond anger and revolt. She simply existed, in all her grace and beauty, as did the moon, the stars, and the sun.

"Today, there are no adults around," Sonia declared. She was a pretty girl, with a slender figure, an oval face and gray eyes. Her dark hair was pulled into a Psyche knot. Glancing at Zica with a half-defiant expression, she suddenly grinned. "What say we eat this lunch with our fingers?"

Zica looked down into her plate of macaroni *à la Bolognese,* and frowned. "But . . ."

"Let's *do* it!" Sigi cried. He was a gawky, adenoidal child, just entering adolescence. Zica didn't like him at all. She didn't like his sudden outbursts nor his Indian whoops as he cavorted about the house. His mother, on the other hand, laughed and shook her head at him, fondly.

"I'd rather eat with a fork," Zica said softly. "It's much easier that way."

Her girl-cousin narrowed her gray eyes and stared at her. "As you wish," she stated indifferently. Then, licking her lips, she plunged both hands into the red sauce. They came up holding a bundle of macaroni. She plopped the macaroni into her mouth and grunted with pleasure. "It's even *better* this way," she explained. "Try it, Zica, and be a sport!"

Siegfried cut in malevolently: "Zica's not a sport, she's a *lady*— haven't you figured this out, Sonia? She won't slide down the banisters, she won't eat with her fingers, she won't sneak into the kitchen for a midnight snack! She isn't any fun at all! Is that how everyone behaves in Moscow, Zica?"

"Everyone my age," Zica replied.

"Well," Sonia declared, raising her brows and pursing her lips. "Since it's so important for you to act like a lady at all times, then I shall take you to see my trousseau. *That* should impress you! It's being assembled this very minute, in the sewing room. Mama ordered twelve dozen sheets, twelve dozen tablecloths, and twelve dozen sets of individual napkins—all hand embroidered. Would you like to see?"

"Yes, certainly," Zica replied, trying vainly to hide her shock. *One hundred forty-four sheets and tablecloths?* How excessive! She didn't know what to say. Dismayed, she wondered at the eccentricity of her Aunt Aniuta. Even in Moscow, she knew of no one with such extravagant pretensions.

"Ready?" Sonia demanded. Having cleaned her plate of macaroni, she was now licking her fingers. "I'll bet you've never seen such a trousseau!"

I'll bet I haven't, Zica thought, rising and wiping her lips with a small napkin. It was then her eye caught someone in the corner, dusting off a display shelf. Wasn't that Yakov, the young driver?

Sonia noticed Zica's glance. "Papa received a bronze statuette today from Paris," she said. "The boy was probably sent by Mama to put it away with the others..."

Loudly, she called out: "Yasha! Hasn't my mother asked you not to come in while we're having lunch? This is off grounds for you, boy, and you know it!"

Yakov stiffened. Zica blushed, acutely embarrassed by her cousin's remark. As Yakov nodded, she looked at him and smiled. He didn't smile back. Instead, he turned his head and moved away quickly.

"That was very harsh, Sonia," Zica chided. "He didn't mean any harm, and wasn't really disturbing anyone..."

The sixteen-year-old girl shrugged in annoyance. "He needed to be put in his place," she observed indifferently. "Now, Zica, wait until you see my pillowcases...!"

Overcome with shame, Zica pressed a hand against her mouth. He hadn't returned her friendly smile. Poor Yakov... What a terrible household! And he seemed like such a nice, polite young fellow, undeserving of Sonia's abuse.

Perhaps, she thought, she would discuss him with her father. Perhaps there was even an opening in their own household for Yakov Pokhis, who was so eager and smart. Yes, she would have to talk to her father! How she despised Sonia, Sigi, and all the Aschkenasys! They *deserved* to have a servant boy snatched from their household. At the Poliakovs', Zica knew, Elizaveta Borisovna and Lazar Solomonovitch would speak to him in gentle tones, as human being to human being.

Nobody deserved to be treated like chattel. Nobody deserved to be humiliated in public.

Zica couldn't remember meeting Yakov Pokhis in Rigevka—but she would take his word for it. She owed him this favor, then, as an old-time acquaintance. Sonia continued to prattle, but Zica was lost in her own thoughts: I wonder whether he still plays the violin, she mused. Perhaps I shall ask him next time—just so he doesn't think we are *all* boors in this family. . . .

When Yakov entered the kitchen, his face was set in grim lines. She had seen his discomfiture, witnessed his shame. He pounded his fist into his palm in frustration. He would have to avoid Zica during the remainder of her visit! *I shall never speak to her again,* he thought. The resolution smarted—but he felt proud.

It can't be helped, if I am a man . . .

Chapter IV

WOULD Kyril ever recover from his grandfather's rejection? Would Elena? And how would God, in his infinite mercy and wisdom, explain it away...?

He had been living in Moscow for just a few weeks now. He and his mother had taken up lodgings in a modest rooming house. Medical school had just begun. Six days a week, that fall, he rose early to walk to the white medical faculty. Surrounded by classmates, he sat in the anatomical theater for his first lecture. The faculty was near police headquarters, in the central part of the city. Kyril never failed to cast a rapid glance over his shoulder whenever he walked by the police building. No Jew in Russia, he was sure, ever passed near a police station without feeling a sudden jolt of adrenaline: for it was known throughout the nation that pogroms were instigated by the Tzar's own police, on orders from "on high."

But Kyril felt relatively safe here in Moscow. His name was "Ostrov"—*island*—and connoted no religious adherence. He had never looked like a traditional Jew. In Rostov, his parents' history was widespread, but in Moscow he was a newcomer. No one knew anything about him, except what they saw—a bright young man, handsome and blond, with cheekbones and the nose of a native Russian. Thank *God,* he thought, for that.

He'd chosen medical school because... why not? A Jewish boy with excellent examination scores—all 5's and 5 pluses—could make the quota. And a Jewish man could practice medicine. Kyril didn't consider himself a Jew, and perhaps he'd escape the stigma: but what if he were not able to? He would need a profession, at least until his grandpa died.

True, his father had also been a doctor. But Kyril did not fault the profession. He would be a doctor totally unlike his father.

Kyril would have been content with his present situation, had it not been for the financial hardships. As he had promised, Yossif had sent a handsome sum of money to his grandson so that he could attend medical school. With this money, Kyril was supposed to live out the year as a student. He planned to eat in student bistros, dressing well but modestly. He knew it would be important not to overspend. That would aggravate the old man. Medical school took six years to complete, and Kyril wanted this relative luxury to continue. The problem had been Elena—she had insisted on coming along, and now he had to support his mother as well as himself on the stipend from his grandfather.

He wished he felt differently, but the honest truth was that Kyril didn't want his mother beside him. She fretted and worried. She waited up for him, beset him with indiscreet questions, and sometimes even went through his pockets. What was she looking for? He wasn't her husband; yet, in some ways, she treated him as though he were. Had her years with Victor been so terrible that the pattern was now irreversible? Had Elena lost her powers of rationality?

What did she suppose he was up to, that would be so terrible? There wasn't much he could afford to do. When he had sent a note to his grandfather, explaining that he felt an obligation not to leave his mother behind, another sum of money had arrived...but a much smaller one. Evidently, the old man wanted his daughter in Rostov, even though he steadfastly refused to see her. If the lad insisted on bringing his mother along—the old man seemed to be saying—he would have to suffer for his kindness.

In Moscow, Kyril had searched out the most inexpensive rooming house that would still be decent enough to accommodate his mother. For in some ways she was always the Princess, as in the Grimms' fairy tale about the princess and the pea: Elena could tell good gold from plated, a cheap reproduction of an antique from a better one, a designer gown from a dressmaker's copy. She saw, she catalogued, she passed judgment—and, most often, she discarded the person upon whom her ill judgment had fallen. Elena had set herself up as the arbiter of good taste, and this plus her mixed marriage was a deadly combination which had kept her from forming friendships all her life.

But Kyril had learned a good deal from her, he had to admit. He'd learned good from bad art, and he could distinguish Bach from Boccherini. Sissy pastimes, his father had called these pursuits. How Kyril still hated the man...!

If only I had money, the young man thought, suddenly angry. His grandfather dwelled all alone in his overcrowded mansion. But he would have to die before his daughter and grandson could truly enjoy life! Kyril now felt like one of the many whose main occupation was waiting for someone else to die. Yes, he was counting on the money.

Yet this realization didn't make him feel the least bit guilty. Yossif Adolfovitch Byitch had rejected his only daughter. In the recent past, he had rejected Kyril, too. If the old man died now, Kyril would not think of him as a sympathetic grandfather. The old man had allowed them both—him and his mother—to be continually abused by Victor, the madman. He had never stepped in to save them. If Elena was, today, a woman obsessed with her idle pretensions, it was because her own father had cruelly rejected her. The Jews are as bad as the Cossacks, her son thought bitterly: I'd like to leave them all behind. I'd like to rise and crush all those who have ever despised me.

But even in spite of his bitterness, Kyril did have hopes! He wanted to find the magic girl of his dreams . . . yet not too soon. He wanted to become a rich and famous surgeon . . . but not really. Another part of him wanted to be an artist in seclusion. He would have preferred a quiet old country home on an estate in the Crimea, with easels and paints and landscapes. But he would have to make do, instead, with his own reality. His grandfather had at least done what he had promised—a first, in Kyril's life. Victor had made it a point to laugh at every one of his own broken promises.

So Elena had fussed, and they'd moved in, and now it was September. He was eighteen and almost free. He had wanted to have one good suit made, something with which to go calling, should the occasion ever arise. His grandfather had thought this a fine idea, and sent him to the best tailor in Rostov. His grandfather wanted him to meet a beautiful, wealthy Jewish girl, a girl such as his mother had once been—to make amends for his own parenthood by bringing this girl home to marry. But Kyril didn't want a Jewish girl. He wanted an irreverent, funny, lewd tavern girl, someone to take into dark alleys to help him explore the seamy side of sex. He wanted someone who was not at all like his mother. In the meantime, he would humor his grandfather and have the suit made. He would even promise to drop off his calling card at the home of his grandparents' friends, the Vaizmans, who lived in Moscow and "knew everybody worth knowing."

But he hadn't been to see them yet, nor had he telephoned. Instead, he wore the suit on Sundays, when he had no school and could pretend to be a gentleman of leisure. He left Elena at home, telling her he was meeting friends from university. (As yet, he had kept too much to himself and had made no friends.) Then he would set forth exploring.

Moscow was an extraordinary city. Outside Red Square, he had visited the Cathedral of Vassili Blazhennyi. The monument was dedicated to Minin and Pozharski, who had saved the Kremlin and Moscow from the Polish siege of 1612, liberating Mikhail Romanov and the Boyars. Kyril had been fascinated by the round Lobnoye Myesto, where rebels, for centuries, had been publicly decapitated. He had wandered inside the Kremlin and meandered through the various churches and monasteries. Today, he was going to the Tretyakovka, on Lavushinsky Lane, where Pavel Mikhailovitch Tretyakov and his family had settled in 1851. This was now a renowned art gallery, specializing in the work of Russian national painters and sculptors.

It was there he saw her.

Illuminated by the sunlight pouring in from the glass roof, a young woman sat demurely in front of the large oil painting entitled *The Rider,* by K.P. Bryullov. She would have been just another pretty young woman, had she not so inexplicably resembled the small girl in the portrait looking up at the rider...

Art and life were blended. The little girl in the portrait was enchanting, with her soft, rounded face, full lips, huge dark eyes, and lush black hair. And the young woman gazing up at the picture, her face in rapture, was like that of the girl looking up at the rider!

The gazer was elegant, Kyril noted: her emerald-green suit was a fine silk, trimmed with bands of yellow. A high-necked, light green blouse reached all the way to her chin. Her closely fitted jacket came over her hips, hugging her snug waist and her slim arms. From the knee to the floor, her green skirt narrowed; black patent leather pumps peeked out beneath the yellow silk hem. A red velvet hat jauntily tilted back, waved its green plumes. Her silk handbag, edged with brass, was slipped upon her wrist with a small silk loop.

How was it, Kyril wondered, that such a young woman happened to be here alone in the museum on a Sunday afternoon? He had never seen such a gorgeous sight—a woman so fine, so richly dressed.

An image of the girl, naked, with full round breasts and that same enraptured expression, flashed through his mind. He blushed as he looked at her—realizing that, yes, he wanted to speak to her. But could he? She looked so removed, so terribly proper, surely words would fail him. Yet, upon closer scrutiny, he saw that she appeared totally captivated by the painting. She had come here to enjoy art, as had he. They shared something already. Wasn't this enough to make her approachable?

I don't have any money, he thought, almost as if his father had rebuked him aloud. The girl looks like an heiress, and a wealthy one. What makes you think she'd even answer you? the Victor inside of him kept taunting.

I am as good as any man, Kyril thought. Yet doubts overwhelmed him. And then she turned, saw him, and her lips parted, as though, *he, Kyril Ostrov,* had been a work of art upon which she had unexpectedly stumbled. He blushed a deeper red and wondered what was wrong: had he put on mismatched socks, or buttoned his jacket stupidly?

She has caught me gazing at her, he told himself. And now I must explain. I have to tell her I didn't mean to be rude to her.

She was blinking at him, her cheeks rosy, her eyes strangely moist. Clearing his throat, Kyril approached. "Mademoiselle," he began. "It's true, as you suspect, I *had* been watching you. It's because you bear such a striking resemblance to the small girl in the Bryullov painting. Did you notice it, too?"

She shook her head. Had he offended her? "Of course, you—you are more stylish than she. And a woman, of course," he continued lamely. His father, Victor, would have known exactly how to handle such a situation.

"You are very kind," the young woman said softly. Kyril looked for a ring on her finger, but she was wearing long kid gloves. Was she married or not? Large, square-cut emeralds gleamed at her ears. She smelled like a garden of exotic flowers—some sort of rich talcum powder, he presumed. "I was not angry," she added, "simply flattered. Please don't be embarrassed."

For a moment, Kyril had a mental image of his own appearance —the new suit: pearl-gray, single-breasted morning coat, sharply cut away, buttoned at his trim waist with two metal-gray buttons. The tails came down to the backs of his knees. He was wearing a white silk shirt with a stiff collar and a gray and white tie. A darker gray waistcoat, single-breasted as well, showed off his strong, large chest; and the striped trousers, tapering below the knees, revealed a pair of well-proportioned legs. A dove-gray, silk top hat completed the picture; this he was now holding in his gloved hands, having removed it when she'd looked at him.

He wanted to win her—he felt the magnetism of his own presence. Yet his mind kept playing tricks, and he thought, malevolently: What do I want with someone like that? She's too well brought up—her family would think me too poor, anyway. Why set myself up? Why even bother?

She was pretty and elegant. She was a *boyarynya* such as the wives of Tzar Peter's Boyars. How could she be attracted to Kyril? Yet, she had spoken to him.

"My name is Kyril Victorevitch Ostrov." He offered his outstretched hand. When she took it, he bowed over hers, hesitating. Married women received a light, imperceptible kiss. But by the way she spoke to him, he assumed she was obviously not married. Or was she?

"And I am Zeinab Lazarevna Poliakova."

This was a shock. She was *Jewish!* He knew the name "Poliakov," knew it from his grandfather, who had outlined for him the great Jewish families of Russia. Lazar Poliakov owned lands, mines, tramways—he owned everything! He was not a Boyar but a mighty important man nonetheless—not one to allow his daughter to speak to strangers.

But how would the pretty Zeinab learn that this stranger was almost penniless? Let her see what was before her eyes—an impeccably turned-out young man, with golden hair and green eyes. Kyril had enough in his pocket to afford a cup of hot chocolate. If his mother later complained, he would simply have to endure her grievances. He had found himself an heiress, with a melodious, cultured voice. How could his mother complain about *that?*

Kyril could see that this young woman found him handsome. Perhaps, then, that was how things went between a man and a woman. Was this what had created the foundation for his father's success? The approach of a young man, the responsive chord in the girl—perhaps that was all that was required, before two people threw themselves into each other's arms.

"Mademoiselle Poliakova," Kyril's voice sounded constricted. "Would you . . . could it be possible to invite you to accompany me to the Hôtel de l'Ours, for a small collation?"

She smiled. Perfect white teeth gleamed between full, pink lips, like rose petals offered for his testing. For a moment, she hesitated. Her eyes misting over, she looked aside, shyly. "It's not that I don't want to, Kyril Victorevitch—may I call you that? It's that my companion—my former governess—went to the powder room and will be back shortly. I cannot leave without her."

Ah... So this explained why she had seemed to be alone. But it presented Kyril with a new problem. He did not have the money to invite two ladies—and besides, the companion would crimp their style. But Zeinab Poliakova was looking up at him, expectantly. His heart turning over, Kyril took a deep breath. "I understand," he said. "I'm so sorry. Perhaps, then, another time?"

Breaking all taboos, Zeinab asked: "Will you call on me? Shall I give you my father's card, with the address? My mother's receiving day is Tuesday."

On Tuesday Kyril had anatomy, precepts of surgery, anesthesiology. Plus lab work. It was a full, busy, taxing day. But all that could be put aside. "Next Tuesday," he agreed.

She smiled. "Fine. I shall be expecting you."

She turned away, then paused. Her brow was knit with concern: "What do you *do,* Kyril Victorevitch? After all... my mother will want to know. Who are you?"

"I am a medical student from Rostov-on-the-Don," he replied. His green eyes were probing. "You have just invented me, and I like it that way. Make of me whatever you wish, Zeinab Lazarevna."

She colored, and bit her lower lip. "The only problem is..." but she didn't finish. He thought: Yes, she thinks I am not a Jew. And, because she is Poliakov's daughter, this perturbs her. Her papa will not approve. But I have come thus far, and I am not about to become Jewish again, just to amuse myself for a few Tuesdays. For what else will come of this, but amusement? She is Poliakov's daughter, and I...? I really know so little about who I am, or what I really want....

Yakov had never seen anything so breathtaking as Moscow. He knew it wasn't unusual in Russia to find a fortified city with a kremlin: the very word *"kreml"* meant "fortress," and many cities had their own. But this kremlin was of another world: its Oriental spires, cupolas, kiosques, and battlements were all crowded together. Their painted splendor touched him as though he'd been transported to a different time and space—to Byzantium in the Middle Ages.

Yet the Red Square, and the Moscow River, and the turreted,

red-brick Kremlin were most assuredly Russian, not Byzantine. The grandeur that belonged to his own country made a strong impression on the young man. He saw all about him evidence of the largesse of spirit—the excessive opulence of his people.

He liked to think of himself as a Russian, foremost: only secondly as a Jew. Being a Jew meant living in the Pale of Settlement; being a Russian meant Moscow, the decadent pull of its twisted, cobbled streets. It meant the awesome *Tzar Kolokol*—the huge bell which had cracked during Napoleon's invasion—and the *Tzar Pushka,* king of all cannon, largest in the world. As a Russian, he felt the pull of the churches and monasteries which beckoned to him from behind their own tinted towers, hinting of miracles and gilded icons. Being Jewish was what he *was;* being Russian meant *what he might become.*

Real Russians enjoyed privileges closed to most Jews. The only exceptions were those captains of industry, such as Baron Poliakov. Or the artistic geniuses, like Anton Rubinstein, the pianist and composer, or Auer, the violinist, who were praised and welcomed by Russians. Indeed, the roster of the Philharmonic displayed a disproportionate number of Jewish musicians. Yakov struggled with his violin because it represented his way out of serfdom—his own escape from being the "little Yid."

Yakov took lessons each afternoon at the Conservatory on Herzen Street, near the Kremlin. He would wend his way from the Poliakov mansion on Tverskaya Street to the music school, drinking in the luxurious atmosphere of the wealthy neighborhood. The twisted streets enchanted him. It was an adventure to imagine life behind the imposing facades of the palatial homes on every corner. Rather than feeling rebuffed—as one on the outside looking in—he felt energized. He felt impelled to push himself a step farther. He wanted to own one of those mansions. It *was* possible, wasn't it? A Poliakov had amassed fame and fortune—why not a Pokhis?

He was lonely, but that was all right. Loneliness gave him time to think, to dream of the other life that he so craved. When he wasn't practicing, he was on duty in the Poliakov household; this was a learning experience. He observed everything going on around him, cataloguing it for future use. Someday, he would own a house like that, and would entertain fine guests. When that happened, he would have to know how to eat, how to dress, and what to say. Of course, he'd have to become fluent in French. For this purpose, he had already found a mentor within the Poliakov household—Senya, the Baron's librarian.

It was September, and Yakov had already been here three months.

The previous spring, his father had announced that Baron Polia-kov himself, *shtadlan extraordinaire* among *shtadlanim,* had requested Yasha's presence in his Moscow residence. Yasha's father had paled when he made the announcement: it was hard to lose his son. Yasha was to go to Moscow and work for *him* in the Baron's household, as a *factotum,* "on call" for anything the great man happened to need. His mother had cried and moaned, not wanting him to go alone... but his father had suddenly straightened his bearing and glared at her. "The boy must go," he had announced. "The boy has a future, Bella. The Baron has seen him, and has not been able to forget him: think of it, Bella! *The Baron* has sent for our son—and you want to keep him here behind your apron-skirts...?"

Yakov had been a little sad to wave farewell to his parents. He noticed how bent and old they appeared, though neither was very old in years—not even sixty. But the marrow in their bones had thinned. Disillusionment coursed through their veins. Mama, with her kerchief, waving from the train station... and Papa, suddenly proud, rearing his basset-hound head and trying to smile, his jowls shaking. Their Yasha was leaving them! He poked his head out to catch a final glimpse of them. Peering out the window of the bag-gage compartment—the car in which he would be travelling to Moscow—Yakov's face was bright with expectation.

What matter that he would be travelling with the luggage, if his destination was Moscow?

Now Yakov felt a pang of desolation, and wondered if, perhaps, he had bitten off more than he could chew. Had it been a mistake to come here alone, knowing no one but the Baron, Zhenya, and... Zica, the exalted daughter? Living in the same house with her, he found Zica so close, at times, that he might have touched her. She always smiled at him so warmly, so sweetly—and then she would turn around and disappear with her friends or with her family. It would have been easier had she treated him like Sonia Aschkenasy, belittling him at all times. It would have been easier, then, to hate her, to distance himself from her in every way. But when he was near her, she endeared herself to him with each gentle gesture, and so, he loved her even more dearly.

She was as far from him as if she had been living on another planet. And yet, close enough to touch, to smell, to hear. It hurt him, because young men came calling and she laughed with them, and sat at the piano and played for them, and served them tea and cakes. And he had to repeat to himself that never—no matter how well he might succeed in his music—would he be anything more than a distant shadow, a servant in her father's house.

Yet he was eighteen—they were both eighteen—and he wanted her with a passion which surprised him. The strength of that passion awakened him from a deep sleep, rushing through his body as though it were a powerful elixir transforming him into someone new—all blood lust, strength, and yes—even violence. He wanted her so much! At the same time, he knew that he would have to forget her. She was inaccessible, for he was a servant and she was Zica Poliakova, a lady born and bred, the daughter of Moscow's foremost Jew.

Yet he knew within his heart, with a calm sureness, that he would never love anyone else. He would love her without expression, until the day when that part of him withered from attrition. One day that love would no longer exist, except as a faint murmur of remembrance. Love was a luxury to which he was never to be entitled. Those born poor but ambitious could not afford to yield to the maddening pull of its destructive temptations. Love was a vortex that drew you in and closed over you, drowning you forever, shutting you off from the means of achieving your goals.

It was his station in life—his poverty and lack of education—which would force the love to die, by preventing him from declaring his feelings. He foresaw that he would change his station and break all the rules, becoming famous and rich. But by then, it would be too late to claim Zica. She would be long gone, but he would, nevertheless, enter her world. He would surprise her! He would make everyone in her world take notice of the "little Yid" from Peredelkino.

In the beginning, the great man, Baron Poliakov, had gone about his business, hardly aware of Yakov at all; whenever he had run into the young man during the course of the day, he had nodded and smiled briefly, an air of abstraction on his birdlike face. *He barely recognizes me,* Yakov had thought, somewhat puzzled. But, if Baron Poliakov could hardly remember that he was there, *why had he specifically sent for Yakov?* This question troubled him.

Not that this issue distracted him. Yakov simply wanted to learn —to learn everything he could. He wanted to know more than how to behave in society, which simple observation could teach him. Coming from a cultural desert, he was now a member of the Poliakov household, where learning could be acquired without anyone's taking notice. He had studied his lessons well at *Reb* Meyer's *ye-*

shiva, and now he had the opportunity to learn even more. For Baron Poliakov possessed a library of over fifty thousand volumes.

On the second story of the white marble mansion were the reception rooms, the master bedroom, and Zica and Zhenya's bedrooms. Upstairs were the boudoir, what had once been the nursery, and a variety of smaller rooms. Under the eaves were the attic and servants' quarters. So far, nothing differed greatly from the houses of other lords of Moscow or St. Petersburg. But below, on the ground floor, was an enormous hallway with statuary and Persian carpets. Opening into this hallway were the Baron's immense, leather-panelled study; the waiting room; and five huge rooms filled with books. The bookshelves, hewn in solid oak, rose thirteen feet high. Each shelf was at least a yard in depth. It was a library that filled Yakov with wonder.

One day, some weeks after Yakov's arrival, three horse-drawn carts covered with tarpaulins pulled up at the service entrance. The young man went into the courtyard to witness the unveiling. Baron Poliakov had just purchased the entire library of philosopher Vladimir Soloviev, who had died without leaving direct heirs. Seeing Yakov nearby, Senya, the librarian, asked him to help unpack the books and classify them.

This Senya was an educated man, who could speak and read several languages. How Yakov envied him! Middle-aged and bent, he walked about with an expression of profound annoyance permanently etched on his features. But behind this expression walked a shy, lonely man. He was more than glad, in his off hours, to show Yakov the books he cherished. The Baron's books included ten thousand volumes on Jewish lore, in Hebrew. Nearby were books in French, Italian, Latin, Greek, English—even, Senya told him, books in Early English and Early French, very different from the languages spoken today. Of course, there were also the Russian books that Yakov *could* read. And so, at night, he would sneak out and take one to bed with him.

"I could teach you languages," Senya said, pleased with the eagerness of Yakov's quick, agile mind.

"I only want to learn French and English," he replied. "The others may be good to know, but will do *me* absolutely no good."

The old man's eyebrows rose quizzically. Here, then, was an ambitious young fellow interested in rising above his station. "Yasha," he sighed, "even if you learn everything there is to know, you have no money and no social standing. All the intelligence in the world will get you only as far as I have come—for I, too, was intelligent and persevering. But you need connections."

"I have my violin. This will get me noticed," Yakov replied.

The librarian shrugged. "Perhaps. But you don't love the instrument. If you did, you would rise to fortune...but it takes passion, my boy, and I've never seen it when you practice."

"Yet it's all I have."

And so they had formed an alliance: Senya and Yakov, poring over crumbling volumes and classifying them in order of subject, time period, language, and author. Yakov was learning. As the weeks lapsed into months, the older man grew to depend on his eager helpfulness, so that, when Sergei, the *maître d'hôtel*, requisitioned Yakov's services for some other task, Senya would miss him.

One day, Senya approached the Baron and asked if perhaps he might be allowed to have an official assistant. Lazar Solomonovitch nodded thoughtfully, saying: "Are you growing tired, Senya? In the twenty years since we have been together, I have always known you to guard the library jealously for yourself alone."

"Perhaps, sir, the time has come to recognize my age. And we've acquired so many new books, Baron..." He hesitated, then plunged ahead: "Actually, I have someone in mind. Young Yasha Pokhis."

The Baron frowned. "My sister's servant? But—he is completely unlearned! Before Odessa, he came from one of our *shtetls* in Podolia!"

"Yes, I realize that. But...he's been helping me these past few months, and I believe he is smart and eager to improve himself. I could teach him many things. Indeed, I already have. The boy can say whole sentences in French—and that, without ever having studied. He has simply picked up phrases here and there, from me, from you, sir—from everyone—and has asked me to translate them for him. Now he can repeat them back to me and know what he's saying."

Soon after that, Yakov witnessed a change in Lazar Solomonovitch Poliakov. Now, whenever Yakov encountered him on the stairs, in the hallway, or by the coach house, the Baron would cock his head and scrutinize his *factotum*. Not in an arrogant, unpleasant fashion, like Sonia Aschkenasy—but with interest, as though intrigued. And he did assign him to Senya full time, almost in an apprentice role, permitting him to give up his other obligations in the household.

The Baron was also paying for Yakov's tuition at the Conservatory. He had turned one of his scholarships over to Yakov and had promptly forgotten all about it. Sometimes, Yakov wondered whether the famous *shtadlan* even recalled the first day they had met, when *Reb* Meyer had brought him to the Poliakovs' in Rigevka for an informal recital. It was clear that Zica had forgotten the event, as she had admitted in Odessa months before. But then, if Lazar Solomonovitch didn't remember... why had he transferred him from Anna Aschkenasy's household to his own? This puzzle remained unsolved.

Senya lived in a small apartment above the stables, and Yasha occupied an even smaller one above the carriage house. The servants' rooms, for the most part, were in the attic underneath the eaves of the main residence—but Yasha, because of his music, had been awarded greater privacy. The Baron did not want him to disturb the others when he practiced.

But the three small apartments that overlooked the courtyard were rented out to three young artists. Part of Senya's job was to collect the rent from these artists at the start of each month. He also heard many of their stories, which they told in a lively, dramatic manner. "Tell me that one again," he would say each time he came to collect the rent. And a tragic story would ensue, to which Yakov listened with interest. Human tales of woe and intrigue fascinated him; later, he would turn them into wry little anecdotes which he would write down and send to his parents, adding touches of black humor. He could almost hear his parents laughing and shaking their heads at the little commentaries he included.

Sometimes, the tenants would ask for repairs and embellishments. They would come to the main house to beg Senya to intercede on their behalf to the Baron. So Yakov came to know them. They would invite the librarian and his young assistant to their apartments, serve them a glass of tea or vodka, and plead their case.

The residents were two young men and a girl; the girl, whose name was Natalya Khazina, quite obviously had a crush on Yakov. He soon began calling her "Natasha," like her intimates, or "Natalya Vladimirovna," the name she used with her other acquaintances. She was older than Yakov, perhaps twenty-two, and her features were sharp, her hair jet black and her eyes large, deep-set, and rimmed with kohl. She powdered her face with cornstarch. Yakov had never seen anything like this. She wasn't Jewish. His mother would have wailed and beaten her breast, and his father would have taken him sternly aside and told him to stay away from such trash, had they known that Yakov was seeing her. This was not a girl to marry! But then, Yakov didn't plan on marrying her—he didn't even want to become involved. He simply hoped that she would teach him the ways of the world—how to behave as a man.

"Go on," Senya urged him, patting him on the back. "Invite her to your room and play a piece for her. Play her part of a Bach sonata, why don't you? She's a nice girl. What does it matter if she's late with the rent once in a while? Everybody is."

Shrugging, Yakov put on his best trousers and shirt and went to Natasha's small apartment, which was opposite his own. He felt very foolish. He didn't really *want* her to come back with him: what could he *do* with her? But she was always asking him about his music, and she wanted to hear him play. "I hear you sometimes across the courtyard, practicing," she'd tell him, narrowing those deep, dark eyes. She hypnotized him with those eyes. Sometimes she looked like a black panther slinking about, proud and sensual and nervous.

Natasha opened her door to Yakov, and stepped back to let him pass into her own apartment. "I wondered," he began, wetting his lips, "if you might like to hear me play this evening."

"Are you giving a recital, Yakov Lvovitch?" she demanded, almost sarcastically.

He felt his throat constrict, his mouth go dry. "No. I meant—I mean..."

"You were about to *practice?* Surely, I'll come. Just let me get a wrap." She smiled at him, those feline eyes narrowing in amusement. That day, she wore a simple woolen dress, with a scooped neck that revealed the tops of small but nicely rounded breasts. She had gold hoop earrings and gold bangles on her wrists. Grabbing a shawl from a chair, she hastened outside with Yakov, closing the door behind her. Once outside, she took his arm.

His small apartment consisted of one room plus a tiny closet-like area where he kept his violin and stand. With Natasha inside, the apartment looked even shabbier and smaller. Yakov was suddenly ashamed of the peeling wallpaper and the stains on the rust-colored bedspread that his mother had sent him from Odessa. "Please sit down," he told her. "Would you like something to drink? Tea?"

She shook her head, looking around. She picked up the violin, holding it gingerly. "This is beautiful." She caressed the wood. "Is it difficult to learn to play?"

"No more difficult than learning to draw," he replied, coming over to her. She was a student at the Institute of Painting, Sculpture, and Architecture. He smiled, and she nodded. She was a wry sort of girl, a little hard, not gentle and feminine like Zica. Yet there was something about her that was appealing. She had an air of knowing what everything was all about—sex, love, the arts, human beings. She came from the Crimea, and smelled of wheat stalks in the sun.

She stood back, and he took the instrument from her, suddenly awkward. It wouldn't do to begin to play now. He replaced the fiddle and turned toward the window, perspiration breaking out upon his brow. *Think, Yasha, think.*

All at once, he wheeled about and faced her, a twinkle in his eye. "What do I have in common with Jesus Christ?" he asked her.

"I don't know. . . . "

He laughed. "We both have Jewish mothers."

She smiled indulgently, her large, white teeth gleaming. "Do you always tell a lot of jokes when you invite women to your private quarters?"

Yakov blushed. "I've never had a woman up here before," he admitted. "You're the first."

Natasha shrugged lightly. "Well," she told him: "I don't know what to say. It's some kind of honor, I suppose. Why me?"

"I like you. You're easy to be with."

Neither spoke for a moment. "Aren't you going to play something for me?" she asked finally.

He shook his head. "I don't feel like it. Why don't we sit here and talk, instead?"

Natasha perched herself on the edge of the bed. "You're very smart," she remarked. "What a shame you're a Jew—how far you might have gone, otherwise! The other night, I was invited to the Moscow Art Theater to see *The Seagull.* Chekhov is wonderful, don't you think? I was reminded of you when I heard the actors. You'd make a good actor, Yakov Lvovitch. You're quick and funny—"

Tears sprang to his eyes, and Yakov blinked them down. Suddenly his life seemed to be going nowhere. He cleared his throat, and sat down beside her. The warmth of her presence, so close to him, was reassuring. "Yes, perhaps I could become an actor. Though that isn't really what I want, either. I just want to make people laugh. So they might forget their cares! But I don't want to be a mime—and I don't want to be a dramatic actor. I just don't see where I fit in—and this leaves me feeling empty inside."

She picked up his hand, and played with the fingers. She turned it palm-downward and reflectively traced the veins with her slim finger. She stared at him, her dark eyes unfathomable. "You must pursue your dream," she finally said. "Look at me: I may never be able to sell a painting, but I'm going to try, anyway, as long as I can last."

"But where would *I* try?"

She dropped his hand on the rust-colored coverlet. "Oh, my dear," she said, "I don't know that. In Paris, they have comedic acts, one-man shows in the theater. But here, these shows don't exist. Maybe you should get the Baron to take you to Paris with the household, the next trip he makes. Senya always goes."

"That's the trouble! If Senya goes, why would the Baron need *me?* The staff that travels abroad is always reduced to a minimum." Yakov's dark eyes probed hers, as he searched for answers he knew she would not be able to provide.

He had made much progress, from the *shtetl* to Odessa to Moscow. But to what purpose? He was still unknown and uncared for in this big city. His only friends were Senya and this girl—whom he barely knew.

"I don't know why I'm here," he suddenly admitted, his anguish cracking the surface of his composure. Could he hold back the tears that were springing to his eyes? "Why would the Baron have sent for me? He only met me once! It makes no sense! *Why am I here?*"

Natasha examined him with a measured glance of incredulity. "Haven't you ever asked Senya?" she asked.

"Senya? But what has *he* to do with this?"

She took a deep breath. "Senya is privy to everything," she observed. "He knows it's not the Baron who had you transferred here. I was certain you two had talked about it . . . that you knew."

Yakov stood up, his heart beating rapidly. "Knew *what,* Natalya Vladimirovna?"

Suddenly she looked away, pursing her lips. "It wasn't the Baron who sent for you at all." She paused, measuring her words. "It was the daughter—Zeinab Lazarevna. She's the one who's responsible."

Yakov's eyes widened in disbelief. But Natasha was angry now. She stood up, gathering her skirt in her hand. "Well, are you satisfied? I presume that's all you wanted to know from me! Well, I've told you: evidently, that *girl* was taken with you. She asked her father to have you brought from her aunt's household to this one."

"But . . . this is preposterous! Why would Zica have done this? Who am I to her?"

Natasha moved toward the door, her chin held high. "I really can't answer that." Her words were clipped. "But whatever it is, you made an impression. The Poliakovs can move mountains: why should they not also move people for their own motives?"

Yanking open the door, she stalked out. Yakov was left staring at the place where she'd been standing, shaking his head. *Zica* had sent for him, and he had believed that she hardly knew of his existence! Zica had gotten him here, under her own roof, all the way from Odessa. But . . . *why?* She had no passion for him. If she had, he would have felt it. She was cool and remote, even when she spoke kindly to him in passing. *What had possessed her* to bring him here?

And now he had blundered his way out of a tryst with Natasha. Somehow, he had vexed her. Women were strange creatures. He might actually have made love to her, had she expressed interest! He had wanted to, and then the conversation had suddenly taken a sentimental turn, making him feel vulnerable and pathetic. He hadn't intended to insult Natasha . . .

Now it was too late. He had lost his opportunity! Yakov was furious with himself. His fist banged into the wall, and he felt the anger bursting from within, bruising skin and bone. He had missed his opportunity with Natasha, who had been jealous of Zica. But there was no *reason* for jealousy. *Zica didn't love him.* How *could* she? Zica was a Baroness!

Yet, she *had* sent for him. Perhaps, after all, there was some hope. Perhaps she had fancied him in Odessa. Perhaps he and Natasha had not been meant to become lovers, even for one night. Perhaps . . .

Still, the futility remained. No matter how Yakov looked at the question, Zica and he remained an impossibility—as impossible as going to Paris to watch the comedians. Disheartened, Yakov closed his curtains and crawled into bed. All at once he was shivering with fear and loneliness. He missed his parents, he missed the *Reb,* he even missed the streets of Odessa. But he didn't miss Peredelkino: and if he possessed a single certainty, it was that he would never return there, under any circumstances.

Every Tuesday, the Poliakov servants prepared the house for the Baroness's receiving day. Customarily, upper-class ladies "received" one day each week; those whose day was the same had to be understanding of one another, expecting that mutual friends would be making the rounds. Nothing about this custom was official, but people knew that they would find the hostess at home that day, and that visitors were welcome.

At two in the afternoon, the tea table was set. It was common for visitors to drop in at any time until six. Most offices and institutions closed at four, and gentlemen had time to go home, change, and pay their respects to at least two hostesses before the end of the day. But, unlike the French custom—where a visitor remained ten minutes and was on his way—Russians liked to sit and talk, relishing this opportunity to visit with mutual acquaintances.

Among the topics that were constantly discussed were the arts, the University, goings-on at the Duma in St. Petersburg (where one irate member had thrown his inkwell at the speaker), the opening of a new flower shop, meetings, conferences, gossip, amusing anecdotes . . . the list continued. Conversation would take place all afternoon, enriched by the interaction of both sexes.

The custom was for the young man or woman of the house, the hostess's son or daughter, to ask friends to drop by for a visit on the mother's receiving day. Sometimes, ten or twelve young people would be gathered together. Frequently, they adjourned into a side room where they would roll up the carpet for dancing.

Zica enjoyed her mother's Tuesday afternoons when her friends dropped in to see her. Often, she would be surprised by the appearance of a new man, brought in by someone's older brother or fiancé. She always liked to flirt—the covert looks, the smiles, the invitations to concerts and balls and gallery openings—even when she wasn't sure she liked the men. She relished the spontaneous nature of these gatherings. But as she thought ahead to being married, she wondered if it wouldn't lead to boredom and endless monotony—always the same faces, the same laughter, the same sense of emptiness that she always felt in a room full of familiar people who were tiring of each other's presence.

At heart, Zica was terribly shy. She felt most comfortable alone, reading, away from society's stares. Yet it was telling, to anyone who heard her speak of it, that her favorite passage in literature was Natasha Rostova's introduction to the Moscow Opera in *War and Peace*. Zica had Natasha's sense of wonder. She was always asking herself what might happen next. So she welcomed social events at the same time that she dreaded them. For they might, perhaps, bring magic into her life.

It was a mild September. The morning of her mother's receiving day, Zica awakened with a thrill. She remembered that the mysterious man from the Tretyakovka had promised to come by. Ever since seeing him there, she had replayed the scene over and over in her mind, relishing every detail. She had never seen such a handsome man. Somewhere deep at the core of her body, she felt a glowing warmth as she remembered the gold-flecked green eyes, the fine-spun gold hair, the proud stance. He had said he would come. She had practically thrown the invitation at him, and he had accepted.

But a receiving afternoon was not considered a binding engagement. What if he didn't appear?

Men as handsome as that could find women at every turn. How easily he had addressed her, approaching her as though she'd been as accessible as a barmaid in a tavern, or a simple peasant girl in a village! He had not seemed awed by who she was.

Then she had doubts. Perhaps, on the contrary, he *had* been awed —and would not have the courage to come to the house.

He wasn't Jewish. He looked typically Russian, and his name did not give a clue to his background. Certainly, in *her* society, he was totally unknown. Rostov was a provincial city. This was not a man by whom her father would ever allow her to be courted.

Yet Zica dressed carefully, singing aloud as she looked through her closet. She picked out the new Oriental dress her mother had sent for, made by the Parisian *couturier* Paquin. It was a long silk sheath, turquoise and black, with pink designs and a narrow skirt. As Zica curled her hair to one side, her young maid, Tania, pinned a huge lacquered comb, studded with turquoises, into the large macaroon behind her right ear. She looked like a Japanese girl this way: the effect, she knew, would be stunning.

At ten minutes before two o'clock, she came downstairs. Most of the ladies chose to serve tea in the dining room, where the samovar simmered all day long. But Baroness Elizaveta Borisovna preferred to be served in the drawing room. Instead of a samovar, there was an enormous white porcelain kettle filled with boiling water. Its lid had been replaced by a tiny teapot containing essence of tea. Heated from below, the tea would continue to brew throughout the afternoon. To make tea, one doled out two tiny teaspoonfuls into every glass and added boiling water. The *maître d'hôtel,* or some other servant, kept constant watch over the little teapot, making sure that it never had a chance to go dry: for the tea leaves, if scalded a second time, would have made a bitter brew. When the kettle was empty, the *maître d'hôtel* would simply refill it in the kitchen and return it to its place in the drawing room.

On the tea-table were platters of *éclairs,* puff pastries, and glazed *petits-fours,* frequently replenished by the ever-efficient butler. It was Zica's duty to serve the tea. Pouring tea to the guests was a sign of hospitality and goodwill, customarily practiced by the daughter of the house.

When she came into the Empire drawing room, her mother was already seated. With an embroidery hoop in her lap, she was engaged in conversation with Fraulein Verlag, the portly German woman who had once been Zica's governess and now was in service to the household. Jewels glittered on Mama's chubby hands, and at her throat and wrists. Zica wondered how the young medical student from Rostov would react to all this opulence. Then again, he himself had been impeccably attired; perhaps there was money in his family.

Often, Zica tried to imagine how other people saw her and her family. The Poliakovs had everything anyone could dream of. Zica's gowns were always more luxurious than those of her friends. Her wealth set her a little apart from everybody else. That was enjoyable, but it also made her just a bit uncomfortable.

The doorbell chimed, and a moment later the *maître d'hôtel* escorted thin, reedy Maria Koestlin into the room. She was accompanied by her daughter Anya. On their heels came tiny Baroness Korff with her Pekingese dog. How Mama hated that dog! But no one in Moscow had the heart to turn it out into the street during receiving hours.

Zica kissed the guests on the cheek. Taking her place by the tea table, she accepted a glass of fine Steuben crystal, engraved with the baronial *P,* from the butler's hands. Pouring the essence of tea from the tiny teapot, she mixed it with water from the kettle, asked whether lemon or cream was desired, and smiled as she looked up into the lined face of Madame Koestlin.

"Anya tells me you are going to hear *Sadko* on Saturday," Madame Koestlin said, stirring vigorously. "I've always loved that opera best of all. It's so . . . *Russian,* isn't it?"

"Yes, Maria Grigorievna," Zica replied. But she was scarcely listening. She was thinking how absurd the woman looked, just like a horse, with her long nose and wide, twitching nostrils. And Anya with her slight stoop, and her moist blue eyes? A basset hound! They were a banking family, very rich. And—Zica thought unkindly—very uninteresting. But one couldn't avoid them.

"Anya said you looked beautiful at the ball last night," Madame Koestlin remarked as Zica poured tea for Baroness Korff.

"Anya, how kind of you," Zica commented, handing her a glass with a slice of lemon. From the corner of her eye, she saw Zhenya walk in with two of his friends and their sisters. She looked beyond the Koestlins and raised her hand in a discreet welcome to her brother.

Now the *maître d'hôtel* was ushering in a very old lady, the Countess Azubova, and her daughter, middle-aged Princess Karyatina. Zica was now overwhelmed with work—pouring tea, smiling at empty faces, and managing small talk which she appeared to enjoy. In fact, however, she hardly even heard what was being said. It was already almost three o'clock, and he hadn't come. Her heart felt like lead.

"What are you going to wear to your brother's wedding?" Tamara Kokhlova asked, leaning toward her. Tamara was a good friend, and very pretty. "How lucky you are," she added, not waiting for the reply: "Petersburg in winter! The wedding will be a fairy tale, won't it, sweetheart? New Year's Eve in the capital..."

"I like to spend New Year's Eve at home," Zica countered softly. "I shall miss the intimacy of being here, Tamarochka—"

But she could not continue the small talk. Abruptly, the room seemed to have stilled—its occupants moving in slow motion. She felt her heart stop.

He had come in. He wore the same gray suit, exactly the same outfit he had worn to the Tretyakovka—distinguished and elegant, but evidently the only one he owned. Zica's heart went out to him. She wanted to cry out and fly to his side—only she couldn't: it would have been unseemly. One didn't make one's feelings visible for all to see! But oh, how handsome he looked, and how alone and dismayed by the company. Now he was seeking her out with those brilliant green eyes—now smiling, as he saw her rising to her feet.

"Tamara," she whispered, "sit here, will you? I must go and greet someone."

"The one in pearl-gray?" Her friend's voice was tinged with envy. "Who *is* he?"

"Someone I met." Zica was unwilling to share Kyril Ostrov with anyone, not even Tamara. She could feel tiny beads of perspiration at the base of her hairline. Panic was beginning to grow in her stomach. What if somebody else reached him first?

She could feel the eyes following her—they almost burned holes in her back: Tamara's, her brother's, Madame Koestlin's. By the time Zica reached the newcomer, she was breathless, her cheeks flushed. "Kyril Victorevitch," she murmured, holding out her small hand. "How nice of you to come..."

"You invited me." He took the small hand, hesitated, then gently dropped it. She wasn't a married woman: a man should not kiss it. He was looking deeply into her eyes; his gaze was hypnotic. And now he was smiling. His face was asymmetrical, his smile crooked, she realized... and she found him wonderful! The circles of warmth emanated from the center of her being; her body tingled. She felt herself trembling; her throat was dry.

"I... Would you like some tea?"

"Yes, please. How have you been, Zeinab Lazarevna?"

"Very well, thank you."

They stood face to face; neither seemed to be breathing. He was a little pale, too. She thought: He is overwhelmed. He owns one suit and here he is, in this house, and I want him to stay here forever.

"You asked me to invent you," she said, looking up. "But how could I? I know so few things about you.... If you had not come..."

"But you knew I would," he replied in a low voice. "Any man who sees you must want to be with you, Zeinab Lazarevna."

Zica cast her eyes down, horribly embarrassed. He seemed to know, with sure male instinct, exactly what to say. She had to avoid his eyes or she would dissolve. He had the eyes of a tortured saint ... or of a mad monk. He was exactly like the characters in her mother's yellow novels: mesmerizing, engulfing, magnetic. What were the other descriptions they used...?

"I don't care about other men," she said recklessly. "There is no romance left in modern society, Kyril Victorevitch. What do I want with men who smile with their mouths and not with their spirits? They are cold automatons, whereas I wish... I want—"

"Zica," her brother interrupted, his voice firm and strong beside her. "Who is your friend? Nobody has met him yet. You have kept him all to yourself, and Tamara is busy at the tea-table in your stead—I am Evgeny Lazarevitch Poliakov," he added, extending his hand toward Kyril.

"Kyril Victorevitch Ostrov."

The young man in gray didn't elaborate. Zhenya's raised eyebrows signified many questions, but Kyril did nothing more than smile. He wasn't about to reveal how he and Zica had met, any more than she was.

Returning to the tea-table, Zica sighed as she sat down. Kyril soon joined her there, a palpable presence, felt even as she poured tea and answered other people's questions. She was obliged to introduce him to her friends. "This is Kyril Victorevitch Ostrov. And this is Tamara Ivanovna Kokhlova, Nadezhda Vladimirovna Bussovskaya, Anna Antonovna Koestlin..." Her voice wavered. She looked at no one.

Naturally, her friends had many unasked questions, but they chattered on about other things. Zica heard their voices buzzing lightly above her head, like a swarm of female bees. She was oblivious. He was here, and had come for *her*. She had never felt this way before. Small shocks pierced her body like convulsions. How alive she felt—yet terribly weak. Her hands were shaking.

"Zeinab Lazarevna thinks that romance has died in the twentieth century," Kyril was telling the group. His voice sounded melodious and self-assured. "But this is distasteful news to a man's ears! Surely, we can resurrect the waning specter of romance...?"

"How would you propose to do it?" Tamara asked.

"Very simply. Zeinab Lazarevna—do you have a minute?" he asked playfully. "We must show these ladies how to resurrect tired Russian romance, which seems to have taken to its sick-bed. Will you rise, please...?"

She set down the glass she had just picked up. As in a trance, she met his eyes. He wasn't smiling now, not at all. His face was serious—serious and a little nervous.

"What is it you want?" she whispered.

"We simply must show them," he stated. All at once, sweeping her into his arms, he began to dance. There in the drawing room, in the midst of all the people gathered in conversation, oblivious to them, he waltzed in time to unheard music. Zica followed, taking little steps, looking all the while into his green eyes.

"Zica, Zica!" her mother was calling. "The drawing room is no place for a waltz, for heaven's sake! Take your friends into the small parlor, and ask Yasha to roll up the rug..."

"Mama!" Holding Kyril by the arm, Zica moved quickly through the crowd. "This is Kyril Victorevitch Ostrov. My mother, Baroness Poliakova."

Her mother's intelligent face was attentive and questioning. "How do you do..." she murmured, extending one jewelled hand to the young man.

"Baroness, what an honor." He raised the small, plump hand,

brushed it with his lips, and released it politely. Zica breathed a sigh of relief. He had known what to do.

"You are a friend of Zica's?" The Baroness's voice was agreeable, not challenging.

"Yes, Madame, I am."

If he was afraid, he was covering his fear very adequately, Zica reflected. She tugged at his sleeve. "Let's find the parlor, shall we . . . ?" she urged in a low voice.

"Yes," he replied. She felt his hand on her elbow. Almost imperceptibly, his fingers tightened around her soft flesh—a small, hard pressure. She did not turn to look at him, but she knew, she *knew,* that she had finally met *him.* Kyril Ostrov was *the one* from her dreams. No matter what, she would fight to possess him.

Yakov was halfway down the hallway when the *maître d'hôtel,* Sergei, called out to him: "We've run out of hot water, Yasha! Bring the kettle into the kitchen for a refill!" He motioned with his chin to his own full hands, which held empty pastry trays to be replenished.

"Right away, Sergei Pavlovitch."

But he dreaded the task. He didn't want to sneak into the drawing room and see the elegant guests, nor Zica. Yakov knew, as always, she would be busy by the tea-table. Yet he had no choice: his was, essentially, a station in life bereft of choices.

Holding himself very erect, Yakov entered the drawing room. Then he saw her, walking away in the direction of the parlor. A superb young man was at her side, clad in pearl-gray, his golden hair slicked back into a fashionable pompadour. Yakov watched, perversely fascinated. This man was like a perfectly etched picture postcard. There was something unreal about him, like an actor on a stage, waiting to be given his next cue. But—why would Yakov even be thinking this? He had no reason to condemn this young dandy! He was seeing him here for the first time in his life. Yakov had no reason to suspect that the dandified young gentleman was a sham—no reason, that is, but his own *shtetl* instinct.

Following Zica and her companion came the usual crowd of friends: her brother, Zhenya, Anya Koestlin, Tamara Kokhlova, and tall, thin Nadezhda Bussovskaya. But Zica seemed oblivious to all of them. Her face was tilted upward, her black eyes fixed on the sculptured face of the golden man. Now he had moved his hand to her elbow, possessively.

At this, Yakov felt such a pang of sorrow that he shrank back against the woodwork of the hallway, his eyes stinging. He did not need to hear the words that passed between Zica and this man. Words were superfluous. Her expressive eyes told all.

Suddenly, for no apparent reason, the young man paused to regard Yakov, who was still in the hallway. Zica did not notice. The man's clear, piercing green eyes seemed to Yakov like the eyes of a jealous lover. The man, for no reason, was appraising him. What probably took less than a few seconds seemed a veritable eternity. Yakov stared back, defiantly.

Who was this new man in Zica's life?

When the little procession was in the parlor, Zica spoke. Her low, throaty laughter resounded in Yakov's ears like so many bells exploding in his head. He could feel himself clenching and unclenching his fists. Sweat broke out on his forehead. He would never forget those reptilian green eyes, silently asking who he was and why he had been staring at Zica.

You are *no one, nothing* to her! Yakov thought angrily. Enraged, he tried to calm down. But his heart was palpitating painfully. He was breathless.

He would not forget his first sight of this chiselled Russian god. Already, Yakov hated him.

Chapter V

ON the afternoon of August 2, 1914, Russia formally declared war on Germany and the Central Powers. It was tradition for the Russian Tzars to start a war by standing on the walls of the Kremlin and asking for God's support. The Imperial Family travelled to Moscow, arriving on the seventeenth of the month in the ancient, historic seat of Tzarist power. The streets were lined with cheering Russians. They hailed their chief as their "Little Father" who would lead them to a quick, easy victory over the Huns.

In the Poliakov residence, the family stood on the living room balcony and waved a Russian flag at the Imperial procession. Behind them crowded the family retainers: Sergei, Senya, the maids, and Yakov. Only Fraulein Verlag was absent. She was in her room, weeping. As a German citizen, she was about to be sent home after fifteen years of loyal service.

Baron Poliakov spoke a lot about the war. Now, he said, the revolutionaries were going to be extinguished merely because an outside enemy had threatened Russia. The Russian people, Jew and gentile alike, would surely unite against the threat of Germany. Bursts of revolt, bombings, and pogroms had sporadically shaken Russia for the past few years: now, Lazar Solomonvitch proclaimed, these internal conflicts would come to an end as sons, brothers, and young husbands were sent to the front. Equals in battle, they would put their lives on the line for Mother Russia and the "Little Father." This, the Baron believed, was the hidden blessing of such a terrible occurrence: now Russia would be healed. Its flagging spirits would be renewed, and the people would march on to victory.

In the months that followed, to Zica's astonishment, nothing changed. Zenya, who was now comfortably managing his father-in-law's bank in St. Petersburg, wrote that in the capital it was the same. The front was far away. Besides, all the eldest and only sons were exempt from military service, as were the managers of banks, large enterprises, and factories. Zica did not have to fear either for her brother or for Kyril. Both were only sons, Kyril that of a widow; besides, her Kyriusha was too young to be drafted. Draftees has to be twenty-one, and he was only nineteen.

Zica's family had interrupted their summer rest and returned home early from Podolia because her father had been worried about the war. Now it was wintertime again. For the first time, Zica Poliakova noticed that the city was crippled. Now she saw evidence that a continental war was taking place. Distant rumblings were felt, ever so slightly, in the big cities of Russia. Though the tramways were still run by men, many of the male servants were now absent from households. Yasha was the only young one left in their own home. The others had all been drafted or had enlisted. Suddenly there were fewer balls, fewer receptions, fewer events to attend during the social season. Her friends' households had shrunk considerably, as had hers.

But the theaters remained open, and many families continued to entertain. As Zica sat in her room and thought about it, she was disturbed. Where was patriotism? During times of national trouble, one had to rally behind the flag and not waste time in idle pursuits. Men were dying at the front. Even if those men were strangers, it seemed indecent that most of her friends didn't seem to care at all. Their parties continued.

It was a bitter-cold December. From the parlor, Zica telephoned her friend, Tamara. "I want to do something for the war effort," she said. "Something to help."

"You could come with me to make bandages," Tamara told her. "Countess Vyrubova has a workshop in her reception hall. We work Mondays and Thursdays, all afternoon."

Zica was pleased. She would be contributing, in her own small way. That night, there was a *soirée* at the Koestlins', and her parents were going. She didn't want to go. Besides, Kyril sometimes called on her in the evening, when she had no plans—especially when her parents weren't home. So she preferred to stay at home, just in case.

Kyril's work at medical school was nearly all-consuming. He stayed up until the wee hours of the morning, studying diagrams of the human body, memorizing thousands of terms with Latin and Greek names. To Zica, this was all rather fantastic. She thought him very smart, and she sometimes wondered that he didn't find her uneducated by comparison. After all, she had only studied at home, with Fraulein Verlag and her brother's tutor. Though she had studied literature, languages and mathematics—with some natural science thrown in to please her father—she felt quite unlearned.

Zica's throat tightened as she thought of Kyril. For the past year, he had made every effort to be with her. He met her at parties to which she arranged to have him invited. On many Tuesday afternoons, he came to her mother's teas; he often went with her and Tamara and Fraulein Verlag to the opera, sitting in the family box with his hand on the back of her seat. He would have spoken to her father, to ask for permission to court her officially, but Zica thought that perhaps it was too soon. Her parents should first become accustomed to him, to his impeccable manners. Later, she thought, they would be more understanding; they would accept his strained financial situation. The fact that he was only half-Jewish would surely be passed over once they recognized his strength of character. Forcing the issue too soon could only ruin things. And half-Jewish was actually better than she had originally feared.

"Who is that young medical student who is around you so much?" her mother would ask. "We know almost nothing about him."

"He's a friend of Zhenya's," Zica would reply. "He's very entertaining."

Her father would look at her circumspectly, and frown. "Zica, if someone is interested in you, I shall have to speak to him. Of course you understand that."

Of course. She understood it and felt afraid. She pushed the thought from her mind, like a stray wisp of hair from her forehead. She felt uncomfortable, misleading her parents. What if they wrote Zhenya and asked him how well he knew Kyril? Thank God her mother had a bad memory: she was unlikely to recall that Zhenya had met Kyril at the same time she had, when he first came to tea in November of the previous year. For a whole year, Zica had kept up the pretense that this was nothing serious—a friendship, nothing more.

Did anyone suspect? Her friends all knew. What if one of them talked to her own mother, and that mother called up Elizaveta Borisovna? But Zica had sworn one and all to secrecy.

In the cold winter evening, the thick walls of the Poliakov mansion seemed wrapped like a cocoon around Zica. Those walls protected her, shielding her from the outside world. Covering herself with a thick blanket, she curled up in her mother's lounge chair in the boudoir. The maid, Tania, brought her hot chocolate. She would be good to herself tonight. She would pamper herself, just in case he did not come.

And if he did not? Well, then, her heart would crack just a little, as it always did when he was unable to meet her.

Zica wondered why Kyril had not yet introduced her to his widowed mother. He had spoken now and then of Elena Yossifovna, yet any talk of her seemed to make Kyril uncomfortable. When Zica expressed interest, he stalled her. "My mother is a little mad," he explained. "She stays home all day and refuses to go out and reads books from morning till night."

"I could do that, too. But they would all have to be love stories."

Kyril had laughed then, and touched Zica's hair with tentative, gentle fingers. His touch was delicate, like feathers brushing against her temples.

That discussion had taken place a week ago.

There was a knock on the door. Zica stirred, pushing the memory way. "What is it, Tania?"

The little maid stepped in, her demeanor apologetic. "Zeinab Lazarevna, Doctor Ostrov is here to see you."

"Show him into the parlor, will you? And offer him a brandy. He must be chilled."

Her cheeks were red. Rushing to her mother's vanity, she powdered her nose. Pulling at her black hobble skirt, she smoothed out the wrinkles. From the small bottle on the vanity, she took a touch of perfume that she applied to her throat, temples, and wrists.

He was waiting for her in the parlor, a small, intimate room, with pale blue walls and delicate Louis XIV furniture. Kyril was standing in front of a painting of a Vrubel icon on a wooden table. When he heard her, he spun around, his green eyes alive with expectation. He was wearing the everyday suit he always wore to classes, with a shirt that was slightly frayed around the collar. Zica's heart tightened with empathy: he sometimes did research for one of his professors, in order to make ends meet, and she knew how difficult it must be for him to come here afterward. What a vast difference in their circumstances!

"Zica!"

She held out her hands as she rushed eagerly toward him. "You came. I thought you might not . . ."

"And I was afraid your parents might be here. Or that they would have forced you to go to Madame Koestlin's."

Zica brought a hand to her throat. "It's this unpleasant cold," she said, shaking her head mournfully. "My throat hurts, and I have the shivers. Mama left strict instructions that I was to be given hot tea, or cocoa, and watched carefully. That's what comes of being a girl: your parents want to think of you as fragile and neurasthenic like a temperamental racehorse." She laughed, her laughter filling the room. "Come," she said, "let's sit on the couch."

He sat down beside her and took her hand. "Aren't you afraid? You know the *maître d'hôtel* or your maid might tell your parents about these visits. What then?"

"Stop being so diffident!" she chided him. "I'm a big girl, and I know the loyalty of my servants. No one would tell."

"*Everyone* would tell. Your father pays their wages, Zica—not you."

They sat silently for a moment. She could feel the distress that had risen palpably between them. "What is to become of us?" he asked. "You will not let me take the next step of approaching your father."

"—How is school?"

"You are changing subjects. School is as it always has been. Better than last year, yet extremely difficult. I don't really want to be a doctor, Zica. But then, you see, I don't know *what* I want to do. I like painting and sculpting—but that's not a living."

"We could move to Rigevka, and live in the country house. And you would paint and I would keep you company."

"Zica, Zica... *Before* the wedding, or *after?* What silly notions you have, envisioning the future... when you won't even let me broach the subject of courtship to your father."

She looked at him, her eyes blazing. "Kyriusha, my father isn't ready to be told. But—but eventually, when you finish medical school, we *shall* get married, of course! And then, you won't ever have to worry again, about money. I have a large trust fund. We could move to the Crimea... and you could become an excellent artist, and sell your paintings and sculptures to the Hermitage and the Tretyakovka. Why is it you always harp on the immediate future—the only part of my life I'm not sure about?"

"Because it is the part that most concerns me. How can we make your father accept me, so he will let us become engaged?"

"There's no need. Not yet. Let things lie, will you, my darling? We are doing fine just as we are."

He gazed at her, caressing her hand, which had grown cold in his. "Are you so very much afraid of your father?" he murmured.

"I am terrified." Her eyes looked enormous and bright, eloquent in their distress. "If Zhenya were still in Moscow, I would ask him to intercede in our favor. But . . ."

"What is it that you're most afraid of? My grandfather is well known in Rostov. He is wealthy and a good Jew. Won't that count at all?" But in the same breath Kyril thought bitterly, *how odd that being Jewish was what mattered most!* The part of his identity that all his life he had sought to shed now seemed to be the most important.

"It *will* count. But Mossia Aronov is courting me, and his father is the purveyor of sugar to the Russian army. His parents built a synagogue in their own home. Papa favors his suit. I know he does."

Kyril's eyes narrowed. She felt him stiffen, pulling away. "Mossia Aronov . . . ? I had no idea! Since when has he been courting you?"

Covering Kyril's hand with both of hers, Zica said hastily: "But it's *nothing*—to *me,* that is. He sometimes comes here with his parents for supper, and we chat, and play four-handed piano. I don't even *like* him, Kyril! It's just that, well . . . you see . . . my father . . ."

Her sentence hung in mid-air. She turned her head away, miserably. "I don't want to marry Mossia Aronov," she stated, her voice small and hurt. "I don't want to marry any of those boys I grew up with. I want . . . I want to marry *you.* Don't you believe that?"

"So this Aronov has had the nerve to propose!" Kyril shot back. "He couldn't have done that without your permission, Zica. He is a wealthy man, a landowner—whereas I have nothing but a little help from my grandfather, and a widowed mother to support. Of course you think you want to marry me . . . because my looks appeal to you! But the fact is that this"—and his hand swept majestically over the lovely room—"is how you're accustomed to living. You would be a fool to give that up for *me!*"

Zica squirmed in her seat. Her face was averted. "I don't care how I live," she whispered. "I care only about being with *you.* But I can't tell Papa this—not now. Kyril, I swear to you, Mossia hasn't done more than ask permission to visit me; besides, I told Papa that I didn't think I could ever love him. Papa won't force me. He, of all people, would not compel me to marry a man without being in love. He loved my mother so much when they were married! How could he expect me to sign a contract with a man who means nothing to me?"

"I don't like this," Kyril muttered, rising. He started to pace the floor. "In the end, you will do whatever is required of you. You are not the kind of woman to fight your parents. You are compliant, you obey!"

Zica leapt to her feet, her eyes flashing. "That's not fair!"

"I'm being thrown away," Kyril continued. "It's only a matter of weeks, or months at most, until you tearfully announce to me your impending wedding to that Aronov—or to some other Jewish robber baron!"

"How can you say these cruel things to me?" Zica cried. Tears coursed down her cheeks, streaking the powder. "Why can't you trust me to manage things right, with Papa and Mama? What must I do to prove that I love you?"

All at once she knew, with perfect clarity, what she *must* do. She walked resolutely to the door and closed it. The lock clicked as she turned the bolt. Approaching Kyril, she lifted his chilled hands and placed them on her hips.

He looked deeply into her eyes—then suddenly pulled away. "Don't be a fool, Zica!" He seemed shaken and angry.

But she was firm. "Look at me, Kyril. I love you more than life itself. Tomorrow, Tamara is taking me to a workshop. I will begin to make bandages for the men at the front. I believe in this war against Germany, and I must prove it. And Kyriusha, it is the same between you and me: I believe in our future. We cannot wait. I love you—I love you."

Kyril was flushed—confused. He seemed almost ready to run from her now. "Zica, you know it would be wrong for me to take you at this moment. Please—please don't compare our love to this war. It is an insult to our feelings! The war is unjust. It destroys lives for a stupid cause."

She trembled slightly, and flicked the tears off her cheeks. "You are so hard," she said. "You are so cynical and hard, refusing to believe in anything! Is life so bitter that you have stopped caring about anything at all?"

He nodded. "Yes, I am bitter, and I am cruel. And more. Your family will never accept me, Zica. You and I may love each other, but that is a dream. For you see, besides my 'good looks,' I have nothing to offer anyone."

She was horrified. "And what about me? Am I worth nothing as well...?"

He shook his head. "You are worth more than I deserve, Zeinab Lazarevna. You are the sunlight that warms me and the breeze that soothes me. You are the God I refuse to believe in."

"Well, then, what of this talk of marriage? Was this all a lie, to lead me on while you amuse yourself?"

His green eyes studied her intensely. "Why marriage? Because if anyone can make me whole, it is you. But I'm afraid. What if I fail you? You do not know my family—my father—" Kyril shuddered. "Perhaps it would be better for me to leave now and never come back."

But he did not move.

Both had tears in their eyes. But finally it was she who moved, closing the distance between them. She placed her hands on his shoulders, kissing him fully on the lips. He yielded, giving way to the soft pressure of her lips on his, as she molded herself to him. Her breasts pressed through the thin material of her blouse and his shirt. He could feel her nipples hardening. The sensation eclipsed all reason. His every nerve quivered with excitement.

Her fingers strong and determined, she took his hands and placed them once again on her hips. "I want you to make love to me, Kyril," she said softly. And this time he could not resist. Silently, he led her to the couch.

The fire blazed in the hearth, crackling now and then as a small twig burst into flame. As Kyril sought the buttons of Zica's blouse, she turned down the small lamp next to them. In the light of the dancing fire, she dropped her skirt to the floor and wriggled out of her underclothes. Now she was facing him, naked, white, beautiful. "I want you to take me," she told him. Her eyes watched unflinching as he undressed—she reached out to him as he stood nude before her. He had been certain she would be afraid, but she showed no sign of fear.

"Oh, how I do love you!" she cried out, holding her arms open. As he knelt on top of her, she placed her hands over his buttocks and brought him closer to her. He kissed her lips, her throat, her breasts, and then he moved downward, tasting the sweetness of her body as he heard her cry out with unexpected pleasure. And yet he was afraid. Deep in his consciousness, below the excitement and the thrill of ecstasy, lay a cold, dark chill. He pressed his lips to hers to make sure she wouldn't cry out, and then he entered her, almost savagely pushing into her, determined to take her now. She had offered herself—knowing full well there would be pain. He penetrated deeply, seeking completion more than pleasure, possession more than response.

Afterwards, they lay together on the sofa, stroking each other comfortably. There was almost a familiarity between them now. "You aren't sorry?" he asked, caressing her cheek.

She shook her head, smiling. "No, not at all. This is what was meant to exist between you and me." She kissed him.

But then the fear took over. Each of them, without looking at the other, turned to get dressed. Zica stood shivering in front of the fire, adjusting the cuffs on her sleeves. All at once she seemed embarrassed. Unreasoning, Kyril felt his heart begin to pound. I've got to get out of here now, he thought. Soon she will become hysterical!

And Zica was thinking: Now that he has had me, what will I be to him . . . ?

But as she unlocked the door, Kyril came up behind her and lightly touched her on the back. She turned slowly to face him. They weren't the same anymore, not after tonight. Realizing it, they were sobered by the thought of what had changed. "I love you, Zica," Kyril murmured. She nodded: "I love you too." But now the words meant something else—and neither knew what the other was thinking.

As Zica opened the front door to let Kyril out into the chill night, she became aware that someone was standing behind her. Startled, she turned, catching her breath. But it was not Sergei, the ever-watchful *maître d'hôtel*. It was only Yasha, the assistant librarian, bringing some books back to her father's study. "Goodnight," she said to him, wondering how long he had been staring at her. She could not tell from his expression whether he'd seen Kyril.

"Goodnight, Zeinab Lazarevna," Yasha replied deferentially. Then he added inexplicably: "I trust you've had a pleasant evening."

She nodded at him curtly. She only wanted him gone. Then, as she turned away, she lifted her skirt and ran toward the staircase. She decided that she didn't like Yasha after all. Something about him unnerved her.

But it wasn't Yasha, of course. It was what had happened between Kyril and her. Now they had become lovers—her life had changed forever. She was no longer an innocent, a virgin. Unexpectedly, this frightened her. She wished she had a friend with whom to discuss how she felt tonight. But such things could never be shared, not even with Tamara. Zhenya? Somehow, she was sure that her brother would not understand. He would tell their parents to marry her off right away—and not to Kyril!

No, there was no one in whom she could confide. Zica would

have to weather this on her own, like a grown woman. This fact gave her little comfort on this cold winter night.

Yakov stood irresolutely in his small room, the image of Zeinab Lazarevna, dishevelled and nonplussed, still vivid in his mind. He knew the blond man had been there—that very night—while Zica's parents were out.

A surge of fury swept over Yakov, like a crimson veil. He found that he had inadvertently grabbed a small penknife from his desk. He hurled it with a cry against the wall.

She was *in love—of course!* The blond man was handsome as a god, handsome as Apollo. But he was not rich! This Yakov could deduce from his clothing. He only owned one good suit. One could tell that he was a student . . . a struggler, like himself. Zeinab Lazarevna was in love with a poor student, and was hiding the affair from the Baron and his wife.

For it *had* to be an affair. Yakov's heart beat faster as he thought of it. *That bastard* was the type to bed every virgin, if only to prove his reputation as a conqueror. Now Zica had fallen under his spell. There was nothing Yakov could do for her any more: he couldn't protect her from the violence of her own passion. God only knew where it would lead her.

He had seen in her face how she loved this man—loved him so terribly that nothing but tragedy could ensue. What could *he,* Yakov, possibly do to prevent this tragedy? If he intimated anything to the Baron—if he so much as cast a shadow over Zica's doings— he would certainly be fired instantly. But he would be bringing another kind of harm to her, the parental kind: irrevocable punishment. So he had no choice. He could only swallow his anger and go about his own life.

To his dismay, the life he once called his own was now swallowed up in hers. His will sought only the pursuit of her happiness; his efforts were aimed only at pleasing her. He wanted to soothe the rough spots of her existence. Whenever he saw her, his heart turned over. But these feelings served only to make her appear more re- mote and inaccessible, to make him feel useless and empty.

He must forget Zica. But who else was there? Only Natasha. Yes, suddenly everything seemed clear to Yakov: He would make the ultimate break with Zica by forcing himself to be with another woman. Natasha liked him. She saw him as a man—not merely as a shadow on the walls of the palace. How wonderful it would be to take her somewhere—the opera!—to spend an evening together. But such an outing would cost him a third of his monthly salary. As assistant librarian, he earned eighteen rubles a month. And if he took Natasha to hear Chaliapin, whom she professed to adore, he would have to spend at least six rubles for a good seat.

No. He would go further. He would rent an entire loggia for nine rubles; and he would invite Senya, and Natasha's artist friends, Misha and Dima, the two young men who rented the neighboring apartments overlooking the Poliakov courtyard. They would go to see *Boris Godunov,* and he would treat her to chocolates at intermission. Then he would bring her back to his own small room and take her to bed and forget there even existed a Zeinab Lazarevna Poliakova. This was how a man healed his heart—by forcing out the spirit of the beloved and quickly filling the space with a love that was less illusion and more real.

Yakov thought how Natasha would look in her brand-new gown. It had cost her sixteen rubles to have that gown made, an exact duplicate of one that Zeinab Lazarevna had ordered from Poiret in Paris. It was made with meters and meters of lace and crepe. As Natasha had shown it to Yakov, she asked nervously, "But Yasha, where will I wear it?" Now he knew: she would wear it to the Opera.

Why was Natasha forever competing with Zica? Yakov already knew the answer. It hurt him, for Natasha always came out the loser.

Still, going to the Opera would be an enormous expense for him. His most lavish extravagance consisted of an occasional meal out . . . for twenty-five kopeks.

He thought: I'll bet the blond Apollo doesn't eat any better than I do—he's just a struggling student, feeding himself for ten rubles a month, just like everyone else, and going hungry at night . . .

Yes, a major outing to a place like the Opera would set him back a long way. Still, he would be gaining a girlfriend from all this. He could do far worse—he, a Jew from the Pale!—than this slender, dark girl from the Crimea.

Now that he was in this expansive mood, another idea came to him: after the Opera he would invite Natasha to the Slaviansky Bazaar, where the rich merchants, the *kupetzi,* took their ladies for supper. They would eat *borsch,* cabbage *pirozhkis,* chicken, *kissel,* the delicious fruit pudding, and wash everything down with a glass of *kvass.* If the others felt like coming, each would have to pay his own way.

Angrily, Yakov pushed the image of Zica out of his brain. It didn't matter now if she got hurt. It didn't matter what this medical student intended to do. As of this moment, it would no longer concern him. Clearing his throat, Yakov began to practice the speech he would deliver to Natasha. The words sounded proud, and intelligent, as he invited her to the Opera—the *Opera!*

How odd it seemed to be standing there at intermission, dressed like a *kupetz!* Yakov felt awkward in the tuxedo that he had borrowed from the portly Sergei, which Natasha had altered in a makeshift way. Yakov felt like a servant dressed up like a rich man. He kept glancing around him, wondering whether anyone else could tell that he felt out of place.

To his right, Natasha Khazina leaned against the edge of the box, eagerly scanning the crowd in the theater with a borrowed pair of opera glasses. Below in the orchestra were bare arms and jewels, a sea of diadems, glittering hairstyles, uniforms, and medals. For a moment, Yakov was stunned by the display.

Behind them, Senya and the two young art students sat silently enjoying the spectacle. Yakov glanced at Natasha. Her dress was elegant and stylish. But it didn't suit her. The pink taffeta sheath, overlaid by a green bodice, was covered with tiers of Valenciennes lace. Beneath all the finery, her small bust appeared even smaller, and her arms seemed skinny and sallow. Yet she had made such a valiant effort that Yakov's heart reached out to her. He took her hand. "You look beautiful," he told her.

Eagerly, she turned to him. "I do?" But a noise from the audience drew her attention away again. She lifted the small binoculars to her eyes once more and peered into the crowd. Suddenly she cried: "—Oh, look, Yasha—over there! Isn't that someone we know, from the house?" She handed him the opera glasses.

Yakov followed her gaze. In the orchestra, among a sea of women in brocades and chiffon, was a man in tails like his own, holding the arm of a middle-aged woman. An unpleasant chill spread through him. "Yes, I do believe that is a familiar figure." It was the blond Apollo—"Ostrov," he called himself—with an older woman, small and quite elegant in black velvet.

"Who is it?" Natasha urged.

"I thought it was someone I knew—but no. It doesn't matter. It's nobody. Listen, Natasha, would you like some chocolates? I'll buy you some, if you'll excuse me." He'd seen Ostrov and the woman moving toward the exit doors.

Behind the loggias ran a small circular corridor; beyond, was a small sitting room with a sofa. Already, a number of ladies were reclining on the sofa, gentlemen at their sides. As Yakov moved restlessly through the small *salon,* he noticed Ostrov entering with his companion. She was small, considerably older—perhaps in her mid-forties—and she resembled him in every way but the hair. Hers was dark, with an occasional strand of silver-gray running through.

Yakov could not help staring as Ostrov deposited the woman on the sofa between two other ladies. The blond man hastened out toward the front vestibule. By the time Yakov caught up with him, Ostrov had picked up a thick coat with a fur collar, and a hat of the same fur. He was headed for the cold outdoors. Yakov saw that he would not be able to follow quickly enough to keep up: he had checked his own coat in with Natasha's, and he could not venture outside in frock coat and tails.

Disconsolately, he stood by the front doors of the Opera. How was he going to explain to Natasha that he hadn't made it to the French confectioner across the street in time to buy her some sweets? He couldn't afford them, anyway. Supper alone would cost him all his savings. The truth was, he didn't want to miss Ostrov when the latter returned to the theater.

The blond man fascinated Yakov—it was as simple as that. He had such power over Zica. His aura was so powerful that no good girl would be able to resist his advances. Ostrov, to Yakov, was like an evil genius who needed to be studied at close quarters. He couldn't help himself from being drawn to the man.

Through the large front doors of the opera, men rushed in and out in a constant flow, returning with packages of candied fruit and caramel creams. A biting draft chilled Yakov's bones; he moved back toward the wall. All at once he saw Ostrov again. His face was red from the cold, his hat drawn low over his ears. He came through the doors and stood a moment shivering, rubbing his arms, and looked around.

It was then Ostrov noticed Yakov. The green eyes blinked, puzzled, and the medical student frowned. He examined Yakov, trying to place him. Finally, to Yakov's amazement, Ostrov approached him with hand outstretched. "I'm sorry," he stated. "I can't recall your name, nor where we've met. But I'm sure I know you from *somewhere*. My name is Kyril Victorevitch Ostrov." He shook Yakov's hand with a hard, precise grip.

Up close, Ostrov had a nice, winsome smile, which made his green eyes crinkle. His features were lopsided when he smiled, and this made him look impish and young. Yakov allowed his hand to be shaken. Under the spell of his surprise, he could only stammer his own name. He had hardly expected this confrontation.

"Where have we met?" Ostrov's tone was polite, in no way arrogant. He had evidently not noticed the ill fit of Yakov's suit—and so he believed that this was a peer, not to be slighted.

"At the Poliakovs'," Yakov replied in a low voice.

"Oh..." Ostrov dropped Yakov's hand, and nodded. Yakov thought: He thinks I was another guest, and I'm not about to tell him any different. Let him ask himself how well I've observed him.... Let him squirm a little, let him worry.

Yakov smiled pleasantly, appraising the other man. All at once he felt very sure of himself. He was not the least embarrassed.

"The Poliakovs are lovely people," Ostrov remarked lamely.

"Indeed." Yakov's eyes were unblinking.

"I am here with my mother," Ostrov explained, ignoring the awkwardness. "She loves the opera. I... well, we can't afford to come here often. But I bring her whenever I can!"

"How good of you," Yakov commented. His voice had an edge of steel. It would do the bastard good to fret like this, he reflected. But knowing that the woman was Ostrov's mother gave him pause.

"I've bought my mother some candied creams," Ostrov said. "Would you like some?"

Yakov shook his head. Yakov enjoyed Kyril Ostrov's embarrassment, his excessive politeness. Since Yakov was *known to the Poliakov family,* Ostrov had to speak carefully, for fear of giving too much away.

Yet there was an earnest, boyish quality in Kyril Ostrov that was so appealing, so direct and charming, that Yakov could not remain impassive. *It was impossible to hate this man!*

What could be wrong with me? Yakov thought with disgust. Aloud, he said, "I wish I could be taking my own mother to the Opera. She lives in Odessa, and has never been to Moscow. In fact, she's never been to an opera, anywhere."

There! He had really done himself in now. He had reversed the tables, revealing his lowly origins. But Ostrov didn't flinch. He merely raised his eyebrows. "Yes," the medical student commented, suddenly quite friendly and at ease. "It's difficult, being a provincial. We're from Rostov-on-the-Don, ourselves. The Opera there is nothing compared to this!"

Yakov began to reply, but before he could utter a single word, the warning bell rang. The theater doors were closing. The second act was about to being! Ostrov smiled, and shrugged lightly. "It was nice to chat with you, Yakov Lvovitch," he declared. "I hope we shall both enjoy the rest of the show." Then he quickly strode off in the direction of the orchestra.

Yakov remained unmoving, visibly shaken. Taking a deep breath, he started to wend his way back toward his box, toward Natasha Khazina and their friends. He felt oddly defeated, drained of all joy and exhilaration. The evening was dead now, reduced to ashes by the charm and dash of Zica Poliakova's young lover.

I wanted to hate him, but somehow, it didn't work out that way, he thought. He was furious with himself, and also perplexed. Now he understood why the world had stopped for Zica, why her face had looked hypnotized that night when he had caught her letting Ostrov out of the house. The medical student was a spellbinder, an enchanter . . . and she had fallen for him. Just so, Yakov had also been dazed, changing from hostility to friendliness. A few words spoken in the foyer of the Opera, a handshake, a smile . . .

You are a fool, Yasha, he told himself. The man's a charlatan, and you know it. There is something about him that isn't quite right, isn't as it should be . . . but I don't know what.

Yakov was determined to find out.

In the hallway alcove, Zica held the telephone cradled against her ear. She was whispering. From his vantage point far down the hall, Yakov watched her moving lips, the soft, apricot curve of her cheek, her luminous eyes. She concentrated on her conversation. Soft wisps of hair curled around her face. The gentleness in this woman was so different, so unique.

She wasn't brittle, like the rest. Tamara Kokhlova, for example, Zica's friend—she had hard blue eyes, like slits of metal gleaming in cold alabaster. And even Natasha, so bony and angular, somehow seemed tough.

Tough like a survivor, Yakov thought guiltily. He remembered her pliant body snuggled against him in the darkness, the smell of musk after they had coupled for hours in his bed. Even now, he could hear the echo of her defiant laughter as their supple bodies sought new positions.

Natasha was *his girl* now; she had taught him everything she knew—about Moscow, about sex and women and how to please them; and about growing up a gentile, a real *Russian,* unafraid of pogroms and persecution. She had taught him, binding him to her, clinging to him for dear life. And yet he felt that she knew how to survive better than he—that if he left her or broke it off, she would cry for a few days and then shrug philosophically and begin anew. She would turn to canvas and palette knife to alleviate her heartache —but all the while her eyes would be glancing here and there to find his successor.

Yakov liked Natasha. But he didn't love her. He loved *this* girl, the one now whispering into the telephone, the frightened, romantic daughter of the master he had come to think of as the "Jewish Tzar." And he loved her in part because he knew she *wasn't* a survivor: she had never learned to fend for herself.

Now that her brother was gone, whom did she have to rely on? Yakov cleared his throat. Zica looked up, frightened and skittish. She put the phone down with a sudden clatter. "I didn't know you were here, Yasha." She sounded annoyed and scared at the same time.

"I was passing through to bring the Baron a pamphlet," he explained. "I wasn't eavesdropping, Zeinab Lazarevna."

"I didn't think you were," she replied defensively. But her eyes said otherwise. They announced that she didn't trust him.

"Well then, I'm sorry I surprised you." He meant to disarm her, to put her at ease: he was her friend, not her enemy. Did she truly see an enemy in everyone around her?

"Please, Yasha," she said now, her voice pleading: "You must give me some privacy. Everywhere I turn, it seems, you are coming at me from a hidden corner. I have wondered whether you mean to follow me."

"I beg your pardon, Miss. I had no intention—"

Suddenly, Zica burst out laughing. But her laughter was a little shrill, with hysterical undertones. Yakov's dismay must have showed in his face. "Oh, don't worry," she reassured him. "I'm not really going mad. It's just that...just that..."

Her eyes were full of tears. "It's just that everything's gone out of control," she murmured quietly. "It's more than I can handle by myself."

Filled with sympathy, he hesitated. He set the pamphlet down on a small table. Boldly, he covered one of her hands with his own. "It's all right, Zeinab Lazarevna. You are not alone. I—I am some-one who cares."

Her eyes opened wide, seeking his. "You do? But why? I am only the daughter of the house. Why *should* you care, Yasha?"

"Don't ask me questions, Zeinab Lazarevna. Just take my word, and let it reassure you. You have a friend near you, someone who will help you if you need it. We all need friends, even if they are only the family retainers we have grown up with. Sometimes a servant can be of real use, in an emergency."

She nodded, silently. Then, embarrassed, she withdrew her hand, and rose awkwardly. "I have to go." She tried not to meet his eye. "Thank you, Yasha."

"Zeinab Lazarevna—"

But she was gone.

Even as she hastened away, Yakov wondered why she was so unhappy. Surely it involved the medical student, Ostrov. *What was he doing to her?*

Perhaps, Yakov thought, he doesn't really love her. Perhaps he is only leading her on. But there was no possible way to find this out. And besides, what if this were true? There was nothing a servant could do.

Nobody had ever loved Kyril like Zica. True, his mother had attached herself to him out of desperation. But this was different. This girl loved him. She loved him so much that her eyes were moist with emotion. Her small hand reached out to touch and caress him; to soothe him; to take away his cares. She loved him more than her own honor, more than the code of values she had been reared with. She seemed to love him more than her parents and her brother.

Yet *I need to be sure,* he thought, adjusting his tie. I need to know she lives for me, that she would die for me. Despite their avowals to each other, Kyril felt a vague but growing uncertainty: he did not deserve her love, so how could she really love him? Wouldn't it slip through his fingers—wasn't this love all a delusion?

Countess Vyrubova chuckled as she patted Tamara on the hand. "You girls have done a fine job today," she declared.

Behind her were row upon row of machines for the manufacturing of bandages. Every Monday and Thursday, men arrived with meters of gauze, which were rolled onto the machines and cranked out to be cut. The cut gauze was then thrown into a tray and passed to the ladies for trimming. Tamara, Zica and their friends sat at large tables, cutting off the excess threads from the frayed edges of the bandages. The threads were tossed into large baskets that were picked up at the end of each day. It was an easy but boring chore: by the end of the day their fingers would be aching. But one felt good. This was essential war relief work. These bandages would help dress the wounds of thousands of patriotic soldiers.

Zica bent down to fasten her galoshes. "I always wonder about the men who will wear these bandages," she commented softly. She tied her hat down with a woolen scarf that almost covered her mouth. "I mean . . . about who they are, and what lives they've left behind." Her voice trailed off. Suddenly embarrassed, she asked, "Are you coming, Tamara?"

"Your driver is waiting outside," the Countess told them. She was a short, plump woman in her fifties. Escorting them into the foyer, she led them to the victoria which stood parked outside. Volodia, the Poliakov driver, opened the door with his usual flourish. The girls pulled the quilted blanket over their shivering legs and arms. The victoria rocked as the driver climbed up on his perch. There was the crack of his whip as he urged the horses into a trot.

"It's all set for tonight?" Tamara asked.

Zica nodded. Her face glowed, pale and haunted. "This is what he wants."

"If your father finds out—"

"Nobody will find out. I know that the man who will drive us can be trusted. It is the assistant librarian, Yasha. He owes me this: I had him transferred from my aunt's household in Odessa, where he was being badly treated. Besides . . . he says he's my friend."

Tamara shrugged. "No servant is ever your friend, Zica. Especially now, with the revolutionaries planting bombs under rich people's noses."

Zica didn't reply. She simply shivered under the quilt, and shut her eyes.

Yakov's face was earnest as he spoke to Dima, Misha and Natasha. They were all sitting on the floor in his little room, drinking *kvass.* He was praising the beauty and fascination of women's breasts in such a hopelessly boyish style that everyone in the room was convulsed with laughter.

Finally, Natasha crossed her arms over her chest. "Don't you boys know that such a topic of conversation isn't to be raised in front of a lady? Where are your manners!" she shouted in mock horror.

"Natashka, my darling, the best thing about you is that, thank the Lord, you are not a lady," Misha told her.

Yakov smiled and touched her cheek. "So listen: I used to worry that I was sick or something. All through my childhood, I would dream of breasts, the larger the better. I didn't care if they were shaped like melons, peaches, or pears—"

As Yakov continued with his oration on female beauty, Dima chuckled, rocking back and forth on his haunches.

"Mine are very small," Natasha suddenly interrupted. She made a gesture with her hands that made everyone laugh even more loudly. When they caught their breath, Misha turned to Yakov. "With you, Yasha, one never knows what is the truth and what is a joke. Your jokes sound serious, and when you're serious, it sounds like a joke."

"But this wasn't meant to be funny," Yakov declared. "It was meant to illustrate a point—two points, actually—" And he was off again.

But he ended on a more serious note: "—Do you know why they call the Jews 'the chosen people'? Because the Tzar chooses us as his scapegoats, and the gentry chooses to exploit us, and we choose to accept everything and bless the ones who oppress us. The Jews are born victims, in this country. But I, for one, have decided to make a life for myself in spite of this."

"You should abandon the violin and make people laugh," Dima told him.

Yakov shook his head mournfully. "I try to tell this to the backs of the Baron's books," he said. "But they never laugh like you, my friends." Yakov's hand was still on Natasha's cheek.

Suddenly there was a rap at the door. "Who is it?" Yakov asked. "Senya, is that you?"

Instead, a feminine voice requested shyly, "It is I, Zeinab Lazarevna. Please let me in, Yasha. I need to speak to you."

Yakov's hand dropped. Natasha flashed an angry look about the room. "What does *she* want?" she demanded in a low voice.

"How should I know?" Yakov shot back. But already, his hand was on the doorknob.

Zica stood on the threshold, hugging herself in a thick woolen coat trimmed with black seal. Yakov looked her up and down, and all at once his heart was filled with empathy. She seemed so small and miserable, so vulnerable. He cleared his throat and made a motion for her to pass inside.

Zica peered around her in alarm and bewilderment. "Oh..." she sighed. "I didn't mean..."

"It's all right. Please sit down, Zeinab Lazarevna."

"And we shall leave," Dima announced, rising. He extended his hand to Natasha and pulled her up unceremoniously. "We shall disturb you no longer."

Zica nodded at them, but her face held fear. She walked to the small window and looked out, clasping her hands together. She listened as Yakov ushered his friends out; she heard Natasha's irritated goodnight; then the door closed. Turning to Yakov again, Zica noticed that his face was full of compassion. "I need your help," she said to him, and leaned against the wall. "You told me I could count on you..."

"And so you can. What do you want me to do?"

She closed her eyes. "I need to be driven somewhere tonight. At midnight, when my parents have retired. I don't want Volodia to do it. This is a private matter. I don't want anyone to know where I'm going, or with whom. Will you take me, Yasha?"

He felt a terrible premonition of loss, of danger. "But if the Baron..."

"If my father finds out, he will fire you. Will you do it anyway?"

Yakov's black eyes sought hers. He saw the panic just below the surface, threatening to explode. He suspected something irrevocable was about to occur—something which would surely alter his life for the worse, forever. A certainty crept over him, telling him that he would surely lose her, whether or not he complied with her heartfelt plea.

"Yasha, *I beg you*," she whispered, and in that instant the die was cast.

He nodded mutely, feeling his body grow rigid with foreboding.

Zica touched his hand for one brief second. She smiled, but the smile was empty. He could tell that in her mind she had already left him. She had already moved away to her mysterious destination. At the door, she paused.

"Thank you," she told him. And then: "I'll never forget you, Yasha Pokhis."

And those words announced the bitter truth—that after tonight she would never return. Beyond their midnight *rendez-vous,* he would never see her again. Still, he could not refuse: for, long ago at Rigevka, she had enthralled him.

Chapter VI

KYRIL waited outside the Medical School, wrapped in the old sealskin coat that had belonged to his father in Rostov. If she didn't come, it would mean that she didn't love him. Only that afternoon, Kyril had confided in Igor Panevsky, a friend at the Faculty of medicine. Igor had noticed that whenever the two of them went out together, women flocked to Kyril; but Kyril didn't know what to do with his apparent success. He flirted, he smiled . . . but, eventually, he let most of the pretty birds fly away from the aviary, admired but never captured.

Once in a while they went to a whorehouse, in a side street off Grachovka Road lit by oil lamps. But for the most part, Kyril was circumspect about his women. He had someone special, he explained—someone whom he hoped to marry. She was some sort of princess, Igor gathered—somebody wealthy beyond imagination, cloistered and guarded, as all heiresses were, by their jealous fathers. Kyril would never marry her under normal circumstances, for he possessed neither the money nor the social standing that parents of such girls considered of much more importance than their daughters' emotions.

"And of course, she loves you," Igor had ventured, a twisted smile lighting his rather gaunt face.

"I believe she does." But there was much that Kyril could not explain to a stranger—his childhood, the beatings, his father, the fears within himself. How could he describe his grandfather's coldness and rejection, or convey the fact that his mother didn't love *him,* but rather had invented in her fertile imagination a "perfect son" to love. Kyril was forever a disappointment to those near him, and, most of all, a disappointment to himself. His attractiveness was the candy wrapper that fooled his public: beneath it, he feared, he was just a tasteless morsel.

The whores didn't expect perfection, and weren't disappointed. But *he* was disappointed, sick at heart for going to them in the first place. So they paid for his anger when he caused them to cry out. Igor would hear them through the thin walls and laugh, praising him for causing them such heightened pleasure that their shrieks reverberated throughout the brothel. Only Kyril knew that the cries went beyond pleasure—to pain.

But he would never want to hurt Zica. "She loves me," he explained to Igor Panevsky. "She is a sweet girl, and a shy one; but for some reason, I have unleashed something wild and powerful within her. She does things I would never have expected. Perhaps there's hope for us then . . . through the strength of her love."

"You are looking for a redeemer," his friend told him. "That never works out."

"I am looking for someone who will make me feel that I am a man."

Now Kyril felt his heart twisting inside him. He remembered kissing Zica and holding her. He remembered how his virility had pierced to her very center, how she would never be the same. How could either survive after that enduring closeness? Now it was Christmastime in Moscow. The streets were knee-deep in powdered white snow, glinting in the moonlight like *pavé* diamonds encrusted in fine, gleaming platinum embankments. She belonged to him.

Kyril heard the crunch of horses' hoofs. An elegant troika was gliding toward him; he pulled the collar of his coat higher to ward off the chill. The troika slowed, and a small man cloaked in several layers of wool dismounted from the driver's perch.

"Kyril Ostrov?" the chauffeur inquired.

He had heard this voice before; it sounded curt, somewhat challenging—not the tone he might have expected from a Poliakov servant. He nodded, peering into the man's face as the driver opened the carriage door. He had seen that face somewhere—and recently.

Zica was inside, a fur blanket pulled clear up to her neck, her head half-hidden by a beaver hat. "You came . . ." he murmured, bending to kiss her.

She nodded silently. Her hands remained tucked inside the fur muff.

"Rabbi Signer has found a house outside the city limits," Kyril told her. "It belongs to a bookbinder he knows. He is waiting there, with the host and his family. He has been paid, and will marry us within forty minutes. After that, you will be my wife. Zica—my love—we can face anything as man and wife!"

"It is all wrong, Kyril. This isn't how I saw it. . . ." Her voice broke.

Kyril squeezed her hand. "It's the *only* way, sweet my darling. Once we have been formally wed by a rabbi, your father will not be able to stop us from being together."

Her sigh was like the moaning wind. "This rabbi . . . have you told him who I am?"

"He is someone I met at my grandfather's friends' house—the Vaizmans. He is an acquaintance of theirs: don't worry. No, I have not told him the name of the bride. I have paid him twenty rubles —a lot of money. I assure you, he is not asking questions. He will find out soon enough."

"What if—what if he refuses to go through with the ceremony? He'll be afraid of my father's wrath; he will be afraid to lose his post!"

"Don't concern yourself with problems: I've thought of everything. *Reb* Signer is not from Moscow: he's a scholar who has no temple of his own. He teaches and lectures all over the country, going from salon to salon and from lecture hall to lecture hall. Beside, his home is far away, near Kiev. Your father may not even find out his name!"

"Papa knows everybody," Zica said. Then she stopped. Kyril noticed that her teeth were chattering. He slid his arm around her shoulders.

"If you are so afraid after being married, we shall have your driver drop us off at the train station. We shall go to Rostov, to my grandfather. He will arrange for us to travel at once to France, or to England."

"So you are afraid as well . . ."

He ignored her question. "Will the driver tell?"

She shook her head. "That's Yasha, the assistant librarian. It wouldn't behoove him to talk about this, for he would be directly blamed, and would lose his place."

Yasha. That would be "Yakov." Now Kyril knew where he had met the man—at the Opera! Yakov, then, was nothing more than a Poliakov retainer. And Kyril had been afraid that Yakov would speak to the family about him. Suddenly he wanted to laugh. The more he thought about their meeting at the Opera, the more giddy he felt. He, Kyril, had shaken the hand of a servant and quaked at his touch, fearing the worst . . . of a simple assistant librarian!

"You trust this Yasha?" he asked, trying to stop laughing.

"Yes, I do. I don't understand why you think it's funny . . ."

"It's nothing, my darling, just a passing notion." Kyril turned serious. "If you trust him, so I shall I." He pressed her cold fingers and kissed her in the vulnerable crook of her neck.

The house was small and low. To Zica it resembled nothing so much as an Eskimo igloo: when she looked out from the troika, she saw only a mound with window-eyes in a panorama of white-on-white. Icy fingers gripped her insides; she felt panicked. *Her parents would never forgive her.*

Tears welled up, but she blinked them away. "Why are you weeping?" Gently, Kyril reached out to cup her chin. He peered into her eyes. "Are you not happy to marry me?"

The image of Zhenya, of her father and mother, of the house on Tverskaya Street, passed before her eyes like a distant memory. Zica gazed back at him, glimpsing the gold flecks in his green eyes and the worry lines in his brow. *He was surely thinking that she didn't love him enough.* Kyril always needed proof of her love, more and more proof. It was as though he were asking her to make up for all the pain he had ever experienced. Sometimes, Zica thought, this was truly a frightening prospect.

"I am happy to marry you, my beloved," she replied. "But you must try to understand: I have a brother, parents . . . I have a whole *life,* Kyriusha, which you have asked me to set aside, and which I am leaving behind forever. I am doing this, darling, because I love you; but it is hard to have lied to those I love, hard to think that I shall never face my father again. I shall never again be welcome in my brother's arms. I know I am causing them much pain."

"My mother and father eloped," declared Kyril. "That is why my grandfather wouldn't take care of us when my father died. Yet my mother didn't hesitate to throw everything aside for the man she loved!" Kyril's voice sounded harsh. "Only *he* wasn't worthy of her sacrifice! It was *I* who was made to pay for it."

Zica was stunned. She had not heard this part of the story—yet, all at once, Kyril's actions—his insistence on this marriage—made new sense to her. A bolt of anger shot through her: how *dared* he have recast her in Elena's role? Would Zica's future be as full of anguish as Elena's past? He had pressured Zica, she now saw, in order to exorcise his own pain. Her parents mattered to him only because of her willingness to leave them. Did he stop to think that these were the people she'd held so dear through her entire existence?

Kyril had lived his mother's loneliness, his mother's relative poverty. After this secret wedding, he wanted to go home to Rostov, to throw himself and his new bride at the mercy of his grandfather. Was this all that mattered to Kyril—getting his grandfather to accept him? Was Zica to be nothing more than a peace offering to Yossif Adolfovitch Byitch? It looked like a cruel manipulation. She drew back from Kyril, appalled. And she said to him: "This is not love! We could have waited, and done this right! Why did you force me into this, Kyril?"

"I want you to belong to me," he answered. His eyes were full of fear.

"People don't 'belong' to each other, like material things," she declared angrily.

But the troika door was already opening. Yasha was holding out his hand to help her down. A sense of the inevitable engulfed her. She stepped into the snow, Kyril following close behind.

Impulsively, averting her face from her lover, she laid her muffed hand on the arm of Yakov Pokhis. She felt better, walking by his side.

"Are you all right, Zeinab Lazarevna?" Senya's assistant asked in a low voice.

She nodded. Inside her coat, pressed to her breast, was a small signet with an etched pattern. It was her personal seal—that she pressed against hot wax when sealing an envelope. She touched it now—glad that she had taken it with her.

"I can always drive you home, if you aren't sure," he murmured.

Tears rolled down her cheeks. She touched the signet inside her coat, thinking it was all that connected her to her family, the family she might be rejecting forever. "Oh, Yasha," she cried, "what am I doing? Will I regret this all my life? I'm so . . . muddleheaded."

"It is still time to undo this, because nothing has yet been done," the young man said in a low voice.

But Kyril was coming up behind them, and, with assurance, plucked Zica's hand from Yakov's arm and inserted it in the crook of his own. Zica felt Fate pulling the blanket over her head. Defenseless, she submitted.

They entered the house.

The rabbi was small and thin, with a wizened face like a bleached prune. He smelled of old parchment and desiccated leather, mixed with an odor of brine, an odor which Zica thought might be typical of the Pale of Settlement. She looked about her at the furniture and the shabby wallpaper. Everyone had now gathered around the enamel stove in the middle of the room. Zica felt herself grow dizzy.

"It will be all right, it will be all right," the rabbi said, hastening to them. A taller man came to his side. There were introductions all around—to the host and hostess, and to their small children. In the commotion the rabbi turned to Zica and asked: "What is your name, young lady? Your bridegroom did not tell me when we arranged this at the Vaizmans'."

Zica swallowed hard. "Zeinab Lazarevna Poliakova." Now, surely, he would end all this. The rabbi would know what her father might do.

Instead, the small rabbi scratched his head. "Poliakov...? But *certainly* not *the* Poliakovs of Moscow?"

She said, "I am the daughter of Lazar Solomonovitch Poliakov. He knows nothing of this marriage."

"Zica refused to allow me to petition him for her hand in marriage, *Reb* Signer," Kyril cut in. Zica glared at him. If the rabbi chose to stop all this, so be it. She was now fully prepared to respect his decision. Her heart was pounding painfully.

Gently, the rabbi probed: "And what if he disinherits you, Zeinab Lazarevna? Have you two children thought this through...?"

"Zica doesn't care about riches. She loves me," Kyril announced. In that instant, Zica saw Kyril's face take on resolve, saw the anxiety ebb away. It was as if her love mattered so much that it could nullify poverty and loneliness.

The rabbi's brows rose. "How hopeful life is when you are in love."

"Zica's love makes me feel invincible."

A moment of silence ensued. Zica felt embarrassed and ill at ease. She felt that Kyril was oppressing her. He needed her to love him, almost more than she needed him to be her Prince Charming. She saw that he needed her steadfast loyalty, the power of her emotion. How, then, could she betray him and not go through with the ceremony? *His need had trapped her;* his need had cancelled out her own desires and wishes.

Would she always have to yield, in order to give him sustenance?

At that moment, her instincts rebelled. *Do not marry him,* called a small voice inside her—a voice too faint to still her emotions and the instincts of her body. But she was too weak to turn him down.

"Come, my dear." *Reb* Signer placed a bony hand, speckled with age spots, on her slim arm. "I want to proceed. It is late and I have somewhere to travel tonight."

"Blessed are Thou, O Lord our God, Ruler of the Universe, Who has created all things for Thy glory."

Yakov shuddered as he watched the little gathering. Once, in Peredelkino, he would have admired their appearance—the men in their neat shirts and yarmulkes, their shoes shining and clean-shaven faces; the women with their kerchiefs and colorful skirts and blouses. But now, after living in Odessa and amid the regal household on Tverskaya Street, he found them sad and wretched. The bookbinder's family seemed only a step above the denizens of his *shtetl* in the Pale.

Zica was beautiful in her silk gown. Her fingers were manicured and be-ringed like those of a princess. Those hands had never touched dishwater, and never would. Yakov had to admit that the groom looked as if he came from a similar background. He was glamorous, with that special charm that rendered his imperfections endearing. With his grace and presence, Kyril seemed like someone who was easy to like and easy to love.

At that moment, Yakov felt pure hatred for the medical student —not only was he marrying Zica, but he was naturally endowed with charm, beauty, an aura of greatness. He was *graced:* the kind of person for whom everything is easy.

Zica's face was pale and drawn. She looked ill. But her hands gripped Kyril's fingers, holding on for dear life. Yakov couldn't figure out whether she wanted to be here or not, whether she wanted to marry this man or run as far from him as possible. Suddenly, he caught her eye and understood. She was in love, but her love had trapped her into being where she didn't wish to be.

Zica, he knew instinctively, had dreamt of a white wedding. She was a woman who dreamt of walking down the aisle of a fine temple on her father's arm, admired by her friends. She would have dreamt of roses, orchids, pearls and diamonds—of a dinner-dance with full orchestra and long tables set with Meissen china and cut-crystal goblets... of waltzes and orange blossoms. Yakov couldn't blame her. She had been reared to expect these things.

Understanding her thoughts, her expression, Yakov felt a renewed stab of pain. An ache pierced his heart. For, if Kyril Ostrov was failing, how much more would he, Yakov, have failed! Zeinab Lazarevna was so far beyond his reach that all he could do was to act the loyal servant. To hope for any other role would have been laughable.

His love had trapped him: in his heart of hearts, this was the place he least wanted to be.

"Grant, O Lord, that the love which unites this bridegroom and bride may grow in abiding happiness. May their family life be ennobled through their devotion to the faith of Israel. May there be peace in their home..."

Kyril Ostrov was staring at Zica, his green eyes embracing her, as if by absorbing her soul he could give substance to his own. Almost in agony, she fully averted her face and looked down at her boots.

Above them was suspended a hastily contrived *huppa* of make-shift wiring adorned with paper flowers. It looked drab and ill-conceived. Yakov felt such sorrow for Zica. *She was throwing her life away.* Men such as Lazar Poliakov disowned their disobedient offspring with a mere stroke of the pen. Didn't she know what lay in store for her?

Of course she did.

But she didn't—not really. How *could* she know?

"As you, Kyril, place this ring upon the finger of your bride, speak to her these words: 'With this ring be thou consecrated unto me as my wife according to the law of God and the faith of Israel.'"

Yakov's eyes filled with tears, surprising even himself. The young blond man took out a gold ring and slipped it on Zica's slim finger, repeating the words. Kyril Ostrov had a beautiful, deep voice, like a cantor's, resonant and mellow.

"And you, Zeinab..."

Yakov tried not to hear. The rabbi's voice faded. Yakov tried to close his eyes as well, but found he could not. Blinking, he watched Zica take the gold band as she said, "I am my beloved's and my beloved is mine."

The words seared Yakov. He felt bile rise in his throat.

"In the presence of this company—"

But suddenly the rabbi's eyes widened. A sudden look of horror distorted his face.

With a crash, the front door burst from its hinges. Three huge men lunged into the small room, dishevelled and red-faced from the cold.

Uttering a shrill cry, Zica fell against her bridegroom. The mother rushed to her small children and pulled them aside, cowering behind the enamel stove. The owner of the house called out, "Who are you? What does all this mean . . .?" His voice was almost a sob.

"You are Yuri Simonov? Bookbinder by profession?" one of the intruders demanded.

The man nodded, his face a white mask. "Wh-why are you here?"

"We have come to arrest you, in the name of the Tzar and the Tzarina. We know you have associated with traitors to the Empire. You have plotted against the life of our Tzar—"

"What are you talking about?" Simonov cried out. "I am a peaceful, law-abiding citizen, a member of the Artisans' Guild of Moscow—"

"You are a *subversive*. You have been engaged in a criminal activity for the past ten years. You participated in the plan to kill the Tzar's uncle, the Grand Duke Sergei, in 1905. You are and have been a member of the Socialist Revolutionary Party. We know you have been meeting every Thursday in the home of one Andrei Ukhtomsky on Petrovka Street in Moscow—"

Ears throbbing, Yakov could hear his own heartbeat. He looked at the terrified faces of the Simonovs, but his mind flashed back—to the Cossack invasion of his village, when they cut off the ear of *Reb* Meyer Zlotkin. Suddenly Yakov saw the body of the *reb,* left for dead in the street that January 1905. His pulse quickened. His mouth went dry. But now he was no longer Yakov Pokhis, young and ignorant and afraid of power, a Jewish boy in the wrong place at the wrong time. He was a man outraged—a man faced with injustice.

"What is the meaning of this?" he protested. "You would arrest a man for a crime committed ten years ago by another person?" he asked. "Surely we all know that the Grand Duke, Governor General of Moscow, was murdered by a man called Kaliayev?"

"And who are *you?*" the largest man demanded.

"It does not matter. This man—Yuri Simonov—is not a dangerous revolutionary. He is just a bookbinder, who leads a simple, well-ordered family life—"

"—and I can personally vouch for him," Zica's voice interrupted. All eyes focused upon her, and she cleared her throat. Emboldened by Yakov, she stepped up, proudly lifting her head. "I am Zeinab Lazarevna Poliakova." Her voice was strong and certain. "I am the daughter of Baron Lazar Poliakov. Surely you know of my father. . . ."

Her words, arrogant and emphatic, hung in the air. Yakov dared not take a breath. The tall intruder said: "Yes, Mademoiselle, of course we know of you, and of your father. But . . . the crime of treason . . . this man, Simonov . . ."

"In ten years you have not managed to find Kaliayev's accomplices? I cannot believe this! You are agoing on a witch-hunt—at whose bequest, I do not know. You have come to arrest a Jew, because that is easy. The arrest will earn you accolades, even if the man is innocent as a newborn. Shall I inform my father of your actions—your intrusion into Simonov's home? I will, then—as soon as I return to Tverskaya Street. Rest assured of that, gentlemen!"

Another one of the men demanded: "What proof do we have that you are indeed the Baroness Zeinab Poliakova?"

Zica's face blanched, but only momentarily. With a quick gesture she plucked the gold chain holding the signet—her personal seal, clearly imprinted with the mark of the Poliakov family. Without hesitation she handed it the official.

The man studied the seal without a change of expression. But as he handed it back to Zica, his face looked perplexed. "Baroness," he hesitated, "I was ordered to arrest this man and all of you in this assembly—"

"You cannot arrest the Baroness Poliakova," Yakov objected. He took a step closer to Zica. "Her father instructed me to bring her here tonight—"

"For what purpose?"

"For the purpose of bringing money to the Simonovs," Yakov declared. His knees felt weak, but his voice remained even and clear.

Confused, the first intruder said sneeringly: "But this piece of cloth—I know what it means!" He pointed to the *huppa* as though it were a rag.

"Surely, you do not think Zeinab Poliakova would marry in a place such as this, away from her parents and brother?"

"Of course not," the rabbi suddenly spoke up, bright spots springing out on his cheeks. "We were preparing for the wedding of one of my congregation. I asked these visitors to rehearse with me. They were kind enough to agree—"

"If you wish to arrest the Simonovs, perhaps you'd like to arrest me too, and deal with my father tomorrow," Zica interjected. Her tone was clear and firm. Yakov was so proud of her that his heart swelled.

The three men looked at one another. Finally, the first one sighed and shook his head. He scrutinized Simonov before turning to Zica. "Very well, Baroness. But we shall return tomorrow. In the meantime, you are free—all of you. But we shall of course check on your story, and speak to Baron Poliakov."

As they strode out through the broken door, Yakov looked at Zica and saw, to his amazement, that she was gazing at him, a half-smile on her face. "You were wonderful," he told her.

Outside, there was a neighing of horses, shouts. And the intruders vanished into the night.

"Yasha, it was you who thought to step up and save these poor people," she murmured. Her hand touched his arm. "How brave you were! You gave me the courage needed to speak up—the courage my father and my brother have, when they are protecting the Jews. I had to do what I could."

She faced Yuri Simonov and the rabbi. "You must all come home with us, to Tverskaya Street. Tomorrow these men will return. They will arrest you for certain. Tonight you will sleep in my father's house. He must be informed of what has taken place."

To her surprise, the rabbi demurred. "Thank you, Zeinab Lazarevna," he said to her. "I'll just be on my way; but my friends will go with you. Your courage tonight has saved many innocent lives. May God bless you and keep you." Then, before she could protest, he gathered up his paraphernalia, struggled into his coat, and disappeared out the door. They heard the whinny of a horse as his small troika started up, bearing him off to an unknown destination.

In the house, as they prepared to depart, Yakov watched Zica help the Simonov woman bundle up the children. He felt his heart melt. Zica was like one of the women from the Pale after a pogrom. Poliakov, Simonov, or Pokhis—it did not matter—when the Tzar or his cohorts lusted for the blood of Jews, a Jewish woman had no family name, only her heritage to guide her.

Timid little Zica, the woman he loved, had made a choice the moment Yakov had spoken his piece. She had chosen her father's side, the side of the just and true. She had taken the side of the oppressed, and laid aside her personal welfare, like a true daughter of the *shtadlan of shtadlanim,* Lazar Poliakov.

Only then did Yakov remember they had been in the middle of a wedding. He found himself staring at the face of Kyril Ostrov, who stood alone in the middle of the room, motionless beneath the makeshift *huppa.*

Ostrov's face had frozen. His green eyes were glazed over like those of a dead man. He looked half dead with fear.

Kyril Ostrov was a coward, Yakov realized. For the first time, he felt compassion for the other man, who had, in one instant, lost his bride by a mere accident of destiny.

Then Yakov thought how close he had come to losing everything: his life, his love, in one tiny moment. Perhaps there *was* a God, after all, who watched over him and kept him safe. Could this be the same God who had saved him from the Cossacks, ten years before? Perhaps this God was on Yakov's side.

But he was not on the side of Kyril Victorevitch Ostrov.

Driving up twisting Tverskaya Street, Yakov saw that a full array of lights had been turned on inside the Poliakov mansion. The white stone edifice, built by the classical architect Kazakov in 1783, jutted out into the street like a midnight guest poking his head out to learn what was taking place.

Adroitly, he pulled into the driveway and made room for the Simonovs' *lineika* to park behind him. Yakov jumped down, threw the door of the troika open, and extended his hand to Zica. Behind her came Simonov's wife, Mania, and one of the small children.

"You must be cold, Zeinab Lazarevna," he said, guiding her gently toward the front door, his hand on her elbow. He knew she must be in a state of apprehension and guilt, having to face both her father and Kyril Ostrov, who had followed behind in the *lineika.*

As Sergei opened the front door, Yakov saw, in back of him, the forms of the Baron and Baroness, in their dressing gowns. He felt Zica falter, and steadied her. Behind them crowded the Simonovs and their children.

For a moment, defiance filled his spirit: surely, Yakov thought, Poliakov would fire him and blame him for Zica's escapade. The young man thought: I don't care! If I lose this job, I shall simply find another. There are many jobs available in Moscow!

But the Baron's face, stricken and white, shook his resolve. When Poliakov rushed to his daughter, Zica took an involuntary half-step backward. She stumbled against Yakov.

"Zica," the Baron cried: "What is the meaning of this?! Where have you been?"

"I—"

"It was my doing, Lazar Solomonovitch," Yakov heard himself say. Zica whipped around, her lips parting. There was a pinched look around her eyes. He had to continue. Now the Baroness, Elizaveta Borisovna, came up as well. Sergei stood a few paces behind her, holding her shawl. Suddenly Yakov was surrounded by a semicircle of curious, attentive faces. "All this was . . . my idea . . . "

"*Your* idea, Yasha?" The Baron sounded incredulous.

"I . . . You see, we received a call around nine o'clock. I happened to be the one who took the call. It was . . . Simonov, the bookbinder. His child was ill and he needed help immediately. I didn't know what to do—but Zeinab Lazarevna overheard me. She decided that we had to go there and help, right away."

"Who is *Simonov?*" the Baron demanded. His voice sounded strident and harsh. Yakov had never seen his face like this—his long, straight nose so sharp and stark against the white of his cheekbones, like the mask of death.

"Simonov is an artisan of the First Guild, who resides on the outskirts of the city," Yakov replied. He was amazed how calm and clear he sounded, in the midst of this confrontation with his own master.

"Zica, is this true?"

"No one was home," she replied, her voice hesitant and small. She avoided her father's stern, questioning look. "I acted on impulse. Yasha and I jumped into the troika, and we went to the Simonovs' to help."

"This is true, your honor," the bookbinder said, stepping up for the first time. "We had a sick child, and Zeinab Lazarevna helped my wife take care of her. It was Murka," he added. He held his tiny daughter aloft for the Baron and Baroness to see. "She's much better now."

"While we were there three men of the Secret Police forced their way into the Simonov house. They were going to arrest him and his wife on charges of conspiracy against the Tzar. Zeinab Lazarevna intervened."

"There was a call just half an hour ago from Lubyanka Street." The Baron's voice had the menacing ring of disbelief. "The inspector demanded to know where my daughter was. It was then that we discovered that her bed hadn't been slept in, and that the troika had disappeared, with Yasha."

"We didn't know what to think . . ." the Baroness said. Her voice, like Zica's, had a hysterical edge. "We thought perhaps—perhaps a kidnapping . . ."

Suddenly, her voice trailed off. She had just noticed Kyril Ostrov in the corner. "You?" she asked. "What are *you* doing here, Kyril Victorevitch? How are *you* involved?"

Zica almost began to speak. But her voice caught in her throat. It was Yakov who answered, shrugging as he did so. "Zeinab Lazarevna remembered that Kyril Victorevitch was a medical student. We called him to look after the child—and picked him up on the way there."

"I see. And now you have brought back the Simonovs, and this 'sick child.' I —"

"Papa, we could not leave them behind for the Secret Police to arrest! We must hide them here! Yasha and I—and Kyril—we only did what we hoped *you* would want us to do, under the circumstances. It was so frightening—they broke the door down. Those men just strode in . . . I . . ."

"*I'm* the one who insisted," Yakov interjected. "You see, Lazar Solomonovitch, the scene reminded me of the pogrom we had in Peredelkino in 1905, when the Cossacks cut off *Reb* Meyer's ear. I was afraid the policemen would return and slaughter everyone in that little house!"

"Yes, Papa: that's what we both thought." Yakov could hear the gratitude in her voice. It enveloped him completely. For indeed, he had saved the situation, not once, but twice: first, with the men from Lubyanka Street, who would have taken the Simonovs away —and now with the Baron, her father.

Zica looked at Yakov with new trust and confidence. Her appreciation was like a gentle balm to him.

"Well," the Baron sighed, "I am distressed, truly distressed by this series of events. It's apparent that the Secret Police are once again singling out Jewish families to persecute." He glanced at the baby. "We must care for this sick child." The harshness had left his features. "Zicotchka," he said: "You did the right thing. And you too, Yasha. You shall receive a bonus this month, with your wages.

I like to see my servants show humanity toward others. You are a good boy, Yasha, and have served us well."

Then his gaze lit on Kyril again. "You have performed a service, too, young man, and for that I thank you." The Baron's voice was tinged with coolness. "You and I are not well acquainted—yet, whenever I take Zica to the Opera, you usually happen to be there. When we go to a gallery opening, you are there as well. Do you not know that you are compromising her by giving the appearance of courting her without my permission?"

The Baron's tone had turned icy, his black eyes piercing. Yakov spoke up once more, impelled by an inexplicable compassion. "Kyril Victorevitch was only trying to be of help," he explained. "We could think of no one else who would come on a moment's notice and know what to do with a sick child. Zeinab Lazarevna suggested several other doctors who might help, but I insisted on calling Kyril Victorevitch, since I know him."

Kyril seemed too shaken to utter a single word.

"Well now, you have been warned." The Baron's eyes narrowed, giving him the appearance of a Renaissance prince appraising his foe. "Again I thank you, but I must also make clear the rules of this household: Zica has no reason to socialize with you without my permission. When you have explained yourself to me and I have spoken with your family, you will be most welcome."

Kyril nodded mechanically, as though entranced.

Zica looked away, unable to face the visible hurt in his eyes. Unable to bear any more, she suddenly ran from the room, bursting into tears.

Elizaveta Borisovna addressed her husband, angrily: "See what you have done, Lazar? It is the middle of the night, and she is exhausted. Now you have upset her with your threats, and she will not sleep!" Lifting a panel of her voluminous velvet dressing gown, she glided after her daughter, her fine gown hissing as it brushed over the gleaming parquet floor.

The Baron scowled at everyone. There was color in his cheeks. "Very well," he stated. "Sergei, please take the Simonovs to the servants' quarters and give them proper lodgings. And you, Yasha —I shall see you tomorrow morning in the library." Without addressing Kyril Ostrov again, he turned around and exited, his steps resounding on the marble floor like the thin taps of a walking stick.

Sergei looked Yasha up and down, questioning him with his eyes. But the young man smiled back innocently. Finally, he said: "Kyril

Victorevitch, perhaps I might give you a ride back to your residence?"

"I would be most grateful." His voice quivered when he spoke.

Outside, the two men regarded each other frankly. "Why did you defend me?" Ostrov asked bluntly.

Yakov shrugged. "You are my age; you are in love; and you have as little chance of gaining your objective as do I. Tonight has proven that, has it not? Why do we need to be enemies, do you suppose...?"

Then, without looking back at the stricken man, Yakov led the way to the troika and opened the passenger door. "She does not love you anymore," he remarked as Ostrov climbed in. "And for this, I have much to be thankful. For I, too, love Zeinab Lazarevna."

Then he closed the door of the troika.

Book II:

Compromises

Chapter VII

As Kyril leaned over the stone parapet, he noticed that the throbbing in his head had increased. He shut his eyes instead, blocking out the sight of the smoothly flowing Seine River below him. This city should have been heaven to him. After all, it was Paris, the City of Light—the city his mother had dreamed of visiting since her youth. He was out of Russia, away from the place that had been the site of so much humiliation. Why was he so alone?

Opening his eyes again, he watched the pigeons dive for bread crumbs. Small children passed by, laughing with their nannies. In 1916, Paris was deserted of all able-bodied men. The blind dragon of war now devoured everything. What a difference from Russia. There, thousands—perhaps millions—of young men like himself were exempted from service.

The fall trees were dropping leaves that swirled in eddies of gold, red, and brown around his feet. But fall brought him no glad memories. He had met Zica during the fall. Suddenly, just thinking about her made him dizzy with pain. The shock stunned him.

In the not quite two years since he had last seen Zica, he had often thought about her. He had relived every detail of their last encounter, even as he sought to put a continent between them. It was almost as though he dared the pain not to flow. He dared Zeinab Lazarevna Poliakova to fade into the colored nothingness of a reproduction, of a still life.

Yet her memory had not faded at all.

Kyril recalled sitting in the troika, numb with hurt. Yakov Pokhis, the Poliakov servant, had driven him back to his lodgings; that was when Yakov had told him that he, too, was in love with Zica. Kyril could not deny the truth—that Zica did not love him anymore. He thought how she had bundled up the Simonov children without looking at him . . . how the rabbi had looked sideways at him before taking his leave, not knowing what to say to him. *Kyril had almost had her!* Had it not been for the Secret Police . . .

Kyril recalled how Zica had trembled in front of her father. Worst of all was the way Lazar Solomonovitch had insulted and belittled him. He had felt her fear. It had enveloped him, too, sending chills up his spine. Kyril had been incapable of formulating a single intelligent thought. Zica's fear had paralyzed him.

Had he loved her *that* much? In the beginning, he had toyed with her. Her ardent passion amused him. If a beautiful debutante like Zeinab Poliakova found Kyril so irresistible, then he was truly powerful. She had redeemed him from all fears and doubts about his masculinity.

And she was so rich . . . ! It was impossible to separate the girl from her surroundings. Even in his grandfather's house in Rostov, Kyril had never believed anyone could live like the Barons Poliakov. So he had conceived the plan to marry her. If Zica married him, she would cast out the malevolent ghost of his father. He would show all the Alyoshas of his youth—all those who had beaten him and called him names!—that he was more successful than they.

Only it hadn't worked out that way.

He had returned home to the boarding house. The next day, when he'd come home from the Faculty, his mother had been scented and well-dressed when she met him at the door. "We have a guest," she had announced, with a sweep of her hand. "The Baroness Zeinab Poliakova."

She has come to apologize, Kyril had thought. Relief swept over him. During the night, he had wept and rocked upon his haunches, grief shredding his guts. He truly did love her, more than life.

But Zica had not come to beg forgiveness. She was dressed in black, wearing a little black toque, bedecked with egret feathers. An odd little figure in mourning, she stirred her tall glass of tea.

"I must speak with Kyril privately, if you do not mind," she told Elena Yossifovna, her tone almost peremptory. His mother had left the room, closing her bedroom door behind her.

"I like your mother," Zica had told Kyril as he sat down facing her. "She is very like you: passionate and obstinate, with haunted eyes."

"Yes, Mother has suffered a great deal." He waited.

"Kyriusha—"

"What?"

They gazed at each other mutely, their eyes fixed. Hers were clear and lucid; his, bloodshot from tears he had shed during the night.

"You could have been my wife," he said simply.

"Yes, you're right." Zica busied herself with her spoon. "But it didn't happen. And—and I'm glad it didn't. Running off to get married in the middle of the night was wrong, Kyriusha. It might have killed my father! The moment I walked in, and I saw his face —*he knew,* Kyril. But he said nothing. If he had, it would have broken relations between us forever. This way we can each cling to the illusion that my story—Yasha's tall tale—was the truth."

"If he loves you so much, he would have understood."

"No. He is a proud and stubborn man too, just like you. He would have crossed me out of his life."

"And so," Kyril said, "you had to choose between me and your father. Ultimately, he won."

"No, Kyriusha. You *put* me in the position of choosing. I asked you to let things lie, to trust me. I knew that, soon enough, the time would come for you to speak to my father. But you couldn't wait. You forced me to go with you. You were oblivious to the pain I was feeling, breaking up my home. Believe me, Kyriusha, that pain would have been too terrible for either of us to bear. It was *you,* not *I,* who forced a choice: now my choice is to let my father have his way. We must not see each other behind his back. Just for a little while, Kyril—until his eyes stop accusing me. Then you and I shall see each other again. We can plan again."

"So I must not be allowed to see you—indefinitely—until His Holiness puts down his defenses."

Zica blinked at the sharpness of his words. Tears sprang to her eyes. "Oh, Kyriusha—just for a few weeks! A month or two, at most!

"And I'm supposed to understand—as I was once supposed to believe that you loved me more than all others in your life! *You're a liar, Zica!* You never loved me! You used me for your pleasure, but you never thought to marry me. I wasn't good enough! You are a Poliakov—how could I have thought otherwise? You played me for a fool, because I was romantic enough to fall in love with you. But now I see that you are cold; you are possessive. You want nothing but to live with Papa and his millions of rubles." Kyril paused, out of breath. Only Zica's shocked expression gave him the courage to continue. "You can wait forever, Zeinab Lazarevna—*because I never intend to see you again!*"

Her lips parted. Her face was white, stricken. He plunged ahead. "Now do us both a favor and get out of here." His tone was metallic. "I want to forget I ever knew you."

Striding to the door, he flung it open. She had said nothing more —nothing that he remembered. When she left, she was sobbing.

Later, his mother had found Kyril seated in the dark. The tea tray was still in place. Her glass was still full. "I don't want you to mention this girl again," he had told his mother, his voice dull and even. "Not if you wish to remain with me."

Elena had nodded, cowed into submission by the cold finality of his words.

He had kept his promise. He had never seen Zica again.

Kyril took a pack of cigarettes from his breast pocket, and plucked one out. With a look of abstraction, he lit it, and began to smoke. After the breakup, he had never returned to Tverskaya Street. On two occasions, she had sent Yakov to him with a note. Each time, Kyril had sent the messenger back with her seal still unbroken on the vellum envelopes.

Kyril could not pinpoint his feelings about Yakov: the man was bright and quick, that was certain. He was unforgiving and judgmental—a real Jew from the Pale, to be watched with caution. Kyril thought Yakov the kind of man who would not cheat you without reason. But his conscience operated like Robin Hood's, with a morality quite his own. Kyril could not figure out the little *shtetl* violinist-librarian—and now, of course, he had no reason to suppose he would ever see Yakov again.

The first time Yakov had come with a message, though, Kyril had invited him inside. He had to ask Yakov one question. "You say she doesn't love me anymore: but, how do you know?"

Yakov had leaned back in his chair, a quizzical expression on his small, dark features. "She's a good daughter. She was taken with you. You embodied passion and romance; she saw you as the man of her dreams. You were everything that she could not find within her own home. And so there was the promise that you could act out all the impulses she was terrified of expressing herself. You set off the rebellion brewing within. But, when the time came, she wasn't ready. That night, she made a choice. She could have asked the rabbi to finish the ceremony—but instead, she took the Simonov children home. *That* is the Poliakov in her: it was more important to help the Simonovs, poor dispossessed Jews, than to continue with her own elopement. She had to save them." Yakov's eyebrows shot up. "She has returned home, Kyril Victorevitch."

"Then deign to tell her not to contact me again." Kyril was furious at the servant's cool insight. He stood up, shaking. "Go, now!"

Yakov, embarrassed, left quickly. And the next time he came, the assistant librarian stayed only a few minutes—moments that were awkward for both men.

On that occasion, Kyril asked Yakov how long he planned to be Zica's messenger boy. His voice had dripped sarcasm.

But Yakov had merely scratched his head and laughed. "My days at the Poliakovs' are numbered," he declared. "I am about to finish my stint at the Conservatory, and then it will be time to start something for myself."

"You are not afraid of being on your own . . . after so many years with the Baron and his family?" Kyril taunted.

"I was not a servant by birth," Yakov replied with quiet dignity. "My father sold second-hand goods in the *shtetl* where I was reared. We were poor as dirt, but we were indentured to no one. I preferred it that way. I am looking forward to going back to that kind of freedom."

"But a Jew is free nowhere in Russia," Kyril said softly.

Yakov examined him. "So it goes," he commented. "But at least, I shall be coming and going on my own. There is nothing worse than a Jew who is indentured to another Jew."

Now, smoking as he leaned over the parapet, Kyril shook his head, at the memory of Yakov. An odd little fellow, sharp as a blade . . . and perhaps just as treacherous. Where was he now? Kyril wondered. Still with the Poliakovs? If indeed he loved Zica, as he professed, how could he bear to be a servant in her own house?

He himself had not been able to stand Moscow for long. He had lasted out the scholastic year, then gone back to Rostov with his mother. In Rostov he had enrolled at the Faculty of Medicine. He had watched Elena reconcile with her father. By the end of 1915, he and his mother were sharing the old man's Sabbath supper at least once or twice a month.

Still, Kyril's grandfather remained unforgiving in many ways. Yossif Byitch was rigid, intensely religious, and very pragmatic. He viewed life as a way to thank the Lord for having made him a Jew.

But he also wanted to hold on to his money. Kyril found the two attitudes incompatible.

"Being a Jew in Russia is the worst misfortune a man can be born with," he once said to his grandfather. "It is a fact to be cursed, not welcomed with thanks."

"But we are 'the chosen people.' It is our *lot* to bear the burdens of the world. Eat, my boy. This roast beef has been cooked for your benefit in the finest red wine."

There was no use arguing: the old man always cut him off in mid-sentence. Elena would plead with her son from across the table, her blue eyes expressing a fond hope of peace and reconciliation. Sighing, Kyril had yielded. For his mother's sake, he would pretend to accept the old man's views, but inwardly he deplored their narrow scope.

He wanted to escape.

That summer, he found the means. He asked Yossif Adolfovitch to send him and his mother to Paris, where he would continue his studies. He knew exactly what tack to employ, too. "We are in the middle of a war that is going ever more disastrously," he told his grandfather. "Mother does not wish for me to enlist. She thinks I would be signing my own death warrant. Be that as it may—if I *don't* enlist, then I shall soon be drafted into the Tzar's tired army."

"We wouldn't want that, son," Yossif stated, shaking his head. "This war is useless to Jews, and will accomplish nothing for Russia, either."

"Well then, Grandpa, how would you presume to stop this? With every day that passes, I am rendering myself more conspicuous by my continued presence at the Medical School."

"I could send you abroad. I could send you to Vienna. You could study psychiatry, like that fellow Freud: he's one of us, you know."

Kyril smiled. "It wouldn't work, Grandfather. The Austrians are at war with us Russians—remember?"

"Ah, so they are! You shall go to France, then, my boy. And you shall go as soon as possible—this fall, for the start of the school year."

It had been so easy, Kyril could not help but smile at the recollection. And Elena had promised to visit him, for her father had been adamant about not allowing her to accompany her son abroad. Yossif Adolfovitch had finally restored his relations with his daughter, and he was not about to permit a long separation between them.

Now, Kyril lived as he had always dreamed of living. He had a small apartment on Boulevard Montparnasse, on the Left Bank, just below the eaves of an eight-story building. "Apartment" was a brave word for the tiny kitchen, bedroom, and sitting room as small as a kopek, with a bathroom which consisted of nothing more than a hole in the concrete floor. But he had managed to furnish the place quite adequately on his grandfather's budget. The bed, dresser and chair were from the Samaritaine store; various small rugs and curtains had been purchased at the Flea Market. Kyril liked the sense of adventure that went with being in Paris on his own. He loved the bold, direct way women looked at him. What contrast to the demure, lowered lashes of Zica Poliakova and her well-bred acquaintances. French women knew what they wanted. During this time of war when there were virtually no young men available, he noted that their hunger was palpable even in their eyes.

Yet he had met no one to take the ache away. As Kyril leaned over, smoking his cigarette, he yielded to the sense of futility which came over him whenever he contemplated his loneliness.

And yet . . . on good days, the magnificent city charmed him. He wandered about whenever he could find time off from his studies. His neighborhood fascinated him. In the morning, chilled and clutching his frayed textbooks, he would walk northwest on Montparnasse to the long Rue de Rennes, and proceed northeast to the Boulevard Saint-Germain. The Faculty of Medicine was near the winding Rue de l'École-de-Médecine. There he found himself ensconced in classicism, especially in the older section of the building which faced the smaller street. Only the facade on Boulevard Saint-Germain, and the newer additions, bore the marks of the nineteenth century. The rest of the school, and the impressive courtyard with its statue of the anatomist Bichat, represented eighteenth-century classicism at its most imposing.

Here, everything was genuine. The musty smells inside the stacks of the library signified the passage of time immemorial, of medieval scrolls and scriveners writing fourteenth-century medical opinions. The museum on the premises was also fascinating. The tender part of Kyril's soul yearned to connect with the romantic past of his science, for he felt himself rooted in so little that bore personal meaning to him.

Did he really want to become a doctor? The idea of cutting open diseased bodies filled him with dread. Yet . . . what else was there? He had already spent three and one half years learning this profession. People admired doctors for their dedication. He had seen the praise his father had reaped, and how he had used his popularity to form friendships throughout Rostov. Kyril, for the most part, had never had friends. True, there had been Panevsky in Moscow... but even then, Igor had only been a sometime companion, a man whose opinions mattered little to Kyril—neither an intimate nor a confidant.

"It is a beautiful afternoon, is it not?"

Kyril turned to see a beautiful woman leaning against the parapet. Her fine, gloved fingers tapped the stone ledge. She was clothed to shield herself from the fall chill: an enormous tent-shaped apricot wool coat ended in balloon-shaped sleeves and large ermine cuffs. The round patch-pockets and large round collar were all decorated with ermine. Two-toned high boots of white and tan peeked under the hem of her coat. A peach hat with a large, flat brim and a bowler-shaped crown completed the outfit, some sprightly feathers adorning the grosgrain ribbon. Beneath the hat, her hair was a light, chestnut brown.

Her face was triangular, with large blue eyes and a small, up-turned nose. She was stunning. How old was she? Thirty, he supposed—her face had a healthy glow and there were no crow's feet at her eyes. Yet, she appeared mature, as was the wont with French women. Their experience breathed through their very pores, he thought.

He was strongly attracted. In Russia, only whores were permitted their worldly wisdom. The world of accessible women was divided into two categories; the ingénues whom men wed, and the experienced whores to whom they went for carnal pleasure.

Perhaps this woman was one of the *demi-mondaines* he had been hearing about: this strange, in-between class of kept women who "belonged" to the rich and powerful men of the city. Their caste was as indeterminate as their backgrounds. Frequently, women such as these inherited vast fortunes upon the death of their protectors.

"Where I come from, it would be unheard-of to be walking around in late October with only a jacket for protection," Kyril replied.

The woman smiled, her blue eyes appraising him. "I do detect an accent. And I would have predicted one even without hearing it. Who else but a foreigner would deign to walk through Paris in the middle of a ghastly war, appearing *insouciant* and contemplative and, above all, *unashamed* . . . ?"

"But I am not ashamed," he smiled back. "This is not my war to fight. It is a matter between the Serbs and the Austrians, and should never have concerned anyone else."

She lifted her brows. "You have strong feelings, Monsieur. And not necessarily popular ones."

"How can I not? Even in my country, I had to make a choice—to enlist, or to allow my deferment to stand. I did the latter, of course, as any sensible man would."

"You must be Russian! How very interesting! And what have you been doing here, Monsieur...?"

"Kyril Victorevitch Ostrov. You are quite right, Mademoiselle. I am Russian. I am also a student of medicine, in my fourth year. That constitutes exactly the midpoint of my student's career."

"How fascinating..." Her eyes played lightly over his face, his chest, his waistline, his hands. He could sense her appraisal—as if she were stripping him naked. It was almost physically arousing. But her eyes returned to his face. A delicate hand, encased in long kid gloves, was extended to him—not shyly at all. *"Madame,"* she corrected gently. "I am not a Mademoiselle, nor have I been for many years. Ten, to be exact. I will call you *Monsieur Cyril*—the French equivalent of 'Kyril'. If I may!" she added almost mockingly.

So she was married. This threw out the possibility of her being a courtesan. Kyril remembered how his father used to toy with women, allowing them to make advances toward *him*. Now he saw why. It was so pleasant: he would make this woman come to him as well. This was infinitely more fun and more rewarding than the chase.

"Cyril, it is, then. And what might your name be, Madame?"

"I am the Marquise de Huitton. My friends call me Lorraine. I was named after a much disputed province of France, where they also make fine cheeses. My father always adored controversy, and wondered whether men would fight to possess me the way the Germans and the French had fought over the Lorraine province since the beginning of the tenth century. In fact, Monsieur, the French are at this moment attempting to recapture parts of my namesake which were taken by Germany in 1871."

"I know very little French history," Kyril demurred. He thought how blue her eyes were: teal-gray, mixed with tiny sparks of cobalt. He wondered what her body must be like beneath that coat, how her hair looked without the hat.

"I could teach you the basics," she suggested, laughter in her eyes. "It's always more fun to learn with a native."

"But—would your husband approve?" The instant he asked, Kyril wanted to bite his lip. But it was too late. Lorraine's eyes glazed over. Her small chin tilted proudly upward. It was as if a cold screen had arisen between them. When she spoke, her voice was devoid of expression:

"He is fighting the Germans, Monsieur. My husband is a Captain of the Infantry. I have not heard from him in some months. But why do we need to discuss this now?"

"There is no reason whatsoever. I . . . just . . . I didn't want to appear . . ."

She smiled. "Appearances? Ah—you Russians. How quaint. Come, it is a beautiful fall day and I am hungry and thirsty. How will it *appear* if we have a cup of tea at the 'Marquise de Sévigné?'"

Kyril felt himself flush. A rush of excitement was followed by a quick let-down: he had no money. He had brought only a few francs with him on this stroll—for, as always, his grandfather had placed him on a budget. How was he to be gracious about such shameful impecuniousness . . . ?

"I am proposing to invite you," Lorraine de Huitton declared, her full pink lips parting to reveal even, luminous teeth. "Will you accompany me?"

He was stunned. Zica would have expired rather than invite a strange man to a public tearoom. But then, Zica was young, naive, and afraid. This woman with the name of the infamous province was older, self-confident, and terribly worldly. She knew exactly how to handle herself.

"It would be my pleasure, Madame la Marquise," he told her, offering her his arm.

Perhaps, as her friend Tamara had warned, she would never get over it. Shame, dread, and horror still pursued Zica. Almost two years later, Zica still recalled every detail.

She couldn't help herself. Now, as she poured the tea for Mossia Aronov, her hands began to tremble. She had to concentrate especially hard, just to avoid spilling. He watched her closely. "You don't seem quite yourself today, Zeinab Lazarevna. Are you perhaps coming down with influenza?"

"I hear it's going around," she remarked, handing him his tall glass in its silver holder.

"There will be a production of *The Nutcracker* in three weeks," the young man offered. He leaned forward, moistening his lips. "Perhaps you would allow my sister and me to invite you to attend the opening performance with us?"

"I must check my agenda, Moissei Yitzhakovitch. Thank you for thinking of me." She took a small cake, crumbled it between her fingers. She wiped her fingers with elaborate care.

"I always think of you."

Suddenly Zica rose. "I really am not well." Her voice was unsteady. "Please forgive me, but—"

"I understand. May I call on you tomorrow, at the same time?"

She shook her head. "No, I mean—I don't think... Moissei Yitzhakovitch, it has been nearly two years since you first began courting me. I don't think it is a good idea for us to prolong this ... ritual. Our parents will be led to expect ... you know ..."

"That we shall marry! But, my dear Zeinab Lazarevna, that is precisely my intention! How could you believe otherwise? I adore you! I have been waiting for the right moment to ask you—no, to *beg* you to marry me—but I had not thought it would be this way. I'm afraid...."

He had a ferret face, she thought suddenly, as she observed the angular features in that sallow face. He was ugly, eager, and so vulgar, beneath his fine clothes. She had sometimes imagined him making love to her—imagined his thin body, all ribs and hair, with tiny, bloodless nipples and a soft white belly. A long, thin penis bursting from a nest of wiry black hair, like a tall white mushroom from a bed of moss. She knew how eagerly he would want to jump on top of her and force her to take him inside; she saw herself cringing, dry and unwilling. The idea itself nauseated her. No! She would have to stop him, and right now, before he could press his suit any further.

"I am so sorry," she said, shaking her head. "I have probably led you on, when I merely wished to be your friend. I do not want to marry anyone, Moissei Yitzhakovitch. I do not *like* the very idea of marriage. I prefer to think of myself growing into middle age here, at home, with my parents and my books. So you see, it is not you I am rejecting, but the mere notion of living with a man, of sharing my solitude with a man ... of having his children. I do not want children, ever."

His face registered stunned, bewildered dismay. "No children— *ever?* I thought this was not possible. I thought all young women wanted to be mothers...."

Zica finally smiled. "All but me. I intend to end my days a spinster lady, with nieces and nephews I shall spoil to death, but no little babies of my own."

There was finality in her voice. Mossia rose as well, white-faced. "Zeinab Lazarevna, I didn't have any idea you felt this way. Why, I—"

"It is better that we remain friends, don't you think? Our parents would find it odd if they believed we'd quarrelled. So perhaps, after all, I shall come with you to the ballet. But you must not treat me any differently than your sister's girlfriends, your other acquaintances. Let people think that we are just good friends, loyal and true but not romantically involved. I *do* like you, Moissei Yitzhakovitch —and I esteem you a great deal."

She extended her hand and he took it. But he refused to look into her eyes. He was confused by her words, and by her determination. What an odd girl she had turned out to be, behind her good looks and fine demeanor. . . .

"Thank you for being so understanding," she told him. With that, she sailed from the room, leaving a delicate scent of attar of roses trailing behind.

On the staircase she encountered Yakov, carrying some notepaper to her father. She couldn't help blushing. "Hello, Yasha," she said. To her own amazement she didn't continue up the stairs. *She was waiting for this man to speak to her!"*

"It is very cold today, Zeinab Lazarevna," he said. "You must take care to wear a shawl, even inside the house."

"You are kind to worry about me."

"It isn't kindness."

Finally they were looking at each other. She could feel his intelligent eyes probing deeply. He knew things about her no one else knew, except Tamara and his own girlfriend, Natasha. And, though she hated him for it, she was also grateful. She would never be alone, as long as he remained in her father's service, sharing those secrets.

That he loved her, however, was no secret. She had figured that out months before. Perhaps she had really known for years. The way he regarded her, fussed over her—she was grateful for such love, for, unlike Mossia Aronov, he expected nothing in return. No reward could in fact be expected. He simply loved her.

"I do not want you to be ill," he said, more forcefully than he had intended.

"You are very kind, Yasha," she repeated.

"No," he said, "I am far from kind. I live my life for my own self, thinking of almost no one else. But I do think of you, Zeinab Lazarevna, because you are so frail and delicate, and you are alone."

"And you too are alone."

"Yes, of course. But I have always been alone. You haven't. Therein lies the difference. I am used to it, and you are not."

"Well," she said, a little breathless, "I must be going now. Have a pleasant afternoon."

"And you too," he replied, smiling at last. "By the way . . . I gave Tania the last book that came in from Paris, to set by your bed. It looks like a love story."

With a quick smile, she hurried up the stairs. Yasha Pokhis, her friend in the house. Her household friend. How odd, for one did not make friends among the servants. Well, he wasn't a *real* friend, just someone polite and agreeable who worked for her father— someone who was solicitous and kind, who kept his mouth shut.

Suddenly she felt chilled. Tears welled in her eyes. Yes, he had kept his mouth shut, hadn't he? And it was good he had. The secrets they shared were such that guilt and shame now made her blush, and she wished she were dead. But she wasn't about to reveal those feelings to Yasha. He was a servant, after all, and a man.

At least, she had ended this absurdity with Mossia Aronov. Tonight, she would have a talk with her father. Her parents would be sad, and they would be sorry. But the vision of Mossia climbing on top of her, ready to violate her . . . it was simply too much to bear, even for the sake of her father and his business. The Baron would have to survive without a link to the Aronov fortune. He would have to make his own business bargains.

She laughed and felt better, instantly.

Kyril looked with wide-eyed wonder around the Place Victor Hugo. The neighborhood was secluded, discreet, and tastefully opulent. Tall, slim townhouses were bordered by equally tall plane trees surrounded by wire pickets. Lorraine de Huitton's green 1913 De Dion-Bouton roadster sped through the quiet Sixteenth Arrondissement as though on a racetrack. Kyril was thrilled by the fact that this woman drove like a man possessed.

Lorraine was French to the limits: she laughed and ate and joked sensuously. She told salacious, funny jokes which would have of-

fended a good Russian *boyarynya.* And yet she exemplified the other
side of the French nobility. Where the Russians were larger than
life—grotesque, almost, in their childlike desire to expose how rich
and splendid they were—the wealthy French were discreet, almost
British in the restraint they showed. One did not flaunt his wealth
in Paris as one did in Moscow. One flaunted *nothing.* In fact, a
French woman left much to the imagination, tantalizing her suitor.
And Lorraine did exactly that. She had toyed with Kyril over tea
and cakes at the *Marquise de Sévigné,* allowing him to guess what
was expected of him. Now his desire was inflamed, teased by her
mystery.

Her house was like her, nothing ostentatious: on the outside,
white marble and tall, patrician windows, with wrought-iron rail-
ings and small balconies. It looked like the Poliakov palace, but
done in such exquisite taste that he could only guess at the splendor
of the interior. As they went in, the doorman led them through a
marble foyer to a thin elevator stall. From there, another liveried
servant took them upstairs, to a marble landing which overlooked
the reception room below. Kyril caught glimpses of huge paintings.
("My Monets are the happiest in Paris," Lorraine had told him), of
Louis XVI furniture upholstered in pale pastel silks, and of fine
Gobelins tapestries. The room was dominated by an enormous
grand piano.

"My Pleyel," Lorraine indicated with a theatrical sweep of her
hand: "I practice every morning before breakfast." She turned to the
servant.

"I would like champagne on ice and some fresh fruit brought to
my sitting room. And you may give Irene the evening off." Turning to Kyril she smiled: "Irene is my Cerberus. She is old enough to
be my mother, my governess, and my witch—and, yes, I believe
she sports three heads, the better to watch me with."

"I'm certain she could write a book about you," Kyril remarked.

Lorraine's features froze. "That would disappoint the public," she
said in a clipped voice. "She would have a paucity of facts to work
with."

Kyril felt duly chastened. He did not want to offend this woman
by overstepping his bounds. But what *were* the boundaries? How
could he know them? He had met no one of Parisian society to
date—no one until Lorraine. The French expected cleverness, but
going a touch too far meant that the clever remark could be con-
strued as rudeness or insulting provocation. It would be a hard

learning process, he supposed. Suddenly he was grim in his determination to succeed.

He had wanted to marry Zica, the Jewish baroness. Now he
thought that perhaps he had been hasty. There were so many delec-
table creatures within arm's reach, available to him because of his
looks and his naive charm. Lorraine de Huitton was married; he
could expect nothing from her. But maybe he could learn, and meet
others through her. Perhaps this was the destiny intended for him
—to slip into the right milieu and become rich and famous.

But could he succeed in this, following the vocation of doctor? In
Paris, the most eminent physicians and surgeons were called "Professor"; they were treated with enormous regard. A man *could* become rich and famous, but only if he made important discoveries,
performed miraculous operations, held a prestigious teaching chair
at the Faculty or found cures for rare ailments. Kyril did not have
the heart for any of these pursuits. In truth, he was bored by the
practice of medicine.

Lorraine led the way into a minuscule sitting room furnished
with a small sofa, a chaise lounge, a low tea table, and tiny lamps of
leaded glass. The atmosphere was cozy and feminine, full of her
scent. Bowls of cut flowers surrounded him on all sides. A Degas
painting of a ballerina in repose adorned one wall, surrounded by
tiny etchings of young ballerinas.

"Do you like ballet?" Kyril inquired, then immediately felt stupid
for asking.

Lorraine sank into the love seat, motioning for Kyril to sit beside
her. "I adore it," she told him. "We *fêted* your own compatriot,
Diaghilev, every year until the war. Now we have fallen in love
with his prima, Tamara Karsavina—not to mention his protégé Nijinsky. I have never seen anything like Nijinsky's leaps...though, I
must say, he is quite simple when one tries to engage him in conversation. What Diaghilev sees in him is no cause for wonder, however."

Kyril, quite lost, attempted to fight down his panic. He didn't
know how to proceed in this conversation without appearing to be
as simple as Nijinsky. "Oh?" he asked with raised eyebrows.

"Surely, my dear, it seems self-evident! Sergei Diaghilev is more
than a businessman. He knows genius when he sees it, and Nijinsky
dances as no man ever has. But, besides that, of course, Diaghilev is
deeply in love with the man. Their affair is no secret. Didn't you
know?"

"Homosexuality is quite taboo in Russia," Kyril stammered. "It is considered a shameful taint."

Lorraine's eyes sparkled. "I see. Well, what a pity! In Paris, it is regarded as part of life. No one can live without love, and whom one loves is one's own business. Diaghilev is a charming man. He has brought us much joy and excitement through his Russian ballets. We are quite pleased with him, and his *amours* are hardly worth comment."

She launched into a discussion of the Paris theater, but her discourse was interrupted by the arrival of a valet with champagne, glasses, and fresh fruit. The champagne flutes were frosty. The valet popped the cork and poured. Then he exited with a bow, closing the door behind him.

Lorraine raised her glass, inclined her head and smiled. "To you, *Cyril!*" she pronounced. "May you enjoy Paris the way Paris is sure to enjoy you!"

He blushed, not knowing how to respond. He clinked glasses with her and drank deeply. At first, relief spread through him as the bubbly wine settled inside. He had always loved champagne, but now it made him think of Zica. And that thought was an unwelcome intrusion that brought him pain. He drank some more.

"You are sad, Cyril," Lorraine commented, laying a gentle hand on his arm. "Has all this conversation of dance and music made you yearn for Russia?"

"No." He decided to be honest. "I was thinking of a woman I once loved, who lived in a palace and drank champagne too. It brought back memories best laid to rest."

"You loved her very much?' Lorraine's voice was soft, encouraging, feminine.

"More than I had supposed. More than I ever planned to. But she was young and inexperienced, and we wanted different things."

"What *did* you want?" Only a Frenchwoman could be so persistent.

"I wanted to marry her. She wanted . . . to tell you the truth, Madame, I'm not sure what was in her mind. She wanted to make love to me, and to pretend she was in love. But she was the daughter of a powerful, influential man in Moscow. In the end, her family was more important. She would not marry me."

"Oh, my dear, what a sad story . . ." Lorraine moved closer to him and touched his face. The gesture was so tender it stirred a terrible ache inside him. This was a new feeling, another kind of stirring he had not felt before. He knew then that he wanted Lorraine, wanted her sexually, and *now*.

"I adore love stories." She took a sip of champagne and plopped a hothouse strawberry into her mouth. "But this one isn't nice. It doesn't have a happy ending. I like happy endings. Though, in life, there are fewer of those than in fiction."

"There *are* no true happy endings," Kyril said bitterly. "Life's road consists of betrayals. Each one must be met—and crossed—like so many stumbling blocks. Do you not agree?"

"With such a sorry statement? Oh, my . . . I don't know. Perhaps you are right. But my life hasn't been so bad. I am an orphan, it is true. But I have fond memories of my parents and fond memories of my husband, too, before we became bored with each other. Marriage tends to provoke this boredom . . . but I would hardly call that a 'betrayal.' Let's call it rather, life's own attrition."

"You still love him?"

"You are a child! I love him as one would love one's own dear friend. Marc-Antoine is a fine, distinguished man, but somewhat weak-willed. I was deeply infatuated with him when we married, when I was twenty. But, after some six or seven years, he began to grow restless. And so the adventures began. First his, of course . . . then mine. It is the way of the world, the way of common sense. We each made the best of a situation that, in truth, was unavoidable. Marriage represents a companionship of long duration; and to make it work, one needs to be broad-minded and accepting."

"I see." He was taken aback by her frank, unassuming words. She had just revealed her age—thirty—for earlier, she had told him she had been married ten years already. And Kyril was twenty-one. The nine-year gap thrilled him; it represented the vastness of her experience contrasted to the limits of his own.

She would be his friend. He knew it at that moment. She would be the friend to whom he would confide his darkest secrets, as he could never have done with Zica, for fear of shocking her. Nine years and a Parisian education separated the two women as well. Zica, compared to Lorraine de Huitton, appeared unschooled and narrow-minded. . . .

He was enthralled. His knees went weak with the need to kiss her, to explore what lay beneath the blue silk gown she wore so becomingly open at the throat. Her breasts seemed full, like Zica's, but she was longer-waisted, with slim, narrow hips and long legs. He wanted her, and he knew he would not wait much longer.

"Do my words shock you, my young friend?" she asked him now, half-smiling. In her indulgence was a combination of amusement and longing—the longing for her own sweet innocence which she knew had vanished.

"I am not so young as you think," he replied shortly.

She laughed, her laughter tinkling like a Russian *kolokol*. She seemed merry, unrestrained, full of life.

Now he was angry: she was mocking him, as his father and the boys from Rostov had mocked him in his childhood. Abruptly, he stood up. But he sat down again in haste, suddenly conscious of his erection. Lorraine continued to laugh, but more softly, her blue eyes caressing him: first his face, then his chest, then his body.

Finally her eyes rested on his groin. She had stopped laughing. She was regarding him almost solemnly.

"You are young, and you are delicious, Cyril Ostrov," she said, her voice husky. "And what a fine old-fashioned name is 'Cyril' in French . . . ! It suits you well: for you too are a proud boy, who takes life very seriously. You laugh at nothing for fear that someone might laugh at *you*."

"You don't know me at all, Madame," he answered curtly, his face dark with resentment. She had exposed him at his most vulnerable moment, just when he had made up his mind to trust her.

"You must call me 'Lorraine,'" she told him, cocking her head to one side. She examined him closely. "I am too young, myself, to stand on ceremony. But we shall be friends, shan't we? You see, I *do* know you, better than you think. We have had Russians in France since Chaliapin came with Diaghilev in 1908, and you are all the same: impulsive, quick to anger, boorish, and very charming. You are also sensuous and hungry, and we women love you."

"You find Russians good lovers?' He couldn't help it: she had baited him.

As earlier, she abruptly retreated to a cold formality. "I am not a book of reference, Monsieur. We Parisian women have a certain . . . fascination . . . with your countrymen. Interpret that as you wish. I am merely echoing the sentiments of the women I know. Those of us who read, go to the theater, and enjoy good parties find the companionship of charming men most pleasant."

Now she seemed offended, while he only wished to reclaim her good will. Helpless and frustrated, Kyril took a healthy gulp of Perrier-Jouet, *brut*. He almost choked on it.

She allowed him to regain his composure before saying lightly: "Russian men are also the most insensitive. Where a Frenchman or an Italian treads on tiptoe, the Russian goes stomping in wearing his combat boots. Perhaps you can tell me—why is that, Cyril?"

"Probably the cold winters," he replied, laughing. By now, he knew she craved lightness of tone, sarcasm, and drollery rather than honesty. She wished to be toyed with, and to toy with him in return.

Now she joined in his laughter, and placed one heavily jewelled hand on his free one, which was resting on his lap. A huge amethyst gleamed at him like the eye of an impertinent bird. For a moment he was mesmerized by it, and by the sensation of her touch.

"I think you are curious about the rest of this apartment," she said to him. "Come, then, my young swain, and see for yourself."

He could not believe that she had made such a blunt proposition. She, a woman of good standing, a member of the aristocracy whom he had only just met today, was inviting him into her bedroom! A married woman with a husband at the front was entertaining a strange man within earshot of her own servants. It would have been unheard of in Rostov, or even Moscow. The mere fact that she had sent her faithful chambermaid out for the evening testified to her nefarious intentions. *Everyone would know!*

Almost trembling with anticipation, he followed her through a low doorway into a long room. To his amazement, the room contained nothing but musical instruments and old books on tall, polished hardwood shelves.

Lorraine picked up a strange silver flute and handed it to him. "This is a Rumanian Pan flute," she told him. "My father picked it up in Bucharest when I was a child." She sat down at a magnificent clavichord. "This I found in an antique shop in Florence," she said. "It was made in the seventeenth century. I should have been born then. Life was much richer."

Kyril was speechless. He had expected anything but this musical museum. She handed him a pamphlet of old folios. "My Uncle de la Haye-Mentier purchased these at an auction in Vienna. They are first drafts of some of Schubert's works . . . notably, the first act of his opera, *Rosamunde*. Aren't they wonderful?"

Setting down the Pan flute, Kyril picked up the pamphlet. To his eyes the scribblings of the great composer seemed no different from the scribblings his mother made from time to time on musical note-paper. He could think of no intelligent comment about the folios. He put them down on a shelf with a nod. Yes, if she said so, they were wonderful.

Then she could contain herself no longer. She threw back her head, with its topknot of light chestnut hair, and laughed, giving herself up to peals of mirth. After a minute or so, she caught her breath. "You didn't expect a music room, you poor dear thing. But I did ask, didn't I, whether you wanted to have a look...?"

"I didn't think..."

"But I am an accomplished musician," she demurred, her voice soft. "I showed you the best room in the house, and you didn't appreciate it. It isn't every young Russian who's allowed within these hallowed walls."

"I—"

She placed her forefinger over his lips. "Come," she said. This time, she opened a door leading to the most beautiful bedroom he had ever seen. A four-poster bed, decked in peach silk—with at least twenty tiny lace pillows tossed upon it—held center-stage in a room all decorated in peach and white. Walls were hung with moiré silk, the sofa upholstered in the same material. Over the bed stood a portrait of the Marquise de Huitton in a white and peach dress, signed "Henri Matisse." Small crystal vases adorned shelves and desks. All were filled with tiny fresh flowers, out-of-season blooms. The room smelled of youth, of intimacy, of powder and lilac and apricot.

Zica would have committed murder to sleep in such a room.

And so, thought Kyril, *would I.*

Silently, Lorraine took his hand and led him to bed. In the distance, he could hear birds chirping and a small child crying. These were the sounds of Paris at twilight. All thoughts of war were stilled for the night.

Lorraine unfastened the buttons on her dress and shrugged it to the floor, revealing the prettiest lingerie he had ever seen, all trimmed in pastel-colored Belgian lace.

Still, he could not move.

She unhooked her brassiere. Now she stood before him, her full breasts ready to be touched, but still she was at arm's length. She watched him, serious and wide-eyed. And he thought: *If I am not careful, I could fall in love.* He came forward and placed his hands upon her sloping shoulders, enveloping her in his arms. Her skin was soft and smooth. He stopped thinking. Held in his embrace, she submitted as he toppled with her onto the bed, tearing at her pantaloons and panties like a man possessed. It was obvious that she liked that, liked the brutality of his hunger and the urgency of his strong, blunt fingers.

Already, Lorraine de Huitton had nimbly undressed him, exposing his wrestler's compact body to her voracious exploration. She lay back on the silk coverlet and ran her fingers across his chest, over his belly. She clutched the base of his large, engorged penis, and made stroking gestures along its rigid shaft, culminating in gentle manipulation of the head. Her fingers seemed gently, acutely aware of the sensitive area where he felt the most exquisite pleasure. He closed his eyes, swaying above, not yet ready to plunge inside her. This was excruciating delight, pleasure such as he had never experienced with a woman—the pleasure of holding back in order to delay the orgasm.

Then she did the unexpected: sliding her smooth, white body down, pressing close to his muscular thighs, she took his penis into her mouth. She sucked it down into her throat, until all but the last centimeter seemed to have been swallowed. The pressure of her lips and her urgent tongue was not as great as that of a woman's tight vagina, but it teased him even more than her fingers had. He thought that he might not be able to hold back much longer, but he wanted to—he did not want her to be the disappointed one. And so he pulled himself out of her mouth and lifted her to the pillows, settling her down with greater gentleness than he had ever displayed with a woman. He probed her open and slipped himself in, mounting her as senses overwhelmed reason, shutting his eyes to block out everything but the sensations playing along the shaft of his penis as he thrust ever more deeply.

She was as tight as he had hoped, but welcoming, responsive. She did not cry out, but pulled him deeper inside, thrusting her pelvis upward in a motion that matched his own rhythm. Then she moaned, gasps of female pleasure, then longer cries, pleas for him to make it last, for him not to stop—until at last her whole body shuddered and she screamed, her face contorting in a grimace of sheer ecstasy. Then at last he gave way to his own need, and slid into his climax, the storm exploding.

When it was over they were both wringing wet. Her hair lay matted over the lace pillows, the pins scattered about, reminders of their unchained abandon. She smiled at him, and he touched her cheek with fingers listless from the totality of his exertion. He wanted to sleep—to sleep next to her, smelling the scent of her perfume mixed with sweat and semen. She sighed, a sigh replete with contentment, and settled against the crook of his arm.

In the middle of the night he awakened. Panic gripped him. He had been dreaming of Moscow burning, of his mother screaming, caught in a house without windows. He had dreamed of Zica with her hair on fire. Fitted like a finger inside the glove of his own body, Lorraine de Huitton continued to sleep.

Suddenly it came to him that he had never spent the night with a woman. He had never lain with someone until sleep swept over them in a gentle, warm wave, cradling them till morning. He sat up in bed, rubbing his eyes, feeling chilled, uncertain, and a little guilty. The horrible dream still hovered in his consciousness. He could feel his heart hammering inside him. But again he lay down beside her and cupped his hand around her breast. Its soft, vulnerable warmth reassured him. Slowly, the memory of the dream began to seep away. He pulled Lorraine's quilted blanket over both of them and lay listening to her even breathing. Moment by moment he felt himself relax, as the terror at last ebbed away. And then he fell asleep, pressed tightly against her.

Zica sat up in bed, clutching the small, oblong pillow desperately. Every three or four nights, she awakened abruptly from a deep slumber to a memory that lay transfixed in her subconscious. She groped for the light switch and turned on her bedside lamp, the lump in her throat too painful to swallow, the tears fresh on her cheeks.

It would never go away, she thought, trembling. It seemed that her entire life would end on that two-year-old memory. At twenty-one, she was already old.

When she had ended things with Kyril, she had made a conscious choice. Seeing the panic in his eyes, she had been frightened. She had understood that he expected her to make the pain go away. She had felt herself divide in two, her mind floating above her body during that awful little ceremony in Simonov's house, and she had recoiled, thinking: *This was not my dream.* Kyril was still her golden prince, but he was a fearful prince, a damaged Apollo. Something was not as she had planned, nor as she had hoped when they had first seen each other at the Tretyakovka.

She had felt so guilty, letting Yasha drive him home without ever speaking to him about what had happened. And that last time, when she had gone to see him at his boardinghouse, he had sent her away before she could say what she wanted to express. His face had haunted her for days. She had felt strangely disquieted, longing for him at the oddest moments. When she took her bath and soaked in the warm, soothing water, she would dream of his hands over her hips, of his body close to hers, touching her like magic. At night before she went to sleep, she would recall the excitement of lying beside him. But she shied away from the memory of his brute force, of the way he had penetrated her with his hard penis. That first time it had hurt so much, making her bleed. She wasn't sure how much she really liked sex, because it still hurt her, and her insides were seared and raw.

Yet she missed him—missed his eyes as they widened with desire for her, missed the perfection of his face and limbs, the pleasure of beholding him. She had loved the fact that such an angel belonged to her, that he was hers to touch and fondle. He was a man with a man's need, and she responded fully, with a woman's joy. Even suffering the pain of penetration was pleasurable if this brought *him* pleasure and assuaged his hunger. She missed being *his woman*. What she did not miss was the role of *nyanya,* the one who was supposed to soothe away all the anguish of those years before she had been a part of his life.

Zica had felt confused, and terribly sad. But she had also felt relieved.

Nearly two months had passed since they had last made love when she began to notice that something was not quite right in her body. Her breasts were swollen and painful. She sometimes felt dizzy. And after the holiday season, she had begun to use a corset to contain her bloated stomach. Her mother had teased her about indulging in too many sweets, and had placed her on a diet. But of course nothing had worked. Instead of losing weight, she kept steadily gaining. Zica felt panic like a disease within her: she had arranged to meet her friend Tamara Kokhlova alone in a small tea room.

"I think I'm going to have a baby," she blurted to her friend as soon as she had sat down.

Tamara looked stricken. "You *think* . . . ? Or you're certain?"

"I think I'm certain." Zica laughed a shrill laugh that broke into a quick sob. "What am I going to do?"

Tamara sighed, shaking her head. "Zica, Zica. The blond angel did this to you. Don't you think he'll make it right?"

"Do you think I want to marry him on the run and spend the rest of my life in Rostov, hiding away? Look at his mother! This was her lot, and her life! She is the loneliest woman I've ever met! Besides,

Kyril has no idea of this—and I *never* want him to know. He said
... he told me he never wanted to see me again, never wanted to
hear from me ever again..." Zica's voice cracked. Embarrassed,
she turned her face away from her friend's concerned look. But she
could not stop the tears.

Tamara's voice was reasoning: "If you don't marry him, you'll
have to tell your mother, and she will send you off some place to
have the baby. Perhaps she will be able to keep the story quiet. But
you know how it is, Zica. Word can spread. You are so bright and
beautiful. You could have the man of your choice—but not if he
learns you had a child out of wedlock."

"I know." Zica tried to wave away her friend's words. "But you
see, Tamara, I don't want to get married. I *know* all the men who
are considered eligible in this city—especially the Jewish ones my
father prefers. They are all flat-footed and stoop-shouldered, smelling of herring. I *can't* fall in love! The only time I ever fell in love, it
was with him—and it was wrong, so wrong!"

"Maybe you didn't give Kyril a chance," Tamara said softly.
"Write him and tell him you are expecting his child. He will behave
honorably: you'll see!"

"What makes you so sure?"

Tamara cocked her head and smiled. "Human nature, my dear. A
man is weak only until his woman needs his protection: that is
when the most frightened man takes heart and thinks of responsibility. Besides, little one, it can't hurt to let him know."

But it *had* hurt. Zica had sent Yasha with a message. Kyril hadn't
even read the letter. He hadn't deigned to open it. She had wept
then, bitterly, right in front of Yasha; he had placed his hand on her
shoulder, whispering silly things, such as: "There, there," and
"Please don't weep so, Zeinab Lazarevna."

When she sent Yakov a second time, he had returned, equally
unsuccessful. He seemed as stricken as she. Zica was comforted by
his friendship—if only because there was no other comfort in her
life. This time, when she wept, she let him take her in his arms as
though he hadn't been a servant. She let him comfort her as if he
were just an old friend, holding her, letting her sob her heart out,
then wiping her nose like a gentle father.

What a strange alliance they had formed!

She hadn't known what to do. Tamara had told her once of a
farm girl on her parents' property who had gotten rid of a baby by
sticking something sharp inside herself. Zica was terrified. She was

afraid to call her friend and ask her all about it. But she was desperate, so desperate, afraid her father would realize what had happened and send her away. She knew the outrage he would feel! And so, one night, when the household had gone to sleep, she had tiptoed to the kitchen. She had boiled water. With hands that shook uncontrollably, she had dropped a thin metal ruler into the pot to sterilize it, as she heard midwives did with their own instruments before delivering babies. You had to sterilize everything in boiling water, or the mother could die from the infection.

Then, she had gone upstairs carrying the pot and the metal ruler. She had gone into her bathroom and shut the door. She had tried sticking the ruler inside her. Fear had nearly paralyzed her, but she had continued. Better to suffer now than to give birth later, in shame and loneliness, held in contempt by her own family. It was a guilty spirit pushing through to her tender insides, telling her that she owed this to her parents. It was guilt, hurting her so much more than Kyril's penis ever had, until blood poured from her like milk from a jug, onto the tiles of her bathroom. She couldn't respond to the need to get up and sponge herself off. Suddenly she wanted to vomit, and then she was vomiting. She fell against the bathtub and the room spun wildly around, and she was hot and dying, she was *sure* she was dying, all alone, shivering on her bathroom floor.

When she fully regained consciousness, she was in a room she didn't recognize, with strange people looking down at her. A thin, dark girl was mopping her brow. When finally she heard Yasha's voice, she felt relieved, so relieved, for she knew she was safe at last. Where *was* she? She did not have the strength to ask. She did not even have the strength to sit up. But she could hear bits of conversation. The girl and Yasha were talking together in low, urgent voices.

"She's going to be all right. I've called Countess Tamara Kokhlova, and she has told the Baroness that Zeinab Lazarevna has been with her. Tamara Ivanovna said they spent the night together because Zeinab Lazarevna didn't feel well after the play. The Baroness wanted to send the victoria for her, but Tamara Ivanovna said no, they wished to be together a little bit more, and so on. The Baroness has known Countess Kokhlova since the girls were babies together."

Yasha was speaking. Then Zica heard the dark girl's voice ask anxiously: "What about her maid—the one who found her? Won't she talk?"

"Tania is devoted to Zeinab Lazarevna. But she is also very stupid. She has no idea what happened. I told her Zeinab Lazarevna wouldn't want anyone to know. I said she was having a hemorrhage that *you* could take care of. I also gave her three gold rubles I had been saving. Tania won't talk."

The voice of the girl: "Three gold rubles. You must be insane, Yasha!"

And Yasha's voice, furious and cold: "What I *am*, Natasha, is my business!"

Natasha. That was his girlfriend, the woman who painted landscapes and strange icons, who lived in one of the rented apartments near Yasha's room. Zica felt a new wave of weakness overcome her, and she yielded to it, all consciousness leaving her.

After that, fragments of reality zigzagged into focus. Someone had made her eat chicken broth. She was spoon-fed by Natasha and when she could sit up, sponged off by her. Yasha made a series of visits, bringing little delicacies from the kitchen. Though Zica thought days and weeks had passed, she later learned from Tamara that only thirty-six hours had gone by. Her faithful little maid, Tania, had found her; Tania had summoned Yasha at once, because she knew that Zica liked him; and Yasha had taken her, unconscious, to Natasha's room. He had telephoned the news to Tamara Kokhlova, and left the Poliakovs up to her resourcefulness.

When Tamara had spoken to Zica's mother, the Baroness had believed her, for she had always been somewhat naive. The Baron, thank God, had been out of town, so the situation had been taken care of by the time he returned.

After Zica had regained enough strength, Yasha had taken her back to her own room. There she had rested, nursed by her mother and Tania, who had kept quiet about finding her passed out in her own blood. The Baroness had fed her sweets and read to her, thinking her illness nothing more than the common "female problem." And so the incident had been dismissed, like a bad memory, pushed aside by everyone save Zica herself... and, she was certain, by Yasha.

Surely he had never forgotten the horror. And she had never forgotten that he knew of her shame—and that his girlfriend knew. But he was already privy to so much!

She owed him her life, the very breath she breathed—because of his passion to always be near her, within reach. He always wanted to talk to her. He would bring her small presents, the food and books she liked, whenever he could. Had he loved her less . . . she hated to contemplate what might have happened—or rather, not happened. She would not now be alive—or, if alive, her reputation would have been forever ruined by public scandal.

Two years later, he was still in the house. And *she* was there, still unmarried, still unhappy. She had heard her father talking about Yasha's music. She knew he had finally graduated from the Conservatory and had tried out unsuccessfully for a place in the string section of the Philharmonic Orchestra. When she'd raised the subject to him, Yasha had smiled and shaken his head. He simply said: "I was not good enough." He had failed at his life's work, and she had been unable to give him the slightest comfort, for he had not allowed her to do so. After all the care he had demonstrated toward her in the past, he had not allowed her to care in return.

Strange little fellow, Yasha Pokhis. Zica liked him—but she understood him not at all.

Taking a gulp of water from the goblet at her bedside, she shivered again at the memory of the time she had nearly died. When would she stop reliving that bad dream? When would she earn her peace and be able to sleep soundly? Suddenly she felt tired, weary to her bones. She was lonely, and her existence was empty. She had killed her baby, Kyril's child, and now it seemed likely that she would never have another. Women who did such things were most often punished by never being able to conceive again.

She didn't *want* children, anyway. She had told Mossia Aronov the truth—that she would never have any. She didn't want to marry, either, nor did she want to fall in love again, only to relive the pain of longing and of loss. Nothing was as dreadful as love—nothing at all, not even loneliness.

Zica turned out the light and snuggled under the blankets, wondering where he was now. And were there times when he still remembered?

Chapter VIII

*Y*AKOV paused for a moment in transcribing the document he was helping Senya draft for the Baron. As he pushed an unruly shock of curls off his forehead, he felt the perspiration drip onto his hand. The library was hot and stifling; it smelled stuffy and unaired. In mid-November, no one opened windows that would let in the bitter cold.

Yakov had come to Moscow to be a musician, and had ended up becoming a scribe and a librarian. He rather liked what he had learned to do: he was certainly set apart from the other boys from his *shtetl*, most of whom could hardly read a word of Russian. He could even speak passable French now. He practiced it sometimes with Zica, who often came into her father's library with a small tea tray loaded down with pastries and hot tea. Over tea, they would converse in the language of Rousseau and Voltaire. She would smile as she corrected his accent, then hand him another cream puff to sweeten the reprimand.

So naturally he was hungry to improve, to gain her approbation. It was now November 1917. He had remained in the Baron's employ against the counsel of his mentor Senya, who saw how limiting such a life could be. Yakov clearly knew that he stayed in order to be near Zica and to make sure that no harm would ever befall her again. He loved her as he had once loved his parents—unquestioningly, without bounds or limits. He knew that his destiny was to be her shadow, her silent protector. He could hope for nothing more, but that was enough—or at least sufficient for the moment.

His life was split in two. On the one hand he lived the predictable existence of a middle-level household retainer, aged twenty-two. Somehow he tolerated the daily routine of his job, enduring its

156

rigors with poise and adeptness. He had friends, he had a lover. He had his moments of joyous release just like everybody else. Even his ambitions were not terribly uncommon to someone with his native intelligence and exploring nature.

But always, he observed—always his eyes saw opportunities for bettering his situation. He needed to remain with Baron Poliakov, needed to be around Zica...but he searched for every chance to improve himself and learn something which might serve him later. One day, he realized, Zica would surely marry; she would cease to need him. And then it would be time to leave, to start his own small business, or go abroad (God only knew where!) and see how actors fared in other countries.

And he knew what he wanted. He yearned to perform in front of a live audience. He had visions of entertaining people with his quick mind and rapid-fire speech. His clever rendition of life's inequities could make people laugh and forget all their sorrows.

In his daily life, Natasha, his girlfriend, was always eager to please him. Natasha took great care not to become pregnant. She'd had experience with men before him, which was why he liked her. She was sexy, amusing, and petulant as a woman could be—pouting when he was impatient, yet always eager to return to him when he was ready to apologize. She kept him rooted firmly in the present.

Yet she liked that he was constantly improving himself. She encouraged him to learn French and write perfect Hebrew and perfect Russian. At times Yakov was reminded that she fancied herself becoming *Madame Yakov Pokhis,* his partner through life, the mother of his children. But she was already twenty-five, and he hadn't proposed yet. Natasha had been growing irritable and sullen these past few weeks, watching the days flow into one another with no change in her circumstance.

She loved him; and he loved Zica. One day, when Zica married, he would marry Natasha. Even though she was not Jewish, and this would hurt his parents; *especially* because she was not Jewish, and would give him real Russian children. Only, how to explain to Natasha that she had to wait until the other married, so that he would no longer be needed...?

As for the other half of Yakov's life, it revolved solely around Zica Poliakova. This aspect of his life was inexplicable, yet as strong as his need to breathe. He would have been ashamed to discuss it with Senya, this oh-so-rational man who believed in the logic of

Socrates and Aristotle. Yet Yakov could no more dismiss his need to stay near Zica than he could dismiss his craving for the stage, or for self-improvement. He was there because she was there, pure and simple.

They had become friends. Over the years—especially after he had saved her life—they had ceased to be servant and daughter of the house, serf and *boyarynya*. They had become mates of sorts, comfortable with each other, able to converse.

...But never too freely. Zica had never explained the affair with Ostrov, and of course Yakov had never asked her about it. Their companionship depended on a strict observance of decorum. Although they took mutual comfort in each other's presence, they were of different worlds—worlds that could never mingle. So they talked of books, of their childhoods, of teas and plays and funny things that each had heard rumored. And, lately, they talked of the terrible events that were taking place right here in the city.

Yakov was afraid, deeply afraid. The "Little Revolution" that had deposed the Tzar the previous March had scared none of the members of the Poliakov *entourage*. Yakov had taken strong tea into Senya's room and sat up nights discussing it with him. Senya pretended that the Provisional Government was composed of wellmeaning intellectuals who did not know what was truly going on with the Russian people. The factory workers and, to a lesser extent, the peasantry of this huge country were now in revolt. Its army was routed. Two million deserters were spilling into the streets, clogging the train stations and railways as they made their way home.

The Provisional Government was as far removed from these folk as Nicholas II has been. Senya reflected the Baron's very thoughts when he told his young assistant not to be afraid of Lvov and Kerensky, "those poor bastards in Petrograd" who had taken over the government. This "bloodless Revolution" could not hurt anyone they knew, could not disband the Poliakov household.

Those words had been spoken in March. By the middle of April, Senya had begun to feel disquieted. A man by the given name of Vladimir Ilyich Ulyanov, who called himself Lenin, had come in a sealed car from Germany to Petrograd. Senya feared this Lenin would do much harm. He was a Marxist, a believer in the system of one for all and all for one. He could sway the masses to follow him and overthrow the peaceable government of *Gospodin* Alexander Kerensky—and *then* what would occur?

Now, November 12, 1917, history was being made right in front of their eyes. This past week, Yakov had been chastising himself: He should have left already, taken Natasha with him and fled at once to Odessa. He should have found his parents and helped them escape to France. The people he most loved would soon be in peril. The Aschkenasys and Poliakovs were so conspicuous in their palaces, the blood-crazed mobs would surely slaughter servant and master alike, indiscriminately. And what had Yakov done about the situation? Nothing! He waited, hoping the tide would turn back, that sense would prevail—that Lenin would back down and the world would return to the previously established order.

But now that Lenin and his Bolsheviks had seized control of Petrograd and imprisoned the ministers of the Provisional Government inside the dreaded fortress of Peter and Paul, Yakov knew that all of Russia was doomed. Presently, Moscow too would be turned upside down. The flow of blood would reach these very doors.

Why, then, was he still here, waiting for doom? Why was he stupidly transcribing this useless old document, when soon enough, the Poliakov mansion would itself be aflame? Only days remained before all these precious books would be burned to a crisp by the Bolsheviks.

And why was he, a servant and a Jew, siding with the deposed Tzar and the nobility of Russia? Why was he not out there with "the People"? Surely he was among the oppressed masses against whom the Romanovs had machinated all three hundred years of their reign.

But even as he asked himself these questions, Yakov knew the answers: Because he loved Zica, because he had been helped by the kindness of Baron Poliakov, and because *he wished to become like them* rather than see the whole world turn into mediocrity. He identified more readily with the haughty lords who lived in grandeur and in style than with the poor, uneducated factory workers and peasants. He had once been like them, and found their condition intolerable.

Of course they did not understand the value of good taste, of art and elegance. They were too busy trying not to starve—whereas he, Yakov, had already passed that point. The moment he had entered the service of Baron Poliakov and found out that Senya could read and write in several languages, he had discovered that, if he tried hard enough, he too might learn wondrous skills. He had seen how the other half lived, and *he wanted to live like that,* the sooner the better. This was the strange truth which Yakov now admitted to himself.

Lenin didn't share his views, and neither did the other, the Menshevik leader who called himself Trotsky. A Jew, that one, like Marx, like himself—but a Jew whose discontent was like Lenin's. Trotsky, too, wished to reduce the world to a level of general monotone, where all men were equal but *equal in their shabbiness and squalor*. Yakov was certain the Communists could not erect a world of wealth and grace out of the abject poverty that now prevailed throughout Russia. Rather, they would strip the rulers of their opulence and render them powerless. Society would be leveled to its lowest common denominator. Where would this leave those who aspired to *more*... where would that leave *him?* For Lenin and Trotsky would be crazy to expect him to set aside his personal dreams and ambitions. Yakov would never opt for Peredelkino over the palace on Tverskaya Street.

There was nothing shameful in being rich. In fact, rich men were needed to make the world go round: the world in which Yakov longed to participate, where talented young artists received patronage from men such as the Baron.

Besides, in Lenin's vision, it was not only the patrons who would be killed off: it would be art itself, the soul of the artist and his medium. Yakov understood that a world of uniform mediocrity would mean the end of art, the death of poetry, the annihilation of entertainment and of laughter. Lenin's thirst for power had shown him how to manipulate numbers to his own advantage. Russia possessed a legion of men who wanted bread, vodka and good, solid jobs—a legion willing to overthrow a government of the bourgeoisie and upper classes in order to achieve their ends. But his own needs had changed since his early *shtetl* days. Now he possessed greater ambitions—ambitions that would have no place in a world of Lenin's creation. Where would be the rapture of listening to Chaliapin? Where would be the grace of a ballerina? Where would there be room for the man who wished to earn his living on the stage—dedicated to making others laugh?

In the midst of these reflections, his pensive mood was interrupted. There was a loud crash as the library door was flung open. Senya, usually meticulous and solemn, appeared looking dishevelled, his eyes bulging.

Yakov rose unsteadily, suddenly afraid. "What's happening?"

Senya pulled out a chair, and sagged into it. "Yasha, the cadets are trying to hold the Kremlin a little while longer. Dukhonin, the Commander-in-Chief, is refusing to negotiate for an armistice with the Bolsheviks. But the Bolshies have sent a new commander; there will be bloodshed when he takes over."

"Perhaps Dukhonin will manage to stave him off." Yakov grasped at a straw.

The two men stared at each other, mutely refuting this pipe dream. "Where are the Poliakovs?" Yakov asked. "It's time they escaped to their country home or to the Aschkenasys' in Odessa. They must leave *now,* before there's general rebellion!"

"The Baron won't budge. He says he will not leave his home under any circumstance. And the Baroness will not leave *him.* In Petrograd they say Zhenya's in-laws have been captured. The old banker was killed. Zhenya has been sent to the fortress as a prisoner. The Baroness won't think of leaving until she has had news of her son."

"And Zeinab Lazarevna?"

Senya's eyes narrowed. He scrutinized Yakov with a thoughtful expression. Measuring his words, he replied: "She is in her room. Tania is with her. They are praying together. God is both Jewish and Orthodox at a time like this, but I don't believe he'll answer their prayers. The Bolsheviks are stronger even than God."

Senya stood up unsteadily and laid a hand upon Yakov's shoulder. "My dear boy," he said softly, "I have come here out of concern for *you.* When the Reds break in, they must not find us on the premises. You must come with me now. Natasha and her friends are waiting for us in my room. There's no time to waste!"

Yakov rose, his cheeks flushed. "You must go without me, Senya." His voice sounded calm, sure, surprising even to himself. "I cannot leave her here, unprotected. I cannot abandon her."

"You stupid young fool! This is no time for tender feelings, nor for unrequited love! You have your own skin to save. Your own girl needs you!"

The two men glowered at each other, the older one shaking his head in futile anger. Suddenly, Yakov embraced Senya, holding him close. "You must not blame me, my friend," he murmured. "This woman means more to me than life itself. I must do whatever I can to make sure she is not hurt. Tell Natasha good luck—that I shall see her as soon as I have settled this other business. She must not tarry on my account. My priorities were defined long ago, when I first fell in love with Zica in her aunt's house in Odessa—or maybe even earlier, when I first met her in Rigevka."

"You are indeed a fool, Yasha," Senya declared, pushing him away. But his eyes were moist and he regarded Yakov with concern. "This is no time for far-fetched loyalty. I, too, am dedicated to this family. But if they wish to stay with their heads buried in the sand like ostriches, thinking they can protect their empire, I must think of my own life. Zeinab Lazarevna will never want to part with her mother. You will die at her side."

"Then so be it." Yakov's dark eyes revealed no emotion. He paused, and his face softened. "God be with you, Senya," he said. Then he recited: "'If I forget thee, O Jerusalem: let my right hand forget her cunning.'"

"'If I do not remember thee, let my tongue cleave to the roof of my mouth.'" Senya passed a hand over his eyes, shielding them from Yakov; then, abruptly, he turned on his heel and hastened away.

After that, the hours melted into one another. Afterwards, Yakov would remember only vague impressions. Servants ran in and out; the Baroness, with her hair undone, wandered through the house, screaming that they had killed her son. The Baron, in his frock coat, more than ever like an ascetic raven, shouted aloud that his forefathers had fought for their rights to this house—and he'd be damned if he would now flee like a coward.

Then Zica appeared in the doorway, pale and silent, terror painted on her face. Yakov rushed up and took her aside, a little roughly—not at all with the respect of a servant toward the lady of the manor. Lenin had levelled the two of them as well, reducing them to a man and a woman in a state of panic, equals in peril.

"My parents' names are on the Black List," she whispered, as he led her under the staircase for a private conversation. "Sergei has seen it. When he went to town this morning, the Koestlin's butler, who has gone over to the Reds, stopped him and showed him a copy. That means they'll be killed!"

"And you?"

"I cannot leave. Mama needs me!"

Yakov shook his head, his eyes red from lack of sleep. Two days had passed since Senya had left, and the new Bolshevik commander, Krylenko, had taken over the Kremlin. He had immediately ordered the assassination and mutilation of Commander Dukhonin, whose bloodied remains were even now displayed on Red Square.

"Zeinab Lazarevna, you must come with me. I shall hide you at my friend's apartment. I have a friend from the Conservatory—Vladimir Nichayev. He lives on a side street off Grachovka Road, in a tiny two-room flat. We shall be safe there for the time being."

Zica shook her head wildly, growing hysterical. "No, no! I cannot leave my parents!"

"Very well. Then Senya was right. I shall die at your side."

They stared long and hard at each other—each stubborn and high-minded, neither giving in. "I want you to be safe, Yasha, and not to think of me," she finally declared.

"But that I cannot do. I love you, Zeinab Lazarevna. You know I do. I cannot leave you here."

"Oh, Yasha . . ." Her fingers strayed toward his face, touching his cheek like the wings of a butterfly. Then the mood was suddenly shattered, as Tania erupted on the scene in tears. There were noises in the yard, a mad, frantic rush toward the kitchens. But it had only been the dogs, let loose by some ne'er-do-well, hurling their frightened bodies on the heavy front door.

Yakov had to get Zica out. But she refused to comply. She had moved into her parents' bedroom, Tania in her wake, and spent the night on the reclining chair with Tania on the hassock at her feet. As Yakov paced outside the door, he had recited phrases from the Bible, Chekhov, and Pushkin to keep himself awake.

This was madness, pure madness. He had to get her out, before it was too late.

The next day, all hell broke loose early in the morning. Wild men battered down the front door and attacked Sergei, the *maître d'hôtel,* with clubs and machetes in the foyer. Yakov heard the commotion and peered down the shaft of the staircase. He could not respond to Sergei's piteous pleas for help. It would have done no good to try to save him. Yakov had no weapon, only his wits. He could not commit suicide by facing the mob.

Bursting into the Baron's room, Yakov lifted Zica from her reclining chair and rushed toward the side door leading to the dressing room of the Baroness. Behind, he could hear the Baron going the other way, toward the hideous yells that were the death song of his old, faithful servant.

Zica shrieked, "Papa! Papa!" Yakov only clung to her more tightly.

He glimpsed the Baroness, rushing in pursuit of her husband. An instant later, Yakov heard her cry as something struck her. It was a horrid, blood-curdling cry—worse, by far, than Sergei's. Zica tried to scream too but Yakov pressed her face against his chest—pressed her so hard she was stunned into gasping silence. Still, she struggled to free herself from his embrace. But it was futile. His strength, as he clung to her, was superhuman. They had only one slim chance of escape.

From the dressing room, Yakov plunged on to the landing that led to the service staircase.

Tania now appeared on his heel, crying in small muffled gasps. "Come with us, but for God's sake shut up," Yakov hissed at her. "Go down to the stables. Unhitch the small cart. Bring it to the back door—and make sure no one else takes it—do you understand? Otherwise, we are *dead!*"

She nodded, her teeth chattering. Then she darted away on her assigned mission. Flying ahead of him down the back stairs, her braid bounced over her shoulder blades like the tail of a young mare in flight. Behind her, Yakov struggled with Zica in his arms, pressing her hard against him to keep her quiet. He took the steps two at a time, his heart hammering like a snare drum.

Her tears wet his shirt, but he paid no attention. Then, suddenly, she ceased fighting him and lay limp in his arms, whimpering softly. He had no time for words of comfort, though he whispered, urgently, "We're going to make it," because he needed to hear the words as much as she did.

Yet, even as he spoke, he could hear the blood-curdling screams of the Baroness in the distance.

He shoved his shoulder against the swinging door that led to the huge tiled kitchen. No one was there. Probably, the screams had terrified the servants and sent them scurrying to the back yard. Yakov lunged through the open back door, onto the porch where an icy wind whipped him. Shocked, shivering, he had no time to grab a jacket. In his wool shirt and pants, he felt naked in the bitter chill. Zica wore only her velvet robe with a nightgown underneath.

To Yakov's joy and surprise, Tania had followed his directions more promptly than he would ever have thought possible. The small lumber cart was rounding the corner, drawn by a single horse. He saw Tania sitting in the driver's seat, huddled under the driver's lap quilt. She reined to a stop. Gently, Yakov lifted Zica beside Tania. Hastily, the young maid covered her mistress and moved over. Yakov leapt into the driver's seat alongside them, seizing the reins from Tania.

"Where are we going?" Tania asked, her voice tremulous with fright.

"To safety!" He whipped the horse to action.

"But my parents . . ." Zica's voice was so small he hardly heard them.

The horse took up its quick trot.

Zica's teeth chattered. She had never felt so cold in her life, but in a way she was grateful. The cold numbed the pain inside her, stilled the dull ache of certain death.

She could still hear Sergei's horrible scream, loud in her ears. She hid beneath the quilt, pressing against Tania as Yakov adroitly maneuvered the cart through the service postern. She heard rather than saw him crack his whip, and the horse galloped forward onto the cobbled side street behind the Tverskaya.

Suddenly a horrible jumble of voices broke through the air. Shots resounded. Yakov rose in his seat, still holding the reins, and whipped the horse again. Turning, Zica saw ragged men standing by the small gate through which they had just passed. A mob of men with muskets, knives, and lame pieces of wood were pointing and shouting. The horse reared, then resumed its frantic gallop. They turned the corner, leaving the men so far behind that only the echoes of their clamor remained in their wake.

It was then that Zica noticed Yakov, slumped against Tania, holding the reins and the whip in his right hand. On his left shoulder was a stark red gash. More red kept seeping through the gray wool of his shirt. She screamed, crying out, "Tania! Yasha's been hit!" Yakov straightened up, his face white and streaked with sweat. His eyes told her to be quiet—he was still in charge.

Silently, tears began to run down her cheeks, freezing to her skin like thin icicles. Beside her, Tania pulled the quilt up over them, and rubbed Zica's hands in her own.

"We're safe, Zeinab Lazarevna," Yakov said, but this time he did not turn to look at her. His eyes were intent on the road ahead. He did not want to see her pain. He could not have answered her questions. She understood. She huddled mutely against Tania, knowing that her fate and her life rested in his hands.

In the driver's seat, Yakov had begun to feel nauseous and feverish. His shoulder was aflame with molten agony reaching all the way to his fingers. He had not felt the impact of the shot. The bullet had lodged in his shoulder, somewhere between the bones of his shoulder blade. He dreaded to think that perhaps it was more than a flesh wound—that the bones themselves might have been fractured. It would be impossible to get medical attention. If they reached Grachovka Road, he would let Tania wash out the wound, and perhaps Vladimir would cut the bullet out for him. But this luxury would not occur unless he were able to reach his destination—until all were safe under his friend's roof.

Only then did he give a thought to Natasha. He was sure he would never see her again. She would curse him for having chosen Zica. Senya would have told her, by now, why he had not joined them. His old friend's anger and hurt were a source of pain, but Yakov's actions had told the truth—the woman in his heart was Zica! He knew he had saved her life—that his quick thinking had prevented her from being killed along with her parents.

One day, she would want to thank him; her gratitude would make everything worthwhile. Until then, the love he felt for her was strong enough to sustain him, through trial and fire, through pain and fear and cold... through a revolution and a blood bath. Even he was surprised by the intensity of his emotions, and of his resolve.

Like dull silver, the sky loomed above them—menacing, dark clouds hovering in proximity. Yakov directed the horse off Trubny Square onto Grachovka Road, then onto a smaller side street with tall, narrow buildings lit by gas lamps. No pedestrians appeared on the narrow sidewalks; only an occasional proffered insult, shouted from deep within an odd apartment, attested to the fact that human beings were alive within these buildings. Next to him, the women sat silently, shivering in the dreadful cold, their eyes wide with apprehension.

In front of a narrow, gloomy passageway, Yakov cracked his whip again: the horse balked at going in. They passed through an alley into the back yard of a building, and there, under the eaves, Yakov reined the horse to a stop.

Gingerly, with the hesitant movements of a cripple, he tied the horse to a ragged post. He could not help the women down from their seats. Tania clambered down first, and held her hand out to Zica. Quickly, Yakov led them through the back door into what seemed to be a dank and foul-smelling apartment building, redolent of rotten vegetables. They climbed a creaky staircase to a third-floor landing. Yakov knocked on the first door and waited.

A hirsute young man, his wool shirt open at the collar, met them at the door and beckoned them in. Glorious warmth surrounded them. Zica seemed mesmerized by the surroundings. There were books on the floor, a violin stand, clothes strewn about, and half-eaten *pirozhki* on a dirty dish on the floor. The host, too, seemed to startle her. Vladimir Nichayev, Yakov's friend from the Conservatory, personified the bohemian Artist. Covertly, Zica examined him from behind lowered lashes. He was unkempt, abrupt, with no social graces. Under different circumstances, she would never have met such a man. Yet here she was in his home—a sanctuary from the hell outside his door.

"Yasha is hurt," she said to him, as soon as he had closed the door on the cold air. The three of them were clustering around his stove. "Do you have some hot water to wash his wound?"

Vladimir Nicolaevitch Nichayev raised thick, bushy brows above small eyes of piercing china blue. He turned Yakov around, examining the seeping gash in his shirt. "Some war decoration, my friend..." he commented. His voice, low and raspy, was tinged with amusement. Zica bristled: this was hardly the moment for fun, and she was quick to take offense. But immediately, the young man hurried off to the small kitchen to boil some water. She took Yakov's good arm and gently escorted him to the sofa.

When Nichayev returned with rags and water and what looked like a scalpel, Zica stepped back. Suddenly she felt weak. Yakov had taken his shirt off and was sitting in his undershirt. The wound displayed behind his shoulder looked like chopped meat. A wave of nausea swept over her. As she turned her head away, the room started to spin. She felt her knees buckle. Tania eased her down, then resolutely took the water from Nichayev, knelt down behind Yakov, and set busily to work on his shoulder. Sponging it off, she made a clucking sound as she shook her head in dismay.

Zica felt the tears come to her eyes. She let them fall. Her shoulders heaved in mute sobs.

"Zeinab Lazarevna is exhausted," Yakov said, motioning for her to sit down beside him on the worn plush sofa. She did as he indicated, numbed into blind obedience. The horrors of this morning, followed by the bitter-cold ride in the lumber cart, had robbed her of all sense of reality.

When Tania had finished cleaning the wound, Nichayev took her place, scrutinizing the bullet wound. "It's just a flesh wound," he told his friend, his gruff voice hiding his concern. "I've sterilized this knife in boiling water," he added. "I won't have to dig very far. But take a deep breath, for in I go." With that, he plunged the scalpel into Yakov's shoulder. Zica felt the bile rise in her throat. She shut her eyes and leaned back, trying not to hear Yakov's soft cries as Nichayev extracted the bullet.

All at once it was over. Brushing the sweat off his forehead, Vladimir Nicolaevitch held up a tiny lead cylinder, declaring proudly, "There it is!" His face radiated success and relief. Yakov, on the sofa, looked white and ill, but he too offered a small, feverish laugh.

"I'm sorry, old man," said Nichayev. "I have nothing to take the edge off the pain. But I do have some bandages. Tania can dress this cut. Fortunately for you, I had a broken ankle last summer and I saved the bandages."

While he was fetching the thick gauze and tape, Zica said, tentatively: "I hope you'll be all right. Yasha. We should really get you to a doctor."

"Is that so?" Nichayev stood looking down at her. His eyes glittered a moment with pity and derision, as though she had just uttered a complete inanity. "And where, my dear lady, do you propose to go looking for a doctor in the middle of a revolution? Doctors are *bourgeois* capitalists to the Bolsheviks. I'm sure they have all fled in anticipation of being killed. Or they have been drafted by the Reds to take care of their own casualties!"

Why was he ridiculing her? And why was he so arrogant? The tears welled up, and Zica hid her face in her hands. Vladimir Nichayev said consolingly: "We are a nation turned upside down; of course, none of us knows where to turn. I myself don't know whether to return to my home town of Simferopol in the Crimea, or whether to stay here."

"Are you a Bolshevik, Vladimir Nicolaevitch?" Zica asked, raising her head to look at him, curiosity winning out over humiliation.

He snorted, shrugging. "'A Bolshevik...'! Do I know what I am? My father is a butcher, and makes good money. The Reds would take his shop from him and force him to sell at reduced prices. No, Zeinab Lazarevna, I am not a Bolshevik. If I were, why would I be trying to help a *boyarynya,* even if she is my own friend's sweetheart?"

The notion that she had been mistaken for Yakov's sweetheart struck Zica as so incongruous that she did not respond. Surely he could *not* be speaking about her and Yasha? Here she was, for the first time witnessing Yasha's life outside the Poliakov enclave. She had never actually considered what he did in his time off, when he wasn't with Senya or Natasha, and she found herself ashamed of this lack of curiosity about a man who had done so much for her.

She turned to survey the young librarian, thinking too that she had never *really* looked at him: he had always simply *existed,* a busy presence around her or around her father. Now Yakov was sitting gravely beside her, his small face feverish from the wound. With an expression alive with intelligence, his dark eyes watched her.

Vladimir had said: "my own friend's sweetheart." Did Yasha, in fact, consider *her* his *sweetheart?* She imagined kissing him, his full lips on hers. What would it be like? She still loved Kyril, or, at least, the memory of him, framed in gilt edges. Kissing Yakov would be...

My God, she thought: I must be mad! My parents have been slaughtered—I myself might lose my life. And here I sit, wondering what it would be like to kiss our librarian! She said, softly: "Vladimir Nicolaevitch, I am grateful to you for helping me. But I am not Yasha's sweetheart. We simply...we're simply..." And here words failed her. "Servant and mistress?" No! "Friends?" Yes—yes. But his love, his caring, his faithfulness had made him more than a friend.

"You could do worse than to marry Yasha," Nichayev said, spitting the words out. He was now reclining in his easy chair, a cigarette between his thumb and forefinger. "At the Conservatory, we all thought a lot of him. We didn't think he'd make the Philharmonic, because he just wasn't that dedicated. You truly have to *live* for your music to qualify for a position in the strings. But we knew —how to put it?—that he'd succeed at something. Something of his own making. He could have, too," he added, a sudden resentment thrust into his words and into his eyes as he narrowed them at Zica. She felt impaled by the look in his face, and also bewildered.

So Yasha had been popular at the Conservatory...He had never shared this side of himself with her. She had always thought of him as a rather lonely person, darting there for a quick lesson and then returning to his little room, to work on his French or on his reading. He had followed Senya's instructions, dutifully obeying the learned old retainer who had been around for as long as she could remember. And she had seen him with Natasha.

Natasha! The image of her all at once struck Zica with guilt. She said, hastily, in part to cover her own embarrassment, in part because she thought it was the truth: "Yasha has somebody already, Vladimir Nicolaevitch; Natasha Khazina is Yasha's girlfriend—not I. Didn't you ever meet her?"

"Yes, I've met her. But Yasha is a fool. Instead of her, a perfectly decent woman with good common sense, he preferred to daydream about you. It's you he loves, and you he aims to marry. You should let him do it, too, because otherwise, much harm will come to you in this city. You are a Poliakov. The Reds don't like rich girls, especially ones like you, that don't know what to do with their ten fingers."

Now she felt truly insulted. Apart from trying to throw her on the mercies of Yasha, this man was calling her an idiot. She stood up, suddenly furious, wondering why Yakov hadn't spoken up in her defense—why, in fact, he had hardly spoken at all, letting his rude friend do all the talking.

"Yasha," she said, her voice trembling: "I want to leave now, if you please. It is obvious Vladimir Nicolaevitch has taken a strong dislike to me, though for what reason I can't imagine."

"And where would you have Yasha take you?" Nichayev asked. He had slid down even more in his chair. An expression of mirth was outlined on his face. His small blue eyes crinkled at the corners as though he might at any moment burst out laughing, just to mock her.

"Anywhere at all! Yasha," she pleaded, "please get me out of here! I will not stay where I am being laughed at, for no other reason than that I am...I am what, indeed? I myself don't know! He hates me without even knowing me—and he...and he..."

"Poor little princess," Nichayev teased, sitting up. "Go on, Yasha, tell her you love her and will marry her in the morning, whether she likes it or not. It's the only solution." He was all seriousness now. "Your parents are both on the Black List, and perhaps you too. Only if you marry someone poor, someone of the people, will you be safe. No one would look for a Poliakov around the likes of us, that's for sure! They will see papers listing you as 'Zeinab Pokhis,' and that will probably be the end of it."

Yakov was avoiding her eyes. "Zeinab Lazarevna," he finally said, his voice even and dignified, as though he had always been on equal footing with her. "Vladimir's point is well taken. Only by marrying someone of the people will you escape detection. Marry me, quickly, tomorrow morning. We'll make our escape through the South, until we reach safety. This marriage will mean nothing once the Reds are behind you, and then you can annul it as you wish."

His voice sounded emotionless, almost hard, and caused her to regard him with sudden fear. She had never heard him like this before—never seen him so decisive and uncompromising. Any tone of respect or caring was missing from his voice. Even when he had saved her life after she had tried to get rid of the baby—even then, he had treated her as a lady, far above him. He would never have dared to propose to her, especially not in this abrupt, matter-of-fact fashion.

Yet, what choice did she have? "My parents..." she faltered, her voice quivering. Perhaps if she waited, she might find out what had happened to them. Maybe she was not, in fact, so alone. Maybe they were still alive and in a position to help her. She kept staring at Yakov, imagining becoming his wife. She thought how absurd the situation was, how unreal.

Yet there was that closeness she felt with him—so precious to her now. And he had saved her life once before, expecting no favors in return. Even now, he did not take advantage. He made this seem like nothing but a business proposition. She would not have to sleep with him; this was no declaration of passion. In fact, the marriage would only be a formality. He was offering her his name, in order to save her. And he was her only hope if she wished to stay alive long enough to get out of the city, away from the Bolsheviks. She had to accept.

But when she opened her mouth to speak, no words came. So she simply nodded, her face as white as his, her hands shaking as she twined them together.

"Well then, perhaps you'd like some soup to celebrate this engagement," Nichayev declared. "Come, Tania, help me prepare it."

Zica wanted to weep. But she could not give in to weeping—not now, when her fate had been decided. She had to show a brave front. She had let a man go, whom she had loved, because she had preferred her father—and now, in all probability, her father lay dead somewhere, butchered by the Reds.

And what of Kyril Ostrov? Surely, he was married by now to somebody else. He was probably safe and comfortable. If she had married Kyril, she might have gone to Rostov with him, and from there to Turkey and France, as hundreds of thousands had gone a similar route. They might have escaped with some of his grandfather's fortune. But as it was, he had surely forgotten her, relegating her to his painful past.

Zhenya, she knew, was dead in Petrograd. Kyril was long gone, and she was alone. Even Tamara had departed, for her father had moved the family to the Crimea some months before in anticipation of this revolution. No one could help her but Yasha Pokhis, and she had to face this graciously. He was all she had and he was a good man.

She realized that she'd forgotten something, in the delirium of the moment. And so, with great shyness, she inched close to him on the sofa, and planted a small kiss on his cheek. "Thank you," she whispered.

To her dumbfounded amazement, he seized her chin in his good right hand and covered her lips with his own. The kiss was violent, startling, his tongue parting her lips and exploring her mouth with hunger and need. When at last he released her, she moved back, her eyes distended, a little afraid. But he said nothing, and lay back, closing his eyes to wait for the soup.

Her heart was pounding wildly, and she wondered whether this time, she had not misinterpreted Yasha. Perhaps, to him, this would be a real marriage. Still, she had no choice: her fate lay in the palm of his hand, to do with as he willed.

And in the sudden violence of his kiss there had been something more tender and more searing than anything she had experienced before—even in the hot, impatient embrace of her lost Kyriusha.

Chapter IX

*A*CROSS the room from Kyril, Lorraine de Huitton was leaning against a silk screen hand-painted by a Japanese artist of unknown origin. She had purchased it in a small antique shop in the Marais, one afternoon when they had gone exploring Paris together —she incognito in her goggles and hat, he resplendent in a new sports costume her tailor had confectioned for him. Watching her, Kyril thought how beautiful she looked, how fine and distinguished. She was like a tall, blooming white lily, her bare shoulders reflecting the soft light from the chandeliers, her chestnut hair gleaming with strands of gold and red as she moved.

"Darling," she called suddenly, "come over here and answer some of the Count's questions. I've told him how lucky we are to have a genuine Russian in our midst." Turning to her companion, she said, "There! Ask the man of the moment!"

As Kyril rose from the love seat, he felt somewhat unsteady, having already drained three champagne flutes *à la Russe*. Now he would have to muster extra concentration to conduct an intelligent conversation with Count Rappel, Lorraine's friend, a member of the Quai d'Orsay, the French Foreign Ministry.

Count Rappel was aristocratic and elegant, a man of a certain age, as were all of those who had not been sent off to war. Even Lorraine was now a war widow—and Kyril thought wryly, certainly the most elegant widow he had ever laid eyes on. She wore only white or black . . . but how well those colors became her . . .

Her friends had called on her when she received news that Marc-Antoine had been killed in August in Verdun. Indeed, they made a great fuss over her loss, especially since Marc-Antoine had died a hero's death. She had let them cluck like mother hens. Sincerity was

173

less important than form, and she knew this better than anyone. Wars were a great testing ground for men, but also for their women. It revealed each woman for who she was and took the gilt off many a relationship by stripping it of its essential polite veneer. You learned who your friends were, who your enemies, and who were the indifferent cronies of no importance to you.

When she had first walked in to society on Kyril's arm, it had been at a *première* at the Comédie Francaise, to see Molière's *Tartuffe*. Kyril had neither read it nor heard of it. Surely an unforgivable lapse on the part of the bookish Elena...

"It's the ultimate statement on hyprocrisy," Lorraine had told him. "A play for the French, if ever there was one!" The moment they'd walked in, Kyril had felt a hundred opera glasses trained on them. He'd felt the flow of blood rising to his cheeks, suffusing his neck. He'd hated that feeling, and hated her—while, at the same time, feeling proud that such curiosity was being displayed on his behalf.

By now however, he'd grown so accustomed to this feeling that his essential self had split in half. He knew what the women thought of him: that he was Lorraine's little Russian doll, to be wound up as she pleased, and when she pleased. He was Russian, therefore exotic. While Frenchmen were absent, fighting for the honor of France, their women could play, without fear of reprisal. Some of them had made it quite clear that if he were to grow tired of his Marquise, there were Viscountesses and Countesses, Baronesses and Princesses who found him interesting. Most of them, poor things, were now alone in their gilded palaces.

Kyril felt ashamed. If his grandfather had only known how he was spending his life, he would have disowned him. Even as it was, communication with his mother and grandfather was infrequent. This Revolution was shaking Russia to her foundations. Tzarist Russia was being reshaped into a Bolshevik configuration. So Kyril felt ashamed. He'd stayed in Paris like a coward, not fighting the Great War and not returning home when Kerensky had taken over the government of Russia. He had ignored his mother's letters and replied that things would soon settle down... and why not come to France with Grandpapa? He, Kyril, was certainly too busy with his medical education to interrupt it and return to Rostov.

Yet he'd given up that education without a second thought when Lorraine had asked him to move into her townhouse on Place Victor Hugo the previous month. He'd hardly thought about his career as he had moved out of his small apartment and signed over the lease to a fellow student. Only Lorraine had mattered—but not Lorraine herself. It was *life* with Lorraine that he loved. Everything about that life was a contrast to the relative poverty of his parents and even the Orthodox restrictions of his grandfather's house, with its provincial narrowness. Compared to the way Zica had sought to hide him from her parents, Lorraine was proud of him, wearing him on her arm like a ribbon of the Legion of Honor. Where Zica had gone to great pains not to publicize their relationship, Lorraine went everywhere with him, introducing him to everyone. The people he met in Paris—people at the epicenter of the world—would have smiled in ridicule of Zica's behavior. After all, who, outside Russia, really cared about the Poliakovs, Muscovite Jewish merchants two generations removed from the Pale?

In Russia, no matter how handsome and talented, he would never have been able to penetrate the innermost sanctum of high society. He would always have been recognized as a Jew from the outback. This was what Zica had feared, and this, he thought, was why she had not married him.

No, in Russia, he hadn't stood a chance. Like Andersen's little Match Girl, he had been out in the cold, looking in at the party, hungry for an invitation that would never come.

But Lorraine didn't seem to care that he wasn't like her, a member of the oldest French nobility. She'd never asked him his religion. She *just didn't care*. He had never met a woman who cared so little about the things which, back in Russia, had loomed as essential in the lives of the rich and powerful. He was her companion, her lover, her partner: it didn't seem to matter that she had the money and paid all the bills. The social order, as decent people knew it, was in fact reversed where they were concerned. Lorraine didn't care, and Parisian society didn't care either. He was astonished and delighted and intrigued. What a place he had unwittingly stumbled into . . . !

Lorraine had moved him right into her bedroom. It didn't matter that she had learned of Marc-Antoine's untimely death at Verdun less than two months before. Her husband had been killed in August; by the middle of October, she began to complain of never being able to get hold of Kyril at his apartment because he had no telephone. She told him how she often awakened in the middle of the night, restless and feverish, prey to horrid anxiety attacks. She wanted him with her. "Come live with me," she'd said. When he'd countered, shocked: "But what will people say?" she had only laughed, thrilled by his innocence. His question was stilled with a kiss.

"Tout est permis," she had told him, winding her arms around his neck and fluffing his hair. All was permitted, when one was young, charming, and very rich. When one's family dated back to the Crusades and when one's dead husband had kept a mistress for years on Place Wagram, using his wife's dowry to pay her expenses, all was indeed permitted. So Kyril heard the determined voice of a woman who knew her own mind, who liked what she'd made of her own life, and who accepted things as they were.

Some day, when he felt better about life, when perchance he had accomplished something truly his own, he would ask her if she loved him. Meanwhile, he didn't think much about love. He was simply glad she had opened her world to him, and laughed with him, pushing the demons as far back as possible. Those demons were his memory, and his shame.

It was December now, more than a month since the events of Red October had devastated Russia. Still Kyril had heard nothing, not a single word, from his mother and grandfather. Now he regretted that he had not gone back to fetch them. And Zica? She had, most likely, been killed by the Reds. More likely her than his mother or grandfather. More likely her than anyone he had known in his homeland.

Now, however, Lorraine's soft white hand, with its ruby solitaire sending refractions all the way across the room, was beckoning toward him. Kyril straightened his bow tie and touched his hair, smiling automatically.

Count Rappel inclined his head. "Yes, my dear Kyril," he said, continuing a conversation he'd been having with Lorraine, "we are wondering about this Cossack, Ataman Semenov, who has allied himself with the Japanese and is said to be ridding Eastern Siberia of the Bolshevik scourge. It is said he has the help of only a few White officers."

Kyril took a deep breath. He felt Lorraine squeezing his hand encouragingly. In truth he knew little or nothing about Lenin and his band of Bolshevik upstarts, for he hadn't been in Russia during the Revolution. He knew less than most well-informed Frenchmen, because, with Lorraine, he often forgot to read the newspapers. He had slowly grown slothful and hedonistic, living each day for its moment, like a well-fed cat in the sun. He knew Semenov was a Cossack, but little more.

"I can tell you that the Whites will have to depend on the Czech forces, which have rebelled against the Soviets," he said, grasping at straws. An annoying bead of perspiration had formed right on the tip of his widow's peak.

The Count seemed satisfied to let the issue of Ataman Semenov slide out of sight. He turned to the Czech question. It seemed to animate him. His cheeks flushed as he lit his cigar and puffed vigorously. "Yes, yes! But the Czechs are in it for only one reason: to reach the French front." Like a triumphant general, he regarded the two young people with a look of proud chauvinism. Sententiously, he explained to them: "The Soviets, as you call them, are trying to prevent the Czech trains from getting there. So the Czechs have no choice but to throw their weight behind the Whites."

"This is good news for France," Kyril smiled.

"Yes, naturally, dear boy. We are quite fond of our Czech allies. This war...Ah, my children, this war...If we don't win it..."

"But we shall, Count Rappel. We shall." Lorraine's voice was edged with silk. "We shall, or men such as my husband will have given up their lives in vain."

By bringing up Marc-Antoine's heroic death, Lorraine had cleverly clinched the argument. Count Rappel blushed, embarrassed by his own *faux-pas*. "Yes, naturally, my dear. We shall win, of course." Lorraine smiled her bright hostess-smile, all the while holding Kyril's hand in her own, as if to protect it.

Suddenly Kyril wished to weep, like a little child. Instead, he stopped the liveried footman carrying trays of flutes filled with freshly poured champagne, and plucked one from his tray. He drank it down with desperation, hoping he would pass out, hoping he would die, hoping that God, who didn't exist, would all at once materialize and swallow him back into the earth. This little interchange with Count Rappel, capped by Lorraine's swift handling of his own ineptitude, had all at once provided a clear mirror by which to view himself: he was nothing more than a two-dimensional painting, the painting of a pretty boy with no substance.

When he had finished the champagne, Kyril broke away quickly from Lorraine and Count Rappel. He was dimly aware that he was committing a dreadful *faux-pas*. But he didn't give a damn. He stumbled out of the reception room and into the corridor, and pushed his way, half-blindly, into the oak-panelled study. It was blessedly dark; only a single light gracefully illuminated Lorraine's leather-bound first editions. He leaned against the bookcase, filled with self-loathing.

It took him a moment to realize that he was not alone in the room. At first he felt a pinprick of alarm, as though a ghost had entered; then he realized that the presence was benign. In the shadows, a young man was standing by the closed velvet curtians, a champagne flute in one hand and a cigarette, in a silver holder, between the fingers of the other. A silver cane was propped up next to him.

"Hello," the man said. "You don't look very festive." His voice sounded ironic, amused. Yet, beneath this tone, there was a strangely tender lining, as though Kyril's evident turmoil had touched him. "I'm Laurent de la Haye."

Still feeling shaken, Kyril simply nodded. The man seemed older by a few years—perhaps three or four. He was tall and graceful, like a dancer, his body long, elegant and slim. As he leaned against the window, one leg crossed over the other. His tuxedo outlined the width of his shoulders; and the cummerbund, the narrowness of his waist. He wore a very pale pink, frilled shirt and pearl studs.

His face was triangular, crested with dark, longish hair. He had almond-shaped eyes of an impenetrable ultramarine; his nose was chiselled and aquiline, and he sported a thin mustache above full, tender lips. Kyril felt his beauty like a wound, felt it transpiercing him to the very center of his being. He blinked, and kept looking at Laurent de la Haye, not even breathing.

Laurent wasn't smiling. He was staring back, his dark eyes wide and probing. Then he moved, and, to Kyril's surprise, when he did so he revealed an infirmity: his other leg was held up by a brace. It looked withered and deformed. "I am Lorraine's brother," he said softly. "And you are...?"

"Kyril Ostrov." In France, one wasn't encumbered by patronyms. Life was more straightforward, and one stood on one's own merits.

"You must be the Russian," Laurent said, and he smiled. There was nothing offensive about how he'd said this, because of the smile. It was an odd smile, a little like Lorraine's: detached by habit, friendly by volition.

Kyril still found it difficult to speak. The emotions he had felt with Count Rappel, the memories of Russia which their conversation had precipitated, continued to churn within him. And now there was this new emotion, the pull toward this stranger. Kyril wanted to say something and didn't know what to say. "Why haven't I met you before?" would have seemed too rude, though, of course, the question could not but have been in his mind.

"My sister and I haven't been close for years," Laurent said, settling himself on the ledge of the windowsill, and positioning his bad leg in front of him, like an object he was accustomed to working around. "We used to be friends, long ago, when we were children."

"What a shame," Kyril said. An only child, he had often felt a sense of yearning when he would hear siblings speak of their childhood. To him, having a sister seemed like a blessing not to be wasted.

"Yes," Laurent agreed, "we used to share a lot, she and I. But you see, now she has her own set of friends, and I have mine. Our lives hardly touch anymore." His limpid eyes shimmered in the night, and sought Kyril's. "I am an artist, Monsieur Ostrov. My sister is simply herself, and she is beautiful and confident. Widowhood fits her like a glove, better than marriage. I myself never liked Marc-Antoine, but then women are expected to marry, and men aren't."

"Oh?" Kyril said. "Is that how it is in France?"

Laurent laughed. "It's like that when one is *very, very wealthy*. Our family is *very, very wealthy*. If I marry, my bride would have to fit into the scheme planned by our forefathers and bring a large dowry; but that is less important, for male heirs control a larger part of the inheritance. Lorraine had no choice but to marry well. Marc-Antoine was a decent choice, and he wasn't a bad sort of chap, actually. It's just that he and I were nowhere alike. He was a hunter and a skirt-chaser, a man's man. And I am not that sort."

Kyril wanted to ask, "And what sort are you?" but again, this would have been an intrusion into the other's privacy. Instead, he coughed, cleared his throat, and said: "I am fascinated by all the differences I perceive between Russia and France. There is a great deal more freedom here, is there not?"

Laurent smiled. His dark eyes were sad, and full of experience. "There is no freedom here, Monsieur. There is only the semblance of it."

"How so?"

"Perhaps I've already said too much," Laurent observed. Abruptly his tone changed, growing cooler and more distant, as though he had already departed. "It's time I went home," he declared. "I have enjoyed our meeting, but now I must find the person I came with, and make my *adieux* to Lorraine."

"Shall I see you again?" Kyril asked. "Surely you will come here soon, to see her."

"Surely I shall, now that I've met you." The smile returned, briefly, casting a glow on the young man's pale face. Then, dragging his bad leg expertly behind him like a prisoner his ball and chain, he opened the door and departed, helped along by his cane.

Kyril shook his head as though to clear it. In a moment, he followed Laurent, hoping to catch a glimpse of him as he passed through the foyer on his way out. He saw him don a velvet cape held out by the *maître d'hôtel*. He was leaning on a silver walking stick. Next to him, a tall man waited, ready to exit.

The *maître d'hôtel* said, deferentially, "Your car is waiting, Monsieur le Comte." The tall, elegant man nodded and answered something Kyril didn't catch. Then he gave Laurent his arm, and they walked out together. Laurent was leaning slightly on the other man's arm.

"Ah, my sweet, I see that you have met my brother," Lorraine declared, throwing the corridor door open and holding her hands out to him. Kyril grasped the hands and brought them to his lips. She smiled at him. She didn't look a bit like Laurent de la Haye; he would never have guessed them to be siblings.

"Who was that other man?" Kyril asked, motioning with his chin toward the front door, through which Laurent and his companion had just passed.

"Orlando, Count del Arno. He's Venetian." Then, touching his cheek, she said, softly: "Let's mix with the guests."

Moscow, capital of the Soviet Union, was no longer a beautiful, feudal city, but a crowded place filled with angry, hungry people vying for attention. The entire city was filled with a sound like fishwives at a market. It was a hot, humid June day; Zica felt oppressed by the dusty, windless atmosphere. Her skin felt gritty and soiled. A thin film of perspiration clotted her hair beneath the cotton kerchief. Her full figure, clothed in a long skirt of combed cotton, struggled against the confining fabric. Her feet felt rubbed raw by the cheap sandals. She looked across the busy street toward the Passport Office of the Moscow CHEKA, the name given to the Extraordinary Commission for the Suppression of Counterrevolution, which the Whites had nicknamed the Red Terror. She had to get there early, before the lines reached the outer doors of the building.

A man wearing a leather jacket (a commissar?) jostled her.

"Watch where you're going!" a woman yelled at her as Zica stumbled on the cobblestones and felt herself slipping in the flimsy sandals. Zica caught her balance and ran across the street, breathless and humiliated. The lines were already beginning to form. She clutched her bag to her chest, knowing that inside it lay the key to freedom — her only hope, her only possession.

Six months had passed since her life had been cut in half, altered beyond redemption. Back in November, she had gone with Yakov to the marriage license bureau. A small, wizened man with white spittle in the corners of his mouth had looked them over. "Want to get married?"

Yakov nodded. Zica, beside him, said nothing. She held onto his hand for dear life.

"Names?"

"Yakov Pokhis. Zeinab Poliakova."

The little man frowned. He was obviously new to this, a factory worker suddenly elevated to the role of commissar. He wasn't quite sure how it worked. But he did appear to recognize the name "Poliakov." Turning to Zica, who had swept her hair into a simple topknot, and was wearing Tania's clothes, he barked out: "Poliakov? You from the family that owns the button factory on Novinsky Boulevard?"

He had mean little eyes and a face like a weasel. When Zica stared at him, uncomprehending, he repeated his question, spitting it out like chewed tobacco. She began to shake: "I . . . I don't know. . ."

"Of course she's not from *that* family!" Yakov cut in, impatience tinging his voice. "Do we look like people who have money?" He'd already figured out that this little official had once had a job at the button factory. In fact, Lazar Poliakov had owned it, but Yakov doubted that Zica had ever visited it, nor been told much about it.

"Place of birth?"

"We're from Podolia," Yakov said. "I'm from Peredelkino, she's from Rigevka."

"Papers?"

Zica felt her body go soft. As she began to shake her head, she heard Yakov saying, pleasantly: "I have mine. My fiancée lost hers long ago. She's an orphan. We're Jews, you know, from the Pale.

We came here by special permission, because I had a scholarship to the Conservatory. But, you know, things changed. I got myself kicked out for causing trouble..."

"What kind of trouble?"

Yakov made a face, and said, confidentially: "I was a Social Revolutionary. The Secret Police came after us and found my friends making a crude bomb in a cellar on Lubyanka Street. I was implicated, though I wasn't present at the time."

The official scrutinized Yakov, then turned his attention to Zica. In her simple smock, she looked like a young Jewish girl from the Pale, intimidated by authority. "All right, then," he declared. He recited a few phrases, asked them to repeat a few words, and pointed toward a large register. "Sign here."

Yakov signed with a flourish; Zica could barely move her fingers. She had a lump in her throat the size of an orange. "Come on, little wife," Yakov said, and he placed his arm firmly about her shoulders. They walked out like that. He held her close to him until they were safely across the street. Then Yakov let her go. She looked at him and burst into tears.

This had been the beginning of their marriage.

That night, in Vladimir Nichayev's flat, Tania had gone to sleep in the small closet, curling up on the floor like a puppy, her head on a pile of their host's dirty laundry. Vladimir (Yakov called him Vova) had settled down on the sofa, saying: "You two can have my bed. It's the only gesture I can make in *lieu* of a wedding gift. Sleep well, my darlings..."

Zica had blushed so hard she thought her cheeks would turn to flames. How lewd of him, how terribly crude.... Did he not remember that this was to be a white marriage, in name only? Yet Yakov had merely smiled, an enigmatic half-smile, saying, "Thank you, Vova. We could use a good night's sleep."

She went into the bedroom, which was itself hardly bigger than a closet, and waited. What to do? Sleep in her clothes, on top of the covers? It was cold. She'd have to crawl under the quilt.

Yakov was sitting on the bed, doing nothing. He watched her expectantly, as if he were waiting for her to do something. And all the while *she* was waiting for *him* to do something. She wanted him to give her an idea of what was expected. How did one behave in such a situation?

But this situation was beyond tradition.

Then all at once he broke the ice. "I must use the toilet," he said, and she winced. You weren't supposed to *say* "toilet," though you meant it. You said, "I need to wash my hands." She remembered a funny episode from Zhenya's past, when he'd been a young man travelling to Paris, and he'd asked one of his hostesses if he might wash his hands; she had shown him to a powder room with nothing but a sink in it, and he'd been mortified, having to return and explain what he needed. Now she giggled.

"What's the matter?" Yakov asked. Since the wedding ceremony, he hadn't called her anything: not the formal "Zeinab Lazarevna," not "Zica," not anything. He, too, didn't know how to behave.

"I was just thinking of your needing to use the toilet," she said, her chin trembling; then she started to weep. And he came over and held her, gently, without saying a word, without bothering to point out how absurd she made this sound, this weeping over the mention of a toilet.

Yakov had to go outside on the landing to use the common toilet, which six other people shared—all students with tiny rooms and apartments like Vova Nichayev's. Zica had been touched. She understood that he'd given her the room to undress by herself, modestly. She'd taken off her clothes and rummaged in Nichayev's closet, finding an old nightshirt. This she put on over her drawers, then crawled into bed and pulled the covers way up to her chin, like a virgin.

Only she wasn't a virgin, and he knew it; he, better than anyone.

When Yakov came back, she turned on her side to let him undress too. Then she felt him getting into bed, and she had stiffened, afraid—afraid he would suddenly ask for his payment in this dubious marriage. For it was his due after saving her life. But she had cried instead of thanking him, she had behaved like a spoiled little rich girl. And she had probably hurt his feelings. Suddenly she was deeply ashamed.

"Yasha," she whispered. "I'm sorry."

"There is no need, Zeinab."

"Yasha . . . ?"

"Yes?"

"You've been so kind . . . I haven't thanked you . . ."

"It has been difficult, I know. You have lost everything . . . your beloved parents, your brother . . .

"I wish I had died too!"

"No, Zeinab, no. You are young and beautiful. Life will smile at you again, you'll see. You're feeling hopeless because of your loss. You feel small, and all alone."

She was silent. He seemed to be able to peer directly into her heart.

"I love you, still. I shall love you, always. Now, go to sleep, for tomorrow we must find a place to live. We cannot keep abusing Vova's hospitality—and besides, he's thinking of leaving the city."

There was silence. Then, suddenly, the fear rose up in her— black, voracious, ferocious as a wild animal from hell. She'd felt its gripping power around her neck, smothering her—she'd cried out. And then, only then, he had come over, sliding close to her and holding her, letting her cry. When the wave had washed over her and dispersed, she'd felt warm, and grateful, and tender in his arms. And she'd fallen asleep.

She couldn't remember at what point in the night she had awakened, her feelings transformed. She felt stronger, with greater resolve, even a tiny bit happy. In the light of the guttering candle by their bedside, she'd seen him lying there asleep, like a little boy, his fist in his mouth. Affection had overwhelmed her. She'd snuggled close, so full of love she couldn't breathe.

He had awakened. So close, so comforting, their lovemaking had come naturally then. It had simply *happened,* one step at a time, without a conscious act of volition. Two young people holding each other for dear life . . . and then she felt him pressed hard against her belly, so sure and insistent. Instinctively, she had opened herself to receive him. He was very gentle with her; in his arms, she felt her body become a gift. He took it gladly, but with love and compassion. She came alive beneath his touch—gladness flowed through her, more binding than passion.

And so she had become his wife, Citizen Zeinab Pokhis. That had been over six months ago, in Vladimir Nichayev's tiny flat. They had proceeded with caution, because of his wound; but she had given herself to him, making a decision, the first important decision of her adult life. And somehow, while she'd made love to him, she hadn't once thought of Kyril Ostrov.

The official behind the long wooden desk barked out: "Citizen Pokhis!" Zica was startled from her memories back to the reality of the moment. She came forward, her heart pounding. The man in the rimless spectacles looked her up and down before addressing her. "You've applied for a foreign passport for you and your husband?"

Why was he asking, if he already knew? It was just another way to humiliate her, by making her beg for it again and again. Dutifully, she answered, "Yes. We have relatives in Paris, and they are sending for us."

"Your husband's papers are in order," the man said. "But yours . . ." The sentence hung in mid-air. Zica's blood froze. "You were married without papers, Citizen Pokhis?"

"What would you like me to do now?" she asked. She had to muster all her strength to face him, without letting her fear show.

"Perhaps if you wrote to Rigevka for a copy of your birth certificate, it would help us here."

Zica nodded. She was entranced by the man's soft words. The official had hypnotized her into docility, and she could only comply.

She stepped out into the muggy June sunshine, and looked at the linden trees lining the boulevard. How Moscow had changed! It was full of ragged people hurrying along. She realized with a tremor of self-awareness that she was one of them. Yakov had found a job at a bakery and was working twelve hours a day. They had split up from Tania and Vova. Her young maid had gone off to join a cousin on the other side of town. The violinist had relinquished his apartment and was returning to his parents in the Crimea. Now they shared a flat with four other couples, strangers to both of them. The women were constantly arguing over the two-burner stove, like cave women over a single piece of meat. Their toilet was a hole in the cement. Each of them took a bath once a week in what most often turned out to be rusty, cold water. Yet, she and Yakov were alive; he was earning a living, and they were together.

How it mattered that she was not alone! At night, in their minuscule, windowless room, she would sit on her haunches and look at him, and tears would well up. She loved him—she truly loved him. He had saved her life, had bound himself to her. She was not alone: a strong man was beside her, and he was wise and smart. There was a roof over her head and someone who remembered what she had been like, long ago, six months before, a lifetime past. To all appearances, she was no different from any of the nondescript women of Moscow. But in Yakov's eyes, she saw that she was Zica Poliakova with spirit intact.

Yakov never spoke sharply, the way the other husbands did. He never drank. Little Marfa Bitova sometimes wailed during the night, waking everyone in the house and making Zica's hair stand on end: her husband beat her. But Yakov treated Zica the way he'd always treated her. He loved her so carefully, so gently, that sometimes in bed she forgot that she hadn't chosen this man. She remembered only what counted: that he was keeping the wolves at bay, that he was protecting her. To him, Zica Poliakova was always somebody special.

She ducked into a side street off Tverskoy Boulevard. There, in front of her, stood their dirty-white apartment house. She was just about to cross the street when an old woman came up and pointed, and Zica saw a long black car—a truck, really—pull up in front of the door. "See?" the old *babushka* said. "No windows. I wonder what poor devil this Black Raven is picking up now. Today I went to visit my daughter, and there was another one on the Boulevard . . . on Tverskoy, I mean. Somebody said they picked a poor woman right out of her family because once, long ago, she had a White boyfriend."

"Where do they bring the prisoners?" Zica asked. Her voice was weak with fright.

The old woman shrugged. "Some to jail. Others . . ." With her hand she made a motion across her neck like a razor blade. "Cross yourself, little girl," she said. "A Black Raven from the CHEKA is an omen of bad fortune."

Zica remained standing as the woman crossed the street. A sixth sense was telling her that, if she didn't want to be squeezed into the windowless black van, ominously covered by a large tarpaulin, she had better stay out of sight. When at last the vehicle rumbled away, rounding a bend in the road, she made her way to the building and walked up the stairs to the apartment.

Marfa Bitova was standing in the kitchen, making a mushroom *pirog*. "Zica," she cried. "You're in great danger. They came here looking for you. We said we didn't know where you had gone. But they'll be back."

"I haven't committed any crime!" She pulled a stool out and sat down, her shoulders drooping.

"Crime? Oh, no . . . it's not only the criminals they come for. It's anybody with a past. The Red Terror is like that. Don't you know?"

She nodded mutely. When Marfa had finished kneading the

dough, she came over to sit down next to Zica. "Look," she said, awkwardly. "We don't really know each other. But you know about me, about the night beatings. I know something about *you,* too. You used to be *somebody.* Don't ask me how I know. It's something we've all learned, living in such close quarters. But not everybody will protect you as I will; there are those who are envious. It isn't safe to trust anyone, Zica. You might be trusting a CHEKA informer."

"We have an informer living here, in this apartment?"

Marfa sighed. "There are informers everywhere. Nothing is sacred any more. No one believes in anything. We have turned into a country of godless people, and this is the result: every man for himself. They'd hoped to make it one for all and all for one, and I thought we would be a great nation. Instead—isn't it strange—they've created the reverse."

Impulsively, Zica bent down and kissed Marfa. "Thank you," she whispered, "for warning me."

She entered the small bedroom and began to pack a suitcase. She and Yakov would have to leave that night, before the Black Raven returned. But, who would have "told" on her? Who could have wanted to hurt her that much? She reviewed the apartment occupants and shook her head, helpless against the enormity of the machine. There were the Bitovs, but even Mishka wasn't a *bad* man, except to his own wife when he was drunk. Then Arkady and Olga Mirkin, a Jewish couple. He was a printer and she was nice enough. The last couple was called Dinutsin: she was soft, plump and harmless, he a railroad official with his head forever stuck in some Bolshevik tract. Perhaps them, perhaps Marek Dinutsin—because he believed in the Communist system more than the others. She could think of nobody else.

A month ago, after five months of silence, they had received a letter from Bella and Lev Pokhis, Yakov's parents, sent to General Delivery. Seeing his father's ill-formed handwriting, the chicken scratches he so well remembered, Yakov had wept unabashedly. Amazingly, the letter had been postmarked "Paris, France." The Aschkenasys, in Odessa, had decided that the Bolsheviks would eventually reach their city and head straight for their house on the Boulevard. So they had booked passage for themselves and their servants, Bella and Lev, on a French freighter. Typically, Anna could not conceive of emigrating without a competent cook and seamstress, nor without the services of a decent butler. After all, she had trained these two, had accepted them right out of her brother's miserable *shtetl*—and now she counted on them to get through the day.

The elder Pokhises wanted Yakov to join them. They promised to send money from their savings as soon as he informed them his passport was ready. Bella and Lev had no idea that their son had married their employer's niece, but Zica had written them a nice letter, introducing herself to them and including a long letter to her aunt and cousins.

Thinking of that letter, Zica suddenly realized what had happened. Someone had intercepted that letter, and understood. Whether this someone turned out to be Marfa's husband or Marek Dinutsin, the fact remained that someone in this household had read her letter and put two and two together, concluding that she was the daughter of someone who had been powerful.

Yakov had told her not to write. She had done so, anyway, giving the letter to Olga Mirkina to mail. She hadn't understood that it was dangerous, that she had done the most foolish thing in the world. Yet she had written nothing more than that she wished everyone well, that she was so glad their families were safe. To the Bolsheviks, this would mean treason, however. Now a Black Raven had come for her. She had narrowly escaped being taken.

Why hadn't she listened to Yakov?

She had thought she would surprise him by endearing herself to his mother. She had also thought that her aunt and uncle would surely send money for the trip, once they learned she was alive and married. She hadn't written anything incriminating. She hadn't said anything about the Poliakovs, her parents and Zhenya. What, then, had given her away?

Marfa had said, "There are informers everywhere." Perhaps it was even Yakov who had told someone about his young wife. Perhaps he had boasted a little. But this seemed unlikely. Yakov was tight-lipped, a loner. He was circumspect and trusted no one. He was a *shtetl* boy who had witnessed pogroms and knew what human beings could do to one another. No, it had been the letter, she was sure of it.

Almost overwhelmed by terror, Zica continued packing until she heard Yakov's footsteps outside the door. She rushed to open it and threw herself into his arms, bursting into tears. "We have to go!" she cried, between sobs. "The CHEKA sent a Black Raven here today. At the Passport Office, the official told me I would need to produce a birth certificate from Rigevka. Yasha...I wasn't born in Rigevka. I'm from Moscow."

"I know," he said, "I know. Calm yourself, Zeinab."

"Are you crazy, Yasha? How can I be calm, when a Black Raven came for me? Had I returned five minutes earlier from the Passport Office, I would have been seized!"

He sighed. His arms were tight around her, and he began to stroke her back in little circles. "We're going to have to find a way out of here," he told her. "Tonight, I know a place for us to hide. Soon we shall have to leave Russia...with no exit visas. I don't know how we'll do it, little one, but we shall. I promise you that!"

She looked into his face, and saw the resolve. And all at once she felt that he was right. Somehow, they would find a way to leave Russia.

Chapter X

*B*UT for the two drunken militiamen on the corner, the street appeared deserted. Yakov could hear them laughing and swapping dirty jokes. Tremors ran up his spine.

The truck that Yakov drove was an old German relic in great disrepair. Mishka Bitov used it to make delivery runs all over the city. He worked for a factory which bottled milk, and in the early morning, it was his job to collect thousands of empty bottles to bring back to the factory for renewed use: that was the only reason why he was allowed to keep the vehicle overnight. Yakov had simply stolen it, taking the key from Mishka's pocket as he lay passed out on the sofa in the common room. By morning, of course, everyone would know who had done this and why. Marfa would have to tell them that the Black Raven had paid a call—that Yakov and Zica had been forced to flee.

Behind him, in the cargo section covered by some rumpled blankets, Zica lay hidden. If only she weren't so naive, he thought. She had placed them both in jeopardy through her naiveté.

"Halt! Who goes there?"

One of the militiamen jumped out of the shadows in front of the truck. Yakov braked abruptly. Zica uttered a muffled cry which died just as soon as it had been uttered. Yakov opened the window and stuck his head out. He smiled. "Just the delivery run for the Gurdjievitch factory. Mikhail Bitov, your Excellency."

"Aren't you a little . . . early?" The militiaman sounded drunk, but not too drunk to know the time. It was only two-thirty in the morning.

"A little, yes. Emergency run." Yakov flashed a smile, hoping his unshaven face would not be noticed.

"What's the emergency?"

This time the second man had spoken. He wobbled on his feet, but he looked belligerent, ready to challenge anything Yakov told him—a mean drunk. He was large and beefy. Suddenly Yakov knew there was going to be trouble. He got out of the car. His words, when he spoke, were uttered in a tone ingratiating and whiny, typical of the small-time Communist wheedling used to avoid red tape: "Ah, brother . . . my friend is sick. I was just going to bring him medicine. I thought I'd start my run just as soon as I saw him. . . ."

"Is that so? Let me see this medicine."

Yakov shrugged, still smiling. "It's in the back." He went around to the cargo section of the milk truck and opened the door. Both men crowded around him, one on either side. Each was twice his size but quite unsteady on his feet.'

Yakov's face was drenched in sweat. If neither man noticed Zica, perfectly still under her blankets, they might hope to leave there alive. He peered inside the back of the truck, seeking inspiration. And there among some empty milk bottles and soiled blankets, he saw the half-empty bottle of vodka. Brightening, he reached for it. Looking from one to the other of his would-be assailants, he held out his prize to the man who had first spoken to him. "See, comrade, what good medicine I have here inside?"

"Where's the *real* medicine?" the beefy man demanded. But the other was already drinking, his head tilted back. Desperately, Yakov searched through the rear of the truck, his hands pushing aside the empty bottles and soiled rags. Suddenly he felt something cool and hard, something metallic. He grabbed it, and lifted out a large pair of pliers. In the same gesture, he seized the pliers in both hands, swinging the tool with his arms. Steel cracked on flesh and bone, as Yakov smashed the second militiaman square between the eyes with the full force of his pliers.

The first man dropped the vodka. The bottle crashed to the ground. The second man, screaming in pain, fists clenched over his gushing wound, collapsed to the ground, swearing. Yakov sprinted around to the driver's seat, jumped in, slammed the door, and started the engine of the old milk truck. The first man was at the window, trying to stick his hand in. Yakov started up with a loud roar and a squeal of tires.

Shots resounded behind him. But the militiaman was drunk. One bullet struck the fender. Yakov, his voice urgent, shouted, hoping she would hear through the partition, "Keep down, Zeinab. For God's sake, don't get up yet. . . . "

Down one street, up another, across a tree-lined boulevard, Yakov drove like Orestes pursued by the Furies, his breath coming in short, violent gasps. After a while he slowed down. There was no way those two militiamen could have alerted any of their compatriots in such a short time. They'd probably been off-duty as it was, looking for some diversion.

He began to head south. But he would not stop the car until they had driven for another hour, and he saw that they had reached Golitsyn Hospital on the outer edge of the city. Then at last he parked the truck along the side of the road. "You may come out now," he said, opening the door of the cargo section.

"Oh, Yasha, I'm so frightened," she whimpered, emerging from the covers dishevelled and weeping. But he had no time for sympathy now, and so he sighed, frustrated, and snapped: "We're alive, aren't we?"

"Tomorrow they will come after us in full force," she said. "They'll put this assault together with the stolen truck and our disappearance. What will we do?"

"I have no idea," he told her. And all at once exhaustion came over him like a down quilt, threatening to smother him. He sighed, shut the door on his wife's trembling form, and got back into the driver's seat. And she sat quietly behind the metal partition too afraid to think, listening to the motor starting up again.

Tenderly, Lorraine passed her arm through Kyril's, and said with regret: "What a shame . . . The most beautiful season in Biarritz used to be the Russian one, in September and October. You should have seen what the town was like, then: it was a time of uninterrupted parties. The grand-duchesses came to show off their costumes, and the princes came to spend. All the hotels, casinos, and villas were decorated with beautiful people . . . and I loved it. But alas, your Monsieur Lenin has transformed all this, and now Biarritz is different, duller." She made a funny face, and laughed. "What an empty-headed woman you must think me," she remarked.

He smiled, but did not answer. The end of the war was approaching; it was October 1918, and Germany was faring worse and worse. Lorraine's group of friends had decided to take refuge in the villa she owned, on the embankment overlooking the Grande Plage, the most spectacular of Biarritz's three beachfronts. The villa stood near the Casino and the luxury hotels. To their right, a promontory pushed forward into the sea, with a lighthouse that picturesquely blinked all night long. Behind it, some distance away, was the majestic Hôtel du Palais.

"Shall we go down?" she asked. "It's such a splendid day."

"You can't go without me," a cheerful voice piped up behind them. Kyril turned and bowed slightly to the woman who was approaching them. She was a tall blonde with laughing green eyes. Though not beautiful like Lorraine, she seemed healthy and wholesome. She was English, and Lorraine's best friend.

"Fresh air's just what you need, lovey," the newcomer said. Affectionately, she linked her arm around Lorraine's waist. The three of them contemplated the sea and the azure sky. "Look at those waves!" the Englishwoman said. "They must be six feet tall!"

"Do you swim, Lady Charlotte?" Kyril asked. He himself swam badly. He was ashamed to try in front of Lorraine's friends. But he wanted to start a conversation with this woman. She intrigued him. She played tennis indefatigably every morning, then croquet on the villa lawn in the afternoon. She spoke French with a funny accent.

"I was born a mermaid, my sweet." Charlotte Maple-White took a deep breath, then unexpectedly pulled off her shoes. She closed one eye and took aim, and the pair of perfect suede pumps landed one after another in adjacent flower beds. Lorraine laughed.

"Race you down, Lorraine," Lady Charlotte said. Lorraine demurred, but already her friend was bounding ahead of them like a gazelle, scampering down the stone steps to the long, sandy beach. They watched, fascinated, as she ran away from them until her candy-pink dress was only a bright dot on the wide expanse below them.

"Lottie's such a rebel," Lorraine said fondly. "Just look at her!"

"You've been friends for long?"

Lorraine descended the steps demurely, holding onto his arm. "Lottie and I go back to early childhood," she answered, her voice a little wistful.

Kyril wanted to ask more, but the moment didn't seem appropriate. They had reached the sand, and Charlotte Maple-White caught up with them, motioning with one strong, athletic arm toward the murky sea. "Let's sit on the big rock and feel the waves crash about us," she suggested.

"Not me!" Lorraine's eyes met Charlotte's and held them. Both burst into laughter. They laughed and laughed, holding each other's hands, until Lorraine collapsed in Charlotte's arms, out of breath. Next to them, Kyril stood awkwardly chewing on the inside of his lip.

"I'll swim if you do," Lorraine said to Charlotte.

"But your suit—"

"I have it on beneath my dress. See, darling? I come well prepared when my best friend is with me. Nothing's left to chance." She unbuttoned her dress, letting it fall to the sand as though the silk had been nothing but cheap combed cotton. Beneath, she was wearing a dark blue bathing suit trimmed with dark braid, its demure skirt hiding her thighs.

"I'll be just a second." Charlotte hastened to unbutton herself. But then, instead of letting her dress fall, she stepped carefully out of it and handed it to Kyril. "Would you mind, dear? I'll be back in a second. Feeling sand on wet skin is not my idea of comfort. Be an angel and hang onto to it for me." She was standing not in a bathing costume, but in a simple silk teddy, seemingly devoid of self-consciousness or modesty.

As the two women disappeared into the waves, Kyril stood holding Charlotte's pink dress, with Lorraine's in the sand at his feet. He was furious. He wanted to dump both garments in the waves and be done. Perhaps, instead, he'd go back up the stairs and see what she'd think, elegant Lady Maple-White, when she returned from her swim and found no dress at all to put over her teddy. Well, *damn* her, he didn't care!

"I see you've met Lottie," a wry voice commented. It sounded soft, almost disembodied. Kyril started. Next to him stood Laurent de la Haye, Lorraine's brother, in a tweed jacket and tan knickerbockers, heavy woolen hose and spats. His bad leg was tucked behind his good one; he was resting his full weight on a silver cane. A sports cap with a wide visor was pulled low over his forehead. He looked pale, even gaunt, his large ultramarine eyes enormous in the white triangular face.

As Kyril opened his mouth to speak, he felt strong emotions pulling at him. "I—"

"It's all right. You don't have to like her. She appeals to noisy, earthy Latins, and to her own kind—the equestrian set with their jodhpurs and whips. I'll bet she whips *them,* too, until their poor little bottoms bleed. Don't you think so?"

Kyril stared at Laurent, incredulous. Then, slowly, he started to laugh. They laughed together, looking at the sea, the waves, and the two women whose heads they could see bobbing up and down in the foam.

"Are you here to stay?" Kyril asked. He wanted to say: *"Where have you been?"*, but that would have been wrong: they hardly knew each other.

Laurent shrugged his shoulders eloquently. "I always come here in the fall," he said. "The air's good for me. But I don't stay with Lorraine. I have my own place."

Now the women were getting out of the sea, shrieking at each other. They shrugged off excess water like seals fluffing their fur. Soon this would end, and they would be here. The last time, Laurent had made a veiled promise to come to see him, and *that* had been *months* ago. Kyril felt his throat knot. He wanted to know when he would see Laurent again—wanted to prevent him from leaving. But he did not know how to ask.

"Will you . . . will we . . . ?" he began awkwardly, twisting his hands until the knuckles grew white.

Laurent looked toward the sea, and sighed. He nodded, briefly, without looking at Kyril. Then, "Goodbye," he said, "I must get back." But he didn't tell him where he lived, didn't tell him when he'd see him next. *I shall never see him again,* Kyril thought, wondering how he could feel such dark despair. Laurent was a virtual stranger. Yet something in Laurent tugged at Kyril—something naked, vulnerable and mysterious.

And then the women were upon him, laughing and talking, each struggling into her day dress. "Your brother was just here," Kyril declared. "I didn't know he was in Biarritz."

"It's hardly news of great import," Lorraine said, matter-of-factly. "Laurent is no different from us all, dear heart. We are birds of a feather, all of us who grew up together, and we do tend to migrate to the same places."

"Why hasn't he been to the house?"

As Lorraine regarded Kyril, her face now showed interest as well as irony. "Because, my darling, Laurent de la Haye does not like me. And now, Lottie and I would like something to eat. Will you drive us to the Hôtel du Palais for a little tea?"

"I'd be delighted." But he could feel his body tensing, as his anger began to swell. To his surprise, the image that came up before him was of Lorraine, naked and spread-eagled on the bed. He could feel a sudden rush of passion, a sudden need—but not to make love to her. He wanted to hurt her, to bring tears to those periwinkle eyes, to mar that perfect white skin.

He had never done this to her; but he knew, as sure as she was breathing, that he was capable of hurting her very, very deeply, as he'd once hurt the whores of Moscow.

Between Yakov and Zica there was enough money to last a week. Yakov's pay would take them that far. Yakov had an old map of Russia that Vova had given him; it was somewhat antiquated, but it would have to do. He spread it out by the side of the road to show her.

"We could go to my grandparents in Tiflis," Zica said. "My mother's parents. The Bolsheviks haven't reached there yet. They will be able to help us get out of the country. Tiflis is just a hair's-breadth away from Turkey. They can give us money to take a ship from Constantinople to France. Aren't you glad you learned French?"

Yakov nodded. His young face now looked aged with worry. "My French leaves a great deal to be desired. But, listen, Tiflis is more than fifteen hundred kilometers from Moscow. We're bound to run out of gas. Outside the big cities, I doubt we'll find petrol anywhere."

"Then, what shall we do?"

Yakov's face looked grim. "We'll take the truck as far as it will go. Then we'll walk to the nearest village and try to rent some kind of vehicle. We'll take back roads, so no one from the milk plant can follow us. The Bolsheviks will begin looking too, as soon as the Black Raven comes back empty from the apartment. If we leave now, by the time this truck runs out of petrol, we'll have gained some valuable time. Tiflis is due south, a little to the west of us. It shouldn't be hard to get close to it as long as no one stops us along the way."

Zica nodded. It was early dawn. The sky was rosy, almost pearlescent, as Yakov helped her to get back inside the truck. They were about to leave Moscow behind them. The gas tank was almost full, and Yakov seemed to know the way. But *did* he? She was certain he was as confused as she, but he succeeded in hiding his fears. She was hungry. But she wouldn't bother him with this. Instead, she closed her eyes and fell asleep.

In the soft, downy bed, Lorraine stirred. Even asleep she smelled of apricots and honey. As he looked at her, Kyril wondered how it

had been possible to hate her the way he had the previous afternoon. He hadn't felt such violent emotions since his childhood,
when he had wanted to kill his father almost every day. It's me, he
thought, not her. I'm doing nothing with my life, and I'm blaming
her for my own shortcomings.

She made a small, purring noise. He saw her eyelids flutter open.
He took a finger and placed it on the curve of her cheek, feeling its
lovely shape. "Good morning," she mumbled, her voice hoarse
with sleep.

"It isn't morning yet, Lorraine. It's only five o'clock. I just
wanted to touch you. Go back to sleep."

She smiled. "You do love me, don't you?"

"Do *you* love *me?*"

For an instant she said nothing. "I love being with you," she said
carefully. "I love having you near me, taking you places, sleeping
with you. Yes, I suppose this means I love you. I'm hardly used to
loving anyone. The men around me haven't exactly been the lov-
able sort, Kyriusha." She'd long ago stopped calling him 'Cyril.'

He nodded. "But surely not *all* the men. Your brother, for
instance... surely there was a time when you and he loved each
other."

She sat up, her brown hair falling like a lace mantilla over her
white shoulders. "Laurent was my little treasure, when I was growing up. I protected him from everything, from everyone." Her eyes
flashed, and her voice vibrated with passion. "He fell off a horse
when he was ten, and was badly injured. The specialists my parents
called in could do nothing to save his leg. It... it atrophied. He
wore a brace and learned to get around, but—well, he was never
quite the same after that. He grew moody and withdrawn. Only his
paintings seemed to matter. He found my concerns and my friends
silly and beneath him."

Her eyes had grown moist. Self-consciously, she turned to the
night table and took a cigarette from the silver dispenser. She lit the
cigarette, then leaned back in bed. Her eyes closed as she inhaled. "I
suppose he felt he could no longer participate in our games, in our
life. But I felt... rejected. For a while I was hurt and angry. I didn't
bother trying to include him any more. He had friends of his own,
all artists, many of them sickly like him. My rowdy crowd bored
him. He found us too 'social.'"

"And that's the reason you don't see each other now, twenty
years later?"

Lorraine's eyes were closed. Tears edged out beneath the lashes.

Kyril looked at her, horrified. "What's the matter?" He wanted to reach out and touch her, but couldn't. It was as though, suddenly, he had been turned into a pillar of stone. He couldn't move. "Why are you weeping?" he asked softly.

She shook her head. "Because, long ago, something happened between us, which makes it impossible for us ever to be friends again. Laurent did . . . something . . . to me. I cannot forgive him, nor can I forget. We see each other twice a year. And we run into each other now and then. But that's all. He betrayed me! I loved him and he—well, it hardly matters how. I'd rather not discuss it any longer."

"He doesn't like Lady Charlotte."

"He doesn't like anyone who loves me! If I were you, Kyriusha, I would simply forget you ever met Laurent. He can do you nothing but harm. He knows that you and I are together. And he'll do you harm, for that reason alone."

She crushed the cigarette in a crystal ashtray and turned on her side. Kyril lay silently beside her, not touching her, just thinking. None of this made any sense. Yet he felt a yearning and a sorrow. Something came to him from the past, some regret or a longing that he could not quite identify. Every time he saw Laurent, that longing would inexplicably recur.

Tomorrow, when Charlotte and Lorraine went to the Casino, he would find a way to contact Laurent. Lorraine didn't own him; he had a right to his own life. Perhaps he felt this attraction to Laurent because he, too, had once painted landscapes. Or perhaps it was that he, too, had been small and weak, the little chick, the *tsyplionok*. But while Laurent had played out his dreams, Kyril had taken the easy way out. Now he was nothing but a pawn, a toy, to keep Lorraine amused. I am worth more than that, he thought angrily: it's time I proved my worth to myself.

The heat was now unbearable, and Yakov felt the truck beginning to falter. Its tires were inadequate for the rough country road. Several hours before, they had stopped for food in a small town. Zica had bought bread, fruit, cheese, and water. Now she lay slumped against him in the small cab, her breathing labored. Yakov wondered whether she was getting ill. Her face felt clammy against his bare arm.

He had removed his shirt and neatly folded it into the cargo area.

His beard had grown; he knew that he looked unkempt. But what did it matter? Zica probably just needed some water and a rest. The sun beat down mercilessly on the roof of the truck. Soon, it would be time to abandon this vehicle. Better to reach a village where they could find a cart before they ran out of petrol. They didn't want to get caught on some deserted side road.

Zica sat up, rubbing her eyes. "Yasha," she said, her voice strangely thick. "I think I'm going to be sick."

He pulled over to the side of the dirt road and got out of the truck. As he helped her out, he felt her shivering. Beads of sweat glistened on her broad forehead. With his help, she reached the embankment. She leaned over, retching. He held her as the violent spasms shook her body. Still white and trembling, she untied the kerchief from her brow and wiped her neck and cheeks.

"Probably just nerves," she said. "The Black Raven . . . those militiamen . . ."

Yakov nodded in sympathy. They climbed back into the truck, but now it wouldn't start. Panic built like a coiled spring inside him. "Wonderful!" he groaned. "We must be empty."

Zica looked at him, knitting her brow. "What shall we do?"

Grimly, he said: "We'll have to walk. I don't know where the next village is. Only the large towns are marked on the map. Zica, are you strong enough?"

"I have little choice," she answered drily. Without waiting for him, she opened her door and jumped down, then helped him gather up the small bundle of clothes and food out of the cargo area. It was so hot that she rolled the sleeves of her blouse all the way up to her shoulders. Nowhere, on the horizon, could they see anything but fields—dry fields with tall, burnt grass, swaying in the sun.

Kyril scrambled down the cliff, his feet slipping on rough rocks between tufts of wild grasses and dunes. The third beach on the waterfront, called the Côte des Basques, was completely wild. There was no staircase leading to it, as there was with the others. Devoid of cabanas, this beach was deserted, for no bathers dared to face the tumultuous waves that crashed against its rocky shore. But the spectacle was magnificent, awe-inspiring. When Kyril found out that Laurent rented one of the few villas that overlooked the Côte des Basques, he had been certain of finding the artist deep in contemplation of the sea.

The October day was gray and threatening. Thunder resounded on the outer edges of Biarritz. One lone figure stood facing the sea, sketch pad in hand. Immediately, Kyril knew that his premonition had been correct, that this was indeed Laurent, contemplating the wildness of the scene before him. Kyril felt like an intruder breaking in upon an intimate scene . . . wondered if perhaps he should retrace his steps. But suddenly Laurent turned around, as though sensing an alien presence on the beach. As his glance fell on the Russian, he raised his hand and saluted.

Kyril caught up with him, and Laurent smiled, that funny de la Haye smile, so wry and aloof, which Kyril had once interpreted, in Lorraine, as snobbery. Now he knew it *was* part snobbery, but it was part shyness too. "Well," the artist said, "have you come here to observe the beauteous landscape? Bored with the tamer beaches?"

"Bored with everything," Kyril replied, surprised at his own honesty. "I'm glad you're here."

"You're especially bored with the goings-on at the Villa Martias, I imagine," Laurent said. Tucking his sketch pad beneath his arm, he started to walk along the shoreline. His bad leg dragged, and he leaned on his cane.

At Laurent's mention of the Villa Martias, Lorraine's house, Kyril grinned. "To tell you the truth, Count de la Haye, I am bored with *life*. Sometimes I think that dying a heroic death might be more exciting than living as I do, from day to day, doing nothing at all."

"That is very sad. You're young, aren't you, Ostrov? Twenty-three, twenty-four? What were you doing when my sister found you?"

"I was in medical school in Paris. But I didn't like that, either. It seems that I don't like much of anything these days. Perhaps it's *myself* I don't like, but I'm too much the coward to admit it."

"I used to dislike myself too," Laurent said, his voice seeming almost disembodied—light, airy, without fire. The irony in his tone had turned inward now. He added: "I wasn't ever much good at *boy* things. My parents were disheartened. The things that meant the sun and the moon to me meant less than nothing to them. So I decided to leave Paris, and the world I'd grown up in. They had a life planned for me which didn't fit in with what I wanted."

"Such as—?"

Laurent motioned to the sketch pad he was carrying. "This is what I've always loved best. I went to Florence and Sienna. I met people there—and then I went to Venice and settled down. I lived there for five years."

"What made you come home?"

Laurent laughed. "My father died. He left me a huge inheritance and I decided I deserved to enjoy it."

"You despise your whole family, then? Surely his death touched you in some way."

"I don't know whether I despise them—or just their society. I despise people who don't think, people who don't feel. I despise people who stay together without real love, like Lorraine and Marc-Antoine. I myself could never live like that. And I never have."

Kyril saw color rise for the first time in Laurent's pale cheeks. He remembered the tall man who had left Lorraine's party with Laurent. A Venetian, Lorraine had said. Laurent had lived in Venice. Still: "You must not be so harsh about your sister," Kyril began, licking his dry lips and wondering whether he were committing another of his inevitable *faux-pas*. "She . . . well . . . she is . . ."

"She told you that I betrayed her? Is that it?"

Laurent's unusual eyes, their dark blue irises hardly distinguishable from the pupils, focused on Kyril. Kyril looked away, embarrassed. "I shouldn't have mentioned it," he stammered. But at the same time, he was terribly curious.

Laurent de la Haye stopped talking and leaned on his cane. "You are like Bluebeard's wife, aren't you, Ostrov? I am a mystery to you, a challenge to your imagination. That's why you're here, actually—I know! You wonder about me, about Lorraine, about our relationship. Why don't you ask *her* to explain it, then?"

Mortified, Kyril turned a deep crimson. "Because she won't reveal herself, any more than you will. It . . . it makes her cry. She says you hate her, and yes, that you betrayed her. She hates all men, but if that's so, why does she want me? I don't understand any of it, Count de la Haye. I no longer understand my own life, and the people in it."

"I'm afraid you've come to the wrong party," Laurent declared. "I'm not a detective, nor a psychiatrist. But I *will* tell you this: Lorraine and I come from a rotten family, Monsieur Ostrov. We come from degenerate roots. How else could we have turned out except degenerate? There you have it: the golden clue. The rest is of little interest but to her and me. If it pains her, I am sorry. But I doubt whether, today, knowing what I know of the world and of life, I would alter my behavior then. And what does it matter? I'll never have the chance to relive that moment when I took the fatal misstep. I am a cold and selfish man, Ostrov. Perhaps it would be better if you didn't try to know me."

Laurent's beautiful, heart-shaped face had grown impassive, withdrawn. Kyril opened his mouth to speak, but no words came. He didn't want Laurent to leave him on this note. If he did, Kyril knew for certain that he would never have the privilege of seeing him again.

"You are hard on yourself, Count," he finally remarked. "Perhaps I'd like to know you nonetheless. Your family doesn't matter to me. My own family has skeletons locked in every closet . . . and I don't have a lovely sister, as you do. I have a mother who's a neurotic recluse, a grandfather who's a religious fanatic. . . . My father killed himself to escape his gambling debts. Whatever the De la Hayes have done, it can't begin to match the Ostrovs."

Then Laurent smiled. "Very well then. Why don't you come up to the house and have some tea with us? I'll show you the painting I finished this morning, at dawn. It's not half bad, if you'll forgive my lack of modesty."

Enthralled, Kyril nodded. Who was the "us" Laurent had mentioned? He couldn't help but feel that a great honor was being conferred on him. At the same time, a nagging worry gnawed at his consciousness. He was exhilarated and depressed at once. He understood neither feeling. But already, Laurent had found the pathway leading to his house, and had started the tortuous way home. Kyril followed.

The small village reminded Zica of Rigevka, except that it was much less attractive and less well kept. The roads were unpaved. Dry ruts were flaking in the merciless sun. The houses were narrow but deep, each with its barn, its hen house, its stable and cow shed. They were made of simple wooden slats, and the ground was their only floor. "These people won't have a cart to give us," Zica said, hopelessness flooding her. "They need everything they've got."

Her heart was beating so fast, she could hear its pounding in her ears. Yakov walked resolutely ahead. As she looked at his slender backside, she thought, he is all I have. Right now, nothing mattered but staying alive.

At the first house, Yakov knocked. An old woman opened the door. She stood wide-eyed on the threshold, her toothless mouth gaping. *"Babushka,* we need your help," Yakov began.

"No help. No money. Nothing. The Reds came yesterday." And with that, she started to wail, as only old folk knew how to do, rocking back and forth as if taken over by an evil spirit.

"They came *here?*"

"They took my four hens, and the cow, and my dog. They took the icons from the walls and the silver samovar. Who are you, anyway, young man?"

"We are refugees, *Babushka.* Our truck ran out of petrol on the road, and we hoped to find a cart and a horse somewhere. Any old mule would do. Surely, the Bolsheviks haven't taken the mules."

The old woman was weeping now. "Ask the Chaikovs up the street, four houses from here. I have nothing left." With that, she shut the door in Yakov's face.

"My God, Yasha," Zica cried. "How will we get to Tiflis?"

"You mean, how will we ever get out of *this* place," her husband replied. But he regretted the sharpness of his tone. He extended his hand to her; together, they walked up toward the house the old crone had indicated. It was a wooden cabin, painted blue, with cheerful trim. Once again, Yakov knocked.

A young man in his shirtsleeves opened the door. He looked like a nice Russian farm boy, with ruddy cheeks and a growth of chestnut beard. "Yes?" he demanded. "Who are you and what do you want?"

Behind him, a young woman in a pink kerchief peered out anxiously. "What is it, Igor?" she asked nervously. "Is it *them* again?"

"Are you folks Bolsheviks?" the man inquired. His tone was neutral, but Yakov heard a tinge of fear.

"We're trying to escape from them," Yakov explained. "Our truck stalled in the middle of the road. We need to reach Tiflis—my wife has relatives there. Please . . . we need something to travel in: a cart, an old horse . . ."

The man swung the door open and motioned them in. Gratefully, Zica followed on Yakov's heel, glad for the sudden coolness of the house. "Look." The young man made a sweeping gesture with his hand. The large main room stood in complete disarray. The walls had been scraped with knives, the furniture maimed. "They did this, yesterday. They're not far from here. I have no horse for you, only a very old *lineika* and an ass. But she doesn't travel quickly, and she's temperamental. Perhaps you'd like to wash up and have a bit to eat before you go?"

Zica nodded, her eyes filling with tears. To the friendly young woman who was grasping her hands with concern, she said: "You are both so kind, to let us in, to let us have your cart. I wish there were a way to show you our appreciation . . ."

"There is money, Zeinab," Yakov said. "We are not asking for charity. How much will you take?"

Chaikov scratched his head and pursed his lips. His wife, who had gone into the kitchen, returned with tall glasses of water and some black bread. The man said grudgingly: "No. We are glad to help. You're going far; you'll need all the money you can lay your hands on. As for us . . . frankly, one system's as good as the next. We don't really care whether it's the Tzar or the Kerensky regime or Lenin's people, so long as they let us work our animals and harvest our orchard. But the Reds made their point, regardless. They've stripped the village clean. The ass—well, nobody needed her. So she's yours."

Yakov sat down in an old broken-backed rocking chair. "Tell me," he said. "I would have thought the Reds would have come here long ago, or left such a small township alone altogether. How is it that they came *yesterday?*"

Their host sighed. "They first came in November, last year. But they left almost as soon as they'd arrived. We're only fifty miles from Moscow, and they just cared about the big cities and county seats. But now and then, they raid the countryside to make sure we remember who's in charge. You're right, by the way, to flee southward. In the Crimea, the Caucasus and Georgia, the Reds haven't come yet. I hear that the White Army is reorganizing. Later this fall, there will be bloody battles. But perhaps you'll be out of the country by then."

"We plan to go to France through Constantinople," Zica said. She drank some water and set the glass down. The room was spinning all around her.

"You'll be lucky to reach Tiflis in one piece," the woman told her grimly. She held out some sliced tomatoes on a chipped earthen dish. Zica took one and placed it on her slice of brown bread. She could feel the dizziness begin anew, along with the fear and anguish. Tears welled up. She busied herself with her food, so the others wouldn't notice. But the woman laid a warm, freckled hand on her arm, and said, "You have a strong young husband. And you have hope. Perhaps I'm wrong, perhaps you'll get there within the month. Then . . . you'll have your dream and be off."

"We had dreams once, didn't we, Inna?" the bearded man said.

His voice suddenly grew soft and wistful. "We dreamed of having babies, and of acquiring another piece of property to add to this one. We dreamed of going to Moscow for a vacation, and letting Inna's brother watch the animals while we were gone. But then the war came, and our baby was stillborn, and Inna's brother died at the front. And the Bolsheviks don't want us to grow prosperous, because we'd only be more trouble. They want us weak, hungry, and begging."

"I think I'm going to be sick again," Zica stammered, standing up. "Please, please tell me where to go!"

Before Yakov could reach her, Inna already had her strong arm around Zica's body, and was leading her away. The men were left alone. "My name is Igor Yureyevitch Chaikov," their host told Yakov. Somewhat shyly, he extended his hand. "And my wife is Inna, Inna Vassilievna."

"Yakov and Zeinab Pokhis," Yakov said, grasping the hand warmly. "You've been very good."

Igor Chaikov smiled and winked. "Well," he said, his voice dropping an octave, "you mustn't worry so about your little wife. How far along is she, anyway?"

Yakov shook his head, blinking. But Chaikov continued. "After two months they usually stop being ill all day long. Inna stopped being sick right after the second month, when she was carrying our little son."

Yakov laughed. "You mean you think Zeinab is *pregnant?*"

"Don't you know?"

Yakov thought for a moment, and considered. "But . . . she never told me . . ."

"Is this your first?"

Yakov had a momentary vision of Zica on the floor of her tiled bathroom on Tverskaya Street, awash in blood. Goose bumps rose on his arms. Shaking himself back to reality, he said gravely, "I'm not sure whether she can have children. I think she's ill because of nerves, because of the Reds. Surely you must be wrong, Igor Yureyevitch."

"I could be. But I don't think so. I come from a family of eight. I'm the oldest. I watched my mother go through seven pregnancies. Believe me, I know the signs. Whoever told you your little wife wouldn't be giving you babies?"

"Nobody," Yakov answered. Then he fell silent. If indeed this were true, how ironic was life . . . ! How ironic that, now he was finally married to the love of his life, they had to flee for their very lives. They were only one step ahead of the Red Terror. How ironic that if she were pregnant, this pregnancy would be spent on the road, an added burden to their shoulders. And yet, my God, a *child of their very own!*

"Nobody told me that," he repeated, a lump forming in his throat. "No one at all."

Chapter XI

*T*HE house on the cliff was tall and dark, appearing ominous beneath the cumulus clouds. There was virtually no garden. The steep slope beneath the house was rich with purple heather. A small pebbled pathway led to a massive oak door studded with brass. Laurent took a key from his pocket, unlocked the door, and walked in ahead of his guest. He stood aside to make room for Kyril.

They now stood in a large foyer with a tall, sculptured ceiling adorned with a rose-window. Through the window bleak light penetrated in metallic sheaths, casting odd shadows over medieval armor displayed against the walls. Laurent continued through this room: and suddenly Kyril found himself in a glass peninsula. Three walls out of four were all leaded glass, overlooking the sea. The furniture in this room was sparse and dark, in the style of Louis XIII, each massive piece hewn out of rich old mahogany and ebony, with little decoration. By the window stood an easel. Mechanically, Kyril directed his footsteps there.

Before him loomed an enormous, oversize canvas on which an ocean foamed out of control, hurling itself against a tall, steep cliff. Laurent had captured the vista below with the eye of a magician distilling reality. The canvas held all the violence of passion unleashing its energy upon creation itself. The colors were dark—purple and green and gray and taupe, dark rose and pewtered silver.

"This is beautiful," Kyril said. "It makes me feel small and inconsequential. Nothing matters beside nature, does it?"

Laurent smiled and shrugged. "I don't imagine. I used to feel angry about this when I was younger. I wanted to make a difference. But you see, none of us does—not even a Goya or a Michellangelo. For there is a cosmos out there that doesn't care whether

there is beauty on earth, whether we are all still living in caves—
whether we are living at all!"

He sighed and went to sit on the windowsill. Looking at him,
Kyril was struck by the beauty of the man, by his physical grace in
spite of his handicap. "Well," Laurent declared. "We should have
tea, don't you think? English tea, with scones and all the rest. That
would do us good, for it's a cold October by the shore." He
plucked a small silver bell from a low side table, and rang it.

A manservant materialized, bowing. *"Monsieur le Comte?"*

Laurent said: "We shall need tea for three. Make it nice and
strong, Aristide. The way Count del Arno likes it."

"Of course, Monsieur."

Once again they were alone. *Count del Arno.* Kyril thought: That
must be the Venetian who had come to Lorraine's party. Kyril had
only caught a glimpse of the man, but was aware of his tall stature
and elegance. The man had an ease which true, blooded aristocrats
always displayed in the ways they walked and talked. The more
recent members of the nobility, such as the Poliakovs, had not yet
acquired this air. It was a mixture of heredity and environment;
generations of inbreeding were necessary to produce such a result of
refinement.

All at once, Kyril felt depressed. Was it because he'd thought of
Zica, or because he knew that no matter what, he himself would
never be mistaken for a nobleman? He'd forever remain a Russian
provincial of dubious lineage, a man with no religion and no vocation. And there stood Laurent, born and bred for the pursuit of finer
things, an artist with all the fire and verve it took to achieve greatness. All his life, Kyril had hungered for someone to admire. Now
he was face to face with a man only a few years older than himself
who already had accomplished so much!

"You are brooding, Ostrov," Laurent commented, lighting a cigarette and handing the crystal dispenser to his guest.

As Kyril took one, he noticed that his fingers were trembling. At
that moment, Laurent bent toward him with the silver lighter,
which he held to the tip of Kyril's cigarette. For a few seconds, the
two men's faces were within inches of each other, illumined by the
orange flame. Laurent's translucent face appeared so intense, so real,
his long black lashes fringing the ultramarine eyes. Kyril thought:
He reminds me of a Christ figure; he is tormented like a saint,
tortured and in pain like myself.

Then Laurent drew away, and leaned back, inhaling quietly.
Kyril, anxious not to break the mood, said nothing. Suddenly

Laurent's face relaxed, softening as Kyril had never seen it do before, and Kyril knew that someone had walked in—someone whom Laurent's eyes sought and welcomed. Kyril turned to look at the doorway; there stood the tall man from the party.

This time Kyril got a clear impression. The Italian was taller than Laurent and broader. He had a thick crop of dark brown hair and a brown Van Dyke beard. His forehead was tightly creased; there were laugh lines around his hazel eyes. He gave the impression of being a sea captain from antiquity, but his informal sweater and slacks seemed oddly incongruous with the man they contained. Kyril thought: Well! He looks as big as a Russian. With that, he felt an aversion to the Italian which he attributed to his childhood memories of another large, muscular, virile man: his father.

"I didn't know we had a guest," Del Arno said, inclining his head politely toward Kyril. "How do you do . . ."

"Orlando, this is Kyril Ostrov. He's . . . my sister's friend. Kyril Ostrov, Count Orlando del Arno."

The two men shook hands. Del Arno's was hard, dry, and warm. Kyril watched with interest as the Italian sat down on the low sofa, comfortably lighting a cigar, completely sure of himself. "Aristide will be in presently, with tea," he announced. Turning to Laurent, he remarked: "You didn't take a coat with you when you went out. It was brutal out there. You might catch influenza."

"Come now, Orlando, you don't catch influenza from the elements. The worst I might get is a head-cold. My jacket is warm enough."

"We went through pneumonia last year, and you almost died."

"Perhaps," Laurent said lightly, "it wasn't my time to die then. And when it is, my dear, I shall die no matter what precautions you take to guard against it."

Kyril looked from one to the other expectantly. Both seemed to be ignoring him. They were exclusively involved in their repartee. At this point the manservant entered, rolling in a fully loaded tea tray. It was Orlando del Arno who proceeded to act as host, and to serve the hot tea and cakes.

"What do you do, Monsieur Ostrov?" he asked. His voice was a beautiful, deep baritone, tinged with a Latin accent. "Besides accompany the Marquise, which is of course a job in itself . . . ?" He was being playful, his tone amused and warm. But the question depressed Kyril. Somehow, he wished he could let the others know that he did not like what he had become.

"I seem to be doing nothing these days," Kyril replied. "Once, in

Russia, I liked to paint, like Count de la Haye. Then, in Paris, I was
a student. I read medicine at the university."

"Lorraine likes her men to pay attention to nothing but her,"
Laurent remarked with some bitterness. "It's always been like that,
my dear Ostrov: don't feel as though you are responsible. She picks
out the man she wants, and cajoles him into abandoning all his
other activities until, finally, he has no life left outside of my sister."

"Perhaps, Laurent, Monsieur Ostrov does not wish to be reminded of these other men . . . ?"

Kyril felt himself blushing. He had never thought about any
predecessors. Now, suddenly, he felt cheap and disposable, like a
container already half-empty. "Lorraine wasn't free then; she was
married," he said, but his statement came off like a question. Laurent laughed. "Well?" Kyril demanded, suddenly needing to know.
"It was different then, wasn't it? Less serious?"

Neither man replied. Instead, Count del Arno, munching on a
crumpet, declared: "Today I saw the Empress Eugénie in town. We
chatted for a few moments. I think she's rather lonely in her beautiful villa on the embankment."

"Certainly she is." Laurent reached over and helped himself to
more hot tea and a slice of lemon. He stirred lightly. "Kyril," he
said, "you haven't told me how you like Biarritz. The natural
beauty of the seaside, I mean. Isn't it spectacular: the wind, the
waves, the tumult of it all?"

"It is quite magnificent. I wish we lived closer to it, as you do."

"Laurent knows how to pick the perfect spot," Del Arno declared. He wiped his lips on a monogrammed napkin bearing Laurent's initials. "In Venice, we lived in my home, of course, but
everywhere else, it is he who picks."

"Orlando's home, as he says, is an ancestral palace on Piazza San
Marco, all tiled and marbled as palaces were in the Renaissance.
Outside, it is decorated with statues of princes and popes. But it
was cold there, and we often left for short trips to Florence and
Rome. Kyril—" he added, "won't you taste the scone with some of
Aristide's own pear jelly? It's one of the true wonders of the world,
I think."

But Kyril no longer wanted to stay. He felt himself in danger. He
remembered Lorraine's words of warning. Count del Arno was
easy and charming, but nevertheless Kyril felt apprehensive, as
though something bad might develop in this austere living room. It
was different when he and Laurent had been alone. But these two

men together had a history, an intimacy, which his presence marred. He felt like an intruder, the same way he had felt around Charlotte Maple-White and Lorraine earlier in the week—as though, in effect, *he had ceased to matter.*

"You've been very kind, Count de la Haye," he said, setting his plate down. "But the truth is, I'm expected at the Villa Martias for a game of gin with the ladies. I'm already hopelessly late . . ."

Orlando del Arno smiled. "But you'll be back, of course?"

"Perhaps I shall. It was a pleasure to meet you, sir."

Kyril allowed Laurent to lead him out of the salon and back to the front door. Orlando del Arno did not follow them. Now Kyril felt the silence settling between him and Laurent as a presence in the room. It held possibilities—like a raffle or a game of hide and seek. Either he could leave with pleasant formality, and return home without a backward glance . . . or he could pull the ghost between them out of the air, giving it form. This ghost seemed to float between them every time they met.

"I enjoyed myself," he said, holding out his hand. "Count del Arno is a pleasant and friendly man. . . ."

"Orlando and I have been living together for many years."

"Really?"

"Indeed. Orlando is my family now, if you know what I mean. It would be difficult for me to survive without him, although sometimes . . ." Laurent's eyes had a faraway expression; his tone was airy, caressing and lingering. Kyril stared at him, mesmerized, wanting to understand. All at once he was pierced with a fierce jealousy of the Italian, this "loving family" to Laurent de la Haye.

". . . 'although sometimes' . . . ?" he echoed softly.

But Laurent shook his head. "No, that is silly. I am glad that I have Orlando, and pleased that you came here. Do call on us again, Kyril. Come whenever you like."

Kyril nodded. "Thank you. I shall." Then, quickly, he walked out the door into the cold, windy twilight.

Zica stirred the pot, her roughened fingers clutching the wooden spoon. The secret was to stir quickly, before the dry millet absorbed all the water. How she hated the way her body had distended like a ripe watermelon, full of seed. She was four months along, almost five. Already she was huge, her breasts voluminous, her stomach a little round globe beyond which she could barely see her toes. She moved awkwardly, one thick leg maneuvering around the other in circular motion, avoiding her own fat like an obstacle. She had gained fifty pounds, she felt certain, although no scale existed in Strashnyi Selo.

"Move it, fat girl," the woman said, her voice loud and grating. Zica turned around, no longer surprised, no longer shocked. "Hey," the woman said, "I'm tired of waiting to use the stove. How long does it take to prepare hot cereal?"

"It takes as long as it takes," Zica replied. She continued to stir. She had learned to talk back harshly, to say her piece. In the old days those words from the woman would have reduced her to tears. But today, no one was going to wrest from Zeinab Pokhis what belonged to her, especially not her five full minutes at the stove cooking supper.

She lifted the lame aluminum pot from the stove and placed it on the counter. It seemed she was always hungry. She ate six times a day. Yakov didn't see how much she ate, nor did he know how this hateful woman, Olya, talked to her. And she didn't want to tell him. She just wanted to leave Strashnyi Selo, the sooner the better.

It was September now, three months since they'd left Moscow . . . three months since Igor and Inna Chaikov had given them the ass and their old, dilapidated *lineika*. And they had only progressed as far south as Strashnyi Selo, this little township hardly bigger than Rigevka. Here they'd been forced to stop, to earn more money for the rest of their voyage. But it hadn't happened. Yakov's meager earnings at the lumber mill hardly allowed them to make ends meet. And they were still only halfway to Tiflis.

They were paying a few kopeks a week to *Baba* Vera, the old widow who rented out her rambling farmhouse to seven people, all of them refugees. *Baba* Vera made it a point not to ask questions. It was better not to know where her boarders came from. But Zica knew. Oksana and Pyotr were here because Pyotr had killed a man in Kiev; the horrible Olya, the woman who always wanted to use the stove, had gotten drunk and hit her husband on the head with a sack of potatoes. (He'd been someone important in the Moscow CHEKA.) The last couple were gentry, hoping to make an escape through the Crimea, due South. They were distant and kept to themselves. Zica, though she would have liked to have some friends of her own background, kept away because they spoke only to say "Excuse me" as they passed in the hall, or "Did you see the salt?" when she encountered them in the kitchen. They roamed like pale shadows around the old farmhouse, reminding her of the ghosts of her childhood nightmares.

Zica stirred the millet and added salt. If only there were milk! Her mouth watered, thinking of how she liked to stir milk into her cereal. Yakov wouldn't be happy if she ate now, before he came home. He'd expect his dinner; he'd want her to sit beside him, and then she'd get hungry again and he would wonder why they were always running out of food. *I am piddling our savings away on food,* she thought, resolutely turning away from the aluminum pot where, already, the millet was congealing. He had better get home quickly.

The front door swung open, and he entered, letting in the darkness. Zica saw a splash of stars, like the tail of an ephemeral comet falling through the sky. For a moment, her heart hungered to go outside, to smell the evening and the countryside. For though she hated the village and the fact that they were stuck there, she was a Russian, with a love of the land.

"Well," Yakov said, setting down his empty lunch box, "how's my girl?"

She leaned over the counter and kissed him. It was awkward. Olya was staring at them, and Zica felt grotesque, leaning over her own stomach to touch her husband's cheek. "What say, skinny boy?" the woman called out.

"Work is still work; the lumber mill is still standing, thank God. At least we have that."

"Yes," Zica said. She took two plates and two spoons from the cupboard, and brought over glasses of water. She began to dish out the cereal. "Are you hungry?" she asked, hesitantly.

"If not, the fat girl will eat your slop," the woman told him.

"She can eat what she likes," Yakov answered mildly. They were too poor to argue. Life had been reduced to this essence, stripped of all but the bare bones of communication. Zica sat down heavily, bringing her plate closer to herself. She was so hungry that she could think of nothing else. She dreamt of lifting the spoon to her lips, of tasting the salty millet and swooning from the ecstasy of its taste. If she didn't start, she would soon faint. Slowly, deliberately tantalizing herself to extend the anticipation of her pleasure, she dipped the spoon into the cereal and waited.

"Well now," he said pleasantly, "aren't you going to eat your supper? I'm going to start." He took a healthy bite, grunting with enjoyment. Suddenly she wanted to laugh: every night they went through the same ritual; every night they would eat the same thing, and he would wait for her and she would delay things, to make it last. They could almost pretend that this was a ceremonial dinner in Moscow, at her father's table—that she was about to taste Beluga caviar on toast, with tiny lemon wedges and minced onions. They could pretend it was a feast instead of the only thing they could now afford: cooked cereal, sometimes with a thin vegetable soup. Tonight they would have millet and nothing else. It had been a lean week.

Suddenly there was noise outside. Rushing to the door, Olya opened it a crack. Zica rose to her feet and craned her neck to peer out. Yakov continued eating. It didn't matter to him who was there: in Strashnyi Selo people came and went, and nobody asked questions. It was as much a place of transit these days as an old-time village. The Communists had arranged it so few Russians stayed in their own home towns. Either they wanted to go somewhere more exciting, or they wished to migrate for financial gain—or, like Yakov and Zica, they were on the run.

Instead of giving in to curiosity, Yakov helped himself to some more porridge and sat back, relaxing. This was as close to a home as he had come with Zica in the course of their brief marriage.

A group of people pushed past Olya, bringing in the evening air with its faint scent of cooking, of onions and lard. There was a striking, very thin woman, about their own age, with short dark hair and angular features, and two men, both older and bulkier than the woman. They were all dressed as commissars. Suddenly Zica felt terribly frightened. They looked like Muscovites. She could feel the hair rising on her arms. Her feet felt like cubes of ice inside the simple wooden clogs. "Yasha," she whispered.

He turned around. He always wore that mildly curious, friendly expression on his face. But she knew it was a facade. Inside, he trembled just as much as she did.

"Hello," he said, inclining his head.

"Hello, comrades. We are looking for a place to sleep. We were told your landlady would put us up." The woman who spoke had a strong, vibrant voice. Zica felt envious of the stranger's vitality, of the sinuous passion which her body conveyed as she stood poised like a dancer, waiting to be informed. There was something oddly familiar about her, but Zica knew that she hadn't met *this woman* before. It had to be someone who simply *reminded* her of this female commissar.

"Vera Semyonovna is out getting milk," Yakov declared. "Please, sit down. We were just having our supper." His voice sounded confident; he was a good player, Zica thought, suddenly envious of him as well.

"Don't mind if I do." The woman moved toward the table, and pulled up a chair. Both men joined her. Zica realized they smelled of venison—not because they'd eaten any, but because these were beefy men with poor bathroom habits. How she detested this: the meanness of their lives, the people they were forced to sit with and eat with in order not to be murdered in the night.

But the woman was attractive. She was examining the millet on Yakov's plate. Wordlessly, Zica brought out another plate and set it before her. "Help yourself," she said.

"Thank you." Coal black eyes held hers, challenging her. Zica blushed and looked aside. She sat down again. But to her amazement, she wasn't hungry anymore. At least Olya had disappeared. She had smelled the CHEKA at her heels; she was afraid of being recognized by one of the commissars.

"Tell me, comrades," Yakov began. "What are you doing in our neck of the woods?"

One of the men wiped the spittle from his mouth with his sleeve: "We're on our way to Rostov-on-the-Don. The CHEKA is sending us out there to round up the workers. We'll speak to them about the New Order. We are to reorganize the local Zemstva, because the Rostov area is rich in metals. We cannot afford to have the gentry vanish across the border with our metals, can we?"

"Indeed, we cannot." Yakov wiped his own mouth on his sleeve. Zica winced. His cheeks looked flushed, as if he'd been drinking. She wondered why. Sometimes he looked like that just before sex, as if he'd been thinking about her in that certain way. Zica strained forward to look at the strangers, and at her husband.

The girl was staring at him, and he at her. Their eyes, so black, were locked in a silent battle, Zica thought. She wondered what it was all about. Yakov's nostrils flared once, and he looked down at his plate of millet. "I wish you godspeed, comrades," he said softly.

"There is no such thing as a God to give us speed," the girl retorted. Abruptly, she stood up. She was good-looking, except for the commissar's uniform which made her seem even sharper than she was. Looking down at the diners, she announced, "We are leaving tomorrow. We have a car."

"Any room for passengers?" Yakov was still seated. His question, like his pose, seemed almost insolent toward this woman. "We were travelling to Tiflis when we ran out of funds," he continued. "We would appreciate a ride. Rostov would put us due west of where we're headed."

"Why not?" the woman tossed off. She scanned the faces of her two companions, but it was obvious she outranked them in such decisions. "We need a better driver than Boris here, who likes his vodka a little too well for those curves on the road. D'you drive, comrade?"

"My husband is an excellent driver," Zica stated. Moving next to him, she laid her hand on his arm. But he wasn't paying attention to her. He had his eyes on the girl.

"Your husband is lucky to have you to speak for him," the latter remarked drily. Her black eyes played over Zica's body, resting on her abdomen just a little too long. "So, if we want a driver, we must take a whole family," she commented ironically. "This means three mouths to feed, I suppose." Staring at Zica, she added, so softly that the words were almost lost: "I had not thought it possible."

"What's that?" Zica asked.

"Everything!" the woman replied, her face setting into ugly, sharply etched lines. She marched to the door, and made a motion for her companions to follow her. "Tell Vera What's-her-name to give us a room," she ordered Yakov. "If I'm going to take you on, damn it, you'd better start earning your keep!"

After the commissars had departed, banging the front door, Zica took the pot and the plates to the sink. Yakov sat down at the table and put his head into his hands, massaging his temples. "You don't know how lucky we are," he said, almost dreamily. "Rostov is a few hours from here by car. We won't even need to go to Tiflis. Rostov is on the River Don, which empties into the Sea of Azov. That's next to the Black Sea. We can sail from there."

"But my grandparents—"

He threw her a scornful glance. "Your grandparents, my dear Zeinab, will be of little use to us now. If these commissars are on their way to Rostov, they will soon proceed east to Tiflis. We may as well do what we can by ourselves in Rostov. It's a much larger city than Tiflis."

Her eyes filled with tears. Seeing this, he sighed, half-annoyed, half-sorry. "Zica, Zica," he murmured, "do not take this so hard, my little one. Don't you know to whom we owe this unexpected breath of good fortune...?"

Bewildered, she shook her head.

"The woman who was here was Natasha. Didn't you recognize her? *Natasha Khazina!*"

Zica stared at him, dumbfounded. Now that he said it, she realized it was true. It *was* someone from her old life—*Natasha Khazina,* who had already saved her life once before. The thought of that other time made Zica turn away and lean against the sink, tears falling over her plump cheeks. God had been good to her. And Natasha was lucky, too, in another way: she had become a Soviet commissar. But did she ever regret Yakov, and their affair? Did she ever think of him with longing, as Zica sometimes thought of Kyril Ostrov?

"Come, Zeinab," Yakov said to her. She felt him approach from behind. Quickly she raised her apron to her wet cheeks, and nodded without turning around. It would be better not to ask, even with her eyes. The past was the past.

Restless and hot, Kyril could not sleep. In the moonlight which filtered in through gossamer drapery, he could see Lorraine lying at his side, her light brown hair spread around her. She slept as soundly as a child, her perfect features translucent and at peace.

Tonight he couldn't sleep at all; he thought of Laurent de la Haye and Orlando del Arno, and wondered how they lived, what kind of relationship they shared, what they did together. He visualized them at night: Orlando going from room to room turning off the lights in the lonely house on the cliff, then stepping resolutely into their bedroom and looking at Laurent sitting up in bed. Kyril imagined Laurent's naked torso, lightly muscled and hairless, like that of an ephebe... here, the image would flicker, wavering like a candle's dying flame. The vision left Kyril breathless and perspiring, his nerves jangled.

Of course Laurent was Orlando's lover. This was tantalizing to Kyril—exciting and yet terrifying: he didn't dare think beyond the moment when, inevitably, Orlando would stride toward the communal bed and approach Laurent.

Whenever he dreamt of them, he would awaken with his heart hammering inside him, his erection pressing against the bed sheet.

Tonight he couldn't sleep at all, so there had been no dream— only the terrible worrying, the fear that Laurent would forget him. He wanted to be near the artist, to look at him and hear him speak with that odd diffidence which indicated detachment and otherworldliness, and at the same time, pain and anguish. Laurent de la Haye wasn't a happy man, Orlando del Arno notwithstanding. Kyril felt a bond.

He knew, now, that he wanted to be with Laurent as once he had hungered to be with Zica. But Zica he had wanted in a different way: he had wanted to possess her, soul, spirit, and body. With Laurent it was the opposite: the Frenchman dominated him, and Kyril yearned to feel himself possessed, swept off his feet by something swirling and hot. Zica had appealed to him by the impossible naiveté of her innocence; Laurent mesmerized him by his ironic rejection of the idea of a fair and just world. Kyril had hoped to be redeemed by the woman; now he longed to be corrupted by the man. He wanted to be dragged far down, into the depths, where he belonged.

Rising from Lorraine's bed, Kyril turned away. Naked, he padded into her boudoir, a dark mood following closely, like a cloud. He flicked on the small light over her secretary, and went to the delicate rosewood bookshelf. After a moment's search, Kyril found a slim volume of Shakespeare's *Sonnets*. His English was that of dusty Russian classrooms, of Elena's boudoir, but he could read it fairly fluently, if laboriously.

He opened the book: to his surprise, it fell open of its own accord at the "Twenty-ninth Sonnet." At first, he hesitated over its meaning. Then, slowly, it dawned on him that Shakespeare must have written this sonnet in just such a mood as possessed him now. What coincidence! Pulling closer to the secretary, Kyril sat down in Lorraine's swivel chair and read the haunting poetry once more, his eyes filling with tears:

> When, in disgrace with fortune and men's eyes,
> I all alone beweep my outcast state,
> And trouble deaf heaven with my bootless cries,
> And look upon myself and curse my fate,
> Wishing me like to one more rich in hope,
> Featured like him, like him with friends possessed,
> Desiring this man's art and that man's scope,
> With what I most enjoy contented least:

My God! Kyril thought, his heart pounding faster: Shakespeare himself was envious of other men, of artists he considered better than he! Shakespeare himself had awakened in the night and penned these very thoughts, with much the same despair as Kyril was now experiencing. Kyril's eyes followed the lines to their conclusion:

> Yet in these thoughts myself almost despising,
> Haply I think on thee, and then my state,
> Like to the lark at break of day arising
> From sullen earth, sings hymns at heaven's gate;
>> For thy sweet love remembered such wealth brings
>> That then I scorn to change my state with kings.

The greatest poet in the English language had once been possessed with self-loathing and self-doubt. Kyril felt oddly vindicated. Suddenly he could breathe more freely. But "Haply *I think on thee,*" the Bard had said; and all at once, Kyril, whose eyes were full of tears, knew what he must do. Seating himself at Lorraine's secretary, he withdrew a piece of her embossed stationery. He copied the "Twenty-ninth Sonnet" and folded the paper neatly into an envelope, without bothering to sign his first name.

He addressed the envelope to "Count Laurent de la Haye," at his villa. Laurent would know who had sent this to him; he would know and he would smile that slightly derisive smile which meant he understood. Yes, Laurent understood the way of the world and the way of men.

Exhausted and relieved, Kyril lowered his head to the desk. It didn't matter what Laurent would do; it mattered only that he, Kyril, had sent him this sonnet. For he knew he had fallen in love with Lorraine's brother. He knew he had to declare this passion before it was too late, before Laurent went back to Paris to resume his normal life. Nothing about this was normal—perhaps that was why it felt so wonderful and so painful at the same time.

Even if nothing further resulted from this act, it mattered that he had taken this step.

In the car, nobody spoke. Yakov sat in the driver's seat, next to Natasha, his eyes on the road. Behind them, the two men crowded on each side of Zica. Through the early morning they drove southward, their grim faces tense with exhaustion.

Natasha had changed. Gone were the artistic touches which had rendered her attractive to Yakov in the old days. Gone was the restless, nervous energy she had radiated. Today she was a Soviet commissar, full of purpose, a leader of men and women.

Yet he felt the closeness of her, and guilt flooded his heart. This was the girl who had loved him while he had loved another. This was the girl he'd made love to, dreaming she was another.

There was nothing fair or unfair about how their lives had changed. Communism had taken over the country; each had taken sides. He was running from her side, but he owed it to her that he could now escape to freedom, with his pregnant wife.

Yakov felt all the more uncomfortable because of the cold impersonality of her demeanor.

Around midday, they pulled into another small town like Strashnyi Selo—like all the other Russian towns and hamlets along the way. "Stop at the inn over there," Natasha told him. "We may as well eat and stretch our legs."

He did as he was ordered. As they stepped out of the car, Yakov saw how quickly Natasha opened her own door, not waiting for the usual chivalry. Yakov felt his wife tugging at his hand, and for the moment his heart softened: she was so frightened. He knew she was uncomfortable because of the baby, sad that they had not talked in ages, had not made love in weeks and weeks. He sighed. All day long he had worked; all night long he worried. There had been no time for lovemaking. He had married this lovely girl and now she had become a housewife. He prayed that their future would offer something more.

"I want to talk to you." It was Natasha, her voice harsh and commanding. With a sideways glance at his wife, Yakov joined the commissar. The two men entered the wooden inn, with its pretty red roof. Reluctantly, Zica followed them inside. Natasha and Yakov remained alone by the road.

Natasha kicked at a dry mound of earth. "You never tried to find me," she said. "Senya went looking for you at Nichayev's; but by then, everyone had spread out. You were nowhere to be found. You were with *her*."

"You knew I would be." His face was grave and calm.

"I knew. But I didn't *want* to know. I always thought you were worth more than the others—but you weren't. You *owed* me—you owed me an explanation, and at the very least, a farewell!"

"Yes," he admitted. "I did. But we were nearly caught. After we left, I had no way to find you. I had obligations of my own. I love her, Natasha," he added softly. "You always knew that."

"And what was *I?* Your whore?"

"No—*never*. I owe you many things. I can say this now, because we have chosen different paths. No—not chosen. We have been ploughed aside, Natasha, by what is happening—what is happening to Russia."

"You make it all sound like destiny, Yasha . . . and you are such a bastard. You loved her all along. . . . "

"Yes," he said. "I did." He paused. "But I loved you too. Not in the same way—yet I did care for you, very deeply."

"Much good it has done me." But Natasha couldn't look him in the eye. Hers were filling with tears. Suddenly she lifted her head—she was the commissar once again, firm and commanding. "Let's go in. I'm hungry. I want a pirozhok."

As she strode forward, he stopped her with a touch of his hand. "Natka," he said, "thank you."

"Go to hell," she replied lightly. Then she laughed. For an instant her black eyes gave off the fire of earlier, happier days, and he was reminded of the girl he'd shared his life with in his small mansard room at the Poliakovs'. But then the smile faded, and her eyes glazed over. And as he followed her into the tavern, he was very grateful for its noise and confusion. He wouldn't have to dwell on the past, nor question his own conscience.

Now that he had sent the poem, Kyril waited. The day passed. Evening came. After supper, the guests at the Villa Martias retired, some to the library to read, some to play bridge in the drawing room. Lorraine remained in the drawing room. Kyril felt grateful when she laid her hand on his cheek and murmured softly: "You don't have to play cards tonight, darling. You're tired, aren't you?"

"Yes. I think I'll take some time by myself . . . maybe go for a walk."

"Midnight tea will be in the drawing room. If you feel better, you can join us here."

Her solicitude made him feel guilty. Other men would have killed to lie beside this beautiful and charming woman, while he felt like a leopard caged in a small box. Sometimes, like tonight, he wanted to slap her, for no reason. I am growing to hate her because I love her brother, he thought—and an unfamiliar exultation filled his soul as he thought of Laurent. He deserved to die a thousand deaths for the betrayal he was contemplating—but, strange to say, he didn't really feel the abysmal shame he should have felt. Like a young boy, he felt a thrill beyond any words, a thrill which rippled through every nerve ending.

In their bedroom, Lorraine's diary rested on her bedside table. It was open, a pen in the binding. Kyril hesitated. Resolutely, he removed the pen and closed the book, replacing it where it belonged.

Restless, he walked to the window and looked out over the sea. Red and gold light from the villas was reflected onto the black foam of the waves that crashed against the unforgiving cliffs. Their rhythmic, nighttime death-dance reached abrupt, exultant climaxes as they hurled themselves at the craggy rocks. Tiny particles of spume glistened in the inky sky. The splendor of this spectacle stilled his anxiety for a few minutes. He allowed it to absorb his entire being, spirit and soul.

The sea offered mythic redemption, almost like a woman. For a moment he was swallowed by remorse. The women in his life had all suffered in some way from the love he had given then. Ultimately, he had not been capable of making any of them happy—not his mother, not Zica, nor Lorraine. The first he had squirmed away from; the second he had sought to possess without understanding; the third he had not loved. He was the cliff against which their emotions broke. He was not good for women; they were not good for him. Now he felt horribly alone, proud and impassive.

Kyril let the curtain drop, closing off the sea view. He stepped out of the room. The hallway was dark and gloomy. He decided to go to Lorraine's boudoir to find a book. He could see that the maid had left the light on inside, for it filtered beneath the door onto the corridor's parquet floor.

Kyril turned the knob and entered the room. In the shadowed light were two people, who now looked up at him, startled. Lady Charlotte Maple-White, wearing nothing but a black lace merry widow that pushed up her cupped breasts, black lace stockings, and black sandals with needle-sharp stiletto heels, was half sitting over the nude form of a man in handcuffs. Kyril's jaw dropped. Lady Charlotte stared him down, her eyelids narrowed. She remained astride the man, whom Kyril recognized as the Duc de Fagnac, a relative of the Comte de Paris, heir to the throne of France. The Englishwoman was holding a riding crop.

Suddenly Kyril remembered Laurent's joke. Perhaps it hadn't been a joke after all, that she whipped her men.

Quickly, Kyril wheeled about, closing the door behind him. He was out of breath, disoriented. Never in his life had he thought of a woman whipping a man; the effect it created in him was one of acute revulsion. All at once, he knew why he had always disliked Charlotte Maple-White: she was a praying mantis who devoured her men after lovemaking. She was the black widow. Her garb was oddly appropriate. How he hated her!

He was trembling.

But why had the scene affected him so deeply? Merely that he hadn't thought that the British noblewoman would be capable of such depraved acts. In Russia, she would have been condemned! In Russia . . . in Russia, Laurent and Count del Arno would have been ostracized as well.

Profoundly disturbed, he emerged from the villa onto the porch. He went out to stand by the bougainvilleas, outside the drawing room. The *maître d'hôtel* had lit up the porch with miniature candles, which cast their pink and orange glow over the outer walls of the house. He could see inside, to where Lorraine and her guests had been playing cards.

Now the drawing room appeared deserted. The bridge tables were abandoned, as the guests stretched and wandered into the dining room for a bite to eat and a short conversation. He peered inside, through the gauze curtains, and tried to forget what he had just seen in Lorraine's boudoir.

He could hear Lorraine's disembodied voice as she talked to someone. Trying to see her, Kyril pressed his face against the glass pane. She was standing to the right, near the next window, smoking. Her bare shoulders shimmered under the soft light of the chandelier. He thought her very beautiful. Perhaps he was wrong not to love her; perhaps he ought to force himself, to make a greater effort. She had done so much for him . . .

Facing her was a man Kyril hardly knew, dressed in evening clothes. He was an Italian who had only arrived the day before. Kyril thought the man's first name was Ettore but he couldn't remember the surname. He was a professor of literature, a poet and, of course, the inevitable titled aristocrat. This was the sort of man one learned to expect in Lorraine's entourage. "So, it's not marriage, then, *cara mia?*" the man was asking.

Lorraine laughed. Her throaty laughter was as soothing as a dove's call. "Marriage? You can't be serious, Roberto!"

So it wasn't "Ettore"—his name was "Roberto." All at once Kyril was drawn to hear more. A sudden anxiety rose within him. Marriage? Why would Lorraine be discussing marriage with this virtual stranger—stranger to Kyril, anyway?

"I'm as serious as they come. The man is attractive. You enjoy him. Why, then, not marry him? Make it some sort of morganatic marriage, witnessed by your attorneys: you will keep your title, and he will have claim to none of it. One has to go with one's senses, *carissima*. After all, you were married once for convenience and money; this time you can marry for love."

"Love? But Roberto, Kyril is an amusement! Surely you didn't think I was *in love?* Kyril is worth another year, or perhaps six months. I grant you Kyril is extremely handsome, something of a fallen angel—don't you think? But, after a bit, the charm wears thin. He eats too fast. He does not know how to play instruments. He cannot converse about the arts, because he knows less than nothing. How could you think I would love such a person, much less consider *marrying* him?"

Kyril blinked, flabbergasted. Surely he had not understood correctly. Lorraine did not speak this way: she was gentle and kind. She lay in his arms and gave him her passion. She had told him she loved him! She had confided in him, told him her special stories, told him about her falling out with her brother.

No, no—Kyril felt certain he had heard incorrectly. It could not be true!

"Come now, Roberto; in a moment bridge will be resuming. Will you partner me?" Lorraine pressed the Italian's arm. "You know," she shrugged, "I was growing tired of the Russian already. He is cloyingly childish. He even asked me whether I loved him! He has grown too much like a mistress who clings to you beyond the point when her beauty has become an annoyance, and you are considering the odd shape of her toes. You understand me, don't you, dear?"

"Why perfectly, perfectly. Who, of our sort, would not...? Come, let me bring you a glass of champagne."

Kyril stood trembling by the window, tears veiling his eyes. She had betrayed him. And her betrayal was far worse than any that he himself had considered. She had spoken contemptuously of him to a stranger. She had betrayed him as Zica had, abandoning him at the very moment he had begun to feel safe with her.

He had wanted to leave her, but in his time, and gently. He had wanted to leave her, to move on without her. But...he had never thought her insincere. He had never thought her ugly.

Zica, at least, had been in love. She had betrayed him out of weakness, the weakness of a devoted daughter. But Lorraine's words were unforgivable. He thought how much she was like that other, Lady Maple-White, who whipped men for her pleasure.

They were all the same: they used a man until they tired of him, and then they threw him away. Well, thought Kyril, I shall never again allow myself to be tossed aside as someone's refuse: I shall never trust a woman again! And he wept bitter tears, feeling like a lost traveller in an alien land, where every shadow is an enemy.

Chapter XII

*R*OSTOV lay beneath a mantle of dust so fine that it stuck to one's skin like sweat, clogging the pores. Zica looked around her curiously at the tall trees with their bright fall colors, which dotted the landscape like points on a Seurat canvas. "It's pretty here," she said to her husband.

Already, Yakov felt safer in the large provincial capital. He and Zica were completely anonymous. "Perhaps we can find a room in a boarding house," said Yakov. "How are you feeling?"

Zica looked at him and smiled. He had asked—that was what mattered.

Earlier that morning, Natasha Khazina and her two companions had deposited them in the middle of the park. The woman commissar had abruptly pushed some paper money at Yakov, without even looking at him, her face grim and defiant. "Be gone with you!" she'd said brusquely. Then she'd marched off briskly, like a soldier, leaving the two of them stranded like children lost in the wilderness.

"I have an idea," Zica now said hesitantly. "We could try to locate Kyril Ostrov's mother and grandfather. They live here."

Yakov looked at her sharply.

"We have no other alternatives," she said softly. "We're complete strangers."

Yakov seemed lost in thought, his brows arched over eyes that were as dark as coal. With his thin, somewhat beaked nose, he looked exactly like a man from the *shtetl*. Suddenly she felt alienated from him. What was she doing here in this strange town with this strange man? "I want to find them," she declared.

Yakov's nostrils flared. "You are nothing to these people," he told her roughly. "Why should they wish to help us?"

Zica shook her head. "Maybe they won't help, but it's worth a try. It's all we have going for us." In the enveloping silence of the woods, her voice rang pure and true, suddenly sure of itself—a woman's voice.

"Very well," he replied. But as he started walking, he did not touch her. "Do you know their address?"

"I remember only the grandfather's name: *Yossif Byitch.* Kyril told me they live on a street with a lot of other Jewish merchants near the synagogue. Perhaps if we ask around, someone will direct us."

Yakov clenched his hands into fists. "I always hated Kyril Ostrov," he declared with passion. Zica was shaken by the intensity in his voice. How he must have suffered all the time that she and Kyril had been playing out their love affair!

"Oh, Yasha," she cried, grabbing his hand. "You don't have to be afraid any more. Kyril Ostrov means nothing to me now! That was the past—the far distant past. It was I who refused to marry him. Don't you remember? Instead, I married *you.*"

As he glared at her wordlessly, her eyes filled with tears. If he didn't believe her, she could hardly blame him; their marriage vows were based on need. How could he know that her love for him had matured and grown? What she had felt for Kyril—that was different—it was passion, romance, illusion. For a moment she felt Kyril's presence. What had she wanted that had made her reject Kyril? But she knew. And so she said: "Kyril is a weak man, Yasha. He could never have done for me what you did. You must believe that I understand this."

"I don't know *what* you understand," he answered. But he allowed his arm to slip about her shoulders. She sighed with relief. *It would be all right.*

The narrow, gabled house loomed ominous and gloomy in the night, outlined by a single gaslight situated near the oak door. Winds from the sea swirled about Kyril like invisible whips that scorched his skin. The gaslight flickered.

The young man stood trembling on the threshold, out of breath and vaguely disoriented. His heart was pounding from the climb up the cliff. He was still shocked from the horror of what he had just overheard in Lorraine's house.

But there was no hesitation as he raised his fist and banged on the thick door. He felt for the knocker and banged that too, banging it again and again violently. He could feel rivulets of sweat making gullies down his flanks and temples; he knew that he was feverish, though the wind had chilled him.

Finally the door opened. Laurent de la Haye, blinking and sleepy, stared at him for a moment without recognition. His gray foulard bathrobe was loosely belted over silk pajamas. He stood barefoot, his hand on his cane. "Who...? What the hell?" he muttered, passing a tired hand over his eyes. Then he recognized Kyril. "Ostrov? *Ostrov!* What's going on?"

"I need to speak with you." Kyril's voice was trembling as he stepped inside and allowed Laurent to close the door behind him. The foyer was illuminated by a rose light from a sconce, giving it the appearance of a cathedral vault. Kyril followed Laurent into the living room, where the painter turned on several Tiffany lamps with molded brass stems and jewel-colored shades. All at once the strange, glass-panelled room, with its view of the severe cliffsides and the demonic sea thrashing against the rocks below, was warmed by multicolored reflections in every hue of the rainbow.

"Sit down," Laurent said. "D'you want some brandy? Hell of a night to be walking about paying a visit to your friends."

Kyril's mouth was so dry he could not speak. Laurent peered at him, frowning. Shrugging lightly, he went to an ebony sideboard and withdrew two huge snifters and a cut-glass decanter filled with cognac. He poured for both of them. "Cheers." He handed his guest the snifter of cognac. "This'll warm you up."

"Thanks." Kyril gulped gratefully, feeling the jolt almost at once. "Laurent..."

"I received your letter." Laurent had settled in a leather-backed wing chair. Kyril's breath stopped; the dark, ultramarine eyes galvanized him, magnetizing his every sense. "It was a lovely thought, Kyril."

All at once, Kyril felt he should minimize everything. "I... well ... late at night, you know..." he started, laughing self-consciously. Then he caught himself; he had sent the poem for a reason. If he turned it into the joke of an insomniac, all would be lost.

"You must not build me into what I'm not," Laurent was saying. His tone was gentle, almost a caress; Kyril had never heard him speak so softly.

"Then, what are you?"

"A man, with selfish motives and a headstrong will. You've been curious about the falling out I had with Lorraine. Let me tell you now. Before she married Marc-Antoine de Huitton, my sister was engaged to an Englishman, the Duke of Marley. He was Charlotte

Maple-White's brother. Aubrey was handsome and fine. He was very blond, like Lottie, and he played the piano and violin. I was only fourteen, but already I knew who I was and what I wanted. I wanted Aubrey Maple-White, the Duke of Marley."

Kyril felt a thrill shoot up his spine. "And...? What happened?"

"They had everything in common—their love of music, their enjoyment of society, their good looks. They were beautiful together. But you see, what I wanted mattered more to me than my sister's happiness."

Laurent's face was grave. A Tiffany panel of red glass illuminated his hair and part of one cheek; he seemed to be on fire. Kyril edged forward on the couch, sipping his cognac. "That summer, Lorraine and I went to Britain, to visit the Maple-Whites. I seduced Aubrey. I waited for him in his bedroom, and told him I loved him. I wouldn't let him get away. In truth, I don't think he much wanted to escape; like you, he had felt an attraction to me from the beginning. But he couldn't face his own feelings. Afterwards, he became withdrawn and remote. He began smoking opium and drinking heavily. Lorraine couldn't figure out what had happened to her wonderful romance, and when she confronted him, he wept and told her that he didn't love her anymore." Laurent's features hardened. "Shortly after, she married Marc-Antoine."

"But... why was she angry with *you?* She didn't know!"

"She found out, a few years later, from Charlotte. Aubrey kept on deteriorating, until he had to be taken to a sanatorium in Switzerland. One night, they found him hanging from the ceiling of his room. He left a letter to his sister, explaining to her about the affair we'd had the summer of my fourteenth year. He said he couldn't live with the realization that I was the only person he had ever loved."

"Is it so bad... to love another man? Why couldn't he have lived with you, as Count del Arno does?"

"Because Orlando is a mature man, and he is strong enough not to care about what other people think. But in England, you don't openly declare your homosexuality—not when you bear a title."

"Lorraine told me that Diaghilev is accepted everywhere."

Laurent smiled. "That's because Diaghilev isn't interested in her fiancé. Diaghilev is a great impresario, whose sexual predilections are of little consequence compared with the rich art he can bring to Paris and London. But Lorraine, my dear Kyril, isn't the open-minded woman you think: she relies on convention far more than you suppose."

Then the anger and the hurt returned, pushing Laurent's story to the back of Kyril's mind. The brandy had risen to his head. Now he told Laurent what he had overheard from Lorraine's patio. Tears sprang to his eyes. Fury poured out of him. He clenched and unclenched his fists as he repeated everything to Laurent. Laurent's own admission of weakness and of guilt had unlocked all of Kyril's feelings, all the pain he had discovered in himself, all his fury at women.

"She never loved you," Laurent commented when Kyril had finished. "But surely you knew that, Kyril?"

"I thought she was different. I thought she cared, that she was proud of me. I—"

"You didn't love her either, my dear. You, like Aubrey Maple-White, enjoyed her and enjoyed the illusion of being a couple. But love is something more than that, isn't it? It's a dark and mysterious passion. It tears you apart when the other eludes you. It brings you magic incandescence when the other returns your love. Enjoyment is *bourgeois* emotion, a contentment we feel when there is predictable pleasure and relatively little insecurity. It is the food of married couples: nourishing but bland."

"But there was more! She *wanted* me!"

"There was her hunger. She consumes men because she is defective: she cannot love. She loved Aubrey, and she loved me, and in her heart, we plotted this affair to ruin her life. And who knows? Perhaps we did."

Laurent sighed, and steepled his fingers under his chin. "You will leave her," he said softly. "You will leave her now, without feeling guilty, and you will begin to live your own life. She did not break your heart, Kyriusha: she set you free."

"But . . . what will I do?"

"I cannot answer that. You must decide. My own life is hollowed out in peaks and valleys of pain and ecstasy. I am no blueprint for another."

For a moment, the two men gazed at each other. The room was warm and intimate, the Tiffany lamps throwing dazzling colors upon the severe Louis XIII furnishings. Outside, the wind howled. Laurent's robe lay open at the front. His chest, unblemished by hair, looked exactly as Kyril had already imagined it in his dreams. A man had killed himself for love of Laurent.

"What did you wish me to do about the sonnet?" the Frenchman presently demanded. Once again his tone was like a breeze, gently grazing Kyril's consciousness.

"I want you to make love to me," Kyril said. The words were heavy, yet he knew that he had better speak them now. The bough of a tall tree cracked against the large front window; both men ignored it. Laurent sat in his chair, breathing deeply, his robe moving like a silk sheath around that pale, firm skin. His delicate triangular face remained impassive. Maybe Kyril had been wrong to be so honest; perhaps Laurent was about to throw him out into the wilderness, sending him home like a foolish puppy.

But instead, Laurent stood up, grasping his cane. He walked to the sofa and stood over Kyril, looking down at him, his eyes enormous. "You think you love me," he whispered. "But you don't. You are simply curious, that's all. Curious about me and about what it's like to make love to a man."

Kyril's lips parted. "I—"

"Shh. . . . Be quiet, Russian boy. I'm curious, too. You are young and eager, as I once said, and I find this refreshing. You're lucky, pretty boy, that Orlando never found that sonnet. He'd have killed you."

"But tonight—I mean, now . . . "

"Tonight he might kill you, too. But, like all honest men, he sleeps the whole night through. . . . "

Laurent gave Kyril his hand, and pulled him up. He was taller than the Russian, but built more slightly. Keeping his eyes on the younger man, Laurent de la Haye placed both hands upon Kyril's shoulders. Then, with unexpected force, he pulled the Russian toward him, seeking his lips with his own. Kyril shuddered as the kiss became deeper and more passionate. He had kept Kyril's hand in his; suddenly it was guided beneath Laurent's robe, around his erect penis. There were tears in Kyril's eyes, tears of ecstasy as he touched the velvet skin and felt Laurent's powerful hardness in his own fingers. This was what he wanted; this was what he had come for. Laurent's syncopated breathing matched his own, and when he felt the artist's hand upon his head, pressing him down, he knelt before him and took the desired penis deeply into his mouth. It was as if they had been lovers all their lives.

Suddenly, a tremor went through Laurent's frame; he withdrew almost violently.

Kyril had already felt Laurent's body stiffen and pull back before he became aware of the overhead light. Without thinking, he stepped back on his haunches and looked up, terrified. In the brightness, Lorraine de Huitton stood staring down at them, her beautiful face drawn into a grimace of mockery and disdain. Next to her stood Charlotte Maple-White. Both women wore furs and evening gowns, their hair disarranged by the wind.

"Well," said the Marquise. "I should have known. . . . "

"Known what, Lorraine?" her brother demanded. His erection had fallen. He pulled his robe around him, his face insolent and angered. "How did you get in?"

"You didn't lock up when you let in Lover Boy. Ah, well, Lottie, what can I say? You two deserve each other!" She turned her face away, but not before Kyril could see her agony, saw the tears she sought to hide.

"Come, come, Lorraine. It was a mistake to look here for him! Let's go home!" Lady Maple-White put her arm around her friend. Staring at them, Kyril was filled with fury. He wanted to punish Lorraine for what she had said about him to her friend Roberto, for what she was doing to *them,* to him and Laurent, at this moment. He felt the blood pounding in his temples. He leapt up like a coiled spring, bolting toward the women, his face contorted and red. Charlotte Maple-White drew back, horrified, but she was not his prey. Kyril hurled himself upon Lorraine, pummeling at her head with his fists, beating wildly, uncontrollably. . .

Suddenly, he felt himself being pulled away. He felt Laurent's arms tighten around him, preventing him from moving.

"My *God!* He's *hurt* her," Charlotte was saying. Her voice was muffled as if it came from a great distance. Kyril felt as though he had sunk down to the bottom of a vast pool, as if he were about to drown, and she were above water. His vision was blurred. He could barely make out her frantic gestures as she knelt down on the rug. She was sobbing, cradling some object to her breast. Was it Lorraine?

Kyril slumped in Laurent's arms. The fury, the blood thirst, was suddenly quenched. He was spent and dizzy. "What have I done?" he asked, his voice a mere whisper.

Laurent didn't answer. The only reply came from Charlotte Maple-White, crouched on the floor, whimpering. All this was unreal, *unreal!* Kyril's head hurt awfully. He felt Laurent setting him on the sofa, gently but firmly. He closed his eyes, brought his hands to his temples, and pressed with all his might, trying to blot out the dreadful throbbing.

No one spoke. The room was strangely silent, bathed in the bright yellow overhead light. Then Kyril made out the robed forms of Orlando del Arno and the butler, Aristide. "What's going on?"

the Italian demanded. "What are all these people doing here?"

It was Charlotte Maple-White who answered him. Sitting on her haunches, she cried out: "Go ahead—*ask Laurent!* You are all murderers—all of you! Isn't it enough that Laurent caused my brother to kill himself? Go on, Count, *do something*... because *Lorraine is dead,* and *they are both responsible!*"

Abruptly, Charlotte stopped screaming, as Orlando faced Laurent. In the hush that ensued, Kyril felt the room begin to spin. Everything was closing in, the objects, the people, the hot yellow light. Only the throbbing persisted, the throbbing in his head. He felt himself suffocating. Then the room floated into nothingness, the sounds dimmed, and he fell forward into darkness.

When Zica saw the house, standing tall and proud like a thin, gaunt old woman, thought Zica, her heart hammered with sudden apprehension. She and Yakov had stopped several places to inquire where they might locate the residence of *Gospodin* Yossif Byitch. An old cantor in the synagogue had finally told them.

When Zica and Yakov, holding hands like lost children, found themselves in front of the severe old mansion, they looked at each other apprehensively. "You knock," said Yakov.

Zica banged hard with the brass knocker. Presently she heard footsteps, and the door opened. A woman dressed in black stood on the threshold squinting at them. Her iron-gray hair was pulled into a severe topknot, and her eyes were very blue and large. With a shock, Zica recognized Kyril's mother. She was taken aback by how the years had transformed her.

"Yes?" the woman inquired. Her face was almost lifeless.

"I... we are the Pokhises, of Moscow," Zica declared. She prayed the woman wouldn't recognize her. They had met only that one time, when she had come to Kyril's boarding house. That had been nearly four years ago—*the last time she had ever laid eyes on Kyril's face!* "We... we were friends of Kyril Victorevitch Ostrov, and we are looking for his mother and his grandfather," she said, her voice trembling.

All at once the woman's face came alive. Her eyes brightened; and her parchment skin took on some pink color. "Kyril's friends!" she cried. "Come in! *I* am his mother—Elena Yossifovna Ostrova. Please... excuse the mess...."

She held the door wide. Zica and Yakov passed inside, still holding hands. Zica felt relieved the woman hadn't recognized her.

The house was dark and crowded with boxes and crates. Thread-bare old tapestries lay rolled up against the walls; paintings stood propped up by large ebony sideboards and tables. Dusty velvet curtains were closed to keep out the sun.

"We're leaving," Elena Ostrova said, indicating the disarray. "In two weeks' time, we shall be sailing to America on a British ship bringing refugees to New York. That's where my father wants to go," she added, almost defensively. "*I* wanted Paris."

She gestured them toward a sofa between two half-packed boxes of books and mementos, and took a seat facing them. "What a sweet young couple you are." Her voice had a girlish lilt. "And—there's a baby on the way, I see."

"I'm five months pregnant," Zica told her.

"What are you doing in Rostov? How were you friends of my son's? I want to know so very much—because we haven't heard a thing from Kyril, not in a long, long time."

"Neither have we," Yakov said. "We are in Rostov, Madame Ostrova, because we are on the run from the Moscow CHEKA. Like you, we are hoping to emigrate. My parents are in Paris."

"My son was in Paris, too," Elena said. She pressed tired fingers against her eyes, and Zica saw tears. "But Papa—he won't think of going to Paris! He says the war has destroyed the factories and the buildings, that France lies devastated. But we must leave, before the Bolsheviks invade this part of the country. May I get you some food? Some tea?"

"Yes, please," Yakov said. "We haven't eaten since last night. My wife is very tired. Do you suppose that you could let us stay for a couple of nights, until we resolve what to do? The Bolsheviks aren't far," he added, sighing. "We rode down with three commissars from Moscow, who . . . did us a favor."

Elena Ostrova didn't ask how fugitives from the Moscow CHEKA had come to be helped by commissars from the same city. One didn't pry, these days, into such unhoped-for blessings. But she rose to her feet. "We keep a kosher house," she said. "I'll make some *blini,* with sour cream and apple compote. I'm sorry the house is so cold; my father doesn't want to waste electricity, and we don't have servants anymore. Everyone's gone off to join the Reds."

"Let me help you," Zica offered. When she looked at Yakov, he nodded imperceptibly. So she followed Elena Yossifovna down a bleak hallway into a narrow kitchen that must have once been splendid and bustling, in the days of cooks and scullery maids. Now it was still clean, but its emptiness was chilling. Not a single pot hung from the wall, not a single basket of onions adorned the counters.

Elena busied herself lighting the enamel stove. She knew exactly where everything was, and soon she had retrieved flour, eggs, a spoon, a bent old fork, and some butter. Zica could feel her mouth salivating. She hadn't tasted butter since November 1917. How had the Byitches managed to obtain it? And eggs! Whole *eggs!*

Elena, blending the butter into the flour, suddenly looked at her. "What did you say your name was?" she asked.

Zica's heart skipped a beat. "Pokhis," she replied slowly. "Zeinab Pokhis."

"What an unusual name, 'Zeinab,'" said Kyril's mother, in a sing-song voice. She broke two eggs, one after the other, into the bowl, and began to rotate the mixture adeptly with a large wooden spoon. "Tell me, Zeinab—I may call you this, may I not? What is your patronym, my dear child?"

"Lazarevna," Zica replied, her voice almost inaudible.

"...Zeinab Lazarevna. I am Elena Yossifovna. Well then, you haven't told me about your friendship with my son. How did you and your husband know my Kyril?"

"We..." Zica could think of nothing to say. Tears had started to well up in her eyes. Quickly, as if remembering her manners, she asked: "How may I help you? Perhaps if I got the compote...?"

But Elena would not be distracted.

"Kyril is my only child, Zeinab Lazarevna. He departed in 1916. He went to Paris to study medicine, and I knew in my heart that I would never see him again. Please, *please* tell me about your friendship! I need to know everything I can about what took place in my son's life! In all probability, I shall never find him again. He has forgotten us. His grandfather thinks it would be useless to go to France, such a demolished country, without having any idea where to look for Kyril...."

As the words came tumbling out of her, she stood back, flushed and trembling. Tears poured from her eyes. "I beg of you, Zeinab Lazarevna... tell me *something!* How did you know him? Did your husband read medicine with him in Moscow?"

Elena's pain was so naked that Zica felt her own dam was break-ing within her. All at once she burst into tears. She couldn't help herself; sobbing, she turned away, hiding her face in her hands.

Then she felt Elena's hand on her shoulder, gently stroking her. "My dear, dear child... now I see who you are," she murmured, practically into Zica's hair. "At first I wasn't sure. The pregnancy has altered your looks—so has the peasant clothing. But I see now. You are the girl he loved, the baroness, the girl in black with the egret feathers. He refused to utter a single word about you, but I knew. You are *that* Zeinab, the Baroness Poliakova—and that is why you're here, isn't it?"

Zica turned around slowly, stunned. Her face was pale, the tears on her cheeks glistening like frost snowflakes. "I . . ."

"Tell me the truth," Elena said, setting down the spoon as she sat down on a wooden stool. "Tell me why he didn't marry you, when you loved him with all your heart. Tell me *why,* after your visit, my son was never the same again!"

Yakov had been right: this had been a mistake! How could Zica have convinced herself that Elena Ostrova would not recognize her? *They should not have come!* But now, here she was, in this freezing kitchen with the passionate widow Ostrov beseeching her for the truth. Elena was tearing into the past like a ravenous she-wolf seizing a small, helpless rabbit. Kyril's mother deserved to know, and yet... this was Zica's most private heart, that part of her which she held intact within her, not even discussing it with Yasha... *especially* not with Yasha.

"Kyril wanted to marry me in secret," she said. "It was all my fault, Elena Yossifovna. I should have told my father the truth— that I loved Kyril and wanted to be his wife, even if... even if he was only half a Jew, and not... from Moscow or Petersburg. But you see, I was afraid."

"You knew your father would find my son wanting," Elena commented. "I know. My father found Victor Ostrov wanting, too, and for the same reasons. Vitya was a Cossack, and he wasn't rich. And my son was half-Cossack, and a provincial. But he was a good boy, Zeinab... a good man. He loved you!"

Zica nodded. "I made that mistake. And then Kyril grew desperate. He wanted us to be married right away. We planned a secret wedding, but..." She shook her head, remembering that dreadful night. "After that, nothing ever worked for us again."

Zica sank down onto a stool beside Elena.

"Is that all?" his mother demanded.

"*All?* What more do you want?"

"*You broke his heart! He never heard from you again!*"

"No, he *did* hear from me. He heard from me, Elena Yossifovna, and he chose to ignore me! He chose to put aside whatever feelings he had, in order to make me pay for not going through with the wedding! Your son wronged me, too!" Zica's cheeks were bright. "I was *pregnant, and he refused to see me!* I sent him a letter and a second one after that—and he never replied! Instead..." But she could not continue. Wracking sobs took the place of words. She cowered, hugging herself and crying. *"He didn't even bother to open the letters!"*

Elena Ostrova was too stunned to speak. For a minute Zica continued to weep. Then she rose, wiping the tears with her fingers. "Don't worry," she said, her voice harsh and ironic. "There are no little Kyrils. No one will come begging for his inheritance. The child was never born!"

"My poor, dear girl... You must not think I blame you for this," Elena spoke softly. "It was just that his heart never mended from you. Whom was I to blame...?"

"We were both to blame," Zica stated wearily. She leaned against the white tile counter. "But that's the past, Elena Yossifovna. Today there are Bolsheviks at our heels. Kyril has disappeared from both our lives. If you allow Yasha and me to stay here a few days, I can promise you that we shall cause you no further trouble. It was just that Yasha and I knew no one else in this strange city, and... well..."

"You are welcome to stay, Zeinab Lazarevna. You are welcome to stay." Briskly, Elena resumed blending her dough into a ball, her features intent upon what she was doing. But there were tears in her eyes, blurring her sight.

From the tiny dormer window in the small rooming house, Kyril could see nothing but a dirty French courtyard. Sitting on the bed, he shivered, hugging himself. Ugly flowered wallpaper was peeling at the corners. He had wrapped himself in the maroon and white chintz bedspread which now bunched up around his hips.

He was waiting.

Laurent de la Haye had said he would come. Kyril could hardly remember the sequence of events that had taken place in the gabled house on the cliff—but he knew he had attacked Lorraine. Afterwards, Orlando del Arno had faced him like a silent messenger of death, brandishing a hundred francs to tide him over, expelling him into the cold with an imperious scowl.

Surely, Lorraine was dead. Had she been alive, Laurent would have come by now. But then, Kyril reflected, Orlando was jealous. Charlotte Maple-White would have told every detail of what she had witnessed. More than three days had passed, and Kyril was full of pressing, agitated questions: What were they going to do? What if the police came? What of Laurent? What if Orlando threw *him* out, too?

The difference between them, of course, was that Laurent was rich and Kyril owned nothing but the clothes and jewelry which Lorraine had give him—belongings which were still at the Villa Martias. After Orlando's curt dismissal, Laurent had come out to the foyer with him, and had stated, *sotto voce:* "Go to the Hotel Tardieu. I'll find you there."

So Kyril had gone out into the storm with Orlando's hundred francs. In the darkness of his soul but a single candle had glowed— the promise of Laurent's forthcoming arrival.

But he hadn't come; the rich forgot what they promised. Their love meant nothing but a moment's pleasure. The rich belonged to one another: Laurent to Orlando, Lorraine to the next wealthy baron or count who would come courting, Lady Charlotte to her Duc de Fagnac, whose white skin craved the welts from her whip. *Hadn't he learned this lesson from the Poliakovs . . . from Zica's betrayal?* His own moneyed grandfather had abandoned him and his mother, leaving them to the degradations of Vitya Ostrov and the humiliations of poverty.

He had hardly eaten these past three days. The innkeeper had brought him bread and a crude red wine, then some sort of watery stew. He imagined himself in his silk suit, with a gold fob watch from Cartier's dangling from his breast pocket. How he had treasured those marks of good fortune! He had thought Fate owed this fortune to him, to make up for the pain he had been caused in the past.

Kyril Ostrov let the shabby bedspread fall to the floor. He walked naked to the window, pounding on the shutters until the side of his fist ached. There were tears in his eyes, tears that slid into his three-day-old beard, mixing with the sweat that caked his face. He wondered what was happening to the people he had left behind in Russia—his mother, his old grandfather, Zica. The blackest of moods enveloped him like a shroud.

A knock resounded. Kyril started, and he padded to the door, gathering the bedspread around him again. On the threshold stood

Laurent de la Haye in a creamy silk double-breasted suit, wearing a derby hat and carrying a gold-tipped cane. Kyril let him pass, afraid to let him know just how abandoned and angry he was feeling.

The artist sniffed as he entered the dusty, airless room. "Ostrov," he declared, "what a mess this place is!" He turned and faced Kyril, and his features softened. "Lorraine's alive. She's not badly hurt. You bruised her face and her neck and her left breast. She does rather resemble an eggplant . . . but she's alive, and won't be pressing charges."

A flood of relief poured over Kyril. He sank against the wall, suddenly exhausted. "She never wishes to lay eyes on you again," Laurent added. "But, my dear, we already knew that, didn't we?"

"What else?" Kyril touched his prickly unwashed skin with embarrassment.

"Charlotte told Orlando what she saw. But as she detests me, Orlando didn't choose to believe her. Orlando's theory on infidelity is simple enough: as long as he isn't made a fool of, and as long as it's not love, he'll pretend nothing happened. An affair becomes a problem to him if the third party interferes in my life . . . our life. Then, you see, he would be forced to get personally involved to the tune of far more than a hundred francs."

"I'm not quite sure I understand."

"Oh, but Kyriusha, you do, you do. Mind if I sit down?" Laurent lowered himself carefully into a cane-backed chair, easing his bad leg forward. When he looked at Kyril, his face appeared graceful and delicate in the morning light, the ultramarine eyes direct and penetrating. "I cannot allow Orlando to leave me," he declared, his voice almost a whisper. "We've been together for so long, you see. Alone"—he held out his hands and shook his head slowly from side to side—"alone, I cannot make it. I am a cripple, Kyriusha. I need the love of a strong, healthy man. My connection with Orlando goes deeper than all sensual connections, deeper than the appeal of novelty and mystery. We . . . belong to each other."

"So . . . between us . . . *nothing?* You will simply let it end?"

Laurent sighed. Kyril felt as if his heart were tearing in two. Suddenly he knelt in front of Laurent, touching his knee. "You don't care, do you?" he asked.

Laurent closed his eyes. "I must continue my life," he said simply. Opening his eyes again, he gave Kyril a measured stare. "Did you think I would leave Orlando?" he asked. "Didn't you see how things stood between us?"

"So you and Lorraine are really no different!" Kyril rose to his feet, trembling with anger.

"I didn't *ask* for you to be attracted," Laurent replied. "It was you who came to me. It was you who sent the sonnet. I tried to tell you from the beginning: Orlando del Arno is my family. And yet you persisted."

Kyril's wounded eyes, eloquent in their hurt, remained on the artist's face. Laurent looked away, clearing his throat. He arose unsteadily and leaned on his cane.

"Kyriusha," he said carefully. "I came here to bid you *adieu*. I came to tell you that you must leave Biarritz, because Lorraine will blackball you from the house of any decent person. She is my sister. I cannot continue to befriend you in this city while the whole of society knows the details of what occurred between you! She is injured in both body and reputation—and she is my only living relative. Even if she and I are not close, appearances must be preserved. I cannot be seen with you—ever again! So it is not merely a question of Orlando," he added softly. "It has to do with reality, and the world we live in. Soon there will be an armistice, and we shall be returning to Paris. Don't think of going back there, either. Lorraine's friends are many, and they will all side with her, the obvious victim."

Kyril's lips had parted in utter disbelief.

Laurent de la Haye took out an envelope and placed it on a small wooden table. "Ostrov," he said, "there is an American freighter stationed in the port of Bayonne right now. It's due to leave in three days for New York. I've made arrangements for you to be on board."

Kyril shook his head, dazed.

"You won't need much more than your passport, which I've fetched from the Villa Martias," Laurent told him. "I've made all the requisite arrangements. There's a bit of cash to tide you over in New York... all I could take out of the house without arousing Orlando's suspicions."

"You must be mad," Kyril whispered. "I have no intention of going to *America!* I... I don't know a soul there, and I... I don't ... I mean, my English is inadequate..."

"You have no future in France, Kyriusha. So you have little choice but to get on that freighter. Otherwise, you will finish your days under a Paris bridge, drinking cheap red wine out of paper bags. This could have been a matter for the police, but... well, Lorraine was keeping you. And she did not want to be thought ridiculous for keeping a lover who would beat her to a pulp."

"But it was she—*she* said . . ."

"It does not matter what provoked it! *Don't you understand?* We are in France, Kyril! And in France there are appearances to be maintained!"

"Appearances? What about Charlotte, who whips people? What about Lorraine, who took up with me in plain daylight while her husband was off fighting the Germans?"

Laurent smiled. "That, my friend, is the way things go. Some sins are considered venial, others mortal. To raise your hand against a Marquise de Huitton is mortal; to sleep with whom you please, merely venial. The French are a depraved lot, but their feet remain firmly on the ground. Their code of morality has the stern logic of self-preservation."

"And what about *you?*"

"I slip up now and then. I am a homosexual, don't forget." Laurent shrugged. "Kyriusha, I have written down the name of the freighter, and where you may find it. I have also given you the names of some friends I have in New York. Pay them a visit, with my compliments. I'm afraid that's all I can do. You must understand that, between my sister and Orlando del Arno, I have my hands full of obligations."

Rage welled up inside Kyril. He let the bedspread fall, so that he stood naked before Laurent. Throwing open the door, he leaned against the doorjamb, his chin jutting out arrogantly. "Go, then, and be damned!" he cried. "To hell with you and your *obligations!*"

For an instant, Laurent de la Haye hesitated, licking his lips. He looked at Kyril, magnificent in his golden nudity. Laurent's lips parted. Then he shook his head and walked out. Behind him, Kyril slammed the door until the frame shook. "God damn all of you!" he exploded.

For the first five days, Yossif Adolfovitch Byitch had circled Yakov and Zica like an old buzzard watching two fresh young corpses. He had spoken little to these unexpected guests that his daughter had implored him to shelter. But Yakov had known that, all along, the elderly merchant had been appraising them carefully. Why the interest? he wondered. *What does he want with us,* anyway?

Now Yakov sat opposite him in the old library. He leaned forward, listening to the old man with white hair and piercing blue eyes.

"It was hard, at first. Nobody would sell to a Jew, and nobody would buy. Furniture is a funny business, sonny, and there was no one to give me a hand."

"How did you begin, Yossif Adolfovitch?"

"I learned cabinet making from my father, the *shtetl* carpenter. But I always wanted to find the easiest way out of the *shtetl*. Know anything about *shtetl* life?"

Yakov suppressed a smile. "Yes, sir. I grew up in one. Peredelkino, near Rigevka in Podolia. Zica's father was the local landowner. That is how we met."

"Childhood sweethearts?" The old man grinned. He had long, yellow teeth and bright red gums.

"Not exactly. We were only ten years old then, of course, and she was the *barinya,* so she hardly noticed me. But later, her father brought me over to their estate in Moscow, and I became Lazar Solomonovitch's assistant librarian."

"I see." The old fellow had sharp, aquiline features. His mind was like Senya's, Yakov thought. Yossif Byitch winked at Yakov. "So you're a self-taught *shtetl* boy, just like me! You know, sonny, I wanted to *be* somebody. I built this house with the sweat of my efforts, but first I had to learn to speak the Russian tongue. You and I, we speak Yiddish together—but over there in the kitchen, your Zica and my Lena are conversing in French. D'you have any notion how hard it was for me to acquire the money to let my daughter have a French tutor, back in the seventies? But my wife and daughter wanted to *parler Français,* and so, what the hell, I went along with it." He laughed, throwing out his hands in mock helplessness. "In fact, I sat in on the class myself. I had to learn. It was required of a gentleman to speak French in those days."

"Yes, indeed, sir. I learned it too, from the Poliakovs' librarian. He taught me everything I know." Yakov's eyes suddenly misted over. "I wish I could find him. Senya was the best friend I ever had."

"Ah well, we lose and lose, in this life of ours. The wandering Jews shall always be the world's homeless. Look at my grandson, Kyriusha! The war came. He was 'reading' medicine in Paris. D'you think we heard one word from him since then? Nothing! Lena is sick about it. As for me, I always knew the boy would turn out badly—just like his father, I said to her. Half a Cossack is too much Cossack for me!" He scrutinized Yakov, then added: "You were friends, you say?"

"Well, Kyril Victorevitch was a visitor in the Poliakov residence. Zeinab—Zica—told me he was a friend of her brother Zhenya. I only met him once or twice."

"Oh?"Nothing escaped Yossif. He would not take his watery eyes off Yakov. "Kyriusha was a handsome fellow, wasn't he? The girls... they liked him, *hmm?*"

"I suppose so, sir. I really wouldn't know. I worked for Baron Lazar Poliakov, but I didn't attend the dinner parties nor the dances. But yes, I recall he was quite charming. People seemed to enjoy his company."

"But not you. *You detested him!*" The old fellow rubbed his dry hands together merrily.

Yakov's mouth fell open. "I... sir?"

The old man chuckled. "I gave Kyril enough money to get by on—that's all. He was a spendthrift: I could tell it right away. Like that father of his! So I kept him on a strict allowance. I didn't want him to spend too much on his pleasure and not enough time at the books. He never did become a doctor—I can assure you of that. Too much hard work!"

Yakov didn't want to discuss Kyril. He wanted to forget there had ever been such a person. He began to shift uncomfortably in his chair. "Yes!" continued Yossif, "you disliked my grandson because, in your eyes, he had it all! But that wasn't so, sonny. *You* had it all: the ambition and the gumption. And so you won the girl! *Ha-ha-ha,*" he laughed, clapping his hands. "*You* won the girl!"

Yakov said nothing. But the old man's merriment only increased. "Your girl is a pretty, fine little doll," Yossif said at last, regaining his breath. "And she will bear you a healthy child. The Poliakovs? I remember them. I never met them personally, mind you, but every Jew in Russia knew about them. I would have liked for Kyriusha to marry her—don't get me wrong! But he would have done her no good. They would have starved, like Lena and her Cossack! Your Zica, she needs a real man."

"Thank you, Yossif Adolfovitch."

"Why d'you want to go to Paris, like a fool?" the old man suddenly demanded. He had a habit of changing the subject abruptly, spearing the listener with his eyes. "The New World's the place for young people! *America! The United States!* Come with us," he added. "Lena could use a companion. And we shall start a business, you and I. A business for *shtetl* boys, hmm?"

"But, sir, my parents..."

"Parents? In Paris? What d'you want to be, Yasha, my boy? Some old person's servant, like your father? Or perhaps you'll be lucky— you'll be handed crumbs, like the proverbial poor relative, and live on the good graces of Zica's aunt and uncle? Come—have your own business, like me. Give your child an education in the New World!"

Yakov inhaled deeply. "I'd never even considered the New World," he said slowly. "I don't speak English..."

The old man shrugged. "So? Neither do I! But Lena does, and so does Zica. They'll translate for us! Think of it—a land where there are no *shtetls* and no Pales of Settlement, where the Jews can walk side by side with the *goyim* in the sun... where you don't have to bribe government officials for travel permits and permits of residence in the big cities. What do you say, Yasha? I need a young man, a strong and courageous fellow. I need a business partner!"

Yakov ran his tongue over his teeth, thinking. Then he looked at Yossif Adolfovitch Byitch. "Well, sir," he declared. "I'll have to discuss it with Zica. But... perhaps you're right! Perhaps it would be a good idea to make a complete change, to start fresh when the baby comes."

The old man stood up. He was frail and delicate, and every time he took a step, Yakov wondered whether he might fall and break. Yossif Byitch placed a gnarled hand on Yakov's shoulder. "Good thinking, sonny!" he lauded him. "Good thinking. I'll tell Lena to serve us that soup right now, and we can ask your Zica. But she's a good girl—she's not the type to oppose you. And tomorrow, I'll see what I must do to get you two on board the ship we're taking. Seems to me," he added, "that there were some spaces left on the lower decks. You young people can sleep anywhere, can't you? So long as the baby's born in the New World..."

He shuffled out of the room, humming to himself an old Yiddish lullaby. Yakov remained in his chair, staring straight ahead, unaware of the tasselled curtains and the view from the big window. He was thinking of life in a land without a Pale of Settlement, of his own business with an old, old man whose only heir would be a middle-aged woman of fragile health, unlikely to marry again.

Zica had been right to push him to overcome his reticence about the Byitches, he thought. She was turning into a right proper little wife. Smiling to himself, Yakov saluted the memory of Kyril Ostrov, whose benevolent ghost had led them here.

Book III:
Deceptions

Chapter XIII

THE lurch of the ship threw Kyril against the wall of the cabin. Determinedly, he plunged ahead, his stomach churning. He swallowed bile. But he knew that if he didn't reach the deck, he would lose his sanity.

The American freighter had remained docked in Bayonne for several weeks. The captain had warned Kyril not to leave his tiny cabin for any reason; they would pull anchor at a moment's notice—and if he didn't want to be left behind, he had better stay put and not cause trouble.

Forlorn in his cabin, with no one to talk to but some American sailors, he had felt sadness engulf him, and his old sense of alienation had surfaced with a vengeance. He was a Russian whose country had changed hands, an alien in France who had thought himself accepted. But, in the end, the De la Haye-Huittons had been laughing behind his back, like the Alyoshas of his past who had taunted him on the streets of his native Rostov. He belonged nowhere—so perhaps going to New York wasn't so far-fetched an idea. Perhaps, indeed, it was the only solution.

Now, after four days on the high seas—four November days of drizzle and fog, with the promise of a tempest—Kyril felt himself going stir-crazy. At meals, which he took with the sailors, he listened with dismay to their slurred accents as they chatted in their odd American English and joked with each other. But apart from those times, he had not yet been outside his cabin. Now he was resolved to get on deck and see the ocean that had been rocking him back and forth until he thought his head would explode.

Gingerly, with great clumsiness, Kyril made his way through the dark ship's corridor and up two staircases to the main deck. Toward the front of the ship, he could hear the voices of the sailors accosting one another as they worked. As he reached the deck, the freighter heaved precariously. Thrown forward, he pulled himself up and gauged his bearings.

The wooden surface of the deck smelled of sea salt and brine. To the side, enormous gray-green waves sprayed the ropes and the masts. Kyril saw no one. Trying not to slip, he made his way forward to the railing. After a few concerted efforts, he arrived breathless, and grabbed the wooden bar.

Below him, the North Atlantic Ocean unfurled its mighty anger. Powerful waves whipped the hull of the freighter. Wave upon gray wave broke upon the ship's hull. Now that he had reached the rail, Kyril felt his nausea begin to subside. The waves mesmerized him. They were beautiful, demented, frightening. For a few moments he forgot his pain, and turned his face to the salt spray.

"How do you do?" a man said in French. Kyril whirled around. Through the fog, he saw someone a few years older than he was coming his way. The man hugged his coat with one hand, holding on to the wooden rail with the other. When he reached Kyril's side, he gave a curt nod. The two men looked out at the spectacle in silence.

"The Captain tells me you are Russian," the man finally said. "Me, too. I was very lucky to book passage here, at the last minute. My name's Malenkov—Count Kyril Vadimovitch."

Kyril smiled. "Kyril Victorevitch Ostrov. Pleased to meet you." Malenkov had a beautiful face, with haunted eyes.

"What an odd coincidence," he observed. "Two Russians aboard an American freighter—with the same first name!" He continued: "My wife and I made it from Petersburg across the Finnish border in 1917. There she perished of pneumonia. I found a way, through Sweden, to come to France. But I was terribly unhappy in Paris. I'd been there many times with Lara. To be there alone, facing scenery that was part of *our* past, tore my heart apart. My friends suggested New York. It seems that the Americans have a passion for exotic Europeans, especially those with tragedy in their lives!"

"Oh? Do they really?"

Malenkov uttered a sardonic snigger. "Look, Ostrov—don't take me seriously. I know absolutely nothing about New York, except that it's not Paris. And let me tell you, I hate Paris. I spent my days in the cabarets, weeping for Petersburg and drowning in vodka— D'you know who I am?" he questioned abruptly.

Kyril shook his head. "I—I'm afraid not. But then, you see, I'm from Rostov-on-the-Don. The only other city I know is Moscow. I've been in Paris for two years . . . studying medicine."

The slender man with the haunted face smiled and this smile was so sad, so melancholy, that Kyril found himself inexplicably touched. What tragedies had this man suffered, besides his wife's demise?

"The Malenkovs—well, my mother was a close friend of the Tzar's . . . almost a member of the Imperial Family. And now . . ." he sighed, and his eyes misted over—"now I am the only one left. I came one step ahead of the Reds, leaving everything behind but my beloved Lara and a small cache of her jewels. You would not believe what I once possessed—my palace on the Nevsky Prospect, an estate in the Crimea near that of Felix Yussupov. In Paris, I couldn't face any of my French friends from the past, and even less, my poor exiled compatriots. Most of them are living like paupers! There is no way I could help them all, and I know they desperately need help. If I'd sold all my jewels, I would have had nothing—not even to pay rent on my suite at the Ritz. How was I to support others in need?"

"I understand," Kyril said, for want of a better reply.

"So you see, it is desperation which has driven me out of France. That, and fear. Fear of poverty . . . as well as the certainty of having no profession. How am I to earn a living? I do not even have the skills of a cook or stablehand. I'm twenty-five . . . and already, I feel fifty!"

Malenkov was only two years older than he! Yet he looked far older, and very frail. For a while, they bent over the railing, watching the crazy antics of the waves, neither saying a word. Kyril wondered at the strange coincidence of meeting Malenkov. Had he ever heard of him? How odd that Lorraine would not have mentioned the rich, exiled Russian. She knew everyone of good family, everyone who was a "somebody" somewhere in Europe. Was it really possible she had not known of Malenkov's presence in the city?

"I had some very good friends in Paris," Kyril said tentatively. "The Marquise de Huitton and her brother, the Comte de la Haye. I wonder if you might know them . . . ?"

Malenkov smiled. "Lorraine de Huitton . . . I met her when I was an adolescent, and my parents sent me to Paris for a winter. She was already a debutante—the kind of "older woman" a boy dreams of when he goes to sleep! But you see, Ostrov, she was among the ones I avoided after Lara's death . . . I could not have borne her sympathy."

That explained it, then. Kyril asked curiously: "What are you planning to do in New York? Do you know people there, too?"

Malenkov's eyes seemed dark and troubled—but Kyril, looking into them, thought how very like him the man was . . . how hopeless and vulnerable and full of sorrow. It did not matter that one was a Jew and the other a boyar. They were both expatriates.

Malenkov shook his head, and sighed. "I don't know. I have some jewels left. Lara had some family heirlooms, some necklaces and rings and a few bracelets. And I have a couple of Fabergé eggs from my father's collection. I shall have to sell them. But I'm told that the rich American industrialists love everything exotic and expensive. The problem is my health. I suffer from heart trouble. My lungs are weak. I cannot work. After I run through the money from the sale of my precious pieces, I shall have to think of some other way to live, shan't I? They say that America loves investors. Perhaps I shall invest!"

Kyril smiled, but he felt uncomfortable. The future that loomed before them seemed as different as their pasts. He had only a small sum of money from Laurent. How long would that tide him over —three weeks? a month? "I, too, have no idea what shall become of me in the New World," he said, his voice unsteady. "I have only a list of names that the Comte de la Haye gave me. Apparently there are five New York socialites who know him."

Malenkov coughed—a racking cough that continued for a full minute. Noting Kyril's concerned expression, he merely shrugged. "We can perhaps help each other, my dear Ostrov," he finally said. His voice sounded weak and breathless. "Your socialites might want to buy my jewels." But even as he smiled, Malenkov's face contorted into a grimace of pain. He placed a hand over his heart.

"Let me help you to get back down to your cabin," Kyril offered. "I, too, have grown chilled and wet from the spray."

The Count smiled at him, the trusting smile of a child. "How good that we have met," he declared, letting Kyril take his arm.

The confusion and noise of Ellis Island was like heaven to Yakov. He had grown up in a *shtetl*, had witnessed a pogrom, and his life had been hard almost without cease. He felt himself filling with joy as he regarded the thousands of immigrants amassed for their processing into the United States of America. He wanted to click his heels and raise his arms in a giant salute to the Statue of Liberty and the idea which she represented. Freedom! Opportunity! Perhaps—no, surely!—fame and fortune. In this great, young country, he would be his own man. His child would be born an American—would never know the constant fear of the Cossacks. In this country there was religious equality. The poor and uneducated had as great a chance of succeeding as those born to wealth and prestige.

Not quite, he knew. But still, he would make his way, under the tutelage of this wise old man, Yossif Adolfovitch Byitch. Together they would work hard to start a business. It didn't really matter *what* business, as long as he made money. With money, he would make a grand life for Zica and his child. She would live as comfortably as she had in Moscow. But here, there would be no distinction between her circle and his. The fact that he had been her father's servant would never be mentioned.

Yakov stole a look at Zica, huddled near Elena Ostrova. It was the first time he and Zica had seen the Byitches since boarding the British ship in the Rostov harbor. Yakov and Zica had travelled in the hold, squashed together with hundreds of other penniless immigrants. Yakov cursed the old man for not having provided better for a pregnant woman. But the old man had done this to teach Yakov a lesson: nothing in this world came easily. You had to earn your way to comfort. You had to prove yourself. Well, he would do it! He'd prove to the old man that he could endure any discomfort. Yakov was *determined* to succeed.

The old man had wanted to establish protocol: he would be the boss, Yakov merely the junior partner. It was up to Yakov to be Yossif Adolfovitch's flunky. Well then, so be it! He had been a servant in the Aschkenasy house in Odessa. He had been the assistant librarian of the Poliakovs. It had paid off, hadn't it? He'd learned to read and write French and Russian—he, a young man who had spoken only Yiddish till that time. And Zica was his wife!

When they arrived at Ellis Island, Yakov had a difficult time finding Elena Yossifovna and her father. Zica's feet were swollen from standing so long in interminable lines. She needed to rest. But just then, some Immigration officers with uniformed blazers, badges and ties—looking fresh and clean—announced something to the expectant, weary Russians.

"What's going on?" Yakov whispered to Zica.

"They're going to divide us." Her voice trembled slightly. "The men that way, the women and children this way. I . . . Yasha . . ."

"Don't worry. We'll meet up soon enough, *zhyonushka,* my little wife. They won't be rough with you: this is America!"

"They're going to give us medical examinations," she told him. "What if . . . ?"

"We are all healthy," Yossif Adolfovitch cut in. "Even I am only old, not ill! Go on, get going, you two," he growled at Elena and Zica. "The boy and I have somewhere to go, and so do you."

The line of women was forming. Elena and Zica moved forward. Little children tugged at their mothers' hands, some whimpering. Yakov gave his arm to the old man, who shuffled his feet and took his place at the end of a long column of men. All looked tired and rumpled. As they marched forward, Yakov caught Zica looking toward him, just as her line proceeded into a large room. Her face, full from the pregnancy, touched him with its great beauty. His beautiful Zeinab, the girl of his dreams! How many of those dreams had been deferred during the dreadful first months of their marriage. Survival had been of the essence. They'd had no time for romance and luxuries.

Now he'd make it up to her. He would be gentler, less abrupt, less condemning of her small faults. He would buy her flowers, pet her, and whisper sweet nothings. He would play music for her. Overcome with emotion, his eyes filled with tears, and he turned away quickly, clearing his throat so the old man would not suspect his sentimentalism.

The men were waved into a large waiting room. Yakov took his passport from his breast pocket and stole a look at it. How great were the wonders that money could buy! Yossif Adolfovitch had gone to a forger in Rostov and arranged for false papers for Zica and Yakov—fake birth certificates and passports for both of them. The forger had even provided them with the necessary seals and photographs!

"Is it true," he whispered to Yossif beside him, "that in America, the Immigration service lets you change your name?"

"Why would anyone want to do that?" Yossif Adolfovitch countered.

"Because, well . . . 'Pokhis' might be difficult to pronounce in English. Zica says the *'kh'* sound doesn't exist there."

"Suit yourself. Call yourself anything you want. I only care that you come to work on time, every morning. That's why I brought you here to America."

"Yes, sir." Yakov looked around at the men sitting on their haunches and leaning against the walls. He needed to find a toilet soon; in all the excitement that morning, he had not urinated since leaving the ship. "Yossif Adolfovitch," he murmured, "would you excuse me for a moment? Nature is calling, and most urgently!"

"I'll wait for you right here," the old gentleman stated. His blue eyes twinkled, and he grinned. "We aren't going to lose each other now, are we? The future beckons to us, near enough to touch!" And he waved Yakov away.

The toilets . . . Yakov had no idea where to look for them, nor how to ask in English. A uniformed guard intercepted him as he prepared to leave the waiting room. Yakov, unabashed, pointed to his crotch and began jumping up and down eloquently, making a funny grimace. The guard laughed, and pointed him down the hall. Yakov was pleased that his pantomime had made the guard laugh. His first "show" in front of an American had been a great success. And language was no barrier—at least for some things!

Yakov pushed open a huge metal door, and found himself in an immense, evil-smelling room. Dozens of urinals jutted out from a gray wall. There were stalls beyond. Yakov rushed to the nearest urinal. As he relieved himself, he looked around. The place was nearly deserted. One aging man in a black homburg stood at the far end of the row. He was busy in the same endeavor, and Yakov smiled. Everyone ended up with his pants unbuttoned, many times a day, in the United States as well as the Soviet Union. In this position, every man was an equal.

The metal door swung open. From the corner of his eye, Yakov saw two well-dressed young men walk into the enormous bathroom. He looked again, intrigued. The men were speaking French in a low voice. One of them wore an astrakhan coat, and he was holding a large, square bag. He leaned against the other man, who had solicitously given him his arm. The man in the astrakhan coat looked sickly and weak, but he was strikingly good looking. Russian! Russians of good family, speaking French.

Brothers? Friends?

Yakov buttoned his fly and went to the washstand nearest to them, to steal another look. The men had similar faces: brothers, surely. Something tugged at Yakov's memory. Surreptitiously, he moved closer to them to listen in on their conversation.

"It's in the case, Kyriusha," the sick man was murmuring. He sounded in pain. "Look in there, will you?"

Kyriusha?

No—impossible! It couldn't be Ostrov! Elena had been quite clear that her son was living in Paris. Nevertheless, Yakov pulled his cap low over his forehead as he turned around. He could not help staring at the two men. The sick one was leaning over a sink, coughing. His face was gray, contorted with pain. Yakov looked at the other, busy with the latch of the bag...and froze. *It was Kyril Ostrov!*

What should he do? Of all men to meet, this was the *one man* whom Yakov least wished to see now. What if Kyril and Zica should see each other again? What if their love should be rekindled? Please, dear God, let Kyril Ostrov remain far, far away, a relic from the past to be forgotten....

Then another thought struck Yakov, making him gasp. If Yossif and Elena discovered that Kyril was here, they would quickly wash their hands of Yakov Pokhis. All their attention...all the money they had brought from Rostov...would be lavished upon their own son and grandchild. Yakov's chances to make it in the world would be reduced proportionately. He envisioned himself in New York—penniless, unable to speak the language, with no connections to anyone of importance in America.

He hardly reasoned. There was no time. All he knew was the electrifying, sudden fear. He could not—*would not*—acknowledge Ostrov. He had to turn around and continue to wash his hands, pretending never to have recognized him. The secret now was to hurry up and get back to Yossif Adolfovitch as quickly as possible, to steer the old man—at all costs—away from his grandson. He had to use every ounce of ingenuity to ensure that those two were kept separate until they were off Ellis Island.

Perhaps, many months later, the old man would run into Kyril. So be it! By then, Yakov would have established himself as indispensable to his boss and mentor. By then, Zica's baby would be born, and they would have a comfortable house of their own.

But even though he was in haste to get away, Yakov listened closely to what the sickly looking man was saying to Kyril.

"Kyril, please hurry!" the darker man pleaded, his voice agonized. Yakov felt a pang of remorse. Conscience dictated that he should go to Ostrov and ask, in a clear Russian or French, what he might do to help. *What if the other man died* while Yakov stood by? Yakov hesitated. But reason told him to keep his distance. As he wiped his hands now on a rough paper towel that felt like sandpaper, he rationalized that, yes, the man might die. But it was

Kyril's responsibility to help him—certainly not Yakov's.

"I can't find the pills, Kyra," he heard Ostrov replying. He sounded panicked. "When did you last see them?"

". . . Can't remember. Kyril . . ."

Yakov was ready to leave. He had to go—now! Then it happened: as Yakov moved away from the washbasins, Kyril Ostrov happened to look up. Their eyes met. For an instant, Yakov was transfixed by Kyril's clear, green eyes. Kyril stared at him—too long. Had he recognized Yakov—the new Yakov, in his worn immigrant clothes, with his tangled beard and mustache? Yakov knew he looked much older, and far less distinctive than the other small, nimble Yakov from the Pale that had been Zica's servant.

But Kyril Ostrov's face was unmoving. If he recognized Yakov, he gave no sign. Yakov could only stare back, caught.

Then, abruptly, it was over. Yakov realized the Kyril was not going to challenge him. Ostrov's eyes moved in another direction, back to the other man's bag. Not a single word had been exchanged between them.

Yakov left the bathroom, letting the heavy metal door clang shut behind him. He was *free!* He hurried back to Yossif Byitch and the line of refugees. Still, there was danger. He would have to keep an eye out for Ostrov and the friend he had called "Kyra."

The next few hours were nothing but waiting. Yakov and Yossif Byitch held their places in a line that wended its way through several rooms, where different doctors and medics carefully checked them out. They were turned about this way and that, their eyes scrutinized and their reflexes tested. It wasn't that the Americans were brutal, but they were methodically thorough. Entrance requirements for aliens were stringent. But no one seemed to mind; Yossif Adolfovitch, leaning forward, tapped Yakov on the knee and whispered to him: "Better to be examined by Americans than Cossacks, don't you think?"

Yakov merely smiled. *Anything* was better than being a Jew in Russia, living in daily fear of the dreaded Cossacks.

It was after their eye examinations that Yakov again caught sight of Ostrov. Fortunately, Yossif Adolfovitch was four men ahead in line; he had already left the room when the golden-haired Russian passed through, papers in hand. He did not see Yakov, who was about to exit.

Yakov hesitated, watching. Better to have his enemy in sight than to worry about where he was.

"Name?" the doctor demanded of Kyril. Ostrov handed the doctor some papers. Yakov noticed that Kyril was clutching the bag in which, hours before, he had searched for pills for his sickly companion. When Kyril handed over his papers, the ophthalmologist read aloud: "'Kyril V. Malenkov, Petrograd, Soviet Union.' Now look here, Mr. Malenkov—right here, at my instrument. . . ."

Yakov blinked, thunderstruck. *Count Kyril Malenkov?* Kyril must be using the name of his companion. But if so, then *where was his friend?* Yakov could not turn away from this mystery. Inconspicuous, hanging by the doorway, Yakov watched Kyril from beneath lowered lids.

It makes no difference to you, he tried to tell himself. *Just get out, quickly!* It was time to find the women. Whoever Ostrov *said* he was, he had to be kept away from Elena, from Yossif Adolfovitch, *and from Zica!* The nightmare vision of Zica seeing Kyril brought sudden dryness to Yakov's mouth. After a year of marriage to Zica, with a baby of their own on the way . . . No! It must not happen! He could not allow Kyril Ostrov—or Kyra Malenkov—to ruin his future. Yakov Pokhis would make it his life's endeavor to keep this man separated from the woman who was most dear to both of them.

Quickly, Yakov caught up with Yossif, and they went to find Elena and Zica. When Yakov saw Zica, he threw his arms about her shoulders, pressing her close to him. "Did your doctor tell you when to expect this child of ours . . . this little American?"

"You're silly, Yashka," she answered giggling. She looked up at him with a shy, proud smile. "You know it's due in March! But the doctor did tell me: 'This is going to be the first U.S. citizen in your family, young lady!' And I looked him right in the eye, and said: 'Yes, *sir!*'"

"—Did you hear about the dead man they found in the lavatory stall?" Elena Ostrova asked, her face suddenly serious. "It was a young man, they say—dead of asphyxiation! They think he had severe lung trouble, maybe heart failure. They were just talking about it in the other room!"

Unable to understand English, neither Yakov nor Yossif Adolfovitch had learned anything about a dead man. But the instant Elena told him, Yakov knew with perfect certainty that the dead man could only be Ostrov's companion. But he asked: "Elena Yossifovna, do they . . . do they have any idea who the poor man was?"

"Oh, *yes!* That is the strangest thing of all. He was from *Rostov,* the doctors were saying. Just some man from Rostov—they didn't know his name. He was young, but very sickly. They think he would have failed his medical examination. If he had consumption, he would have been sent back, or so they say."

"Poor man," Yakov said softly. But a grim thought had crossed his mind. Why hadn't Kyril reported the death? Why had he taken the man's bag—stolen his identity. Yakov himself was the only witness to what had taken place in the lavatory. But his lips had to remain sealed. To give away what he knew would mean confronting Kyril. And that was now unthinkable. The man might be a murderer—he might intentionally have let his companion die—but Yakov could say *nothing*.

He wished he had never seen Kyril—never recognized him. Suddenly, Yakov's heart constricted with guilt. After all, Elena and Yossif had not seen their son and grandchild since 1916. Elena talked about her son all the time, she wept bitter tears—and now that very man was practically in the same room. But Yakov could not tell her—he *could* not. For the more Yakov thought about it, the more he was certain in his heart that Kyril was a murderer. Kyril Ostrov had Malenkov's bag, and his identity. *I have only kept these good people from having to face a murderer within their own family,* Yakov rationalized. *They need never know that their child is as evil as his Cossack father.*

But to be fair, the death posed a question. Malenkov had died of asphyxiation; who could tell whether, in fact, Ostrov had killed him? Even if Yakov took the bold move of offering himself as witness, it would be his word against Ostrov's . . . and Ostrov, after all, had studied medicine. . . .

Yakov's arm tightened around Zica. He looked out toward the skyline of New York. And his future—their future—lay right there within view, within touch, within taste . . . He would not endanger that future now. "We're going to be happy here, Zeinab," he whispered softly.

Chapter XIV

*A*s Kyril gazed from his bedroom window over the lush green spaces of Central Park, he realized that he hadn't expected to be so moved, nor to feel such thrills of excitement at arriving here. He found himself expectant and nervous, on the threshold of something new and wonderful.

Below him, seven stories down, women with parasols strolled through the park on the arms of their admirers. A horse-drawn carriage unloaded two small children, accompanied by a nanny in uniform and a man with a walking stick. From his north-facing window at the Plaza Hotel, the people below appeared like tiny tin soldiers.

But superimposed on this scene was the disquieting image of Zica Poliakova. She had loved him. She had wanted him. Yet, in the end, she had rejected him for the same reasons as Laurent—her family, her social prestige, had been more important. Then, as now, he had run away from his own broken heart.

A twinge of regret passed through him, and he sat down. He wondered at the poignancy of his memories. Four years ago, Zica had sent him two notes via her servant, Yasha. Each time, Kyril had sent the notes back unopened. How foolish! Now he wished he knew what she had tried to tell him then. Why did Kyril feel such a desire to uncover the past? Perhaps only to understand why that affair—like the one with Laurent—had ended in failure and loneliness.

And again, he felt like a social outcast, either too Jewish or not Jewish enough, with never enough money to buy himself a place among the *ne plus ultra*.

He cast his glance toward the park, shaking his head. He wanted this life at the top. He wanted revenge against the Alyoshas of his youth, against his grandfather who had turned his back upon him, against the Poliakovs and the De la Hayes. The only way to make the bitterness disappear would be to rise higher than all of them, and then to thumb his nose at them from the height of his own glory.

He smiled. For once, he had an edge. He had stolen Malenkov's papers. A theft, it was true—but a small theft that could not possibly harm the dead man. Those papers effected a transformation. He had *become* Count Malenkov. He had left behind the ineffectual little Jew, Kyril Ostrov, whose undignified father had ended his life at the end of a noose.

Until this moment, Kyril had lived out a mere dress rehearsal. Now he would step onto the real stage. He knew his lines. He would play out his future!

From the opposite window, he appraised Fifth Avenue to the east. Crowds were gathering, lining the street, men and women holding flags. Police had cordoned off the street. The absence of motorcars was highly unusual. Probably some kind of parade. But the notion of a parade bored him, and he let his eye wander up from the street to the majestic buildings that lined it. At once, his mood changed.

Marble palaces with imposing facades met his hungry eye, and he smiled. These were the palaces of the captains of industry, who ruled the New World. One day, he resolved, he would erect his own!

But . . . how to accomplish such exalted dreams? The mere price of this room in New York's most luxurious hotel was more than he could afford for long. He had only the Count's name and his case of jewels. What if nobody here was interested in Fabergé's craft or in the Russian gems that had been Malenkov's sole legacy from his past? The thought sent a chill through Kyril.

His attention was distracted by the sight below. Up Fifth Avenue marched a parade of women and uniformed soldiers waving banners. On the sidewalks, the crowd was cheering wildly, pressing forward. *What was this all about?*

His curiosity ignited, Kyril grabbed his coat and made for the elevator. Striding through the lobby, he emerged onto a crowded sidewalk. An elegant man in a bowler hat with a thick fur-trimmed coat was standing near the door. Kyril asked, his English tentative, "What's going on?"

The man frowned at him, perplexed. "You mean, you don't *know?*"

"I am not an American," Kyril replied.

"It's the Armistice!" cried the man. "The end of the war! Every-one is celebrating! I'm from Cleveland," he added, smiling. "I'm glad I'm in town for this. My boy fought in France! Came back with one leg shorter than the other—a bullet in his spine. He fought for his country. I'm damn proud of him."

Eyeing Kyril, he asked: "Didn't *you* fight?"

Kyril shrugged, overcome with sudden shame. "I am from Rus-sia," he explained. "For us, the war ended early. Lenin stopped it after he took over the government. I have pulmonary disease," he added, "and a heart condition."

The man didn't answer. He couldn't in any case, for the roar of the mob was deafening. The crowds were waving American flags and singing American songs. Kyril felt acutely uncomfortable. De-spite what he had told the man from Cleveland, Kyril himself knew why he hadn't fought in the war. He had not fought because he had not believed in it. Being the only son of a widow had been a conve-nient excuse—and it had exempted him from service. But he'd known all along that he didn't want to die in battle, not for Sarajevo nor for Russia.

Of course, the elegant man from Cleveland could not possibly have peered into Kyril's heart right at this very moment. But if he had, he would have seen the shadow of his shame.

Looking across the street at the happy faces of New York's cheer-ing patriots, Kyril remembered the argument he had had with Zica in her house in Moscow, about the war and commitment. Perhaps *she* had been right: though he was a Russian, he had turned his back upon his own country.

Without saying a word, Kyril wheeled about and retreated inside the Plaza. He had never wept for Russia, but now he wanted to. His beloved country, beset with wars and now with communism, ex-isted no more. It had been ransacked by Lenin and his band of hooligans! He would never set his eyes upon it again—of this he was certain.

In the elevator, thoughts of his family kept recurring to him. Even after he returned to his room, the memories continued to haunt him. He hadn't even written to his mother! He had aban-doned her. Nor had he tried to find her and his grandfather when news of the Revolution had broken. Other Russians had moved heaven and earth to locate missing relatives; yet he, who had known people of influence at the Quai d'Orsay, hadn't even bothered to do anything on behalf of his own mother . . . !

Now his mother was lost to him, like his country, like Zica, like

Laurent. He was alone in this strange new world of overgrown children, alone with his old shame and his new resolve.

He would turn his life around and become the success he knew he could be! He would do good things and redeem himself. He would think of others, minister to them, and he would love and be loved in return. Then, perhaps, one day he would have the courage to look for his family—and to face them without shame and anguish.

Was it too late? How could he begin to find his mother and grandfather again?

Correspondence with Russia was all but nonexistent. He might never set foot in his motherland again—might never see his mother. Yet he still had his own life. He could honor her by fashioning himself a code of ethics, and learning to live by its dictates.

A plan had formed. He would use Malenkov's name to gain entry into New York's cosmopolitan high society; but then he would create his own success. Thanks to the dead man, he had an important advantage; but that was all. In all other respects, he was still Kyril Ostrov, the orphan. And he was determined to bury this Ostrov forever. As Malenkov, he would be strong, good, and brave. He would make Russia proud of him—and his mother proud of him—though both worlds were now out of his reach.

Somewhere in the world, Zica existed. He was sure of it in his heart. He would keep alive the memory of her honesty. And he would bring honor to himself for her sake too, because she had loved him. He knew she would have wanted him to make something good of his own life.

Kyril lifted his jacket from the chair beside the dresser. From its breast pocket he withdrew Malenkov's passport and the entry papers from Ellis Island. In the passport he found what he was searching for—the list of names that Laurent de la Haye had given him. Five New York socialites.

The neatly folded vellum was embossed with the Renaissance dragon representing the De la Haye crest. Kyril read through the list. There were three men and two women. If they ever wrote to Laurent and thanked him for sending the charming, debonair Count Malenkov, friend of Tzar Nicholas, Laurent would certainly not disclaim his role. The real Malenkov knew Lorraine and her brother; Laurent would simply assume that his name had been used as an entrée. He would not waste time pondering the why's and wherefore's. Any acquaintanship with a Malenkov could only raise him in the sights of these New York socialites.

"Mr. Herbert Hauser, Fifth Avenue." Kyril mouthed the first name.

Then he gazed out his window toward the rococo palaces across the street. One of them belonged to the man with this name, *Herbert Hauser*. Kyril would call on him first.

The operator put him through quickly. Even before anyone answered, Kyril's heart began to pound very fast. An officious male voice announced, "Hauser residence: may I help you?" The voice had a lilting accent that Kyril had never encountered before.

"I need to speak to Mr. Hauser," Kyril declared. He could hear his own accent, very clearly Russian. It sounded exotic and pleasant, and also a bit brutal and masculine. It was good: he would impress the Americans with his Russian ways, and they would adopt him readily.

"Whom may I say is calling?" the manservant asked.

"Tell him I am Count Kyril Vadimovitch Malenkov," Kyril declared. "Tell him Count Laurent de la Haye, of Paris and Biarritz, told me to telephone with his compliments. I have just arrived from France."

"Very well, sir. Hold on, please."

Kyril began to panic. He had given this butler too much information, betraying that he was nervous and apprehensive.

A horrible thought occurred to him. *What if Hauser had already met Kyril Malenkov?* But Kyra had told him that he had never been to the United States. Still . . . Hauser might have met him while travelling through Europe.

"Hello?" A low voice with a nasal twang came on the line.

"Mr. Hauser? My name is Count Kyril Malenkov, of St. Petersburg . . . Petrograd. My friend, the Comte de la Haye, recommended that I call you. I am afraid I know no one in this city." Polite, yet self-confident, Kyril sounded to himself like a real aristocrat accustomed to having doors opened to him.

Hauser's voice warmed. "Laurent? How *is* the old boy? Well, well—haven't heard from that family in years! And you're a Russian? Malenkov, did you say?"

"Yes, sir: Malenkov."

"Of all the funny things! Just last week, my friend, Anna Voorhies, was wondering what had happened to all of you in the Revolution. She mentioned some names, and yours was one of them. D'you know Anna?"

"No, sir, I'm afraid I don't. Although perhaps she knew my parents."

"Ah! Of course! You must be a young man, like Laurent! And I am old as the hills. So is my friend Anna. Ah, well... so much for friends. Tell me, young man, where are you staying?"

"I'm at the Plaza temporarily," Kyril answered. "Of course, I shall have to find myself a permanent suite before long."

"Look," Hauser said, "I'm just half a block down from you. Tonight, I'm giving a dinner dance for little Jennie Arnold, the opera singer. Would you come? My guests would love to meet a genuine Russian lord. You would be a hit! What do you say? Cocktails will be at seven-thirty—black tie, of course. You did bring a tuxedo, didn't you? Or did the Bolsheviks take all your clothes away, as well?" Hauser's rumbling laughter echoed over the line.

"Yes sir, that would be fine. I think, yes, I have my tuxedo with me. Seven-thirty."

"Okay... you'll have a good time. New York is a fine place to be when you're young. The girls are pretty. You'll like Jennie, especially. She sings like a nightingale, and she's as pretty as a picture. So it's arranged: you'll be here tonight for my little *do,* and we can talk some more about Laurent."

After Hauser had hung up, Kyril sat for a moment with the receiver in his hand, sweat pouring from his forehead. Thank God that was over—and he had performed well. Hauser had been convinced. So much that Kyril had been invited *for that very evening!*

Suddenly, relief gave way to exhilaration. Somewhere in Malenkov's bag was a tuxedo. He would call the hotel staff and arrange to have it pressed, and to have the frilled shirt starched. He would have a splendid time, flirting with the opera singer and old Madame Voorhies, whoever she was. Surely she was important, if she was familiar with the Tzar's acquaintances. Kyril would convince her that he was Kyra Malenkov. She would adopt him for the sake of Countess Malenkova, Kyra's mother... *his* mother now—and old Count Vadim, *his* father.

He would so charm the guests of Mr. Hauser that the old man would certainly take Kyril under his wing. Perhaps Hauser would give him a job with his company—or maybe he would help Kyril sell the Count's jewels. However it worked out, Kyril would come out a winner—that much closer to having his own house on Fifth Avenue.

If only Zica could witness all this, he thought, yearning for someone to share his excitement. He now longed for her.

I must not think of Zica, nor of the past, he admonished himself. *This is the New World, and I am about to conquer it.*

Kyril glanced at the clock on the mantelpiece, and sighed. It was time to take a warm bath and soak all regret from his aching muscles. It no longer mattered who Kyril Ostrov had left behind, nor whom he missed. Kyril Ostrov was gone, replaced instead by Count Malenkov.

Zica dropped the scrub brush into the wooden basin. It bounced off the metal ridges of the washboard. She shook her wet hands in the sunlight, wiped them quickly on a threadbare towel, and hastened to the window. Eagerly, she slipped the rusty latch from its hook and pushed the panes apart. Tucking her skirt under her knees, she wedged herself on the window seat to observe the scene below her.

Somewhere far off, above the din of Essex Street, strains of band music reached her ears. Zica thought she recognized "The Long, Long Trail." A sudden hunger seized her—how she wished she could grab the baby and push her way to Fifth Avenue! She longed to join the parades celebrating the return of America's heroes from the European front! Makeshift shrines had been set up all along the Avenue. There was a plaster arch at Madison Square, and, farther north, near the Public Library, the Court of the Heroic Dead, a monument of pylons and palm trees. The sight of that monument had moved her in spite of its grotesque appearance. Seeing that monument, she had thought how America's pride in its own contrasted with the shame of the disbanded Russian army—betrayed by Lenin when he had signed the separate peace treaty at Brest-Litovsk the previous March.

She was a Russian no more. The Russia of her youth did not exist any more, and the Soviet Union meant nothing to her but deprivation, enslavement and murder. She was grateful for the fresh start America had offered her and Yasha.

Their life had been hard in America, and at times they suffered desperately in their noisy, crowded lodgings. But already she loved the spirit of this new land. Americans were a noisy lot, but they were free and full of life.

Zica sat on the ledge and smiled, suddenly as happy as a little girl. She gloried in the noise and confusion that filled the busy intersection of Hester and Essex Streets. She loved to watch the vendors calling out their wares as they set up their carts along the sidewalk. The squalid conditions in which she and Yasha lived mattered little to her; it was the bustle of the street that she liked.

She saw Katya Silverman crossing the street, holding her small son's hand. Katya was Russian, but she spoke mostly Yiddish, which Zica did not understand. She'd come to America some years ago from her *shtetl* near Vitebsk, and had met Manny Silverman, a German Jew, who had made the crossing to New York a year before Katya. Now they were married; neither spoke the native language to the other, but that didn't seem to matter because both spoke Yiddish, the language most often heard on Essex Street. Zica felt embarrassed because she had never learned it.

Yakov, on the other hand, had been reared in the bastard dialect of the Jews; routinely, he conversed in it with everyone, making people laugh. She was pleased that people liked him so much and found him so funny and companionable. But she felt timid, because she alone could not understand Yiddish. She blushed a lot and smiled a lot, but she was tongue-tied around Katya and Manny Silverman and Aron and Rose Nimoy, all of whom were her age, all of whom were married with small children. She spoke Russian to those who could speak it, and Katya was the nicest girl on the block . . . but she knew that as soon as her back was turned, they would comment on the fact that she was a *barinya,* a girl from high society, one of the ones who had had everything while the rest had starved and lived in hovels in their *shtetls.* It wasn't her fault; she never spoke about her Poliakov family, and never boasted about the past. But somehow, people *knew.* They knew, and they were wary, whereas they treated Yasha like one of the boys, a regular fellow with whom to smoke on the stoop and to share a glass of vodka when the sun went down. Zica was the outsider.

But when the landlord came round, they came to her door and asked her to speak to him in her good, though clipped, English. She spoke like a lady, saying, "Please, Mr. Netter, Aron promises to have the money by Tuesday. Please, Mr. Netter, let Manny bring you the last five dollars tomorrow. It's been a hard month, Mr. Netter. Milk costs fifteen cents a quart, and eggs have gone up to sixty-two cents a dozen. It's very hard, Mr. Netter. My husband won't be paid till the end of the week, and our baby needs her milk . . ."

Mr. Netter was a Jew like the rest of them, but he wore a gold fob watch with a chain extending from one vest pocket to the other, and carried a silver walking stick with a carved lion's head for a knob, and he liked to smack his red, moist lips, like a wolf on the prowl. Zica would speak for all of them, and he would watch her, his watery eyes narrowed to slits, his breath smelling of brine, until she had finished. No matter what she said, his eyes would always be narrowed, aiming a foot below her face. And she would blush, and place an awkward hand over her collarbone, her breath coming in short, hard gasps. He would let her speak on and then, most often, grant the offending tenant a brief—ever so brief!—reprieve.

But sometimes he didn't. He'd thrown the Zeligs out of their miserable one-bedroom flat, because Izzy Zelig had been laid off at the factory and had been two weeks late with the rent. One afternoon, Zica had come home from her errands and had found the apartment across the hall vacated, the front door wide open. She looked in and saw Mr. Netter fingering his gold fob and smiling, his red lips glistening, his nostrils flaring in and out. "Well, well, well," he had intoned, his eyes resting on Zica's shirt front, "it looks as though you're going to have new neighbors, Mrs. Pokhis. *Solvent* new neighbors, who don't leave their landlord high and dry, like the last. . . ." And he'd added, seriously, opening those watery orbs and looking at Zica's face for a change: "I'm sure *you* understand, dear Mrs. Pokhis. . . . Mr. Netter has a family to support. Just like the rest of you. Mrs. Netter has to buy butter at sixty-one cents a pound, and sirloin steak at forty-two. . . ." He'd mocked her openly then, and she had felt the hatred inside her welling up like a tidal wave.

Mr. Netter was the sort of Jew whom her father, Lazar Poliakov, had most despised—the kind who gave his co-religionists a bad name and engendered gentile prejudice. He was that oily, uneducated *nouveau-riche* Jew who has bribed or cheated his way into money, and who uses his new-found power to crush his better brothers. Such Jews, Baron Poliakov had often asserted, were the most dangerous: for their ruthlessness was based on fear, on the fear of losing their money and having to regress to the squalor of their origins. They didn't give anyone else a chance to get a foot up in life, for fear that another's rise, another's success, might threaten their own safety and comfort.

But there was nothing the Pokhises could do about Mr. Netter. Thank God, Yakov was almost never late with the rent. He was managing Yossif Byitch's pawnshop up the road, on Hester Street, and was paid a percentage of the profits. He hated his job and was growing to hate the old man for keeping him down, for not having advanced him the money to get a decent apartment in a decent part of town. But Zica didn't mind. Elena was good to her, almost like a mother, and, after all, the old man, Yossif Adolfovitch, had made it possible for them to escape from Communist Russia and come to America. It was up to them, the young people, to make it on their own. At least Yasha had a job, and if he hated bartering with tired old Jews and weeping, dispossessed women, he was, nonetheless, more fortunate than Aron Nimoy who worked in a fish store ten hours a day, and Katya's husband Manny, who worked in a badly lit shoe factory packing boxes. Yakov was a *manager,* and, in truth, it was he who ran the business and made it prosper.

"But we didn't come to America to live this way!" he would complain. His bitterness was palpable, hanging in the air like kitchen smells. "I didn't come here to barter like a fishmonger with every *schlemiel* who has something to hock. I—"

"What *did* you come here for, Yasha?"

"I came to become *someone!* I came to make money and buy a house with a garden for my daughter. I didn't marry you to have you take in laundry—other people's laundry!—in order to make ends meet! That old man promised me a slice of the action, a piece of the pie—and he lives in a lovely large apartment overlooking Washington Square, while *we* live *here!* Junior partner, indeed! The business is in his name alone, and I fell for the line he handed me in Rostov and *believed* him, for God's sake! What a fool you must think me, Zica!"

"But you are *not* a fool," Zica answered Yakov. "You are the man who saved my life—the man who runs Yossif Adolfovitch's business. He considers you both smart and trustworthy. No, Yasha, you are no fool."

To Zica, truly, her own dreams had become one with those of her husband. She was proud of Yakov—proud that he was the father of her baby. And he was a hero—though not a vain one! He had taken her out of Russia just in time and had brought her to safety. True, she didn't love him the way Katya loved Manny, blushing every time he looked at her, holding hands with him beneath the dinner table. But what was that—only silly, young love, fresh but untested. And, yes, Zica had known that giddy kind of love. She had been artfully wooed and loved; she had been crushed to someone's chest, had made abandoned love with frenzied passion. Like Russia, this was best forgotten; it had no part in her present life.

From the crib, two-month-old Victoria began to cry. It was a tiny bleat. As always, Zica felt a thrill of joy when she heard her daughter. She went to the crib and gently lifted her out. Her diaper was wet and smelled of ammonia. Zica brought her to the table and undid the pins, throwing the dirty cotton diaper into the washbasin. She cleaned off the baby, rubbing the tiny round stomach lovingly, and fitted her with a fresh diaper.

Cradling Victoria, Zica returned to the window seat where she settled comfortably, crooning to the infant. She spoke in English: "See the street below? See the old Hassid with his long black beard? See the little boy near the orange stand? Once, long ago, Mama lived in a very pretty house in a faraway land, and Mama used to sit on a window seat and watch what was happening in a magic fortress called the Kremlin. But that was a long time ago, Victoria. Now Mama is a grown woman, and the Kremlin is full of very bad and dangerous people."

Suddenly Zica could no longer hear the band playing. She remembered all the laundry still to wash. Lifting Vickie high in the air, she murmured: "Mama has work now, *detochka*. Mama must put you down."

She would not get to visit the library and the Court of the Heroic Dead today, nor tomorrow. Doing laundry brought in money, and the rent was due the fifteenth of the month.

Kyril stepped onto the marble terrace and peered out at the placid waters of Newport harbor. The June sun shone through puffy white clouds, its rays making the waves glisten like lacquer. He breathed in the salt air and closed his eyes, savoring being a guest of honor in the fashionable resort during the height of "the season."

How much had happened since the previous November, when he'd first arrived in New York! He recalled the party at Herbert Hauser's Fifth Avenue mansion as the magic turning point. There he had met beautiful women in low-cut gowns drinking champagne, all of them curious about "poor Nicky and Alix"—Tzar Nicholas and Tzarina Alexandra, executed in a cellar in Ekaterinburg in July 1918. He had met blunt, plain-spoken financiers and intellectuals who wanted to ask him about the Soviets, to find out from a real expatriate whether they were actually a threat to the United States. Speaking in his halting English, he had held their full attention while they drank in his words. Amazing what prestige he had, just being "associated" with the Imperial Family of Tzarist Russia! The Americans had absorbed his words like hungry sharks. Truly, he might have told them *anything*—anything at all, spinning them a tall yarn if he had felt like it. They would still have nodded, their eyes widened with naive credulity.

He had become Count Kyril Malenkov. It wasn't a role now any-more: he had grown into the man himself. At first he'd felt uncom-fortable with his lie, but eventually he had accepted his fate philosophically. These people wouldn't have given Kyril Ostrov the time of day. As Kyril Ostrov he would have starved, but as Count Malenkov, he had become one of the most sought-after bachelors in New York.

As for Herbert Hauser, the old man had accepted Kyril as Kyra Malenkov without a moment's hesitation. His friend, Anna Voor-hies, had scrutinized Kyril's face, quickly found a resemblance to Count Malenkov's mother, and had nodded with great sadness. On the ship, the real Kyra had talked about his parents, and Kyril had remembered every detail. So he had spun his tall yarn, and Anna's eyes had filled with tears as she listened to him recount their dra-matic murders. He had sighed as he told about the desecration of his palace on the Nevsky Prospect and mourned the loss of his estate in the Crimea. And he had wept openly at the mention of his wife, Lara, who had died of pneumonia in Finland two years before. Anna Voorhies had embraced him and patted him on the back, mur-muring "Poor child . . . ," and shaking her magnificent head of curls. She had believed every word.

Hauser was visibly moved. As Kyril concluded his tale, his host had coughed delicately and led him resolutely toward a group of his nearest and dearest friends. "Let me introduce you to my young friend Count Kyril Malenkov," he said to them. "Kyra was lucky enough to escape the Bolshevik massacre, but I'm afraid his family fared much worse. He needs champagne and some good cheer, and I'll leave him to you!"

And so the change of identity had worked like magic. Anna Voorhies and Herbert Hauser had opened every door for him. The day after the party, three well-heeled ladies in fur coats and elegant hats had appeared at the Plaza Hotel to take a look at his cache of jewels. He had regretfully parted with one ten-carat emerald ring, a pair of pearl-drop earrings with diamond studs, and a bracelet con-taining seven gold chains dotted with lapis lazuli, rubies, and pearls. Three days later, Hauser himself had purchased a platinum brooch covered with pavé diamonds "for a lady friend." Later, a wealthy industrialist came to take a quick look on behalf of his wife and daughter; he'd left with a sapphire necklace for the former, and a small Fabergé egg for the latter. In a single week, Herbert Hauser had enabled Kyril to net more money than he had ever dreamt of.

He had moved out of the Plaza Hotel into a flat on Central Park

West, overlooking the Park. Not the most prestigious location, but one which Hauser's friends found perfectly acceptable. He was pitied. Anna Voorhies sighed for him. And pity had served him well. Jennie Arnold, the *diva* nightingale, had sent him an antique dresser that she thought might suit his taste. Mrs. Tulliver, the young woman who had purchased the ten-carat emerald, had sent him her *maître d'hôtel's* brother-in-law, Oliver Mason, to become Kyril's butler. She said he was a "top-notch butler, a real gentleman's gentleman, recommended by none other than Prince Christophe of Greece—you know, he married the Leeds widow from Cincinnati...?"

Kyril had never heard of the Leeds widow, but he did have enough presence of mind to be dismayed at the notion of how much a gentleman's gentleman might cost. On the other hand, if he wished to be accepted by New York's elite, he had to have a suitable servant. Oliver Mason was tall, angular, and perfectly groomed. After an hour's interview with the man, Kyril concluded that the butler would be a great asset, teaching him society English, and improving his manners. So he took him on. He showed Oliver Mason the naked apartment on Central Park West with its lone Chippendale dresser in the master bedroom. "The Count mustn't be concerned," Mason told him, surveying the rooms. "Tomorrow I shall take care of everything."

Kyril shuddered, remembering the lavish winter garden inside Herbert Hauser's house, a garden replete with indoor trellises and exotic plants. He thought of the priceless Persian carpets, the polished sideboards and the gilt mirrors. He could afford none of these. If Mason went on a spending spree, the sale of the jewels and the egg would be consumed by antique furnishings. "Mason," he said, licking his dry lips, "I am new here, a refugee. I... well, it is not the same for me as for Madame Tulliver. In Petersburg, life was... things were... different. *Here,* I am a refugee. I am without... *property.*"

Kyril found himself sweating, his cheeks aflame. Mason coughed delicately; his grave, dark eyes fastened on his master. "The Count means that he has not yet *established* himself, and is concerned about, *ahem*... his *situation*. But of course, sir, I understand. Of course, it would be desirable to have a chef and a sous-chef, a scullery maid, and perhaps a chauffeur to add to the Count's *staff*. But one realizes that is *impossible*." Mason had the habit of emphasizing certain words, almost invariably the ones that were fear-inspiring. Sighing, the butler shook his head. "Later, when the count shall be *settled,* we shall worry about his *staff."*

Kyril had handed the man a wad of bills, without counting. But Mason shook his long bony head, very gently. "The Count shall be *billed,* of *course.* Tomorrow I shall open an account at the Chase National Bank. In Russia, perhaps the custom of *billing* was not yet common practice...?"

"Oh, yes, yes," Kyril had demurred, his face turning red. He had added with forced bravura: "I did not know if, in *America,* stores were accustomed to billing their patrons."

"I understand the Russians are *insular,* your Excellency. One bills *everywhere* in the *civilized world....* " Mason had the habit of letting his sentences trail off until only their essence hung in the air, like the Cheshire Cat's disquieting smile. Kyril, thus reproved, had been only too eager to send the man on his errands. He prayed that the new butler would not *bill,* in a single afternoon, more than the income from the Tulliver emerald. Kyril had hoped to live modestly on the income from this single gem for at least a year.

Kyril spent a few nights at the Brevoort Hotel on lower Fifth Avenue (more modestly priced than the Plaza) while the new apartment was being furnished. He returned to find the apartment vastly improved. The moldings had been replaced in the Wedgewood style. Hardwood floors had been polished to perfection, tiny Persian rugs scattered artfully about the rooms. Oliver Mason had furnished the apartment in the French neo-classic style of the late eighteenth century. There were oval-backed chairs, a "confidante" sofa with its angle seats at either end, and a commode of veneered satinwood. Kyril's heart sank as he surveyed the splendor.

"Mason," his voice sounded hoarse. "This is very nice. Very... elegant. You went to too much trouble."

"I am glad your Excellency approves of my taste. I...uh... attempted to remain within the *boundaries* prescribed by the Count. The moldings were touched up by an Italian-American painter I have sometimes had occasion to employ."

"And...the furniture? Madame Voorhies mentioned a *Sotheby? Southbee?"* Kyril's heart was pounding.

The gentleman's gentleman smiled, his long face lighting up. "Ah, the Count flatters me! These are not, of course, the *real thing.* I know some excellent craftsmen—European immigrants of the *highest talent*—and I purchased these reproductions from their workshops. Your Excellency *approves,* then...?"

Relief flooded through Kyril. He could have embraced this man for his tact. "Well, Mason," he declared, with an elaborate gesture, "what is there *not* to approve?"

Thus Count Kyril Malenkov prepared his stage, from which he had taken New York by storm. The lucky young man forbore to tell his butler that this was the first real apartment he had ever possessed, for his student rooms in Paris hardly counted. *What luxury!* After Mason excused himself, he had gone from chair to sofa to sideboard, running his fingers along the woodwork, touching the soft velvet cushions. These pieces belonged to *him,* to Kyril Ostrov, the son of a poverty-stricken widow!

What a strange route his life had taken, Kyril thought. He wondered how he might have fared if he had never encountered Lorraine de Huitton. Would another *grande dame* have swooped him up from his student's garret—or would he have succeeded on his wits alone, remaining in France to become established as a doctor? None of that mattered now. The past was the past. *Kyril Ostrov died on Ellis Island. Long live his Excellency, Count Malenkov!*

Now, on the terrace above Newport harbor, Kyril was jolted from his reflections by the arrival of Elsie Tulliver, his hostess. He smiled, his eyes lingering on her delicate face and violet eyes. "I was just admiring the view from your beautiful home."

"It *is* lovely, isn't it?" She looked out to sea, her dainty hands grasping the wrought-iron railing. For one instant, Kyril thought to place his palm over her hand. She was beautiful, like a small doll. She had smoky gray eyes, translucent skin, and glistening brown hair that swept low on her forehead, covering her ears.

Seven months in New York had taught Kyril that American women were unlike the French. Whereas a French woman considered a man a boor if he *failed* to flirt with her, in America a married woman belong to her husband. Even a lingering look could be taken for a sign of boorishness.

And Elsie Tulliver was *very* married. The wife of an industrialist, she was also the mother of a three-year-old girl named Consuelo. Kyril judged Mrs. Tulliver to be about twenty-four or twenty-five.

"Mr. Tulliver will not be coming today?" Kyril inquired.

Elsie sighed. "I'm afraid not. You see, Henry works very hard. He can only come on weekends. I wish—"

"Yes?"

"I wish that things could go back to the way they were, when we were courting." Elsie Tulliver's voice trembled slightly. "He had just graduated from Yale when we met. I was home after two years in a Swiss finishing school. We fell in love here, in Newport, at the home of Mrs. Vanderbilt. He came to me each day, with flowers and funny little poems. Now... well, now we are an old married couple, Count Malenkov, and we must be *responsible.*" She tossed the word off with acrimony. Kyril knew instantly, by her intonation, the word was Henry Tulliver's, not hers—and that she loathed it.

"You *will* come and play tennis with us on the lawn, in half an hour?" she asked, resuming a pleasant, conversational manner. "My cousin absolutely demanded that you join her in a game of doubles against me and my sister. The weeks grow so long here, my dear Count. You must realize what a valuable companion you are to us. We have all become quite fond of you, I must admit."

Her eyes were twinkling. Kyril laughed, feeling at ease in her company. She was simple, amusing and uncomplicated. She added, somewhat anxiously: "Are you quite pleased with Mason? If you're not—"

"—Oh, but I am, I am! Mason is what you call a para... a parag..."

"A paragraph?" she supplied with incredulity.

"A *paragon!* He takes care of me better than my mother ever did."

"Tell me about your mother."

"I'm sorry," he said, looking at her gravely. "I'm afraid that would be difficult. My mother was murdered by the Bolsheviks. I cannot think of her without remembering—everything. Please forgive me, dear Mrs. Tulliver, but I cannot."

"I'm terribly sorry." Her gray eyes were full of compassion—so much so, that for a moment Kyril felt an acute sense of shame. She added softly: "Everyone in your family is gone, I hear. I wish... I wish there were a way to make the loneliness less acute..."

The truth of what she was saying went beyond her understanding. Yes, it was true. His family was gone. His loneliness was a presence, a living shadow attached to his being. Perhaps his mother and Yossif Adolfovitch Byitch were dead. No news of them had ever reached him.

"Thank you for your kind words," he replied, trying to shake the sorrow from his spirit. Resolutely, he brightened. "Please tell your cousin that of course I shall partner her in the doubles. In this way, I shall be forced to look at you all through my game, my dear Mrs. Tulliver!"

She was blushing, but he knew he had not offended her. She even laughed, shaking her head. "Oh, goodness!" she exclaimed. "I've let the time pass, and have forgotten to speak to the cook about tea! Shall we go in now?"

"Perhaps I'll stay out here for a few more minutes," Kyril said to her. "If you do not object...?"

As she turned to leave, he could not help turning around to watch her. Elsie Tulliver was not only a pretty woman, she was a consummate hostess. But she was out of bounds, sealed off by her marriage vows.

Kyril sighed. No, he would not trouble to court her, however delicately she complained about her husband's neglect. He knew all too well the danger, and he did not intend to be *blackballed* from her world. *That* was a word he knew in all its ugly strength. He knew he would hear that word yet again if he yielded to his appetites. No! This time, he would keep a rein on himself. He would remain blameless!

Elsie Tulliver, sweet as she might be, was a bauble he would have to give up. And he could do so with hardly a second thought.

Breathing in the fresh salt air, Kyril followed her steps to the house.

Chapter XV

*A*s the subway roared through the dark tunnel, Yakov felt the sharp impact as the man standing beside him was thrown against his shoulder. In the close confines of the packed subway car, the acrid stench of day-old perspiration assailed his nostrils. His pores were clogged with the dusty grime that seemed to cover New York.

It was seven o'clock. Yakov was hungry and bone-weary.

It was the end of another year, however, and business was booming. Yossif Byitch had bought the entire building on Hester Street and had set up a wholesale jewelry business next to the pawnshop. All day long, old women in threadbare black shawls pressed their liver-spotted knuckles toward Yakov, begging, "Please, give me a good price for this sapphire ring! It belonged to my grandmother." Or, "This was my engagement ring, but I have no use for it here. In the Crimea, when I was young..."

Many told the same stories, whether they hailed from Turkey or Italy, from Russia or Germany. They had all known much better days. They spoke of their pasts wistfully, their old eyes half-closed, entranced by memories. For most of them, America had proved a bitter disappointment, yet none spoke of returning to the countries from which they had come. Many were like Elena Ostrova, who discoursed on her glamorous life in Rostov for days on end, her voice breaking at dramatic moments. But Yakov knew that, in fact, Elena's life had been sad and lonely. Here, at least, she had friends who shared the same existence which she was so constantly bemoaning.

The year 1920, now almost over, had been a momentous one for the United States. In the summer, the Volstead Act had initiated

Prohibition. The nation had been divided into two camps—the "Drys," who favored the act, and the "Wets," who called it an infringement on personal liberty. The presidential election had effectively decided the issue. On November 3, the nation had elected handsome Ohio Senator Warren Gamaliel Harding, a Republican "dry," over another Ohioan, Governor James M. Cox, a Democratic "wet." The vote had been sixteen million to nine million.

Yakov marvelled at this. Russia was so different from this nation of children! They worried about drinking, when in Russia, you worried about the boot-thumping arrival of the Cossacks. Here women went on hunger strikes in order to be given the vote—whereas in Minsk, Pinsk, or Odessa, voting was a fairy tale.

As the subway car came to a screeching halt, Yakov was thrown forward. People pressed from behind, urging him to get out. But this wasn't his stop. He saw an old man leave his seat and elbowed his way over, reaching the vacant seat a split-second before a large, fat man with an unlit cigar. Yakov sank down between a pregnant woman and an old man who smelled of raw onions. Crossing herself, the pregnant woman raised her eyes to the ceiling of the metal car and whispered, "Santa Maria, Santa Maria . . ."

Yakov felt a wave of pity. Seeing a pregnant woman reminded him of Zica during that dreadful time when they had been fleeing from the CHEKA. All pregnant women seemed to have that look of resolution on their faces: whatever happened, *they were going to have the baby.*

Zica had not given up—not for an instant. His hothouse princess, his Muscovite baroness, had stood beside Yakov: it was she who had held his hand and urged him forward. How much their relationship had changed! Now they were comfortable with each other. Little Vickie was beautiful—a happy, irrepressible child who delighted in baby dolls made out of colored rag clothing and laughing when her father teased her.

Yakov felt a surge of pride as he thought about the house that he now owned. It was in Brooklyn, beyond Washington Square, well removed from the center of Manhattan. The bank owned most of it and Yossif Byitch a part. But still, Yakov and Zica thought of that house as *theirs.*

Of course, Zica had lived in a palace. Yakov knew it couldn't compare. But for him, the little house on Midwood Street—with its pretty front lawn dressed up in bright flowers, was a world away from the *shtetl* he had known. Thinking of his past life, he was sometimes struck with awe. He had married the princess of his dreams, his *barinya!* He had a daughter and a little house. Now he was gong to be a real American living with people he loved, moving forward toward a gilded dream of fame and fortune.

But until fortune came, life continued in the big city. Every morning and night he rode the crowded subway, in the midst of this bustling nation filled with orphans.

Yakov pulled the rolled-up tabloid from under his arm and spread it over his knee. He never had time to read the paper at home or at work. He was always busy. Yakov detested his job. But he was grateful to be able to pay the mortgage and the installments on his bedroom furniture. He had even bought a washing machine for Zica.

Though he chafed under the tutelage of the old man, Yakov knew that without Yossif's help he'd still be living in the tenement on Essex Street, always fearing a call from Mr. Netter.

Yakov read The New York *Daily News* to improve his English, memorizing any new words he came across. And his English *was* improving. Zica said she was proud of how well he could speak. "Like a real American," she told him in her neat, clipped British English, with its lilting Russian rhythm.

His eyes scanned the headlines. There was news about the Hardings, and the President-elect's campaign promise to bring the country back to an era of "normalcy." In France, Alexandre Millerand had taken the Presidency over from Paul Deschanel, who was now in a mental institution. The poor man had gone mad.

Yakov smiled and opened to another page at random. It was, he discovered ruefully, the society page—which Zica liked more than any other. Yakov could not have cared less about the glittering life of Manhattan society—he was about to turn the page when suddenly he froze, staring at a two-column society photo. The photograph portrayed a young man by the side of a very old lady with the Metropolitan Opera House in the background.

The caption read: "Count Kyril Vadimovitch Malenkov and his Manhattan mentor, Mrs. Anna Voorhies." The old woman was bedecked in furs and pearls. The young man had his hand beneath her elbow, as he was helping her into a taxicab. He was wearing a tuxedo and smiling mischievously. He almost seemed to wink at the camera.

It was Kyril Ostrov, beyond a doubt. But this was a new Kyril, resplendent in his finery, his light hair gleaming. He appeared to radiate success. Kyril's large, almond-shaped eyes held Yakov's attention like a magnetic spell. What had he done to attain the height of this fantasy?

Yakov remembered how they had met in the lobby of another glittering opera house, in the heart of Moscow. He recalled when he had recognized that Kyril was Zica's suitor—and had wanted to hate him. And instead, he'd come away liking Kyril.

Closing the tabloid Yakov tucked it under his arm. All at once he was very weary from his day's work, from his long trudge to the subway station. Why did Kyril Ostrov have to appear again? The very Kyril whom Zica had loved with all her heart. And how did she love her husband? She was so quiet, so reserved. She seemed grateful and happy, but perhaps that was only because he was Vickie's father. There was contentment in her face now. But the look she had borne then, seven years ago, during Ostrov's courtship of her, had been a look of rapture.

Would that rapture return if she saw him again?

Yakov felt the blood pounding at his temples. He was trembling with anger. Wasn't Kyril a *murderer?* What other conclusion could anyone draw from that encounter on Ellis Island? Yet, now, the murderer paraded up and down Manhattan, using his victim's name and title! *Dear God,* Yakov prayed, *I hope Zica hasn't seen the paper today!* For Yakov knew she would recognize Kyril in spite of the name and in spite of the ridiculous title.

And what would she do then? Yakov wondered. *What would Zica decide to do if she knew that Kyril was in this very city?*

No! She must not find out!

Pausing in her daily walk with Vickie, Zica would step up to the small shop and look in, with one hand pressed against the windowpane, the other clutching the tiny hand of her little daughter. "Look, Vickie," she would say. "Look at the pretty ladies inside!"

Holding the child about the waist, Zica would lift her up to show her the magnificent interior of the hair-dressing parlor. Through the window mother and daughter gazed at the operators with their shears and curling irons, the row of seated women beneath bell-like hair dryers.

Vickie didn't think they were pretty at all. She shrugged and wiggled free. She wanted to continue to the subway station, where they went every night to meet her father. It was a ritual with them each afternoon: Zica's stop outside the hair-dressing parlor, and Vickie's eager dash to the "magic tunnel" which brought her father back to her each night. Even though he wasn't due home for hours, and Zica would explain this, the little girl kept hoping that this time, he might come early.

Once, while serving Yakov his supper, Zica had told him she wanted to cut her hair. To her surprise he had been adamantly opposed. "You are not a woman of today, Zica," he said. "Your hair is beautiful just as it is. You are a real woman. Why would you wish to have short hair and resemble a man?"

"You're being unfair, Yasha. I am as much a . . . a modern woman as . . . Rosalind!"

He knit his brow. "Who's that?" he asked.

She sighed. How could she explain? "I have been reading a book by Scott Fitzgerald," she explained. "There is a debutante in the novel—*her* name is Rosalind." She took *This Side of Paradise* from the single half-empty bookshelf and handed it to him. "I'm young, too," she added, her voice taking on a resolute tone. "But old enough to make up my own mind!"

Zica had felt wounded by Yakov's indifference. It sometimes seemed that he didn't even try to understand her. He had married her during a time of trouble; now, triumphant, he kept her sealed off from other people, like a treasured *objet d'art* displayed behind glass. She had liked the hustle and bustle of Manhattan, even though they had been poor. She detested Brooklyn. It didn't matter that they owned their own house. She felt isolated and forgotten in this ancient neighborhood of neat brick homes, among little old ladies and working class shopgirls with bright red rouge on their cheek bones. She missed Katya Silverman and Rose Nimoy, her old neighbors. Here, there was no one at all but Vickie.

Did Yakov believe he *owned* her? She remembered a conversation with Lena Ostrova, who had been speaking of her late husband. "He was a liar, a cheat, and a vulgar, loud-mouthed boor, but he was all I had. My family would have nothing to do with me. A Jew married to a Cossack! I was ostracized by everyone." Zica felt the anger rising within her as she thought: So it is with me. Yasha is all I have. But why? Something is missing. I know he loves me—but why does his love feel like a trap to me now?

Lately, she had been weeping in bed, late at night—she had wiped her tears silently with the back of her hand. She wept at the trap she had been caught in. Worst of all was the feeling that she *should* have been happy with the man she loved in so many ways— as a brother, a friend, a companion. Why, then, did she feel such desolation at times?

Only Sundays were different for her—so different that she longed for the end of every week, just to share that day with him. On Sundays he listened to the radio while she sat beside him sewing. Sometimes they went to the neighborhood theater to see the latest two-reeler from Charlie Chaplin, or Ben Turpin as an athletic, cross-eyed Keystone Kop. Yakov loved the comics; he watched the screen intently, studying the antics of these great comedians, while she sat back and laughed. And when they came home, still laughing at the slapstick scenes and funny lines, they would play with Victoria, enjoying her chortling joy even more than the cinema.

But Yakov would grow sour and resentful in a moment. He didn't like Lena and Yossif Adolfovitch; he resented their wealth and he wasn't grateful for their help in buying the house. Yakov, Zica realized, wanted to *be* something else: he wanted to *be* Ben Turpin or Charles Chaplin. (How intently he would watch the screen, memorizing every move they made, every mad antic!) Zica's needs were simpler, perhaps, but just as hard to fulfill. She wanted to have friends, to go dancing. She wanted to take long walks in the park, to giggle, gossip, and tell her friends stories, as she and Tamara always had in Moscow. You didn't need a lot of money to have nice friends! To Zica it seemed odd that Yakov kept to himself. He didn't seem to want or need close friends. Zica remembered Senya, the librarian: her husband had been close to him. But then again, Senya had been more of a teacher than a real friend.

Sometimes Zica wished that she could leave home every day and go to work. She had read articles by prominent women who believed that a woman could hold a job outside the home, even if she wasn't pressed for money. But the question remained—what job? She wasn't prepared to follow any particular trade. But then again, she reflected, she hadn't been prepared for the Revolution, for rearing a child, for doing her own dishes and cooking her family's meals. The real obstruction was that Yakov would never allow her to work in a store or an office. He would think her crazy.

More and more often she felt as if she and her husband were two strangers living in the same house, creating a future that only *he* wanted.

And what did *Zica* want? She didn't have a ready answer.

Feeling guilty about her hidden thoughts, she moved into the tiny foyer and picked up her heavy coat and Vickie's tiny one. Calling out to her daughter, she bundled Vickie into her wrap, like candy in cellophane. "Ready for a special treat?" she asked.

"Soklit cake?"

"No, darling, not *that* kind of a treat," Zica laughed, opening the front door. "This one's a treat for Mommy. Vickie gets to watch Mommy have her hair cut."

"Mommy cut 'air?"

Zica laughed as she gulped in the cold, crisp atmosphere. But her laughter sounded nervous and hesitant.

Zica grabbed Vickie's hand more tightly as they approached the steps of the hair-dressing parlor.

"Go in?" Vickie asked.

"Mommy and Vickie can go in now," Zica replied.

The young, red-haired woman behind the small counter looked up from her register and smiled. "What may we do for you, Ma'am?" Her cheeks were rouged and she wore deep coral lipstick. All at once Zica felt naked and out of place, with her pompadour of coiled hair and her plain unpowdered cheeks.

"I want," Zica swallowed, "an Irene Castle bob." Her eyes held the woman's gaze—held it for dear life. What would Yakov do when he saw her? What would she herself think of her own looks, once the step had been taken? She was about to plunge into American modernity. It was a step out of the past, into the here and now. Clara and Isabelle and especially Rosalind—Fitzgerald's fictional women—would have applauded and encouraged her.

"I want to have that look, you know, like the dancer, Irene Castle." Zica's voice gained strength as she repeated her request.

"Yeah, lots o' wimmin do," the woman answered, in her thickened, nasal accent. The woman gave Zica a smock, while Vickie watched, fascinated by the sight of her mother being readied for a real haircut. She seated Zica in a chair that leaned back. "Shampoo time!" she exclaimed. "Lissen, d'ya want me to put yer little girl over there in the corner, by the magazines? That oughter keep'er bizzy!"

But Vickie wouldn't budge. She wanted to watch—stare actually —as the woman washed Zica's long black hair. Vickie's eyes widened as the woman lopped off the hair just above shoulder length.

Her mommy's face was white, and she looked scared. *Why was this supposed to be a treat?*

But, later, Vickie found out. The red-haired woman wrapped

Zica's hair in strange little metal tubes and put something funny-smelling all over her head. Zica laughed, but her laughter sounded brittle. The operator tapped her on the shoulder and said: "Yer supposed ta feel wobbly on yer feet, the foist time!"

She put Zica in one of the leather chairs, and Vickie saw the girl clamp something over her mother's head that made lots of noise. When Vickie began to cry, the young woman hoisted her into the chair next to Zica, where she promptly fell asleep. After handing Zica *True Story* magazine and the *Daily News,* she padded off. *Oh, God,* Zica thought, suddenly terrified: *what if I've made a terrible mistake?*

Her hands trembling, she began to flip through *True Story*. She usually delighted in its tales of love among shopgirls and hairdressers. The lurid tales made Zica dream of a life outside Brooklyn. Perhaps she would go by herself to a tearoom in Manhattan to meet a gentleman in tails and a top hat, who would invite her to visit his art gallery. She dreamt of strange fingers caressing her flesh, of someone who smelled of musk and leather, of love letters being sent in secret. Indulging in these stories, she usually felt guilty—and tried to shut out her daydreams, locking the lid so tightly they would never escape.

But today she was too nervous to concentrate on the stories. She dropped *True Story* on the table and picked up the tabloid newspaper. When she came to the society page—the only page that truly held her interest—she pulled it out. Suddenly the room receded.

Even the sleeping Vickie disappeared.

Staring at Zica from the page was a young man with a wide smile, dressed in evening wear; his hand was on the elbow of a fashionable, regal old lady wearing a sable coat. Zica's heart stampeded.

Many times she had pictured meeting him again; many times she had rehearsed what she would say! And whenever he came into her mind's eye, she forgot that she was a respectable married woman with a child. Forgotten, too, was the fact that he had never called on her after he sent back Yasha, twice, with the unopened envelopes.

The man in the picture frightened her with his power. He was still, after all these years, her Golden Prince, her knight in shining armor. And the flame seemed unquenched. She had loved him the way Guinevere loved Lancelot, the way Juliet loved Romeo.

Why had she rejected him? She'd been not quite twenty, and terrified—still tied to her family, to her tight circle of friends and acquaintances. Kyril Ostrov had represented everything outside that cocoon—the danger of a new life with new risks. Zica had needed her safe life with other people whose good opinion had given her an image of who she was. At the thought of losing all that comfort, she had balked, afraid, rejecting the intruder.

But she had loved him, even then. If he had only read the notes and learned about the baby, what then? Perhaps she would have married him in spite of the cocoon.

And what of Yakov—the man who had loved her forever, who had dedicated his life to making her happy? Yes, she loved him. But if that was so, how could Kyril stir such powerful feelings in her?

Confused, tears pressing at her eyes, Zica brought the tabloid closer. The caption bewildered her. It referred to Kyril as "Count Kyril Vadimovitch Malenkov." But it *was Kyril, her Kyril!* What could this mean? Then she remembered a conversation she had overheard, between Yossif Adolfovitch and her husband. Yasha had asked if they could change their name in America, and the old man had scoffed at the very notion. But at the same time, he had allowed that this could be done. Perhaps, then, Kyril had changed his name to "Malenkov" at Ellis Island.

She looked for the article accompanying the picture. It described a performance of *La Traviata,* with Jennie Arnold. The benefit performance at the Metropolitan Opera House had been organized by Mrs. Clinton Voorhies. The article described Mrs. Voorhies as a wealthy widow with a magnificent mansion on Fifth Avenue and Fifty-second Street. Then it mentioned *him* briefly, just briefly. Zica held the paper up close, so no one in the beauty shop would see the tears.

Mrs. Voorhies' escort last evening was Count Malenkov, a new figure on the New York social scene. This dashing young man hails from the fabled city of St. Petersburg, now known as Petrograd. The Count's parents were friends of Mrs. Voorhies in Russia and the Malenkovs were familiar figures at the courts of Alexander III and Nicholas II.

Zica let the paper fall. She didn't understand. The old lady, Mrs. Voorhies, professed to have been friends of this Malenkov family, and yet to Zica's eyes, the man was Kyril. How could this be?

"It's time to come out," the operator said, turning off the hair dryer. Zica looked up, numbly. "Yes, I know," the woman said, mistaking Zica's expression. "The first time, it's always scary. But don't worry, we'll make a flapper out o' you!" She proceeded to remove the funny little rollers, rinsed Zica's hair of the evil-smelling solution, and then set it once more with large metal tubes.

Ensconced under the hood of the hairdryer for a second time, Zica reviewed the conundrum. Who was the man in the picture? Kyril, or some other man who resembled him closely? Then she thought of Lena, who mourned for Kyril, her son, almost daily. Lena had a right to see this picture; his mother had the right to know that Kyril Malenkov existed—a man who, in all likelihood, was her Kyril. *She,* above all, would know beyond the shadow of a doubt. He was the child to whom she'd given birth. There was no way a mother would fail to recognize her own child.

Yes, Lena would know. But was it fair to offer hope when in fact it might be nothing but a mistake? Was it fair to make her grieve, to feel her loss all over again, if indeed the man were not her son at all? Perhaps Zica would wait and discuss this with Yakov. Perhaps—if she brought the matter up coolly, as though concerned only for her friend Lena—her husband would not suspect that Kyril Ostrov still posed a danger to him. Perhaps she would be able to convince Yakov that Ostrov meant nothing to her today, now that she was a happily married woman.

But Yakov wasn't stupid; Yakov would know. He would hate Kyril for appearing here—of all places—to spoil the happiness of their marriage.

A half hour later, the operator brought Zica out again, and combed out the set. Zica looked in the mirror and gasped. Her black hair, set in a wave, seemed to have a life of its own. Without the weight of the pompadour, she felt lighter by pounds. Her shoulders felt bare, her head strange and weightless. She did not look like herself at all, but the picture was pretty, nevertheless. She looked like one of the models in the advertisements for Woodbury beauty soaps and Camel cigarettes. She thought, *I look like an American woman.*

She awakened Vickie, who touched her mother's new hair in great excitement. All the way home, Vickie prattled on about her pretty mother, and the snow, and Hanukkah, and her favorite old rag doll, Tweety. Zica hardly listened. She was thinking of Yakov, who liked to read his paper on the subway home. He would see the picture! And then she began to worry about what he would say when he saw her—that more immediate concern temporarily pushing aside her concern about the picture in the *Daily News*. What if Yakov hated how she looked? She trembled at the thought of how he might behave. She had openly, wilfully, thwarted his wishes.

Yakov came in the door, looked at her long and hard . . . and said nothing.

Zica sat through dinner, quaking inside while he told funny stories about customers who had come into the store. He played with Vickie before putting her down for the night. It was inconceivable that he hadn't noticed. She was so afraid of his odd silence, wondering when the explosion would take place.

But it was not until they were in their bed that he remarked at last, "It's really not so bad, Zica." His tone was gentle, conciliatory. Zica's stomach untied itself. Relief flooded her senses. "I mean," he said, "if it's what *you* want. . . . "

Tenderness filled her, and she smiled, taking him in her arms. With his head against her breasts, she whispered, "Thank you. Yes, it's what I want. I want to be an American woman." And suddenly she felt as if he had given her permission to bring up the unmentionable, to say what was really in her heart. "I want to be more than just a housewife, Yasha. I would like to do something, like the women here—something else besides taking care of Vickie. I want to be a real American woman, in every sense!"

He nestled closer against her, still oddly calm and content. "What do you want to do?" he murmured. "We are managing fine now. We have a washing machine. Next month we're even going to get a car. And now"—he looked up and smiled—"now you've cut your hair and given it strange waves. Yes, I like it, Zica!"

"But . . . I would like to work. Think how much more we can do then, Yakov. I know I could get along with elegant people. What do I see every day? Just the girl at the cash register of the Piggly Wiggly grocerteria!" Zica was becoming excited, her voice rising.

Yakov sighed, pulling away to lie on his own pillow. "Zeinab," he said deliberately, "you are my wife. I shall hear no more of this absurd conceit of yours, to work outside the house! Who would clean *our* house, and take care of Victoria? You aren't *thinking*, Zica!" But his voice was calm. He wasn't angry.

Later, he wanted to make love. She let him. But after he had fallen asleep, she wept silently, wiping away the tears with the back of her hand.

The next day, she retrieved Yakov's *Daily News* from the trash can outside, and brought the society page into the kitchen. There, with the scissors she used to mince parsley and dill, she cut out the photograph of Kyril Malenkov. She was glad that she had not asked Yakov if he'd seen the picture. Probably he'd missed it entirely. He never read the society page.

And she wouldn't show the picture to Lena, either. Only if Zica were sure that this was Lena's son would she tell her friend—*only* then.

Holding the clipping in her hand, Zica tried to think of a secret place in which to hide it. Finally, she seized on her cookbook. Yasha would never look there, for certain. Opening it to "Devil's Food Cake," she laid the picture carefully between the pages.

Kyril set his tea cup down on the translucent Meissen saucer and regarded his hostess. Anna Voorhies, seated in a tall, straight-back damask chair, resembled a great Roman prelate draped in Schiaparelli silks. Her arms and neck were dripping with heavy antique jewelry.

The first time Kyril had visited her, she'd said to him *sotto voce:* "See this emerald? It's three hundred years old, dear heart, almost as old as I am."

He loved this majestic old woman, who, at eighty-three, still enjoyed the pleasures of the palate, patronized the arts, and held court in her vaultlike salon—a dowager empress scowling down upon her petitioners. With him she was always an interested friend, perceptive and devoid of pretense.

"You haven't touched your cake," she now remonstrated. Her skin was a criss-cross pattern of fine wrinkles, her nose a round button, her unplucked brows a forceful statement. When she rouged her lips, she always managed to smear the rouge. But, as she said, "At least I'm a modern woman, worthy of the vote."

When Kyril teased her about not having bobbed her hair yet, she answered, "Later. I'm still adjusting to the Marcel wave. One thing at a time, sweet boy. I have all the time in the world."

But now she seemed concerned. "Something's wrong," she said, noting Kyril's expression. "Tell me what it is."

As his heart began its arrhythmic dance, he pushed back the panic.

"Hurry up," Anna told him. "Elsie will return from the powder room, and we shan't be able to talk."

"It's Mason." Kyril's mouth felt dry and woolly. "I—I can't afford him anymore."

Anna frowned. "You can't afford *not* to have him," she stated. "You're dependent on him. Mason is much more than a regular butler!"

"I know, Annushka. But however shall I find the money for his next year's salary? Everywhere I turn, I face expenses. My personal expenses have all but eaten my savings away. Yesterday, I went to a jeweller recommended by Herbert Hauser. He could not guarantee the sale of the last remaining pieces. He said they are the least desirable in the collection. The second Fabergé egg has a fault in it, and the amethyst choker is badly made. Besides, amethysts aren't worth much. There's the ruby ring—but honestly, Annushka, how far will it get me?"

Despair reverberated in his voice. "I know it's bad manners, to say the least, to speak of money to one's friends. But there's no one else I can turn to for advice. Even Herbert would turn his back if he knew how close I am to bankruptcy. With the others, I wouldn't even get a chance! America is a hard country: if you run out of money, you run out of friends."

"It's no different anywhere else," the old woman observed. "You know what I always advise all my young friends: you must have the strength of your convictions, and the money to back it up!"

Kyril smiled, but the smile was thin. "So what would you advise *me?*"

But just as Anna was about to answer, Elsie Tulliver entered the room. Her once-long brown hair was bobbed to the chin, and her tube dress of soft gray wool showed off a rounded calf and slim ankle. Kyril could not help noticing how her figure had flattened; she now resembled a lithe young boy.

He rose as Elsie took her seat across from him at the coffee table, next to the old lady. "Well," Anna said. "Now you must tell me, Elsie dear, what's new with you?"

"I've been boning up on this Émile Coué," Elsie replied brightly, motioning for Kyril to sit down again. "You know, his system really works! I've been repeating the slogan, 'Every day, in every way, I'm growing better and better.' Believe it or not, I actually *feel* myself getting better every day!"

Anna turned to Kyril with knitted brow. "Who *is* this Coué, Kyra? A doctor?"

"A French pharmacist, actually," Kyril replied. "A hypnotist of sorts. This 'Every day, in every way' is a form of self-hypnosis he's developed. We read about him in medical school, in Paris."

"Medical school? I didn't know you'd gone to *medical school*,"

Anna Voorhies said archly. Abruptly, her expression held bewilderment and wariness. "What's *this* story?"

Dear God, thought Kyril, *now* I've done it! For two years, he'd been careful not to bring up any part of Ostrov that might have conflicted with the Malenkov persona. He'd watched every word. No one had ever doubted him. Now suddenly, here, lulled by these two friendly women, he'd let his customary vigilance slip.

Pearls of perspiration tickled his hairline. *Stupid,* he told himself, *you stand to lose everything you've gained, by one thoughtless remark!*

Forcing himself to take a deep breath, he smiled at Anna. "Annushka, I *had* to find a way to occupy my time, those first six months in Paris. I never intended to become a *doctor;* but all my life, I'd been fascinated with the subject of healing. So I took some classes. It helped, you know, not to spend my days thinking of Lara, mourning for the past."

"Well," Anna remarked, "I can't say it was a bad idea, though I must admit it was a strange thing to do. Medicine... well, young people certainly are a curious lot, I must say!" She sighed, then turned to Elsie again. "This Coué of yours—is he a follower of Freud?"

"No, no," Elsie shook her head. "Freud reduces life to the sex complex. It's all too complicated for words. Although you, perhaps, Kyra, can understand it. I mean, you're a *scientific* man...." And she gave her most engaging smile, her gray eyes half-closed.

"Ah yes, psychiatry is the science of the moment," Anna Voorhies declared. "But do we really need it, Kyra?"

They were asking *him!* All at once he thought, *My little error, which could have cost me everything, seems, instead, to have added to my worth! Now I've become a "scientific man," no less.*

"It depends," he told them. "Some people have neurotic disorders. For example, there was a woman in Paris who possessed a terrible fear of travelling. She refused to go anywhere outside the city. One of Freud's disciples came all the way from Vienna to treat her and discovered that when she'd been a very young girl, her uncle had molested her on a train from Paris to Rome. Only she'd forgotten all about it: her conscious mind had refused to accept what had happened!"

"Really? How utterly fascinating!" Elsie cried. She leaned forward, eyes shining. "So how did the psychiatrist handle this woman? Was he able to help her?"

"Quite so. He took away the guilt she still felt. He helped her recognize the uncle's behavior had not been her fault. The woman is well now, thanks to Freud and his disciple. She travels regularly, in fact, like any normal person."

"What a fountain of knowledge you are, my dear Kyra," Anna Voorhies commented. "To think you kept this aspect of your life a complete secret from us all . . . !"

"Kyra is just too modest, that's all," Elsie said, smiling at him. Her angelic face radiated admiration. "Henry would have boasted of his knowledge of medicine, if indeed he'd had any. But of course," she added tartly, "Henry only cares about stocks, bonds, and investments. Science leaves him cold."

"You judge him too harshly, darling," the older woman cautioned.

Elsie Tulliver regarded the elder woman with an intent expression. "Anna," she said, her voice hushed but steady. "I'm going to get a divorce. Henry and I are far too different *ever* to be happy together. It was a mistake to marry him, but it's not too late to rectify it."

"A divorce? But, my dear, your parents . . . ?"

"My parents have nothing to say about it," the young woman scoffed. "I have money of my own, of course." Then she explained: "I've rented an apartment on Madison and Fifty-fifth, until my lawyer can untangle my financial situation and I can purchase a house. I'll be moving in with Consuelo, the nanny, my maid, and our butler, two weeks from now." Turning to Ostrov, she asked: "Would you escort me to an art show next month? I've just received the invitation, and I'm dying to go . . . but with someone who knows how to have a good time, for a change!"

Kyril feared his voice would betray him. "I . . . well . . . Elsie . . ."

"Do say 'yes'!" the young woman pleaded. "No one will speak ill of you for escorting a woman about to be divorced. Everyone will know the news by then, and no one will be shocked. Even if they are, *I* don't care! I'm tired of being Good Girl Elsie."

Still stunned by the rapid turn of events, Kyril glanced at pretty Elsie Tulliver, model wife and consummate hostess. What he saw was, instead, a flapper with a tubelike dress, pressed-down bosom, bobbed hair and makeup.

Once he had thought about courting Elsie Tulliver, when she had been forbidden fruit, a happily married woman. And now, almost a free woman, she was turning to him . . . as a good friend, or a potential lover? He couldn't tell.

Elsie Tulliver's father was richer than Henry Tulliver, and Elsie's settlement from her husband was bound to be enormous. She had just announced that, apart from all this, she possessed independent means. Besides, she was a sweet, charming woman, and had been a good friend. Obviously she had been miserable ever since marrying that prig of a Henry Tulliver. What would be the harm in escorting her?

"It isn't done, my darling, to go out with a man so shortly after moving out of your husband's home," Anna Voorhies announced from her empress chair. "Think of Consuelo! You wish to receive a large settlement from Henry, do you not? Well, if you aren't careful, you might embroil Kyra in an ugly trial. Should Henry decide to sue *you* for divorce, he might name our friend here as co-respondent! This would ruin you, Elsie, and it would do Kyra no good. *I* shall go with you to this art show," she stated, ending the subject. She drew her bulk to her feet. "Now, you *both* must go home, because I have an important matter to think about. I must think about the matter we discussed earlier this afternoon, concerning business," she added pointedly, addressing Kyril.

She turned her cheek, which was kissed first by Elsie, then by Ostrov. Then, unceremoniously, she shooed them out into the vestibule. Elsie Tulliver was blushing; she avoided Kyril, hastening toward the butler who held out her coat.

"I need a taxi," she told the manservant. And then, in muted tones: "You needn't offer me a ride, Kyra. I'll see myself home."

Anna's remonstrance had embarrassed her. But he could only feel a blessed relief at Anna's timely interference. He wasn't ready to become Elsie's escort. He wasn't ready to court Elsie—at least, not yet. Let her settle her divorce—and her financial affairs—first of all. Then he would see.

Their old friend had fixed this in her usual direct, blunt style. Perhaps he would lose Elsie's friendship, but he was determined not to give in to foolish notions anymore.

But what would he do when his money ran out? This issue was far more pressing than Elsie Tulliver's need for companionship. If Anna didn't help him, he might have no choice but to marry a woman who was well off. He didn't want to give up being Count Kyra Malenkov!

Chapter XVI

KYRIL sat at his desk, hunched over the accounts book with the meticulous list of his expenses that had been pencilled in by the exasperatingly correct Mason. Just thinking of his gentleman's gentleman made the young man feel a rush of sorrow. With his accounts in this state, Kyril wondered again how he could continue to afford this paragon of a gentleman's gentleman.

Discreetly, a tap sounded, breaking Kyril's thoughts. He started and cleared his throat. "Come in!" The angular form of his *maître d'hôtel* appeared in the doorway.

"Your Excellency has Mrs. Voorhies on the line," Mason announced. "And," he added, looking away, "Mrs. Tulliver phoned three times. I told her the Count was out for the morning."

"Thank you, Mason." Kyril smiled: Mason had learned to read him like a book.

He picked up the receiver of the elegant black telephone.

"Annushka? Good morning, my pretty. How are you today?"

The Dowager Empress came straight to the point. "I've thought of something. Or, to be precise, something quite literally came to *me*. I've received so many calls about our picture in the *Daily News* that I've had to ask my secretary to take most of them. And all because a charity workhorse like me needs to be listed in the phone book...! People are such gossip mongers! But my darling boy, there have been several calls concerning *you*. No one knows how to reach you, because you're unlisted so they've all called me. It seems your photo has created quite a commotion."

"What do you mean?"

"Well, dear heart, Sol Hurok has been on the phone, wanting to know if he could meet you. I would have mentioned it at tea, but

291

Elsie was here, and she spreads tidbits around town faster than the *Daily News* itself. You see, I've had to decide whether Hurok might do you any good. I've decided he can."

"But who is Sol Hurok?" Kyril enquired.

"Aha. He is quite a prodigious individual. He is, first of all, a Russian. He has made a name for himself as an impresario. He brings musical talent of the highest quality to the Hippodrome. You've heard of the 'Hurok audience. . . . ' No? Well, the Hippodrome provides music for the masses. It's all very lively—for those who can't afford to go to the Opera House. Recently, he's been expanding. He brought Fokine and Fokina to the Metropolitan. He introduced Diaghilev's first choreographer and his *prima ballerina* wife to the American public. I hear that Pavlova has befriended him—she's going to become his client, too."

"That's all well and good, Annushka, but I have no talent. I am neither a musician nor a dancer, as you know, so I don't see how he could possibly help me."

Anna Voorhies was silent for a moment. "John Barrymore may or may not be a dancer, and if he plays an instrument, what difference can this make in a silent picture? My dear child, Barrymore simply *is,* like his brother Lionel, and that seems to be enough for his fans."

"You mean . . . Hurok thinks that I could be an *actor?* But . . . I've never acted in anything in my life, Annushka!"

"Really? It seems to me, Kyra, my sweet, that you are the best actor I know. You *act* from the moment a woman enters the room, even if, like me, she's three hundred years old. Your eyes speak for you. I've never seen eyes like that, and believe me, I have seen eyes of every form these past three hundred years. Hurok's specialty is finding talent, particularly among his countrymen. He's brought Mischa Elman to the American public. He had great success with Zimbalist. If he wishes to meet you, darling, then I believe you must jump for joy. Anyway, you have no choice. You're to come to the Palace tomorrow at three. He's coming at three-thirty."

The Palace was Anna's nickname for her mansion on Fifth and Fifty-second. Kyril was overwhelmed, but no one refused a summons from the Dowager Empress. "Very well, Annushka," he conceded.

As he prepared to set down the receiver, Kyril heard the imperious voice crackle once again through the line. Kyril raised the receiver to his ear. "I almost forgot," she added. "Someone else called me—a man, with a Russian accent, who claims he knows you. Yakov Pocus? Or Pokas? Does that ring a bell?"

Mystified, Kyril shook his head. "I don't think so. Why would he call you?"

"He was interested in knowing how to get in touch with Count Malenkov. He said you had some mutual friends in Moscow—the Baron and Baroness Poliakov. Why does this name sound so familiar?"

Kyril's heart leaped to his throat. Panic washed over him. Of course... Yakov Pokhis, Zica's houseboy! The thin little *shtetl* librarian she'd sent over with her messages, after telling him she wouldn't marry him! So Pokhis was here, in New York, and had recognized Kyril from the photo. He'd found him out!

But immediately, Kyril began preparing his objections. Who was Pokhis, anyway? Nothing more than another impoverished immigrant. Kyril knew that his resemblance to Kyra Malenkov was striking enough to have convinced Anna Voorhies that he was indeed the son of her friends. *Anyone* could be mistaken. And who would believe an impoverished immigrant, just off the boat?

"Annushka, I'm afraid this man must have me confused with somebody else," he stated. "I look very Russian, you know. If he should call you again, you need only tell the butler not to bring you the 'phone. There's no need for strangers to be importuning you for no reason."

"I quite agree," the old lady answered. Then, just as she was about to end the conversation, a thought crossed her mind. "Oh, my!" she cried. "I suddenly remembered why the Poliakovs sounded so familiar! I've had *another* inquiry. And this was from a very nice young woman who says she was great friends with you back in Moscow. She quite convinced me. The voice was charming and cultured, and she was so shy and afraid to disturb you. *Her* name is also Poliakov, and of course I asked her if she knew this Yakov, since his call preceded hers by about a day. The coincidence was quite remarkable, I think, but she told me that she couldn't remember any Yakov Pocus. She said she is the *young* Baroness Poliakova. She must be about your age, judging from the things she told me over the phone." And Anna went on to relay some further details of the conversation.

Kyril's complete silence surprised Anna. "Hello?" she called. "Are you still there?"

"Yes," he murmured, his voice just a hoarse whisper. "I'm here,

Annushka. Tell me, did she give you a number where she might be reached?"

"Of course she did. Here it is—" And Anna gave him the Brooklyn number. "Perhaps, if you'd like, you could bring this girl to me. I'd like to meet her."

"So would I," Kyril said softly. "So would I. . . . "

Long after he hung up, the young man remained at his desk, lost in thought. How was it possible that Zica was here, as well? So close, yet miles away. And what was she doing in Brooklyn, for God's sake? To see her, touch her, talk to her—the mere thought of being with her again filled Kyril with longing, with nostalgia. Did he still love her, or just want to recapture something lost from his past?

If he phoned her, what would happen? *She knew who he was.* But perhaps she had no intention of revealing his identity. He could swear her to secrecy—and tell her the truth.

It would be good to tell someone the truth, at last. There were times when he hated the burden of his false identity. Zica had loved him. She would understand his desire to "become" Count Malenkov. Perhaps now, she even regretted the break-up she had instigated. And perhaps, now, he would forgive her.

But this was all daydreaming. He hadn't seen her yet, nor spoken to her. What if the Bolsheviks had changed her, and she'd grown fat and unattractive? And besides, he was so low on money he could not even think of courting a woman.

Somehow, he was certain she had never married. But how strange it was that she'd forgotten Yasha, her father's little librarian from the Pale. . . . As he remembered, they had been quite friendly. Oh, well, thought Kyril, New York is enormous, and Yakov Pokhis is a man I have no intention of meeting. I shall call Zica, but I certainly shan't remind her of her former servant.

And then, tomorrow, I shall meet the great impresario, Sol Hurok! Who knows where such a connection may get me . . . ?

It was ten-twenty. He had nothing to do for the rest of the morning. Why don't I call Zica now? he wondered, reaching for the phone.

The telephone rang four times. No one was picking up. Kyril was about to hang up when suddenly he heard an out-of-breath female voice, calling: "Hello! Hello?"

For a moment he couldn't speak. She said: "Is anyone there?" Her voice sounded tentative, the accent clipped, British with a tinge of Slavic. It stirred him just to hear it.

"Zica?" he asked hesitantly. His eyes were burning.

"Kyriusha?" She whispered this, as though to hold on, however disbelieving, to the distant sound of his voice.

"Zica. I . . . didn't know you were in New York." His words sounded stupid.

"I saw your photo in the paper," she answered softly. "But it gave you a different name. Mrs. Voorhies calls you 'Count Malenkov.' Is that how people know you here?"

He gulped down his nervousness. "Yes," he said. "That's my new American name." He tried to laugh it off, but the chuckle sounded hollow. "Zica? May I see you?"

At first she didn't reply. He thought, I've got to be truthful with her. "When I see you," he told her, "I'll explain everything. *When* may I see you?"

"Any time. Now. No," she contradicted herself, "not now. I . . . well, I can't leave the house for another few hours. Perhaps we could meet somewhere. I don't live in Manhattan," she added, as though he might hold that against her. "But you must have guessed from the number."

"I have a car," he reassured her. "I'll come to you. Just tell me where to meet you."

"Yes. *No!*—no, you must not come here." She sounded panic stricken. Bewildered, he asked, "But why?"

"Because! There are people here—I have things to do. I can't leave until . . . well, until I can find somebody to watch . . . well, there are just things I must do."

He sighed. "All right, then. Where would you like to meet me?"

"In Manhattan," she said, decisively. "Pick somewhere we can talk quietly—somewhere people aren't going to interrupt us."

He thought a moment. "There's a restaurant on Seventh Avenue in the Twenties. It's called the Castle Cave."

"I'll meet you at . . . one-thirty?"

"We'll have lunch together."

"Kyril . . ." She hesitated. "I . . . I don't have pretty clothes any more. I'm just a refugee. Maybe you'd rather not see me this way?"

"I'd see you any old way, Zica," he murmured softly. "Any old way . . ."

After she had hung up, he remained by the phone, receiver in hand. A lump the size of an egg was choking him, and he could not gulp it away. With a sudden shock, he realized that he could not remember the particular details of her face. He simply remembered that she had been beautiful.

Well, he thought, rising to change his clothes, that was enough, wasn't it?

As Zica peered into the restaurant, she thought to herself, This is truly a cave. But she couldn't *see* him.

She could hardly hold her purse. Her fingers, in their wool-lined leather gloves, were shaking, unable to respond to the commands in her brain. *Dear God,* she thought, *what if he doesn't come?*

In a rush, she had taken Vickie to Mrs. Patchulnik, next door. Her explanation to her daughter had been hasty and abrupt; she could see in Vickie's eyes that she didn't want her mother to go. But Zica had run off to the subway like a madwoman.

And now—*where was he?*

A florid man with a big smile was making his way toward her, hand outstretched. "Baroness Poliakova? I'm Bardush, the proprietor. Count Malenkov is waiting for you in a booth at the back. He wanted a place with...privacy. But he asked me to look out for a lovely lady with dark eyes and hair."

She nodded mutely. Self-consciously, she conjured up an image of herself—her black wool coat with large sleeves and a chin collar, ears and forehead covered by her black felt *cloche* hat; her comfortable old second-hand boots polished to a high sheen. Zica had no jewels but her simple wedding band—and that she had removed, leaving it at home in the cutlery drawer.

Her heartbeat was pounding in her ears; her face was red from the cold, and from embarrassment. Kyril was known here. What must the owner think of her impoverished appearance? Yet he had spoken to her as to a lady. She hadn't heard such a genteel tone since before the Bolshevik Revolution. She'd almost forgotten what it had been like to *be* the Baroness Poliakova, now that she lived and breathed the drab existence of Zica Pokhis.

Seeing *Kyril* sitting alone in a booth, Zica was struck dumb, as when she had first seen him at the Tretyakovka. Seeing the gold of his hair, the green light in his almond-shaped eyes, the radiant smile, she wanted nothing so much as to weep. Her emotions were a jumble. He was the Golden Prince she had recalled to memory ten thousand times. She could blot out that horrible winter night six years before, when they had stood together under a *huppa* of make-shift paper flowers in the simple suburban home of Yuri Simonov, the bookbinder. She could blot out the feeling she'd once had so strongly that his love would stifle and oppress her. *What had she known, then, of real life?*

He rose, extending his hands to her, and murmured, "Zica..." She gave him her hands. There was an awkward silence until Bardush coughed and cleared his throat. "Ah, yes," Kyril said. "We'll have oysters over charcoal, and . . . some tea."

"Yes," Bardush repeated. "Tea." And then he was gone. They were alone—very much alone, neither knowing what to say.

Finally Zica unbuttoned her coat. Kyril helped her remove it. She had worn her cowl-necked white blouse, which Lena had sewn for her, and her black skirt. Zica pulled off her hat, shook out her hair, and sat down, embarrassed by his long, intense appraisal. "I've changed," she remarked softly. "I know."

"You've changed; but I like it. I like your short hair. You're very thin, though, Zica."

Then he won't guess I have a baby. "You haven't changed at all. If anything, you're more splendid than ever."

"It's the clothes," he said.

"You're more . . . self-confident," she remarked. "And you seem to be . . . well . . . established."

"That's just an illusion," he smiled. He sat across from her, clasping his hands just centimeters away from where she had laid hers, now ungloved. She was drinking him in, fascinated, curiosity gaining over self-consciousness.

"Tell me a little about Count Malenkov," she said. "Wasn't there a famous family with that name back in Petersburg? Zhenya used to visit them, I think . . . unless I'm mistaken. An old *boyar* family, I seem to recall."

"It's a long story, Zica."

"I have all afternoon," she replied, her black eyes suddenly penetrating him with a gentle insistence. He looked down at his hands before addressing her once more.

"I was living in France for some years. I moved there after . . . after we ended. You have to know I couldn't bear to remain in Moscow after that. The idea of being in the same city with you, yet shut out from your life—"

"But it was *you* who shut *me* out! I sent you two letters by messenger, and you never bothered to open them!"

"You didn't want to be my wife. What possible message could

you have sent after that? A message that you wished to remain my friend?" His tone had hardened into bitterness.

Her jaw hardened. "Go on," she said, "tell me about France."

"Yes. France. I met some interesting people there and I gave up my medical studies. I lived a life of intolerable sloth and no accomplishment whatever. Two years ago, I could bear it no longer. I was in Biarritz when I decided to try my luck in America. It was on board ship that I met Kyra Malenkov; he was a charming and kind young man, of the highest Russian aristocracy—" And Kyril went on to tell Zica of all that had happened on shipboard . . . and afterward, when they had arrived at Ellis Island.

"I have very little money, Zica," he concluded, having told her about selling the jewels. "But now, a lot of important people think I am someone worthwhile—a mind, a wit, and a presence. There was a time when all I could boast of was being the son of a provincial Jewish woman and a loud-mouthed Cossack who killed himself. People here respect me, Zica."

"Yes," she remarked. "I understand that. In Moscow, until the Reds took over, I was somebody, too. After that I became a cipher —as I am here. I am just one among thousands of Eastern European refugees."

"I thought for sure the Reds had killed you." Kyril's voice was suddenly husky. "What happened to you when they came?"

"They murdered my parents." She said this harshly, her eyes averted. "In Petersburg, they got my brother, his wife, and her whole family. I'm the only Poliakov who survived."

"But . . . how did you do it?"

"I got help. One of the household servants was kind enough to save me. Tania, my maid . . . she soon went over to the other side of town, to be with her own people."

"Who was the generous one?"

"Oh, no one you'd remember. He got me out one step ahead of the Bolsheviks, and then he himself disappeared. I was able to find a small room. Much later, I escaped with the help of an unexpected friend, Natasha—the young artist who used to live in a room overlooking my parents' courtyard. She was a member of the CHEKA, and she got me out."

Zica could tell that the large gaps in her story puzzled him, yet she had no intention of providing details that would allow him to guess her present circumstances. "That's all," she added. "I came to New York from . . . Odessa, two years ago, like you. Someone kind helped me put together the money for my passage."

A pang of acute guilt pierced through her. She *couldn't* tell him about Yossif and Lena—*his own family!* If she did, he would want to see them at once. Then he would learn about Yakov as well! He'd find out she was married, with a baby. She would lose him all over again—would lose any chance at a fleeting moment of happiness.

For a few hours at least, let him belong to her alone!

She would have to tell him about his mother soon enough. She had to be fair to everyone. But not, she reasoned, right away. He had survived without Lena for many years, and Lena had adjusted to the idea that she might never see her son again. In a short while, Zica would bring them together. She'd think of some way. But right now, all she could think of was how glad she was that he was here, gazing at her, his eyes probing her soul.

"I never thought I'd see you again," he told her.

"And I thought you'd forgotten me."

"Sometimes I did put you out of my mind," he said honestly. "In France, there were moments—" He let his sentence drift off with his thoughts, and she felt a pang of jealousy.

"There was . . . someone else there?"

"There were people. There were adventures. But there wasn't anyone like you—no one I could dream with, no one I could trust, no one who made me feel valued the way you did. No one I could have married," he concluded gravely.

"What a mess we made of our lives," she said, her eyes filling with tears. "How young we were, how foolish, and how falsely proud!"

"Yes," he agreed, reaching for her hands. "We were both young fools. But with some hope, we're not anymore. Perhaps now, Zica, there might be a chance for us. What do you think?"

His words hit her like blows; without thinking, she pulled her hands away. He retreated to his side of the booth, his face mirroring shock and hurt. "Oh, Kyril!" she cried, suddenly at a complete loss. "You don't know, you'll *never* know, how very much I prayed for this moment! But my life—it's complicated. I'm not what I used to be."

"I don't know what you mean," he said, defensively.

"I . . . just can't explain! I live with these people. They have a small baby. I've grown attached to the baby. I couldn't leave her."

Kyril blinked, shaking his head in disbelief. "A baby? You are telling me you can't make a life with me on account of *someone else's baby?*"

Mutely, she nodded.

He stood up, fury mottling his face. "You say you wanted me, that you hoped we'd meet again...then you mention some stranger's child!"

"I...I want you too," she said, bursting into tears. "But...I have to think of some way to make sense of my life. You have to give me time, Kyril! You never would give me time, and that's what came between us! Please—"

Kyril struck the table with his fist and cried out: "Why? We're young, Zica! *This* is our time—this is our chance. We must seize it!"

Zica let the tears flow down her cheeks. Then she said the words she had sworn that she would never say to him. "I was—with child—when you left me, Kyril. That's what I wrote you six years ago. Only you wouldn't read the notes, and so...I got rid of the child." Then Zica dropped her head into her hands and began to sob soundlessly, her shoulders heaving.

He could not speak. His face was a mask of tragedy. Slowly he sank down onto the banquette, shaking his head. He murmured: "No. You aren't telling me the truth...are you, Zica?"

"I'm telling you the only truth I know." She raised her face to him. "I swore I'd never let you know...but it's in the past, Kyriusha. Don't think about it. It was a bad time, and we were both hurt. But yes, we did create a child, and sometimes I think about that child and wonder what it would have been like. And then I push the thought away, because it only brings me pain and regret."

"I'm so sorry," he said tonelessly. "So...sorry."

Zica went on in a rush. "If you think you might love me again, please—give me time now. I need to think things through."

"What, Zica—what stands in our way?" he pleaded. "I've told you the truth, haven't I? Why can't you trust me?"

"Because I can't trust myself," she replied, standing up. "I'm afraid. Afraid of you, of myself, of...other people. I've made a greater mess of my life than you have, Kyril. And now it's up to me to straighten it out. Give me some time."

"Do I have a choice?" he asked.

"No," she answered softly. "This time you don't." And before he could reach out to embrace her, she grabbed her coat and hat and rushed toward the front of the restaurant. She could no longer bear to see his beauty, to hear the deep sound of his voice caressing her senses. He had stirred up the darkest moments of her past, and her strength was seeping out through the reopened wounds.

By the door of the Castle Cave, she stopped to put on her coat and hat before facing the cold. Bardush was just emerging from the kitchen, holding a tray. "Hey!" he called out. "Don't leave yet, pretty lady. Look what I'm bringing you!"

He lowered the tray so she could see. Two plates full of steaming broiled oysters emitted a delicious odor; beside them were two tall glasses. "Your tea, Madame," he whispered conspiratorially. "Bootleg champagne, which I get specially for the Count."

"He always was a *bon vivant*," she remarked, smiling in spite of herself. "But, still, I must leave. There's someone waiting for me at home."

"You'll be sorry," Bardush told her. "No one 'at home' could possibly compare to the charming Count Malenkov."

"No one ever could," she answered, fighting down her tears.

She pushed open the door, hoping the freezing wind would numb the searing pain in her heart.

The great impresario was as well-scrubbed as a rotund little baby emerging from his bath; Kyril was immensely reassured upon seeing him enter the room. Sol Hurok's appearance, unprepossessing and friendly, dispelled the dark foreboding which had been gnawing at Kyril since the previous night. The young man had been picturing a Russian larger than life, and he had imagined that this huge impresario would shake his head with exasperated disdain and dismiss Kyril without so much as a single polite word.

Instead, Hurok appeared well-fed and neatly attired in an elegant three-piece suit. He had clear eyes, a dimple in his chin, and he was already semi-bald. He was a courtly man, given to hand kissing and much smiling; he openly admired Anna Voorhies. "How often I have wished to meet you, Madame," he said to her as he bent over her outrageously beringed fingers. "You are one of the great art patrons of New York."

"I thank you, Mr. Hurok. And I accept your compliment. Yes, in my day, I have met many great talents on both sides of the Atlantic. Diaghilev was my friend, and also Picasso. And it has been my good luck to discover a number of young artists. So I bring you my latest find, Count Kyril Vadimovitch Malenkov. Is he not absolutely splendid?"

Kyril sat speechless, staring at his benefactress. Hurok laughed. "Yes," he said, "the Count is indeed very handsome. I thought so the moment I saw the photograph of the two of you together, in the *Daily News*. How do you do, Your Excellency?"

"Please," Kyril demurred, shaking the plump little hand that was being thrust at him. "Call me, 'Kyril Vadimovitch.' I am glad to meet you."

Anna Voorhies' butler entered with a magnificent tea tray, and began to arrange platters of *petits-fours* around the coffee table. "I know a little about your family," Hurok was saying to Kyril. "Please accept my sincere condolences upon the untimely deaths of your wife and parents."

Kyril's eyes misted over; he was thinking of Elena. "There are deep sorrows in the life of any adult person, sir," he declared. "Mine have sometimes appeared overwhelming. In Paris I gave in to my grieving, but here, I'm afraid I must pull myself together, and quickly. I am in a new country now, and it's essential I *do something* with myself."

"The United States rewards hard workers," Hurok replied. "And I'm afraid the Bolsheviks have changed the world around. Our most exalted countrymen—such as yourself—have been brutally thrust out, with no preparation for their new existence. As for myself, I came from a humble background, so I never harbored the slightest illusions about my destiny. But any member of our aristocracy is now like a fish out of water these days."

"It's all right, Mr. Hurok." Kyril started to laugh. "I don't really mind the notion of a job. It's just that I've had no training in anything theatrical. I'm prepared to do just about anything—only who would hire someone as inexperienced as me?"

Anna Voorhies was now pouring the tea while the butler passed out the cakes. For a moment nobody spoke. First Hurok, then Kyril, filled their Wedgewood dishes with delicacies from the silver platter. "Cream, Mr. Hurok? Or lemon?" Anna asked.

"Lemon and two sugars, please, Madame." He smiled at Kyril and added: "In our country the samovar used to run all day long in every household, whether that of a peasant or noble. It's a custom I sorely miss."

"I, too," Kyril replied. He bit into a minuscule glazed éclair and gazed helplessly at Anna. When would Hurok get to the point? Almost moment by moment, Kyril could see his revenues diminishing. Each day, new expenses were cropping up. Yet, one could hardly push the man before he was ready.

"Tell us a little about the artists you have represented," Anna said,

smiling graciously. "I understand your newest acquisition is the incomparable Anna Pavlova."

"Yes. This is my good fortune. And I've been managing the Isa-
dorables since 1917."

"I have met Isadora Duncan's young protégées—Lysel and Gretel
—*lovely* girls," Anna commented.

Hurok acknowledged her compliment by inclining his head. "I've
presented quite a few musicians, among them Titta Ruffo, the baritone, and Luisa Tetrazzini, the great coloratura. She is a charming
woman. The only trouble she ever caused me was due to this very
charm. She loves to be in love. In every city there must be someone
to make her heart throb, or her nightingale's voice will not resonate
to its full capacity. Ah, well, with a great artist, one must be prepared to make unusual allowances . . . don't you think, Madame
Voorhies?"

"Quite so," she conceded. Then, clearing her throat, she observed: "I quite admire you for bringing music so successfully to the
masses, Mr. Hurok. At two dollars a ticket, any working man can
go to the Hippodrome to hear your great concerts. That was a brilliant idea, don't you think, Kyra?"

"A splendid idea, Anna." But Kyril's stomach was so tied in
knots that he had to set down his plate, unable to continue eating.

"Do you like Douglas Fairbanks?" Hurok suddenly asked. His
intelligent eyes fastened first upon Anna, then upon her young
guest.

"Well, yes, of course," Kyril stammered.

"He's a romantic hero, like the Barrymores," said Hurok, "but he
possesses other talents as well. He's an athlete, a right proper
swashbuckler. He performs difficult feats as though they were quite
easy for him. Women," he added, "find him irresistible."

"Indeed," Anna assented. "It's little wonder he commands all the
great scripts and great directors."

"Of course. Anita Loos has written for him, and her husband,
John Emerson, has directed. He owns his own production company; this means he can control the material in which he appears.
But the most remarkable thing about Fairbanks is the range of his
roles. To play that many roles takes an unusual sort of personality. It
takes intelligence, beauty, and charm—and it takes humor. In a
word, it takes versatility."

Silence greeted his pronouncement. Then Hurok's face began to
smile. "Kyril Vadimovitch, after having the pleasure of meeting you

in person, I am convinced that you too possess such versatility. To be honest, you are a more handsome man than Fairbanks. You're as good looking as Valentino, with a range of expression in your body that remind me of Fairbanks. I would like you to give me permission to represent you."

"As an actor?" Kyril's tongue felt glued to his palate.

"As an actor. I have an idea. There's a brand-new production company in Hollywood, going by the name of Star Partners. They've purchased a small studio. The partners involved are Sam Unger and Aaron Schwartz, businessmen with no previous experience in films. But they have money behind them, and they're looking for talent. I'd like to fly you over to Hollywood and have you meet them. They could give you a screen test, hiring the best director available for this . . . and if your work can convince them, I see no reason why you shouldn't become their number one male star within a few short months. They've already signed up a well-known female star."

"I don't know what to say," Kyril answered, blinking. "Yes, thank you, Mr. Hurok. Of course, I shall be glad to do whatever is required."

"Then I shall telephone these gentlemen tomorrow morning. Thank you, Mrs. Voorhies, for arranging this informal meeting with Count Malenkov. It has been of infinite value to me."

"And to me as well," Kyril added.

"Well then, how about a toast? I have bootleg champagne stashed away in my cellar for just such occasions as this. Shall I ring for some?" Anna asked.

"We should be delighted," Hurok replied, bending to kiss her hand. "And I say Valentino has reason to sleep badly tonight."

Kyril Ostrov tried to smile, but found himself overcome with emotion. He was afraid to say another word, for fear Hurok would change his mind. How on earth, he wondered, could a few polite sentences have so impressed this knowledgeable impresario? What had made Hurok think that Kyril would be able to compete with Fairbanks? It made no sense whatsoever.

After Hurok had departed, Kyril posed the question to Anna Voorhies. "I'm *not* a Fairbanks," he told her. "I can't see myself swinging from a tree or climbing four stories to rescue a maiden in distress. I'm not funny. I'm not Fatty Arbuckle or Mack Sennett."

"He didn't say you had to be a comic. He said that you had flair, and magnetism. A little training with a sword will quickly restore your fencing abilities. Of course, you did fence as a young man, didn't you, dear?"

"Oh, yes, of course," Kyril lied, swallowing hard. Kyra Malenkov had probably been a master fencer, but he, Kyril Ostrov, had never held a sword of any kind.

"Then you have nothing to worry about," his old friend declared. And she flashed him a brilliant smile.

Kyril maneuvered his flint-gray Pierce-Arrow runabout into Midwood Street. As the cold air beat about his ears with a hissing noise, he thought dreamily of Southern California with its mild weather, its blue skies, and its ocean breeze. He couldn't wait.

As he parked the car in front of the house and got out, he was suddenly nervous and apprehensive. To lessen his discomfort, he stood a moment looking at his automobile. It had cost him seven thousand dollars, a thousand down and the rest in monthly payments. He'd been satisfied with it up till now. It was a two-passenger roadster with a sleek, low-slung body, and its engine was a powerful six-cylinder. Nevertheless, it could not compare to Herbert Hauser's Phaeton nor Anna Voorhies' Bugatti. Those were champion automobiles!

"It will *do,* your Excellency," Mason had declared, handing him the keys as though Kyril were a small boy.

He shook his head and sighed. He wasn't an actor! He had never thought to *be* one! The owners of Star Partners would smile and send him on his way before the first day was over. Agonizing over what to do with as yet unearned riches was as stupid as dreaming of being a knight in shining armor. There was always a dragon to slay before reaching great fame and reputation.

He took a deep breath as he looked at the house. It was small and neat, wedged between two other homes, one larger and more venerable, the other of like stature. Kyril could feel his nervousness mounting as he walked up the stone steps to the front door. His hand hesitated before ringing the doorbell. Perhaps he shouldn't have come.

Zica wore no makeup. She had on soft wool household slippers and a blue skirt that was too long for the fashion of the day. A simple apron was tied around her waist, and her blouse was wrinkled. "Yes?" she asked a trifle nervously, peering out into the winter glare and shading her eyes.

Then she saw who it was. "Oh, my God..." she moaned. *"Why did you come here?"* She took an involuntary step backward into the foyer, the color draining from her cheeks. "My God!" she repeated, *"this is my worst nightmare come true!"*

Kyril was flabbergasted by the violence of her reaction. "I don't understand," he stammered. "Zica, it wasn't so hard to find you. I pulled a few strings to find the address that matched your phone number. It was as simple as that."

"I asked you never to come here," she whispered, her eyes harsh with anger. Then he saw that she was shaking.

"Will you let me in?" he asked. "I'm sorry if my coming has caused such a commotion in your life. I thought... well, after last time, I thought nothing mattered but our being together. I know, you didn't want me to see how you lived... you wanted me to remember you as the Baroness Poliakova in her magnificent palace ... But we're in New York, Zica, and I don't care how poor you are!"

"I care," she said, her voice trembling. "You don't belong here."

Her body blocked the entrance. He hesitated. "Zicotchka," he murmured, "I have guessed it already. This isn't your house. You work here. You didn't want me to know you were working for a family and taking care of their child. But there's no shame in that, you know."

Her dark eyes glared at him, her face closed, tight and stricken.

"Zica," he whispered, "we are immigrants. You're doing what you must to make ends meet. I don't care. I love you, and I've come to ask you... well, to make a voyage with me." His green eyes implored her for forgiveness as he added, humbly: "Please don't let me *freeze* to death on the stoop, darling. I'll come in for ten minutes, and then I promise to be gone—and I'll never visit you here again!"

Silently, she moved aside. As Kyril stepped into the tiny foyer lined with blue wallpaper, he noticed the only furnishings—a costumer and a small mirror. Zica preceded him into a small parlor, where he saw children's toys scattered about and a half-finished square of embroidery on the sofa.

"What do you want, Kyril?" Zica demanded, seating herself on the edge of the sofa.

"I wanted to share something wonderful with you," he said, gently. "I've been invited to Hollywood for a screen test! I thought ...I thought you'd be excited too. Think how many men would give their life savings for a chance like this! It could mean a whole new direction for me!"

For a moment her face softened. She exhaled deeply. "Kyriusha..."

"Yes?"

"I'm very glad for you," she stated, her voice warm and yet detached, as though it had been someone else sitting there in the large wing chair.

"Is that all you can say? Zica, the world is opening for me. Think what that means for *us,* as well! Aren't you happy?"

Instead of replying, she stood up, her face masked with pain, and rammed a fist into the pocket of her apron. "I'm happy for *you,*" she said. But this time her voice broke. She turned aside, beginning to sob. "Oh, Kyriusha, go away! Go to California, go wherever you want...just leave me in peace!"

At that moment a child began to cry. She picked up a fold of her skirt and ran into a corridor. Perplexed, Kyril followed her. The corridor was short and dark. She had opened a door on the left, and had gone in.

As Kyril came to the threshold, he saw her standing in a child's room, the wallpaper bright yellow, decorated with colored animals. She was bent over a crib. More curious than ever, he stepped in quietly behind her. She was lifting a little girl out of the crib. When she turned and saw him there, her face took on a feral look of pure, haunted terror.

"Get out of here!" she hissed, her voice a semi-whisper. "You don't belong here!"

"Mommy no cwy" the little girl said. She was round and robust, perhaps two years of age, with huge chocolate-brown saucer eyes. Her dark, curly hair tumbled about her rose face. "Mommy smi','" she ordered. "Smi' *now!* "

They stood staring into each other's eyes, Zica holding the little girl, Kyril facing her. Zica's features no longer appeared fearful; they were defiant. She was daring him to say something.

Kyril was at a loss for words. He looked at the child, then back at Zica. "She's exquisite," he murmured. "What's her name?"

"Victoria," Zica said. "We call her 'Vickie.'"

"I see." He remained staring at the two of them, feeling time come to a stop. The world balanced on the head of a pin. He could feel the pain, the sense of disembodiment. "She looks just like you," he finally stated, his voice uneven.

"You may go if you'd like," Zica said. "I must give her a bottle."

"I'd rather stay," he answered. "For a little while, at least."

"Suit yourself." Zica pushed past him, holding the small child, and proceeded into a tiny kitchenette. He followed some steps behind.

In the kitchen, she secured Victoria in a wooden high chair, set a bottle of warm milk in a double boiler on the old stove. She addressed the child gently: *"Mmm . . .* Vickie's going to get good, warm milk. And then we can go for a walk. Would you like that?"

"Bick an' Mom. Go bye-bye? Man come too?"

"No," Zica answered smoothly. "The man must go home."

Without looking at Kyril, she took the warm bottle from the stove, dried it, and popped a few drops of milk from the nipple onto the back for her hand. Satisfied with the temperature, she handed the bottle to the child. Vickie grabbed it and began to suck hungrily on the rubber nipple.

"Why didn't you tell me?" Kyril asked. "Vickie is *your* child— not just a child you were paid to take care of?"

"I did not tell you because you are no longer part of my life!"

"But surely, Zica, you could have told me that you had a child! She's a lovely little girl. I would have wanted to meet her."

"Why should you care?" Zica tossed back, but there was exhaustion and defeat in her voice. She turned toward the stove and let her head drop. "I have another life, Kyril. This child is my life. You are a playboy in society. I could see that in the newspaper picture. It's been years since I went to a society party, Kyril. But I don't miss those parties. I am glad to be out of Moscow—thankful to be alive. I am grateful to be safe from the Black Ravens who took good men and women to their deaths, from the CHEKA, from cockroaches and roast millet and misery. You have no idea what happened after the Bolsheviks took over. We were *all* their slaves, to do with what *they* willed." Zica took a breath. "I love being here in New York. I'm not going to apologize to you for anything! You told me, Kyril, that you never wanted to see me again. You wanted me to forget I ever knew you. Well . . . this is the result!"

"That was *six years ago,"* he said, in a hushed voice. "Can't we go beyond that mistake? I wanted you then, and I still want you now. Can't we try to start again?"

Without speaking, Zica took the now empty bottle away from Vickie, released her from the high chair, and let her slide down to the ground. The little girl looked up at her mother, tugging on her small jumper, for all the world a tiny little woman. "Go bye-bye," she declared.

"Not yet, angel," Zica answered. "First, the nice man is going away, and we must walk him to the door."

Kyril shook his head, as though to delay this. "But you didn't explain—"

"Explain what? That I have a child? Yes, Kyriusha, Vickie is my child. After what happened to *our* baby, I never believed I would be able to have another. But you see, I did. The gods were kind to me after all."

"And the father?"

"A Russian man. None of this is important." Zica waved the question aside with a shrug.

"Is he . . . are you . . . married?"

She began to tremble. "You no longer have the right to ask me anything," she stated, her voice low and vibrant. "It was my mistake for calling that woman, Mrs. Voorhies, and giving her my number. It was a bigger mistake to meet you in that restaurant. But now we can correct these mistakes. You can leave me alone, Kyril Ostrov, or Malenkov, or whatever your name is! *I am not yours, Kyril*—do you understand? And you are never to come back here," she added.

"Zica, I love you. I'm sorry if I hurt you long ago. You have a beautiful child. I don't really care who her father is. It's you I want. If that means this child comes with you, I'll take her and gladly!"

In Zica's eyes was an ineffable sadness. She shook her head. "It's too late," she whispered. "It's years too late. I'm sorry if I misled you the other day."

"You gave me hope because you wanted this, just as much as I did," Kyril said, urgency in his tone. "You can throw me out, but your eyes tell me different. Why can't you come with me to Hollywood? Is it the man . . . the father? Is he still in your life, here in New York? Or is he back in Russia?"

"It doesn't matter," Zica repeated, her eyes filling with tears. "You must go to Hollywood. You will be successful and you will soon forget me. I *want* you to forget me. I have a life here, Kyriusha, and other obligations."

"We'll get you a divorce, if that's the problem. Is it?"

She shook off the question. "You must leave me alone. You must go to the West and meet your film people. I wish . . . yes, I do wish I could just pick up Victoria, and follow you to sunshine and glory.

But I can't hurt *this man!* He was there when I most needed help, and he has never let me down. I can't walk out of his life, just because—"

"—you're in love with someone else? But yes you can, Zica. This is not like Moscow, where you had a reputation to preserve. Here, nobody knows you. You will be my wife, and no one will ask for your history. Zica—I beg you—come with me!"

The little girl was tugging at Zica's hand. "Man go bye-bye?" she asked.

"Yes, Vickie," Kyril replied, crouching down beside her. "I'm leaving now." He touched her small cheek tentatively, with wonder and regret. "Good-bye again," he said, turning toward the door.

"Good-bye," Zica said softly, as he stepped out into the cold. She pulled the door shut behind him and fastened the dead bolt.

When Kyril reached the Pierce-Arrow, his eyes sought the living room window. He could see two faces gazing out at him. The two looked almost identical, framed with dark hair and the backdrop of gauze curtain. The child's face was softer and rounder, her eyes filled with wonder. The woman's eyes were sad—so sad that he could not bear to look back for long. They were the saddest eyes he had ever seen.

Chapter XVII

*I*N the heart of the Hollywood hills—between Hollywood "proper" and the San Fernando Valley township of Burbank— Star Partners Productions had set up its studio. Originally, the lot and some crude sound stage sets had been constructed by a comic actor to start his own production company. Bad luck had plagued that endeavor. On the verge of bankruptcy, the actor had sold his land and buildings to two businessmen from Florida, Aaron Schwartz and Sam Unger.

Schwartz and Unger, two middle-aged Jews reared in the rougher neighborhoods of New York City, had possessed no previous experience in running a film studio. But they knew a great deal about investments, contracts, and the gambles required to turn one's business from a moderately successful enterprise into big money.

Aaron Schwartz, born in the Bronx in 1880, had managed, by the age of twenty-two, to turn his father's dry goods store into a small chain of grocery stores. By the time his father died in 1910, Schwartz had sold the concern to the Piggly Wiggly grocerterias, on condition that he would become a junior partner. With the phenomenal profit he reaped in two years, he took his wife Naomi, a Brooklyn school teacher, to Orlando, Florida, where he invested in a land development company that built retirement homes for couples in their golden years. On the side, he began dabbling in the stock market.

A tall, wiry, good-looking man, Schwartz had met Sam Umger at a promotion party given by an Orlando realtor in 1919. Unger was a short, soft-spoken man with prematurely white hair. His appearance was that of a gentle, lazy white cat sunning itself on a terrace; but in fact, he had a sharp, legal mind and was one of the brightest students ever to graduate with a law degree from New York University. A Brooklyn boy who had made his way on scholarships and hard work, he had been on retainer for many years to a number of important firms around the country. Unger had passed the bar in New York, California, Texas, and Illinois; his clients included public utilities, resort hotels, restaurants and department store chains.

Most recently, he had become counsel to the Orlando realtor who threw the party at which he met Aaron Schwartz. He had moved to Florida to escape the hustle and bustle of New York City. He conducted the majority of his business on the telephone, and when he had to make a trip, he carried his work with him on the train. The Florida sunshine had seemed a good idea at the time.

Thus businessman had encountered lawyer: an immediate bond had developed. Aaron Schwartz knew a good thing when he saw one, and the soft-spoken, gentle-mannered Unger seemed a definite "good thing." So Schwartz had convinced Unger to drop most of his other clients and form a partnership.

The two men then embarked on a new field of endeavor, an enterprise which, if successful, would pay off a-thousand-to-one. They decided to enter the burgeoning film industry. Backed not only by their own money but also by that of former clients of Unger's, they moved their operation to Los Angeles. They would open a film studio to rival Metro, Paramount, Vitagraph and Biograph—and they would produce one- and two-reel shorts as well as quality features. All they needed was a dynamic star in the Fairbanks mold, and a *femme fatale* to stop men's hearts.

The first step had been the purchase of the land and the construction of a modern studio. The groundwork was all set. All that remained was to find talent for the films. Unger felt that new talent would be easier to develop than hand-me-downs from the other studios, although he had been more than happy to "steal" Harry Walsh, one of Adolph Zukor's prize directors, from Paramount. He also had the foresight to steal the nubile Adrienne Lance from Metro. What was most needed now was a romantic male lead—and perhaps also a comic actor like Chaplin or Keaton to expand their *repertoire* of scripts. Star Partners needed actors that had that magic element—mystique. To create such mystique, they had hired Melodie Warren, a bespectacled public relations expert in her early thirties. Melodie knew how to play the news-hungry tabloids and magazines for every last ounce of publicity.

Star Partners was now prepared to begin its search for the next male heart-throb of America.

Unger and Schwartz had let it be known that they were on the lookout for some as-yet-undiscovered star. And this was why Sol Hurok thought of them when he opened his *Daily News* to the startling photograph of Count Kyril Malenkov. The morning after his meeting with Kyril at the home of Anna Voorhies, he telephoned Aaron Schwartz at his new home in Beverly Hills.

"I have someone for you," Hurok told Schwartz. "He's everything you say you want—young, but with enough experience in his face to give him range of expression. He's genteel and elegant, dresses like a prince, and has as much innate charm as Fairbanks."

"Who is he?" Aaron Schwartz asked cautiously. He knew Hurok by reputation, and respected his ability to pick out talent at a concert, opera, or ballet. But how would the impresario know about an as-yet-untested actor?

"His name is Count Kyril Malenkov. A *real count,* Aaron. Think of the mileage you can get from *that!* His family has been on intimate terms with the *Tzars of Russia!* Better yet, Aaron. He's a victim of the Bolsheviks! Now look what I'm giving you: a Count brought low, impoverished by a terrible injustice. What moviegoers won't be thrilled to see him on the screen—foreign nobility with an *exotic flair. Aaron,* this is too good to pass up!"

"You haven't told me how he looks," Schwartz interjected.

"Wait till you see. Cross a Cossack with a Greek god, and you've got the picture. I won't keep you guessing. I'm having photographs made—they'll be coming to you, by special mail. In the meantime, I'm sending a newspaper clipping which appeared in the *Daily News*. My man is the darling of the East Coast blue bloods. He got here two years ago, and they've idolized him ever since. This can't hurt his reputation, either."

By the time Anna Voorhies had arranged for her photographer to take head shots of Kyril—as well as several full shots to display his physique—Aaron Schwartz and his partner were already tantalized by the charming newspaper photo of the tuxedoed Russian count. Sol had not been wrong. Malenkov was "the genuine article," an elegant man with the face of a fallen angel—tragic yet amused and sensitive. If a newspaper photographer could catch him unexpectedly, and still reveal his splendor, how much better the count would look when "done up" by the studio. The camera was his friend.

The following week, the Star Partners Productions received an airmail manila envelope from the office of Sol Hurok in New York. Sam Unger looked over Schwartz's shoulder as his partner slit open the envelope. Together, they hunched over the eight-by-ten glossy photographs of Count Kyril Malenkov in various poses. As they flipped through the twenty photographs, the partners did not utter a single word.

Finally, Schwartz set them aside and wheeled his chair around to face Unger.

"We've got our man," he declared softly. "This one's a winner."

Unger nodded. "Shall I place a call now?"

"Careful," Schwartz countered. "Let Hurok know we've got our reservations. We don't want this society kid thinking he's hot stuff before the screen test comes. In fact . . . we don't want him to expect anything at all. We'll send his him train ticket and have Melodie meet him at the station in Pasadena. That way, he'll want to polish our apple, rather than the other way around."

"I'll book Harry Walsh for the screen test," Unger said. "Melodie can take care of the rest."

It was only then that the two partners shook hands, smiling broadly. "Good old Hurok . . ." Schwartz murmured. "He's right on the money, as usual. This time, so are we."

"Not so fast—they're only stills," Unger said soberly. "Our Russian wolfhound could turn into a mutt in front of the camera."

The telephone rang insistently in Zica's little house. After seven rings, she picked up her end and said, "Hello?"

"It's me." Kyril's voice was low and tentative. "I hope you don't mind. I had to tell you that I'm leaving on Friday."

"I hope you'll pass your screen test." Zica's voice was no stronger than his.

"Zica." He paused: "Won't you please come to the station to see me off? It would mean the world to me."

"I can't," she answered, tightness in her voice. "I already gave you my farewell. Kyriusha . . . it's never going to work between us. Every time we see each other, it's either too soon or too late."

"But—you are in love."

There was a pause. When she spoke, her voice was tired. "I've tried so hard, Kyril, to put the past behind me—all the past. The house on the Tverskaya and everything it meant. And above all, *you!*"

"Can't we at least speak to each other on the telephone?"

"You'll be on the West Coast. I'll think of you. I'll—I'll see all your movies . . ."

"My train leaves Grand Central Station at ten-fifty on Friday morning," he said firmly.

"Good-bye, Kyriusha," she whispered, putting down the receiver.

The bloody bastard hadn't returned his call.

Yakov sat behind the counter in the pawnshop, tapping his pencil in frustration. Mrs. Voorhies had promised to give Ostrov—whom she called "Malenkov"—his message. But days turned to weeks, and still Kyril had not called back.

Yes, Yakov knew he was just an unimportant immigrant. Perhaps Anna Voorhies had not even conveyed his greetings to her young friend. Yakov felt his blood begin to boil. Ostrov was no better a man than he. Yet here, as in Russia, he consorted with the powerful, moneyed elite—and snubbed those of lesser station.

Yakov's ill humor was not helped by Zica. She herself had been moody herself lately. She stayed busy with Vickie, hardly bothering to exchange words with her husband when he came home. She was probably resentful about her situation. How hard, thought Yakov, to have been a great lady and now to be forced to live in modest circumstances, like a *shtetl* immigrant!

After three years of marriage, there were still moments when Yakov found Zica very mysterious. He reminded himself that she'd married him without any declaration of love. *He* had forced the marriage. But whenever these bouts of honesty would come upon him, he thought of how much they had grown to love each other and their daughter. True, there were times when she did not seem to love him; these days, she barely seemed to tolerate him. But that was the mystery; how, and why, did she drift away from him?

Whenever her eyes clouded over, Yakov would feel a stab in his heart. Always, he wondered if she were remembering Kyril. Yet how could it be, when that man was so weak—when he had wronged her in so many ways and deserted her in her most desperate hour?

Impulsively, Yakov picked up the black telephone on the counter. Moments later, he was telling Yossif Adolfovitch that he was coming down with a case of influenza. "I'll just have to close up shop," he said, holding his nose as though he had a stuffed head. "I'll try to be here early tomorrow." The old man answered gruffly—he had no patience with anybody else's problems. But Yakov didn't care. His thoughts were already far from his Hester Street job.

Before locking up, he dismissed the teenage boy and girl who worked for him in the pawn and jewelry shops. He could not trust them alone in the building, with all the cash and merchandise.

Bundled up in his overcoat and scarf, Yakov walked to the nearest subway station. Within half an hour, he was at his destination— Anna Voorhies' palatial home on Fifth Avenue at Fifty-second Street.

Was it too much to hope that Ostrov might be visiting her *that very day?* Clearly, the young "Count" had many other pursuits besides visiting an old lady.

Had this been Russia, Anna Voorhies would have had her "receiving day," like the Baroness Poliakova. But Yakov knew that here in New York the practice of receiving days did not exist. And suddenly, his search began to seem hopelessly futile.

It was bitter-cold. The sidewalk was lined with ice patches, and the soles of Yakov's feet began to smart. If he were to wait for Ostrov, he'd have to find a place of refuge where he would be provided with a head-on view of Anna Voorhies' front door.

But where?

Despair washed over him. He was examining the sculpted facade of the imposing mansion, when all at once it occurred to him that only one lone footman paced the pavement in front of the venerable edifice.

Suddenly hopeful, Yakov walked to the corner. On Fifty-second Street was another entrance. Stone steps led up to magnificent double doors of bronze-studded oak, shielded by a splendid red and gold awning bearing the huge initial *V* in scrolled script. Two footmen in gold-braided scarlet marched back and forth from opposite ends of the house, passing each other where the steps began.

Yakov quickly crossed to the north side of Fifty-second Street. Neat brownstone houses flanked each other, elegantly protected by wrought-iron fencing. Suddenly he knew just where he'd wait. There was a small tea room in the bottom half of the brownstone cater-corner to the mansion. He turned the brass handle and entered the tea room.

Immediately, a *maître d'hôtel* in tails came up to him. *"Monsieur* would like a table by himself?"

Aware that he looked out of place in his simple wool coat and bright red scarf, Yakov nodded. "I'd like to sit by the window," he said. Moments later, he had a vantage point for any comings and goings across the street. A quick look around the tea room assured him that, apart from two silver-haired ladies in hats, veils, and furs, he was alone in this exclusive little eatery. It was only eleven in the morning, much too early for tea: probably the two old ladies had taken refuge from the cold during a shopping expedition.

He had little money on him—only a few dollars. Although hunger was already gnawing at his insides, he ordered no food. He nursed his single cup of Ceylon tea for over an hour.

Shortly after noon, cars began to pull up in front of the marble edifice. Immediately, Yakov paid his bill and rushed outside. Automobiles were being parked by one of the footmen, while the other let people into the mansion. It looked like a luncheon party.

Yakov rubbed his gloved hands and shuffled his feet to revive circulation. Phaetons and coupés were already pulling up, discharging well-dressed people of every age.

Finally, a sleek gray car stopped right in front; the eager footman helped a young woman out of the passenger side. She wore a lush fox fur and a trim little hat; underneath, her short, bobbed hair bounced saucily. When Yakov saw the young man emerging from the driver's seat, he realized he had to wait no longer. It was Ostrov!

Yakov barely escaped being hit by a passing Cadillac limousine, which blared its horn. The elegant young man, wearing a sealskin coat with a matching Russian-style hat, had joined the pretty young woman. Arm in arm, they ascended the stone steps where the other footman stood at attention.

"Ah," he greeted him. "Mrs. Tulliver and His Excellency, Count Malenkov!" The man's jovial voice had an Irish lilt. The footman opened the double door with a graceful, deferential gesture.

Yakov took the steps two at a time.

"*Wait!*" he shouted.

By the open doorway, the three people froze, turning to look at him with puzzlement and a hint of fear. The footman was the first to react, jumping forward to intercept Yakov. His bulky body was in the way; there was a frown on his florid face. "What is it ya be wantin'?" he demanded.

The man and the woman stood framed in the doorway. Ostrov's hand protectively cupped the woman's elbow—the very pose he had adopted with Anna Voorhies in the *Daily News* photograph. Yakov noticed she was very pretty, with a chiselled face and soft, dreamy eyes.

"I have something important to say to Count Malenkov!" he blurted to the guard.

The Irishman turned to Kyril, perplexed. Kyril stared at Yakov with a quizzical expression.

"Who is this?" murmured the young woman anxiously.

Kyril stared at Yakov as the intruder tried to edge past the guard. But the guard blocked his way with practiced temerity. "Y'ain't goin' no further till the Count gives his okay," he rasped.

"Kyriusha!" Yakov cried. "It's me, Yasha Pokhis! From Moscow! Don't you remember?"

He saw Ostrov stiffen. The young woman looked quizzically at her escort. "Do you know this man?" she murmured. "He called you 'Kyriusha. . . .'"

Ostrov's eyes narrowed. "Hugh," he said, turning to the footman, "I'm afraid I've never seen this person before in my life." To the woman he added apologetically: "I'm sorry, Elsie. Ever since that picture appeared in the paper, I've been stopped by many Russian immigrants who claim they knew me in the motherland. They're hoping for a hand-out. One can hardly blame them, actually. The Bolsheviks have reduced our beloved country to a heap of rubbish. Those who escaped had nothing but the clothes on their back."

"But he called you, 'Kyriusha,'" Elsie Tulliver insisted.

Ostrov smiled. "'Kyriusha' is the more customary diminutive for 'Kyril,'" he explained. "But my family liked 'Kyra' better. Anyone who knew me wouldn't have made that mistake. And now, let's go in. We were expected at Anna's luncheon ten minutes ago." He addressed the footman: "Thank you, Hugh. We're all right now."

Kyril and the small woman disappeared inside the Voorhies mansion, their footsteps click-clacking on the parquet floors of its foyer.

The instant they were gone, the footman grasped Yakov by the collar. "I'd better never see the likes o' *you* hangin' 'round this place," he warned in a low, threatening voice. His face was so close, Yakov could smell tobacco on his breath. Abruptly, Hugh let him go. Yakov backed away, shaken and defeated.

Descending the stone steps, Yakov pondered. What to do now? Clearly, Kyril Ostrov wanted no one to finger him as an imposter. Yakov felt like a fool, confronting Kyril in a public place, in front of two witnesses. Ostrov had felt safe dismissing Yakov like a small nuisance.

But Ostrov did not know that Yakov held all the cards. Yakov could bring forth Lena and Yossif to confront Kyril and prove he wasn't Malenkov. More damaging still, *he knew what had taken place on Ellis Island.* If Ostrov intended to play that "I-don't-know-you" game (a dirty trick!), then Yakov would be forced to bring out the heavy artillery. He would have to confront Kyril another time—but this time, he would be better prepared.

The problem remained... *Where would he meet Ostrov,* to put the screws to him? Now that Hugh, the footman, recognized him, Yakov could no longer hope to catch Ostrov when he emerged from the Voorhies mansion.

There had to be another way.

Grand Central Station was awe-inspiring. Zica felt dwarfed by its sheer size and cavernous interior and by the hubbub of activity all around her. Lengthy lines of anxious passengers stood before every ticket window while a loudspeaker announced the destinations of trains about to depart, signalling a wild rush toward the tracks.

She had five minutes to catch up to Kyril. Zica wove her way through the people waiting to board, dodging the luggage that crowded the narrow island of concrete.

Until an hour ago, Zica had been firm in her resolve to forget Kyril—to continue with her life as it was. She didn't want to hurt Yakov, but he already knew something was wrong. Ever since meeting Kyril she'd been afraid to talk to her husband, afraid to look him in the eye. She knew how unhappy she was, and she knew it showed. Kyril was right: by compromising her own feelings, she was abdicating the will to be happy in her own right. Why did she still feel this surge of love for Kyril? Why couldn't she stop it from happening? Was her life with Yakov a terrible mistake?

That morning at breakfast, Yakov had leaned over to kiss her. Instinctively, she had placed a hand on his arm to stay him. She'd seen his hurt but was unable to stop herself. The marriage had taken on an image of unreality, as though it were only a play in which she had a role. She wanted that unreality to go away; she wanted Yakov to touch her heart, as he had so many times in their years together. But the shadow of Kyril lingered, like a demon condemning her to unhappiness.

That morning she had been acutely conscious that *this* was the day Kyril would leave for Los Angeles. If she didn't get to the station, he would be lost to her forever—of that she was sure. She didn't know whether or not she had a future with him. All she knew was that she had to see Kyril before he took that train.

Once before, she had ruined both their lives by losing her belief in their love. If only she had married him that night at the Simonovs, and consecrated their love forever, perhaps the strength of this love would have conquered all.

I am not alive anymore, she told herself. I'm twenty-five years old and I feel dead inside; each day is like the next. *I must go to him.*

Afraid to pause or even to think, for fear that her conscience would still her heart's resolve, Zica had scooped up the baby and brought her over to Mrs. Patchulnik's. "I'll be home by noon," she had said to her. She prayed she was telling the truth. But her heart was racing so madly, she could no longer trust herself.

Now Zica glanced quickly at the huge clock. Kyril's train was due to leave from Platform 17. Zica darted ahead, bumping into a child, then an old man, searching for the platform number. She glimpsed number 17 above a dark passageway, and elbowed her way past passengers struggling with their suitcases.

The train was still in the station.

Where was he?

Suddenly, she saw a young man wearing a fur coat and hat, standing on the step of a first-class carriage. His broad face was turned away from her. She recognized his figure with a lurch of the heart—but as she dashed forward, crying out Kyril's name, a burly man with three small children blocked her path.

"Excuse me!" Desperately, she edged past. What if she lost him *now,* in all the confusion?

A loudspeaker announced final boarding. Zica looked all about her for the man in the fur coat. He seemed to have vanished.

A tall, thin man in black livery was just emerging from the first-class carriage. Following immediately behind was Kyril. Zica raised her arm to wave—but suddenly she froze, her greeting halted in mid-voice.

A young woman in a full-length astrakhan coat with a gray felt hat, was holding out her arms to Kyril. In disbelieving horror, Zica watched as the young man stepped from the train, bending to take the slight, elegant woman in his arms. The woman pressed her hands lovingly to Kyril's face, caressing his cheeks. When finally they drew apart, Zica saw the man turn back toward the train and once more ascend the steps.

He disappeared inside and the metal door shut behind him.

Zica could not move or breathe. All around her, well-wishers were waving their handkerchiefs. The train whistled—a series of

long, lugubrious hoots signalling the start of its long journey west-
ward. Zica sought out the young woman in the astrakhan coat. She
was leaning on the arm of the somber butler. Zica could not take
her eyes off her: she looked small, vulnerable... and unbearably
rich.

As the train began to move, Zica edged toward the woman. Who
was she? What was she to Kyril?

Zica approached the center of the platform, where the tall, angular man still supported the woman. *She was beautiful,* beautiful like a
Dresden figurine, in her smart hat and costly fur coat. She had a
heart-shaped face and tiny, perfect features.

Then this small, doll-like woman raised her hand and waved her
square of lace, standing on tiptoe to make sure Kyril could see her
from inside the car.

Unable to bear any more, Zica turned around and followed a
group of elderly women back to the main lobby of Grand Central
Station. Despair flooded her being—a dark, enveloping despair that
seemed to pull her into an abyss. *He'd found someone else.* This delicate little girlfriend had been there all along. It made no difference
that Zica had turned him down. She was nothing to him—just a
bauble from his checkered past!

Suddenly enervated, she sank down on a bench beneath the big
clock. Kyril had given his affections to another woman, a rich
American. He had dropped into *her* arms—to *her,* he had given his
final kiss. And Zica, feeling the fool, had been forced to stare in
open-mouthed amazement while these two people, so much in
love, said their farewells.

Kyril no longer needed Zica: he had already forgotten all about
her.

Then, and only then, did her tears begin to fall.

Chapter XVIII

*M*ELODIE Warren was annoyed. She had been forced to leave the studio to pick up this Russian. Frankly, she thought she had better things to do than to play chauffeur to a would-be actor who hadn't even been tested. She resented the fuss. So what if the man had been a Count in the days of the Romanovs? Oh, she quite agreed that his exotic background would play well in Cleveland and Omaha. Even in Manhattan and L.A. he would draw notice. In fact, she was excited about working on his image. This was her specialty. But sending her out like a messenger to greet the man's train... that was going too far.

Melodie Warren knew her worth. She also knew everybody else's. At thirty-three, she was moderately good looking—if you like a tall, broad-shouldered woman with short, bobbed red hair touched with henna. But she was no beauty. Melodie was myopic, and wore large, round glasses that made her sharp hazel eyes seem almost naively innocent. But few were stupid enough to think her naive. And those who were quickly changed their opinion in her presence.

Melodie, *née* Mirna Weiss, had been born in Pittsburgh, Pennsylvania, where her father and mother were the proud owners of a tailor shop. Since the first time she had gone to the circus she'd dreamt of being a showgirl. She'd even studied dancing, hoping that Florenz Ziegfeld would some day make her one of the chorus girls in his annual *Follies*.

Sometime in her late teens, she'd come to her senses. She wasn't delicate and dainty; she was simply a smart Jewish girl with a hard Pittsburgh accent, who looked nice enough for Hymie Erbst, the butcher boy, to want her for a girlfriend. But she wanted more—much more, and she knew how to get it. Persistent hard work and a clever understanding of people's motivations and desires had served her well.

She'd first gone to New York. There, in a small, cramped room at the YWCA, she had considered her options. Since she'd always had a talent with words, she visited the offices of the Calkins and Holden Advertising Agency in Manhattan, where a new kind of advertising was being pioneered. In the past, agencies had merely placed advertisements, created by their clients, in magazines and newspapers. But in 1902 Calkins and Holden had begun to make up its *own* ads and campaigns on behalf of clients. Mirna thought she saw possibilities. She convinced Ralph Holden that she and his partner needed her talents. It was 1906, and she was barely eighteen years old; but her gumption won her points with those in power.

She was first hired to work on soap ads as an assistant to the writer in charge. The starting pay was small, so she continued to live at the Y. But Mirna soon began to make suggestions—first to her boss, who incorporated her ideas into his own work and appropriated the credit; then to Holden and Calkins, who realized the value of this young woman. By the mid-teens, she had stopped acting shy and had started to send memoranda to the offices of the principals, noting some of her marketing observations.

It had been her suggestion, for instance, to heighten sales of Palmolive soap by making it appeal to a woman's vanity. The slogan "You, too, can have 'A skin you love to touch'" had been her idea. Then she suggested placing a man in the picture, with his arm around the beautiful Palmolive girl, his cheek to hers.

"Everyone wants to be Theda Bara, vamp *extraordinaire* of the movies," she explained. "We're just telling them how easy it can be."

Within a few months, she had been promoted to her boss's position and placed in charge of the agency's most demanding clients. With the job she inherited her boss's salary, which enabled her to move to a pretty apartment in Greenwich Village. She began setting money aside.

She'd bought herself a second-hand fur and a turquoise-and-amethyst cocktail ring, redeemed from a pawnshop on Hester Street. She understood that, if she wanted to be pampered, she would have to pamper herself. Mirna Weiss had neither the time nor the background—nor, indeed, the inbred sophistication—to marry into wealth and fame. She would have to carve out her own identity by virtue of her sharp wits.

Meanwhile, she sought out news articles concerning women for whom everything had come easily since birth. She examined the girls in the society columns. They enraged her, both because of their nonchalant beauty and because she felt they lived useless lives. Since Mirna was brutally honest with herself, she knew that she also hated them for having what she wanted and would never have—a romantic love life and ready access to cash they never had to worry about earning. Last but not least, they had the cameo beauty that came of purebred WASP genes.

Mirna was determined to become a success. But her position at the agency was ultimately a dead end. The bosses owned the company. There was little incentive to stick around waiting to take their place. So Mirna had left New York and moved to Los Angeles with her fur, her cocktail ring, and her suitcase full of books and magazines. Toting her portfolio to Metro, she asked whether she could work in the public relations department. And why not? If she could create myths around a simple product such as soap, how much more challenging to put her brain to work on a human product.

The personnel department at the large studio was convinced. Mirna Weiss was put on Metro's payroll. It was 1918, and she was put in charge of the great comic star Mabel Normand, who had recently come over from Mack Sennett's Keystone Company.

But in spite of Mirna's clever news releases and the press kit she put together for the beautiful actress, Mable Normand could not readily adjust to the fast pace of Hollywood, and her career took the inevitable downward swing. Declaring the experience a loss, Mirna moved to Fatty Arbuckle's company to pump up his already splendid image as one of the funniest men on earth.

It was then she decided to reinvent herself, changing her name to Melodie Warren—a name that might have belonged to a slim, *blasé* heroine of the society page. She hired an elocution teacher to get rid of her telltale accent and acquired the smooth speech of a Vassar girl. She took to bobbing and coloring her hair. She shortened her skirts and began sporting long strands of fake pearls. She told everyone that she came from Boston, where, sad to say, her once-prominent father had died burdened with debts. How unfortunate that he had been incapable of setting up a trust fund for his only child.

But the family, she said, had once been steeped in money. Her father—and his father before him—had never known how to manage it properly. They had both been scholars with heads fit only for writing poetry and reading old Latin texts. That explained why she had had to go to work.

In the evening, Melodie rode the trolley to Vermont and Sixth Street, where she owned a small house. She would sit and file her nails, set her hair, and down her nightly glass of bootleg scotch on the rocks. And she waited for the phone to ring, which happened whenever Cubby Armstrong was in town.

Cubby Armstrong was a shoe salesman from San Francisco, a married man with two children he dearly cherished; but he was handsome and funny, and he liked her company. He'd take her for long drives and out to dinner, and they danced and stayed out late. He was her fantasy of a romantic lover, and she was his escape from the doldrums of his marriage.

She knew that Cubby wasn't the answer for her; but, if pressed, she would have stated that she didn't think she'd ever find a perfect mate. She didn't even know whether marriage was for her. How much more agreeable to be treated like a lady by her courteous lover.

When Unger and Schwartz made their move to Hollywood, they began to gather information about the film business. One day, while chatting over breakfast with a Metro executive who wasn't happy where he was, they learned that Fatty Arbuckle had acquired a talented workhorse named Melodie Warren. Melodie now headed his public relations team.

That very night, from their suite at the Beverly Hills Hotel, they called Melodie and set up a meeting. They hired her at lunch the next day. They recognized at once that Melodie was an intense, ambitious, clever woman, whose desire for achievement far outweighed any thoughts of family. "Consider *us* your family now," Sam Unger had told her. "And baby, we'll make 'em sorry at Metro that they ever let you go!"

She'd kissed Fatty good-bye—on the cheek—and moved into a spacious, comfortable office in the new Star Partners studio. She loved the sense of power that her position offered. Schwartz and Unger respected her judgment, and she liked starting with them from scratch. She'd gotten in on the ground floor. And, as they kept reminding her, "The sky was the limit!"

Now, as Melodie Warren hopped out of the company car, she was prepared for the worst. Malenkov would be ill-bred and arrogant, one of those Lenin types who would reek of bad vodka; or he would be a Tzar Nicholas, effete and ineffectual, his heart in his palace and his wits somewhere around his ankles. Melodie patted her *cloche* hat and sighed as she entered the Pasadena terminal. She went at once to the platform where the train was due to pull in.

But if Malenkov expected to be greeted effusively, he would be sorely disappointed. Irritated, Melodie now wished she had turned Aaron Schwartz down, and forced him to send a young assistant in her place.

The balmy breath of warm air swept over Kyril the moment he stepped from the train to the Pasadena platform. He hadn't slept the night before. Now he felt dazed as he looked about, waiting for the porter to take down his luggage.

"Where to?" the man demanded, when he had loaded the luggage on a cart.

Kyril shrugged. "I'm not sure. I was supposed to be met by someone from the studio." His eyes scanned the platform.

"Count Malenkov?" A tall Amazon in a trim cloth coat and felt hat covering a profusion of red curls, was striding toward him. Her gloved hand was extended. Huge glasses perched on the bony ridge of her nose.

"I'm Melodie Warren," she announced, smiling. He saw large, white teeth and a strong chin, and heard a clipped accent redolent of careful training. The voice reminded him of Elsie Tulliver, but the thought of the small, dainty New Yorker unsettled him. American women were surprising creatures; he still hadn't figured out what to make of the debutante-turned-divorcée.

Kyril returned her smile and sought to raise her hand to his lips. She resisted him, strong fingers gripping his palm and shaking it briskly. "I'm in charge of public relations at Star Partners," she told him. "Come. I'll take you for a hamburger and we can talk. Then I must drive you to your hotel. This evening, you are invited to dine at Mr. and Mrs. Schwartz's. You'll meet Mr. Unger there, too."

"This is too much for me to swallow in one gulp," he replied, grinning sheepishly. "But I'd love a hamburger. I couldn't eat breakfast down in the dining car this morning—the excitement, you know. I feel like a small boy anticipating his first visit to a toy factory."

She nodded, studiously unimpressed by his sincerity. "The company car is parked in the lot." To the attendant she added: "It's a black Porter. You can't miss it. Just load the luggage in the back."

Indeed, it couldn't be missed. It was a sleek black town car. Kyril was impressed by the car—impressed, too, with the tall Amazon who had been sent to greet him. Surely, this meant that Schwartz and Unger considered him a promising prospect.

Melodie watched the porter fit the bags inside the car, and motioned for Kyril to take the passenger seat next to her. She pressed some bills into the porter's hand, revved up the motor, and sped away along a well-paved road bordered by hills.

She drove with the casual ease of an experienced driver. Kyril was overwhelmed by the lush countryside. It was warm and pleasant— a pleasant contrast to the chilling temperatures of New York.

As Melodie Warren drove, she hummed a jazz tune Kyril had often heard at the speakeasies in Manhattan. He did not know what to make of her. Did one flirt with such as person, or would she consider this an insult to her position?

Finally she veered off onto a long, winding road. To the right rose magnificent hills; to the left, the city of Los Angeles. Kyril was, indeed, very hungry by the time they pulled up in front of what looked like a drugstore. Melodie took his arm commandingly as she led him inside.

They seated themselves in a small, cozy booth. When the waitress appeared, Melodie ordered hamburgers, fries, and Coca-Colas. Then she sat back and appraised Kyril, her hazel eyes half-shut as she peered at him from behind her huge, owlish spectacles. What was she thinking?

When Melodie finally spoke, her voice was different from before —just a shade more tentative. "Tell me about the life you led in Russia. I want to understand what you're all about."

"Why's that?" he asked.

"It's my job to send out press releases on the actors we hire." Her voice was clipped and businesslike. "I won't know whether you're hired until *Messieurs* Schwartz and Unger have seen your screen test. Nevertheless, talk to me."

Feeling like a schoolboy in front of the principal, Kyril fumbled for words. "I was born in St. Petersburg," he began. "I married Princess Lara Belikova." And he continued with the carefully rehearsed autobiography of Count Malenkov, concluding, "I . . . lost everything to the Bolsheviks. My wife died. I escaped to France, remained in Paris for about a year, then decided to try my luck in New York. What else can I tell you?"

"Plenty," she said.

At that point, the waitress arrived with their orders. Melodie attacked her hamburger with obvious enthusiasm. Kyril was grateful for the respite. He wasn't used to such direct questioning. In polite circles, people skirted uncomfortable issues such as pain, bereavement, and penury. With Melodie he worried that he might say something out of place, momentarily confusing his two identities. A trickle of sweat wended its way down his temple and over his cheekbone. Self-consciously, he swiped it away with his finger.

"Yussupov," Melodie Warren intoned. Her eyes stared beyond him, unfocused, as though preoccupied with a connection she just couldn't nail down. "Wasn't that one of the men who killed Rasputin?"

"Yes. Prince Felix Yussupov. He was one of the group of Russian noblemen who rid the nation of Rasputin. But not soon enough. Rasputin called himself a monk—but was really just a lecherous drunk. It was because of his influence over the Tzarina that we lost so many lives during the Great War. Rasputin made Alexandra Feodorovna the butt of many international jokes, but I think he did much worse: he created a need for Lenin's return."

"I see. How tragic for your country. I suppose you knew Nicholas and Alexandra."

"I grew up around them. They're much older than I am . . . that is, they *were*. And I am older than their daughters. But my family has been friendly with the Romanovs for a number of generations."

"And the Yussupovs?"

Kyril frowned. Why was she returning to them? "What about them?" he asked, biting into his hamburger.

"Felix and. . . ."

"Irina. Princess Irina was a cousin of the Tzar. Rasputin seduced her, forcing himself upon her. Felix was right to have killed Rasputin, but there were other reasons he felt compelled to do this—sound political reasons." Kyril had rehearsed the speech many times. Rasputin's death seemed to fascinate Americans. In fact, everything about the man seemed to enthrall them.

"Yes. Well." Melodie took a healthy gulp of Coca-Cola, and set down what was left of her hamburger. "The murder of Rasputin was a colorful murder, wasn't it? He didn't die right away, did he?"

"No. He survived poison and then had to be stabbed many times. The men who killed him were heroes. But Yussupov was exiled to the Crimea for his participation. The Tzarina was beyond consolation."

Melodie pushed her plate away and leaned forward, her face suddenly animated. "I've got it!" she declared. "*You* were one of the men who committed this heroic deed! You received no thanks for it, but you were willing to risk your life to rid your Tzar of the man who had placed his wife under an evil spell. You wanted order to be reestablished in the government. You wanted the country made powerful once again. Only . . . your act came too late. You risked your life, your good name, and your friendship with Nicholas for . . . nothing. Unbeknownst to you, Lenin was already planning his return."

Kyril shook his head. "This story sounds most noble—but I had no part in all this! It was Yussupov, and the politician Purishkevitch, and some others I can't even *remember!*"

Melodie Warren daubed the corner of her lips with a cloth napkin. "You don't get it, do you, Malenkov?" she said. "The murder of Rasputin was a romantic deed, worthy of Galahad or Lancelot! Of *course* you didn't do it—but what does that matter? We'll simply say you did."

Kyril's mouth opened. "I see," he remarked. "Just like that . . ." This woman stepped into his territory. He was suddenly afraid that she might trap him by adding one too many strands to his own web of implausible lies. At least, *his* story had steered close to irrefutable events in the real Kyra's past.

"What else are you planning to invent?" he inquired.

With a swift movement, Melodie swept her glasses off. Her large hazel eyes gleamed with cunning. "Whatever it takes to make you a star," she said. "That's what I'm paid for."

Yakov had always liked to go to the movies. Above all, he loved to watch Chaplin; his characters came from the poorer side of life, and Yakov could relate to them intimately. He particularly loved the complexity of Chaplin's Little Tramp, the warmth with which the great comic actor endowed this character.

But he also enjoyed Buster Keaton and Roscoe "Fatty" Arbuckle. The "Keaton Shorts," though less sentimental than Chaplin's work, were full of sight gags that amused Yakov and kept him on the edge of his seat. There was also the ludicrously cross-eyed and mustachioed Ben Turpin; and the serious and earnest Harold Lloyd—that young Everyman in straw boater and horn-rimmed spectacles who regularly endured terrible trials and tribulations.

Shorts ran one or two reels, averaging ten to twenty minutes each. Features ran much longer. But Yakov, who had very little free time, preferred the shorts because he could watch them on his lunch hour. Sometimes, on weekends, he would take Zica and the baby to a feature. Afterwards, his eyes shining, he would tell Zica that his dream in life was to become another Chaplin or Keaton or Lloyd.

"My accent wouldn't matter," he told her one evening, after they had seen Keaton in the wildly funny *The High Sign*. "Since pictures are silent anyway, I could be speaking Greek and no one would know."

"How would you go about becoming a comic actor?" she asked, gently. "You're a pawnbroker who was once a librarian—and you can play the violin! What would be your qualifications?"

"Think about it," he said, smiling. "That creates a funny image, don't you think? A pawnbroker who goes home to play the fiddle and rearrange his library. Sounds like some kind of lunatic. I could work out a routine for him, like the Harold Lloyd character or the Tramp; my fellow would be the little Immigrant from Eastern Europe, who can't adjust to life in the big city."

One evening, during just such a discussion, Zica suddenly took his hand. She played with the raised vein around his knuckles. Something in her silence made Yakov expectant, but she continued to say nothing.

"Everyone in America dreams of being a star," she reminded Yakov softly. "Yet very few make it." To herself she added, bitterly: *I hope Kyril falls on his face in Hollywood. I hope he fails his screen test and comes back with his tail between his legs!*

"Most of the great comedians came from poor backgrounds," Yakov stated. Zica heard the desperate hope in his voice, and her heart lurched. "Look at Chaplin! *His* childhood was as shabby as mine! He's only five years older than I, but look what he's accomplished! He earns hundreds of thousands a year, and now he's even formed a company, United Artists, with two film stars, Pickford and Fairbanks, and a great director, D. W. Griffith!"

"But darling, Chaplin came from a family of vaudeville singers. He was already on stage at the age of nine!"

He sat up, suddenly angry. "Look, Zica," he said to her, "He grew up in Britain and I was stuck way in hell's back yard, behind the Pale! At nine, all I could think of was getting away from the *shtetl* to relative freedom. My rabbi said to play the violin, so I did; my father said to go to Odessa and become your aunt's flunky—so I did. I had no time, and less opportunity, to train for the stage like Charlie Chaplin. But at least, I got out of Peredelkino . . . and, because of you and your father, I even got to Moscow."

She blinked, coloring. "You knew that's how it happened . . . all along?"

He sighed. "Of course I knew. You spoke to your father, and he sent for me. You saw what I endured in Odessa, with the Aschkenasys... and you spoke for me. I felt... embarrassed... when I realized I owed my good fortune to you. I already loved you; now I saw that I had further reason for this love to grow. But," he added, "that was a long time ago."

"Meaning that you no longer love me as much?"

"Meaning that we have both suffered along the way. My love for you is different from what I felt as an adolescent. Now I love a grown woman, not the princess of an adolescent's fantasy. I love you because I know you, because I respect who you are, and because we share a life and a daughter. In the beginning I adored you, I dreamt about you. *Then,* I thought you were perfect—now, I love you for being human." He paused, and looked down at his fingers. "I used to love you because you could never be mine... I was only a humble footman; now I love you because there is no one else in the world for me—I would be poor without you."

Receiving his words, Zica was at once stunned and moved by what he had said. Emotions pushed at her from all sides. Suddenly tears welled up in her eyes. She was trapped by his love, his goodness—trapped by his need for her. Yet, at the same time, his simple declaration freed something in her. No matter how much she rebelled, no matter what she did, this man would still love her. Suddenly she recalled how he had objected to her bobbing her hair—and yet how gently delighted Yakov was when she went ahead and did it.

And she saw, at the same time, how this contrasted with Kyril's love. Kyril was always testing, always measuring. He never gave her time to sift through the passions in her heart. His love for her seemed so shadowy, so thin, compared to Yakov's.

Now she saw that she'd wanted Kyril *because* he was weak. She had always known she would be stronger than Kyril. His need was so great that it empowered her. But at the same time, Kyril's love was the greater trap, far greater than her marriage.

Zica's heart had begun to beat rapidly. Her mouth felt dry. She parted her lips to speak. But Yakov returned to the earlier topic of conversation, the movies.

"It's all a matter of luck," he said. "You have no idea how much I've been dreaming of doing comedy. Back in the *shtetl,* I listened to every joke the grownups told. I would parody it for my school-mates. You didn't know me then—not well, in any case. Even in Moscow, I entertained the servants and the other students at the Conservatory. I lived to make people laugh. And now, I'm a pawn-broker. Here I am. Sennett, Arbuckle, Chaplin... all the others, have moved out to California. You are right—I should adjust to being what I am, a pawnbroker living in Brooklyn. But it's so far from the dreams I've had—so far from what I wished to become, when I was still young. At twenty-five, I feel like an antique ring."

He laughed at the image, but Zica felt the tears rising again.

"And you?" he asked softly. "What do you dream of, Zica?"

She passed her tongue over her lips. Her voice trembled. "I used to read those yellow-backed novels my mother got from France. Remember them? I dreamt of being romanced by a Prince Charm-ing. He would be everything my people condemned—a gentile, a vagabond, an adventurer. I wanted to fall in love and be whisked away by my prince, but I never thought beyond that. I did not ask myself where he might take me; that would have been too frighten-ing!"

She fell quiet, too deeply aware of the cruelty of her words. Yet, he had asked—and she had been honest. Now he stared at her, his face serious and questioning in the evening light.

"Yasha," she whispered, "it isn't working between us. We're both unhappy. We should both stop hiding from the truth. It isn't com-edy that has eluded you—it's our marriage. I haven't been the wife you deserved, because... because, let's face it, we married in haste, because you hoped to save my life. For this, Yasha, I shall always be grateful, I shall always love you. But something is missing for me. This is not the sort of love I wanted to feel."

Yakov shook his head, stupefied. She was still holding his hand, still rubbing her forefinger over the vein across his knuckles. But now her touch brought a stab of pain. *She didn't love him.*

But then, had he ever thought she did? Her kindness, her dutiful tenderness had never been intended to fool him. She had tried to give the most she could... and he had deluded himself into thinking that their kind of love was enough.

Now she had cancelled his hope. She had killed his will to keep trying—to live his life as though, someday, both love and good fortune would come to him. She had taken everything away from him in a single moment.

"What are you telling me, Zica?"

She shook her head, tears spilling down her cheeks. "I'm trying to tell you the truth," she said. "I'm unhappy. Yasha... I've let you support me, and buy me this house. I've always let you do for me, and I've given you so little in return. It's not fair: I can't keep up the pretense that I'm a real wife to you. It's time I grew up, and learned to take care of myself for a change. And it's time you tried to find yourself another girl... another wife."

What was it—why was she suddenly so unhappy? Yakov knew she had not told him the whole truth. But what could she be hiding?

And then, like a bolt of lightning, Yakov remembered the article on Anna Voorhies and his fear that she would see it. She'd been acting strangely for some weeks now; perhaps she *had* seen the article. Perhaps she had found a way to make contact with Ostrov....

But no, that was impossible. It wasn't possible that she could still love that man, so many years after their horrible breakup. Perhaps she had simply met someone new. But... where? Zica did not have a car. Her days were filled with household chores and caring for Vickie. Their neighborhood was filled with old folk. *Where* would she have met another man?

As though guessing his thoughts, Zica rose abruptly, her cheeks aflame. "It isn't what you're thinking! There's no one else! It's just that... I need to feel *alive!* I want you to give me my freedom, Yasha. I want to move out and earn my own living... so that I can earn my self-respect again. I need... I need to think of what *I* want, of what's important to me. I really don't know yet; I've been drifting from day to day—taking and not giving back. I can't do this anymore—I make myself sick!"

"No," he said slowly, "it is I who make you sick. You can't stand the sight of me any more."

She remained standing, gazing down at him, her face contorted with pain; he stared back, impassive with anguish. And then, absurdly, the telephone began to ring. Zica picked up the receiver. "Hello?" she said. Her voice was still shaky.

Yakov watched her, entranced, as slowly she nodded, her eyes glazing over. She nodded a second time. And then, tentatively, she addressed her husband. "It's Lena," she announced, her voice toneless and weak. "Yossif Adolfovitch has just been taken to the hospital. He's suffered a heart attack."

Mutely, she handed the receiver to Yakov.

"We'll be right over," he said, his voice strong and clear, as though the previous conversation with his wife had never taken place. "Just try to stay calm, Elena Yossifovna."

Zica dried her tears on the lace trim of her apron. As she darted to the front closet to take out their coats, she could only think of how she had wronged Yossif. She had never told the old man about his grandson. Kyriusha still had no idea his family had emigrated to New York.

It's all my fault, she thought, blinking back new tears. *If I had done the right thing, Yossif Adolfovitch would have had a reason to keep strong and healthy.*

But perhaps he would be all right. Perhaps it would not be too late to bring his grandson to the old man. She could only hope, and make a silent prayer.

In the afternoon, Melodie Warren drove Kyril through Beverly Hills. Turning on broad, sunny Wilshire Boulevard she headed south to show him the recently built wooden auto raceway, with its one-and-a-quarter-mile track, inaugurated with a two-hundred-lap race only weeks before. From Wilshire she took a right turn on Rodeo Drive. She explained that the developer, Burton Green, planned the houses on this street for the household servants working on the grand estates north of Santa Monica Boulevard.

They drove through elegant, peaceful streets bordered with trees. Continuing north on Crescent Drive, Melodie stopped by an imposing gate. Behind that gate, she said, dwelled King Gillette, the razor tycoon, who had a swimming pool in his garden. "But it's not nearly as big as Mr. Schwartz's," Melodie added.

Then Melodie had maneuvered the Porter across the bridle path in front of Burton Green's pink and green hotel, which had cost five hundred thousand dollars only eight years before.

"We'll check you in now," Melodie announced. She revved the Porter up a curving driveway and stopped beneath a painted roof.

Scampering doormen ushered Kyril into the hotel. Like royalty, he and Melodie had walked up a few steps, then down to the true entrance, where a footman opened the front door with a flourish.

Cool, enormous, and imposing, the inner sanctum of the Beverly Hills Hotel belittled even the Plaza in New York. The rolling hills around the grounds were trim and green, even in the winter. Kyril was overwhelmed by the vastness, but also by the feeling of repose. At the marble desk, Melodie registered him, then demanded that

Count Malenkov's bags be sent up to his suite.

Kyril stepped into a wide living room decorated with antique furnishings; French windows gave out onto the garden below. He was instantly reminded of Versailles. Suddenly he was overwhelmed with apprehension. "Wh-what if I fail the test?" he asked Melodie, who had entered the suite with him.

"You'll do just fine." Melodie took his arm and guided him into the bedroom. It was fit for a king. His suitcase and small toilet bag seemed dwarfed next to the expanse of the bed and the ornate dresser.

When she had announced her intention to leave, Kyril felt positively panicked. "What am I supposed to do until dinnertime?" he asked. "I mean . . ."

"You could stroll around. Or you might wish to lie down a while and rest up. Shooting begins early. You'll be starting at the crack of dawn, and you'll need to be made-up first. So for now, I'd suggest a warm bath and a nap. I'll pick you up at seven-fifteen this evening. Cocktails at seven-thirty." She winked at him. "The L.A. bootleggers love the Schwartzes," she added, *sotto voce*. "They order champagne by the caseload."

When Melodie departed, her springy walk reminded him of a military commander marching off to a parade. Kyril sat by the windows contemplating his situation. Schwartz and Unger were paying to put him up in this magnificent candy-cake of a hotel; they would be expecting him to perform miracles on film. He was very nervous—frightened, even. He had never acted.

But you have, his conscience told him; *you act every day when you pretend to be Kyra Malenkov.*

His pretensions seemed absurd. The Star Partners would surely find him out. They would throw him back into the ocean like Pushkin's little goldfish—only the latter had been returned to freedom, whereas only penury was awaiting Kyril.

He was unable to sleep. Going to the lounge to order iced tea, he left instructions for his tuxedo to be pressed in his absence. He had wandered through the expanse of grounds, attempting to dull his stage fright and soothe his nerves.

At six, he drew a hot bath for himself, where he sat soaking for twenty minutes. Then he dressed meticulously, mentally rehearsing what he would say when he met Schwartz and Unger. He would act like a true aristocrat who had taken time off from the New York season to indulge the whim of these two producers—and to amuse himself in the clement warmth of Los Angeles. He would show

them how little tomorrow's outcome could affect his perfectly or-
chestrated life.

But somehow, this attitude failed to convince him of his ability to
act. He would never pull this off! They would see that he lacked
composure, that his hands were wringing with sweat. They would
laugh at him and send him away, with pity and scorn! Melodie
Warren would shrug with disdain.

Already, the back of his frilled shirt was clinging to his shoulders.
He patted cologne on his face. He wished someone were with him.
If only—*if only* Zica had come to see him off! He'd wanted her so
badly—he'd hoped, with a wild surge of joy, that she might come
with him to Los Angeles! But she had turned him down. He'd let
Elsie come to the station instead—good, sweet Elsie who thought
the world of him.

He needed Zica. He needed *someone*. For a moment, his hand
went to the telephone, and he thought of calling Melodie at home.
But perhaps she would simply laugh at his ridiculous jitters. After
all, wasn't he supposed to have hobnobbed with the Tzar and the
Tzarina? Who were the Star Partners, anyway? Two Jewish men
from New York, whose parents or certainly grandparents had probably emigrated from the Pale of Settlement.

Melodie came on time, at seven-fifteen. She wore a green evening
gown with a plunging neckline.

"You look beautiful," he had said, taking her arm. And she'd
smiled . . . like a woman, not an Amazon. It was her smile of delight
that calmed him down, her awareness of his charms which silently
convinced him that he would not fail.

Melodie veered off to the left on Lexington Road. Kyril saw a
wrought-iron gate with a footman in front of it, illumined by a
gaslight.

"Melodie Warren and Count Kyril Malenkov," Melodie said
brusquely. The attendant opened the swinging gates. At the end of
the long, winding driveway was an immense stone mansion decorated with gargoyles and buttresses. Kyril was once more reminded
of France—this time, the cathedral of Notre Dame. He mentioned
this to Melodie, who simply raised an eyebrow.

The inside of Aaron Schwartz's house was cavernous and formal.
Ceilings rose to lofty moldings and scrollwork, imported, as Melodie explained, stone-by-stone from a French *château*. In the sunken
living room, damask couches on tiny, Louis XIV legs formed a

semi-circle around an enormous fireplace. Its crackling orange and gold flames mingled with the refracted light from five crystal chandeliers. A tapestry depicting a medieval hunt covered the wall facing the door. The melancholy twang of a harp came from the far left corner, where, to Kyril's astonishment, a young girl sat on a low stool. Her pliant body, sheathed in what resembled a lavender toga, leaned forward as she plucked the harp strings.

Kyril hesitated on the threshold, holding Melodie's arm. Below stood a small group of people, the men in tuxedos, the women in bright gowns of shimmering silk. He had seen far more imposing clusters at Lorraine de Huitton's gatherings, yet these Americans filled him with the greatest terror he had yet experienced.

"Come now," Melodie chided him. "They're only good old boys from *Noo Yawk;* their ancestors were probably slaves on your ancestors' Crimean estate. Think of that as you greet them, Count Malenkov!" She said the latter with amusing emphasis, *Count* Malenkov, as though to mark the humor of such a title in the U.S. of A . . . as though this were a funny joke between them. It was uncanny, he decided: as if she had sensed that he was nothing but a fraud to begin with, yet had forgiven him with a couldn't-care-less shrug of the shoulders.

As if on cue, she marched into the room, with Kyril holding her arm.

"Hello, everyone!" she called brightly. She had the brazen assurance of Anna Voorhies.

This bewildered Kyril. After all, could her job *really* be so important? Or was she simply braver than most people?

The small group parted to let them join in. There was a tall man with dark, curly hair, olive skin and small, sharp features; he was wiry and attractive. Next to him stood a medium-sized woman in her late thirties with a generous figure shown off by a frilled *bateau* neckline; her brown hair was long, held in place by a Psyche knot at the back, curls cascading around her full face.

Near the tall man stood a shorter man with a shock of shining white hair and a kindly face. Beside him was a blonde woman his own size; a splendid diamond choker glittered around her neck. All looked expectantly at Kyril.

It was the tall man who moved forward first, extending his hand. "Count Malenkov," he said, shaking Kyril's hand in a dry clasp. "I'm Aaron Schwartz. This is my wife, Naomi. And my partner, Sam Unger, with *his* wife, Judy."

Suddenly the large room resonated with animated greetings. The clamor of voices broke the tension, reminding Kyril that all these people were just human beings—human beings, in fact, who all spoke with undisguised New York accents.

The women looked as awed by him as he was by their husbands. He was amused by the women's childish delight in shaking the hand of a true Russian aristocrat. "How do you do?" he declared, smiling directly at Mrs. Schwartz and Mrs. Unger; and then, "What a marvelous house you have," singling out Naomi as he let more than his usual accent seep into his voice. Beside him, Melodie applied ever so slight pressure on his arm, signalling her approval.

At once a butler entered, bearing flutes of amber champagne. Kyril held the stem of his glass pinched between his fingers. Blushing, Naomi replied, "Yes, we've put a lot of care into this house. Aaron wanted a home, you know—a comfortable place to hang his hat after ten hours at the studio."

Kyril thought, but forbore to say, that this formal decor hardly constituted his idea of comfortable. Instead, he declared: "I am impressed by Beverly Hills. The hotel is beautiful . . . it has a phenomenal garden. Melodie tells me the entire town sprang up only eight years ago. This is fascinating to a Russian."

As he continued, Naomi Schwartz drew Kyril to a sofa. Everyone sat down. Melodie was across from him, between the Ungers; he was between Naomi and Aaron. Seeing a silver platter of hors d'oeuvres, he picked up a tiny crab cake. "How heroic your story is," Naomi commented. "Melodie's been telling us how you helped eliminate that man Rasputin—that rapist and drunkard!—from the entourage of your beloved Tzarina. . . ." She placed a jewelled, manicured hand on his forearm.

Kyril flushed. So Melodie had wasted no time generating the p.r. she wanted. He pictured her dropping him off at the hotel, then rushing back to the studio to give her employers a detailed account of their new find. But she had forgotten to inform Kyril whether Unger and Schwartz had been briefed by Melodie that the Rasputin story had been her idea. Now he was caught off guard.

He cleared his throat. "These are painful memories, Madam. It is never pleasant to kill anyone—even one so disgusting as Grigori Rasputin."

"You *must* tell us all about the last days of the Romanovs," Judy Unger begged him.

"But I was no longer in the country, my dear lady," Kyril demurred. "I had already emigrated to Paris."

"How broken-hearted you must have been. . . . " Judy sighed. She resembled a small, well-fed pigeon. Wanting to laugh at her naiveté, Kyril nodded gravely instead. Across from him, Melodie Warren covered her mouth and pretended to camouflage a cough. He saw that she was actually hiding an amused smile. He flashed with sudden anger: Why should she be amused by a story about a wife's death and a hasty emigration?

The dinner table was set in what looked like a medieval banquet hall, adorned with escutcheons and twelve authentic banners. At table the conversation turned to films. Kyril was excited and curious; he addressed his questions to the two men. Schwartz answered honestly: "Everything depends on your screen test. We at Star Partners are looking for a romantic lead, a *star,* who could sweep every American woman off her feet. We already have a leading lady —Adrienne Lance. She's marvelous. She *oozes* sex appeal. We need someone of her caliber to play opposite her . . . a real heart-throb. I want *fireworks* when they're together. I want the screen to *sizzle* when they kiss—even when they just look at each other."

Schwartz smiled. "Oh," he went on, "we'll sign up other actresses besides Adrienne. Swanson, maybe. But first we've gotta go with what we've got, and that's not bad for starters."

Kyril could only nod. Adrienne Lance was the most mesmerizing woman on the American screen. She had perfect features and the body of a voluptuous flapper, slender everywhere but at her bustline, which billowed out white and soft. Her dark hair was long and flamboyant. Playing opposite her would be like playing opposite the goddess Aphrodite. How would Kyril succeed in overcoming his stage fright?

"Don't be afraid," Naomi Schwartz told him, smiling. "All you need to know is that Adrienne was born out of wedlock to a farm girl in Indiana. She barely finished fourth grade. She'll probably be more intimidated by you than you by her."

Kyril smiled, relaxing.

Unger spoke up. "We tested Fairbanks for the part of the Sultan of Omar just three weeks ago. We wanted to see how he'd do with Adrienne. Well, I must tell you, he *stank.* And he was expecting to get two hundred thou just for signing the goddam contract!" He uttered a low chuckle.

Kyril stood up shakily, his face ghastly white. "Please excuse me," he murmured. Almost knocking down his chair, he turned around and strode from the table, heading for the small room off the foyer where he had seen a sink and some towels.

"You shouldn't have said that, Sam," Judy Unger remonstrated, turning her attention to Kyril's retreating back. "Why d'ya have to scare him that way?"

"Because this is business," her husband replied. "We're not baby-sitters coddling an infant here. The man has to know what he's up against."

"I think he's charming," Naomi stated. With that, she rose, hastening after Kyril like a concerned mother.

Melodie Warren cocked her head to one side, and caught the eye of Aaron Schwartz. Neither was smiling. Melodie narrowed her eyes like a cat and clamped her teeth over her lower lip. Across from her, her boss sat deep in thought, steepling his hands over his soup bowl.

"Charming, shmarming," Unger remarked, taking a sip of wine. "Let's see what the camera will tell us. The female public's gonna look at the screen, not at the person. Let's see how charming Mr. Count Malenkov will be tomorrow morning, when Harry Walsh tests him with Adrienne...."

"Hear, hear," Schwartz said, and at last he smiled.

Ever since Lena Ostrova's call, Yakov and Zica had hardly spoken to each other alone. Zica's candid assessment of their marriage lingered between them like an invisible screen which threatened to stay between them forever. In truth, there had been no time for this or any other discussion. Arriving at St. Luke's Hospital in uptown Manhattan, Zica and Yakov found Lena by her father's side in a private room. Yossif Adolfovitch appeared old and used up, his arms pricked with intravenous tubes. In a rasping voice, he informed Yakov that the pawnshop and jewelry store were now the young man's sole responsibility.

"Take good care of Lena," he added as if uncertain whether he was going to recover.

And indeed, he had not. Later that night, he fell unconscious. With his thin, cold hand clasped in his daughter's fingers, he took his last breath.

Yakov's deep unhappiness was mingled with confusion. He had always resented this old man. Why, then, did his death cause him such pangs of anguish? Was it because of Lena, who wept unabashedly at the loss of a father who had once thrown her out of his life and barred her from his house?

Zica had not wanted to leave her friend alone with her grief. So that night, after dropping his wife and Lena at the Byitch home in Washington Square, Yakov had taken the lonely ride back to Brooklyn to face his own soul.

Zica had left the baby with the old lady next door. The little house was empty and cold, the furnace empty. After stoking the furnace with some coal from the basement, Yakov went to the living room and sat down in the easy chair.

Lena, of course, would inherit everything. But, unlike her father, Lena was a gentle soul and cared deeply about the well-being of the Pokhis family. She loved Zica almost like a daughter.

Since she knew nothing about business, she would expect Yakov to take total control, as the old man had willed it. She would surely increase his earnings and help them to upgrade their lifestyle, provided...

...*provided that he and Zica remained together.* Did Zica love him enough for this?—that was the question.

They were married, for better or for worse, and Yakov knew her to be loyal and grateful. He had hoped—such a fool's hope!—that her love for him would be born of her respect for him. He knew she had stopped thinking of him as her former servant, as a cast-out from the Pale. Now she viewed him as her protector. Yakov saw their future, clearly, as an upward slope—each step a new victory over mediocrity and the strain of poverty. How far they had come, in just two years! Surely she'd noticed and been impressed. But what did that struggle mean to her?

She had said she didn't want to remain his wife. What would she do—move to a single room and work in a factory, just to get away from the home he had bought her?

Tonight Yakov had lost everything. Zica had told him how she felt, and the old man had died, leaving him full responsibility for his middle-aged daughter.

Now he was trapped at the store—the store he hated.

Lately he'd been thinking about the act he was planning—the *shlepper,* the little immigrant with his sad hopefulness. Just thinking about this performance made him feel lighter. It was a concept that would certainly work, bringing tears as well as laughter to an audience. He'd even thought about taking a trip to Hollywood to meet Chaplin, or Sennett, or Keaton. Of course, with no introduction he would most probably be left waiting at the door. Still...he had something to show. If he just remained stuck behind the counter at the pawnshop, he would *never* emerge. If he wanted to carve out a new life for himself, the time was now.

He was sad. Once again his plans had been thwarted.

Did any of this matter if Zica persisted in wanting to leave him? As Vickie's mother, she would get custody of their beautiful child —who looked, thank God, like her mother. He would be left with nothing at all—no dreams, no family, no one for whom to live his life. The old man had trapped him, true... but how relevant was this if his entire *raison d'être* had already evaporated into the mists of oblivion?

Yakov sat up, hugging his thin torso with both arms. He rocked back and forth on the edge of his chair. He felt shooting pains in his arms and legs, radiating out from his heart and his stomach. He felt that he was about to die. Zica, loyal and caring, wanted to leave him. She could no longer bear the empty promise of their marriage.

Could he blame her? Of course not; she had lived beside him without ever uttering a complaint. His goddess of light and beauty had become a laundress and a housekeeper—and all this, with good cheer and decorum. He had no reproaches.

What would become of him? He imagined himself sitting behind that wooden counter ten or fifteen years from now, arguing in guttural Yiddish with old bearded men with payess curls. He saw himself turning gray and then hoary, growing a long white tangled beard. Alone! If Zica left him, he would stay alone, forever, for she was the only woman he would ever love.

He still loved her! Yet dignity and human kindness dictated that he let her go graciously, without rancor—that he give up his soul and let her fly out of his life, taking their baby. Surely Zeinab Poliakova would not remain single for longer than a year. She was so lovely and sweet that some marvelous Prince Charming—her very term! —would bear her off with him on a white horse.

Prince Charming. Yakov stopped rocking. Zica used to call Kyril Ostrov her Prince Charming. Or had it been her *Golden Prince?* It hardly mattered. Suddenly he thought he understood his wife's outburst. More—now he was *certain.* She had seen the article on Mrs. Voorhies. She had recognized Ostrov, just as Yakov had feared.

Rising hurriedly, he turned on all the lights in the house and began to search. If she had seen the photograph, she would have kept it around to look at in his absence.

His search turned to methodical frenzy. He opened all the kitchen drawers, all the desk drawers. He searched among the linens and the baby food. He uncovered pots and pans. He overturned their mattress . . . to no avail.

Perhaps he was insane. Let him face facts: she wanted to leave him because, and only because, she would never love him as a wife.

Was that true? No—no! His heart and brain denied it.

Yet it was no use searching further. Exhausted, he realized he was hungry. He padded back to the kitchen to examine the contents of the refrigerator. She had purchased two steaks and marinated them, probably for their dinner the following night. His mouth began to water.

Yet Yakov was no cook. It was always Zica who prepared the food for the family. She hardly ever even allowed him to come and keep her company in the kitchen. Most often she preferred to have him baby-sit with Vickie, to make sure the child would not interrupt her mother's work.

Yakov stared at the steaks, wondering how Zica had been planning to cook them. Yakov took down one of her cookbooks. She'd wanted to learn basic American cooking; Yakov held one of the books she had prevailed upon him to purchase for her. Yakov opened it on the little table below the cookbooks, where, so frequently, Zica would plan meals for the week.

Flipping to the back of the book, he found an index. "Steak." There it was, page three-ninety-one. As Yakov flipped the pages, all at once the book fell wide open. Something was tucked in the binding. *It was the clipping.* Obliterating "German Chocolate cake," facing "Devil's Food cake," the smiling faces of Mrs. Voorhies and Kyril Ostrov stared back at him.

He began to tremble. She had found the photograph. Alone, opening this very book, she had looked at it every day.

Oh, dear God, he prayed, *let it not be what I fear! Let her not have found him again!*

The tears began to fall, until, at last, he let his head drop on the cookbook, his shoulders heaving. *Let there be nothing between them,* he begged. *Let there still be a chance to hold her. . . .*

Now that his grief had burst, he wanted to feel relieved, cleansed of bitterness. Instead, he felt the totality of his pain like an inner death, filling him with hopelessness. He loved her so much! How could he give her up, after his years of protecting her, keeping her safe from harm?

Ostrov did not deserve her! He had *never* deserved her! He had abandoned Zica when she was pregnant, in the depths of her despair. He had run away from Moscow just when she most needed him. He had *failed* her! Why, then, did she still insist on forgiving him? Dear God, Yakov thought, *I should have exposed him after all,* ending his golden life in one fell swoop, reducing him to the murderous fraud he was . . . !

With a heavy heart, Yakov closed the cookbook and replaced it on the shelf. He wasn't hungry any more. He only wanted to sleep, so that grief, for a few hours, would be blotted from his consciousness. Tomorrow, he would know what to do.

Chapter XIX

KYRIL decided that he liked Melodie Warren. He liked her in the same way he had immediately liked Anna Voorhies. Both women were sure of themselves, and strong.

Melodie was a partner, a compatriot. He couldn't tell why, but he sensed a kindred spirit in this tall exclamation-point of a woman, whose distinction was, he suspected, more a product of will than breeding. But at the same time he knew he could only rely on her up to a point. She would resent too great a dependence.

Kyril was up at five — washed, shaved, and dressed by five-thirty. Melodie called him from the lobby five minutes later. He found her waiting behind the steering wheel of the Porter.

The morning was bitter cold. "Why did I ever leave New York?" he complained. "What happened to your famous warm climate?"

"Get in, and be quiet. Of *course* it's cold. This is the goddamn middle of the night. At least the studio's heated, thank God." She grinned at him. A brown felt hat was pulled low over her right eye. She smelled of dune heather, and of cinnamon.

They fell silent as she drove through deserted streets, illuminated here and there by solitary, yellow gas lights. He admired her sure handling of the large car. His thoughts wandered. Today, his whole future was about to be decided.

After a half hour's drive through the hills, she pulled up to a small guard house near a huge gate. She gave their names to the attendant on duty, the gate opened, and she drove through. She drove through several parking lots and past some low, dark buildings that resembled military barracks. She drew to a stop and yanked on the hand brake.

"Okay, hotshot," she said, tapping him amicably on the shoulder. "Here we go. It's makeup time."

Kyril soon found himself in a small room lit up like a carousel at midnight. Melodie disappeared, winking at him. A man with a huge white apron and pomaded black hair undressed him to his shorts, covered him with an enormous sheet, and began to paint him. He slathered layers of disgusting creams and pastes on Kyril's face, fussed with his hair, and plucked his eyebrows.

Three women came in, wheeling racks of clothes. When the makeup man left, the women began to discuss what Kyril should wear, talking as though he weren't in the room at all. They commented on his coloring and the choice of material that would or wouldn't go. They finally decided on a costume. After numerous tucks, fits, and adjustments, he was ready to go.

When the costumers departed, pushing their three racks, Kyril examined himself in the full-length mirror. To his astonishment, a figure several inches taller than his usual self stared back at him—a figure clad in dark velvet knickerbockers, opaque stockings, and high-heeled men's pumps of Louis XIV vintage. Across his shoulders was a magnificent, swirling dark velvet cape. A long sword swung from a sheath at his waist.

Kyril gazed at himself with numb detachment. His cheekbones had been highlighted, his lips perfection, outlined in grease pencil. He peered at his reflection as though viewing a wax figure in a museum.

The door swung silently open, and Melodie glided in holding two cups of steaming coffee. She handed him one and seated herself opposite him in a canvas chair. "Want to meet Adrienne before Walsh comes in with the script?" she asked.

"I'm not ready."

She burst out laughing. "Don't worry, the foreplay's not over yet. The lady has requested a meeting with you first, to 'test out the chemistry between you.' Her words, cookie-pie, not mine. And since you're the unknown, and she the great star making a hundred fifty thou per feature, I have no choice but to deliver you to her chambers. That's business in Hollywood. Adrienne Lance is always Number One."

"She vetoed Fairbanks," Kyril said, understanding at last.

Melodie simply raised one eyebrow and smiled, crookedly. "Let's go," she said.

Adrienne Lance's dressing room didn't look anything like the place he had just left. Upon entering, he noticed the luxurious sofa, the fine draperies, and the magnificent burled wood vanity. On the wall hung the painting of a shy, vaporous woman, signed "Marie Laurencin."

Adrienne was seated at the vanity, while two women wound her long, rich hair into a coiled *chignon* on top of her head. She saw him reflected in her mirror. He saw her watch him perhaps five seconds, and their eyes met. For certain, this was the most beautiful woman he had ever seen.

She had almond-shaped eyes ringed with long lashes, so dark they appeared impenetrable. Her face was a delicate oval, with high cheekbones. Her nose was tiny and pert, her lips tender like his own. Slowly, dramatically, she rose—ignoring the women fussing about her—and came toward him.

She was of average height, but her slenderness made her appear younger and frailer than she was. Her costume was that of a Spanish infanta, all red velvet, with a plunging neckline that showed off the top half of her dove-white breasts. "Hello," she said, her eyes devouring Kyril. "I'm Adrienne."

Dumbstruck, like a teenager in front of his first naked woman, Kyril continued to stare. Finally he took the hand proffered to him and raised it to his lips. "How do you do?" he murmured.

"I'll do just fine," she said. "It's you I'm worried about—Go away," she commanded, addressing the two attendants, "I need to speak privately to Count Malenkov." Her eyes lit upon Melodie, but she said nothing. Melodie sighed almost imperceptibly and dutifully followed the other women out of the room. Behind her, the door closed ominously, and he stood face to face with the most famous film star in America.

"What do your friends call you?" she demanded. Her voice did not fit the image. It was thin and light, the reedy voice of a schoolgirl, and it bore a distinct Midwestern twang. But of course, this would hardly bother the American public. No one would be able to hear her voice.

Hearing her voice immediately reassured Kyril. It took some of the mystique away.

"Well, my name is Kyril. Some call me Kyra, the nickname I had as a small boy; others prefer the more traditional diminutive, Kyriusha. You may call me whatever you like... Adrienne."

She smiled—a smile that softened the imperiousness of her manner. "Fine. I think I'll call you Cy for 'Cyril.' It's simpler to remember and say. Good old American. I had a boyfriend once called

Cy, for 'Cyrus,' but he drove his Bugatti off a cliff near Siena." She laughed. "Don't drive off a cliff, all right?"

He burst out laughing. "Does that mean I get to be your boyfriend, regardless?"

She examined him circumspectly. "I know you already have a girlfriend." Was her tone defiant—or scornful?

"What on earth do you mean?" he demanded. He wondered whether he were being followed—whether someone already knew about Zica.

Adrienne Lance lowered her lashes, a vixen intent on torturing her prey. "Yes, well," she tossed off, "I found out all there is to know about you. You *do* have a girlfriend—a nice one, I'm told. Mrs. Henry Tulliver. I suppose when her divorce comes through, you're going to propose."

Kyril threw his hands into the air, shaking his head. "Elsie has been a good friend, but that's *all* she is. She trusts me. I've escorted her to a few parties. There's nothing more to it than that."

"I see."

But Kyril was suddenly angry, very angry. No one had the right to chronicle his private life; and this Lance woman, for all her power, had less right than anyone to dig into his life. He didn't even know her!

"Look, Adrienne . . . Miss Lance, I don't need to explain myself to you. I need to perform with you on the screen, and that's all. Whom I date and whom I'm planning to marry should be none of your concern! I consider that invasion of privacy—*my* privacy— and I'm going to tell Melodie a thing or two."

"Melodie had nothing to do with this. I have my own press agent, darling, and *she* does what *I* tell her." Narrowing her eyes, Adrienne straightened, suddenly becoming imperious again. "My dear Count Malenkov," she said, "do you think I give two hoots about your sex life? You're nothing in this town, and I'm at the top! Perhaps you were once important in Russia, but this is Hollywood, and you're not even an actor yet! You're a goddamn playboy who knows he looks good, and that's all! I don't need you—but you do need me. So don't give me your high-handed rich boy speech, because it sure isn't going to make me like you. And you *need* to like me."

Kyril simply stared at her. The ugly way her mouth was twisted made her look like a human viper. At that very moment, he experienced pure hatred. His first impulse was to slap her face, and then tell Melodie he was leaving on the next train out of Pasadena. But he restrained himself. She had stated the blunt truth. He *needed* this insane, self-important woman—needed her to give him a lift up the ladder, so he could get a job in the movies that would pay his bills. Without this opportunity, he would surely be condemned to poverty.

He took one step forward, his face distorted with rage. His fury wiped the smirk off her beautiful face. She stepped back, frightened. Trapping her in front of the vanity, he grabbed her arm. Her eyes were wide with terror. One hand flew to protect her face. He seized it. Now, she was his prisoner.

And then he bent, in a lightning gesture, his lips finding hers and parting them roughly. His tongue invaded her mouth. He heard her moan, felt her become pliant in his arms. He let go of her hands, wrapped his arms around her delicate body, pressed her to him. He knew she could feel his erection, insistent, pressing against her velvet gown.

Slowly her hands rose to his face. She caught his cheeks in fingers that felt like the wings of a frail, gentle bird. She touched him gingerly, with wonder, then wound her arms around his neck and pressed herself against him willingly. At long last he released her, stepping back, his face flushed, the makeup smeared. She stared at him, wide-eyed and dishevelled, her neckline askew—two strangers discovering each other, surprised by what they saw.

"Look," he said, finding his voice. "My past has been filled with big, strong bullies. The boys I grew up with, my father, the woman I lived with in Paris. But this is a finished chapter in my life. You're not going to bully me, Madame, no matter how important you are to Star Partners and the fans of America. My private life is *my* private life . . . and so it shall remain."

She seemed dazed by his kiss. "May I suggest," he said in a low voice, "that we go out and find the director."

The old man had hidden away hundreds of thousands of dollars. Yakov was amazed. Never, at any time, had Yossif Adolfovitch helped direct Yakov's investments so that he, too, could have profited from his savings. All of Yossif's talk, in Rostov, of partnership had been nothing more than that—talk, empty promises.

The young man had many duties in arranging the funeral. He found the appropriate Orthodox rabbi to say the *Kaddish*, and he helped prepare for the service. He did not have to think about Zica all day long. There was the business to oversee, the hospital to pay.

He tried to explain to a mournful, lost Lena how much money was now hers. The widow merely nodded, mutely uncomprehending.

Yossif Byitch had come to America a wealthy man and his wealth had increased. Apart from owning the pawnshop and jewelry store, he had become part-owner of a dry cleaning factory in Queens as well as a prosperous and large Kosher butcher shop in Brooklyn. He had bought stock in a newly developed drugstore chain. Unbeknownst to his junior partner, Byitch had not only purchased his spacious apartment on Washington Square, but the entire building it occupied. It fell upon Yakov to sift through account books and boxes of folded receipts, and to make sense of Lena's inheritance.

He attacked his responsibility fiercely, wanting to dull his senses. For Zica had left him.

She had come home the morning after Byitch's death to collect Vickie from Mrs. Patchulnik. She filled a single suitcase with clothes and toiletries for her and the child. Yakov had been out of the house. She had come home during business hours. Later, she called him at the store to tell him in a weary, listless voice that she and Vickie were going to be staying with Lena.

Then he couldn't speak with her alone. When he came to Lena's place, Zica was often out. Sometimes, she would appear at Lena's side, hugging the grieving woman who had become, in her eyes, a mother figure. It was as though she were avoiding him on purpose.

Finally, it was he who confronted her, about a week after Yossif's funeral.

Zica had come to the jewelry store to retrieve a ring that Lena wanted. It was obvious that she thought Yakov would be gone: it was lunch time and he liked to take a walk and stretch his legs or go to a movie during his free hour. But this noon he'd stayed in the store. He saw her the instant she passed through the doors. Immediately, he came to her side. He instructed his assistant to take a fifteen-minute break.

She wouldn't look at him.

"Zica," he pleaded, "you must tell me what's going on. Are you hiding from me at Elena Yossifovna's?"

She turned away, her fingers playing with a button on her coat. "Yasha, I said all I had to say the night Yossif Adolfovitch passed away. Our marriage... it's no good anymore. I think we'll both be better off on our own."

"We can try to work it out. I'll change, Zica—I'll do anything for you! Just...," he shielded his eyes with his hand, "just don't leave me like this."

"No," she answered softly. Her wonderful black eyes were filled with sadness and defeat. "I don't want you to change. I respect you the way you are. You're a great man, Yasha Pokhis—a good father, a good husband. I can't find fault with you!" She blinked, and tears fell on her cheeks. "It's with myself I find fault, for not being sure of what I want. You were my friend in Russia, and you will always be my friend, and Vickie's beloved father. I shall never take that away from you. But I'm not happy, Yashka; I don't know why. But I can't wait for something to happen that never will. I must begin, myself—"

"What is it you *want?*" cried Yakov in frustration. "Just *tell* me."

"If I could tell you, I know you would try to help me," said Zica. "I *know* you would, Yakov. But, don't you see, it's always that way with us. I always owe you gratitude and friendship. But I can't manufacture feelings I don't possess. I feel trapped, Yashka, by your kindness. I feel enclosed in a cocoon. I'm suffocating for a little bit of air on my own, for an existence of my own choosing!" She stopped, her cheeks warm with passion.

"I think I see," he whispered. "I was wrong to force you to stay home with the baby, like a nursemaid. It was selfishness, and an old-fashioned way of looking at things, an old *shtetl* attitude. In America things are different, women have their own lives, they even have jobs. . . . " His voice trailed off. Slowly, he regained his composure. "I can change," he repeated finally. "Give me a chance."

For almost a full minute, they stood gazing at each other, each feeling more exposed to the other than ever before. Then, slowly, she shook her head. "Lena has asked me to move into her place, with Vickie," Zica told him. "We . . . we're going to buy an art gallery. You know how much I've always loved paintings and sculptures. Well, so has she. She'll invest, and I'll run the business. And—she needs me, Yasha. She's terribly alone, and . . . we're very close. You know that."

"I need you too," he said.

Zica raised her shoulders, sighed, and dropped them. "Please don't," she murmured softly.

"Is it . . . Kyril?" There, he'd said the name. Almost fiercely, Yakov studied her reaction. "You're still in love with him, aren't you? That's why you're going, isn't it? It's because of him!"

Surprise was written on her face. *So he knew!* And now it hardly mattered. Zica bit her lip and nodded. "Yes—yes, I still love him." Her voice had dropped so low that she was practically mouthing the words. "But no. I'm not going to Lena because of him. Lena doesn't even know he's still alive! He...he's got a life of his own, and it doesn't include me. I must live my own life, Yasha, regardless of him, regardless of you. I love Lena because she's been so caring. Maybe I do need a mother—and she's all alone, needing a family. But this has little to do with Kyril. I've grown to love Lena for herself."

"Then you *aren't* leaving me because of him?"

She shook her head, dispassionately and with infinite sorrow. "No," she answered. "I'm leaving you because I've grown up, and I want to be my own woman."

"I wish...I wish there were something I could tell you to make you see things differently. I wish...I wish you would stay."

"I'm going to leave now, Yasha, because Lena's expecting me. But we shall never stop...being friends. We shall never grow bitter or angry with each other. Some day, you'll see, you'll wake up wondering why you gave so much to someone as undeserving as me..."

She couldn't continue. "I have to go," she whispered. Without looking at Yakov again, she hurried from the store, head down. He watched her depart, and suddenly nothing had meaning anymore. He knew he was all alone now, without hope of rescue.

When he locked up the store a few moments later, he did not even leave a "Closed" sign in the window. Nor did he bother to scrawl an explanation to his young assistant. He wrapped himself in his heavy winter coat, stepped into the blinding white light of the December day, and trudged away from the vacant store.

Harry Walsh was tall and lanky, with the easy gait of a Western cowboy. Standing six feet four inches, he had enormous hands and feet and large features set in a craggy, sun-tanned face. He spoke with a Texas drawl. There were laugh lines around his piercing blue eyes.

Whenever Melodie was in the same room with Harry, she could feel a quickening of the pulse, a sudden flash of sexual awareness. The man had *something*—which was probably why he was known, in Hollywood, as a woman's director.

Melodie sat in the cool projection room, picking at her pink nail polish. Next to her, Aaron Schwartz fidgeted nervously, while on his other side sat Sam Unger, perfectly composed. They were all waiting for Harry Walsh to emerge from the projection room. It was time to screen Kyril's test.

A door at the back creaked. Walsh strode in, grinning. "All set," he declared, taking a seat next to Melodie. He swung his long legs onto the back of the chair in front of him and chucked her under the chin. "How ya doin', cookie?"

"What do you think of him?" she asked.

"Well, let's see. Shut up and watch." He winked at her and settled back, slouching in his chair.

The room darkened. Melodie heard Schwartz shifting in his seat. She leaned forward eagerly. She hadn't felt such excitement for a long time; it was a strange excitement, the thrill of pure suspense. Either Malenkov would make it, or he wouldn't; and she knew how difficult Adrienne could be around neophytes.

Malenkov had been intimidated by the entire idea of a screen test—even more so at having to perform with Adrienne Lance. The script they'd worked with had been quickly put together by Walsh. It was a scene of love and betrayal in which Malenkov, a member of the court of Ferdinand of Aragon and Isabella of Castile, must face Adrienne, the daughter of a nobleman whose town has just been stripped of its autonomy. The crux of their confrontation revolved around their divided loyalties.

All at once Malenkov filled the screen. Melodie was now alert. He strode in with elegance and ease, a true Spanish warrior in command of his strong, compact, yet graceful body. His face, in *chiaroscuro,* revealed the exotic planes of his cheekbones, and the depth of his light eyes. Melodie was riveted to the screen. He photographed beautifully. Walsh had captured the intensity of his unusual face.

A shift in angle revealed the sultry Adrienne, her face full of outrage and hatred. Now Malenkov approached her, suddenly shy and guilty. He held out his hands, pleading. As he came a step closer, she made a gesture of rejection and scorn. He fell to his knees, his beautiful face eloquent with passion and naked grief. Her look softened. He rose and touched her shoulders, trying to explain. For a moment she vacillated, then he swept her into his arms, kissing her with complete abandon.

Melodie's eyes widened: the magnetism between them was palpable. Schwartz was sitting forward, elbows on his knees, his head balanced on the palms of his hands. The actors' tension had become the spectators'.

After the kiss, Adrienne recovered her composure and pushed

Malenkov away, violently. Her entire body expressed her scorn. The woman *is* worth what they're paying her, Melodie thought. She is a born tragedienne. But it was Kyril who held her attention, the terrible grief painted on his features. His limbs appeared to shrink as his beloved's diatribe continued. He made you want to weep, even though this was only a small scene, out of context.

Then he appeared to recover his sense of purpose. He stood proud and defiant, the King's emissary addressing a noblewoman stripped of her rights. He held power—and he was not above using it when necessary. Every inch a conquistador, he turned his back on her and marched away, swinging his cape over his shoulder in a casual gesture of magisterial disdain.

The screen went blank. The lights came up. For a moment no one spoke. Melodie, oddly queasy, was unable to find her voice. Next to her, Aaron Schwartz turned to Walsh. He bent forward so that Melodie had to press herself against the seat to let the two men speak.

"How many takes?" Schwartz demanded.

"Two. He was nervous the first time. But all he needed was a five-minute break and a glass of cold water. He was a different man on his second try . . . even Adrienne was surprised."

Schwartz nodded. He looked at his partner, seated in comfort with his hands pleasantly clasped in his lap, and asked, softly: "Do you want to call Hurok?"

Only then did Unger's impassive face break into a smile. "Immediately!" Then he sighed. "We wanna get him as cheap as possible. Malenkov's a newcomer. Let's see if Hurok will agree to a seven-picture deal—a thousand per week, with an outright fee of fifty thou on signing of the contract."

Schwartz grinned. "Try it, Sam. Remember what Melodie found out—the good Count is quite desperate for money. And we have a second advantage: Hurok's in New York, and hasn't seen the test." He wheeled around to address Melodie. "Hey," he said, "he's sexy, isn't he?"

Before she could answer, Harry Walsh spoke up in his slow drawl. "With her, he's terrific. He's just what we're looking for. He'd make a great Sultan of Oman, against her Fatima. It's the chemistry."

"Just don't let them get involved," Schwartz ordered, his tone growing terse. "Mel, this is gonna be your job. If he signs with us, a lot of women are gonna chase him, the way they do Rudy Valentino. Any sign of scandal, and he's out."

"So I'm to be the official baby-sitter?" Melodie cried, angrily. "Wasn't it enough I had to be the chauffeur?"

"Look," Unger said, his voice a balm on Melodie's outrage, "you like the guy. Just do us a favor, Mellie, and keep an eye on him. Hollywood's not St. Petersburg, and the chippies that hang around ain't Alexandra. We don't want this fella to go crazy here, the moment he becomes a household word."

"Don't call me 'Mellie,'" she countered. "And what d'you expect? He's young, he's attractive, and soon he'll have plenty of money. Is he supposed to live like a monk?"

"We just don't want him getting too close to Adrienne," Schwartz said, shaking his head. "You know exactly what that could mean. Think about it, Melodie. If the two of them start palling around, we end up with egg on our faces—all of us. We can't afford to have *two* lunatics under contract!"

"He's not a lunatic," Melodie stated. "He's your average first-time actor, scared and shy. Besides . . . I think he hates Adrienne."

"You wish, you wish," Unger remarked, smiling in spite of himself. "But she has ways *no* one understands. Remember, there are reasons why she isn't still washing dishes in that diner in Indianapolis."

"Come on," Harry Walsh said to Melodie. "I'll buy you a cup of coffee."

Melodie Warren rose, strangely out of sync. Walsh had never offered to spend two minutes in *tête-à-tête* with her before. But all she could think of was her own uneasiness. How was she supposed to prevent something happening with Adrienne, short of keeping watch over him twenty-four hours a day?

"Adrienne's a problem," she muttered to Walsh as they walked out of the projection room into a bright, sunlit courtyard. "You know that, Harry."

"Yeah, well," he replied, "right now she's the hot number and he's new in town. Business is business, ain't it, kiddo?"

"I suppose you're right," said Melodie.

Zica had been told the story of Lena's marriage—and of the lean years before Kyril brought his mother and grandfather together again. Not only had Lena told her, Kyril had told her in Moscow. She recalled his pent-up anger at the wrong done to Lena by the cold, selfish old man.

Oddly enough, Lena had borne no resentment toward her father.

In truth, she felt that by marrying Victor, the handsome Cossack, she had thrown her life away. "Papa was right," she would say, her eyes filling with tears. And so, when her father had at long last summoned her and decided to include her in his life once again, she had come with bowed head, like a penitent child.

Lena was a beaten woman. Zica had always found her beautiful —an exotic, fine-boned beauty with dark hair threaded with pearl gray. Her features were as firm and smooth as those of someone much younger. But she carried herself like a defeated person, weary of bearing her burdens on her back.

After Yossif's death, Lena seemed a woman bereft of moorings. Like a lost child, she had gone from room to room, shyly touching the objects her father had used, weeping all the time.

"What will become of me, now that he is gone?" she would lament to Zica, her face bathed in tears. Suddenly her existence appeared purposeless. She had no one to care for, no one to worry about, no one to *do for*.

But now that Zica had moved in with the baby, Lena rebounded. To the young woman's joy, Lena looked like a happy person at last. She fussed over Vickie like a grandmother, and the child repaid her with tenderness and attention. Often Vickie would run up to Lena with small items she had found. She always wanted to share her food with Lena; she was forever asking to be read to by *"Baba* Lena." Suddenly there was happiness for the older woman—for Lena was someone who needed to be loved in return.

Shortly after the funeral, Zica had come to her with the idea of the art gallery. "We could make a great success at something we both like," she insisted. "Let's at least give it a try!" She had convinced Lena to put up the money. Now, every morning, the young woman made the rounds of the real estate offices in midtown Manhattan, seeking to find a storefront to rent. She knew exactly what she wanted—something with lots of wall space at a passably elegant address. If it was old and the walls needed painting, so much the better. That would hold costs down, and Zica would simply paint the place herself.

Her cheeks were bright red with excitement every time she came home. To date, she had not found the perfect location. But she knew that it would fall into her hands soon. Though she was still new to business, she was after all her father's daughter, and her brother's sister. Both of them had always acted by instinct, the result being limitless financial success.

"How I wish my son had married you," Lena remarked one afternoon after Zica, fresh from another foray uptown, had removed her coat and shaken out her boots on the small balcony of the apartment. "How I wish you really were my daughter-in-law, and that Vickie were truly my grandchild. . . . "

Hearing those words brought back the full extent of Zica's heartbreak. She ran into the bathroom to weep. Had Kyril not given her a chance . . . or had *she* vacillated too much? None of this mattered any longer: their dreams had already evaporated.

Something else kept tugging at her—a deep, dark guilt concerning the fact that Lena knew nothing of Kyril's presence in New York, just as he knew nothing of his mother's. Zica felt she had committed a mortal sin by keeping them from each other for the sole purpose of testing out a romance with him. Yossif Adolfovitch was dead: her omission had caused the old man to die without his grandson. But at least she could bring Kyril back together again with his mother. She owed this much to Lena.

Zica's emotions clashed with reason. She wanted to hate Kyril for having found another lover so fast. Yet, rationally, she had to admit it was she who had given him no hope to begin with. *I always come to him too late,* she thought, weeping anew.

When Yakov came to discuss business with Lena these days, Zica remained upstairs. She even had Lena bring Vickie to her father. Zica wanted a divorce, but Yakov did not wish it. He had flatly refused to "stage" an adulterous encounter so that she would have grounds for filing.

Zica was filled with resentment toward Yakov. He was making everything hard on purpose: defeated, she would have no choice but to come back to him. For the first time since marrying him, she felt her heart fill with hatred toward the man who was still her husband in name only.

Often, Zica and Lena discussed the failed marriage. Emerging from the bathroom, her tears washed away, Zica told Lena that she had seen the divorce attorney that morning between rounds of real estate viewing.

"My bill is beginning to add up already," she explained. "Yakov is doing this on purpose, I *know* it! He's going to make filing an impossibility. Mr. Jenkins told me I could give up all claims to the house and ask for no money whatsoever. He thinks money's the reason Yasha won't agree to set me free. And perhaps he's right! Perhaps I should go to him, and plead." She looked beseechingly at Lena, as though imploring counsel. Then her face fell. She shook her head. "Here I go, fooling myself again. The fact is, he's obsessive about me. He doesn't want to admit that it's over. But I had to tell Mr. Jenkins to table the divorce for now, because I've run out of money."

"You forget that *I* am a rich woman, *devochka,*" Lena told her.

"But you've already taken in Vickie and me. I couldn't possibly let you pay my divorce costs as well."

Lena Ostrova sat down opposite Zica and took her hands in both her own. "Darling, when I was your age, I realized I'd made a grave mistake. But it never occurred to me to divorce Vitya. I was too proud. I had no resources. So I ruined my life, and Kyril's as well. If you are so unhappy with your husband, then I must help you before it's too late."

But Lena was still confused about the reason for this divorce. She addressed the issue with Zica as she poured them both a cup of tea. "My Vitya was a violent man, who beat us. He was a gambler and a womanizer. Yashka is a sweet boy. He's a good father. What is it, Zicotchka, that makes it so difficult for you to live with him?"

"I don't love him. I married him at a time when I feared for my life. Afterwards I tried to change him into a romantic figure. I wanted to love him because I was grateful. But gratitude is not sufficient reason to stay with someone. We both deserve a fuller marriage."

"Times have changed," Lena remarked, sighing. "What I would have given for a kind and decent man...!"

"But you married the man you fell in love with," Zica reminded her. "For all his cruelty, you wanted his arms around you. *That*'s why you stayed, Lena... for no other reason."

"If only I had met you earlier," Lena said, "I could have helped you and Kyril when you were still in Moscow. But Kyriusha never confided in me. I only suspected that he was falling in love."

"We were both so young, and in over our heads.... And my father did not want me to marry a nice Jewish boy of moderate means; he'd hoped to form an alliance with another family like ours. When my brother married Baroness de Gunzburg, my father felt as though his own power had suddenly doubled through Zhenya's wife's family."

"But that's all in the past," Zica mused. "What's important one day can become unimportant the next." She shook her head. "That's why I wish to make something of my life, independent of any man. I want our gallery to be successful, Lena—for both our sakes!"

"Well," Lena stated, "I meant what I told you. I'll pay for this divorce if you decide to go through with it. I have no personal use for all the money my father left me."

Zica found herself unable to answer. Lena had placed her full faith in her, making the gallery more than just a dream. And now, she was even offering to set the wheels in motion for Zica's divorce. Bowing her head, the young woman felt a renewed sense of shame for not telling the whole truth to this dear and kind friend.

I must tell her, Zica decided. I must act *now,* before my resolve disintegrates. And she went into her room to search for Kyril's number.

The telephone rang once only before being picked up. The mellifluous voice of Kyril's manservant came on the line immediately. "The *Malenkov* residence."

"Hello. I—my name is Baroness Poliakova. May I speak to the Count, please?" Zica's voice was a bare squeak.

"The Count has *guests,* Madame. Is this *important?*"

Zica conjured up the image from the train station of the small, dainty woman in the fur coat. "Yes," she stated, "it *is* important. Please tell him I am holding to speak with him."

"Very *well,* Madame." The pompous voice sounded displeased. Zica waited, feeling like a reprimanded child.

At long last, she heard his voice. "Yes? Who is this?" His butler hadn't informed him!

She gulped. "It's me... Zica. How are you, Kyril?"

A beat went by. Then his cool, impersonal voice responded, "I'm quite well, thank you. To what do I owe this telephone call?"

Zica felt herself being rebuffed. Not only had he replaced her— he'd half-forgotten her already. This was hardly the same person who had come to Brooklyn to plead with her, his heart on his sleeve.

"It has nothing to do with *us,*" she said to him quickly. "But I must come and see you right away." She felt her cheeks burning, her heart racing.

"I'm afraid that's impossible," he countered smoothly. "I'm moving to California, Zica. There are many friends I must see before leaving. I have only two weeks to pack up everything I own. There just isn't... time."

His refusal paralyzed her. But it stabbed at her heart in another way as well. He had passed his screen test, without actually bothering to *tell* her.

Still, she needed to say *some*thing. If she didn't, he would hang up, and she would have failed in her mission on behalf of Lena. She tried to empty her mind of the personal hurt. "Oh, Kyril, I'm so glad for you," she said at last, her voice ringing warm and sincere. "So you are going to be an actor—for real?"

He sighed, exasperated. "Yes, Zica. The first feature I am going to do is *The Sultan of Oman,* opposite Adrienne Lance."

"Adrienne Lance?! Kyril, *the* Adrienne Lance?"

"I thought there was only one," he commented coldly. "Look," he continued, "I'm sorry I can't see you, but I have some people over right now. You understand, don't you?"

Taking a deep breath, Zica insisted: "It's really important, Kyril. To you—not to me. Please . . . all I ask is to see you for just five minutes. In the lobby of your building, if you'd like."

A moment of silence followed. "What's this about?" he finally asked, his tone a touch less formal. "Are you all right?"

"I will be if you let me come. I could be there within half an hour. Five minutes, Kyril—that's all!"

She could feel his hesitation. Did he hate her so much that he would refuse such a small request just for spite, to show her that he didn't need her anymore?

"Kyril," she whispered, "do you remember our last phone call, when you asked me to meet you at Grand Central?"

"Oh, Zica," he answered, his voice empty, "if that's what you are phoning about, it's past history. Our whole story is past history, my dear. Perhaps I overdid it when I saw you again at the restaurant. I mistook simple homesickness for passion; whatever it was, you were right to set me straight."

"I wasn't going to set you straight," she said softly.

"You weren't? Well, but it's all right. I don't need a love affair right now. If you had let me break up your marriage, it would have been a grave error. I will have to work very hard in the movies, and the last thing I need is a relationship. So you see, you were the wise one, and I the impulsive fool. History repeats itself," he added bitterly.

She could not reply.

"Listen," he told her. "If you can make it up here in thirty minutes, I'll come down to the lobby to talk to you. But for five minutes—no longer. All right?"

"Yes," she murmured. "I'll be there."

She hung up before he could, so she would not have to hear him break the connection.

Kyril held the telephone in his hands, his head ringing with anguish. He had done well, very well, not letting her know how much he still loved her, how much she still belonged inside his heart. But it was difficult, no matter how hard he tried, to still his emotional rebellion against the cooler reason of his mind.

What was it about Zica that made him want her so much, after all these years? She was bad for him, very bad. One day, she would be the death of him. He couldn't get her out of his mind. At the oddest moments, her image would pop into a corner of his memory.

What was it about her?

He didn't know. But she had entered his heart and refused to come out.

A light tapping interrupted Kyril's thought. "Come in," he said gratefully.

Elsie Tulliver entered. She was wearing a purple silk dress that fell from tiny shoulder blades past the jutting bones of her pelvis, to an inch below her knees, revealing rounded calves and tiny slingback pumps.

"I was getting lonely," she said, pouting mischievously.

"Oh, Elsie! I didn't mean to take so long. I'm going to have to excuse myself for five minutes to meet someone downstairs. But I'll be back in a flash."

"Oh, well," she said, sitting down on an ottoman next to him, and crossing her legs. "Mysterious business, hmm?"

"Mysterious to me, too," he remarked, then quickly changed the subject. "So Henry has decided to meet you in Mexico for a rapid dissolution? What prompted *this* change of heart?"

"He's met the ideal mate, my dear Kyra. Vanda Lane, with the golden mane. Young and twenty, money's plenty. But the lady's father doesn't want to wait. He's terrified she'll turn twenty-one and come into her trust fund without a husband to take care of it . . . and of her. Henry loves being Sir Galahad."

"Poor little Vanda Lane, soon-to-be Tulliver."

"Yes, but lucky Elsie, soon-not-to-be. I believe I deserve a quick, painless divorce along with *lots* of money for being such a sport about it. Henry actually *said* that. He also told me that she was still young enough to be house-trained!" She laughed, delightedly. "But, Mr. Film Star, the question remains: are you going to invite this divorcée to California?"

Warning signals flashed through Kyril's mind. "You wish to come... for holidays?"

"I wish to come for as long as you'll have me." Her gray eyes were soft and gentle. "You know how I feel."

"Dear Elsie. You are very sweet." He racked his brain for something else to say. "I do know how you feel," he said finally. "You're important to me, my dear."

But his film career was more important. He remembered kissing Adrienne Lance, crushing her body against his. She had closed her eyes and yielded to him. While he had kissed her he hadn't once thought of Zica... nor of Elsie.

If I were interested, Adrienne would come to me, he reflected. And Elsie would have me now, right away. Elsie, at heart, wants my baby. Why, then, am I still in love with Zica? Clearly, she doesn't want me.

Anguish flooded him. Every time Zica drew close, it seemed, she would change her mind. She had done this in Moscow, and now again here.

He had wanted to punish her with his coldness when she'd called. Instead, she had manipulated him into agreeing to see her. He had *sworn* he would never see her again—never speak to her again as long as he lived!

He glanced at the clock. A half hour had passed since her call.

"Will you excuse me for just a few minutes?" he asked Elsie.

Elsie regarded him oddly. "All right," she replied, nodding. "But don't tarry, Kyra, because I must be home by seven."

He smiled, but she was already absent from his mind.

As the elevator rolled to a stop, Kyril tugged at his shirtsleeves. He pulled back the accordion grill and stepped into the lobby, a high-ceilinged hall with Doric pillars and a marble floor. No one was there, except the elderly doorman, Andrew, chewing on the remains of a cold cigar.

Kyril patted his hair and smoothed out his eyebrows. *I hope this won't take long,* he thought nervously. He had promised to attend a black-tie affair later that evening with Anna Voorhies and Herbert Hauser.

As he went to the door, Andrew opened it for him. "Yer Excellency," he bowed. His veined nose gleamed crimson. "Goin' out this evenin'?"

Kyril laughed. "Later, yes. At the moment, I'm just waiting for a lady."

The old Irishman laughed, raising one eyebrow. "Yer Excellency is always very popular with the ladies."

Kyril smiled. He assumed that Andrew was thinking of Elsie. Two women in one afternoon!

The two men waited in companionable silence.

Through the glass door, Kyril could see two women hastening down the street. They were bundled up; he could make out neither of their faces.

"Want a cigar, Excellency?" Andrew asked, holding out a fresh one.

"No, thanks."

The two women walked up. As Andrew stepped out to greet them, Kyril pulled back into the shadows by the door.

"Whom d'ya wish ta see, Mesdames?" Andrew asked.

Kyril could now perceive the women's faces, illumined by the gas lamp next to Andrew. One was older—something about her looked vaguely familiar, although her hair was wrapped in a scarf and he could not see her well. The other . . . was Zica.

Shocked, Kyril turned to stare at the older woman, wondering who she was. Why had Zica brought her along? Surely this was not another White Russian refugee, begging for a handout.

As he stared, the blood in his veins slowed. Everything turned to slow motion. The older woman resembled his mother. But this couldn't be. Amazement replaced wonder.

It was his mother!

Just then, Andrew pushed open the door. They stepped into the lobby, arm in arm. Kyril moved out of the shadows. The older woman stared at him, unable to breathe, her face white. Her lips parted and she placed her hand on her collarbone. Slowly, she shook her head from side to side, like someone who has just seen a ghost.

Zica, who had stepped back a pace, was smiling.

Kyril turned to her. "What's the meaning of this?" he demanded. "Who is this—an actress? Is this some sort of sick joke?"

"This is your mother, Kyril," Zica answered softly. "It really is."

"Mama?" he whispered. *"Mamatchka?"*

The woman rushed forward, tears streaming down her face. She threw herself into his arms, sobbing.

"Kyril! Kyril! *Sinok dorogoy, maya detochka!* My darling son, my little baby."

Kyril held her, his emotions in tumult inside him. A veil of tears fell over his eyes. She clung to him, crying little words in Russian, touching him, weeping.

At long last, they pulled away. Kyril noticed Andrew gaping at them from the doorway. Instinctively, he led his mother further into the lobby.

All at once he remembered Elsie, waiting upstairs, and panic seized him. *What was he going to do?*

He couldn't take them upstairs! How could he explain this strange reunion to Elsie? His mother was supposed to be dead! He was supposed to be Count Kyra Malenkov—not Kyril Ostrov.

All at once, he turned to Zica. "How could you do this to me without warning? You know my situation! What on earth am I supposed to do? How *dare* you pull my life apart?"

Zica looked thunderstruck, overwhelmed by this sudden attack. "Kyril, I . . . I'm sorry. I wanted . . . I hoped to give you the most wonderful surprise in the world! I wanted to do something good for you and Lena."

"Lena." She had called his mother *Lena,* not the more formal Elena Yossifovna. How had she come to be so close to his mother? What lay at the heart of this matter? Distracted, Kyril reached over and enveloped his mother in his arms. But his eyes blazed with anger at Zica, as he looked at her over the top of Lena's head.

"Kyriusha, *sinok,*" his mother crooned. He led her to a low, marble bench against the back wall. Then she turned to Zica. *"Devochka,"* she murmured, "how did you find him? What are you doing here, Kyriusha? Are you alone in the city?"

She'll expect to be taken to my place, he thought, even more furious with Zica. *What else can she expect? A mother wants to be taken to where her son is living.*

He couldn't! Throwing his hands in the air, he tried to explain. *"Mamatchka,* I didn't know anything about this. Obviously, Zica has told you nothing of my circumstances."

Lena was touching his face, alternately laughing and crying. "Oh, my beloved boy," she sighed gratefully. "Zica didn't say a word. But what a surprise, what a good surprise. Tell me everything. When did you come to America? *How* did you come? Are you well? Do you have a job? Do you . . . need money?"

He chuckled, pulling her head to his shoulder. "Mama," he said, "try to understand what I'm going to tell you. I've been here two years. I came from France, with a friend, Kyra Malenkov. He was one of the Malenkovs, from Petersburg—remember that powerful family? Well, as bad luck would have it, Kyra was very ill, and he died in my arms. It's a long story—later, I will tell you everything —but he and I looked very much alike. When he died, I did something dishonest. It wasn't really bad, Mama, because Kyra had no people here—he had no heirs . . . anywhere. I used his name—I took it as my own. And I took a bag of jewels that he had brought from Russia, through Paris. I felt that, as Count Malenkov, more doors would be opened to me in New York. And I was right."

His mother's face mirrored her astonishment.

"Remember, Mama," Kyril continued, "when I was a child in Rostov, and the boys would follow me home hurling insults at me? You used to tell me that it couldn't be helped, that a Jew in Russia was bound to be laughed at and cursed—especially *half* a Jew, like me. After Papa died I knew I'd have to leave eventually if I wanted to become *someone*."

Lena listened, then turned to Zica, beseeching her with her eyes. *Is this all right?* she seemed to be asking. *Can I accept these actions of my son's?*

"Lena," Zica said softly, "Kyra Malenkov was a friend of Kyril's. Kyril prevented him from dying alone, on the shores of a foreign state. There was no legal heir to those jewels; if Kyril had left them, the U.S. government would have appropriated them. And he took a name no one else could ever have used." Zica paused, as the older woman nodded. "And now!" Zica concluded, "now he is going to make Kyra Malenkov a household name in America. Your boy is going to become a film star in Hollywood!"

"Is that true, son?" Lena asked.

"Yes, Mama. I leave in two weeks. I've signed a contract with a studio called Star Partners." His face fell. "Oh, Mama, I didn't know that you were here. If I'd known, I wouldn't have planned to leave so soon. . . . "

"The young must do what they must do," Lena remarked, sighing. "You don't need me to pull you down. I'm glad, my boy, that you have done so well for yourself. Your grandpa would have been most proud of you. How he loved the movies!"

"Grandfather? Where is he, Mama?"

Lena shook her head, sadly. "He passed away, a few weeks ago. But he established himself too, just like you. He owned a lot of businesses here. Now . . . Zica's husband . . . manages it for me." She bit her lower lip, suddenly embarrassed. "You see, we all came over together," she explained in a rush. "Zicotchka, her husband, your grandfather, and I. Great friends we became. If it weren't for her, I don't know how I could have borne your grandfather's death. So many years of taking care of him . . . so many years." She sighed again, shaking her head. "You made a grave mistake." She looked from one to the other of the young people. "You should have married when you could, in Russia. Then Vicotchka would be my granddaughter, and Zica my beloved daughter-in-law."

"But people change," Zica said softly. "Kyril has his life now, and I have mine."

Yes, Kyril thought, and now, more than ever, it hurts me to hear those words.

Behind them, there was a clank as the elevator reached the ground floor. Kyril glanced over quickly. Elsie Tulliver was emerging from the box, her elfin figure outlined in its delicate sheath.

"Ah, Kyra!" she cried brightly. "I was beginning to get worried! I see you've found your friends. I thought . . . perhaps . . . that you had told me a story."

"Elsie, this is . . . this is . . . Elena Ostrova. Lena, this is Mrs. Elsie Tulliver. And this is Zeinab Poliakova." He added: "Lena and Zica were friends of mine in Russia."

Elsie's pretty face lit up. She held out her hand, smiling. "How do you do? And . . . what a pleasure to meet some old friends of Kyra's. Any friends of his are of course automatically mine as well." And she clasped the bewildered Lena's hand between both of hers.

With Zica the handshake was briefer and much colder. Zica withdrew her hand almost at once. The two young women appraised each other frankly. "Yes," Zica said. "Any friends of Kyra's are *my* friends too." She gave the surprised Elsie a dazzling smile. "Perhaps we should have lunch in order to celebrate this new friendship of ours . . . Mrs. Tulliver."

Taken off guard, not knowing what to think, poor Elsie nodded like a puppet. "Certainly, Mrs . . . or is it Miss? Poliakova."

"It's *Baroness,*" Zica told her, not smiling at all. *"Mrs.* Tulliver."

Then she rose, and her eyes went to Kyril. *I know what you're up to with that woman,* her steady glare told him. But he smiled in spite of himself. He had never seen Zica be so discourteous to anyone. In a few short sentences, she had decimated poor little Elsie Tulliver. As though—*yes!*—as though she were jealous.

But why jealous? Kyril wondered. She has made it quite clear that she desires no part of me. Why, then, this hostility to Elsie? If she could be jealous, perhaps all was not over between them.

He wanted to speak further to his mother. But Elsie's presence had made this impossible. Suddenly, the little American woman had become an annoyance. Had she come down to spy on him? Very well, then she would receive retribution. He hated possessive women, and this one had no rights at all to his person.

To Zica's amazement he grabbed her suddenly by the shoulders and kissed her firmly on the lips. "Good-bye," he said to her. "It was good of you to come." Then he turned to his mother, and wrapped her tightly in his arms. "Please call me tomorrow," she whispered. "Zica has my number and will give it to you. There's still so much I'd like to ask you—to tell you . . ."

When he released her, he caught the look of cold anger on Elsie's face.

But Zica was smiling brightly—her triumph was so evident that a wave of exhilaration swept over Kyril. He could even forgive Elsie.

"Come," he said, giving the latter his arm. "Let's go upstairs."

Book IV:
"Da Capo"

Chapter XX

*T*HE year 1924 was a momentous one for the United States of America. Yet it was a year of small steps forward, many steps sideways, and some steps backward for its citizens.

It was the year that President Calvin Coolidge won reelection with fifty-four percent of the vote, stressing the "Coolidge Prosperity" which had begun to make America complacent.

Ford lowered the price of the new Model *T* motorcar to a record low of two hundred ninety dollars, and produced nearly two million of these cars for the second year in a row.

Three million people in the country now owned radio sets.

Metro-Goldwyn-Mayer and Columbia Pictures were founded that year.

And in 1924, Star Partners—now a major motion-picture studio—agreed to rewrite Cyril Malenkov's contract to pay him twenty-five thousand dollars a week and an outright fee of two hundred fifty thousand dollars on signing.

In every Main Street of America, women swooned at billboard displays of Cyril Malenkov. And the tabloids went into a picture-publishing frenzy as heart-throb Malenkov married his leading lady, Adrienne Lance, America's Number One "naughty girl."

Inside the new, plush Poliakov Gallery (dropping the Russian feminine from her name as a gesture of Americanization) in a Madison Avenue brownstone, Zica was tired. She had worked all day with the accountant. The gallery's books were now up to date. Tonight there was to be a small reception to launch a new painter she had recently discovered. Afterward, she had promised nightclub

371

proprietor Noel Pierre to dine with him at his club.

Zica sank into the soft Beauvais tapestry that upholstered her desk chair. Her snug, elegantly furnished office was her retreat from the rest of the gallery. In designing this hideaway, she had indulged herself. Soft lighting was ensconced in an oval recess in the ceiling; pale mauve and sky-blue lines wove themselves into a free-form design on the wall. With her elbows down on the huge, ebony desk, Zica kicked off her shoes and let her bare toes squish through the luxuriant white bear skin on the pegged wooden floor.

Noel Pierre . . . He was an attractive man, the sort of whom her father would have disapproved—in other words, the kind who appealed to her. A man of average height, he was graceful and nonchalantly elegant, always dressed in the latest fashions. He favored nubbed, raw silk jackets and wore his jet-black hair cropped close to the sides, romantically drooping over his forehead. His curiously handsome, slanted sloe-eyes were ringed with thick, dark lashes, his mouth forever curved into a half-smile of irony. He had olive skin.

People often speculated about his background. Cuban? Part Arabic? But Zica knew him to be half-Japanese on his mother's side and part French (hence the surname) on his father's.

Noel ran the poshest speakeasy in Manhattan, in the basement of a brownstone in Washington Square. He was reputed to be connected with some powerful Chicago gangsters.

One entered his ultra-luxurious Club Pierre by discreetly knocking at the peephole of the house. The wrought-iron grille remained open until the early morning hours. Unlike the rowdy speakeasies run by his most famous competitor—the boisterous blonde known as Texas Guinan, who greeted her customers from atop a grand piano—Noel's place was quiet and refined. It catered to the upper crust of New York, offering an excellent menu along with the best liquor. If anyone propositioned his cloakroom girl or the cigarette vendor, Noel's bodyguard would whisper something in the offender's ear, place a hand upon the customer's shoulder—and the man would never again be seen in Club Pierre.

Zica had met Noel with a client who had taken her to the Club Pierre to celebrate the purchase of a prized Picasso etching. The nightclub owner sent her roses the next day, at the gallery. The club was close to her home, and she had agreed to meet for a midnight glass of French champagne. She had found Noel enigmatic, terribly gallant, and had loved his smooth voice with its hint of a lilt. She had also been afraid of him—deliciously so. What might this debonair individual do to her? His voice caressed her ears like a soft, teasing feather: his eyes, sultry and impenetrable, made her skin burn.

She hadn't felt such thrilling temptation since Kyril Ostrov—now the film idol "Malenkov"—had left the city, almost four years previously. Zica sighed. *How could the memory still cause her pain?* she chided herself roughly. *He never really loved you! His love was no more than a pastime.*

But she would never forget the small, perfectly dressed woman who had come to find him in the lobby of his apartment building—the same woman he had kissed at the train station. He had turned to *her, Zica*—had kissed *her* in front of the woman. He had done so, she had come to realize, simply to show the other woman that she did not own him.

Still, the moment had been sweet with victory.

But after that, she never heard from him again—not directly, that is. Lena often wrote to him and called him, and her son had come to New York to see her. But he had never tried to contact Zica.

Lena, Zica knew, had told him everything. He would know that Zica was now divorced from Yakov. He certainly knew that she had changed her name back to Poliakov and that she was now recognized as one of the most dynamic young art dealers in New York. Now—more than any other time in her life—Zica was an independent woman, free to make her own choices. But Kyril had never called, written, or spoken to her since that encounter four years before in the lobby of his building.

"You still love my son, don't you?" Lena had asked, some months before.

Zica had not answered. Was it love she felt, or merely the need to go after a man who had rejected her? As time passed, Zica had concluded that when Kyril had loved *her* to distraction, in Moscow, she had sought refuge behind her parents and the cloak of their respectability. Yet she had loved him then, and had missed him when he had turned his back on her. And she had loved him passionately—perhaps more than before—when they had met up again in New York, and she had been trapped in her marriage to Yasha. *She had loved a man she couldn't have.*

Zica had trained herself not to think of Kyril—not to hurt. She had plunged into her work. In the beginning, that work—starting from a tiny gallery on Third Avenue and Eighty-first Street—had been an uphill battle all the way. With her own hand she had painted the small, dark storefront and gone in search of art to fill it. She had attended every major and minor auction in New York, purchasing modest works at first—or those of dubious value that she thought trendy or interesting. She had combed the society section of the newspaper for names of patrons and collectors, in order to compile a list for her first exhibit. Night after night, she had stayed up arranging the lighting and order of the eclectic works that she proposed to show. Then, when all was prepared, she had sent out hundreds of invitations on colorful paper, expensively engraved, in order to draw the wealthy art connoisseurs to her small gallery.

And it had worked. She had ended up with fifty people, and had made five sales—just enough to enable her to continue the arduous process of selecting and displaying the works of her particular taste.

Lena's inheritance had launched the gallery—and Zica was always conscious of how much that woman's confidence meant to her. When Lena had offered to increase her investment, Zica would not accept. She preferred to work from the modest sum she had initially borrowed from her friend.

"I have to prove myself to you," she had explained. "You can't stay partners with an inept beginner. If I succeed, even in a small measure, I'll feel better about having you invest your savings in this enterprise."

Zica, the debutante who had never worked a day in her life—the woman who had known nothing about business—had thrown her energies wholeheartedly into this first venture. She had taste. With her instinctive knowledge of what paintings "worked" and which did not, she simply had to trust herself. At first her success was modest. But after she had sold her first major work to a collector, her triumph became more conspicuous.

The art patrons of New York took to her. Her elegance, her exotic beauty, her Russian title, and her sad history of fleeing one step ahead of the Bolsheviks had appealed to the Americans. New York socialites had adopted her as a "find" of their own. When Lena finally sold her father's holdings, Zica was ready to accept an investment of the majority of that money in the now-thriving gallery.

"Now that we both know I am not a loser, we can form a true partnership," she had laughed, kissing her friend on both cheeks.

But it had been a hard climb. She still needed to work ten hours a day to keep the Poliakov Gallery a going concern. There was so much competition! And her success was still relative: she was still unknown to the majority of art collectors in the United States. Her attorney had advised her to go to Philadelphia and Boston, to Chicago, San Francisco, and even Los Angeles to make important connections. Zica knew he was right, but still . . . she hated the idea of travelling so far from Vickie. She didn't want to leave the gallery solely in the hands of her assistant, Bruno Lesschi, whose tastes she only partially trusted. He had an illustrious background as associate curator of the Pitti Palace in Florence, but Florentine art was a long step from Manhattan Jazz Age tastes. Bruno, at fifty-five, was perhaps too old to gauge New York properly.

So she had little time to think about Kyril Ostrov. And besides, he had taken up with Adrienne Lance. Everywhere, Zica saw tabloids publicizing their "flaming" romance.

"He doesn't love her," Lena had declared, pushing her spectacles firmly back over the bridge of her patrician nose. "I'll bet that p.r. girl, whatever her name is, is forcing them together for publicity reasons."

"She's the most popular actress in America," Zica had remonstrated. "How could he *not* love her? She certainly loves *him:* just look how her eyes devour him!"

"He's weak. It's just a fling," Lena had insisted. "He has his father's weakness."

"He could have anyone he wanted," Zica countered, gently.

"He loves you, I tell you," Lena insisted—"not this *kurveh!*"

But Kyril was a rising meteor. He and his leading lady had beguiled America, like Mary Pickford and Douglas Fairbanks. Adrienne Lance and Count Cyril Malenkov were the most beautiful couple in the world.

So the newly divorced Zica had closed her mind to him. She had closed her mind to *all* men before the advent of Noel Pierre. Noel had in common with Kyril his easy, graceful sex appeal, his quick charm, and his exoticism. But Noel was stronger than Kyril, and therefore that much more dangerous. She didn't love him, and she had as yet not let him seduce her . . . but, trembling inside, she was already aching to let go. She wanted him to make love to her—and, much as it pained her to admit it—she wanted him because she was unsure of him. He was inconstant, a gambler, a man for heated, passionate sex without thought of tomorrow. He was a man for the Twenties—a flapper's dream—sensual and mysterious.

She did not want to marry him or have his child, of course. She simply wished to forget the world in his embrace, to taste his lips and to smell his scent, feel the heat of his desire . . . and lose her pain. *Nothing but that.*

* * *

Tentatively, Kyril opened one eye and surveyed the wreckage of his bedroom. His silk bathrobe lay haphazardly thrown at the foot of the bed. On the Persian rug was the tuxedo he had worn last night, his shorts, and his frilled shirt; one shining shoe peeked out from under a chair and the other was in the corner by the antique secretary.

Fighting off waves of nausea and a vague sense of shame, he turned his head, gingerly, and looked at Adrienne beside him. Her marvelous black hair fanned across the silk pillow. She slept with her arm hanging over the edge of the bed, limp on the coverlet— her torso naked but her evening gown gathered in clumps of beaded chiffon over her hips. Her stiletto-heeled shoes still clung to her toes like apostrophes.

Jesus Christ, he thought. *I can't remember last night. I can't remember where we were,* or how we got home.

Kyril crawled out of bed, his temples pounding. Reaching the large, bevelled-glass bay window, he parted the heavy velvet curtains. The sun glistened on the emerald lawn and flower beds. In the distance he could see the turquoise and lapis reflection in his tiled swimming pool. All this gemlike luxury made his head spin. Suddenly he felt sicker than ever. Just the sight of his property filled him with an odd, unusual revulsion. Letting the curtain drop, he wandered into the connecting bathroom to splash water on his face.

The mirror reflected a handsome, tanned, healthy face with a golden forelock hanging romantically over the broad forehead. He never exhibited signs of dissipation—but God, the signs should have shown, with the lifestyle he led. He was twenty-nine years old, looked twenty-five, and felt fifty.

He brushed his teeth. He knew the source of his morning-after dejection. It was the opium. It felt good when you smoked it—and, later, he would fall into a dull, lethargic sleep. But in the morning he always felt sluggish and depressed, as though the world had collapsed.

He reached for a terry-cloth robe hanging on the back of the door and went out into Adrienne's adjacent boudoir.

Kyril sat down at a guitar-shaped vanity and pressed the button that summoned Mason from the bowels of the mansion. There was a whole panel of buttons, each representing the various servants who would appear if a particular button was pressed. Mason's was polished brass: he was the most important. There was light blue for

Theresa, Adrienne's maid; a red one for Flora, the cook; a yellow one for Antonio, the head gardener; and a green one for the pool man. Surely, Kyril thought ironically, even Kyra—when alive— had never had so many people to fuss over his every gesture.

No other male actor—not even Fairbanks and Valentino— commanded the sort of attention from the press and the fans that "Count Malenkov" did. Every word Kyril uttered was embellished with dramatic context in every tabloid in the nation. Each week, Melodie's staff would bring huge sacks of fan mail. Hundreds of autographed photographs went out daily. Personal secretaries tackled Adrienne's fan mail. The Malenkovs single-handedly supported half the Star Partners staff, including the team of writers who constantly worked on the screenplays that were destined for them.

Why, then, wasn't he happier? Kyril had found a profession that suited him like a glove on a lady's hand. But inside he felt curiously restless—though he would never have admitted this to anyone.

He loved acting. During filming, he was truly satisfied. But between pictures he felt only depression. He was a rudderless ship with no destination.

Mason knocked on the door and entered, carrying a silver tray holding a covered silver dish, a silver coffee pot, and a fluted crystal glass filled with freshly squeezed orange juice.

"Good *morning,* Your Excellency." His demeanor, as always, was impassive. He set the tray down on Adrienne's desk and removed the domed cover, revealing poached eggs, sliced tomatoes and chives, and crisp buttered toast.

"It's not a good morning, Mason. What's on the schedule for today?"

"Two *scripts* arrived from Mr. Schwartz, by messenger," the butler said. "And Mrs. *Voorhies* called from New York. Oh—also, Miss *Warren* wondered if she might *stop by* for half an hour later this afternoon."

"Is it afternoon already?"

"It is one-*fifteen,* Your Excellency."

Shame flushed Kyril's face. He turned to the food on his plate. "What does Miss Warren want?"

"She didn't *say.*"

Mason's words hung in the air. The ominous silence raised prickles on Kyril's spine. "To see me, or the Countess?"

"To see His *Excellency*. She asked . . . that she be allowed to *speak* to you in *private*."

After five years, the *maître d'hôtel* had begun to address Kyril in the second person, some of the time. This was the only sign of familiarity that signalled the devotion he felt for his illustrious master, whom he had followed to the West Coast with lugubrious looks and many long sighs. Hollywood, land of decadence!

Mason had been right, as usual. Kyril's life was decadent, though few outside the motion picture crowd realized it.

"The *Countess* has an appointment at two-thirty, with her *beautician*," Mason declared. "Should I have Theresa *awaken* her now?"

"Probably so. But Mason . . . let it wait. Give me ten minutes to eat my breakfast, will you?" His green eyes told the butler everything. He did not want to face his wife until he had fortified himself with coffee and juice.

"Very *well*, sir. And what *time* should I tell Miss *Warren* to come by?"

"Give me an hour," Kyril replied.

Mason nodded as he backed away. He opened the door noiselessly and slipped out, a thin, dignified raven in black livery.

The blinds were open, and the film star could see the tennis court. *What had happened last night?* he wondered. He bit into his toast, washed it down with juice, and shook his head. His stomach was tied in knots.

Melodie had warned him . . . repeatedly.

The door that connected the boudoir to Kyril's bathroom was opening. Adrienne stood in the doorway, completely naked, her delicate limbs white and perfect. She squinted at him, massaging her forehead. "When did you get up?" she asked.

He sighed, feeling the room close in on him. "Mason was here, wondering when to send Theresa up. I told him to let you sleep a while longer. The beautician is coming in about an hour."

"Let her wait, damn it! She's being paid a fortune to come up here." Adrienne sat down beside him, dangling a well-turned leg that brushed against his thigh. "Let's go back to bed."

"I'd rather not. Melodie will be coming soon. I have to bathe and dress, and . . . would you like breakfast, or do you want one of my eggs?"

"I loathe eggs. Cy, I want to go to San Francisco tonight. I want Mason to drive us there. Will you ask him?"

He could feel the tightness in his stomach. "I have no intention of going to San Francisco," he said quietly.

"But we're out of *stuff!*" She laid her head on his shoulder and cuddled up to him, pleading. "I can't get up in the morning without my *stuff*. Clears my head so I can think."

Abruptly, she rose and walked over to a small sideboard on which lay a small silver tray crowded with crystal perfume bottles. She lifted a small bottle filled with white powder and brought it over to the vanity. Unscrewing the gold top with trembling hands, she dumped a line of powder on the desk. She opened the drawer, withdrew a gold straw, and leaned over the desk. Pressing one side of her nose with her forefinger, she lifted the straw to the other nostril. Placing the lower end of the straw in the white powder, she inhaled deeply. When she was finished, not a trace of powder remained on the polished wooden surface. She looked at her husband, smiling. "I feel better already. Don't you want a little wake-up?"

"I don't want to turn into *you,*" he answered, aware of the cruelty of his words. She winced. "Adrienne, you're hooked!"

She studied him disparagingly. "Are you gonna turn *moralistic* on me, Cy? Because, if you are, you can stop now. You like the stuff same as me, so don't act like I'm just some dumb Dora!"

"I like all of it. But...I'm getting so I can't go to sleep without opium, and I can't wake up without coke. I don't *want* to live my life depending on a series of drugs to get me through the day."

"Forget it," she said, edging toward him. "Why don't you come back to bed with me? There's something I have to tell you."

"You can tell me here."

She lifted an eyebrow, her eyelids narrowed. *"Like hell I can!"* she suddenly screamed, her mouth twisting. "Look, buster, you got where you are because you married *me*. So don't you high-hat *me*. If I wanna go to Frisco, I'm gonna go...and *you* are gonna go with me."

He stood up, his heart pounding. "No," he told her, "I'm going to stay right here and read those scripts Aaron messengered over. If you want to remain Adrienne Lance, perhaps you should do the same. I'm tired of the life we lead—tired of the boredom, the waste...tired of *everything!* You can't intimidate me. Aaron and Sam need me more than you—and you *know* it. It doesn't matter whose star rose first, Adrienne: it matters what the public thinks, *today.*"

She rose again, her perfect round breasts inches from his face. "You go to hell," she said evenly. "I'm getting sick of *you,* and your high-handed selfishness. I like to have *fun*. I like to get high. I like to smoke, I like to drink, and I'm not afraid of men. I'm not afraid of *you,* buddy-boy—not at all! I don't care how much Melodie fawns over you like a lap dog. I've got my plans, and believe you me, if you don't wanna play, I'll find someone else to play with. I thought . . . I thought you'd be different, a real man." Her voice trailed off into regret, then grew bitter again. "I'm pregnant," she spat at him. Now she was facing him, her hands on her hips. *"That's* what I wanted to speak to you about. I'm pregnant, and I don't wanna be, the pessary didn't work, and now I'm gonna have to *do something about it*—and you're no help. All you care about is how many women sent you love letters this week! Well," she added, "it's my career that's going down the drain, it's *me* who's pregnant—so *of course* you don't give a damn!"

He could feel the breath being squeezed out of him. He was trembling.

"Adrienne," he said, raising his hand to stay her arm. "I only said I thought we should both take it easy on the drugs. I can't even remember what we did last night—nor whom we did it with. If you're pregnant . . . well. . . . Are you quite sure?"

"Of course I'm sure. I'm already two months along."

"I . . . I'm sorry, Adrienne. I'm sorry about this. I'm sorry you're angry with me. But the life we've been leading—well, I'm frightened. I'm frightened not to be able to remember where I was last night."

"A little snort might clear your brain, lover-boy. Don't you want some, baby?" She sat down on his lap, playing with his hair, her breasts pressing against his terry-cloth robe. "Wanna play with your little girl?"

"Adrienne," he said, "you don't want to have the baby, do you? I mean, think what it would do to your career right now?"

"Little tiny girls don't have babies," she intoned, pouting, in the voice of a child.

"We need to take care of this. When Melodie comes, I'll talk to her about it."

"She knows someone?"

"Melodie knows everything," he replied seriously. "She and Mason can handle any emergency. Don't worry. There are doctors . . . they take care of this painlessly, and we can pay for the best. Let Melodie find one who can keep his mouth shut better than anyone else. Okay?"

She shrugged. "Do I have a choice?"

He laughed. "I suppose not. Listen, the beautician will be here any minute. And I need to get ready for Melodie. Be a good girl and let me finish my breakfast."

She sighed, and slipped off his lap. Running three fingers abstractedly through her hair, she sauntered off in the direction from which she had come. At the bathroom door, she turned to him, almost as an afterthought. "Last night," she said, "we went to dinner at the Coconut Grove. You were dancing all night with Brian Donahue's new girlfriend, that teen-age flapper from Texas. We ended up at their place, swimming nude in his pool, and then we got high on some hooch and he brought out the opium. I don't know what *happened*—I mean, I don't know if you and this gal ever really *made* it. But that's okay; Brian and I were necking all night in the pool. He says he'll write a screenplay for us, something perfect for the best-looking couple in the world. I told him to go ahead. Aaron says nobody in Hollywood can write better than him. Don't you think?"

"If you think, I think." He smiled at her, and she slid away into the tiled bathroom. He heard her singing in their bedroom. He shut his eyes, pressing his palms against his temples.

Dear God, he thought, *how will I ever get through today?* He pushed his eggs away. His hand moved toward the small crystal bottle she had left unscrewed on the desk. Resigned, he tapped some white powder into the palm of his free hand, raised it to his nose, closed his eyes, and inhaled. Disgusted, he took his napkin and rubbed the rest of the powder off the palm of his hand.

Chapter XXI

ZICA'S office had a walk-in closet with a full-length mirror inside the door. She kept a number of outfits there in case she had no time to go home before an evening's outing, often the case when there was an opening or a reception at the gallery. Adjoining the office was a small bathroom where Zica could freshen up.

She removed her day dress, powdered her body with scent, daubed perfume on her wrists and then, wickedly, in the depth of her cleavage and on the inside of her thighs. She powdered her face and carefully rouged her prominent cheekbones. She touched her eyelids with soft turquoise and her lips with red, finishing the picture with swift upward strokes of black mascara that appeared to prolong her thick, curled lashes. Running a comb through her black, bobbed hair, she removed her small pearl-studded earrings and replaced them with antique coral pendants. After she put on her panties, brassiere, and garter belt, she sat down to roll on her silk, seamed stockings. She slipped coral silk ankle-strap slippers onto her small feet, and stepped into her coral-colored gown.

Finally she paused, contemplating her image in the full-length mirror. She had lost all her roundness. Through strenuous dieting, she emulated the pictures of elegant, bone-thin flappers which appeared in all the issues of the women's magazines. Only her bosom remained round and large, which she liked, in spite of the fact that fashion now required tiny, fruit-cup breasts. Her seamstress had confected long, tubular gowns with ample, low-cut necklines, so that her cleavage always looked inviting. The gown she was wearing for this evening's reception was a sleeveless, floor-length silk sheath with a scooped neckline. A small train ended in a pointed serpent's tail of the same shimmering coral.

All she needed was a necklace. She took a long, dangling string of antique coral beads from a hook on the inside of the closet, slipped it over her head and nonchalantly knotted it below her breastbone. She knew she looked wonderful—knew the reporters would comment on her outfit. Yet her outfit was tasteful enough not to overshadow her artist, Giuliano Perelli, who liked to seize the limelight whenever he could.

Her outfit would also please Noel Pierre, later.

Zica consulted her tiny gold watch and saw that her guests would arrive soon. She stepped out of her office and went in search of Bruno Lesschi, her assistant. He was in the main room of the gallery with Perelli, a small, flamboyant Italian who had recently moved to New York. Both men looked like penguins in their tuxedos. She smiled, extending her long, graceful hand to the artist. "What do you think of the exhibit?" she asked. "Do you approve of how we've set you up?"

He kissed her hand. *"Benissimo, carina* Zeinab. But tell me... whom did you invite?"

"Everyone!" she smiled. Giuliano Perelli was the sort of artist who needed total reassurance, who fretted nervously before every opening. Zica now recognized the type. Patting him on the arm, she went off to inspect the canapés and the bottles of mineral water and ginger ale which now replaced traditional French champagne at gallery receptions.

Perelli's work had first been noticed by Bruno, his countryman. The painter was a bolder Marie Laurencin. Zica had immediately fallen in love with his soft, romantic aquarelles, his flappers, his bathing beauties, his gardens, exotic birds, and flowers. He appeared to have captured the entire epoch with a few swift brush strokes. She had decided that Manhattan socialites would jump for him as soon as she exhibited his work. So she had planned a romantic evening, setting the paintings under soft, pastel lights, complemented by elegant vases filled with fresh flowers. The invitations had been designed by Perelli himself.

She wished that Noel could have come, but he made it a habit to supervise his staff at the club. And, in fact, she wasn't yet sure that she wished to have him as her official escort. There was something illicit about him, something not quite proper. Perhaps it was the fact that his club served illegal hootch; perhaps his exotic background. The fact remained that he was only half respectable, while the success of her business depended solely on respectability. And yet, it was precisely that aura of ne'er-do-well-ness which had drawn Zica to Noel Pierre from the beginning.

She heard voices. People were beginning to trickle in, in small groups or elegant twosomes. Zica was soon in the midst of her guests, explaining Perelli's work to the art critic from the *Times* and then to H. L. Mencken, the iconoclast of the recently founded *American Mercury*. Escorting collectors through the gallery, she eloquently explained why she believed that Perelli's paintings were easily worth their exalted prices. All the while she kept up the chatter that appealed to fashionable New Yorkers, speaking of the latest concert, of Mr. Jones's most recent golf victory, of socialite Elsie Tulliver's recent marriage to radio announcer Brett Morrison. The last item, especially, brought a smile to Zica's lips.

Bruno Lesschi tugged at her arm. "The radio personality is here," he whispered dramatically. Bruno was a little man, very precise and quick to gossip. Zica suspected that he was a homosexual.

"I think it was a mistake to invite him," she confided to Bruno in an undertone.

"He has been on the mailing list from the beginning, *carissima*. You must meet him, Zica, and his lovely wife. They have brought us a most prestigious guest: Mrs. Clinton Voorhies."

Now that she was about to see Elsie again, Zica felt a mixture of emotions. She remembered when she had first seen Elsie Tulliver— now Brett Morrison's wife—at Grand Central Station. And Zica vividly recalled the later time when they had words in the lobby of Kyril's apartment building. What would Zica's destiny have been— had the diminutive woman failed to show up when Kyril left for his screen test? Would Zica have climbed aboard and followed her old lover to California? Would they have married, instead of his tying the knot with Adrienne Lance? Zica felt a surge of fury provoked by memories of Kyril. How could he stir such strong emotions in her?

Welcoming Mrs. Voorhies was a necessity. Having her at this opening constituted a real *coup,* for she patronized the arts and her word was a command among the rich. When she approved of a singer, a dancer, a writer, or a painter, everyone listened. So Zica tried to clear her mind of everything but business. She followed Bruno to a small cluster of well-dressed people standing in front of a huge oil portrait of a woman with her hair a tangle of lilac grapes.

Elsie Morrison looked prettier than ever in a long black gown with elbow-length gloves and an egret feather in her hair. Her husband was tall and stocky, with sandy hair and a broad Irish face. He was more pleasant-looking than handsome, but his expression was hearty and humorous, and Zica found herself disposed to like him.

Mrs. Voorhies, supported by an ivory cane, resembled an aged Dragon Lady from the Orient, though her eyes were round. Her now-shapeless body was draped in a gown of emerald-green damask. She radiated a sense of power, a presence that was undeniable.

Zica forced herself to smile, as she extended her hand. "Mrs. Voorhies?" she said. "How do you do? I'm Zeinab Poliakov."

"My dear girl," Anna remarked, "we met on the telephone some years ago. You called to ask me about Kyra Malenkov. How times have changed since those days. . . . "

Zica nodded. Her eyes misted over. "It was good of you to come," she said, wanting to change the subject.

Bruno spoke up brightly. "Zica, I don't believe you've ever met Mr. and Mrs. Morrison. This is the Baroness Poliakov—my boss," he added.

Elsie put out her hand. She was regarding Zica with frank interest, and some amusement. "*I* have had the pleasure of meeting the Baroness," she said. "Do you remember, Baroness? Those were our salad days, if I might be so bold as to quote Cleopatra."

"Cleopatra only spoke the words—Shakespeare coined them," her husband commented. He shook Zica's hand warmly, his friendly hazel eyes crinkling as he grinned. "We are quite impressed with your gallery. And Perelli's work is fresh and happy. I like painters who entertain. I like humor in art. The woman with the grape hair—she's quite mad, isn't she? I'd love to own this canvas myself."

"Perhaps you'd like to meet the artist," Zica answered. "And by the way, I quite agree with you. I get tired of self-important painters who want to change the course of art. Giuliano wishes to charm the world; he wishes to bring people out of their doldrums, and I think he succeeds very well. Bruno deserves the credit for discovering him, however," she added, making a gracious gesture toward the rotund little Italian.

"Perhaps," Elsie Morrison suggested, "we'll buy this grape woman that Brett fell in love with. You know, Baroness Poliakov, if my beloved husband is going to get a crush on another lady, I'd much prefer that she be two-dimensional." She squeezed Brett's arm, and everyone laughed.

This was going better than expected, Zica thought with relief. Elsie Morrison wasn't choosing to bring up that old rivalry, now that she was married.

"Giuliano would be thrilled to meet you," Bruno said to the couple. "Please . . . come with me. I'd like to introduce him to you." He gave his arm to Mrs. Morrison.

Zica remained with Mrs. Voorhies. As she tried to think of something to say, she noticed the old woman's keen brown eyes fastened to her face. She blushed.

"I miss Kyra," Anna said abruptly. "We were good friends. He telephones me regularly. Once in a while he comes to New York, and I see him. But it's not the same as when we could see each other two or three times a week. He's the one who introduced Elsie to Brett, you know."

Why is she bringing this up? Zica wondered. She cleared her throat. "Oh," she said. "Really?"

"You are a very pretty girl," the old woman continued. "I know that you and he were once in love. I can see why he picked you."

Zica's lips parted, but she was speechless.

"My dear," the other went on, "I could read the boy like a well-worn and much-beloved book. He never told me about you—but when I told him you had called . . . and when Elsie told me about meeting you—I put two and two together. By the way," she continued, "he and Elsie never had anything together, really. They were good friends, and when she divorced that dreadful bore of a first husband, she and Kyra went through a mild flirtation. Oh! Elsie would have liked it to become more—but Kyra was smart enough to keep her as a friend. Elsie and he would have been unsuitable for each other, though I quite adore each of them separately. Brett is exactly whom she needs. As for *him—Kyra—*well, all I can say is that he made a very big mistake by marrying the wrong woman."

Zica blushed, embarrassed at receiving so many details about a man she had been desperately trying to put out of her mind. Why was a dignified lady such as Mrs. Voorhies confiding in *her,* a woman she had met only moments before?

"My dear girl," Anna broke in on Zica's thoughts, "you must forgive me for speaking so frankly. It's just that the boy is in trouble. I know this. He's unhappy. Perhaps he is unhappy because things never worked out between the two of you. When he left New York, he was disconsolate. I knew someone had broken his heart."

"Perhaps he broke it himself." Zica surprised herself with the sudden bitterness in her voice. "Perhaps he will never learn anything about women. I—" She broke off. She was growing miserable.

"You two go back a long way, to the Russia in which you both grew up. You were the girl he loved, weren't you—the one he kept mourning for?"

"Kyra Malenkov was married then," Zica said coldly, remembering Kyril's story of the real Malenkov. "His wife died—he was mourning for her."

Softly, almost inaudibly, Anna Voorhies said: "There was no wife, Baroness Poliakov. You know it and so do I."

Zica's eyes flew to the other's face, shock painted on her features. "But—"

"I don't really know who our Kyra is," Anna Voorhies stated gently. "He is not, and never was, Count Kyril Vadimovitch Malenkov. It doesn't matter. I love him for himself—for the real man behind that charming face and figure. I love him because he is sweet, and because he is young and lovely. And I think you are still in love with him."

Zica's mouth had gone dry. "How long have you known all this about him?" she asked.

The old woman's eyebrows lifted. "Since the moment I met him. I am sure he *needed* to pose as Count Malenkov—who, for all I know—is dead and buried. You see, the real Kyra was a sickly child. His doctors predicted he would die before he reached the age of thirty. *Our* Kyra radiates health . . . even now, when he is consumed with unhappiness. It does not matter to me who he is. And you're the only person to whom I have ever told this—because you knew him then, and loved him deeply."

"I don't know what to say," Zica murmured. "I really don't. He—he doesn't know, does he?"

"That I realized the truth? Oh, no, my dear. It would cause him great embarrassment, and probably fear. I told you: he is like a grandson to me, or a dear godchild. Why would I wish to cause him pain by unmasking him? If he has chosen to wear a mask, that's his judgment. You will not, I trust, unmask *me* . . . ?"

Zica shook her head firmly.

"Because Kyra—whoever he is—is a good man. The jewels, certainly, once belonged to the Malenkovs. I do not know how he got them, but I am *completely sure* that he did not obtain them through some illegal or immoral transaction. I believe in our boy, and I have been willing to accept whatever fantasy he wished to weave about his origins." Anna paused, and her brown eyes fixed once again on Zica. "What's more, I don't *want* to know his real name, nor his true antecedents. These matters will remain a secret between you and him."

"Yes, they will, Mrs. Voorhies," Zica stated gravely. "Kyra is lucky to have you on his side."

The old woman smiled. "You, my dear Baroness, cannot be a fraud. I can smell the purebred in every word you speak, in your every mannerism. You are who you say you are. We shall be friends, you and I, won't we?"

She held out her gnarled hand with its many rings. Zica took it between both of hers, touched by this interchange. "Yes," she replied, her voice a feather's stroke. "We shall be friends."

And she thought: This woman makes me feel the way I used to, in my father's house. But it was more than that: in Lazar Solomonovitch's palatial home, she had been a child, a dependent—a good little Jewish girl reared to become another rich Jew's priceless decoration. Lena, who loved her as a daughter, also viewed her as an attractive, reliable, *good* little girl . . . whereas Anna Voorhies saw her as a woman, an equal—a person unfettered by clannishness and parochialism—a woman of the world.

And how did Noel Pierre regard her? Zica wondered. She consulted her watch surreptitiously. In just a few hours she would be with him. This time, she would not refuse his advances. She was ready to *be* this woman of the world, to be flirtatious and free, to have some fun. Now she felt surer of herself. She knew that no one—neither father nor husband—was sitting at home waiting to scold her. She needed no one's approval but her own.

"I can see why the boy loves you," Anna Voorhies remarked.

The young woman shook her head. "He *loved me,* Mrs. Voorhies. Yes, he did. But Kyril—Kyra—belongs to my past. Let's allow him to remain there."

For the first time her heart felt curiously light as she spoke those words; for the first time her heart did not ache. Their love had belonged to another Zica—a hopeful, starry-eyed young girl with her whole life before her. Now she knew who she was. She was an adult, a person of greater experience. She felt wistfulness as she considered Kyril, but it was the same wistfulness she felt toward all of her past, toward her adolescence and the Russia of her younger years. She no longer felt shattered when she recalled those years. Now, for the first time, she could think of Kyril with the same distant wistfulness, without feeling broken inside.

At long last, Zica realized, she had forgiven him his desertion and marriage. She had forgiven him because she no longer needed him. This came to her as a revelation; she felt an odd sense of release, as though a burden had been lifted from her consciousness.

"He doesn't love me, either, Mrs. Voorhies," she declared gently. "He has a full life of his own. It's hard to let go, hard *not* to romanticize an unfinished love affair. But we're not children any more, neither one of us. We're both almost thirty years old."

"When you're as ancient as I am, Baroness, you will smile to remember that you thought this old. Now lead me to this painter of yours, my dear; it's time I introduced myself to him, so I can solicit one of his works." And the old woman planted her cane forward, linking her free arm through Zica's.

Kyril's study always caused Melodie to wince. Mirna Weiss of Pittsburgh always cringed at the conspicuous display of extravagant wealth. Her own, recently erected house, ensconced in the Hollywood hills, had one glass wall so that she could look out at the birds in the canyon. She liked the wildness of nature.

Few people would have guessed that her vice president's salary from Star Partners had climbed to one hundred thousand dollars. She believed in keeping her money in sound investments. So Kyril's study, with its floor of gray-green, layered mat glass lit from below struck her as disastrously costly. For Melodie liked comfort. But in Grayhall Manor, there was no comfort—only special effects.

Kyril bussed her on the cheek and offered her an apricot-and-rum drink that tasted slightly cloying. In her elegant, cream shantung suit, she looked quite the smart businesswoman. Kyril scanned her from head to toe, raising an eyebrow in appreciation.

"You look quite marvelous," he told her, flinging himself into a curved leather armchair.

Melodie stared at her hands. Then she gave him a level gaze. "Kyriusha," she said—for so he had instructed her to call him—"I didn't come here for a social visit. I came on a mission. I want to remind you of the stars that *were*, who are no more: Fatty Arbuckle was accused of raping a starlet, and implicated in her murder. He was cleared—but who has seen an Arbuckle comedy since then...? Mabel Normand. Her career took a beating after her sometime boyfriend, William Desmond Taylor, was mysteriously killed. You may recall that Mary Miles Minter, another famous actress he'd been involved with, never played in a picture again. And there was

Wallace Reid's publicized drug addiction. It ended his career. These people lived for their art—and the cameras rolled. But then, Kyriusha, something happened to their careers. Their images became tarnished. No studio would touch them with a ten-foot pole. Surely, Kyril, you must be aware of these scandals. You knew these people."

"What are you leading up to?" he cut in, his eyes suddenly hard. "Surely you didn't come here to give me a lesson on morals! We all have morals clauses in our contracts. I assure you, Melodie, I read those clauses. But I haven't killed anyone, and I haven't been accused of rape—or at least, Mel, not that I can remember." His slight, self-conscious chuckle was not lost on her.

"Listen, Kyril," she continued. "We live in a nation divided into sinners and saints. The saints are the good folk from Iowa and Nebraska who lead quiet lives and adhere to the law. The sinners are the hedonistic young who sleep where they please, swap partners, and drink in speakeasies. Unfortunately, the saints far outnumber the sinners—so we bow to their morality. The Hays Office was formed as a concession to the saints. When plain, common folk go to the movies three times a week, they want to know their morals will not be offended. Ma and Pa Smith, in rural Arkansas, do not approve of necking, drugs and drinking."

She paused, taking a sip of her drink. "This country has spoken, and what it's told us is that we must watch out, or our viewers will seek their amusement elsewhere. They want morality plays, not witty comments on what's taking place in our big cities."

"What has this to do with me?" Kyril asked. His hand holding the highball glass had begun to shake.

"When you married Adrienne," Melodie replied, "I warned you that she was trouble. The public went wild, of course, and both of you benefited from this. But lately, she's become more than just trouble. She's a drug addict, Kyriusha. If you don't watch it, you will soon be one too. Her drug addiction has caused a lot of problems for the people who work with her. I can't believe it hasn't started to cause problems between you."

"What kind of problems?" he asked cautiously. "I mean . . . on the set?"

"You know as well as I. She only comes on time when you get her there. She's hung over from opium or morphine. When she sniffs cocaine, she becomes frantic." Melodie waved her hand. "But I didn't come to talk bout Adrienne. It's you I'm worried about."

She shifted uncomfortably. "I'm afraid for you, Kyriusha. Adrienne has thrown herself headlong down the drain, and I don't want her to take you with her."

Kyril pressed his hands against his temples. Then, like a sheepish little boy, he looked at Melodie. "I know," he admitted. "I'm afraid as well."

Containing herself no longer, Melodie asked: "Why did you *marry* her, Kyril? *Seriously* . . . why *did* you?"

He sighed, his face mirroring his confusion. "You just don't know how empty my life was," he told her. "Adrienne was so beautiful, so magnetic . . . ; she wanted me, and I let it happen."

"You're a prop to her, like her drugs and expensive clothes. 'My-husband-the-matinée-idol.' But she's destructive and vengeful. You're silly putty in her hands. Long, long ago, Aaron warned me not to let you get too close to her. One day, she will drive her white Bentley off a cliff, and you'll be with her. I believe she wants to die. Somewhere inside, she knows she's never going beyond being illegitimate and uneducated, and that her past lies just below the surface of Adrienne Lance, the movie star. She knows she doesn't measure up, and she's terrified others will find out. She thought that becoming the Countess Malenkov would make her seem legitimate. But she's a fraud, and she's smart enough to know that."

"We are all frauds," Kyril murmured. "Adrienne and I have this in common. Deep inside, I know that I don't measure up—I'm a pretty boy . . . with nothing inside."

"That's not true!" Melodie cried. "You've got a heart! You've got a brain! You have the talent to play with *both* your heart and your brain. *She doesn't*. That's why you'll survive and she won't. But you *won't* survive if I have to keep fishing you out of these dreadful situations. Last night . . . last night, Kyril, you were passed out cold. Cubby had to drag you into the car to drive you home."

"Cubby?" he asked, puzzled.

"Yes, *Cubby. My boyfriend*. Thank God he was in town. And those people . . . You should know better than to hang around with Brian Donahue. He drinks like a fish and likes to swap partners. Adrienne doesn't seem to care where she leaves her shoes. But Donahue likes to boast about his conquests. If he should decide to describe last night's little foursome in one of his screenplays, he would leave no doubt as to the participants. Discretion is the name of the film game, my pet. And you've got as little of that as your precious wife."

"She's not precious to me!" Kyril cried, suddenly passionate. "She's just the woman I happen to have married. I'm not in love with her, Mel—but I've got to assume some sort of responsibility toward her, or I would really be a louse!" As he remembered the earlier conversation with his wife, a sick feeling crept into him. "Melodie," he said urgently, "you've got to help me! Adrienne says she's pregnant. She wants it . . . taken care of. Could you . . . I mean, *do* you know anyone who could . . . ?"

"Yes, yes," Melodie spat out disgustedly. "I'll find someone for her. Don't worry," she added more gently, "part of my job entails keeping our female stars fit for their performances. Aaron and Sam would pass out cold if they thought their darling Adrienne Lance was about to swell up like a balloon. Besides," she eyed him squarely, "the kid might not be yours. That woman's a hard-boiled little sheba, and she comes on to every man who pays her some attention. I wish you'd get rid of her, Kyril."

"It wouldn't be easy," he answered gloomily. "Besides, I *know* she's bad news—but tell me, what else is there? Adrienne has glamor, she can be funny. . . . Would another woman treat me better?"

Melodie shook her head incredulously. "You are asking *me*? Why, most of the women in America would give their souls to marry you—and they'd treat you with kid gloves! You could have anyone you wanted!"

"I've never had success with women," Kyril muttered. "They like me for a while, until they discover who I really am. Then they toss me out. Once they see the real Kyril, they never want to stay with me."

"But your wife, Lara? Surely she loved you?"

"Lara died," Kyril said, dismissing the subject. "But before her there was someone else—someone I loved even better. She left me at the altar, quite literally. She aborted my baby."

"You truly loved this girl."

"Yes," he said, "I did. And I'd think about her and wonder what had become of her. Well, wouldn't you know, I saw her again in New York . . . she had emigrated, too . . . and she turned me down a second time. I suppose I deserved that: I must have. Otherwise, I would have gotten what I wanted."

"You got your stardom. You have more money than Croesus. You have your friends. You have me," she added, simply. His pain had reached her.

"Yes, you're right; I have you, and I have Anna Voorhies and Elsie Morrison, in New York. You three are my triumvirate of friends. But each of you has more important concerns than Kyril Malenkov." He gazed at Melodie, clear-eyed, wanting her to understand. "Don't you see? I married Adrienne because we were alike: we were both empty and trivial inside. We are terrified that the rest of the world will find it out."

Melodie shook her head. "The girl in New York... what's her name?"

"Zeinab Poliakov... Zica. She owns and manages an art gallery in Manhattan. She's become quite the New York businesswoman, my little Zica. And she was right: if she'd come out here with me, it would have been an enormous mistake. Eventually, she would have become just like me... empty inside."

Melodie sighed. "I don't know what to say any more. This Zeinab—I think she sold a Matisse to Sam and Judy Unger, not long ago. Perhaps she was trying to reestablish contact with you, through them."

"You are sweet and silly," Kyril smiled. "Zica will one day sell you a painting, too. She'll do well. In fact, I met her at an art gallery in Moscow. Love of art is in her blood. As for trying to reestablish contact, she would never do that. I am a married man—and she is very proper. Melodie, if she didn't love me back then, when I was free, why should she love me now? And you know what? I don't love her either, at this point. I don't love Adrienne... I don't love anybody. Least of all myself."

"Poor darling Kyril," Melodie commented, getting up. She stopped in front of his armchair, reached out, and fluffed his hair. "Whatever you do, think about your acting career. You are a true talent, a true artist. Divorce Adrienne. Or let her kill herself. But *stop following* her to her petting parties and opium haunts. Keep your self-respect. It will make you feel better, I promise you."

She leaned forward and kissed the top of his head. "I've got to run," she told him. "Swear to me you'll be good, from now on. No more crazy behavior, no more drugs. No more goddamn waste!"

He couldn't speak. Mutely, he nodded as he watched her leave the room. Her high heels clicked on the parquet floor of the long corridor. Kyril felt as if his last connection to human warmth and kindness had retreated, leaving him abandoned.

It was exactly as his father, Victor, had always told him. He was a *samocer,* an eater of refuse, a man who could always sabotage his own success. But now, he had something special to botch: he had a career about which he cared deeply.

But what was this career, actually? He presented the same facade to the world that he had been presenting all his life; but this time, the public had bought it. He presented the painted shell, and his fans the world over believed it to be him, the real person.

Now he could only hope that this charade would last forever. But he did not want to sabotage the shell, to lose his only link to civilization. He was an actor—not a lover, not a kept gigolo anymore. And he needed to remain an actor if he intended to remain alive.

Zica got out of the taxicab exactly one block from the Club Pierre. As the driver pulled away, she hugged her white mink stole around her shoulders. She always walked to the door of the club. It was better not to tempt the fates and draw unneeded attention to Noel's undercover activities.

The balmy autumn night was scented with garlic and parmesan, a reminder that the Village was largely inhabited by Italian Americans. Zica found comfort in these familiar smells. She felt exhilarated. The reception had gone well indeed: the Morrisons and Mrs. Voorhies had purchased paintings, and the art critic from the *Times* had followed Perelli around like an enamored youth.

Zica smiled to the world at large, feeling buoyed by success. The future vibrated with promise.

She reached the tall townhouse at the same time as two young collegians in top hats and tails. Their eyes told her how striking she looked, and she smiled. With a flourish the first pushed open the grilled gate for her, gallantly tipping his opera hat. When she had passed through, they joined her on the front walk. "It's a beautiful evening," she said pleasantly.

"Indeed it is. But not so safe for a lady to be walking alone," the second man remarked. He was flirting with her, and it gave her an agreeable sensation. These boys were younger than she!

"Not to worry," she replied. "I only walked a single block."

"Will you let us buy you a nightcap?" the first man asked.

"You're very kind, but I'm meeting someone."

"Ah; the lady is attached," the first said, inclining his head. "What could we have expected, Roger? She's too beautiful to be going out alone to a Village nightclub. She's probably married."

"I'm not . . . but, I do have a date, however," she added seriously, "and I think it's time we all went in."

At that moment, a beggar in tattered clothes came up to the gate and leaned over. "Ma'am, d'you have a quarter to spare?" he asked. His breath was hot and winy.

"Look here," Roger cried, stepping up to grab the beggar by the collar. "You get outta here or I'll call the cops. You leave the lady alone!"

"Y'ain't gonna call no cops," the man replied, giving them a toothless grin. He motioned toward the townhouse with his chin. "Y'all gonna go to jail if ya do, an' all yer fancy friends inside! The Feds'll be right on yer tails!"

"I'm going to send *you* further than jail," the second man declared in a loud, aggressive voice, moving between his friend and Zica. He was young, clean-shaven, and flushed.

"Wait," Zica said. Her voice was trembling but strong. She opened her small jewelled purse and held out a quarter. "Here," she told the beggar. "Get yourself a sandwich or something. You're right, of course, we're not going to call the cops."

As the bum stumbled away, admiring the coin, she turned to the two strangers and smiled, extending her gloved hand. "Thank you for trying to save me," she said. "But you needn't have threatened the man. I don't think he was dangerous."

"Bums don't belong in Manhattan," the first man spoke up, shaking his head.

She looked from one to the other, sadly. "Where would you propose to send them?" she asked softly. "It wasn't so long ago that I myself was homeless and hungry like this poor fellow." A moment went by in palpable discomfort. "You look horrified," she said softly. "But I'm not crazy, gentlemen. I was once scared and destitute, with no family, and I was rescued by some very kind people."

Their bland, clean-cut young faces stared back at her with supercilious puzzlement.

Seeing their expressions, she sighed, deciding to end this fruitless interchange. "Thank you again," she told them sweetly. Before they could move forward, she stepped up to the door and, standing on her tiptoes, lifted the heavy iron knocker and banged three times— two short knocks, and one long one.

Someone slid back a panel and peered at her through the peephole. The massive oak door opened a crack. "Ah, Baroness!" a liveried attendant greeted her. "Do come in, please! Your table is waiting, and Mr. Pierre will be with you shortly."

She turned to the men behind her and smiled. "Have a pleasant evening," she murmured, walking in.

The cloakroom girl, Francie, asked if she wished to check her stole. But Zica felt chilled; a pall had fallen over her. She shook her head, mouthing a silent "Thank you." Perhaps the happy atmosphere at the club would restore her earlier sense of well-being.

As she followed the *maître d'*, she felt a grateful warmth reenter her, as she heard the low buzz of chatter and the band's lively music. Put it aside, she told herself; this is the time to have fun—and you, my girl, are brooding.

Her table, decorated with a red rose in a bud vase, faced the dance floor. Slender women in short, clinging dresses and men in trim tuxedos were moving to the rhythm of Paul Whiteman and his orchestra. Whiteman was a chubby violinist-turned-bandleader from Denver with a pencil-thin mustache who commanded twenty-five thousand dollars for a six-night engagement. People called him the "Prince of Jazz."

A waiter pulled out her chair. Zica smiled as she took her seat and ordered a White Rock Ginger Ale. Then she found herself blissfully alone.

As Zica let the mink stole slide off her shoulders, she looked about her, wondering about the dancers who were gyrating to the Black Bottom. There were three couples, all about her age. Most of the women wore pastel gowns held up by spaghetti straps, their skirts in bouffant layers ending at the knee. Their hair was short and bobbed; they had rouged their cheekbones. Most had long, slender legs and no noticeable bosoms. The men were thin and agile. All were in black and white, with evening tails.

When the waiter returned with her drink, Zica took a sip, reassured that Noel had remembered her favorite champagne. She liked Taittinger Brut; it came in a highball glass with a straw, as though it were, indeed, a glass of ginger ale. Holding the glass in her hand, Zica looked at all the elegant men in their frilled shirts and bow ties, at the bright and pretty flappers with their fake pearls and sparkling eyes. New York was having a ball.

It was time to play, to put the bad memories far behind her. Why, then, could she not dismiss the feeling of unease that clung to her? She recalled those early months when she had taken in laundry on Essex Street. And that dreadful old man, the landlord—Mr. Netter! And all at once she thought of Yakov—of those early years when they struggled together to build something, to make something of themselves.

Where was Yakov now? Zica had achieved her dream—she was successful and fairly happy. But he had nothing left. His wife was gone. He only saw his child on certain court-ordained weekends.

Zica had taken so much away—the dream, the ambition, the reason for trying—when she had divorced him and resumed her life as Zeinab Poliakov. Suddenly she felt guilty, and unhappy. She had ruined his life—and for what motive but her own selfish need to be free of him, to be able to live and love as she pleased? She had thought that motive sufficient. But, now, she began to wonder.

Yakov was the kindest and noblest man she had ever had the good luck to encounter. He had loved her with the true, steady passion of mature love—that love which knows when to sacrifice the self for the loved one. He had saved her life more than once. Watching her love another man, he remained her devoted friend. He had never let her down.

But she had let *him* down. She had broken his heart.

True, he had loved the funny movies. But otherwise, what had his passions been? Only Zica and their child. During all those years of work, Yakov had tried to set money aside to build a foundation for their future. At night he had held her close, gazing at her with his sharp black eyes, smiling at her from the solemn center of his soul. And she had thought him boring, prosaic...just one step from ordinary.

Lately, when he had called her on the telephone, she'd made excuses not to talk to him. She'd had Bruno tell him she was with a client or an artist, or the governess say she was out for the evening. She wanted him not to call, and she told herself it was "for his own sake." But it was really for hers. His devotion to her was unbearably pure—more, far more than she felt she deserved, especially now.

Last year, his father had died, after a long illness. And, six months later, his mother, Bella, had followed suit, like so many aging widows who cannot survive the death of a beloved spouse and life's companion. For two years already, the elder Pokhises had been on their own, having retired from their distasteful indenture to the Aschkenasys, and Yakov had been talking of bringing them to America to meet their grandchild. Why hadn't he done it...? Zica knew, deep inside, that he'd been ashamed of the divorce, afraid his parents would think him at fault, for having dared to look above his station. He'd been afraid they would reopen the wound and tell him things he had no wish to hear, things that would bring back the past, and Peredelkino. *They* had never put the *shtetl* behind them, and had continued to serve the aunt and uncle of their own daughter-in-law long after Yakov's marriage had become public knowledge. To them, it had not seemed incongruous to remain servants of their own in-laws . . . because to them, to Lev and Bella, it was Yakov's pretensions they had never understood, and Yakov's aspirations.

And so Lev and Bella had remained in Paris, living meagerly on their savings and accepting only partial help from their ambitious boy. Zica had written to them until the separation, and they'd continued to address her as 'Zeinab Lazarevna,' in the formal second person, plural. Now she felt a renewed pang of shame. She had virtually abandoned them, writing less and less, feeling less and less obligated to these former in-laws she had only seen once in her life, when she'd visited her aunt in Odessa years before. But Yakov must have suffered from her laxity; he must have felt her distance from them, and understood why. These were not her own kind. These were servants, *shtetl* people, while she, fundamentally, had never ceased being a *barinya*.

He had lost his parents. And he had had to bear this loss alone. Sure, she had telephoned him, and offered her condolences. But she had made no effort to see him, to comfort him, to ask him about his deepest feelings at the crucial moment of mourning. And now, besides having lost her and his daughter, his home, he'd lost his parents. He was truly alone in the world.

Zica sighed. She would call Yakov tomorrow, and arrange to have lunch with him. She would encourage him to sell the house in Brooklyn—to sell it and move somewhere exciting—Chicago, perhaps, where he could get a new start and meet some new people.

She would call *him* for a change. After all, he had been a good and kind husband to her, and he was Vickie's father. She had never intended to be cruel to him.

"Well now, don't you look like a princess," a voice murmured into her ear. She turned, blushing, to gaze into Noel Pierre's almond-shaped eyes. She smiled, her face lighting up, as Noel kissed her fully on the lips, his mouth parting hers. It was a brief kiss—a kiss that lasted only the time it took to say "I love you."

"How did it go this evening?" Noel asked. Sitting down beside her, he reached over to taste her champagne. His hand grasped her fingers mechanically, the proprietary gesture of an intimate—a lover or a husband. Chills knit her spine.

"It was a big success, Noel. We made two immediate sales, with eight prospects. The press was all there. Of course they trailed Giuliano like bloodhounds. Just as we planned!" She laughed, reliving the moment. "Looks as if you have quite a turnout here," she remarked.

He shrugged, raising his eyebrows. His eyes rested slowly on her face, and she basked in the look, letting it caress her. "I've missed you, Mona Lisa," he whispered. "It's been a while, hasn't it? Two weeks?"

"Only ten days," she corrected him. She could feel the heat radiating from within her, like the glow from a shot of brandy. He could have this effect with a single, lingering look, with the brushstroke of his voice. She felt waves of gratitude. With every word, every touch, he reminded her that she was a woman, with a woman's needs.

"Ten days seems an eternity," he went on. His ironic half-smile told her that he was in fact teasing himself, that he was laughing at his own boyish passion for her. She liked that about him; his quick, easy humor, his odd self-deprecation. "Will you dance with me?" he asked, as Paul Whiteman made a signal for his band to slow down to a more romantic tango.

Zica nodded, rising as he pulled back her chair. Noel was wearing a gray silk shirt under his tuxedo that, in this light, looked almost lavender. His skin had a bronze cast to it, as though flecked with gold dust. He touched the small of her back as they walked up to the dance floor, and suddenly Bix Beiderbecke's cornet rose, plangent, a human wail, rending the room with its heartbreak. Noel swept Zica into movement, pressing the small of her back so firmly that she seemed glued against him, his breath hot on her neck, the new bristles of a half day's beard rubbing against the downy smoothness of her own cheek.

New York was having a party, and she had been invited.

Later, waiting for Noel to tally up the night's receipts, she powdered her nose in the ladies' room and reapplied lipstick and rouge. She had never before agreed to stay after the club closed its doors for the night. Her heart fluttered; she wondered whether she would live to regret her impulse to stay.

But she also knew this was no impulse. It was a meticulously planned seduction. She wanted Noel to seduce her, that very night.

Then why was she afraid? Zica wondered. With panic she realized that she had only slept with two men in her life—Kyril and Yakov.

In truth, neither her husband nor her lover had known much about how to please a woman in bed. But Noel Pierre had surely made love to many women. He would have learned from them how they liked to be pleased. She knew that was part of her attraction to him: he would know exactly what to do.

But she was afraid. She was the inexperienced one. She was all *wanting*—but how could she meet *his* needs? And what if he only wanted the conquest? What if, the seduction accomplished, he would think of her as yet another flapper, devoid of morality and self-respect?

Hearing a tap on the door, Zica peeked out. Noel was standing outside the ladies' room, a mischievous smile on his face. "I'm all done here," he said to her. "Come, pretty lady, and see my etchings. For a gallery owner, this ought to be interesting, don't you think?"

She blushed, casting her eyes down. "Am I embarrassing you?" he asked her softly.

She nodded, taking his arm and letting the door swing closed behind her. "I'm not used to this," she answered, not looking at him.

"I know," he said.

They walked together past the empty tables, where the staff was changing tablecloths and removing the day-old flowers. A smell of lemon oil and disinfectant pervaded the air.

Ignoring his staff, Noel proceeded across the deserted dance floor and out the back. Zica had never been in the private areas of the house. She peered about, noting the steep staircase with its deep velvet carpeting and a wrought-iron rail. Noel put his arm around her waist and guided her up the stairs, humming a tune she had never heard.

At the second-floor landing, they paused. "These are my offices," he told her. "I live on the top floor." At the top of the second flight, he opened a door and led Zica into a large sitting room illumined with beautiful brass lamps. The room had two silk sofas, cater-cornered to each other, heaped with a multitude of brightly colored cushions. In the corner stood a Chinese sideboard with lacquered inlays, upon which were placed crystal decanters and a tray with cocktail glasses. From a silver bucket a large green bottle protruded. Sinking into one of the sofas, Zica folded her hands nervously in her lap as she watched Noel uncork the bottle and pour two glasses of champagne.

He returned to the sofa, carrying the two champagne flutes, seating himself so close to her that she could feel his thigh pressing against her. The fine Waterford crystal made a singing noise as they clicked glasses. "Cheers," he said. "To the most beautiful woman in New York."

She smiled. "You're too kind."

They drank for a moment in silence before he set down his glass on a low, black-lacquered coffee table. He removed her glass from her fingers and set it down beside his.

"You don't know how many times I've dreamt of holding you in my arms," he said gently.

"I'm afraid, Noel," she stammered. "You know, I'm not... well, used to this. I... oh, dear, I'm making a dreadful mess of this, and I'm sorry. Maybe I should just go home."

Instead of answering, he placed his hands on her shoulders and looked deeply into her eyes. He was terribly handsome, she thought, sighing. He cupped her face between his fingers and kissed her, long and softly, on the mouth.

"There is nothing to be frightened of," he told her gently. "I am only a man, who wants you. There's nothing wrong with that, Zica."

She let him kiss her face as though every feature were a fragile object of adoration. She wanted to continue—but what was one supposed to do with a strange man? When she'd been eighteen, it had been so easy! She and Kyril had been children, bursting with curiosity and desire, surrounded by the pure halo of first love. They had done what came naturally, peeling off their clothes behind the living-room sofa, without thought of consequence or appropriateness. Now she was a woman, a grown-up. And Noel expected her to be a modern woman, one who knew.

He stopped kissing her. He was looking at her steadily, not taking his eyes off her. In the kaleidoscopic light of the Tiffany lamps, his dark, sultry face appeared almost sinister, shadowed in forest-green and highlit in golden amber. She thought that this was the sort of man she would never really know... the volume of erotic poetry she would never get the chance to read from cover to cover.

"Come," he said, his voice a cadent murmur. He held out his hand, and then he drew her close and she lay her head on his shoulder. Like a magician leading his assistant on stage, he guided her toward the back of the room, opened a door, and drew her through a long corridor lit by a few electric candles ensconced in niches in the wall. They reached another door. He turned the brass knob, and they were swallowed into darkness.

"Wait," he told her. He left her standing alone. He turned on a switch, and the room was all at once bathed in soft silver light. The bed, shaped vaguely like a butterfly, stood on a foot-high dais inside an alcove sprayed with interwoven silver and blue forms. A series of recessed lights illumined the design. Zica gasped, bewitched by this spectacle. "This is beautiful," she murmured to Noel.

"It's just a room. *You* are beautiful." He came toward her, holding out his arms, and she obeyed, mesmerized. Soft music rose around them. She felt her senses caught by the plaintive sounds of a jazz quartet emerging from a phonograph that Noel had switched on.

He captured her in his arms, kissing the crook of her neck. As she leaned against him, she felt his hands behind her, unhooking the snaps of her dress. She closed her eyes and the room began to spin. She could feel a heat inside her, spreading from her stomach toward her chest, making her extremities tingle. The most private part of her seemed to burn, aching to be touched. She felt her breasts press against him, yielding at the contact, the nipples hardening.

Her gown fell to the ground and she stepped out of it. Now his hands were on her back, her buttocks, her thighs. She wore only her lace panties, her brassiere and garter, her stockings and high-heeled shoes.

But he was fully clothed. Smiling at her from the penumbra, he moved to the bed and turned down the silver coverlet. Sitting down, he removed his bow tie, the gold-and-pearl cufflinks, and the studs on his crisp white dress shirt. She watched, entranced, like a woman at a matinée, watching her favorite idol spinning a web of intrigue on the screen before her. She was curious now, her fear turning to hypnotized numbness, wanting to see what he would look like undressed.

As he slipped out of his jacket, his pants and his shirt, she saw that his body was hard and muscular. His biceps rippled as he pulled off his silk undershirt. His chest was hairless, the nipples large and dark.

Beckoning to her, holding out one hand, he said, "Come to me." She stepped onto the dais, her eyes never leaving his face, afraid to look down at his erection. He took her hand and pulled her down beside him, tilting her back onto the soft, downy pillows. And then he crouched above her, and she looked into his eyes. He unfastened her lace undergarments, until she lay completely naked below him. Only then did he pull off his shorts. And then they were together, his large, hard penis pressing against her stomach, sending thrills to her fingers, her toes—the sensations traveling like electricity through her body.

"I love you," he murmured. She knew that this was something he had said a thousand times to other women. And each had lain in his room, on the soft cloud that was his bed, and listened believingly to those words. She knew all this—yet she thrilled to hear those words from his lips. It would make the rest permissible.

Closing her eyes, she felt him kiss her nipples, taking them like sweet grapes into his mouth. His lips trailed down to her belly, his tongue darting in and out. When he reached her pubis, she let out a soft moan, arching her back so that he would kiss the soft, tender heart of her sexuality. And he did as she wanted, flicking his tongue around her clitoris, sucking it hard, until she felt ready to explode.

She lost all sense of time. Lying on her back, she felt the room circling, spinning, until she was only aware of the parts of her that were alive to the exquisite sensations of his tongue, lips, and hands. Her body was an instrument, and his tongue and fingers playing with it made it hot and wet, until the heat burning inside her caused her head to toss wildly on Noel's soft pillows.

Then he stopped, contemplating her as she thrashed on the bed. Abruptly, without warning, he lifted himself above her and entered her with a swift, hard movement, diving deeply to the very core of her being. She cried out, hearing her own voice like the voice of a stranger in the distance, and she heard herself begging him to thrust more deeply, to break through to her center.

"I love you, I love you," he said, his own voice breathless as he rose and fell against her, lifting her buttocks off the coverlet, slipping one of the pillows beneath her. She could hear his breath coming in gasps, shorter and shorter, as he pushed and withdrew his penis from the corridor of her vagina, only to glide again inside her with renewed vigor.

Suddenly he began to pulsate—she could feel his thick penis contracting inside her—and then she lost all sense of everything but her own pleasure. She cried out as waves of sensation washed over her and her nipples hardened again. His contractions stimulated hers and she screamed, her hands gripping his shoulders, her pelvis rising and falling of its own accord.

And then it was over. She felt him roll away, his body bathed in a coating of sweat that sheathed him like a shiny cloth. He pulled her toward him, encircling her shoulders as she laid her head on his chest, hearing the angry beating of his heart.

Much later, when she rose to go, he tried to pull her back to bed with a restraining hand.

"I love you, Zica," he said quietly. "Please stay with me tonight."

"No," she told him. "I can't. I have to go to the gallery early in the morning. I—"

"Next time, you must stay. I don't want you to leave, Zica."

"And I don't want to go. But I must." Already the magic was over. She felt pinpricks of shame, lying naked on his bed, slimy and perspiring. She wondered what he was thinking about her, now that it was over. She knew he wasn't serious about loving her.

But did she love him? Had the heat inside her changed her feelings for him? Tears hovered on the edge of her lashes, and her throat felt strained. Her fingers were cold as ice. She felt overwhelmed with self-consciousness. What did one do now?

"I'll walk you home," he told her, raising himself on an elbow. He padded into another room, his taut, ridged backside illumined by the silver light. Zica remained alone, gathering up her underthings as she slipped her gown back on. She balled her stockings into the palm of her hand, knowing that she was blushing from head to toe.

When Noel reentered the room, he looked fresh and clean. His hair shone as though it were newly washed. She felt embarrassed at her own appearance. She could not meet his eyes.

"I'll walk you home, beautiful lady," he said softly. But already she thought she detected a change in his voice, as though the moment for love and tenderness had passed, and he was eager to move on to something else.

"It's all right," she answered. "You don't have to come. My house is close by."

"Don't be silly, Zica. I'd never let a lady walk home alone."

Reluctantly, she gave him her free hand, the one without the stockings. "Next time, I'll make a space for your clothes in my closet," Noel said.

She nodded mutely. But she wondered if there ever would be a next time. Too many feelings were at war inside her. She could neither talk nor think.

"Hey," he said, his voice light and teasing. "I love you."

Chapter XXII

STANDING awkwardly in the foyer of the Algonquin Hotel on West Forty-fourth Street, Yakov tugged at his tie, then rubbed his left cufflink with the fingers of his right hand. It was past one o'clock. Zica was late. He wondered if perhaps she'd changed her mind and wouldn't show up.

"*Monsieur* is waiting for someone?" a dapper man asked him solicitously, coming out of the dining room. "Maybe the lady or gentleman is already inside . . . ?"

"—Here I am!" Zica called breathlessly as she entered, her small, navy feathered hat askew on her head. Her face was rosy from the nippy fall weather. She wore an extremely tight, knee-length navy skirt, a creamy chiffon blouse with pointed tabs on its collar, and a red wool blazer.

"Baroness, how very nice to see you," the dapper man declared, rushing up to take her hand. "Are you coming for lunch today?"

"Yes, Mr. Case." She turned to Yakov, smiling. "This gentleman is the proud *hôtelier*," she explained. "Mr. Frank Case, meet Mr. Yakov Pokhis."

The two men shook hands. Yakov thought that the proprietor seemed surprised that Zica would be meeting an anonymous person such as himself. She hadn't defined their relationship. Was she ashamed to admit that they had once been married?

Mr. Case personally guided them into the dining room. Zica waved toward a group of people who were smoking and laughing around a big round table at the center of the room.

"That's the Vicious Circle," she said to Yakov in an undertone. "See the attractive woman over there? That's Dorothy Parker, the writer; and next to her is Robert Benchley—they're both editors at *Vanity Fair*. So is the man two seats down, Robert Sherwood—"

Yakov nodded; her chatty discourse left him with no appropriate response. Charming and quick-witted, she now seemed the social butterfly, even more so than when she'd been a gay debutante in Moscow. She was a woman now, an accomplished one—a real Poliakov, who ran her business like a consummate professional. Four years had removed all the timidity—all the soft, feminine contours. He could not help eyeing her small waist and flat stomach as she took her seat.

Their table had an unprepossessing location, well removed from the high-spirited group in the center. A waiter deposited celery sticks and hot popovers in front of them. Yakov watched as Zica grasped a celery stalk and bit into it.

"I'm famished," she announced.

"You look it," he said, immediately regretting the tartness in his tone.

She smiled, cocking her head to the side. "You don't like . . . ?" She made a gesture with the celery, indicating her own figure. "Too skinny?"

He shook his head. "You're beautiful. You always were. It's just that . . . well . . . I don't feel I know you anymore, Zica. I feel as though I'm on a blind date with a stranger—a beautiful stranger, but not *you!*"

Her face saddened. "Yasha," she told him softly, "I'm not your wife anymore. We're not on a date. But I am your friend, your dear friend, and I'm glad we're having lunch together. Don't fret about the past. It's over, and thank God it is."

"You've flourished, Zica," said Yakov, "and I'm glad. Of course, I made plenty of money when Elena let me sell Yossif's shop. But what good is that money to someone who has no profession and no place in the world? Zica—" he looked at her solemnly—"I've been at a loss, ever since you divorced me. I keep asking myself—'Why? Why?'"

"Don't be pitiful, Yasha. You are as much a man as you ever were. You're bright and funny—*that's* enviable, don't you think? You're the person I most admire in the entire world—do you know that?"

"I had no idea," he told her simply. "But . . . thank you. It feels good to have you say this."

The waiter arrived with menus, but Zica shook her head. "I want the chicken salad," she said, "and some White Rock mineral water with a splash of lime. I highly recommend this salad," she remarked to Yakov.

"I'll take it then," he said. "But bring me a pot of hot tea with lemon. Preferably in a glass," he added, smiling, "the way I like to drink it at home."

"We don't serve tea in glasses, sir," the waiter responded, lifting a corner of his upper lip.

"I don't care, then. Bring it in a soup dish, if you prefer. Do as you like."

After the man had departed, Zica said, "You tease these simple people and they don't realize you're joking. Why must you do this?"

"To annoy you," he smiled, realizing, as he uttered the words, that he felt suddenly happy—perhaps because he'd shaken her composure just a little.

"Why can't we just be friends, Yasha?" she sighed, shaking her head. "You make things so difficult between us. It makes me not want—well, not want to spend time with you. Why can't we sit and talk with no unpleasantness, without trying to irritate each other?"

"Because we're divorced and you wanted this divorce. Because—well, it's not important why. I wanted to see you because I have something to tell you. I've sold the house."

She leaned forward, her hands clasped over the tablecloth. "You *have?* That's wonderful, Yashka! I was just planning to suggest this to you. You need to make some changes, and then you'll feel differently about a lot of things—me included. I want to be your friend, Yasha, but you make it hard for me. I don't feel . . . at ease with you. And so I make stupid comments, like a fool."

"Half the proceeds of the house belong to you," he told her softly.

"I don't want them. I'm doing fine, Yasha. I'd like to think you would invest this money, along with the revenue from Yossif Adolfovitch's business. You need to find some kind of work that will make other people happy and give you satisfaction. You always hated managing the old man's stores. You were *meant* to be involved in something more fun, Yasha—something, well, like what I've been doing. I live and breathe art and artists. The hours pass so quickly, I hardly know which day of the week it is!"

"You're right, Zica. I've given all this much thought—a great deal of thought, in fact. And I've made up my mind. I've got a plan. Maybe you'll think I'm crazy, but I've got to follow this plan through—even if it doesn't work out, even if I'm reduced to poverty.

"I want to *act,* Zica. I want to act in moving pictures, just like Charlie Chaplin, Buster Keaton, and Harold Lloyd. If they could do it, so can I!"

Before Zica could reply, the waiter arrived with their salads. A busboy came in his wake, carrying a tray with Yakov's tea and Zica's mineral water. When at last they were alone again, she thrust her hands palms-up in front of her.

"Yakov," she said, "you don't need to become another Charlie Chaplin or Buster Keaton. You have such a good head for business! You, and you alone—not that old man—managed to turn Yossif Adolfovitch's shops into profit-making enterprises. You could buy a seat on the New York Stock Exchange, or buy yourself a small company to develop."

"What you really mean," Yakov stated quietly, "is that I can't be a comic actor."

She took a deep breath, prepared to fire something back in frustration. But instead she looked at him, carefully. He was fine-boned, with dark eyes and curly dark hair and a trim beard that gave him a certain sophistication. No . . . he wasn't bad looking. He was lithe and clever and his face was expressive.

How is it that I've never really *seen* him—my own husband? she wondered in shock. He's always just been Yasha, my lifelong companion, my good friend, my family.

"You *are* handsome, in fact," she said, smiling. "The beard makes you quite the figure of an elf. You look like a man who feels deeply! Your face changes with the emotions you feel. I never thought of it before . . . but you do bring different roles to mind. It's just that—"

"I am not a matinée idol."

"Well," she said, "you're not. You're a real person, with genuine passions and genuine responses."

Yakov took a mouthful of chicken and Belgian endive and chewed carefully. "What you say is great encouragement to me," he finally declared. "Because you see, Zica, the kind of acting I want to do *must* come from inside. I want to bring to life a comic character, like Charlie Chaplin's Tramp. I want to move people by making them laugh first. You don't need bedroom eyes for this sort of part —it doesn't matter if I don't look like a romantic hero. I've been thinking about it—and I've already got a character—the *Little Immigrant,* who thinks America is his playground but cannot quite fathom its complexities. He suffers, he stumbles. His spectators will identify with him if they are new Americans, and they will look at immigrants with new understanding if they are Daughters and Sons of the American Revolution. I could *do* it, Zica, *I could play this part,* if only I could find a studio to back me!"

Zica blinked, her fork poised in mid-air, gazing at him with complete astonishment. "Yes," she said slowly, nodding. "Yes, I believe you could; I believe you will." And then, as he began to smile, his face lighting up, she sighed, dropping the fork on her untouched plate. "So you're going to try your luck in Hollywood?"

"Well," he replied, making a funny grimace, "that's the idea. To take my savings and move there, and make my own two-reeler, if necessary, to convince one of the studios."

Zica looked away from him, concentrating on the crust of a popover. Then she regarded him seriously. "Oh, Yasha," she murmured, "if you go, I'll miss you. I mean, *we'll* miss you, *Vickie* will miss you. But you have to try, don't you?"

"Yes," he told her. "We all must follow our dreams. And mine has always been to make people laugh. Ever since I was the school clown at the *shtetl* yeshiva . . . !"

"So this is actually a farewell lunch?" she asked.

"I suppose so. Nobody needs me here anymore. It's time I thought of what lies ahead of me."

She passed her tongue over her lips pensively. "But we shall always need you," she remarked. "You're Vickie's father, and . . . you and I have been part of each other's lives since we were little children. I guess . . . what I'm trying to say is that I just can't imagine a world without you in it."

"You could when you divorced me."

"Perhaps that's true. But I always thought you would remain my guardian angel. Good God, isn't that the thought of a selfish, spoiled girl?" She looked abashed. "I'm ashamed I even admitted it."

"Don't worry," he told her softly, "I'm glad you did. I need to know that I'm still important to you."

"Of course you are," she said warmly. He saw that her eyes had filled. Her lower lashes glistened. He reached across two salad plates and a dish of half-eaten popovers to take her hand.

"There was a beggar in the street the other night, in the Village," she said in a dreamy voice. "He wanted money for food. This man . . . he reminded me of both of us, when we were fleeing Moscow. We were hungry, too, and had no money. And I'll tell you something, Yashenka: only another Russian would have understood. At that moment, I felt closer to the beggar than to anyone else." She paused, studying him. "If you leave New York, it will be... strange. Sad, too. Because you are the only one who truly knows me. You know my life, because yours was lived alongside me; if you go, part of *me* will go with you. Does that sound odd to you?"

"It doesn't sound odd at all," he commented gently, squeezing her hand.

"I'm selfish to say these things. You deserve a life of your own. But Yakov, I feel as if I'm breaking apart...."

"You'll do just fine, Zicotchka," he said. "You won't fall. You're safe now, remember? You've left Russia behind—you're not poor any longer. You are the Baroness Poliakov, owner of the Poliakov Gallery, and you know all sorts of famous and distinguished people." He glanced in the direction of the large round table and smiled. "What was that woman's name? Dorothy *who?*"

"Dorothy Parker," she replied, automatically, shaking her head in puzzlement. "But she's no Yasha Pokhis. Nobody is," she added gravely, looking him in the eye.

He stroked her hand. "You're my sweet girl," he told her. "Always you were, since the day I met you in Rigevka. And don't you worry, you will always be my own sweet girl."

"I hope so," she said, taking her hand away to wipe her eyes. "Though I'm selfish and horrid, aren't I?"

"Shut up and eat your salad," he commanded. "You're too damn *skinny,* that's what, and if you don't start eating I won't be able to see you when you stand sideways."

She laughed, picking up her fork. "You'll kill them in Hollywood," she declared, taking a bite of salad. "But don't marry any naughty movie stars. I hear they lead a fast life, running from nightclub to nightclub. People have swimming pools on their property, for God's sake, and they drink champagne in their bathtubs."

"Don't worry," he demurred. "I'm still old fashioned enough to think bathtubs are for scrubbing oneself. The trouble with Dom Perignon is, it leaves a ring...."

She was staring at him fondly. For a minute, he forgot that they were even divorced. He felt happy and complete, here with Zica, her face so beautiful and tender. Then reality pierced through, sobering him. "I'll miss you," he told her. "I really will, Zicotchka. But you'll take care, won't you? And care for Vickie?"

She nodded. "Good luck, Yasha," she said. Lowering her fork to her plate, she rose from her seat, came around to him, and planted a quick kiss on his forehead.

At that moment, Dorothy Parker looked across at them, raised her hands, and began clapping. Much to Zica's chagrin, the entire Round Table began applauding.

The small house was snugly set at the bottom of a cul-de-sac; it lay low and squat, painted a mustard yellow. Melodie braked the Model T to a stop, and, turning to Adrienne, announced: "We're here."

The actress nodded, too frightened to speak. For a moment she hesitated. Her trembling fingers gripped the door handle. With a sigh, she stepped out into the foggy twilight. She wore a belted raincoat and pumps without stockings. Her long black hair had been pinned up. Her face, devoid of makeup, looked pale and pinched, the tip of her nose tinged with red. She looked young, nondescript; none of her glamor was perceivable through the gray penumbra.

Melodie had been careful to drive in a car that might have belonged to anyone at all; in fact, it belonged to her secretary, Ann Simmons. She had forbidden Kyril to accompany them; his face would certainly draw attention, and inevitably he would be recognized. Tonight it was imperative that no one recognize the two women in the secretary's car.

The tall redhead came around to Adrienne's side. As she did so, her hazel eyes seemed to undress the actress. Involuntarily, Adrienne drew her raincoat more tightly around herself, as if to shield her body from Melodie's stare. "Is this . . . really necessary?" she murmured. "I mean . . . couldn't I simply have gone to a private clinic in Sweden, or in Switzerland?"

Without answering, Melodie took Adrienne by the elbow and led her up to the plain brown door. The younger woman's teeth began to chatter.

"This is just routine," Melodie reassured her. "Just routine."

She rapped the knocker three times. After a moment a woman answered, peering out at them nearsightedly. She was plump, middle-aged, and plain.

"You must be here to see my husband," she said, letting them pass through. "Follow me. He's waiting for you in his office."

They filed behind her. To the left, they saw a shabby, dimly lit living room. The corridor was dark and smelled of cooked cabbage and mothballs. Nobody spoke. The mistress of the house stopped in front of a closed door and knocked tentatively, listening for the voice that finally told her to enter. She turned the knob and stepped aside, making way for the two women.

Adrienne gasped. They were standing in a stark white room decorated with a long table, a dilapidated brown sofa, and a small desk with a single hardbacked chair. The table was draped with a white sheet. The woman had closed the door after letting them in. Adrienne felt like a small child led into the principal's office.

A small, balding man came toward them. He was round-shouldered. His baggy brown pants sagged around his hips and thighs, and he wore a navy blue sweater over a cotton shirt. His eyes were watery, and his hands were sweating. He rubbed them over his pant legs before shaking Melodie's hand. It was a weak handshake.

"You came on time," he said. "You're Mrs. Andrews?"

"I am. Dr. Levine, this is my cousin, Ethel. She's quite frightened and I had a hard time getting her to come here."

The man smiled. His double chin wobbled. "Ethel? How old are you?"

"Twenty-five," the actress replied, her voice shaking. She'd forgotten that Melodie was going to use her real name, Ethel Glough. To Adrienne it was a name better forgotten, along with other memories of that detested Indiana childhood. Why did Melodie hate her so?

"And . . . you're how far along, Ethel?"

"I'm not sure. Six weeks, maybe two months."

"And why do you wish to—how shall I say?—put an end to this predicament?"

The doctor's opaque eyes were like magnets. She couldn't stop following them as they ran up and down her body, finally coming to rest on her chest. "I . . . I'm not married," Adrienne answered, almost ready to burst into tears.

"I see," the man intoned. He looked at Melodie, and smiled again. "Well then, Mrs. Andrews," he told her, "I believe we should begin at once. I would suggest that you go find my wife in the living room. She will prepare you a nice cup of tea, while we take care of things here. As you know, this is a very minor procedure and quite painless."

A panicked expression appeared on Adrienne's face. "Mel—" she began, her hand shooting out to grasp the red-haired woman's arm. "I—don't go. Please don't go!"

Melodie patted her hand. "Don't worry. These little problems get taken care of rapidly, and with relative ease. I'll be just outside, with Mrs. Levine. Nothing will happen to you."

"Will I . . . I mean, will you put me to sleep?" Adrienne squeaked, turning once more to the doctor.

"Not completely. But you won't feel anything, my dear. Now," he stated, his odd little face settling into a hard and cold mask, "you must let your cousin go. We cannot get started until she does, and it's late. Tomorrow I have hospital rounds at six in the morning."

Melodie let herself out of the room, breathing a sigh of relief.

Beside Melodie, on a small pedestal table, a half-drunk cup of tea had grown cold. An oily film covered its surface. "Would you like some raisin bread, Mrs. Andrews?" the doctor's wife asked her timidly.

"No, thank you." Melodie consulted her watch. Almost two hours had elapsed. She sighed; Cubby had promised to telephone her at midnight, and now she would miss his call. Oh, well, she thought, I'm getting tired of him, anyway. Married men seldom leave their wives—and when they did, it was over someone with the looks of an Adrienne, not over the Mirna Weisses of this world. Besides . . . she didn't really need him anymore. She would find someone else.

"How long does this usually take?" she asked Mrs. Levine.

The woman raised her hands, palms-up, in front of her. "It depends," she replied hesitantly. "My husband likes to be extra careful. But she's not showing yet; that should make the procedure easier."

"I see." Melodie fell silent again. But irritation made her rise to her feet and begin pacing the room. This was one aspect of her job that she abhorred. She would ask Aaron and Sam to give her next week off in recompense—and then, perhaps, she'd go to Florida to forget the experience. It wasn't the first time she'd been put in charge of such an expedition, but it was the first time the patient was a top-ranking movie star. The others had all been second-stringers, and anonymity had been easier to maintain. This time, Melodie had had to search far and wide for a doctor who was very remote, without any connections to anyone in Hollywood.

When she first talked to Dr. Abe Levine, in San Diego, she'd told him they were from Fresno. Fortunately, the distraught unpainted face of Ethel Glough had not reminded him of the movies' perennial "Naughty Girl." Such a lack of awareness would have been unthinkable in the Los Angeles area. Perhaps Dr. Levine never went to the movies.

Half an hour ago, the two women in the living room had sat up in shock, as a shrill cry pierced the air. Melodie had wanted to rush into the office, but Mrs. Levine had gently dissuaded her. But as Mrs. Levine had poured Melodie a second cup of tea, her hand was shaking. What was the meaning of that outcry? Melodie wondered.

"Well, Mrs. Andrews, we're finally finished." Dr. Levine stood before her in his shirtsleeves, a trace of blood on the right cuff. "You can take your cousin home with you. I will give you some clean rags for the ride back. She's bleeding, and she'll continue to bleed for a while, even though I've put in packing for protection. But she'll be all right."

Melodie nodded silently, and followed the little doctor down the dim corridor. She realized that she was trembling. But why? she asked herself. And then she realized why this was so difficult. It could have happened to *me,* she reminded herself. It could have been *me* on that slab of a table, *me* whose blood flowed. This was the secret bond all women had: they carried babies inside their bodies, and became united in birthing them. Or, in some cases, in expelling them from their bodies before the time came. The thought of this happening to her, Melodie, was frightening.

In the office, Adrienne sat numbly in the chair, her legs parted, a cloth draped over her. Her eyes seemed enormous and unnaturally bright. She appeared feverish. Her face was beaded with sweat. Melodie felt a spasm of revulsion when she noticed the blood on the sheet over the operating table.

"Are you *sure* she's all right?" Melodie asked.

"She'll be just fine. Put her in the back seat and cover her with this cloth. I imagine you'll stop overnight on your way to Fresno. Tomorrow she'll be better. I've cut up these clean rags for you," he said, handing Melodie a canvas bag.

Then he reminded her: "You said another five hundred after I was finished." His small, watery eyes met her own, and she shuddered. Swallowing hard, Melodie rummaged in her bag and produced an envelope.

"It's all in there," she said, still refusing to look at him. She walked over to Adrienne and held out her hand. "Come, Ethel," she said. "It's time I drove us home."

Like a small child, Adrienne Lance gave Melodie her hand. It felt icy cold. She said nothing. Melodie glanced at the doctor and saw that he was fussing with some instruments on the desk. He was not about to help her bring the patient to the car. She propped her arm

around Adrienne and half-carried her out of the office. The actress'
body felt like dead weight. Melodie had trouble getting as far as the
foyer.

Mrs. Levine was waiting by the door. "Thank you for stopping
by," the plain little woman said absurdly, as she opened the front
door. She stood back to let the two women through. Melodie did
not dignify this with an answer.

Outside, it was dark and chilly. She half-carried Adrienne to the
car and let her lean on the hood while she arranged the rag bag into
a cushion on the back seat. Then she helped Adrienne into the car
and settled her as comfortably as she was able. The younger woman
moaned.

When Melodie got behind the wheel, she pressed her head to her
knuckles, suddenly exhausted. Why *me?* she asked mutely; why not
someone else, for a change? Why did every star in trouble, every
director, have to come to her?

"Melodie," Adrienne said, her voice a mere whisper in the night,
"I don't think I'll see Cy again. Never again."

"Of course you'll see him," Melodie told her. "You're just saying
that because you're afraid of getting pregnant again. But someday,
maybe, you two will decide to have a child, and then you'll feel
different."

Damn! She hadn't meant to come up with such nonsense, such
encouragement. In fact she prayed nightly that Kyril would divorce
this inappropriate specimen of a wife. But Adrienne sounded so
helpless and wounded that Melodie didn't know what else to say.

"No," Adrienne countered, her voice disembodied and ghostlike.
"I'm not afraid of getting pregnant again. Melodie, I'm not going to
make it home. It wasn't the kid he killed in there, it was me, all of
me. I'm going to die, Melodie, and I'm scared!"

"Baloney, banana oil, applesauce!" Melodie answered. "That's the
biggest chunk of hokum I've ever heard."

Adrienne didn't reply. Almost fiercely, Melodie switched on the
headlights and revved up the motor. She wished she weren't so
tired, that she weren't so goddamn weary. Tomorrow she would
sleep all day, covering the telephone with a heavy pillow. But right
now, she needed to get the lady home, to her anxious husband.

Yakov looked out over the city of Los Angeles, his heart swelling
with hope and excitement. It was autumn, but here the weather was

still warm and bright. The trees rustled in the light cross-breezes, the sun sparkled in a clean blue sky unmarred by clouds. Yakov felt a surge of happiness such as he had not experienced in a long time.

He had just turned thirty, yet he felt younger than he had since the advent of the Bolshevik Revolution. Perhaps the old hunger was returning, the desire to explore the world and conquer new kingdoms. Now, all the enthusiasm of his youth was back, the sheer, antic yearning joy that he got from making people laugh.

The small hotel where he was staying was modest, but he didn't care. Yakov didn't want to spend his money on food and rent until he'd reached his goal of meeting a producer and presenting his idea of the Little Immigrant. This task, however, now seemed enormous. Where should he begin?

In New York, he'd read all about the big studios in Hollywood. Now, in his little room, he shook his head, feeling discouraged and overwhelmed. How did an unknown come to meet a rich producer? Such people were guarded by a phalanx of secretaries and assistants, twenty-four hours a day. The mere idea of gaining access suddenly seemed as remote as being granted an appointment to speak to Calvin Coolidge.

The best studio to approach would be Star Partners, Kyril Ostrov- Malenkov's workplace. The two men who owned it did not have a major comedian under contract—no one like Chaplin, Keaton, or Lloyd. He recalled running after Kyril Ostrov in Manhattan, waiting outside Mrs. Voorhies' mansion and calling out to the man from Rostov. But Ostrov hadn't wished to speak to him. Yakov had abandoned his pursuit. He'd even felt ashamed of himself for having thought to gain something by applying pressure.

But now he wondered. Sitting down, he steepled his fingers and thought about his strange connection to Kyril Ostrov-Malenkov. Why hadn't Yakov told the authorities that he had witnessed Kyril and the real Count together on Ellis Island six years ago? What was it about the other man that made Yakov protect him when he needed it?

Back in 1914, he'd lied to Baron Poliakov about the real purpose of his visit to the Rabbi—thereby saving Kyril from the full force of the Baron's ire. Had he done this for Zica? Of course. But a feeling of sympathy or compassion for the other man had animated him as well.

There existed a connection between the two men, and Zica was the link. They'd sparred over this woman, though never directly.

Ironically, neither had won. Yakov had married her, but she had never loved him, and Ostrov had mistimed every opportunity to recapture the past after that failed elopement in 1914.

Now this sinister, three-way connection was broken. Yakov and Zica were divorced, and Kyril had married the love goddess Adrienne Lance. As for Zica herself, she was seeing another man, the owner of a famous speakeasy. The two men had nothing left to argue about, no passions to work out, no griefs to bury. There was only the matter of Ellis Island, and suddenly, Yakov wanted that too settled, to pave the way for a renewed acquaintanceship. Perhaps if Ostrov was reassured that there would be no reprisals from Yakov, he would agree to grant him an interview of a half hour. Perhaps Ostrov would listen to his ideas.

After all, the Russian was now the most highly regarded movie star in America. Everyone listened to him, including his producers.

Yakov sighed. It was worth a try. He would have to reassure Kyril that he did not have to fear exposure—that his true identity would always be safe with Yakov. Yakov felt uneasy. Wasn't he behaving like an opportunist, to patch things up with a *murderer?* For Ostrov had let a man die, hadn't he?

Or had he . . . ? What, really, had Yakov witnessed? Had Yakov assessed the situation for what it really was? Or had he tried and judged Kyril because he *wanted* to condemn him?

Before calling the movie star, Yakov tried to recall every detail of the scene between the dying man and Kyril Ostrov in the men's bathroom on Ellis Island. He remembered Ostrov's face, the concern painted on his features. He remembered how the sick one had begged him to locate his medicine, and how frantically Ostrov had searched through the other man's bag. Ostrov's handsome face had looked anything *but* that of a man plotting murder.

In fact, Ostrov had looked like a person on the edge of panic—like someone who had cared and did not know what to do. He had not looked like a coward or—worse—an assassin.

And the aftermath?

Taking a dead man's name was perhaps unethical—but he didn't think it constituted a crime. It was not as though Ostrov had cheated his friend—for his friend was already dead.

Something else nagged at Yakov, a nebulous memory that he needed to place in clearer focus. That bathroom scene. The two men. He, Yakov, washing his hands. *That was it!* He'd washed his hands, wondering whether to help Ostrov or not, afraid that if he did, Ostrov would recognize him and find him afterwards.

Yakov had hesitated. He wanted to offer his aid, but hadn't wanted to lose his wife, nor to jeopardize his precarious position with old man Byitch. He'd stood there, ruminating—his conscience battling with his selfish desires—and meanwhile, the sick man had been dying almost in front of him. The real criminal had not been Ostrov, who had sought to find the pills, but Yakov himself, who had stood there doing nothing, pondering his own selfish choices.

Deeply remorseful, Yakov now rose, sighing. He'd let a man die in order not to be recognized. And then Ostrov had looked at him, piercingly. Their eyes had met. He'd been certain the other man had recognized him.

But, if he had . . . why hadn't he simply asked for help? Why hadn't he said, "You're Pokhis, aren't you? Can you lend me a hand?"

Tumultuous waves of emotion shifted within Yakov. He found himself inexplicably moved; his fingers trembled over the telephone receiver. Guilt, anger, jealousy—shame, compassion, fear—all filled his heart with their own clamor. Kyril Ostrov, he realized, was someone he knew very little, but one who had played various roles in the history of Yakov Pokhis. And now, perhaps, he was about to play another. *We shall see,* Yakov thought grimly. *It can't hurt to try.*

So he picked up the receiver and spoke to the hotel clerk who placed calls for the patrons. "Get me Star Partners," he said to her. "Put me through to the p.r. division."

Melodie Warren was absorbed by what had taken place at Gray-hall earlier that day. Kyril had called her in the middle of the previous night, hysterical, claiming that Adrienne was bleeding. He said she was having convulsions and vomiting. Cursing under her breath, Melodie called Doc Stanton, the company physician who was himself on the Star Partners payroll. He was on call twenty-four hours a day. They had met in front of the Malenkov mansion and went in together to see the patient.

The household was in an uproar. Lights blazed in every room. Upstairs, Adrienne's bed was soaked in blood. Her maid was beside herself. Melodie led Doc Stanton to Adrienne's room. One look at Adrienne's face told her that this was indeed a very sick woman. Her skin was bright red, her eyes bulging unnaturally from their sockets. The long hair was matted on the pillow, drenched with sweat.

Melodie had no trouble finding Kyril. He was seated in the billiard room, his head in his hands, a glass of scotch before him on a long ebony table. She had never seen him so distraught.

"She's going to die, isn't she?" he cried, seeing his friend. "That man, Levine—he botched it up!"

"Doc Stanton will take care of everything," Melodie said, seating herself across from him.

"Why didn't you call him *this morning?*" Kyril demanded, his eyes bloodshot. "You goddamn well *knew* how ill she was, and you said nothing to me! Just walked in here cool as a cucumber, saying you were both exhausted from the drive. You just told me to *put Adrienne to bed*. Didn't you realize she needed a doctor as soon as possible?"

"I had no idea," Melodie said softly. "Neither did you. You went to a story conference. You met your accountant for dinner, and you didn't call all day. Probably she wasn't very sick until just now, Kyriusha. She's had a bad reaction to the surgery."

"You should've told me," he repeated sullenly.

"There was nothing to tell. All women bleed a little afterward. How would I *know* that she would start to hemorrhage? *And why are you so angry with me?*" she asked.

"Because Adrienne's going to die, and you knew exactly what you were doing. You found some kind of *butcher* nobody had ever heard about, and you got him to chop her up! *You wanted her dead,* didn't you, Mel? You wanted her out of my life!"

"You're hysterical," she replied, rising. "I'll just pretend I never heard any of this. You can't *possibly* believe such nonsense! I wished for you to divorce her—that's true—but since you wouldn't, I have done my job. She wanted an abortion? *I* arranged it. She needed to be driven? *I* drove her. Now she needs a doctor you can trust... and I've brought you Stanton. No, Kyril," she said, her voice catching, "I'm certain you cannot mean what you just said. I'm no more a murderer than you are."

"Perhaps we both are," he had whispered, tears spilling on his cheeks. "Perhaps we both are."

Together, they waited for Doc Stanton to come in and report. As they drank their bootleg scotch, they avoided each other's eyes.

The doctor did not come down. Instead, it was a gray-faced Mason who had entered the room, bringing a tray of strong, dark aromatic coffee. He had told them that the Countess was very weak. Doctor Stanton did not feel it was safe to leave her. He said she would probably have to go to the hospital in the morning.

At dawn, his brow beaded with sweat, Kyril insisted on going upstairs to see his wife. He pushed his way past the young maid, stumbled over the Doc's case of instruments, until he stood, dishevelled and bug-eyed, at Adrienne's bedside.

"Adrie!" he called. And then again: "ADRIE! DO YOU HEAR ME?"

"She's semi-conscious," Doc Stanton said. "Cy, her condition's extremely grave. I would take her to the hospital right now, but I'm afraid of moving her. She has septicaemia . . . blood poisoning. This goddamn butcher probably used some unclean instruments. . . ."

"I'll kill the bastard," Kyril said. But his voice sounded dull. Melodie appeared at the door. With an arm around Kyril, she led him outside, settled him in his wife's boudoir, and enfolded him in her arms. Finally he fell asleep, his head on her breast. She rocked him gently until daylight. Then, and only then, she went home to wash and change her clothes, in order not to be late to the office.

About mid-morning, her office door swung open. Melodie was startled. It was most unlike Ann Simmons, her secretary, to enter without knocking.

But instead of the pert figure of the small woman, it was Aaron Schwartz's tall, lanky form which darkened her threshold.

"Melodie," he said, "how ill is Adrienne?"

"Pretty damn ill." Melodie sat forward. "Didn't Doc call you?"

"No. I guess he's still over there. Cyril had a meeting scheduled with us at ten this morning, but of course he didn't show up." Schwartz sat down opposite Melodie and lit a small brown cigar. "Why did she have to go and get herself pregnant, goddamnit?"

"I did the best I could," Melodie murmured. "I picked someone who who would never associate Ethel Glough with Adrienne Lance. And he came recommended, Aaron. Two of Cubby's pals had sent their girlfriends to him."

"It's not your fault," Schwartz told her. "Don't even think about it that way. This sort of surgery is always risky."

"It's Kyril who blames me," she said softly. "He says I wanted her dead . . ."

"Perhaps we all did," Aaron remarked, his eyes half closed. "She's a chronic problem. She's dragging Cyril down."

"You speak as if you want her gone," Melodie said, wonder in her voice.

Aaron Schwartz sighed, and dragged on his cigar. Then, regarding her squarely in the eye, he cocked an eyebrow at her. "Mel," he told her, "I want her to live—but I don't want her making any more movies. Adrienne Lance stopped making money on her pictures right about when Cy joined the studio. He brought her back up, so we could make a big deal about their romantic partnership on celluloid. And you kept up the legend of cinema's Naughty Girl. But without him, and without you, Adrienne Lance would have been professionally dead back in '21. I'd already considered pairing Cy up with Connie Talmadge, or the Swanson woman, for his next movie. He'll perform better with someone clean, Mel. Adrienne's a sick woman, in more ways than one."

They both fell silent, Aaron inhaling and releasing acrid cigar smoke. Melodie pursed her lips.

Had she wanted Adrienne dead? She had been tired of dragging the star away from various opium dens. She did not want Adrienne to stay married to Kyril. But never—*never*—would she plan such a horrible thing as a botched abortion.

The telephone began to ring. She picked it up.

"Miss Warren," Ann Simmons said, "Count Malenkov is on the line."

"Put him on." Melodie sat forward and mouthed "Cy" for Aaron to decipher. And then: "Kyril? How is she, darling?"

Schwartz stubbed out his cigar, his eyes intent on Melodie's face. She was holding the receiver numbly, nodding mutely. Her eyes closed.

"Oh, my dear, I'm so terribly sorry," she whispered into the receiver. "I'm so very, very sorry."

She hung up, shaking her head.

"Adrienne died." Her voice trembled slightly. She shook her head. "And all I could think of, while he was telling me, was how much publicity we'll be able to milk out of her funeral. Adrienne Lance's death will turn her into a heroine, and Kyril into the most famous widower in the nation. If their wedding made headlines, her untimely death will multiply those headlines by a hundred. "Tell me *why*," she asked, her voice suddenly impassioned, "I seem to be blind to the events around me except in terms of their p.r. value? I measure even my dearest friends in terms of the splash their names will create in the tabloids . . . ?"

"Because you're the best damn p.r. person in Hollywood," Schwartz replied, rising from his chair. "And because your best friend is the biggest box-office star in America."

Melodie sighed. "I never thought he loved her," she remarked, shuffling some papers on her desk. "Do you suppose he did?"

"I never suppose anything," Schwartz told her with finality. "I think he wanted her the way a little boy wants an electric train. He *had* to have her, for his ego. For some odd reason, our young Count Malenkov appears to have a very fragile ego. But as for love... what do I know? Who cares? The press will say they were the closest, most intimate couple on earth. Anything they print will send people flocking to Cy's new movie. So don't worry about it, will you? He'll get over her, and we'll get him working again just as soon as it's decently possible. There's nothing like a film to make you forget your sorrows, let me tell ya. . . . "

As soon as Schwartz had left the room, Melodie let her head sink onto the pile of papers on the desk. She wondered whether she was going to be sick. Poor Kyril, she thought. Poor, dear, lonely Kyril . . . She'd have to go to him, of course, but not right now. This morning had been too much for her.

When Ann Simmons tapped on Melodie's door to tell her that a Yakov Pokhis had telephoned during Mr. Schwartz's visit, leaving a number at a small hotel not far from the studio, Melodie's first reaction was an expressive, drawn-out shrug. "I'm only telling you this, Miss Warren, because he said he was an old friend of Cyril Malenkov's," the young woman said hesitantly. "He claimed they knew each other in Moscow. More recently, he said he managed the affairs of a Mrs. Elena Ostrov in New York."

Melodie started, her eyes focusing sharply on her secretary. "Elena Ostrov? Isn't that the woman Kyril visits in New York—the older woman who owns an art gallery?"

"I've quite forgotten," Ann admitted. "But Mr. Pokhis would like to see Count Malenkov. He wanted his private number, and of course I refused to give it to him. He could be just a reporter looking for a way into the Malenkovs."

"Give me that hotel number," Melodie said. "If it were any other time but now, I'd tell you to throw it away. But let me call this man. If, as he says, he's an old friend of Kyril's, he may be just what we need." She thought for a moment, her eyes growing remote. "Nobody knows this yet," she said to Ann, "but Adrienne Lance just passed away. We have a funeral to arrange. An old buddy from the old country might be just the person to help our young widower to get through it more easily."

Chapter XXIII

*Y*AKOV could hardly believe his eyes when the sleek Dagmar rolled
up the driveway. It was a soft blue, robin's egg color, with sleek
military wings and brass trim.

A chauffeur emerged. "You're Mr. Pokhis?" he inquired.

Yakov nodded. He hadn't expected the studio to send a regal-
looking car for him. In fact, he'd expected to be passed on to some
minor clerk and told that his message would eventually be delivered
to Count Malenkov. But the brisk, friendly woman who returned
his call was none other than the Vice President in charge of publicity, Miss Melodie Warren. And now this car—expressly to fetch
him.

As the chauffeur ushered him into the back seat, Yakov wondered
if they did this for anyone who claimed to be the friend of a studio
star. He gathered they didn't; all the more reason to puzzle over his
reception.

"Where are we going?" he asked the driver.

"To Grayhall, sir. Miss Warren will personally escort you to the
Count."

"I see." Only, of course, he didn't.

As the car rolled smoothly along, Yakov wondered, What if he'd
been a fraud? In a sense, he was; he'd told Melodie Warren that he'd
been an old friend of Kyril's, when, in fact, they hadn't been friends
at all. Vague acquaintances, rivals—not friends. Kyril Ostrov—he
had to begin thinking of him as Cyril Malenkov—the film star—
would certainly be surprised to find him in his home. Yakov sur-
mised the surprise of his visit might be unwelcome. How was he to
explain to Kyril why he'd come?

After an abrupt turn, the Dagmar began a steep ascent. They

turned left and climbed further up the hillside. Yakov had no idea at
all where he was. The mansions they passed resembled the most
majestic estates in Moscow—or, better yet, Baron Poliakov's entire
property in Rigevka. None bore any resemblance to any of the
others; Yakov saw a Tudor mansion followed by a Colonial palace,
then the surprise of a Greek temple set upon a huge green lawn.

"Where are we?" he asked.

"Beverly Hills, sir. We're almost there."

If he succeeded, he would live here, too, Yakov thought. He
could picture himself with Vickie on a stretch of lawn, playing
hide-and-seek among the Doric columns and the twelve statues of
the nine young and the three older Muses. His heart constricted:
when would he have this opportunity? Zica would surely remarry;
and Vickie would be lost to him forever, like her mother.

The car stopped at an ornate black gate. A liveried guard walked
up to the driver's window. "We're expected by Miss Warren," the
chauffeur announced. "I'm Johnny from the studio, bringing Mr.
Pokhis."

What a difference, Yakov thought, from the last time he had
come to Kyril; then, Mrs. Voorhies' Irish Cerberus had threatened
him with bodily harm if he annoyed Count Malenkov.

The guard opened the gate. Suddenly the Dagmar was again on a
steep incline, headed up an interminable driveway. They pulled up
in front of an elegant palace of gray sandstone, four stories high.
Strange dragons coiled around its balconies and bent toward the
huge black front door. Near the door stood another servant in the
same livery as the gate man.

The chauffeur stepped out and opened the passenger door for
Yakov, who felt tiny and inconsequential, standing before this imposing structure. Could this all belong to the young medical student
he had known in Moscow? Yakov distinctly recalled the modest
rooming house redolent of *blinys* and *côtelette Pozharsky* where Kyril
had once lived.

Before he was even announced, the front portal was flung open
and an extremely tall, red-headed woman came bounding down the
stone steps. "John," she called out, "thank God you're here! You,
naturally, must be Mr. Pokhis." The tall woman extended her hand
to him. Yakov took it gingerly, not daring to raise it to his lips.

"I'm Melodie Warren," the red-haired woman declared. "Come,
Mr. Pokhis; we can take a brief walk around the back, and you can
see the Shakespeare rose garden and the swimming pool. We can
talk a little."

Yakov nodded. The woman was so much taller than he, it was awkward to offer her his arm. But she took it anyway, leading him around the mansion, chatting all the while. "It's been terrible," she told him. "Just terrible. Kyriusha won't come out of his study, not even to talk to me. And *we're* good friends!"

Yakov understood none of this. But his feelings of unease began to multiply. Something was wrong with Ostrov. Was that why he had been given the royal treatment—to make things right with his "old friend"?

But as they rounded the corner, he put his doubts aside to admire what lay before him. More lawn—with a gazebo and a trellised arbor into which roses of every hue and color seemed to be woven. Below was a huge swimming pool, its turquoise and lapis water reflecting the sun's rays.

"Nice, isn't it?" Melodie remarked. She smiled. "Cyril Malenkov is the hottest property we have at Star Pictures. You've seen his pictures, haven't you?"

"Yes, of course."

"Well then, you know how well he played with his wife, Adrienne Lance. And that's the reason I wanted you here today, Mr. Pokhis. Miss Lance ... well, she's ... dead. She died this morning. She came down with some sort of influenza three days ago, and by last night, she was delirious with fever. Kyriusha— well, sir, you can imagine how he feels. He wishes to see no one, not even me, but I'm sure he'll feel differently about *you*. It's at times like these that a childhood friend is most welcome ... someone who's known us a long time. You'll go in, won't you, Mr. Pokhis, and visit Kyriusha?"

Yakov was appalled. Now he knew why he'd been summoned and what role he was expected to play. But it was all a horrible mistake. He was no childhood friend of Kyril's. He was no one the actor would wish to see at a time of grave mourning and despair. In fact, Yakov might be one of the *last* people Kyril would wish to see during his hour of need.

He shook his head, retreating a step. "No," he said. "No! I ... I can't. It would be wrong to speak to him at this moment."

"I disagree. Kyril's a Russian through and through. He has something of the Cossack in him. He'll want someone from the old country. He and I are pals, we trust each other, but we only go back four years. He's devastated, Mr. Pokhis. To tell you the truth, his despair is far greater than I would have predicted." She stopped, eyeing him carefully. "Please," she pleaded. "Talk to him. He has no family here, and the friends he has in New York, Mr. and Mrs. Morrison, old Mrs. Voorhies . . . even this Mrs. Ostrov whose affairs you said you managed . . . they're *over there*. He needs someone here *now*. By sheer good luck, you just happened to call. Come!" She grasped Yakov once more by the arm. "I'll take you in, and you can see him now."

There was no arguing with this woman. And suddenly he understood: this woman had made her reputation on Kyril Ostrov, on Malenkov and his wife Adrienne; she'd been with the studio when he had been discovered, and she'd helped build him into the big star he had become. Now, of course, she wished to safeguard her position, and she was using Yakov as a tool to keep Ostrov in line.

"I can't guarantee he will agree to see me," Yakov remarked. But he allowed Melodie Warren to direct his footsteps around the other side of the mansion. How could he possibly avert this disaster?

He knew, fundamentally, that he was here because of a mistake. He had given this woman the wrong impression! Ostrov would have him thrown out; and then, he, Yakov, would lose the chance ever to speak to him about the Little Immigrant. A sensation of impending doom closed over Yakov. He thought: So be it. I've lost my chance. Tomorrow I'll just pack my bags and return to New York.

The heaviness in his heart translated into a lugubrious sigh.

"I'm so glad I've been able to convince you, Mr. Pokhis," Melodie Warren said, her voice unexpectedly soft. Yakov turned to stare at her and realized that her tone of voice sounded, of all things, genuinely grateful. *He had earned the gratitude of a vice president of Star Partners Productions!*

Perhaps, after all, his dreams were not about to end up in the trash can. If he agreed to help her, might she not—like a *mensch*—return the favor? But one never knew about these Hollywood types; few of them behaved like normal people. He would count on nothing but his own sharp wits, as, indeed, he had never counted on anything nor anyone before.

Kyril stood by the window, a tray of untouched food congealing on the sideboard. He looked out over the covered veranda without seeing it, his heart tight with anguish. "Everything I touch begins to rot," he said aloud.

A knock at the study door startled him. "Who is it?" he demanded.

"It's me—Melodie. Let me in, will you?"

Good God, he thought: she just can't seem to leave me alone. But he said, with resignation: "The door's unlocked, Mel."

The knob turned, and Melodie appeared on the threshold. She was wearing a dark gray *ensemble* with a cascade of black beads for decoration. Absurdly, he thought: I'm paying for this Paris elegance! Before me, she was just a functionary, someone eking out a salary. Now she's hit the big time.

"I'm not going to stay," Melodie told him. "But I've brought you someone to talk to. Don't ask me how I found him. Just be glad that I did."

Kyril took a step forward, feeling a momentary surge of interest. Melodie stepped back and someone else appeared, a man Kyril did not recall ever having met. He was short, slight, with dark curly hair and a trim beard. His sharp features radiated alertness and intelligence. The man looked about Kyril's own age and was dressed conservatively in a double-breasted charcoal-gray suit and a bowler hat that matched it.

"Kyril Victorevitch," the man said in smooth, unaccented Russian. "I am so sorry to hear about your wife." And he removed his hat, politely.

Kyril sat down, nonplussed. He couldn't place the man yet, but now he knew he'd seen him before. The man looked Jewish. Had it been New York? Why did his mind keep thinking New York, when, in fact, he'd met a paucity of Russians there?

Oh, my God, Kyril thought: he called me "Kyril *Victorevitch,*" when Kyra Malenkov's name was "Kyril *Vadimovitch!*" *He knows who I am!* For a moment, panic replaced his despair, but then, sudden relief flooded through him: he was an established star, and no one would care. Gone were the days in New York City when he'd relied on his stolen identity to get him places and privileges. Now he was *a star,* and all that mattered was his ability to portray fictitious characters . . . something he'd been doing in real life for quite a while.

In Russian, he replied: "Thank you for your solicitude. I know we've met. But you'll have to forgive me if I can't at the moment place you. It's been a hard day—" and at that, his voice cracked, and he shielded his face with his hand. He cleared his throat and looked up again into the other's coal-black eyes, asking: "Where did we know each other?"

Melodie, checking up, peeked in behind the young man. She waved bye-bye to Kyril, then gently closed the door behind the newcomer. Now the two men were alone. Still, recognition eluded Kyril's memory.

"Please sit down," he said, motioning toward a small love seat. He himself retreated to a chair behind his desk and turned to look more carefully at his visitor.

The young man kept his hands tightly clasped over his thighs. "I really shouldn't be here," he told Kyril, lapsing at once into Russian. He bit his lower lip, shaking his head. "Miss Warren . . . well, I'm afraid, to put it bluntly, that, not having any idea of your terrible loss, I'm the one who gave the impression we were friends. I hope you can forgive me this misrepresentation. I—I didn't know she would insist on bringing me to you like this, at such an inopportune time."

"But you still haven't told me your name," Kyril reminded him. In spite of himself, he smiled. It felt good to speak the guttural syllables of his mother tongue again. And the other's discomfort was so obvious that it touched the actor.

"I'm Yakov Pokhis—Zica's husband. Or ex-husband, I should say. I used to know you in Moscow, when you and she—when I was working for Senya, Baron Poliakov's librarian. He's the one who educated me," the dark man added, fumbling for words. His face reddened. "And I used to work for your grandfather, when we moved to New York."

Kyril blinked. This was too much! "You once chased me on the street in front of Anna Voorhies' house!" he exclaimed, all at once fitting the puzzle pieces together. A surge of anger exploded within him. *"What do you want?"* he demanded. *"Why would you tell Mel that we'd been friends? Why?"* he asked, exasperated. He studied the slighter man. "Wasn't it *you* who went running after me on the steps of Anna's house?"

"Yes, that was I," Yakov replied soberly. "But then and now are two different answers. Then, I was angry with you. I'd seen your picture in the paper with that Mrs. Voorhies—and had read a little about your new identity. I thought: This man has everything, and I have nothing. This man hobnobs with the rich and powerful, while I tend to his grandfather and his mother. And I felt none of this was fair. I came after you," he added, his dark eyes on Kyril, "because I fancied that you owed something to me. I'd married Zica, you see, and our marriage had never gone right, because she kept on loving you even after she and I were married. It didn't seem fair that I would get all the work, and you, all the profit."

Kyril's green eyes remained pensively on Yakov's face. He nodded. "I see. You understand, of course, that I had to deny knowing you. I had no desire to run into anyone who'd known me in the old country. I'd changed my identity. This is a long and complicated story—"

"I already know it," Yakov said. "I learned it first-hand, Kyril Victorevitch. You see, I saw you before...in the men's room on Ellis Island. You...and we...docked in New York on exactly the same day. You had come from France, and we from Russia."

Kyril's lips parted. He shook his head, confused. "That can't be," he said. "I can't believe that."

"Well," Pokhis smiled, "you'll have to change your mind. You were there with Count Malenkov. I recognized you, but I had my own reasons for not wishing to be noticed by you." Embarrassed, he looked down at his neatly trimmed fingernails, then bravely plunged ahead. "Zica, for one. And your family. Your grandfather had offered me a position, and I was afraid that if he knew you were there, he'd offer it to you instead."

Kyril could not help himself—he burst into laughter. "What a pair of scoundrels and ne'er-do-wells we are! Both of us behaving badly, afraid of the other. Both of us hiding a guilty secret! But Yakov—let us dispense with patronyms, shall we?—I would not have accepted a job from my grandfather, even if he'd offered one on a golden platter! It isn't my way. Jobs give me the shivers. This, my dear fellow, is the first real job I've ever held, and only because the fringe benefits far outweigh the negatives. Yes, it *is* hard work —but I get to be whoever I want, and the role only lasts a few weeks or months. But other kinds of jobs—*pfui!* I wouldn't go near them."

Yakov Pokhis examined Kyril with frank curiosity, his lips twisted into a half-smile. "I did rather like you in Moscow," he declared. "Although of course I felt foolish for it. You and I were in love with the same girl, and she'd given her heart to you. After the Revolution, I began to hate you. Zica never did love me, and I suspect the reason was *you:* she never forgot you."

"So how come you're here?" Kyril asked, narrowing his eyes. "How come you don't hate me anymore?"

"Because I resigned myself to the loss of Zica. After our divorce, she began to see someone, a man named Noel Pierre. I believe he is some sort of half-hoodlum, another one of her n'er-do-wells," he added, smiling. "She might marry the fellow, for she seemed quite taken with him. So what is the point of continuing to bear *you* a grudge? You and Zica have each fallen in love with someone else; certainly you are no longer the cause of my misery. The more I continue to blame you for the emptiness inside me, the less I will do to replace it with something meaningful."

"I see." Kyril leaned back in his ebony chair and breathed heavily. "What is it that brought you to Grayhall today?" he asked. "You rang up Melodie at the studio, told her you were an old friend... but I still don't understand why you wished to see me."

"It hardly matters now," Yakov said, lowering his eyes to the floor. "I am so very sorry about your wife. And I'm embarrassed to have walked in on so personal a sorrow...."

Kyril abruptly stood up. His green eyes, bloodshot and moist, fixed on the visitor. "Since you and I have been uncommonly honest so far," he said, spitting the words out, "let me tell you about this sorrow of mine. *I never loved Adrienne Lance!* I never loved her at all! What I felt was lust, of course, and the silly pride of ownership. Since I didn't love Adrienne, I didn't care when she told me she was pregnant. But I certainly didn't want a baby by her. I went along with her desire to have this pregnancy taken care of—in fact, I quite encouraged it. And that's what killed her, Yakov! Not influenza, or whatever nonsense the studio cooked up to tell the papers. She was killed by a butcher-doctor in a badly performed abortion!"

Yakov's mouth opened. "I see. I'm sorry."

"But, Yakov, I would never have deserted Adrienne at this hour. I learned my lesson. You were *there* when it happened to Zica! And Zica I *did* love, Zica I never wanted to get rid of! She left me, practically at the altar, if you remember. When she sent you with those notes, it was my pride that sent them back unread—the pride of a nineteen-year-old boy with no experience in matters of the heart! Later—when she told me about it in New York—I wanted to die. I wanted to feel the pain she had felt. I wanted to turn back the clock! But it was too late. She was already married to you—and that, as far as she was concerned, was as far as it would go."

Yakov looked at Kyril, nodding. "So we both lost her," he said. But Kyril—you are right about Zica—it was *she* who pulled away from you, she who chose her family over you, that December night ten years ago. You acted no differently from the way I would have," he added, grudgingly, "had I been placed in your situation. As it was, she married me because her life was in danger. The Bolsheviks had all the Poliakovs on their Black List, scheduled for execution. Marrying a Pokhis was a way to escape detection. Why else would the only daughter of Lazar Solomonovitch marry a lowly Jew from the Pale . . . ?"

Kyril sighed and his eyes grew misty. "I wasn't good enough for the Baron, either," he commented softly. "In a way, ever since, I've been trying to thumb my nose at his ghost!"

Yakov didn't answer, and Kyril began to pace the floor. "What does any of this matter, anyway?" he asked. "Zica belongs to neither one of us. I'm sorry it didn't work out between you, Yakov— I'm sorry because, like me, you truly loved her." Kyril stopped pacing and stood lost in thought.

"Would you like me to leave?" Yakov questioned gently. "Surely you'd like to be alone for a little while? The press will be at your door soon enough?"

"Yes," Kyril agreed. "Soon enough. But don't go yet. You haven't told me why you wished to get hold of me in the first place. I'm curious—tell me about yourself, Yakov Pokhis. What is it I can do for you?"

"Well," Yakov began, "it's very simple, and yet it is so very much to ask of you. I came here with my savings because I've always wished to be a comic actor. I thought perhaps that you could guide me in the right direction . . . that you could tell me how to go about making a two-reeler to promote myself. I want to approach one of the major studios. I know I can do it—all my life, I've been able to make people laugh. That's what I've done best, and doing it has made me happy."

Kyril listened, leaning forward. "You can begin by telling me your ideas. This is as good a time as any." He consulted his watch. "This may be the only quiet moment we shall have for talking. Tomorrow, I have a funeral to plan. But right now, what I'd like is to have a drink with you and talk about this inspiration of yours."

He felt beneath the desk for the small button that would summon Mason. "Talk, Yakov Pokhis," he said. "I have some Russian vodka chilling in the icebox. Let us drink to old times, to old dreams, and to the girl who left us both!"

The other man's smile was, like his own, tinged with the sadness of melancholy. But Kyril felt heartened. "It's good to talk Russian," he admitted. "We both belong to that great body of political exiles who will never see home again."

"For my part," Yakov told him, "I would never go back. Who could compare the freedom of America with the life I knew in the Pale of Settlement?"

"Yes," Kyril responded. "Or the fame I have here, with the half-caste status I endured in Rostov? Here, it hardly matters where we've come from; all that seems to matter is where we're going."

He eyed Yakov with a half smile. "Melodie was right to bring you," he told his guest. "Why don't you stay and have dinner with me?"

"I have no other plans," Yakov replied, responding to his host's smile. "If you want me to stay, I gratefully accept."

Crossing her legs gracefully, Zica took a small spinach turnover from the platter presented to her. "This is delicious," she commented.

"It should be. I went to the trouble of importing the French Minister of Culture's very own pastry chef, at a ghastly salary of two thousand dollars a year," Anna Voorhies replied. She popped a tiny cheese *brioche* into her mouth and considered its taste with a pensive expression. "*Mmm . . .* not bad."

"I would love to borrow this man for my restaurant," Noel Pierre said, smiling at the old lady. "The man we now have is best known for his roasts. Desserts, as Zica can attest, are the least appealing part of our menu."

"The best part, you naughty boy, are the spirits," Elsie Morrison laughed.

Zica sat back, relaxing. Another pleasant Sunday afternoon at Anna's house. Elsie always came alone, for Brett had sports commentaries to broadcast—but Zica found her amusing and *piquante,* and had grown to enjoy her company. In many ways, Elsie reminded Zica of herself: a good little daughter of the upper class, Elsie too had married young, had a daughter, then awakened to the fact that she did not love her husband and needed her freedom. But the difference was that Elsie had never suffered deprivation, and that, long ago, she'd been in love with Henry Tulliver. Having slid from one rich man to another—this one a flamboyant radio personality—she had never felt those terrible lean times. Certainly, she had never given birth to a child in a public ward, nor taken in other people's laundry. She could afford to laugh, to be perpetually amused . . . whereas Zica had learned to regard the world as a potentially hostile place where one needed to be forever on one's guard.

"I'm curious," Elsie now said, playing Little Bad Girl to the hilt. "You two seem to have such fun together, but I haven't heard any gossip about an eventual wedding." She looked from Zica to Noel. "Or am I badly out of line?"

"It isn't that I haven't asked," Noel replied. His handsome face showed a tenseness that set Zica on edge. "I believe that Zica is essentially opposed to pledging her troth to an underworld figure. That's what the papers call me, anyway," he added, shrugging lightly.

"We find you perfectly delightful," Elsie replied, helping herself to a miniscule serving of Beef Wellington.

Noel smiled at Zica, who smiled back. Why wasn't she sure of him? she wondered. It had nothing to do with his "connections," which mattered very little to her. He made love with the smooth, gliding motions of a dancer, bringing her much pleasure. Still, she wasn't sure of her own feelings. She liked the rush of excitement whenever she was with him—and how charmingly he fit in with her friends—but as for loving him, she balked at confronting the issue. Did it really matter?

"I listened to this morning's broadcast from Glendale," Anna Voorhies broke in darkly. "Poor darling Kyra...I sent a wreath, though I know he wasn't happy with his Adrienne. What an extravaganza that funeral is going to be! They've dressed her in her wedding gown, like a virgin! Does anybody wish to turn it on?" she demanded.

"He asked me to come, but Brett couldn't get away," Elsie stated, fidgeting in her seat. "Truth to tell, I never liked her. We met a couple of times, and she always sounded too crude for him. But very sexy. A beautiful woman. I can see why he married her."

"It was a great publicity stunt," Noel Pierre declared. "I understand her career was beginning to teeter, though the public hadn't noticed yet. He prevented it from taking that fateful slide. But the marriage improved his own status as well."

"Would you turn the radio on, dear?" Anna asked him. "It's three o'clock—noon in California. They're going to bury her at that new place, Forest Lawn. Everyone's going to be there, and somehow, I feel we owe it to Kyra to at least listen. None of us approved of this wedding, but, after all, he is our friend, and she was his wife."

Zica remained silent. Her face revealed no emotion. Noel rose, walked over to the large radio in the corner, flicked it on and located the broadcast. At first, all they could hear was static; then the voice of a female announcer filled the spacious sitting room.

"This is Felicity Powell, speaking to you from Glendale, California, where film actress Adrienne Lance—in real life, the exotic Countess Malenkov—is about to be buried. The crowd gathered here in the Little Church of the Flowers is Standing Room Only—a testament to the popularity of the movie star and her husband. Cyril Malenkov, the well-known actor, is sitting in the cordoned-off first row alongside his producers, Aaron Schwartz and Sam Unger. Melodie Warren, head of public relations for Star Partners, is nearby with a mysterious unknown. This man is young, small, with dark, curly hair, black eyes, and a beard. He has been fascinating news reporters since morning. He had remained steadfastly at the side of the widower, and appears to be some kind of old friend, for he has been overhead speaking Russian to Malenkov. The press has been unable to approach him for an interview."

"Turn it off, Noel," Elsie broke in. "I can't bear it! She's treating this like some sort of social event. Oh, God! How awful this must be for poor Kyra . . . what a terrible travesty."

Noel flicked the knob, and sat down next to Zica, taking her hand. "I know they waited to stage this funeral so luminaries from the East could arrive on time—but I hardly think they cared to gather real friends of the bereaved."

"Elena wished to go," Zica said softly. "But she has a bad heart. A prolonged train ride would have endangered her life."

"I wonder who the little Russian man could be?" Anna Voorhies pondered. "We were Kyril's dearest friends, and apart from Zica and Mrs. Ostrov, there were no Russian folk who knew him. How good that someone from the past is there to help him through."

"It is my ex-husband," Zica said. She lowered her lashes and played with a signet ring on Noel's finger. "I didn't even know he'd found Kyriu—Kyra. They weren't even friends," she added. Knitting her brow, she looked up at Anna, perplexed.

"Death, like politics, brings odd pairs together," the old lady pronounced. "You see who your real friends are, and who are your enemies. Tell me," she asked, peering curiously at Zica, "did Mrs. Ostrov believe *you* should go to California?"

"What for?" Zica asked softly. "I didn't know Adrienne. And I have nothing left to say to Kyra. I'm sorry he's in pain, and perhaps I'll write him a letter. But, unlike the rest of you, my friendship with him has fallen by the wayside."

"How you must have loved him!" Elsie Morrison said to Zica. "I see now why the lady is loath to get married," she added, shaking her head at Noel. "I liked the man myself, didn't I, Anna? And he *is* a darling boy, as Anna loves to tell us. But the next time he marries, it will be Clara Bow or some other actress, just like his wife. He needs the high drama; the rest of us need reality. Listen to me! Get married, you two," Elsie chattered on, looking directly at Zica and Noel—"and forget you ever knew Kyra Malenkov."

Zica stared at Elsie, her face white and drawn. Anna Voorhies stood up, trembling with wrath. "How can you be so dreadfully untactful, Elsie?" she demanded. "Zica's feelings are her own. They're not subject to your scrutiny or anybody else's!"

"I'm sorry, Zica," Elsie said softly. "I was only trying to speak to you from my own experience. Kyra is a man whose heart is fluff, beaten egg whites...and we—we once loved him. But you *still* love him, don't you? Oh, Christ!" she cried, standing up so abruptly she spilled tea on her skirt. I'm going from blunder to blunder, aren't I? Will you ever forgive me, Noel dear? And you, Zica—will you please not hate me?"

Zica shook her head as she put her arm around the little woman. "I'd never hate an honest person," she replied. "And neither would Noel. But I assure you—all of you—that this matter belongs in the distant past. We have all had childhood sweethearts, a first love; he was that for me, a lifetime ago. What I need now is a grown-up man, someone whose life has not always been easy—someone who, like myself, has had to struggle and face disaster. Yes," she turned to Noel, her arm still around Elsie Morrison: "I'll marry you, as soon as you wish. We'll make a good team, you and I."

"Well, I never!" Anna Voorhies exclaimed. "I suppose this means no more tea for now. Zica, be a darling, and reach over there to ring for the butler. We must have champagne, the best there is, to toast the most dramatic acceptance speech I have ever heard!"

Chapter XXIV

*T*HE seven-year-old girl leaned forward in rapt attention, small elbows gouging her thighs, dainty fingers cupping her round face. Zica turned from the screen to watch her daughter, and an unidentified emotion gripped her throat, bringing sudden tears to her eyes. Every Saturday afternoon, she'd made it a habit to come home early enough to take Vickie to the movies. The child clung to this ritual as though the moving pictures she saw were truly bringing her father back to her—if only for an hour or two.

"Let's go watch Daddy," Victoria would announce, waiting beside her governess, dressed in her pinafore and patent-leather pumps. Miss Richard would smile at Zica, kiss the child on the cheek, and retire to her room to write letters to relatives in Brittany. After that, the afternoon belonged to Zica and her daughter.

After the movie, Zica would take Vickie to a large, airy drugstore, where they would order mounds of ice cream covered with chocolate fudge. Vickie always asked what it had been like growing up in Russia. Zica felt uncomfortable telling these stories. Inevitably, Vickie would interrupt to ask eagerly: "So tell me again about the first time you ever met Daddy. What was the name of the village, Mommy?"

"It was called Rigevka. Practically all of it belonged to my daddy. You'd have loved my daddy—your grandpa. Everybody loved him. I still miss him, you know."

"I still miss *my* daddy," Vickie chimed in. "But at least, I can go watch him every Saturday. What did Daddy look like when he was ten years old?"

"He looked the same, baby. He was small for his age, and very serious. He had large brown eyes and curly hair, and he was...

cute. And very talented. He played the violin like a magician. It was wonderful to hear him."

"So you fell in love with him right then and there?"

"No, sweetheart. That came much later. We were only ten in those days, and that's a little young for true love, don't you think?"

"So you were just friends?"

"We barely met. We became friends when he came to work in my daddy's library. We used to have long talks on the staircase."

"And that's when you decided to get married—right, Mommy?"

"Not *quite* then. First, we learned to like each other a lot."

"Daddy told me he fell in love with you the first time he saw you, because you were the most beautiful little girl he'd ever seen. He said you looked just like me, only your hair was longer. He thinks we look a lot alike. Maybe some nice boy will fall in love with me, too, and we'll live happily ever after like you and Daddy did." Then Vickie would inevitably pause, grow pensive, and sigh. *"Before."*

"Your daddy and I are very good friends, and we both love you," Zica would tell her. "But now Mommy's going to marry Uncle Noel. You're going to be the flower girl. Aren't you excited?"

At that point, Vickie would begin to fidget in her seat, playing with her ice cream and letting it drip off her spoon onto the table top. "Don't you like Uncle Noel, sweetie? He likes you a lot."

"He's okay." But that would signal the end of good feelings between them. Vickie mourned her father's absence. She could not understand why her mommy had sent him far away.

The girls at Mrs. Pratt's Academy made a great to-do about Vickie's daddy. They invited her to all their parties, and made her tell them about visiting her daddy in Hollywood and meeting all the famous people like Uncle Cy, Miss Clara Bow, and Charlie Chaplin, the Little Tramp. Her daddy was a funny man, like the Tramp, only he was much, much cuter. His name was Poker Jack and he always played his funny parts with a straight face—which, Mommy explained, was called a poker face.

Grandma Ostrov was good friends with Uncle Cy Malenkov, and Vickie's mother knew him, too. He was a friend from Russia. They called him by his Russian name, 'Kyril,' or his nickname, 'Kyriusha.' When Vickie had gone to visit her father in Hollywood, he had taken her everywhere, bought her new clothes. They had gone to see Uncle Cy in his huge house. Vickie had been awed to see Miss Clara Bow and Miss Gloria Swanson in their bathing suits taking sunbaths. Her father's boss, Mr. Unger, one of the men who owned the studio that made the Poker Jack films, had told her that her daddy was right—she, Vickie, looked exactly like her mother. (He'd met her mommy once in New York, where she'd sold him a painting.) Then Mr. Unger had looked strangely at her father and asked, his voice suddenly soft: "Why'd you ever get a divorce, Jack?"

Her father had shrugged and smiled sadly. Later, Vickie had asked her mommy about it. "Why can't Daddy live with us, like other fathers?"

"Because Mommy and Daddy prefer not to live together," Zica had replied, somewhat sharply.

Now she cringed in anticipation of that question, levelled at her from across the booth in the drugstore.

In the dark theater, Zica got a strange sensation in her stomach as soon as the orchestra in the pit began playing. Soon she was watching the antics of Yakov on the screen— a changed Yakov, in a top hat and tails, attempting to tie a bow-tie for a formal banquet. Poker Jack was always tripping over his own two feet, throwing his expressive hands into the air, rushing out with shirts untucked and spats unbuttoned. It was hilarious—or, it would have been, had the man on the screen not been Yakov. Zica, as she watched him, could only feel a pang of nostalgia, remembering how many years Yakov has suppressed his desire to act in order to support her and Vickie.

"Yes," she whispered to her daughter, "your daddy was always a talented man. Only now he's found his place."

As if to mark her words, a burst of music resounded from the giant Wurlitzer organ, followed by the chimes of bells and klaxons in the pit. Zica leaned back and sighed, amazed at the "rightness" of Yakov's face on screen—amazed, but hardly surprised. In just two short years, America had adopted the funny little Russian Immigrant and taken him to their hearts. Yakov was singing the praises of America, showing the public how dearly he wanted to blend in... and how hard it could be for an immigrant, even when the climate was welcoming. Poker Jack made people look anew at their neighbors, to give others consideration where, before, only asperity and irritation had existed. And Yakov had done it all—Yakov, and Kyril's people at Star Partners Productions.

No wonder Yakov had become an instant celebrity, like Charlie

Chaplin. He made people laugh, but behind the safety of their laughter, he was speaking to their hearts.

Why was it that now, all of a sudden, Zica missed him?

Zica was intrigued and a little frightened whenever she thought about all the facets of Noel's self that were still foreign to her.

"You don't know the man," Lena had told her recently, leaning forward to scrutinize her young friend's face. "You're going to marry a man you hardly know. And you're not in love with him! What you are, little one, is enticed, enthralled, the way I used to be over that no-good Vitya." Her large eyes remained on Zica's face, spelling out the words she wasn't saying: Meanwhile, in Beverly Hills, there is a man whom you *do* love, and who is free for you.

But I don't want Kyril, Zica thought, her breath growing short. She could sense panic, as she did every time she thought about her upcoming wedding. She thought: Kyril is still a child, and I need a man. Besides, I haven't seen him since he left New York to sign on with Star Partners. That had been back at the start of 1921, and now it was already spring, 1926. People changed a lot in five years.

She had changed. She no longer loved the image of the Golden Prince she'd met in 1913, at the Tretyakovka. With Noel, she was dealing with a man who had fashioned his own existence and didn't need her to give him meaning. "I don't want to take care of anyone but Vickie," Zica heard herself say to Lena. "I want...I want someone to let me be *myself*."

"This Noel character isn't going to let you do that," Lena contradicted her darkly. "He likes things to go his way. Yasha was a good boy; he protected you and the child. Your Noel Pierre, my darling, is nothing but a despot masquerading as a suave man of the world. He no more wishes for an independent woman than my father did. That's why I can see through him: he reminds me of Papa."

Remembering Lena's words, Zica paused in the midst of rouging her cheeks. She was sitting in front of the vanity Noel had installed in the small dressing room on the second floor, behind his office. It had been an empty room—the only one in the entire house—and she had appropriated it to change in whenever she was there.

Tonight, they were going to have a quiet bite to eat upstairs, and then he would have to go down to check on the club. She wanted to go with him to listen to the show, Ma Rainey singing the blues. She'd shed her day suit for a short, slinky red silk dress. She was just touching up her makeup when suddenly she had to stop, almost overwhelmed by a feeling of panic.

What could be wrong? Zica wasn't really worried about Noel and Vickie. Noel was kind to Zica's daughter. True, he hardly spent any time with her, but that was only because he had so *little* free time, what with the club and his investments.

People said Noel was tied in with the rackets, but Zica didn't really belive it. *And what if he was?* He was not killing people. He simply owned a restaurant-nightclub, and he didn't believe in Prohibition, so perhaps he had to deal with unsavory types. Bootlegging had become a profitable business. None of the upper crust Social Register-types she knew believed in the Volstead Act!

Noel was received everywhere. As the daughter of Baron Poliakov, Zica realized how important this was. In Moscow, only your family antecedents could get you accepted into the house of an aristocrat. But in America, one had to have glamor, position, and money to be accepted. Yakov, for instance: until two years ago a quiet Jewish businessman of no lineage whatsoever, he had suddenly become a *presence*. Now he was Poker Jack, the movie comedian, and all at once it did not matter that he'd been an obscure immigrant.

What did parentage matter, anyway? It was the person himself who mattered. Again, she thought of Yakov. A finer man did not exist—yet his parents had been servants, he himself a servant. He sometimes made jokes about this, and the reporters laughed with him, for Poker Jack was dearly beloved of the press. They thought him clever and ingenious.

As for Noel, he had simply found another way to become a *presence*—to be successful, prosperous, and well-liked.

So what was wrong? I'm not really in love, she thought, horrified by the thought that had popped into her mind.

Not in love? She loved his hands on her hips, his tongue on her breasts and between her legs, his body against hers. She loved his long, sideways glances, his half-smile, his tapered fingers, his smooth ephebe's chest. She loved making love to him. But, her mind insisted, Lena's right: this isn't love, it's lust. This isn't knowing someone, it's knowing how he moves his limbs. It's loving his throaty voice, without understanding what he's trying to say.

I really *don't* know the man I'm going to marry in two weeks, she thought, feeling nauseous. But maybe if I put off the wedding and ask him to go away for a few weeks. . . . Go *away where?* And, more to the point, how? They both had businesses to supervise, employees they couldn't trust to run the operations on their own.

So I'll learn to know him, she told herself. Don't be a goof, Zica. He's a good man and he loves me. There's nothing more I need to know. I don't care what Lena thinks, I'm going to have a good time in this marriage, and I won't have an adult child to carry through it—as I would have, had I married Kyriusha.

Besides, she thought, I don't love Kyril anymore. He could be right here in front of me, and I'd still want Noel Pierre. I want to be Mrs. Noel Pierre, not the Countess Malenkov.

Zica felt much better. She turned on the small Tiffany lamp behind her. Now her reflection appeared incandescent, like a medieval madonna. She smiled at herself and began to apply mascara to her long, curled eyelashes.

Behind her, the door connected to Noel's office stood ajar, as she had left it coming in . . . she could see the large study by looking directly into the mirror of her vanity. It was dark, as always when it was empty. She continued to paint her lashes. She was about to reach over for her Lalique bottle of perfume when she heard a door opening behind her. Starting, she realized that someone had entered Noel's office from the hallway. It must be Noel, she decided. He was always forgetting his pen, or leaving important papers on his desk.

She picked up the Lalique swan, and uncorked the top. In a moment, he would see the light in her dressing room and come in. No need to disturb him by calling out. In the mirrored reflection she saw him turn on the overhead light and move behind his desk.

Someone else was with him.

"Look," Noel said, speaking in a hard, humorless tone that was unusual for him, "you told me you were dealing for Johnnie Rubio. I've done business with Rubio for the last six years. You don't switch when you're in my line of work."

"I need protection money," another voice cut in—a male voice with a Brooklyn accent. "The goddamn Feds are everywhere."

"I pay Rubio, he pays you. Ask him to increase your living expenses," Noel said sarcastically.

"Look," the other voice whined, "I've bought you everything from the New Jersey still, and the Scotch is *right off the boat!* My boys are riskin' their lives, Mr. Pierre. It ain't fair o' youse not to give me protection money."

"You work for Rubio, or for the boys in Chicago?" Noel demanded. His voice was not only hard, it had an edge of steel.

"You don't understand. Sometimes I work for Rubio, sometimes for Capone and Torrio in Chicago. But they work together, mister —Rubio works mostly for Mr. Torrio in Chicago."

"In that case, you and your boys have nothing to worry about. Chicago will protect you from the Feds. They protect us all, directly or indirectly. You have nothing to worry about."

The other didn't reply. Zica could feel goosebumps rising on her skin. *I shouldn't be here at all,* she thought. He's forgotten I'm here, and the other one doesn't know it.

"Mr. Rubio, he don't like me to bring the stuff myself," the Brooklyn voice went on. "He likes it when his own boys do it. I'm supposed to bring him the stuff, and then his boys deliver it to you. Only, you see, last week you needed it quick, 'an I heard about it t'rough Angel Guccione, an' so I thought, Mr. Pierre he don't wanna wait, I better bring 'im the stuff right off the boat. An' that's what I done."

"I see. So Rubio knows nothing about this. Just a little deal between me and you, with a little extra dough to make it worth your while—and that way I get my hooch more quickly, and you get a bigger cut. Is that right?"

"That's right."

There was a pregnant silence. Zica held her breath, not moving. "Well," Noel commented. And then: "Well, well, well. What you're asking me to do, if I get the gist of your proposal, is to double-cross Rubio's boys in Brooklyn as well as his associates in Chicago. I pay more, and I risk my life—but I get the hooch right off the boat. That doesn't sound to me like a very good deal, Beppo. Not a good deal at all. I'm getting married in two weeks, and I have a mind to be alive for the occasion. Alive, Beppo—and rich. The lady I'm marrying doesn't want me sponging off her, and I can't say I blame her. So you don't have a deal, mister. You'd better get yourself out of my place before I call Rubio myself and ask him to pick you up in a garbage bag."

"Mr. Rubio he don't get you good stuff off the boat," Beppo whined. "He puts a gallon a' Scotch into two gallons a' water, and sells it to youse for the price of the real thing! That ain't fair, Mr. Pierre. But it's your dough, not mine." He paused. "Just pay me the protection money this one time," he said. "'Cause if Rubio finds out, ya won't have ta put me in a goddamn garbage bag. He'll have me thrown into the East River!"

"I want you off my premises in five minutes, do you hear me?" Noel's steely voice commanded. Zica heard the drawer of his desk slide open. Something was slapped down on the desk. "Take your goddamn protection and get out of here!" he added. "I don't ever want to hear from you again, Beppo. From now on, Rubio sends his own boys, and he gets paid as usual. What do I care if the Scotch is diluted or not? I care about my life a whole hell of a lot more, my friend, and I intend to go to my wedding in the bloom of health. If I were you," he remarked, "I'd be extra careful from now on. You'll have the Feds on one side of the street watching you, and Rubio's boys on the other. I'd rather go to jail than have to deal with muscle like that."

"Thanks, Mr. Pierre. Thanks a lot."

Zica heard the scraping of Noel's chair, and footsteps to the outer door. "Don't ever come here again," Noel told Beppo. Then she heard the door slam.

At the vanity Zica began to quiver uncontrollably. What flashed through her mind was the Black Raven, waiting outside her apartment building in Moscow, that June day in 1918. Then, she had known she would die. Now, she could not stop herself from reliving the experience. Behind her, the office was quiet. Noel must have left with Beppo. But Zica couldn't stop trembling. How could she marry a man who dealt first-hand with gangsters and underworld figures? She'd read about Capone. This Rubio sounded like the same type—presumably an associate of the Chicago mobster.

"Oh, Noel," she whispered aloud, heartbroken, "how could you wish this kind of life for me and Vickie?"

"You learn to live with it, my darling."

She gasped in horror. It was *his* voice. Looking up, her eyes encountered his in the mirror. He was standing right behind her—so close, he blocked her way. He laid his hand like a silk glove upon her shoulder. She shivered.

"It isn't nearly so bad as you suppose, my frightened little Mona Lisa. Look," he continued softly, "it doesn't matter that you heard all this. We'll be husband and wife in two short weeks, and it's better you know how this business works. It's not as civilized as running an art gallery, I'm afraid. But it's hardly as dangerous as you seem to think."

"It's you who spoke the words!" she challenged him. "You're the one who's afraid of this Rubio fellow!"

"I'm a careful man, Zica. That's why I sent Giovanni Beppo on his way. I don't need more trouble than I can handle. But I do know how to protect myself, my little darling. No need to worry about you and Victoria."

He knelt beside the vanity and drew her head against his chest. "You belong to me, Mona Lisa," he whispered into her hair. "And I belong to you, forever."

What an odd, mismatched pair were Poker and Malenkov, thought Melodie Warren. Writing publicity for them, she had to use completely opposite approaches: with Kyril, you had to emphasize his enormous sex appeal, to cast his past in romantic shadows; with Yakov, you could be precise in regard to his childhood and his youth under Soviet rule, but you could not, *must* not, intimate the slightest possibility of a love affair.

Melodie set down her pen and considered Yakov Pokhis—or Poker, as he was now known. He was a strange fellow. Melodie still wasn't quite sure what to make of him. Whereas Kyril was all charm, weakness, and decadence, Yakov was his opposite. He was strong, obdurate, and single-minded. He was also terribly intelligent. Melodie loved Kyril because he was a waif in need of her support; but she saw in Yakov a kindred soul, someone who hungered for power as she did. Yakov was highly politic; he knew what to say and when to hold his tongue. He was a businessman, and, as a result, Aaron Schwartz and Sam Unger had listened to him as to an equal, recognizing in him somone who had already struggled and succeeded in business.

Sometime after Adrienne's funeral, Kyril had spoken to the two partners about his Russian friend, and they had granted the New Yorker an interview. At first it was only an act of politeness, for the number-one star. But Yakov had won them over. He drew his character for them and explained his ideas. He also told them a little about himself—how he had come from a simple *shtetl* in the Pale of Settlement to study at the noted Moscow Conservatory; how he had learned to read and write both Russian and French, then married the daughter of a famous *shtadlan* and gotten himself and his wife out of Soviet Russia; and finally, how he had helped his old Russian-Jewish sponsor make a success of the small business on the Lower East Side of Manhattan. He'd told them this to show them just how much like them he was: a Jew of modest origins who intended to work hard enough to catch the star of success. And also to underscore—without ever broaching the subject in words—how alike all three of them were to the character of Poker Jack. Like Yakov, Unger and Schwartz were also sons of immigrants from Eastern Europe.

Sam Unger had mentioned that he'd met Yakov's wife—that, in fact, she had sold him a painting from the Poliakov Gallery in New York. Yakov complimented Zica's taste and accomplishments, then explained that they were divorced. Unger thought this fine and courteous: in this land of quick, flashy divorces, a man who could still have good things to say about his ex-wife deserved a lot of credit. Afterwards, he had said to Melodie and Schwartz: "If Pokhis was once the husband of Zeinab Poliakov, this speaks well for him. The Baroness Poliakov is a real lady. But to tell the truth, I can't quite picture them together . . . He's tough and self-made, and she's charming and romantic."

The two partners had decided to be cautiously optimistic about Pokhis. They'd begun by making five two-reelers, allowing Pokhis, the actor-writer-director, to invest some of his own money in the project. Star Partners had distributed the two-reelers as an appetizer tagged onto a main feature. The public responded with mild enthusiasm, sufficient for the hopeful Unger and Schwartz to sign a contract with Yakov Pokhis—paying him $1,550 a week for six months, during which time he was supposed to write and direct a total of ten more shorts.

It was during this period of probation that Melodie's respect for Yakov had emerged. She'd become his friend. He'd needed someone to talk to, a professional—and not Kyril. For Kyril understood the comedy market very little, and only where it concerned whimsical swashbuckling parts for himself.

"Can you stay late tonight?" Yakov had asked Melodie one evening, with his customary directness. "I'd like to show you some scenes from my last short. I have a problem."

"Tell you what," Melodie had answered. "I'll ask Jimmy in the projection room to stay an extra two hours, and afterwards, I'll buy you both dinner."

So had begun a successful friendship and a successful portrayal. Yakov showed her the last batch of two-reelers he had put together. Then they carefully reviewed the last one. He wanted the Immigrant, Poker Jack, to fall in love with a machine, thereby parodying the sort of hopeless, slavish adoration with which some men pursue the woman of their dreams. Modern love, Yakov observed, could be frustrating and idiotic. It was like the American obsession with gadgetry—which, in this decade, was gripping the country. Poker Jack would be poking fun at all of this.

"The Immigrant is delighted with his new washing machine. In Russia, this machine didn't exist. Of course he's thinking about the three nubile servant girls who *used* to do the washing in his house— and that can be quite funny. But in the meantime, how do I show him *falling in love* with a *machine*? He's *crazy* about it! *He can't let it alone!* And it doesn't give a damn about him. It just continues doing its job. He ends up getting his tie caught inside it, but still, it continues to pay no attention and to have no mercy. What do you think, Melodie?"

"I think it would make a great two-reeler. Let him treat the machine like a real girl. He fawns over it and even goes to sleep beside it. Eventually, you could have him sleeping right on top of it, being rocked to sleep by its spinning motions. The problem," she had added, "is that you're making the Immigrant too wise a man. He should be completely childlike and naive. He's so pathetically well-inclined, so willing to learn and to adapt—but America keeps throwing newfangled things at him, like washing machines, that keep tripping him up."

"You know that funny girl you got playing the secretary in the last batch of shorts?" Jimmy, the projectionist, reminded them over pizza and beer at Melodie's house. "She'd be good here, too. She's in love with him, right? Only he doesn't see it. And so he ignores her shy efforts to reach him. *He* loves the washing machine, and *the girl* loves *him!*"

Thus the character of the Immigrant, Poker Jack, had begun to emerge ever more clearly. By the end of six months, Yakov's screen character had acquired enough idiosyncrasies to distinguish him from any other comic personality. He could touch your heart or make your sides ache with laughter.

Unger and Schwartz declared themselves pleased with the experiment. They'd signed on Yakov for ten full-length feature films at ten thousand dollars a week, and Melodie had been summoned to create an off-screen persona for the real Poker Jack. It was time the public became acquainted with him.

From the onset, however, she discovered that Yakov was intensely private. "I don't date anyone worth writing about," he'd informed her. "I don't like actresses, especially the starlets who throw themselves at you. And I don't want my daughter's home in

New York invaded by photographers. When she comes out to visit, you can have her photographed with me—but no interviews for reporters. I don't answer questions about her mother. That part of my life is a closed book."

Nevertheless, the creator of Poker Jack was winsome and witty. He quickly became popular, and made friends within the industry. Melodie realized with gratitude that this was not an actor to drag her out at night on unexpected emergency calls. No cover-ups were needed to explain his behavior. He didn't mind describing his background in Russia. He talked openly about the cruelty of the Cossacks and the abject poverty of his parents. He made people aware of how far he had come, but how close he still was to the pain of his childhood and youth. His listeners would come away shaken, sensing that, but for the grace of God, there they walked as well.

In his interviews, Yakov was known for giving credit where credit was due. He would tell how Cyril Malenkov had introduced him to Schwartz and Unger, and how the latter had given him a chance. He always enjoyed interviews as long as no one asked about current romances or his broken marriage. On the set, he praised the staff: to the gaffers and grips he was a swell fellow, a regular guy with no false pretenses. He was one of the *them*— a fact which Jimmy, the projectionist, had reported back after that first dinner at Melodie Warren's.

Melodie thought, *If he were any taller, he'd make a good husband.*

But the thought brought only a half-smile to her lips. She respected Poker Jack: he was tough and smart. But she preferred her Cubby, who was soft and malleable and goofy. Cubby's big problem was his wife and kids—though, of course, if it hadn't been for them, he'd have married her and wanted her to become a mother. And that was simply not in the cards for Melodie Warren. Babies and she just didn't mix.

So instead, she'd become Poker Jack's pal and his alter ego. They discussed the film business. They went to dinner at each other's houses. Sometimes one would ask the other to escort him or her to a party or a function. And Melodie never asked him to bare his soul. She knew the wounds were still fresh from his divorce two years before.

With Kyril she could be more open and less inhibited. She had broached the forbidden subject, although with misgivings. He, too, had loved Yakov's wife, and he, unlike his friend, had told her about it.

"How is it," Melodie finally asked Kyril, "that you and Yasha can spend time together, when the specter of this woman is still between you?"

Kyril had stared back at her from wounded eyes. "Zica is like Moscow, Melodie. Neither one of us can return to her now. We are both outside the Pale, and perhaps we can understand each other's pain."

"So the woman has made you friends." Melodie shook her head in wonder.

"Perhaps at first. But now it's something different. We are both Russian boys in the big web of Hollywood. We can't trust anyone —except you, of course. The day the mail arrives with one fewer fan letter, Aaron and Sam will think nothing of terminating the services of me or Yasha. We're out of our elements. So we look to each other for reassurance. In his youth, Yakov knew plenty of boys like me, and I knew lots just like him. Once you have named the stranger, he is less frightening—don't you see?"

Now, seated at her desk, Melodie nodded. It was true: they were two lost little boys caught up in something huge and cruel, something neither of them had the power to control. It was public opinion. Compared to Cyril Malenkov, American's *premier* matinée idol, Yakov Poker was still a neophyte. He did not as yet have the clout to set his own salary and to manipulate the studio. But he was growing more popular each day, as evidenced by his fan mail and box office receipts.

But neither of her boys could forecast public opinion; it could just suddenly turn against them, or find others to replace them. All this was enough to make anyone crazy.

Within the last six years, America had gone through the Harding scandals of Teapot Dome, witnessed the mass production of cars and radios, and seen Negro blues become the music of its era. Its citizens had been subjected to Prohibition, and had plunged through a series of outrageous fads that had begun with Coué's method of self-improvement, and ended in crazes over Mah Jong and—of all things—bananas. Life was fast-paced and exciting, if trivial. If you became bored, you simply left what you were doing and jumped to something else. Flappers casually discarded their boyfriends, and even nice women were divorcing their husbands. Who, then, could predict the morrow—or the tastes of a hedonistic and fickle public?

Melodie could understand how Hollywood's climate of instability had overshadowed all jealousy between Kyril and Yakov. Maybe it made sense. But still, she thought: *still . . .* Zica wasn't dead, and she lived in the United States. If one could not predict the mood swings of an entire nation, could these boys—*her* boys—predict the mood swings of a beautiful and passionate woman . . . ?

Noel's eyes slanted upward, giving his face an expression of shrewd contemplation. This expression came from his Japanese mother, Zica thought; at first it had attracted her like a magnet, but now it almost repelled her. This odd, aloof quality of unreadability and remoteness chilled her profoundly.

"I guess I'm trying to tell you something important," she repeated, clasping her hands in front of her on the table. "And it's something that just can't wait any longer."

"Oh?" The word came out like a rush of breeze, tranquil and soothing. Only it did not soothe the disquiet in Zica's heart: to the contrary, it only increased her uneasiness.

The two were seated at a small table in the empty nightclub. Both were tired. The club had closed its doors a few hours earlier, and Noel had supervised the clean-up crew. Now it was practically dawn; outside, a bleak light was already starting to pierce through the nighttime blue of the Manhattan skyline.

"Noel," she said, "I'm not happy anymore. I'm not sure of myself. I think . . . I think it's best we wait to get married. Right now would be the wrong time."

"You must be joking."

"I would never joke about something as serious as this. I'm trying to be honest, Noel, but you aren't hearing me. Yes, of course, I loved the courtship. It's still fun to meet late at night, to sneak in and out of my house like a brigand. This appeals to me. I guess I want to be less of a good girl than I've had to be. But this isn't a *life*. It's not *real*."

"I love you," he told her, grasping her hands. "I dream of you when I awaken and you aren't beside me; I'm hungry for you in the middle of the day and at night, I tremble with anticipation at the notion of seeing you later. You're like a drug to me, Zica: I have you under my skin."

"Yes, well," she stammered, looking down at the wooden table —now devoid of its neat white linen cover—"that's all very nice, Noel. I mean—it touches me. You know how much I always wanted to be with you . . . But that isn't real love. It's a fad, a thrill

. . . sexuality. Our lives are too different, Noel. After a year and a half, I hardly know you better than I did at the beginning. I'm frightened by your business. It's not the kind of life I want for myself, and it's especially not what I wish for Vickie. She needs stability and safety."

"You aren't telling me you want to *wait*," he said, his voice beginning to quiver. Suddenly his face reddened, and he stood up. "What you are saying is that you don't want to marry me *at all*— not now, not *ever!* Is that it, Zica? You don't love me?"

She made herself gaze into his eyes, trying not to flinch. "I don't feel the way I used to," she murmured.

"Because of Giovanni Beppo? You've been acting strange since the night he was here. Is *that* what's been bothering you?"

"Yes," she said. "That, and the certainty that there will be other Beppos, other . . . Rubios? I once thought your business was exciting, that you always lived on the edge . . . but now I see that it's not exciting to be scared all the time!"

She had never see such darkness in his face. His eyes were slits. There was a meanness about his features that she had never noticed until now.

"Look," his voice was dead calm, "you agreed to marry me. I never lied to you about who I was. I wish for the moon, and I'd like to bring it home to you; but, to reach it, I've had to make some compromises. Not all the money I make is 'clean'. This should not concern you. I haven't asked to see the books of the Poliakov Gallery."

"If you had, you'd see how simple my accounting is. It's *completely* 'clean.' This is how I live, Noel."

"You drink my bootleg liquor without complaining," he countered.

"Half the country drinks behind closed doors. But half the country doesn't deal with characters like Beppo. I'm frightened, Noel . . . and that is why we must break up, before more danger comes along. I'm responsible for Vickie. Please try to see it from my point of view."

"Let's go for a walk," he told her abruptly. "You've *thrown* me, Zica . . . I don't know what to think anymore; I need some fresh air." His voice sounded raspy and hard. He wasn't looking at her.

Grateful for the chance to escape the claustrophobia of the nightclub, Zica rose. Noel stalked out ahead of her, seemingly oblivious of his manners. She followed him into the foyer, her heart pounding.

What if he refused to let her go home? She was seeing a different Noel tonight, someone angry and hurt who might retaliate by hurting *her.*

When he pushed open the front door, she rushed past, into the cool early morning breeze.

"Here." Noel removed his smoking jacket. "I'm not cold." He placed the jacket around her shoulders. "You're killing me, Zica," he said, with the voice of a willful child who has been rebuffed.

His baffled tone stirred her compassion. "Noel, don't take it this way. I didn't mean—"

"—*What,* Zica? You didn't mean that you won't marry me?"

His eyes were probing. She turned aside. It was so painful to be hurting someone she had believed she was in love with; but, in truth, she had little choice. She'd failed in one marriage; she couldn't do it a second time.

"Noel," she said, "I don't know. I need some time, I need to be alone for a while, to concentrate on other things—my child, my work. My life has gone out of kilter. I can't get married at this point."

"I don't think I could ever live without you."

They walked on in silence. Dawn had daubed the sky with mother-of-pearl. Zica hugged the smoking jacket more tightly around her. They were walking at a brisk pace. For a moment Zica allowed the atmosphere of the Village to enchant her as it always did—the narrow, winding streets, the low houses with wisteria vines adorning their stone gables. An Italian grocer had hung sausages and garlic in strings over his doorway. She could already smell the rich aroma of Colombian coffee beans being ground at the small French café on Bleecker Street.

A Borden Company wagon, loaded with crates of glass milk bottles, was headed toward them, the horse clip-clopping along the cobblestones. It stopped and she saw the driver get out to make a delivery.

"Some things won't ever change," Noel said, his voice sad and wistful. "Milk wagons will always be driven by horses, won't they?"

"Let's hope so," she answered, smiling shyly at him. "I like them; don't you?"

"Ah, Zica, Zica...I don't want to lose you," he said, his voice breaking. Suddenly he stopped and turned to her. "Don't leave me," he implored her. "Don't do this to me!"

Across the street, the milkman returned to his wagon, empty-handed. He climbed back into his seat and touched the horse gently with his whip.

Zica looked into Noel's face; it was dark with despair. For a moment she felt sick, not knowing what to do. She had hurt Yakov very deeply by leaving him. Years before, she'd walked away from Kyril at the moment of becoming his wife. Could she do this *again* —now, to this man whom she was supposed to marry in barely a week? Was it to be her destiny to break the hearts of good men? For Noel Pierre wasn't a bad man—he simply led a frightening life.

But I don't wish to marry him! her spirit told her. He was bending toward her. Vanquished by the task of resistance, she looked up at him. When he came closer, she closed her eyes, more from exhaustion than from acquiescence.

He pressed his lips upon hers and parted them, finding her tongue. *Dear God,* she thought, *please let this end. I want to go home.*

All at once, something broke the silence. She heard a noise, then another, like a car backfiring. Noel dropped forward into her arms.

Zica staggered, suddenly bearing the full weight of his body. "Noel! Noel!" Her voice rose in a scream. The Borden wagon was turning the corner, the horse clip-clopping rapidly, too rapidly—a nightmare of rhythmic, hollow sound.

The wagon turned the bend and disappeared from sight.

"Noel!"

He sagged in her arms.

Zica moved back toward the lamppost, dragging Noel with her, and lowered him to the pavement. She shuddered, repeating his name again and again.

His eyes were wide open and glazed. A trickle of blood oozed from the corner of his mouth.

And then Zica screamed.

Noel's lifeless eyes stared up into the sky. His mouth hung open.

Zica backed away, gripped by fear. She stopped screaming, but her whole body shook like a leaf in the wind.

Someone had killed Noel—someone who had seen *her!* That car backfiring had been *gunshots!* This was the way men like Rubio punished people.

And what did they do to witnesses?

Noel was dead. There was nothing Zica could do for him. She had to go, quickly, before the killer returned to gun her down, too. She had just been witness to a murder.

Zica Poliakov began to run. She had not been this frightened since seeing the Black Raven waiting for her, in Moscow. These men would be back to finish the job, just as surely as Black Ravens in Soviet Moscow returned to fetch the victims that escaped their grasp.

She had been earmarked for death. Anyone who knew Noel would surely know about her, too, she realized, with unreasoning fear. And the killer had seen her in the light of dawn.

Zica stopped at a street corner. Nausea made her dizzy, but the nausea only increased. Suddenly, violently, she vomited into the street. Before her eyes swam the image of Noel's body, his eyes staring up at the sky.

Only when it was over did she begin to weep.

Chapter XXV

*A*NNA Voorhies stood over Zica, liver-spotted hands gripping the young woman's shoulders. "Listen to me," she said, her sagging jowls quivering with emotion. "*Noel is dead*. No one can change that. The police will look for his killer. They will come up empty-handed, whether you tell them what you know, or not. If it was a gangster, you can be certain the killer was a hired gun. He won't leave a trail, my girl. He'll cover his tracks."

"But the cops will have to investigate this Rubio, whoever he is," Zica insisted.

"And what will that accomplish? They won't be able to pin the murder on him. But *he* will take plenty of notice of *you*—the concerned citizen who caused him to be investigated. What if he decides to use Vickie, to warn you to back off?"

Zica hugged herself. "Don't!" she cried. "Don't even think it, Annushka!"

"*Someone* has to think about these matters; *you* certainly haven't got your wits about you. Zica, get out of the city! If you go to the police, they will begin to ask you questions. You won't be the successful gallery owner, Baroness Poliakov, any more. In their eyes, you'll just be the gangster's moll. You will lose all that's dear to you, Zica—your success, and the income it generates; the high regard in which people hold you; and your friends. Even Elsie won't be seen with you if the police turn you into some kind of cheap tramp. And what of Vickie? Doesn't she deserve better than to be ostracized from society at such an early age?"

Zica began to cry. Anna sighed, shook her head, and sat down next to her. "Darling," she murmured, "don't out-stubborn me. I'm older and much, much wiser. Let the police handle it their way;

they don't need you. More to the point, *you* don't need this publicity. It could cost you your life. At the very least, it will cost you your hard-earned reputation."

Anna took a deep breath. "But you can't stay in New York. You have to leave as soon as possible, with Vickie. Bring her to her dad for a visit. Call the school and tell the headmistress she's ill—the doctor wants her to go to California. Then call Yakov." Anna considered a moment. "It would be better for you and she not to be together. Leave her with Yakov, where she'll be safe. You'll have to find somewhere else to wait it out. Let this Rubio figure you for a frightened woman who will never open her mouth. No one knows you overheard Noel with his visitor that night—all you saw, as far as they're concerned, was a milk wagon pulling away."

Zica nodded, biting her lower lip. "You're right," she whispered. "But—where will *I* go? Should Yasha find me a small hotel?"

"Nonsense," Anna Voorhies declared. "You'll go to Kyra's. He has the proper security around him. Ask your friend Elena: Kyra will take care of you for a few weeks, until this whole thing blows over. I'm sure she and that Bruno of yours will be able to take adequate care of the gallery till you return."

Zica sat bolt upright, shaking her head. "Oh, but I can't go to Kyra. He and I—no, I just can't! You know that, Annushka!"

"Yes, you can, and yes, he must take you. It's a matter of survival. I'll call him myself, and tell him to expect a present from me within the coming week. You call Yakov. Tell him the child is feeling tired and peaked, and the pediatrician wants her to spend some time with him in the balmy California sunshine. All right?"

"But a train ride? Rubio could send someone—"

"You won't be travelling by train," the old woman told her loftily. "I'm on the Board of Directors of the Robertson Aircraft Corporation. We have three planes!"

"Airplanes carry mail, not people," Zica countered.

"I'll make the arrangements. My people at Robertson will schedule this for you; airline companies do favors for one another."

In a gentler voice, Anna Voorhies added: "We have an excellent pilot at Robertson; his name is Charles Lindbergh, who's had much experience piloting a DH-4 biplane."

"Oh, Anna," Zica cried, "A DH-4 biplane? It sounds ominous. *You'd* never travel in one of these, much less with a seven-year-old child!"

"That is because nobody ever saw fit to threaten my life," the old woman said. "You will go where I send you, Zeinab, because, in truth, you have little choice. Someone must look after you. I've come to love you, and that little replica of you. . . . "

Zica shook her head, speechless. Anna said: "If the man who had Noel murdered suspects that you have left the city, he won't ever think to look for you on a series of mail planes."

"That's because no one in her right mind would travel in one, let alone nine or ten of them across the country."

"Send me your Elena while you are away," Anna told her, brusquely. "She'll keep me company in your absence. Tell her to come for tea next Tuesday. I'm to have Grace Vanderbilt, back from Europe, and Mrs. Borden Harriman, who is a prude. Mrs. Ostrov will be amused by the former, and bored to tears by the latter; but that can't be helped: they are both old friends."

Zica opened her mouth, shook her head, and shrugged helplessly. "That's right," Anna Voorhies told her. "You'll do as you're told! Kiss Kyra for me and tell him to call once in a while. I miss him."

Impulsively, the young woman flung herself into the old woman's arms, clasping her tightly. For the first time in twenty-four hours, she felt safe.

Melodie reclined on the lounge chair, and sighed peacefully. Yakov's house made her dream of what it must have been like to have dwelled in Paris at the turn of the century. He had adopted a mode of living that was harmonious and old-fashioned. You could hardly believe you were in Los Angeles, once his front gate shut, enclosing you within the sanctuary he had created for himself.

The decor was simple. He had not wished to insert himself into the glittering *nouveau riche* society that had built up Beverly Hills. The magnificent palaces, such as Aaron Schwartz's and Kyril's awesome Grayhall Manor, made the comedian uncomfortable. "Everything there is a fake," he'd told Melodie. "Fake colonial homes, fake Doric columns, fake Mediterranean villas."

Indeed, the new aristocrats of Southern California were the film colony. Their wealth was as phenomenal as that of the sugar barons in Kiev at the turn of the century, and of the warlords of Europe during the Middle Ages. Old money tended to pale by contrast, and its subdued elegance was dwarfed by the obvious splendor of the Twenties' producers and film stars.

Yakov had built his house in a nameless section of Los Angeles, caught between Whitley Heights and Beachwood Canyon—a section that rose from Franklin Avenue into the Hollywood hills near upper Ivar Avenue. The Vedanta Society, which had built a comely Indian temple on Longview Drive, owned most of the surrounding land. Yakov had purchased a large lot from them, and had erected his home at the corner of Vine and Longview, cater-corner from the little Vendanta temple.

The house was white sandstone, with simple, graceful lines, like a French townhouse. It had shutters, small balconies, a ground floor and two upper stories. The floor plan was relatively simple. There was a living room, a formal dining room, a comfortable den, and several bedroom suites, including a child's suite for Vickie. Behind were some servants' rooms for his relatively small staff of a butler-chauffeur, a gardener, a cook, and a chambermaid. A small pool house stood by the discreet swimming pool in back.

In front of the house was a goldfish pond with lily pads, and a small fountain. A circular driveway curved around the pond and fountain to reach the main residence.

One became serene upon entering this haven, Melodie thought— an odd sensation in the home of a film star.

From Yakov's house the magnificent view encompassed central and eastern Los Angeles. A visitor could easily distinguish the two main arteries of the city, Sunset and Hollywood boulevards, which stretched busily for miles on either side.

Although Yakov had not chosen Beverly Hills, he had not selected a completely unknown and singular paradise, either. In his area lived two other famous actors, Mae Marsh and William Boyd. Sometimes they would be sitting by his pool when Melodie came by for a Sunday afternoon, because, as good neighbors, they visited one another.

But, usually, Yakov could be found in his den, reading, or outside in the sun, jotting down ideas for his skits and scenarios, blessedly alone in his retreat, a Coca-Cola bottle in his hand. He was the most private individual Melodie had ever encountered.

Melodie saw Yakov frequently. She lived nearby, on the other side of Whitley Heights, and it was easy to drop by for a chat.

Other times, they saw each other at the studio. The night before, he had come by her office to share a pot of strong, black coffee. His face had appeared drawn and tired.

"Something odd's happened," he had confided in her. "My ex-wife called. She's sending my daughter out to visit me. Someone is travelling with her to bring her to me."

"That *is* strange," Melodie agreed. "It's not yet the end of the school term, is it? Is she ill?"

"Zica says she is. But I spoke with Vickie last week, and she was perfectly fine." Yakov wet his lips tentatively. His sharp black eyes held her gaze. "Zica's fiancé was murdered last week."

"That Manhattan nightclub owner, Noel something? *That* was her boyfriend?"

Yakov nodded. "They found him on the pavement, dressed in formal attire, without his dinner jacket. The police think he might have been carrying a list of bootleggers—or the phone number of a powerful gangster. The jacket is still missing. What if the killer never found what he was looking for?"

"I don't get your point."

"Zica was engaged to him—and he was definitely dealing with the rackets—even if he wasn't directly involved."

"You believe Zica is sending you the child because she's afraid of trouble?"

"That's right." Yakov gulped the rest of his coffee. Then, in a faraway voice, he added: "She always did need someone to watch over her."

Melodie did not respond. It was unnecessary to underscore the fact that he was not speaking about his daughter anymore.

That had been Friday evening. She'd had a date with Cubby, who had stayed well beyond midnight at her house. In the morning, Melodie had driven to the studio to check up on some figures she needed for a report; then, on impulse, she'd telephoned Yakov and invited herself to lunch. They had eaten on the patio, by the pool. Neither brought up the topic of Yakov's ex-wife, or the dreadful murder of the man she'd been about to marry. Nevertheless, Yakov's preoccupation weighed on the atmosphere of Melodie's visit.

The child was expected that very day. So, after lunch, Melodie had stayed. Yakov busied himself with a screenplay while she sunbathed in a sleeveless dress—both of them waiting.

At one point Yakov had looked up and smiled at her, his gentle face illumined with a real, touching beauty from within.

"Thanks for staying," he'd said, his hand reaching out to touch her cheek. And she had smiled back, silently. He was her friend and he was worried. She would do him the favor of not leaving until the child arrived. Perhaps the missing pieces of the puzzle would fit together for him. He didn't even know who would bring Vickie to the door.

"I just heard the gate open," Yakov said suddenly. Melodie sat up, shielding her eyes from the sun. She could hear sounds of crunching gravel, then of voices and car doors being slammed shut. "I'll go check it out," he told her. "If it's Vickie—" He rose hurriedly, dropping his screenplay face down on the table, and hurried toward the house.

Melodie waited anxiously. She wondered, as she so often did, about Zica Poliakov. How was she dealing now with the pain, with the loss, with the fear? Melodie shivered. Better not to dwell on this; after all, she didn't even know the lady. She only cared for Yakov's sake, and for his little girl.

All at once the back door was flung open. Vickie appeared, running into the sunshine, her arms outstretched. Yakov followed close on her heel. "Oh, boy!" she cried. "My favorite pool, my favorite yard, my favorite Daddy!"

She twirled around and flung herself into Yakov's arms, giggling as he lifted her high into the air.

Melodie rose, smoothing out her dress, and smiled at them. "Look who's here!" Yakov said to Vickie. "It's Aunt Melodie! Remember how you two went all the way to Santa Barbara together to eat crab cakes?" He set his daughter gently down on the lawn.

"Hi, Aunt Melodie. Are we going to go somewhere fun this time, too?" the little girl asked. As Vickie dashed forward, Melodie crouched and spread out her arms. Vickie crawled into her embrace, laying her smooth cheek against Melodie's tanned face.

"I'm glad you're here," the girl told her. "I like you lots." And then, in the same breath: "Guess what? We got to ride in an *air-o-plane*—a real *air-o-plane* that flew in the sky like a giant bird, and we got to look into the clouds to see if we could find God, sleeping. But he wasn't there."

"An airplane, Vickie?" Melodie echoed. Holding the little girl, she peered up at Yakov from above Vickie's head. Why would a child travel by plane?

"'Cuz Mommy said this would be more fun, like a 'venture," Vickie replied. She struggled out of Melodie's arms, bounding back toward the house, just as a woman emerged from the back door.

The woman was clothed in a three-quarter-length fox coat. She had long, slender legs. Her hair was short, dark, and bobbed, her face like an antique cameo, smooth and creamy-white. Large brown eyes studied Melodie with hesitation and sudden shyness. Melodie stared back, her lips parting. Then she looked at Vickie, who was now standing next to the pretty lady. The small girl's tiny face was a mirror of the woman's, even to the same exact form of her dainty, upturned nose.

Melodie turned to Yakov. He was gazing at the woman and the child. His face was naked, his eyes filmed with tears. The woman's hand moved to the top of the small girl's head and remained there, caressing the child's hair. Melodie tried to read the expression on the woman's face as she regarded Yakov, but all she could make out was a wrenching vulnerability. And so the two of them continued to stare at each other, the man and the woman, her hand on the child's head, their dark eyes unblinking. Melodie felt intensely moved as she watched them gazing at each other wordlessly, the child absorbing their silence.

At length, it was Yakov who spoke. "Come, Zica," he called out. "This is my friend, Melodie Warren."

The woman was beautiful, impeccable; yet Melodie saw that she walked with uncertain steps, as though light-headed. Up close, she was even lovelier, her clear complexion almost translucent. But her features seemed frozen in apprehension and worry.

"I'm a new old friend," Melodie stated. Breaking into one of her famous grins, she stretched out her hand. The woman took it, her own gloved fingers almost frozen. "If you're Zica," said Melodie, "I have heard lots about you."

It was the wrong thing to say. For a moment, the woman's face registered even greater anxiety, and she almost pulled back. Of course, Melodie thought: she thinks I mean *I've heard of her from Kryil!* So she laughed, and added: "Yakov and Vickie have told me some funny stories. Haven't you, Miss Victoria?"

"I met Aunt Melodie last Christmas vacation," the small girl told her mother. "I told her lots of stuff about us in New York. She seemed real interested, too."

"I hope you didn't bore Miss Warren too much," Zica said. For the first time, she smiled. Next to Melodie, Yakov smiled too. Melodie relaxed. The moment of awkwardness had passed.

"I am never bored with Vickie," Melodie said. "Some day, when I need a new assistant, I'll know just where to look for one. I do the p.r. at Star Partners," she explained. "Your charming daughter would make a great spy. She picks up gossip faster than a hidden microphone!"

Zica Poliakov laughed. She was everything Melodie had envisioned—pretty, smartly dressed, and sweet. How could "her boys" have loved her otherwise...? Ah, to be a girl like that...! Melodie thought. To be a true lady, utterly feminine and modern! Mirna Weiss would have traded a year's salary for a week of being Zica Poliakov. But would Melodie Warren...?

I certainly wouldn't want to be her *now,* Melodie thought, remembering the frozen hurt on the young woman's face when she had first ventured out into the garden. That look had struck a chord in Yakov, and in herself, too. This was a sweet, sad young woman —one who had suffered many losses in her life. No, thought Melodie: I'd rather be plain, gawky old me, comfortable with my life, my friends, my work and my guy. The Zica Poliakovs are too damn breakable, and you can never glue them back together when their souls are shattered.

"I've heard about you, too," Zica said. "I know that there are many you have helped, Miss Warren."

Yakov cleared his throat. "I'll order tea," he announced. Vickie followed him toward the house, running up to grab his hand, and they went inside together.

Melodie remained alone with Zica; above their heads, a blue jay cawed raucously, the lonely sound underscoring the silence. "This is a beautiful house," Zica remarked. "It's my first time out here; I didn't know how to imagine Yasha in his new surroundings."

"He's a well-loved man," Melodie declared, "—a consummate professional, who loves what he's doing. You should come out to the studio and visit one of the sets some time."

Anxiety returned, full force, to Zica's features. She took half a step back. "I can't," she demurred quickly. "I mean...I'm sorry, I'd love to—but I have somewhere else to go. I can't stay here. I—"

"It's really okay," Melodie told her. "You don't owe me any explanation. I thought, since you'd both come for a visit out here, that you'd enjoy seeing how a Poker Jack picture gets made."

"You're very kind," Zica smiled tremulously. "Vickie *has* come to visit with her father. I—I'm expected somewhere else."

Suddenly Melodie had a vision of this scared, sophisticated woman as a very young girl, dancing the cotillion in Moscow. She would have been rounder and softer, perhaps, with longer hair twisted into a topknot. A beautiful, lively young girl whose future beckoned invitingly. And she would have been in love, for the first time—blindingly, dazzlingly in love. Of course, not with Yakov: he would have been too serious about getting ahead, and besides, in those days he'd been dirt-poor and of the wrong social background. She would not have taken a great deal of notice of him.

So the object of her desire must have been Kyril. She would have loved the golden boy, and he would have loved her—passionately, ardently, with wholehearted idealism. He still loved her. They *both* still loved her, Melodie thought, gazing at Zica with admiration. To be the kind of woman to sustain the love of two men for so many years...!

Melodie's eyes narrowed. If Zica was not planning to stay at Yakov's with their daughter, then she must have plans to be with Kyril. He hadn't confided in Melodie, but that was all right: perhaps this visit was too important to jinx by discussing it with a third person.

Resentment surged up within Melodie, and she thought: Not only do two men love her here, but there was that other in New York, the fellow that got murdered! If she had lost one fiancé, it surely wasn't taking her long to replace him with one from her past.

"I hope you will enjoy your vacation," Melodie said. But she couldn't entirely screen the sarcasm out of her voice.

Suddenly, inexplicably, Zica Poliakov burst into tears. She covered her face with her hands. Melodie stared at her, perplexed.

"Oh, I'm so sorry," Zica cried, raising her tear-stained face. "It's just that I'm so very tired, tired of *everything,* you see...."

"Yes, of course," Melodie said gently, laying a hand on Zica's shoulder. "But it does no good to cry. The bad guys win anyway, whatever we do to fight them off." Then, realizing how this must have sounded to Zica, she caught herself: "I'm sorry about your boyfriend; it must have been a terrible shock. And here I am, making absurd small talk like this...."

"It's the small talk that helps," Zica replied, attempting to smile through her tears. "Sometimes real life is just too hard to bear. Don't you think so, Miss Warren?"

"It's always hard," Mirna Weiss told her. "But sometimes, we're weaker in the bearing of it." Putting an arm around Zica's shoulder, she drew her back toward Yakov's house.

"So," Yakov said, "you are going to stay with Kyriusha. Does he know about it?"

Yakov was sitting in his comfortable Chippendale sofa. Zica had sunk down on the window seat by the great bay window which commanded a view of the city below. Dusk was falling gently on the hillside and valley. Sitting there, looking up at him, Zica reminded him of the ten-year-old girl he had first glimpsed at Rigevka. His heart constricted.

"It's not what you think," she told him softly. "You see, I *know* who killed Noel."

He wheeled about. "What?!"

"It's a long story." And Zica began to explain. Her voice was subdued. But he remained attentive, listening intently. At the end, she raised her eyes to his and said: "So it's a matter of laying low for a while, until these gangsters decide I know nothing—or that I'm not going to tell if I do."

"Where's the smoking jacket?" he asked.

"Annushka had it burned. I know—the police think it's missing because the killer was looking for information in its pockets. Anna says, 'Let them think it.' "

"But in the meantime, doesn't Rubio suspect that someone else took it? Won't he send someone to look for it?"

"The killer knows I was with Noel. He knows I was wearing his jacket. But you see, the killer was unrecognizable. If I hadn't overheard Beppo the other night, I'd have had no way of knowing who shot Noel. No one but Noel and I knew that I'd overheard Beppo. Rubio will think I saw a milkman from the Borden Company—but in no way does that point to *him,* nor to his cronies or hired gunmen."

"So I'd say you're safe." She could read concern in his eyes. "And Mrs. Voorhies, your guardian angel, has sent you to Kyril."

"She did think it would be best to go far away, and . . . not to stay in the same place as Vickie. It wasn't just Anna," she quickly added. "Lena, of course, urged me to go to Kyriusha as well. The place is well guarded. I'll be safe there."

"Naturally. Lena Ostrov would like you to finally become her daughter in the legal sense as well. It must really hurt her that he doesn't publicly claim her as his mother."

"That isn't fair, Yasha." But she smiled at him, a little shyly. "At any rate, no, he doesn't know I'm coming. Anna was afraid the FBI, or Rubio's people, might be monitoring the phone lines to see what I'm going to do. She just told him she was sending him something special."

Yakov pulled a straight-backed chair opposite her, and straddled it, folding his arms over the top of the back.

"He won't be disappointed," he replied, his voice low. "There hasn't been anyone in his life for a long time. He wasn't even in love with his wife."

"I see." She looked down at the floor, sucking in her lower lip.

"And you?" he asked. "What will you do, now that you lost this man you were going to marry?"

"I had just broken the engagement." Zica lowered her head. "I'd come to this decision, and I knew it was right—"

"You don't know what you want, do you, Zica?" he observed distantly.

"Perhaps I don't. I—I know I wronged you, Yasha—and I'm so sorry. You'll never know how deeply I regret the pain I caused you."

"Ah, well, that's all in the past. Would you like a cup of tea?"

She shook her head. He thought: How lovely she is, how gentle and sweet and fine. But below the surface of his composure, a web of anguish was growing. Suddenly he cried out, unable to help himself: "What have we done with our lives, Zeinab? *What have we done?*"

Her pretty face reflected back his agony. She clasped her hands together and said, her voice trembling, "*You've* done wonderfully. You've achieved your childhood dream. Yasha—you are a real success, because you always knew what you wanted. Don't you feel that?"

"From my eleventh year on, I wanted your love," he replied, seriously. "I could have lived without any fame; in the shadows— but it was *you* I wanted most of all. Once, for some years, I had you in name—but I never had your love. And it was that I wanted most of all."

Tears glistened in her eyes. "I was too silly for you, my darling Yasha—you wasted your love on someone immature and unworthy. Perhaps now you will let me go, and find someone *real*, someone grown-up like yourself."

He gazed at her, his intelligent face intent on trying to decipher her jumble of words. "I once thought if I brought you the world on a platter that you'd be grateful and *have* to love me then. I was wrong. Now I think that maybe Ostrov is the right man for you, after all. Maybe you've both matured, in the thirteen years since you first laid eyes on each other. I think you should see for yourself." Yakov was measuring his words. "I think you and he deserve a try, now that neither of you is involved with anyone else. You owe it to yourselves, after all this time..."

Zica stood up. Tears had spilled onto her sculptured cheekbones. She blinked. How vulnerable and small she appeared. Yakov fought down the urge to take her in his arms.

"Oh, Yashka," she said, "you may be right. But—I don't know. I don't know anything any more. I only know that you're the dearest man I've ever met, the kindest—"

"Enough, Zica—enough." He turned away to hide his own tears. "You have already decided—you are staying with Kyril. It's time for you to go to him. Would you like my chauffeur to drive you?"

"No, thanks," she murmured. "I'll call a taxicab if I may. It's better this way. Please give Vickie a kiss when she wakes up tomorrow morning. Tell her that her mommy loves her more than the world."

"I'll do that," he told her. And then he took her in his arms, holding her close to him with all his might.

Chapter XXVI

As Zica stared at the enormous mansion, she felt oddly dwarfed and ill-at-ease. She had expected to be greeted by Kyril, not by this monument to Hollywood stardom. All at once she wondered if maybe Anna and Lena had led her astray, if she should go back to Yasha's or to a hotel.

"Ain't ya comin' out, lady?" the taxi driver growled. He was holding the door open. She nodded, embarrassed, grabbed her small suitcase and her handbag and scrambled out onto the driveway. The driver muttered something and slammed the door shut behind her, leaving her alone in front of the edifice.

Swallowing her trepidation, Zica marched up the walkway and the porch steps to an enormous front portal, which was immediately opened from within. She gasped. The black-clad figure of Oliver Mason stepped back, blinking. *"Madame!"* he cried. "I had no idea the *Count* had been expecting the *Baroness!"*

She smiled. "It's nice to see you, Mason," she told him. "No, Count Malenkov wasn't exactly expecting me. I told the gateman I was bringing a gift from Mrs. Anna Voorhies. He let the taxi through."

"Mrs. *Voorhies*—although of course she never *comes*—is on the permanent *list,"* Mason explained. "But, dear God, *Baroness,* please, *please,* come *in!"* With his usual style, he picked up her suitcase, moved back, and let Zica through.

She found herself standing in an immense foyer that reminded her of a *château* in the Loire valley. The hall had an immense, vaultlike ceiling. On the wall were hung enormous tapestries of medieval origin that appeared to be genuine Van Eycks from Flanders. She stared, fascinated, professional interest momentarily eclipsing her apprehension.

"*Impressive,* isn't it, *Madame?*" Mason murmured. "But the *rest* of the house is *modern.* I'll get the *Count,*" he added, disappearing.

A moment later, Kyril stood before her—in a maroon silk dressing gown, staring at her, his eyes wide with surprise. She stepped forward and so did he, both of them speechless. Mason was nowhere to be seen. They stared at each other.

"Zica," he said finally. "*You?*"

She nodded.

"Then *you* are my mysterious gift from Annushka!"

She nodded again, her enormous eyes filling with tears.

Then he laughed. "Zica," he cried. "It's wonderful! They sent you to me! What a marvelous, stupendous surprise! Why did it take them so long?"

Her eyes drifted away from his face while she tried to find the breath to speak. "I need to stay here for a little while, if I'm not in your way," she told him. "It's this business with Noel Pierre—I don't know whether you've read about it in the papers."

"Pierre? The man you were going to marry?" His face fell, and the joy seemed to seep out of his expression.

Without thinking, she flung down her handbag and in the same motion, cupped his face in both her hands. Pressing her lips on his, she felt his face and touched his hair and began to cry—small weeping sounds escaping her. And then she leaned against him like a child, seeking refuge in the folds of his bathrobe.

"Don't send me away," she begged him. "Don't judge me for what happened before. You don't know what my life has been, you don't know what I've felt, you don't know how lonely I have been in New York all these years. Noel Pierre was attractive, he was exciting, he liked Vickie—he was *there,* Kyriusha, he was *there!*"

"What are you trying to tell me, Zica?" Obviously bewildered, he moved his hands awkwardly to her back, to her head. He began to stroke her. "What are you saying, Zicotchka?" he asked—only this time, his voice broke, and he began to sob, holding her.

"I'm only trying to explain," she murmured, "why it took them so long. You asked, didn't you?"

"Yes, yes; I asked. And I really didn't care about that man. I wanted to die when Yasha told me you were going to marry him. But of course I had married Adrienne. I married her because, like you, I was alone. But it was no good—the marriage was a failure. I felt lonelier than ever with her."

"We don't have to talk about it," she whispered. "Please, Kyriusha, say it's all right. You'll let me hide out here with you, for a little while?"

He pushed her gently away from him, taking her chin in his hand. "Zica," he told her. "I want you to hide out with me forever. We belong together, you and I. How could you ever suppose that I would not want you?"

She shook her head. "I haven't slept in days. Vickie and I came together, by airplane—several of them, in fact." She laughed, nervously. "We flew with the U.S. mail—can you picture that? Vickie kept staring out the window asking where God was sleeping! I left her at Yasha's."

Stumbling and starting again, she told him the whole tangled story.

When she had finished, he pulled her toward him, brushing the hair from her face. "It puts us right back in Moscow, in 1914," he told her softly. "It puts us back where we were first in love, where nothing, and no one, could keep us apart. I've never stopped loving you, Zica—and I believe you've never stopped loving me, have you?"

"I suppose not," she answered, laying her head on his chest and closing her eyes. "I suppose not . . ."

She was so tired, so full, so tender; maybe it was all possible, she thought, maybe one could recapture what had once been thrown away, carelessly. God was going to give them another chance.

A sound of footsteps made them both start. Instinctively, they straightened and moved apart. Mason was standing before them, a big black bird with a serious expression. "I have put *Madame's* suitcase in the *ivory* bedroom," he announced, clearing his throat. "*Theresa* is right now *putting her things* away, and turning down the *covers.*" He looked at them expectantly, then added: "The *Count* is expected at *Mrs. Schwartz's* tonight, if he *remembers.* Perhaps he wishes me to *call in his regrets,* and send over a basket of *flowers?*"

Kyril chuckled. "Good idea, Mason. And see if Cook can throw something together for us here. Something simple, with lots of bootleg champagne. And candles, Mason—I want lots of candles!"

Possessively, he drew Zica against him, and she rested her head on his shoulder. "Ask Theresa to draw a bath for the Baroness," he ordered. "With those special salts from France! She's had a rough voyage, Mason, and she'll need to rest a bit before supper."

Against his custom, Mason was smiling too. Suddenly Zica felt overwhelmed with joy—the fiery joy of a hope realized, of a dream about to come true. She wanted to dance around the medieval foyer, to laugh out loud, to kiss that dear old Mason on both cheeks. Instead, she leaned more snugly into the crook of Kyril's arm, replete with satisfaction.

"I take it that the *Baroness* is here to *stay,*" Mason remarked.

"You take it correctly, old boy," Kyril said, and then, as the butler stood blinking at him, he started to laugh again. "Give the staff champagne too!" he commanded. "In honor of my perfect lady!"

"But of *course,* Your *Excellency,*" and Mason's smile broadened.

As he walked away, his footsteps beating against the marble floor like a measured drum roll, Zica said, shyly: "But I'm not, you know . . . I'm not perfect, by any means. I'm just, well, *me!*"

"You're all I ever wanted," Kyril told her passionately, "and nothing else matters now, does it?"

A soporific calm permeated a morning that held soft cotton clouds. Kyril could hear birds chirping, ever so far away, and the soft breeze of Zica's breathing on the pillow beside him. He felt like someone wrapped in sunlight, being slowly brought back into the real world—softly, gently coaxed into opening his eyes and facing reality.

Yes, she was here, right beside him, her lovely face peaceful and trusting. He sat up, remembering. She'd lain in his arms in the early days, in Russia, when she had thought of him as all-powerful.

She stirred, turning on her back and opening one eye, tentatively. He bent over her, smiling at her. "Do you still love me?"

"Who are *you?*" she asked, laughing and sitting up, the sheet slipping off her breasts. "I don't know you, do I?"

"Just another man in the night," he informed her. "My name doesn't matter. Just the number."

"You're so silly," she murmured sleepily, snuggling up to him. "I guess that's one of the reasons I like you so much. The other is, you promised me breakfast."

"Another promise I made in the heat of passion. Gets me into trouble every time!" Holding her close, he reached across to press a button underneath the nightstand. "Still," he told her, "I'm an honorable man. If I give my word, I had better keep it. It should take Mason about ten minutes to arrive here with Your Majesty's breakfast. Eggs, homemade muffins, lingonberry jam, orange juice, and coffee. Okay with you?"

"Is that how you keep on your diet around here?" she quipped. "We'll need exercise." And she pounced on top of him. Straddling him with her lithe young body, she bent down to bite his neck. "See if you can get me off," she goaded him. "Bet you can't!"

He took her at her word. She was unusually strong for such a small girl. Turn as he might, she resisted his effort to pull her off and wiggle away from her. She laughed delightedly. What a difference, he thought, from the frightened girl who had tumbled back into his life last night, fearful of her life . . . She'd needed to be loved, he decided; she'd needed *him* to love her, to lay claim to her, to reaffirm his need and his devotion.

"Get off," he told her. "I have to make a phone call." As she slid aside, a question painted on her lovely face, he picked up the white telephone receiver from the nightstand and recited a number into its mouthpiece. It was the Star Partners exchange. "Melodie Warren," he told the operator at the studio. "It's Cyril Malenkov."

More puzzled than ever, Zica propped her head upon her hand, staring at him.

"Hi, Mel," he greeted the head of the p.r. division. "Listen, kid, I have *very* good news to tell you! *I'm getting married!* As soon as possible, in fact. I understand you've already *met* my good news, at Yasha's house, yesterday, so you'll hardly be surprised to learn that I'm marrying Baroness Zeinab Poliakov, the most beautiful, most talented, sweetest girl in the whole wide world! You can send this to all the papers, my dear. I'm happier than I've ever been in my whole useless, misspent, dissipated life!" He laughed, looking at Zica and noting the look of joyful surprise on her face.

On the other end, there was a measured silence. "What's wrong, Mel?" he demanded, annoyance seeping through his voice. "Aren't you glad?" But he could feel strange stirrings in the pit of his stomach, warning signals that dampened his fiery joy.

"Of course—I'm very glad," Melodie Warren replied deliberately. Kyril could picture her licking her upper lip as she attempted to couch her reserve in the proper words. "Perhaps I ought to say that the timing surprised me. You're about to do another romantic comedy, and . . . well, I'm not sure if getting married off the set will do much to whip up the public's enthusiasm for the new film."

"Who gives a damn?" he retorted angrily. "I've been waiting thirteen years to marry this lady! One of us was always married to someone else. And there were other complications—such as the Bolshevik Revolution!"

"Kyril," Melodie's voice was measured, "you missed Naomi and Aaron's dinner last night. But I was there. So was the female star of your next picture. You were supposed to meet her; that was the whole point of this little supper. The Schwartzes were embarrassed and angry about your absence."

"Mason sent flowers on my behalf," Kyril retorted. "Look, I had more important matters to discuss than my next picture. Besides, I didn't think anyone had been picked for the female lead. Who *is* it?" he asked.

"Karen Quarnstrom."

"The Swedish actress? I thought she didn't want to be imported," he said, intrigued in spite of himself. Zica was looking at him expectantly, wondering what was going on. He covered the receiver and told her the news.

"Sam convinced her," Melodie declared. "She always wanted to do a romantic picture with you as co-star. *That's* what really convinced her. That, and many thousands of dollars—but she cared more about playing opposite you than she did about the latter. You see, she's getting top money for every picture she does, and she's already a wealthy woman. But she thinks you're the best actor she's ever seen."

"What a pleasant compliment," he said. "She's an excellent actress. I'd be honored to play opposite her."

"Aaron and Naomi were hoping you'd tell her this in person last night. She's recently divorced her French director-husband, Henry Châtel, and she's a bit—well—*troubled*. She's lonely here, Kyril. She needs to be shown some attention—the Schwartzes have had her as their house guest. But they're afraid she'll change her mind and go home before doing the picture. There's some kind of clause permitting her to pull out at the last minute, it seems. Frankly, Aaron and Sam were depending on you to prevent this from happening."

"God*damnit,* Melodie," Kyril burst out, "what you're telling me is that they expected me to get involved with her! Who do they think I am, anyway? Star Partners' number one actor, or their number one stud?"

Zica was staring at him, eyes wide, her lips parted. He made a motion with his hand as though to tell her he was in control, not to worry.

"We are going to make a picture," he said steadily. "A *picture,* Melodie. And I am going to get married, whether the timing pleases Miss Smorgasbord or not! If she changes her mind, there are a hundred other actresses who would jump at the chance to do an Anita Loos story, directed by Harry Walsh!"

"But Aaron and Sam have been after *this particular* actress for several years," Melodie countered. He could hear her growing impatience. "You know the quality she exudes on screen—no other actress has it, not even Adrienne at her best. Everybody *wants* her —Zukor, Louis B., Fox! If Star Partners can tie her down for a seven-picture deal, think what a *tour de force* that would be for us!"

He closed his eyes, despondency washing over him. Zica took his hand and began tracing the bumps and ridges of his knuckles with the tips of her fingers.

"Melodie," he said wearily, "it's not my job to woo prospective members of the Schwartz and Unger stable. I'm committed to someone now, and she's the most important person in my life. I'm not interested in other women, Mel—please understand. I'm only interested in Zica." His voice began to quiver with intensity. "So tell your bosses to jump in the proverbial lake!"

"You can't possibly mean that, cookie," Melodie said. Her voice dripped acid.

"Try me. March yourself into Aaron's office and tell him that Miss Ingeborg Smorgasbord will have to learn to like L.A. without any help from me, unless she feels like trailing along beside us as we visit bridal boutiques. Do I make myself clear?"

"Perfectly," Melodie answered coldly. "But you're expected tonight at the Coconut Grove, at Sam's table, at eight o'clock sharp. I wouldn't be late if I were you, after last night's no-show. Naomi was fit to be tied. And the prim Swedish beauty kept her lip buttoned the entire evening. She's been to Russia," Melodie added, "and she even practiced the Russian words she knew . . . but you sent flowers instead—a slap in the face."

"I didn't even *know* she was in L.A., much less at the Schwartz's," Kyril said defensively. "Nobody bothered to fill me in."

"It was going to be a surprise. She's beautiful, Kyril. You were going to walk in and be introduced to your co-star at dinner—a co-star who is sought out by every major actor in America. Barrymore and Fairbanks would turn somersaults to play opposite her!" Melodie hesitated. "Zica is a lovely woman," she finally said. "I'm sure she'll understand. Ask her—you'll see. She's smart and she runs a business, so she will know exactly why this is not the time to rush into a marriage."

"Surely," Kyril said, "you are not telling me that Miss Karen Quarnstrom will only be my co-star *if I am single?* That would even defy *common sense*. Surely, Melodie-of-my-dreams, this . . . is . . . not . . . what you're really saying."

Melodie sighed. "Oh, dear," she breathed. "Nobody ever told me how hard a job I'd have making myself clear. Karen Quarnstrom is a strange lady, Kyril. She's lonely and she's aloof as a Swedish iceberg. I'm not asking you to sleep with her—I'm only asking you to be her dinner partner at studio functions, at least until pre-production begins—at which time she'll be in breach of contract if she gets up and goes home. *And,*" she added portentously, "*that includes tomorrow night.*"

"I'm not going to the Coconut Grove without my fiancée," he answered furiously. "If Sam wants me to be his guest, I'll come, but only with Zica!"

"She won't wish to come," Melodie said acerbically. "She's here to hide out, not to be presented left and right. Just ask her, will you?"

"Go to hell, Melodie," Kyril spat out, and he hung up the telephone.

"Trouble in paradise?" Zica asked softly, kissing the fingers of the hand she was holding.

Just then there was a knock on the door. Breakfast had arrived. "Go back to your own room, and let me put on a robe," she murmured to Kyril. "It wouldn't do for Mason to catch us together like this before the wedding."

Kyril beat a hasty retreat through the connecting bathroom.

He hated Melodie Warren. She'd ruined his joy, as surely as if she'd poisoned his champagne with a dose of vinegar. She had tarnished his triumph. He'd be damned if he forgave her this, now or ever. Her loyalty to her job had obviously been greater than her devotion to their friendship, and the thought of this wounded him profoundly.

Standing in the marble bathroom, Kyril tried to control the churning revolt that was rising within him. After all, wasn't it more important—that Zica loved him, that she promised him her life . . . ? But all Kyril could hear were Melodie's ominous words. For the first time in his life, he'd gotten what he most wanted and desired —and his friend, his best friend, had negated his joy. He wanted to strangle Melodie Warren, to kick Aaron Schwartz in the groin, and to smash his fist into the pudgy face of Sam Unger.

Yakov was amused by the Coconut Grove. To him this nightclub in the luxurious Ambassador Hotel represented everything that spelled out "Hollywood"—the wide grand staircase leading to the tables, the *papier-mâché* coconut trees, and the real coconuts and palm fronds that decorated the room overhead, with stuffed monkeys swinging from their branches. The ceiling was a star-studded blue. The painting of a moonrise over a splashing waterfall completed the atmosphere of an island paradise.

Yakov was present, in black tie and tails, because he had been summoned by Sam Unger. Towering above him, Melodie, her red hair held back by a band of velvet from which sprouted some proud egret feathers, peered up at the staircase, her brow knit with concern.

"I hope Kyril shows up," she whispered. "We're going to have one giant problem on our hands if he decides to stay home with Zica. No Kyriusha, no Quarnstrom. No Quarnstrom, no bonus for little Melodie."

Yakov winced. He couldn't adjust to it—couldn't remain impassive. *Zica and Kyril!* He shouldn't have been surprised: Nevertheless it hurt, hurt deeply, and he couldn't stop imagining them together.

"You'd better get tough," Melodie had told him. "He says he's going to marry her."

She was right. Yakov had to get tough. That translated into: *Forget her.* But it wasn't that simple. She was the mother of his child, and Kyril had become his friend. He liked the charming, sentimental boy with his golden hair and his terribly expressive green eyes. Still . . . their friendship had been based, in part, on the fact that neither possessed the woman they both loved. A new imbalance would ruin the delicate structure of their relationship. Perhaps they would lose their tenuous friendship altogether.

It's up to her, he thought. But of course, she'd made up her mind years ago. Yakov could feel a well of tears inside him, tears which would never fall—for he was first and foremost an accomplished actor, someone to be relied on to provide entertainment, not self-pitying sadness. He'd loved her more than life, but tonight he was here to help amuse Miss Karen Quarnstrom.

As always, he had a job to do.

Sam Unger sat at the opposite end of the table, an anxious frown on his cherubic face. Next to him, his plump wife, Judy, nervously toyed with the silverware. The Schwartzes—Aaron elegant in his tails and Naomi overdone in her blue taffeta gown—did not hide their displeasure. Kyril had promised to pick up the Swedish actress on his way over, as a gesture of courtesy, and the Schwartzes had gone ahead, leaving Karen powdering her nose and pacing the floor in the den of their mansion.

"There they are," Melodie announced, her hand darting out to press Sam's arm. Yakov's eyes, like everyone else's, flew to the plush grand staircase. The *maître d'* and the bell captain were leading a couple down the stairs. Yakov noted that a hush fell over the tables and dance floor. People were star-struck at the Coconut Grove, and nobody missed the entrance of anyone famous. The *maître d'*—trained to promote this effect—was in cahoots with the bandleader to help set the stage.

Sweeping down the grand staircase, Kyril looked his usual self—graceful and aristrocratic. He was resplendent in tails, his carriage as proud as that of a real count. His large shoulders gave him an air of power, enhanced by slender waist and long legs in their tuxedo pants. No wonder Zica loved him; how could a woman of flesh and blood resist this paragon—this exotic face with its high cheekbones and liquid eyes?

Jimmy Grier and his orchestra were in the midst of a lively fox trot when suddenly "smiling" Jack Smith called out, "Here's to the incomparable Karen Quarnstrom!" and they switched to Gershwin's "I've Got a Crush on You."

Melodie laughed. Aaron and Sam smiled, too, and the women craned their necks to catch the grand entrance of the two stars. Karen Quarnstrom was tall and willowy: she literally floated beside the handsome blond Russian. Her golden hair fell in a sweeping pageboy to her collarbone, and her heart-shaped, pale face shone like a jewel above the soft, tubular gown of ice-blue muslin which sheathed her body like a second skin.

She was splendid. Yakov's heart soared at the sight of her.

She held Kyril's arm demurely; pausing on the staircase, she looked up at him with a tentative half-smile, something subtle and full of the promise of intimacy. Yakov felt a jolt, and his eyes jumped to Ostrov. But all he saw on the actor's face was the acknowledgment of this woman's admiration. Kyril's eyes remained impassive, cool. Was he thinking of Zica, even now, waiting for him at Grayhall?

When the *maître d'* arrived at the table, with his little company, the band resumed its fox trot. Karen Quarnstrom, her blue eyes narrowed, appraised the other guests. Aaron and Sam sprang up to greet her; chairs were pulled out. Naomi and Judy, leaning over the table, began separate welcome speeches.

Yakov was highly amused. Like the other men, he had risen politely. To his astonishment the actress looked his way.

"Poker Jack," she stated in a lilting, singsong voice with Scandinavian inflection. "We like you very much in Sweden. Your... antics?... make us laugh through the bitter cold of our long winter. It is nice to meet you."

Yakov noted that a grateful expression passed from Kyril to him. *Goddamnit!* Yakov thought: he is thankful that I am taking the attention off him, so he may remain true to Zica—*my own wife!*

But, at the same time, he felt a grudging relief. One never knew with a lightweight such as Ostrov: he was always susceptible to flattery and to flirtation.

The couple sat down. Their seats faced the dance floor, where men in white tie and tails swung sequined women over the parquet strips. Yakov found himself surreptitiously looking at the Swedish star, noting the asymmetry of her cheekbones.

One of her eyes was slightly less open than the other. She was imperfect—not really beautiful the way Adrienne had been—but the glow which emanated from her made up for it. She was a woman with a mystique, whereas Adrienne had been a naughty girl, representative of semi-decadent Twenties flappers. Quarnstrom had a presence—a rare quality in an actress or in any woman.

The waiters came to take orders. Kyril produced a silver flask from his pocket, and took a discreet swallow. Aaron Schwartz regarded him with surprised disapproval, but the actor smiled back charmingly.

Naomi said: "This place is a bit garish, but they have amusing entertainment. They have dance contests and chorus lines, you know. Mae West was here last week with a huge black hat and feathers all about her neck and neckline. They've had the mentalist, Sidar Rammi Setti—that was fun, wasn't it, Aaron?"

"It sounds very... *mm*... hotsy-totsy," Karen remarked. She seemed about to laugh, but didn't. "This is a swanky place," she added. "Very ritzy, no?"

"Has Cy been teaching you American slang?" Judy exclaimed, delighted.

"I've done my best," Kyril told them. "There's no better teacher than another foreigner, I think. Yasha and I learned everything the hard way—didn't we? In my case, my American friends were so amused by my mistakes that no one bothered to correct me. I went around mixing up expressions, saying 'What a raspberry!' instead of 'That's the cat's meow,' and calling an important person a 'Bronx cheer' instead of a 'big cheese.'"

"I didn't even get to speak much English, my first few years here," Yakov said. "I was running a pawnshop on Hester Street in the old Jewish section of Manhattan. Most of my customers spoke less of it than I did. Yiddish was the native tongue there."

"I have read articles about Poker Jack," Karen commented. "Rags to riches, no? They call that in American?"

"Yakov was never exactly in rags, Karen," Melodie corrected gently. "He was actually a serious businessman. But his story is certainly one of the more interesting success stories I've come across—and I've come across a good many in my line of work."

Kyril looked at her with an unmistakable coldness that surprised Yakov. "I think you make half of them up, Melodie. You take a little girl from Dubuque, Iowa, and turn her into a nightclub *chanteuse* from Paris. No one cares about Dubuque, but everyone wonders what it was like in the bohemian sector of Paris. So she starts granting interviews, and makes up all sorts of amusing anecdotes about a place she's only visited in her dreams. Only none of the readers has been there either, and they fall for it like a ton of bricks."

Everyone stared at him, momentarily stunned by the seriousness of his tone and by the hard, metallic glint in his eyes as he regarded his old friend. But, just as things threatened to grow awkward, he burst out laughing. Naomi and Judy, relieved, started to laugh as well, and Melodie joined in.

"*Touché,*" she replied graciously.

Bewildered, Karen Quarnstrom glanced from one to the other, trying to piece together what had just occurred. But Kyril continued to laugh. Bringing out his silver flask again, he took a nip, right in front of everyone at the table. This time, there was nothing discreet about the gesture.

Karen Quarnstrom looked at him. "Give me a sip, please," she demanded. She was sitting proudly in her chair, shoulders back, head high over her swan's neck. Kyril passed the flask to her and, amused, watched her tilt her head back to take a swallow. She handed the flask back to him, nodding her approval. "Good gin," she announced. "Booth's, no?"

Kyril's eyebrows shot up, surprised, and he grinned at her. "I didn't expect you to be such an expert," he told her.

She placed her small white hand over his arm. "In Sweden," she said, "we drink to keep warm. Here, you drink to keep amused."

"Would you like to dance?" Kyril asked her.

"Yes. Naomi promised me you were a good dancer, Cyril, but I already knew that. You danced so well in *Dolly's Dilemma,* with your wife, Adrienne. I was jealous when I saw the picture. I thought: Here is a real artist, a man for—what?—all seasons. Someone I wish to act with, one day."

"Well, you shall have your chance, and very soon," Sam Unger quickly replied.

"I test you out. Come," she told Kyril, and the smile she gave him was ironic. Yakov thought: She's testing him, all right, and he's being as outrageous as he can without becoming rude; so far, she's keeping up, step for step. But Quarnstrom will be furious when he turns her down. Ultimately, he will have to do this, or he'll be betraying the woman he's pledged to.

"God, how I hate it when he acts like the bad boy," Melodie whispered as the couple walked off toward the dance floor. "I wonder how many drinks he had before coming here?"

"You put him in a difficult position," Yakov replied. "If I were he, I'd have stayed at home."

"That's because you're a comedian, and he's a romantic lead. He needs to do the films we tell him, because we know what's good for him. You have more freedom, Yasha: all you need to be is funny. But he needs to set every woman on the edge of her seat. That's what being a matinée idol entails. There's just no getting around it."

"Then don't blame him for being naughty. He's giving Karen what she wants. Good guys," he added with a hint of bitterness, "never keep a woman's attention for long."

"We asked him to escort Karen to this dinner. We didn't ask for more, Yakov."

"Are you sure?" Yakov's expression was unfathomable. "Well, never mind. Frankly, I wish that he would fall madly in love with the enchanting Swedish Ice Queen. It would suit my own purpose *perfectly.*"

"Still in love with her, are you?" Melodie asked gently.

The sympathy in her eyes suddenly made him furious. It was sympathy for a loser. He shrugged off her question and turned his attention to the appetizers.

"I think she has a crush on him," Naomi Schwartz remarked,

smiling indulgently as she watched the dancers. "They're cute together, aren't they?"

"I think they make an excellent couple," Yakov suddenly declared, enthusiastically. Melodie stared at him, perplexed. "Hey," he added, turning from one to the other around the table: "this is exactly what you all were praying for. Magic between the leading lady and her romantic heart-throb."

"The last time, you warned him not to get too close to Adrienne Lance, and he ignored us," Melodie told Aaron. "Now, you wish for *these* two to become an item. He's promised to marry someone else, however. How on earth do you think you can pull off a romance between him and Karen?"

"Quarnstrom will do the job for me," Schwartz replied evenly.

"Karen's okay. She's a consummate professional and a crackerjack actress," Sam Unger added. "She'll do a whole lot more for him than Yakov's wife will," he continued, glancing apologetically toward his leading comedian. "I'm sorry, Yakov, but you know the business. Zica Poliakov is classy, she's attractive, she's a nice young woman. I liked her plenty myself, when I bought that painting from her. So did Judy—didn't you, honey? But a movie star she ain't. She's a private person, whereas Cy's a public figure. He needs to be with a woman who will interest the gossip columnists and the photographers."

"And Zica, in all of this?" Yakov asked softly.

"Zica can wait till the picture gets done. All Karen needs is a little romance—not the love of a lifetime. Let him take Zica to Mexico for their honeymoon, if he so wishes—as long as they wait till the end of the year. She'll see it our way, if she loves Cy as much as you say."

"Perhaps she won't," Yakov muttered. He looked toward the dance floor, his feelings confused within him. He felt angry, cheated, outraged—yet oddly hopeful. He wanted to protect Zica, yet, at the same time, he wished for her to be terribly hurt by Kyril, so she would stop loving him. *Damn!* he thought. I want her to be happy, but I also want to have one last chance with her—one last moment to vie for her love . . .

The dancers parted, leaving the floor to Karen Quarnstrom and Cyril Malenkov. Kyril was twirling Karen around, her gown clinging to her fluid figure. At the end of the number, he tilted her way back. Her blonde head almost touched the ground; her supple waist bent over Kyril's arm. Then she rose gracefully, as the audience applauded all around.

The band leader ordered a drum roll. On her tiptoes, Karen came toward her partner—who still held his arm about her waist—and deposited a kiss on his lips, quick and fluttery. The crowd gasped with delight.

Then, unexpectedly, Kyril Ostrov pulled her back to him. In public view, he bent over her and kissed her long and hard, the kiss of a man who wishes beyond anything to possess a woman. It was a trademark kiss, the sort for which he was well known to his audience. They applauded with glee.

Triumphantly, grinning broadly, the pair left the empty dance floor and made their way back to Sam Unger's table.

Yakov felt nauseous. He glanced at Melodie. Her face was set in harsh lines, but her eyes seemed to hold approval for the actor. Aaron Schwartz was starting to smile. Sam Unger nodded to himself, squeezing his wife's hand.

"Excuse me, please," Yakov murmured, rising as Malenkov and Quarnstrom approached the table. With Melodie's eyes on his back, he walked briskly out of the Coconut Grove, anger and disgust making his head spin.

He was angry—angry at Kyril for his flirtatiousness, but above all angry at the producers and at Melodie Warren. They had planned all this, using the weakness of Kyril Ostrov to their own advantage. It wasn't Kyril's career, it was their own, to do with as they pleased! Right now, their pleasure could destroy Zica. But what did it matter to them—as long as their machinations led to a blockbuster box-office success.

Kyril's final playacting had made him their boy again... and perhaps it hadn't all been playacting. Karen Quarnstrom was beautiful and famous, and she had kissed him first, hadn't she? Perhaps he'd simply responded, like any warm-blooded male to a female who liked him. No one but Zica would be hurt.

It was Hollywood; it sickened Yakov. But business was business. Perhaps Kyril was playing his own game. Perhaps he'd merely wished to please the men who controlled his career. It didn't matter, did it? Zica would merely be hurt and humiliated, but she might as well learn now how the game was played.

Kyril had caught the snap of a flashbulb. He knew that the Malenkov-Quarnstrom kiss would make the front pages of the next day's tabloids. Perhaps an item would even appear in *Variety,* to bolster interest in Star Partners' upcoming film.

Zica, he thought: I must go to her. I must not let this town destroy her, the way it's trying to. *She's still my girl,* and I can't let this happen! Retrieving his top hat from the cloakroom girl, he rushed out of the Ambassador Hotel to claim his car.

Chapter XXVII

*I*N the center of the enormous reception room on the ground
floor of Grayhall Manor, Zica paced the floor in front of the
radio set, rubbing her hands together in agitation.

She was wearing a long white silk robe embroidered with pink
and white pearls. When Mason announced to her that Mr. Poker
was here, wishing to see her, she ran her fingers through her hair
with an expression of confusion, and nodded. What was Yakov
doing here at this hour? It was almost eleven o'clock.

He appeared wearing his white tails. She was immediately startled by his elegance. The clothes fit him perfectly, and he walked
with ease, as though accustomed to black-tie affairs.

"I thought you might want someone to talk to," he said by way
of greeting. His face, in the light of the lamps of veined alabaster,
was open, kind, and good-looking. How was it possible that for so
many years, she had taken this pleasant face absolutely for granted?

"This is odd." Turning off the radio, she motioned for him to sit
down. "How did you know I was alone? And...where are you
coming from?"

He smiled as he took a seat. "Kyriusha and I were invited to the
same party," he explained. "When he came without you, I assumed
you were here by yourself."

"Yes, he thought it might not be safe for me to be seen in public
yet. But all this has changed, Yasha! Annushka called—you know,
Mrs. Voorhies—to tell me that Johnny Rubio had been arrested!
He's been charged with violation of the Eighteenth Amendment,
evasion of taxes, and the murder of Noel. The fellow who shot
Noel confessed to the police, in exchange for immunity from prose-
cution. I guess I don't have to be afraid anymore. I was just now

listening to the news on the radio, and they mentioned Rubio's arrest."

Yakov's face lit up with joy. "What tremendous news!"

"Perhaps now I can go out like a normal human being, and... well, plan my wedding," she said hesitantly.

"Are you really sure you want to marry Kyril?" He asked the question coldly—almost as if he were disinterested.

Zica pressed her teeth on her lower lip. "It's awkward to be discussing this with you, Yasha," she murmured.

"That's all right. We're good friends, aren't we? Just pretend we're still eighteen and standing behind your father's big staircase. You used to confide in me back then, remember?"

"Yes," she answered, "but in the meantime, I became your wife. Things changed."

"Perhaps things did; but I hardly have. I still care about you, Zica."

She sat down across from him, on a love seat. "Kyriusha didn't tell me the truth about tonight," she said carefully. "I felt it. You know, last night, everything was perfect. I knew he loved me. But this morning, he had a conversation with Melodie Warren. I know she doesn't want him to get married—at least, not to me. Today, he began to behave strangely. He drank a lot of wine. He told me he had to meet his producers—but I shouldn't come along because it wouldn't be safe to take me to the Coconut Grove. But he was edgy. He couldn't look me in the eye. Do you know what's going on?" she asked, turning to Yakov.

"It's not my place to comment," he told her. "You should ask Kyril to explain things to you."

"But he refused! He told me I was jealous, that I wasn't used to being alone, that I shouldn't try to crowd him.—Is there another woman?" she demanded.

"Not exactly. The studio would like to encourage him to court Karen Quarnstrom, the Swedish actress. She's arrived here to do a picture with him. It wasn't his idea," he continued. "I don't think he was pleased about being put in this position."

"I see." She brought her hands to her face, rubbing her cheeks, abstractedly. "Karen Quarnstrom's a beautiful woman," she said gravely, "and so was Adrienne Lance. I suppose the studio is looking for another magic couple."

"How should I know?" Yakov demanded. "Maybe Aaron Schwartz's just sick of entertaining the prima donna, and wants

Kyril to help out. I'm sorry, Zica, but I can't really help you there. You should have a long talk with Kyril tonight, when he comes home—or better yet tomorrow morning when you are both refreshed. Ask him what all this means. If his career is going to stand in the way of your happiness, tell him he must be frank with you."

"I'll do that," she said. But suddenly she was sobbing. "Goddamnit!" she cried. "I don't know what to believe any more! Kyriusha's so *easy*. He flirts the way other men say 'Good morning.' I know, it's his job to be a charmer, but if wants to marry me, he'll have to be my *husband*—in public as well as in private." She bent her head into her hands and sat weeping for a full minute in the empty silence.

"Kyriusha doesn't know how to handle these people," Yakov explained, measuring his words. "When a studio head comes to him, or sends Melodie, he simply caves in to their demands. He's afraid of power."

"Doesn't he see that *he's* the one with the power? *He's* the reason the studio's making money! He could go to another studio or form a partnership with you and some other famous actors, and develop his own projects!"

"Yes, well, that's true... but he doesn't understand this. He thinks Schwartz and Unger know everything about the marketplace. He believes he has to toe the line and do everything they wish."

"I want to go to parties," Zica said softly. "I want to meet these people. I don't wish to be cooped up at home while Kyril escorts his female stars around. That's not right!"

"No," Yakov agreed, "it isn't. What are you going to do about this, Zica?"

"This Quarnstrom—she was there tonight?"

He nodded. "She's very cool." He was fumbling for words. She caught his hesitation.

"What is it, Yasha?" she asked him. "Did something happen? Is that why you came over here tonight?"

"Nothing happened, Zica," he replied. His eyes were dark and caring. "Well, something *did* happen, but it didn't mean anything. I came... because I was afraid you'd learn about it from the paper tomorrow—and that you'd be hurt and would assign too much importance to a simple actor's gesture. He danced with Karen Quarnstrom, just for the sake of the crowd. And then, just to end the show, he gave her a small kiss. It wasn't anything, but someone took a picture. The tabloids are going to blow it up into a romance. They always do. Even Melodie will help play it up—that's her job."

"He didn't *have* to kiss her, Yasha," Zica said furiously, "—and you know it! He wasn't on a set—he wasn't reading from a script! This morning," she continued, her voice starting to break, "he told me how much he loved me, that we would never be apart. He said he wanted to marry me. I believed him."

"Zica, if he does marry you—it could be different between the two of you. You'd be true to him—a real wife; he'd have to honor this commitment to you."

"Perhaps; but perhaps not." She sat down and stared at him, interlacing her fingers on her lap. "Why are you so keen on defending him?" she asked. "Have you two become Siamese twins this past year and a half?"

"It's not that at all," he replied. He stood up abruptly, strode to the fireplace. Then he wheeled around to face her, his features tight with passion. *"It's that I don't trust myself!"* he cried out. "You wish to marry this man, who is now my friend. But you were once *my wife! I love you, Zica!* Don't you understand? You want me to behave as your confidant, but it is breaking my heart! Can't you see this?"

Her lips parted. She half-rose, then sank back into her seat. "Yasha," she murmured. "Yasha...I told you it would be awkward. I told you I didn't really want to discuss Kyril with you. It was *you* who encouraged it, you who kept pressing me! I'm sorry. I'm sorry I hurt you. But I didn't mean to."

"Yes," he admitted, "I thought I was strong enough to talk about ...you and him. But I guess I'm not. I *love* you, goddamnit. I wish you'd stay in California to marry *me!* I wish you'd let us be a family again—you and Vickie and I. I was wrong not to let you go to work for yourself, back in New York. But I've changed! I would let you do anything you pleased—I *swear* I would. Only, for God's sake, Zicotchka, give me another chance!"

This time she stood up, her cheeks aflame, tears in her eyes. "This is too much!" she cried out. "All of this is too much! Yasha, I came here to get away, to put my life in order—and instead, I am more confused than ever."

"I should never have brought up how I feel about you." Yakov's voice was anguished. "I didn't come here with this intention! But it just came pouring out of me, it couldn't be unsaid....I must leave," he concluded, picking up his top hat from a side table.

"No!" she countered, her voice oddly hushed. "I'm not going to let you leave. You are the kindest man I know. Yakov Pokhis— Poker Jack!—and I have never been loved by anyone as much nor as deeply as by you. Maybe I've been blind all these years. I took you for granted, Yasha, time and time again. And it was wrong, wasn't it? For you were always faithful and true."

"Goodnight, Zica," Yakov said. He placed a hand on her cheek and stroked it. "Go to sleep now. I'm delighted they caught that gangster, and that you're permanently out of danger. But it's time I went home, to check up on Vickie. I'll call you in the morning, if you wish, to see how you are."

"Oh, yes," she caught his hand. "I do wish it! Goodnight, Yasha. Goodnight." She kissed him briefly on the lips, then turned away as he left the room.

Kyril felt drunk, ill at ease, and unhappy. Beside him on the soft white sofa, Karen Quarnstrom extracted a silver cigarette holder from her small evening bag, pulled a long, thin cigarette from a silver case on the coffee table, and stuffed it into the holder. The intimate den at the Schwartz mansion was close and warm. Karen sat back, waiting while he fumbled for the silver lighter on the table, awkwardly lighting her cigarette for her.

"I make this Anita Loos picture with you," she announced to him, inhaling deeply. "Then, we make *The Beautiful and Damned;* I love Fitzgerald—don't you?"

Kyril shrugged. "I suppose so." He sighed. "Karen, I'd better go home. It's after two."

She laughed—her laughter was a pure cascade of sound. Her thin hand reached out to touch his. "Cy," she stated in her lilting voice, "you can't drive home now. You almost killed us coming back here. You are . . . *ossified?* Spiff . . . *spifflicated?*"

Through the haze of gin and misery, he heard her laughing at him.

"Do you always drink so much?" she asked. "I did a film with Barrymore and it was not nice, he was drinking and drinking. I don't want you to drink," she added with mock sternness. "We drink together, maybe, after we shoot. But when we shoot, no drinking."

"I don't drink on the set," he said angrily. "Just when I'm un-happy."

"And why are you so unhappy, Count Malenkov? Don't you like me?"

He turned to look at her frankly. Her thin, translucent skin shone pink and white in the light of the leaded glass lamp; her mouth was a pure heart-shape—pink, too, with almost no lipstick. And her eyes were the color of morning. He sighed again, covering his own eyes with his hands. "I *like* you," he replied, almost moaning the words. "I *like* you, but you remind me of my wife."

"Adrienne Lance? But she was dark, and I am fair. We are not alike at all," Karen declared, puffing on her cigarette.

"You both want me to perform," he told her. "You want me to be your playmate. I want to do a film, and you wish to flirt. Adrienne always had affairs with her leading men. Otherwise, she couldn't kiss them on screen."

"Oh," Karen said. "But I want you to *love* me. That isn't the same. I think you are a great actor. I want you to find the heart of Karen Quarnstrom, the center of her being, and *make* it vibrate."

"That's ridiculous," he answered, staring at her incredulously. Her features were blurred, but he could see the swinging blond hair like a golden halo behind her neck. She was beautiful. The coolness of her reminded him of Lorraine. But Lorraine had used him and cast him away, thinking him unworthy, whereas Karen thought him desirable, an artist, a man to admire. He breathed in deeply, thinking. How good it was to be admired, looked up to, respected. For once, someone wasn't treating him like a *samocer* or a *thing*. "It's ridiculous. How do I find the heart of you?"

"You explore," she informed him, taking his hand and playing with his finely manicured fingers. "We go to Palm Springs. We spend a few days. You talk, I talk. We swim together. We sleep together. We wake up together. You find the heart of Karen Quarnstrom. Others have tried and failed—my ex-husband. But not you. You will find it."

He laughed. "I can't," he said, surprising himself with the regret he felt at his own words. "But you are very beautiful," he added. "Like a painting."

"Then come away with me."

She stroked the palm of his hand, and the inside of his wrist. It felt good. Though woozy and a bit nauseous, Kyril suddenly relaxed. He tried to think of Zica—of his unhappiness at being here with Karen—yet he couldn't summon the features on the face of his absent beloved. "I love someone," he said softly, "only I can't remember what she looks like."

"You can't love her that much, then," Karen told him. She brought his hand to her lips and deposited tiny kisses on his knuckles and on the pads of his fingers. "You haven't found the heart of her."

"Oh, but I have," Kyril countered. And suddenly he could visualize Zica, the triangular face, the enormous brown eyes, the sleek brown hair. His beloved Zica! "—What am I doing here?" he asked, a sense of panic overcoming him. "I must go home!"

"I'm not going to drive you, and the Schwartzes and their servants are asleep. You stay here tonight, Cy," Karen announced. And then she leaned over and kissed him on the chin, on the Adam's apple, in the crook of his neck. "Stay with me," she said softly. "Learn to touch my heart. We make *The Beautiful and Damned*. We make love and drink gin together and find each other's hearts. Feel," she added, taking his hand and placing it over her left breast. "Karen's heart is right there."

He wrenched his hand away. "I didn't want to come tonight," he told her, his eyes filling with tears. "I wanted to stay with the woman I love. Aaron and Sam and Melodie *made* me come! I want to go home to Zica, and stay in her bed. I can't stay with you!"

"But you are here, and she is not," the actress said. "If I did not want to come, I would *not* have come. You liked me, Cy. You really want to hold me, but you are afraid. Why? We sleep together, then we make the two pictures. Come upstairs with me. I don't want to be alone."

"That's not my problem," he told her.

Unsteadily, he stood up. The den appeared to tilt on its side. He felt his forehead. Karen was peering anxiously at him, leaning forward, the blue muslin pressed tightly over her breasts.

"You are so beautiful," he said. "You make me crazy." He sat down again, put his head in his hands, and began to weep.

"*You* are crazy," Karen replied. She put her cool white hand on his head, stroking his golden hair. "You are crazy-drunk. Me, I only drink a little. You drank all night long."

"Ah..." he sighed, "what is happening to me? You smell so good, Karen Quarnstrom. You make me dizzy. If we make this picture and also that other one from the Fitzgerald novel, you'll be driving me crazy all day long—day after day, week after week, for *months*."

"And why is that?"

"Because, damnit, I want to sleep with you!" he told her, raising his tear-streaked face from his hands. "I want you to make love to me. But I cannot. I have Zica."

"But you must forget this person, and come now to bed," the actress said firmly. "No more drink, no more strange talk, no more Zica. We go upstairs, to my pretty bedroom in Naomi's monstrous castle, we make love, you find my heart. Maybe I find yours," she added, standing up.

"No," he said, shaking his head. But even as he did so, he felt the misery welling up, the misery of knowing this beautiful woman would have her way.

"*Yes,*" she insisted. She held out both hands to him to pull him up.

It wasn't his game anymore. He'd lost it, anyway, but the rules had changed. "Yes," he echoed.

"And I promise I won't tell *anyone,*" the actress said, pulling him up with all her might. Her tinkling laughter rang out like bells—small, silver bells, soothing the white-hot fire in his head.

Some noise awakened Zica abruptly. She sat bolt upright in the wing chair, rubbed her eyes, and peered around her. The alabaster lamps were still lit. She'd fallen asleep in the living room. Now cold, she rubbed her arms, wondering what had awakened her so suddenly.

The large clock, mounted in cut crystal, showed five thirty-three in the morning. Alarmed, she thought: I was waiting for him. *But he isn't here!*

Had he found her asleep when he'd come in the house, and deliberately left her in the wing chair? That made no sense!

She listened. In the foyer down the hall, she heard other noises. She stood up, smoothing her silk dressing gown, and started toward the foyer. Her heart beat wildly with apprehension.

Steady, she told herself. *Rubio's gone! He can't get to you where he is now.* Suddenly Kyril appeared in front of her, swaying slightly on his feet, his blond hair dishevelled, his bow tie undone, his pleated shirt half-buttoned. She started, stifling a cry, and covered her mouth with her hand.

He appeared equally startled. He almost bumped into her. "Zica," he said, his voice sounding thick with drink or sleep. "What are you doing?"

"Waiting for you," she answered quietly.

"It's late," he said. "I need to sleep." But instead of moving away from her, he just stood there, dully, staring at her. "What do you want?" he asked. "Go to bed!"

Feeling incredibly small and unwanted, she turned aside. Her whole world seemed to be crumpling before her. Why was he sending her to bed? She looked up at him—at the bruised eyes and the flushed skin.

"You're drunk. Where have you been?" she asked.

"None of your business," he answered truculently. But she saw the pain in his face, and moved toward him. And as she put her arms about him, he fell against her, trembling.

"What is it?" she asked softly. "What's going on, Kyriusha?"

He shook his head, pushing himself away from her arms. "I'm so tired," he sighed, "so tired. So sick. Please let me go to sleep, Zicotchka. We'll talk in the morning."

"But it *is* morning," she reminded him gently.

"No matter. Leave me alone." This time, he did push past her, going up the stairs. She followed anxiously. He dropped the bow tie on a marble step and let his pearl studs fall to the floor. Zica picked them up, her heart in her throat.

They proceeded up the grand staircase until they reached the second-floor landing. He shuffled down the hallway to his room, opened the door, and practically let it slam in her face.

Undeterred, Zica turned the knob and entered his bedroom. He was seated on the edge of his bed, trying to pull off his patent-leather pumps. "Oohh," he groaned, looking up as she closed the door quietly behind her, "my head hurts."

Silently, she crouched before him and pulled off his shoes. Tears fell on her hands. She ignored them, but they kept on falling.

He lay back on the bed, his shirt now completely unbuttoned, his tuxedo trousers half off.

She said, "Lift up," and pulled the trousers down over his feet. Folding them neatly, she placed them over the back of a chair. But the tears kept falling, forming patterns on her cheeks.

"Zica, Zica," he moaned her name. She climbed onto the bed and moved his torso to pull off the shirt. But where was his jacket? As he lay back, she noticed that he wasn't wearing any undershorts. The realization stopped her.

"Where are your briefs?" she asked.

"None of your damned business. Do we have coffee?"

"Mason's asleep," she said. "He'll be up in half an hour. Want me to run you a bath?"

"Mm-hm." He closed his eyes, spreading his arms out, and she crawled off the bed and walked into the adjacent bathroom. She turned the light on, put the plug into the tub drain, turned on the faucets, tested the water as it first poured in, and, last of all, sprinkled in some bath salts. Then she returned to his bedroom and sat down in a chaise lounge, facing the bed.

He appeared to be sleeping. She continued to watch him, as though entranced, her mind shut off to all but the sound of the bathtub filling. A sweet scent of fragrant flowers permeated the air; as though on cue, she rose to turn off the faucets. When she walked back into the bedroom, he was sitting up, rubbing his eyes.

"You're so good to me, Zicotchka," he said to her. Rising, he took some tentative steps into the bathroom. He was now completely naked. She watched him dispassionately, with exhaustion, following him in to make sure he would not slip as he stepped into the warm bath. But he sank down without trouble, and then relaxed, his head tilted back, his eyes closed.

Dejected, Zica left the room soundlessly. The tears were beginning to fall again. She walked into the hallway and proceeded to the ivory bedroom reserved for her. Her shoulders were heaving. At the door she slid down to the floor, hugging her knees, and began to sob.

Through the bevelled glass window at the end of the carpeted hallway, a ray of pale pink light fluttered in shyly. Dawn had risen.

Zica was unaware of how much time had passed. But when she finally stopped crying and looked about her, a beam of golden sunshine was highlighting a design on the Persian carpeting. She rose, went into her room, and summoned Mason to order breakfast. The small ormolu clock on her bedside table indicated that it was seven forty-five.

She had to think. Karen Quarnstrom had shattered her dreams. Zica still felt stabs of anguish, recalling Yakov's account of the previous night's festivities at the Coconut Grove nightclub.

It was relief to think of Yasha. He had come to her so loyally—to prevent her from experiencing pain and humiliation. Kyril, on the other hand, had behaved badly. He'd gone out and made a public announcement of his availability, by kissing another woman—a famous one—in front of witnesses! Zica felt herself turn furious with anguish and outrage. Was this love? It was only a child's desire to possess everything in the candy store!

Mason knocked discreetly. When she called out "Come in!", he entered formally, clicking his heels. He held a silver platter loaded with breakfast food.

"Good *morning,* Madame," he said to her, placing the platter on a small writing table. "And how did the Baroness *sleep?"*

"Very badly, I'm afraid," Zica replied, sitting down in front of her breakfast. "By the way, Mason," she asked him, "is there a car that I could use later this morning?"

His eyebrows shot up. "Oh, *certainly,* Madame. There's the gray *Stutz* that the *Count* likes to use as a *sports car;* it's quite *fast,* but it's *easy* to *drive.* The *Baroness* will surely *like* it. The *Countess* used to drive a *similar* one of an *earlier model.* I daresay that a *woman* can *maneuver* the Stutz without *trouble.* Although *perhaps* Madame would *prefer* to be *driven . . ."*

"No," she replied. "I'd like to go on a few errands alone. Listen, Mason, can you arrange for me to take it out around eleven o'clock?"

"Why *certainly,* Madame."

He left the room. Zica lifted the glass dome over her shirred eggs, and buttered her toast. But her mind was elsewhere. She was thinking of life without Kyril. Now that she'd found him again, what would it be like to give him up?

He'd been drunk. One could forgive a man for behaving foolishly under the influence of alcohol. But, no, she wouldn't forgive him!

Zica was furious. Her stomach rebelled. She pushed aside the entire platter and sat lost in contemplation. How had Kyril been able to make love to another woman—barely a day removed from the night they had spent together—in such bliss and ecstasy?

He'd come home dishevelled, without his underwear, without his tuxedo jacket. He'd walked in, stumbling, at five thirty-three in the morning. He'd stayed out till dawn, knowing that she, Zica, had been waiting for him. Wasn't it obvious what he'd been doing?

He'd gone home with Karen Quarnstrom and had made love to her!

I must break up with him; I must leave him at once! Zica told herself, standing up abruptly, filled with righteous anger.

She picked up the small telephone on her bedside table and asked for Yakov's number. Surely, he would be up by now, breakfasting with Vickie. On the second ring, his butler picked up. She asked to speak to her ex-husband.

"Zicotchka?" his voice came on the line.

"Tell me something, Yasha," she said without introduction.

"That woman, Karen Quarnstrom—you say she's staying with the Schwartzes? Do you have their number?"

"Are you about to do something foolish?" he asked her. "Don't make things worse than they already are. Just leave the woman alone. Talk to Kyril. Don't bring the actress into this."

"But I have to, Yasha. It's between her and me. I want to know where I stand, and he is never going to tell me. Kyril's an emotional coward. He won't explain why last night occurred. Maybe she will."

"I think it's a mistake," Yakov cautioned her.

Nevertheless, he gave her the number.

Kyril sat up in bed, his head in his hands. The memory of last night flooded back into his consciousness. The images horrified him.

How—how was it possible? With Zica waiting here at home, he had made love to Karen Quarnstrom!

He rang for Mason. It was a quarter to eleven already. His head wouldn't stop pounding. Why had he had so much to drink? He'd wanted to provoke Aaron and Sam, to let them know how angry he . . . but also, he'd wanted to blot out the pain and confusion. He'd hoped to eclipse his guilt at leaving Zica alone at Grayhall. He'd hoped his drunkenness would discourage the actress, make her think he was a hopeless lush, not worth bothering with.

Only it hadn't worked that way. Karen had liked him even better in person than she had on screen. She'd been terribly attracted to him—and in the end, her liking him had ovewhelmed his conscience.

Mason knocked on the door and entered, bearing his breakfast. Kyril sat up in bed, bare-chested and groggy. "Good *morning,* your *Excellency,*" the *maître d'hôtel* said brightly, smoothing down the covers in order to place the tray on his master's lap.

"Good morning, Mason. Has the Baroness risen yet?"

"Yes, sir. She *left* about *ten minutes* ago, in the *Stutz.* I offered to have her *driven,* but she *refused.* Said she *preferred* to drive *herself.*"

"I didn't even know she knew how," Kyril commented. "Mason . . . did she look upset to you?"

"She didn't eat her *eggs,* sir. And she looked rather *tired.* But she *behaved* the way she *always* does: spoke nicely to *Theresa,* and to the *gardener* on her way *out.* I did *ask* when we would expect her *back,* but she said she had *no idea*. Will that be *all,* your *Excellency . . . ?"*

"No one else called?"

"Just Miss *Warren,* sir."

Kyril nodded. "Very well, then; thanks, Mason," he said. "You may go now."

When the butler had departed, closing the door noiselessly behind him, the young man drank his grapefruit juice and thought about his life.

Had he *meant* for Zica to find out? Kyril wondered as he drank his coffee. Perhaps he wanted to announce to her: *This is how I am: I can't resist a beautiful woman who offers herself to me! Know me, and love me in spite of it!* But what woman in her right mind would accept a marriage based on such a premise? Certainly not Zica. She was proud—rightfully proud—of who she was and what she had accomplished. Zica had a thriving business in New York, and a coterie of friends and supporters. *And she still had the undiluted love of Yasha Pokhis. . . .*

The telephone rang. He picked it up.

"Miss Karen *Quarnstrom* is on the line," Mason announced from the main extension.

Oh, Lord . . . "Put her on," he told his butler.

"Cyril,"—her singsong voice made him cringe—"I trust that you slept well this morning?"

"Passed out was more like it," he retorted. "And what about you?"

She described her feelings in detail. She seemed thrilled by all that had transpired between them. Kyril felt a miserable weight upon his shoulders.

"Look," he finally interrupted, "Karen—"

"It's all right." A warmth in her voice surprised him. "We take time. Explore around each other. We drive through Hollywood, eat in small restaurants, and tell secrets. Being lovers cannot happen in just a single night."

"No," he agreed, "it can't. That's what I've been wanting to tell you. Last night was spontaneous and exciting and all that, but, Karen . . . my life is somewhere else. There is this other person I told you about—remember? I can't just let her go. I need her."

"You need me, too." The voice was cold and hurt. "We make two pictures together. Maybe more. Maybe I move to Los Angeles permanently. I like the weather! Mr. Schwartz—Aaron—he wants to make these pictures with us. Your other girlfriend can't help you there. You need an actress. You need *me."*

"I'm going to marry Zica, Karen. You and I can still do the pictures—but we can't repeat last night's performance. I'll be a married man."

"I don't wish to kiss another woman's husband, on screen or off," she declared stiffly. "I cannot give my soul if I do not want the man I'm supposed to kiss."

"That's what Adrienne used to say. That's baloney, Karen. Acting is acting, and real life is real life."

"And I am disagreeing. By the way," she added, her voice steely, "your little woman is on the way over here as we are conversing. She called me this morning, wanting to meet with me. So, if I am you, I leave it up to us, me and her, to resolve between us. Women understand love so much better than men!"

Kyril felt his blood run cold. "I beg your pardon?" he demanded. "My 'little woman' . . . ?"

"Zica Poliakov. She has a beautiful voice, Cyril. She sounds very nice. I'm sure she'll understand, if she truly loves you, that your career must come first, or you will surely die."

"I don't want you to speak to her!" he cried, panic-stricken. "Karen," he commanded. "If you wish ever to see me again, do not—I repeat, *do not*—engage Zica in any conversation! Tell her you made an error, that you have reconsidered and do not wish to speak to her after all! It's between her and me, and you and me— not between the two of you. Let me resolve my own life's dilemmas, will you please?"

"I'm afraid it's too late," Karen Quarnstrom commented. "The *maître d'hôtel* has just come in to announce the arrival of Baroness Poliakov. She gave him her card, and it's lying here on a small silver tray. . ."

"Don't you *dare* tell her anything she doesn't already know," he told her roughly. But Karen had already hung up the receiver. Kyril found himself listening to a dial tone.

Desperately, Kyril rang for Mason. Finally the butler entered, concern on his narrow, patrician face.

"Mason," Kyril told him, "get me my clothes—anything will do! Get the Rolls ready. I want you to drive me over to Mr. Schwartz's. I'll finish getting dressed in the car. *Hurry,* Mason. For God's sake, *hurry!*"

Chapter XXVIII

ZICA knew that she looked her best, even after a sleepless night.

The skirt on her turquoise suit was very short, displaying her perfect legs. Her cream blouse was cinched at the waist with a wide belt of tooled leather embossed with real turquoise and silver. She wore a wide band of turquoise silk around her head—and earrings of turquoise set in silver. Her pointed, high-heeled shoes and matching bag were off-white alligator, with silver buckles inset with more small, perfect turquoises.

Karen Quarnstrom, waiting for her in the Schwartz's solarium, was wearing a black silk robe over a black Belgian lace negligée which revealed itself whenever the panels of her robe separated. The robe was trimmed with marabou feathers at the collar, wrists, and hemline.

Seated among exotic plants, on a wicker armchair with a footstool, the Swedish actress wore no makeup. Her skin was iridescent perfection, the color of mother-of-pearl; her heart-shaped mouth was pink like a child's. She appeared to be languidly enjoying herself, for she had just put down a copy of the year's best seller, *Why We Behave Like Human Beings*. She looked up at Zica with a pleasant smile.

"Please sit down, Baroness," she said, indicating a small wicker love seat facing her armchair. Looking at the butler who had brought in Zica, she asked: "Could you refresh this coffee for us? And, Andrews, see that we are not disturbed."

Zica sat down, crossing her legs. In truth, she felt intimidated. Perhaps Yasha had been right—she should not have requested this face-to-face meeting. Karen Quarnstrom was almost thirty, but her beauty was compelling, even though her features were not really symmetrical. There was a *je ne sais quoi* about her that was undeniable. Zica bit her lower lip, wondering how to begin.

"It was gracious of you to agree to see me," she finally remarked. "After all, we are complete strangers and what I wish to discuss with you is intensely personal. Believe me, Miss Quarnstrom, it's not my habit ever to disclose myself to someone I don't know. But the subject matter is too important not to be brought out into the open."

Karen nodded, turning to a tray at her side to pour a cup of coffee. "How do you take yours?" she inquired. "With cream and sugar?"

"I take mine black, thank you."

For a moment neither woman spoke. Karen handed Zica her cup and refilled her own, diluting the coffee with two lumps of sugar and some cream. At last she returned the fullness of her gaze to her visitor.

"I know why you have come," she stated. "It is because of Cyril. He has told me a little about you. What he didn't say, I learned from Miss Melodie Warren at the studio. You own an art gallery in New York?"

"I love him, Miss Quarnstrom. And I believe he loves me as well. We were sweethearts long ago, in Russia, before the war. Then events intervened, and we met again in New York. It was the same thing between us then—wonderful, frightening, terribly emotional. But once again, there were problems. I was married, and Kyriusha and I miscommunicated."

"You were married to that charming actor Jake—or is it Jack?— Poker. I met him last night at the Coconut Grove. He is a fine, distinguished man. A kind person. I can tell from his eyes. You were wrong to leave him, Baroness. A man of such talent and wit is hard to find. And you have a child together, don't you?"

"Yes, we do. But I didn't come here to discuss Yakov. It's Kyriusha—Cyril—that concerns us both. After so many years, he and I finally have a chance to be happy, to fulfill a dream both of us have kept alive for thirteen years. I beg of you—don't destroy this chance! There are so many handsome men in this town, so many wealthy, successful, handsome men who would die for a chance to love you! Leave Kyriusha to me . . . leave him in peace. I entreat you, Miss Quarnstrom, woman to woman: please do not go after him now. You will be ruining the lives of two people. I am certain," she added, her large black eyes fastened imploringly on Karen's oval face, "if things do not work out between us this time, we shall never have another opportunity to make them come out right! This is our last attempt before we both give up—and things were good between us until he met you."

Karen raised her delicate blonde eyebrows, and took a sip of coffee. "Doesn't this tell you something, Baroness? It took such a small event, his meeting me, to disturb the peace between you! I, too, wish for his love. At this time I do not yet have it. He still loves you. But I am certain I am better for him than you are. You see, he loves his work, and he is immensely talented. Most of his critics think him only a sexy man, a charmer, as you say in this country— but I see the heart beating inside his characters. I see Cyril's intelligence at work each time he meets the eye of the camera. Such a man needs someone who can talk his own language."

"I have always understood him," Zica countered. Her voice was trembling. "Kyril can be himself around me, because we were lovers when we were young and unformed, and there are no secrets between us. Why must you go after a man who has already promised to marry another woman?"

"Because for years, I admire Cyril Malenkov. Because it is the soul of him I wish to touch. We find each other's souls when we make films together."

"Why can't you just make films together and be friends? Yakov —my ex-husband—made a film with Edna Purviance, and also with Marie Dressler. They became friends. But he had no need to become lovers. Why are you after Kyril? He is just one man, one simple man, and we had plans to marry and make a home together. . . . "

She knew her voice was breaking, that tears were forming in her eyes—this could not happen. She took a deep breath, meeting the eyes of Karen Quarnstrom honestly: "I beg you to reconsider," she said, her voice low and vibrant, "because Kyril does not know what to do. He is weak, and he is flattered by your attention and your admiration. But that is not love. If you persist in going after him, each one of us will lose. I shall return to New York with my little girl, because I shall not remain involved with someone who is unfaithful to me. But you will lose as well; Kyril will never love you, and to him you will always be the symbol of our break-up. He will not forgive you, even if, one day, he decides to marry you. In his heart, Miss Quarnstrom, he will always love me."

"You appear very sure of this."

"After thirteen years, I am completely sure. But I am not sure of the strength of his commitment. Had it been what I hoped it was, he would never have gone to the Coconut Grove without me—and even if he had, he would have left alone."

"But, my dear Baroness, if not I, then some other woman, later ...! Your love had not the power to keep him away from me, the first night we met! Does your ego not flinch at such a realization—that you are not woman enough to keep your man faithful?"

There: it had been said—stated plainly, openly, no holds barred. Zica felt the hot flush of shame, followed by outraged fury. Quarnstrom had hit home. In a softer tone, the actress said: "I do not care whether a man I love remains faithful to me or not. With Cyril, I leave the door open. He breathes freely. I am certain that if he steps out, it means less than nothing. I won't wait in the shadows, fearing other women. I do not own him. If he came home with me last night, it was because he wished to do so. Make no mistake about that, Baroness."

A tap on the door brought in the Schwartz's butler with another silver coffee pot. This he exchanged for the empty one. With a bow, he departed.

Zica thought about what the actress had been telling her. Finally she said: "Perhaps he was afraid to displease the studio. He believes, erroneously I think, that *Messieurs* Schwartz and Unger are in complete control of his professional future. He did not wish to go out last night, Miss Quarnstrom. He did not wish to be your escort. But he went to please his producers, and he stayed—because he was drunk."

"He got drunk to give himself the excuse to stay. He *wanted* to be with me, Baroness Poliakov. Cyril liked Karen, Karen liked Cyril. Perhaps we fall in love. You make him feel guilty, and no man likes to marry a woman who gives him a bad time. I suggest you leave this house and return to New York. I further suggest that you reconsider that adorable man who was your husband once. Jack Poker is too strong-willed for me; I prefer to love a needier sort of man. You are needy too, and your needs conflict with Cyril's; but with Jack, you are protected."

Zica could feel the room beginning to dance around her. Her throat was painfully constricted. "You are attracted by the actor, Cyril Malenkov," she said, her coffee cup rattling against the saucer as her hands shook. "You find it appealing that he's a Russian count. But that's *not* who he is, Miss Quarnstrom! He's a simple boy from provincial Russia, not from Leningrad, but from Rostov-on-the-Don, near the Caucasus. His name is not 'Malenkov,' but 'Ostrov' —Kyril Ostrov. He is the son of a Cossack who committed suicide, owing thousands of rubles, and of a good Jewish woman who lives in New York—kept in the shadows by a son who refuses to acknowledge her publicly. That is who I know—a real human being, not some celluloid doll with a fancy name and an invented pedigree! And you will never be allowed into his past. You will forever wonder who he is—because he will not share himself with you, only with me!"

Karen Quarnstrom stirred her coffee calmly, taking a measured sip. "My poor dear lady," she declared, "I have no wish to know the man he was . . . I do not care who his parents were, nor what his real name is. My name isn't Karen Quarnstrom, either. Nevertheless, I *become* Karen Quarnstrom, just as he *becomes* Count Cyril Malenkov—the great, the splendid screen actor! That is the only man I need to know, the only man I need to understand. We stay together, we share secrets . . . in time, all lovers do. I am not worried."

"Then I wish you good luck," Zica said, setting her cup down abruptly. Standing up, she strode out of the Schwartz's solarium.

It wasn't until she had reached the ground floor that she burst into tears.

Kyril jumped out of the Rolls-Royce, his heart leaping at the sight of the pearl-gray Stutz neatly parked in the driveway beside Naomi Schwartz's enormous Heine-Velox touring car. Mason hastened out of the driver's seat, asking whether Kyril expected him to wait.

"Go on home," his young master told him. "The Baroness is still here. I'll drive back with her."

Clearly, he was already too late. Since Zica was nowhere in sight, she had to be inside, speaking to Karen Quarnstrom.

Sadly, Kyril watched Mason drive away, his last thread of hope fading as the elegant roadster vanished behind the Schwartz's acacias.

Kyril trudged up the porch steps to the massive front door, remembering the first time Melodie had brought him here. That had been in the winter of 1920—six years ago! In six short years, he had matured into a real actor. He was not just a pretty boy. His heart had found its haven in motion pictures, and when he played a role, he played it for all it was worth, with his body and soul.

He raised his hand to the doorbell. But to his shock, at that very moment, the door opened from within and he found himself face to face with a turquoise apparition—Zica, in a turquoise suit, tears streaming down her cheeks. The two stared at each other, stunned. Then, with a little cry, she ran past him out of the house, her hand flying to her mouth.

Kyril whirled around, catching up with her just as she reached the gray sports car. Her hand was already on the door handle when he stopped her. "Zica," he said, "we have to talk."

"There's nothing left to say," she answered. He had never seen her like this—her face ravaged by tears, the mascara clotted beneath her lashes. She tried to open the door, but his hand resisted, hurting her fingers. "Let me go!" she cried.

"Godamnit! I want to talk to you!" he shouted, prying her fingers off the handle. He pressed her against the car with the force of his own body. "You either come inside the Stutz and talk to me like a civilized person, or I'm going to force you to listen to me *here,* like *this.* You can't just run away from me!"

She looked up at him, her wounded face reflecting back the shame he felt. "You can no longer hold me," she told him tiredly. "That was yesterday."

He took her by the forearms and began to shake her lightly, his face contorted with pain. "What does this mean?" he demanded.

"It means that Karen Quarnstrom was right. You and she share a common passion—acting. I can never share that. And you will always be tempted by other women. That isn't something I could bear. A man has to love me when he is away from me as well as with me—or I will feel cheated."

"It was only a mistake," he countered. "One mistake, Zica!"

She regarded him with serious eyes. "One mistake? After you and I spent *one night* together? No, Kyriusha, it was *my* mistake. I dreamt of you for thirteen years, I thought you my golden prince, I ruined my marriage because of those dreams. *And I was the fool!* You were living your own life, going from woman to woman. You will always fall into the arms of women who want you because you are charming—and now you are a matinée idol! I want a home, a husband, children. I want to be the single shining star in my husband's horizon. I want to *trust* the man I'm married to; *I don't want to be hurt again!*"

"I won't hurt you," he whispered, tears forming in his eyes. "I promise you, Zicotchka, I'll never hurt you again! Please—let me prove myself to you! I'll go in there and tell Karen I'm going to leave Star Partners and marry you, that I don't care whether I ever act again! Just say you'll give me one more chance, Zica—my beloved Zica."

Wrenching to one side, Zica pushed him away with all her strength. He stumbled backward. She flung open the door. She was halfway into the driver's seat before he blocked her again. He grabbed her arm in a viselike grip, bending down to shout at her through the open door.

"I'm not going to let you go!" he cried. "You can't leave me!"

"I can do whatever the hell I please!" she shouted back, twisting her arm to free herself. She collapsed against the steering wheel, her head on her arms, sobbing. "Why?" she cried. "Why wasn't it enough that I love you?"

"But it was, it was!" Seeing his opportunity, Kyril dashed around to the passenger side, flung open the door, and jumped into the seat beside her. Closing the door, he leaned toward her, his arms around her waist. "It was just *foolishness!* I don't know what came over me! I didn't mean to do it—you know I didn't. Oh, Zica, for God's sake, don't listen to Karen! She's just another willful actress! I was an *idiot.* I should never have gone to the Grove—I should never have listened to Melodie! Zica, I'm sorry, I'll do *anything,* believe me—just give me another chance . . . !"

"No." She shook her head, refusing to look at him. "You've broken my heart. You've taken away my pride, and my dignity. No man is worth that. I *can't* love you after this, Kyril."

"Zica—please listen—I'll do whatever you please, Zicotchka, so long as you do not leave me, so long as you stick by me this one time!"

"Just let me drive back," she sighed, shaking her head. I have to pack, I have to go back to the gallery. I have another life, Kyril—a good one. It was a mistake ever to think of giving it up for you." She turned the key in the ignition, pressing her foot on the accelerator. The Stutz shot forward onto the graveled driveway.

Now that the car was moving, Kyril felt as if he could reason with her. "Anna sent you to me," he said to her, as she maneuvered the sports car down the driveway and out through the open gate. "She thinks we belong together, as do I!"

"I belong to no one," Zica said. She turned right, and the Stutz shot forward on the narrow road that curved around the hillside.

"You're going the wrong way," he told her.

"That's right," she answered. "We're going into the hills, Kyriu-sha. Not far—but far enough that you'll have a very long walk home. And no one will be holding your hand. No one will pity you. I need time to pack and get away from this place—and you need time to think about how you're living your life." She pressed her foot hard on the accelerator, and the car sped up as she pulled around a bend. "All you think about is the present and your plea-sure! You have no heart! Melodie Warren doesn't want your happi-ness—all she cares about is signing up Karen Quarnstrom! And all Karen cares about is bedding you down, to improve her on-screen performance! But watch out, Kyril: she will surely dump you, once you've done those two pictures with her. She'll go on to the next star, onto Barrymore or Fairbanks or Valentino! And you'll be all alone—until the next girl comes along, the next bright starlet on her way to stardom. That is how your life will go. Think of it— just think of it!"

Zica laughed giddily.

She was becoming hysterical. Her breath came in syncopated gasps; her eyes shone strangely; and her cheeks were unnaturally flushed. For a brief second she turned to him, nostrils dilated, and cried out: "I should never have come to you! You have broken my heart! *You have broken my life!*"

He was horrified. She was driving faster and more recklessly— but even as she drove she began to sob again, her chest heaving. Had he hurt her that badly? Overcome with compassion, he laid his hand gently on her arm.

Violently, she shrugged it off.

"Zicotchka," he pleaded, "it doesn't have to be this way.... Your heart isn't broken, it is merely bruised by my foolishness. Please ... give us both the chance we deserve!"

She would not look at him. She was panting for breath, her cheeks bright crimson. Her fingers trembled on the wheel. The car spun round another bend, and she jerked it toward the side of the hill, away from the outer rail. For an instant, as she swerved, Kyril glimpsed the sheer precipice beyond the guard-rail.

"Kyriusha," she said, "you do not know what grief I am feeling. I was young when we met, a virgin. I gave you my heart! But I made a mistake—I didn't marry you—and so I lost you. I lost you and my heart broke into tiny fragments.... I killed our baby, but I was really trying to kill myself, I think.... But I loved you so much, I would have died to be near you."

He could feel his own heart breaking. He had never heard anything so heartrending. No one had ever loved him like this! He could not help it: the tears fell from his eyes, and he asked, in a hushed voice: "You loved me this much?"

"I loved you *more!*" She turned her face to him.

For an instant, the car was out of control, swerving toward the cliff. Wildly, she jerked the wheel. It rocked back onto the road, into the curve. Her face was bloodless, ashen. The flush had vanished. She looked like death—a death mask—like one who had ceased to care whether she lived or died. He was terrified by her wild abandonment of all hope.

"I loved you *more,*" she repeated in a tremulous voice. "I loved you to the point of distraction! I could not stop thinking about you. I went to Noel Pierre—I tried to lose myself in him, drug myself with him—I closed my eyes and closed my heart so that all I could feel was the thrust of him inside me. . . . Oh," she cried, "you do not know how hard I struggled to forget you, to forget I had ever loved you! But *you*—you threw my love and my devotion in the gutter. You let *that woman* trample them with her bare feet! Kyril Ostrov, *you rotten bastard,* last night you killed me, you *killed me.* . . ."

The car was slipping out of her control.

Lunging across, Kyril seized the wheel, whirling it. Tires squealed as the car found the road, turning back on course.

Immediately Zica pressed her foot on the accelerator, and the car sped forward, the violence of the motion throwing him back against his own seat.

"For God's sake, Zica," he breathed, "stop the car! Let me drive!"

She shook her head, knuckles whitening as she gripped the steering wheel more firmly.

Zica was starting to cry again. The road was steeper, climbing toward the top of the hillside, toward the house that Fairbanks and Pickford had built. They were far from Grayhall.

She was weeping piteously, silently, her shoulders heaving.

"Zicotchka," Kyril told her, "I love you. You aren't giving me a chance to mend things between us. All I ask is one last chance—a chance to make good, to make you forget Karen, and last night!"

"Oh, Kyriusha, what would be the use?" she asked. "You'd only do it again with somebody else. Karen is right—I'd have to live in fear of other women, the rest of my life."

"Don't go back to New York," he told her. "Don't break up with me!"

"I have no choice." She drove quietly now, maneuvering the small sports car with renewed ease. Her moment of hysteria had passed. He thought: it is hopeless. She has turned from me, once and for all.

"Stop the car!" he cried. "I want you to listen to me now, godamnit!"

"It's no use." She made the car go faster, around a bend.

She no longer sounded desperate, only determined. Her calm composure made him more uneasy than her former hysteria. The frenzy of her loss had passed with the violence of her hysteria. But Kyril could not accept that she had terminated their affair once and for all.

"Stop the car!" he shouted, his face turning red. "You've talked, and now I want to!"

"Don't be silly," she said, continuing to drive. As though to taunt him on purpose, she sped up as she came to another curve in the road. The speedometer read sixty-five, seventy, seventy-five . . .

Her voice, so calm and obdurate, drove him insane. He was going to lose her. He had to do something, quickly.

Lifting his leg over the shift, he jammed his foot down on the brake with all his force. She screamed as the speeding car squealed to a halt, fishtailing wildly.

The scream ended in a horrible crash as her body shot forward against the windshield.

Blood splattered on the glass. But the Stutz was still running. It bolted forward toward the embankment. Kyril reached for the hand brake.

Zica's bloody, unconscious body fell on top of him.

"No! *NO!*" he heard himself scream as her blood seeped onto his shirt.

"Goddamnit! *NO!*" The panicked scream died in his throat, as the gray Stutz rolled over on its side, then toppled over the cliff in a somersault.

It came to rest halfway down the embankment, in a cloud of sagebrush and dust.

A door flew open, and an arm fell out, hanging over the rubble like a drooping flower.

Above, high in the sky, a white-hot sun baked the tinted landscape.

* * *

The hospital room that Yakov entered was a large single room, where flowers fought for shelf space but could not mask the cloying smell of disinfectant. The figure in the bed was heavily bandaged and appeared to be in repose. But as Yakov spoke, the eyelids fluttered.

The pupils were dilated, but clear. The bandaged head on the pillow shifted almost imperceptibly as the patient awoke.

"Hello, Kyriusha," Yakov said, pulling up a chair.

As the hand on the covers moved, Yakov took it between his own. "How are you feeling?"

"Yashenka." The murmured voice, speaking Russian, sounded disembodied, as wispy as a soft breeze. "Please, Yashenka, don't pretend. There's nothing more the doctors can do for me. The morphine"—he paused—"I know, they are trying to dull the pain . . . until the moment comes."

"Lena is here," Yakov told him gently. "She came yesterday, but it was after visiting hours. I've had her at my place. She and Vickie have been keeping each other company."

"How is she taking this?" Kyril asked softly.

"Like a true Russian. More valiantly than I'd expected. She'll be in to see you this afternoon. I just wished to come in before going to the studio, and Doc Grayson said it would be okay. Everyone sends love."

Kyril forced the shadow of a smile. His eyes went to the windowsill, then to the small table beside the bed.

"The nurses keep reading me telegrams from fans," he said weakly. "And from the film community, too. These aren't half the flowers I've been sent . . . ! Angela—my day nurse—has been giving most of them away, by the potful, to the children's ward. I never would have pictured this, in Moscow, when we were youths. In those days, even my own grandfather would not have sent flowers."

"Those days are past," Yakov told him. "Melodie says the scripts are piling up on Aaron's desk, waiting for you to get well."

The weak smile returned. "But I won't get well. Aaron and Melodie know this. Tell me," he said, "about Zica."

"She's doing better." Yakov looked down at the floor. "They've moved her to another ward, two floors down. She's starting to walk again, very slowly."

"Thank God." A long silence followed. Kyril turned his tortured, hurt eyes toward the ceiling. "And . . . what else has been happening?"

"Karen Quarnstrom is going to do the Loos picture with Richard Barthelmess."

"Is she still at Aaron and Naomi's?" The eyes remained on the ceiling.

"Not since last week. She bought herself a house way up in the hills, off Laurel Canyon. Says she needs solitude. To contemplate her navel, I suspect—or maybe the stars in the firmament."

"You don't much like her, do you?"

"Given the harm she's done—" Yakov's voice vibrated with passion. "I wish she'd go back to Sweden and leave us all in peace!"

"I wish so too," Kyril said sadly, his voice a bare whisper. "I wish none of this had ever happened. . . . It was all my fault."

"Oh, it was the fault of everyone: Aaron, Sam, Melodie, Karen . . . you, Zica . . . each of you thinking only of yourself! But what use is it to weep about it now?" Yakov asked, his tone suddenly bitter.

"I never wanted any of it to happen!" Kyril cried out. "I never asked for Karen Quarnstrom to come here. *I only wanted to marry Zica!*" Tears ran from his eyes, darkening the bandages.

"Well, it doesn't matter any more," Yakov declared. "Stop blaming yourself, okay?" He pressed Kyril's hand between his palms, then let it down gently to rest on the coverlet. Then he arose and stood over the dying actor. "Farewell, Kyriusha," he murmured. "I have to go to work."

He left the room, grateful to be spared those hurt, wounded eyes that would never again look into the lens of a camera.

The young woman looked like a teen-age girl in her white hospital gown. Her hair glistened in the sunlight, and, from the back, one might even have thought her healthy. But when she turned around, the picture changed. There was a bandage over the bridge of her nose. The hollow cheekbones below bruised skin were tinted various hues of purple and yellow. Her right arm was in a sling and there was a brace on her left leg.

The nurse was saying, "He's extremely ill, Miss Poliakov. The morphine no longer seems to keep the pain away. He keeps asking for you, Miss."

A spasm passed over Zica's face. "I don't want to go," she said, her voice tense. "Don't make me go!" Her eyes filled with tears.

"No one's going to make you do anything," the nurse said gently. "However, Dr. Melton wants you to try a few more steps today with the brace and the crutches. I thought. . . . Well, Angela, his day nurse, said he was fighting not to lose consciousness, telling her over and over that he needed to see you. *Needed to see you,* Miss Poliakov," the young nurse repeated, her hazel eyes on Zica's face. "I thought we might try to walk over to the elevator, go up two flights to Count Malenkov's floor, then take a few more steps down the hall to his room. I'll be right beside you."

Zica shook her head, her face flushed. Panic was mounting inside her. "I'm not ready," she stated, her voice quivering. "I . . . I can't see him, Helga!"

"Miss Poliakov," the nurse said gravely, "he's *dying*. He won't last the week!"

Zica's large brown eyes filled with tears, and she made a strange grimace. "Take me to him," she whispered at last, holding out her one good hand. It trembled like the wing of a frightened bird.

"There," the young nurse stated, helping her up and arranging the crutches. "Dr. Melton will be proud of you, and so will I."

But Zica's blazing eyes stopped her in mid-track. "I wish we had both died!" she cried out fiercely. *"I wish we had both died!"* And her entire body began to shake.

In Kyril's room the shades had been drawn up to allow afternoon sunlight to penetrate, shedding a golden glow upon the flowers. Slowly, very slowly, Zica followed as the young nurse drew her inside.

Zica's face was white with concentration. Beads of sweat clung to her hairline. It was the first time that she had walked so far. The bad leg in its brace trailed behind. She had been forced to summon up all her might, just to plant the crutches down, take a step with the good leg, drag the other behind it . . . and start all over again. Helga, her private duty nurse, had encouraged her all the way, her round face creased with smiles.

Now the smiles were gone. Helga's face reflected only the grave fact that they had entered a room where a patient lay dying. His day nurse had moved out of the room, making way for Helga and her patient. Now Helga herself prepared to leave.

Zica felt panicked. "What if . . . ?" she whispered, her enormous eyes beseeching Helga not to abandon her. In the bed, Kyril appeared to be asleep or unconscious. Zica felt her precarious strength ebbing from her.

"Don't worry," the young nurse reassured her. "Angela and I are going to be right outside. He wants to talk to you alone," she added meaningfully, her hazel eyes stern in the round face.

Didn't anyone understand that *she just wasn't ready?* Helga's strong arms lowered Zica into a chair, lifted the bad leg, and placed it on a footstool. The nurse concentrated on rearranging the crutches, then patted Zica's good hand, and strode relentlessly out of the room. Zica was alone—but for the man sleeping in the bed!

Fear gripping her by the throat, Zica felt a spurt of bile shoot up from her knotted stomach. Perspiration clotted her forehead; she could hear her own heartbeat. With a true effort of will, her whole torso trembling, she lowered her eyes to the bed.

His head was bandaged around his face and down over his jaw. She could see wisps of his long eyelashes, the good cheekbones, the pointed nose. The Cupid's bow lips, always so perfect—Zica felt a sob rising within her. She hadn't expected *this*—not his own face, peeking out from the wounds. She'd thought—well, that he'd be unrecognizable, as she had been when they had lifted her from the debris. But only one cheek seemed blotched and bruised. The rest was *him*.

Could it be, then, that they'd been *wrong?* That he *was* getting better, after all...?

A soft moan arose from the bed. Zica brushed her tears away. His eyelids began to flutter like butterflies. Suddenly he was looking at her with eyes large as his soul, immense as death itself, green with flecks of gold.

"Zicotchka," he whispered. She could hardly make out the words. "I didn't think you'd come...."

She nodded. Her throat was so tight she could not speak. She tried to smile. "I'm not going to make it," he said weakly. "You know that, don't you? They've told you?"

Again, Zica nodded. Then, with great effort, she reached over to touch his face.

He smiled at her. "I love you," he told her, in an odd, raspy voice that grated like sandpaper. "I've always loved you. Since I first saw you at the Tretyakovka, a lifetime ago—" He paused to catch his breath, and the concentration beaded his forehead with dewdrops. "I've ruined your life. But it's because I'm bad, I'm a *samocer,* and I can't help being bad. God is punishing me now."

"God doesn't punish in this way," she said softly, finding her own voice. "God is good. He doesn't bring His children pain. The pain happens in spite of Him, I think."

"Maybe so. I don't really believe in Him, anyhow...."He

grinned, and she felt her heart flop over. "Zica," he said, "Zica, my own darling. You were all I ever had, and even you I couldn't keep. My father was right: I'm no good."

In a minute, she would once more burst into tears. Zica felt her body trembling all over. She touched his face, his nose, the eyelids, the bruised cheek, the delicate mouth. "Oh, you are wrong!" she told him. "You were never evil. You never loved yourself enough, that's all! You haven't changed: you're still magical like the apparition that came to me at the Tretyakovka—the boy I turned into my Golden Prince! Only now, you are *everyone*'s Golden Prince, and you belong to the whole world!"

"So you still feel something . . . ?" he asked softly. The green eyes mesmerized her, held her to him.

She did burst into tears. But her hand remained on his face, as she caressed it with her fingertips. "Of course I do. . . . " she told him. "I shall love you all the days of my life—like no other man, no other love. . . . "

"Can you forgive me?"

"There is nothing to forgive," she answered, her voice cracking. "We always misunderstood each other, you and I. You gave me your heart, but I didn't really know what to make of it. I tried to fit it into the mold I had prepared for it, never realizing that no human heart can be molded. I was wrong—as well as you!"

"No," he told her, "you were never wrong. You were all good, all tenderness and kindness. I wish you well, Zica, when I am gone. . . . "

For a moment, neither could speak. And then, "Go to sleep, Kyriusha," she murmured. "Go to sleep. Zica still loves you, and always will." She began to hum a lullaby from her childhood, her hand on his brow.

Then, as his eyelids grew heavy, she kissed her own fingertips and placed them against his burning cheek. "Good night, my one and only darling," she whispered. "May God bless you and keep you. . . . "

As he grew still, she brought her good hand against her eyes and began to sob silently.

The younger woman was slim and attractive. Dressed in black silk, her beautiful black hair pinned behind her ears, she wore a small toque hat with a lace *voilette* shielding her pale face from the winter sun. But she walked with difficulty, favoring one leg and leaning heavily on a cane. The older woman beside her looked very old, beyond her true years. Her gray hair was tucked beneath a wide-brimmed hat adorned with a black velvet ribbon; her intelligent face was creased with small lines, her sharp blue eyes were shadowed with anxiety. The two women held onto each other, making their careful way between the headstones and the pots of flowers that graced the graveyard.

"You really were going to get married, weren't you?" Lena asked. She stopped to catch her breath and to adjust Zica's suit jacket, tugging at it maternally.

Zica turned to her seriously, the hollows in her cheekbones underscoring the wideness of her dark eyes, and the sadness in them. She nodded.

"But you won't talk about it—not even now."

Zica sighed. She reached out to Lena, clasped her hand—but said nothing. The two women resumed their trek, the older woman matching her steps to the younger one's more hesitant ones. It was still an ordeal for Zica to walk without crutches and a brace.

Around the bend, a large marble monument arose before them. Instinctively, Zica caught her breath. It was always the same reaction—it couldn't be his, it simply couldn't . . . , because at heart, she did not wish to believe him dead. Silently, the tears began to flow.

But Elena Ostrov would not pause this time. Keeping a firm grip on Zica's fingers, she urged her forward. Grimly, she continued upward toward the monument, clutching the flower pot in her other hand.

"Believe me, *detechka*," she said to Zica, "no one prepares you for outliving your own child. There is nothing in this world to teach you how to grieve. Each one must do it in his own way, *maya devochka*, in his own time."

Once more, Zica just nodded. They had come to the marble archway. "I'm going to go in," Lena said. "Do you want to take the flowers?"

"Yes, thank you." Gingerly, Zica took the small pot from Kyril's mother and walked carefully to the other side of the mausoleum. She waited until Lena had gone inside, then approached the wall. There was a niche at eye level for fresh flowers; it was now empty. She placed the white poinsettias inside and stepped back, her face veiled with tears.

White poinsettias. White, for purity and for death. I wanted to be your bride, she told him silently, her eyes suddenly reproachful and angry. I wanted to live with you and to have children.

"Why did you have to die?" she cried to herself, choking on a sob.

The two of them, she and Kyril, had always acted at cross-purposes. Often, during the months of her convalescence, Zica had wondered whether she would have forgiven him Karen Quarnstrom, and ever trusted him again. She thought not.

But of course, Lena needed to be reassured, Lena needed to hear that "her beloved children" had been headed for a blissful life together. And so, whenever the question came up, Zica always nodded: yes, they had planned to get married, they would have been married right away and lived happily ever after.

And now it was winter, and it was time for the two women to pack their bags and return to New York. This would be their final farewell to the man they had both loved.

Kyril's will had left Grayhall to Zica. After the funeral, she had moved in with his mother. The two women had lived almost in seclusion, recuperating, trying to sort through the past and the present. The two grieving women had given themselves time.

Zica couldn't remember the funeral. She could only remember Yasha holding her up—and the open coffin with its myriad flowers, the thousands of fans who had trailed by to pay homage to him for three days. Lena had brought her the newspapers and the magazines, many of which had featured her photograph alongside his, labelled the star's fiancée.

But now it was time to go home, back to New York.

She felt the marble with her fingertips, as though it were a lover's fair skin. "May you rest in peace," she whispered.

She took a step forward, detached a single white petal from the poinsettia plant, and held it to her cheek. "May you rest in peace, my beloved Kyriusha," she said softly. "For you will always be the prince of my dreams. . . ."

A stiff winter breeze suddenly lifted the veil off her forehead, and she looked about her, startled. Lena was coming out of the mausoleum, holding her coat together against the gust. As Zica moved forward toward her old friend, a woman's voice made her pause.

"Excuse me," she heard. When she turned around, she saw a young girl wearing a scarlet coat, carrying a long-stemmed rose in her hand. "Is this where Cyril Malenkov is buried?"

"Yes," Zica told her. "It is."

The girl squinted at her. "Aren't you. . . . ? Aren't you Zeinab Poliakov?" she asked. "The woman he was going to marry?" Her face lit up.

Zica nodded, feeling the tears begin anew. The girl touched her arm respectfully, a little awe-struck. "So you really knew him well," she said. "You knew what he was like?"

"I knew him, yes," Zica replied. "I'd known him many years. He was a sweet and loving man, and a talented actor."

The girl smiled again. "Oh," she breathed, "you are so beautiful! I've seen your picture several times, you know. Didn't you also go with that New York gangster who was shot down?"

This time Zica scowled. "He wasn't a gangster," she said carefully, "and I believe my past belongs to me alone."

"Well, geez, I'm real sorry," the young girl stammered, fumbling for words. "It's just that, you see, your life is like a storybook. Back in Oklahoma, where I come from, you don't meet people like you every day. . . . "

Zica reached over and touched the girl's hand. "It's all right," she reassured her. "I know the way it all sounds in the papers. But I'm going to grow into one of those boring old ladies you see in tea rooms in every city, munching on crumpets and chatting about their grandchildren. No one will remember what happened to me when I was young."

"You're wrong about that," the girl retorted. She held the rose out to Zica. "Here, I've brought a rose to lay before *his* gravestone. I thought he was the greatest actor in the world! But I think he'd prefer for me to give it to you. He loved you lots, didn't he, Miss Poliakov?"

"Yes," Zica answered, smiling through her tears. "We loved *each other* . . . lots."

When she walked away, she was holding the rose the girl had given her—and the white petal she had taken from Kyril's poinsettia.

Epilogue

SITTING behind her large desk, Zica propped her spectacles over the ridge of her small nose and looked coolly at her assistant.

"Surrealism is the coming thing," she told him positively. "You may find it garish and crude, but you'll see. Don't think *I* like it! But Salvador Dali is a young man I've been watching for five years. Exhibiting his work in an *avant-garde* show—alongside some new Paul Klees and Henri Matisses—will prove to be a great move for the gallery this year. We'll be seen as *the* people who smell out a trend even before it becomes fashionable everywhere."

"Americans will laugh at the vulgarity of this artist," Bruno Lesschi sneered, his upper lip raised in disdain over his long, yellow teeth. "Limp clocks over desolate landscapes.... What does it mean, anyway, Zica?"

She sighed, twisting her lips into a funny grimace. "It simply means that our poor, sad world is barren and empty—save for the technology man keeps trying to impose on his own environment.... The point is, this young Spaniard aims to shock the complacency out of people's souls—and he's succeeded, hasn't he?"

"The Great Wall Street Crash achieved this more effectively two years ago," Bruno stated ironically. He shrugged eloquently. "It's a good thing your ex-husband got us all to invest in films. Everyone else I know was in the market—and lost everything."

"I don't know what Yakov does better—comedy or business," said Zica, tapping a pencil on her desk. "Maybe he's successful because he thinks they're the same thing." She smiled.

Bruno cleared his throat. "So you want me to compose a letter to Dali's agent?"

She nodded. "I'd like to see a transparency of his new work, *The*

Persistence of Memory. Draft the letter and show it to me this afternoon."

As the small man exited, Zica smiled at his retreating back. Bruno was sweet but hopelessly old-fashioned. He still chose the Venus de Milo over Jacob Epstein, and Rembrandt over Picasso.

She stood up, and went to the long mirror to survey herself. For a woman of thirty-six, she was holding up well. She wore her black hair in a longer bob which softened her face. Her figure was still willowy and supple, the large breasts delineated by her narrow sheath dress. With its huge sleeves, padded shoulders, and long hem, she looked demure in the green silk dress.

It was already winter, 1931. Many things had changed besides the hemlines. The Volstead Act had been repealed. Al Capone was in jail for tax evasion. People travelled by air from coast to coast, and many pretty, personable women twenty-five and younger had chosen to become airline stewardesses. The handsome young pilot, Lindbergh, had attained world renown, much to the excitement of twelve-year-old Vickie who had once flown in the back seat of the young pilot's mail plane. In Hollywood, "talky" films had been introduced, on a new, wider screen.

But the greatest change in America had been caused by the Great Wall Street Crash of October 24, 1929. The entire world was still reeling from this tremendous economic devastation. Only the ultra-rich had been little affected—and, for Zica, this had meant that most of her clients continued to buy expensive art pieces for their many homes.

In the rest of the nation people sought solace in the movies. Poker Jack, with his exaggerated Russian accent, had turned into a national hero. He had made it his job to boost morale on a wide scale—not just among children. While watching his antics, the unemployed could temporarily forget the harshness of their daily existence.

Zica looked at the telephone on her desk, hesitating. She wanted to call him. Last night, she'd gone alone to a dinner-dance at Anna Voorhies' and listened indolently to Elsie and Brett Morrison as they discussed the latest eligible bachelor to whom they wished to introduce her.

"I don't like blind dates," she told them. "It's not dignified."

"Sitting by yourself at a dance isn't dignified, either," Elsie had retorted. They meant well—but the truth was, Zica did not feel like meeting new men. She hadn't felt like it for some time now.

Impulsively, she lifted the receiver and asked for the familiar number of Star Partners in California. It was still morning in Los Angeles.

"Can you put me through to Poker Jack?" she asked the receptionist. "I think he's somewhere at the studio."

"He's on Lot 13," the young girl told her. "But they're in the middle of shooting and Mr. Walsh doesn't like to be disturbed—unless," she added, "it's some sort of emergency."

Yakov was filming a serious picture, his first. It was an experiment, with a large budget, which he'd presented to Schwartz and Unger with some trepidation. It told the story of a man wrongly accused of murdering his immigrant girlfriend.

Yakov had written the screenplay himself. Karen Quarnstrom played the girlfriend. It felt odd to Zica, knowing that, on a daily basis, this woman was shooting love scenes with her ex-husband.

"She's not such a bad egg," Yasha had told Zica. "She knows how to act, and the role requires subdued energy and fire."

The part Karen played was fitting, Zica thought—a woman who betrays her lover for a moment of thoughtless passion with a stranger.

"Well?" the receptionist demanded. "*Is* this an emergency, Ma'am?"

"Oh, no, no," Zica stammered. "Thank you all the same." Feeling sheepish, she hung up quickly.

Her face was on fire, her hands were trembling.

What was it that she'd wanted to ask Yasha? Vickie hoped he would buy her a pony, so that she might ride with Melodie Warren on the beach at Malibu whenever she visited him in L.A. Zica still resented Melodie for her part in what had happened the summer of 1926. Kyril had needed her to support his marriage plans, and instead she had sided with her studio bosses.

But the past was the past. Thinking about it now would only reopen old wounds that, slowly but surely, had begun to heal.

But Yasha knew about this wish for a pony. Vickie had told him herself, on the telephone, some time ago. Zica could feel the pressure in her chest, the breathlessness; she sat down again behind her desk, dropping her face into her hands. She'd just wanted to call him—that was all—for no particular reason.

Karen Quarnstrom had a couple of love scenes with Yakov in this new picture, which was entitled *Deception*. Zica imagined the blonde actress looking enticingly at Yakov, her ice-blue eyes devouring his face. She could picture Yakov's own dark eyes turned passionately toward the Swedish woman, his nostrils slightly flared, lips parted with desire. Zica clenched her fists, a sudden cry escaping her. The notion of Quarnstrom and Yakov together in a love duet, even an on-screen make-believe one, disturbed her greatly.

But why? Yakov was only her ex-husband, the trusted friend she'd had all her life.

Yes, she answered herself, *but he is mine, not hers.*

What do I want? she wondered. Her face was inexplicably bathed in tears. She'd had excitement living on the edge, with Noel Pierre; she'd had romance and passion with Kyril. Oh, how she'd loved him, from the first moment they had set eyes on each other at the Tretyakovka! But this love hadn't nurtured them.

Whenever she thought of Kyril Ostrov, she would feel pangs of sorrow and remorse—remorse at the waste of his young life, at the way she had participated in ending it.

And now, Zica was lonely. She was lonely in her gallery, lonely in her house, lonely with her friends. Anna and Lena attributed this to 1926—the year Zica had thought would never pass, the year she had wished she had died alongside Kyril. But then other years had followed, and the pain had dulled, and she'd seen how impossible a reconciliation would have been. She would never have married her Golden Prince; such a marriage would have been doomed to failure.

She had pushed Yasha away. Some time after the funeral, Yakov had withdrawn. He'd told her, "I can well understand how badly you feel. But I can't keep looking at you when you keep seeing *his* face, *his* eyes. I, too, must put the past behind me, with its obsessions. I've been obsessed with you, and you with him. This led us nowhere, don't you see?"

She'd seen. She had let him go, and returned to New York. He still telephoned her, advising her on business matters when she asked. But he wasn't the same. He'd had enough.

Her hand returned to the telephone. This time, she spoke to her own secretary in the outer office.

"Blanche," she said, "I want you to book me a flight on United Airlines, to San Francisco. Then a shorter flight from San Francisco to L.A. Make that for next week, any time. No," she corrected herself, "make it for tomorrow! Pay extra if you need to, but get me on."

The sun, the color of lemon curd, shone through a hazy blue sky that told Angelinos it was winter; but, to Zica, the weather was a perfect balm, compared to the whipping winds of Manhattan.

Zica wore a square-shouldered suit of heavy burgundy silk, with a feminine blouse of cameo pink that softened the severe, tailored lines. Theresa, the lady's maid she had inherited in 1926 with Grayhall, always travelled with her. Thinking this was a business trip, Theresa had packed accordingly. But Zica didn't mind. She wasn't exactly sure why she had come. It was only an impulse of the heart that had pushed her to see Yakov again, in his own environment.

A light breeze swirled around her ankles, lifting her skirt a few inches above the knees. When Zica had called from New York, the studio receptionist had said that Jack Poker was shooting on Lot 13. It would not be an easy task to find him. Star Partners had grown into an immense studio, especially since the advent of "the talkies," and a stranger could easily get lost searching for a single lot.

Zica looked about her, at a quaint Parisian street now empty of actors and extras. Painted backdrops simulated a bridge overlooking the Seine River. She found herself marvelling at the accuracy of this facsimile of a Left Bank corner. Moving around the corner, she came upon a Western saloon from the 1850s. There, some men who looked like Central Americans were sweeping up some debris. She went up to them and asked, hesitantly, "Excuse me, but where is Lot 13?"

A young man with an Indian face peered at his older companion. They both shrugged. "Sorry, lady, *no entiendo,*" the younger said, leaning on his broom. She blushed and moved on.

The studio seemed interminable. After wandering through several back lots, she came upon a medieval palace. Gingerly approaching one of the stagehands who was bringing in a box of doughnuts, she asked, "Could you point me toward Lot 13? I'm hopelessly lost."

The boy smiled at her. "Looking for Poker Jack?" he queried. When she nodded, he swung his arm around. "You go back out toward Lot 3, the Western town, and circle toward the right. You'll see it in the distance. It's Hester Street in Manhattan—you can't miss it!"

Hester Street. . . . How well Zica remembered the time after Victoria's birth when she'd lived on the corner of Hester and Essex streets in Mr. Netter's ugly tenement, with the Silvermans and the Nimoys, haggling over the rent . . . ! She'd been elected the building's official translator. While she'd been taking in other people's laundry, Yasha had worked a few blocks over, on Hester itself, in Yossif Adolfovitch's pawnshop. They had both hated that time, he especially, their lives and the misery of their condition . . . yet they had also been thankful to God for having spared them a far worse fate in Russia.

Rounding a corner, Zica knew at once she had reached her destination. She had ambled onto a Hester Street that looked exactly as she had left if back in 1920. Clotheslines hung from tenement to tenement. Housewives in long skirts with *babushkas* tied round their heads were milling on the pavement, arguing over prices with street peddlers. The setting for Yakov's script was that very environment where Zica and he had lived when they got off the boat in 1918.

Zica stared, fascinated. It amazed her how well the *papier-mâché* facades duplicated their own street—just as she'd seen it from her kitchen window. She was transported to another time and place.

In their own, struggling way, they'd been happy together then. Vickie had forged a bond between them. Zica glanced at her finely manicured hands and sighed. How far they'd both come! And yet, how pathetically lonely they both were. In the early days, they had had each other, their hopes and dreams entwined. But Zica had broken the spell by deciding that wasn't enough.

She'd wanted glittering romance, and Yakov had offered hard work and the common goal of a good life. How long ago all this seemed now, how fresh and naive all their wishes, all their hopes and fears! They'd been so young then, all three of them . . . : Kyril with his jewels, terrified of running out of money; Yakov slaving for old man Byitch, disgruntled and discouraged; and she, with her daydreams and the baby, trying so hard not to smell the cabbage that the other tenants insisted on cooking each day.

Zica could see several cameras, and a tall, rangy man barking out orders. Assistants were running around with boards and loudspeakers. She strained to see if Yakov was nearby, but this scene appeared to have only extras in it—old women, young girls, men with long, untrimmed beards and top hats, and street vendors shouting out their wares in Yiddish. Yakov was making a movie about his own arrival in New York!

She moved forward, transfixed. "All right!" the rangy man called out. "Yasha! Karen! We're ready to do Scene 123. *Where are they?*"

"Mr. Poker's around here somewhere; Miss Quarnstrom's in her trailer," one of the assistants responded. "Ann's gone to get them."

Zica could feel her heartbeat quicken. The tall, lanky man had to be Harry Walsh, the famous director. She knew he'd been to Kyril's funeral, but they hadn't met; she'd been too distraught to meet any of Kyril's colleagues. Now she could feel the excitement of being on a set, part of the action of making a motion picture. So *this* was how Yakov felt. . . . She closed her eyes, enveloped by the sounds of rolling dollies, of orders shouted out among grips and gaffers.

Zica felt uncertain. She didn't belong here. If Walsh were suddenly to turn around and see her in her city finery, he would be furious—rightly so!—and throw her out. But she wanted to stay. She was fascinated at the prospect of seeing a love scene between Yakov and Quarnstrom—the woman she had come to hate more than anyone in the world and the man to whom she owed her very life.

And she wanted to see him as the whole world saw him, as a professional actor. Why had he decided to leave Poker Jack behind for this unexpected foray into high drama? She was curious and a little anxious. This Yakov was not the man she knew so intimately—but another, more worldly figure, who had left her far behind.

"Okay, kids. Ready?" Harry Walsh rasped out.

Zica opened her eyes. Immediately her gaze was drawn toward the actors coming forward in the make-believe Hester Street. Yakov, dressed in simple work clothes and a cap, was moving toward her. And there was Karen Quarnstrom, the elegant, the refined Swedish beauty, a *babushka* hiding her golden hair—a long brown skirt and apron eclipsing her royal figure. She had left *herself* behind, and in her place stood a poor young girl. The two looked totally convincing as immigrants from the Lower East Side of Manhattan.

"Scene 123, Take 1!" somebody called out, clicking a board with numbers on it.

Zica took a step forward, entranced by the scene.

Yakov began to walk toward Karen Quarnstrom, his hands held out to her. He was terribly handsome in his working-man's clothes, Zica thought, admiring the expressive, even features, the dark eyes. Quarnstrom advanced toward him as well, but her face showed indecision, reluctance. Zica gazed at them, completely convinced, wondering who they were and what was their story.

In the middle of the street, the two met. Karen laid her hands in Yasha's, and he moved to kiss her. At the last moment, the actress turned her cheek. She took a step back.

"Where have you been?" Yasha asked, half-angry, half-imploring.

"I had things to do. Mama needed me to buy her some eggs."

"But we had a date," Yasha countered. "I was waiting for you!"

"You are too demanding!" the actress cried out, withdrawing her hands and bursting into tears. "You don't let me breathe! I'm not ready for such insistence, I'm not ready for all you expect of me. I'm not even sure if I love you anymore, Zhenya—"

Zhenya! Zica's brother's name!

Yakov moved forward a step, grabbing Karen's forearms and shaking her. *"You don't know if you love me?* What kind of nonsense is this, Lifa? You and I have been lovers all our lives—we've shared everything, since the first time I saw you in your father's field, in our Russia! I brought you and your family over here! And now you say you aren't sure of me? That you aren't sure of your feelings anymore?"

There were bright tears in Yakov's eyes. He brushed them away with a swift, instinctive movement with the back of his hand. "But you might as well kill me, Lifa! If you stop loving me I shall surely die—don't you understand?"

"I want to be a real American—not an immigrant," Karen sobbed. "I don't want to wait for you to save money from your pitiful wages as a bus driver! I want—oh, Zhenya, I'm not sure what I want, but I know it's not this! *This isn't why I let you take us out of Russia!"*

"—All right—*cut!"* Harry Walsh broke in. "We need to take ten here, kids. You're fine, Karen; you, too, Yasha. But we need Emily to do a quick rewrite. I don't like it. It sounds too melodramatic. It isn't coming out the way I'd hoped. Don't you agree, Yasha?"

Now Yakov was leaving Hester Street. He walked right up to the director, only yards away from Zica herself.

"Hey," Yakov demurred amiably, "so I'm a lousy writer. . . . I'm an *immigrant,* Harry, for God's sake! This was my best effort, but you're right, you're absolutely right. Emily—tone that down, will you, love?"

This was the moment to step forward and speak to him. But Zica's feet remained glued to the pavement. Too many feelings were in conflict inside her. She had seen an interchange between two people, one with her brother's name, the other with her *mother's*— but she'd been watching Yasha, the *real* Yasha, who had come over in 1918 with her and Kyril's family, to give her a better life.

She looked at her ex-husband, who was laughing at something Harry Walsh had just said. Yakov was handsome and terribly sexy in his immigrant work clothes. His face was tanned; his eyes sparkled with vitality. How was it that she'd never thought him sexy while they had been married? How was it that she'd lived with this talented, intelligent, kind man—and had looked right past him all along?

Karen Quarnstrom joined the director and script writers, pulling off her kerchief and shaking out her blonde pageboy. Easily, Yakov threw an arm around her and gave her a hug. . . .

"You were great," he said to her. "Just great! I don't know how you do it, baby. For me it's easy, I'm just playing myself. But you? You don't know Hester Street, you don't know Jews, you don't know poverty!"

"Lifa's Russian, not Jewish," Karen countered. But she gave Yakov a small kiss on the cheek.

"That's only because we don't want to spell it out," Yakov told her with annoyance. "Jewish stories don't sell. The *amorphous* immigrant stories—Horatio Alger stories—always do well. We don't *have* to say she's Jewish. But the Jews will know—they all see themselves. Don't you doubt it."

"I think you are a marvelous actor, Jack." Karen Quarnstrom gazed at him fondly. "You are also a strong man. I like that."

"Strength isn't enough to win," Yakov declared ironically. "Is it, Harry?"

Suddenly, Zica could contain herself no longer. With small, hasty steps, she ran up to the small group, her face on fire. If she did not speak to Yakov now, they would start the scene all over again. Minutes—maybe hours—would roll by. She'd come all the way from New York for the chance to see him.

Coming up behind, she tapped him on the shoulder. "Hello, Yashenka."

Karen Quarnstrom stepped back, visibly paling. Harry Walsh blinked at the intrusion.

Yakov's eyes widened; his lips parted. Then he smiled. "Zica!" He seized her hands. "I can't believe it! What are you doing here?"

"I came to see you. I thought—well . . ."

"Never mind—don't explain!" Yakov told her softly. He squeezed her hands tightly. "It really *is* you. I'm so glad you're here! My friends," he said to the others, "this is my ex-wife, Zica Poliakov. You know Karen—but I don't believe you've ever met the *Maestro,* Harry Walsh. . . ."

Karen Quarnstrom simply nodded. But Walsh extended his hand. "Well, well, well . . ." he declared as he took her hand in his grip, "how nice to meet you! I never had the pleasure of meeting Victoria's mommy. You are a lovely lady, Miss Poliakov. Will you be joining us for lunch in the commissary?"

"No, no, it's all right, Harry," Yakov broke in. "Zica and I have much to catch up on. I think we'll slip off somewhere for lunch—"

Karen Quarnstrom had drifted away, without a word, and was talking to one of the extras. Harry Walsh cleared his throat. "Well then, okay, you two . . ." He settled with Yakov on a time to resume.

When he was gone, only Zica remained, staring into the dark eyes of her ex-husband.

He touched her cheek. "I *am* glad to see you. And what a surprise."

"Yes, well... here I am." She didn't know what to say next. It was as though she were meeting a stranger.

His fingers lingered on her cheek. Finally he said, gently, "You look so good, I swear to God. But then, you've always looked good to me, Zica."

"I'm surprised you're not calling me 'Lifa,'" she remarked, her voice trembling. "This is our story, isn't it?"

He raised his brows and chuckled. "Perhaps a little. But it's really just a story, Zicotchka. It's about two people who really are in love, even though the girl doesn't realize it till the end... when it's too late. She gets killed, you see, and he's left never knowing how very much she loved him!"

"How terribly sad," Zica whispered. "And so he never understands the role he played in his girl's life. . . . "

"It's a good story, don't you think?" he asked lightly.

She shook her head. "No," she told him, "I don't like it at all! You've used my family's names: Lifa, Zhenya—to write a story that makes everyone come out the loser. Is this what you believe happened to *us,* Yasha? To you and me?"

"Never mind the names, Zica. They just came to me—Russian names, that's all." He seemed very disturbed by her tears. "If you wish, I'll take you to the commissary after all," he said, smiling.

She'd flown three thousand miles to speak to him. "I like it right here." She looked around at the familiar street.

He shrugged. "They don't like us eating on the set. Listen, we'll get a private table in the corner somewhere. Don't worry. We'll have time together."

He doesn't love me anymore, Zica thought, hearing indifference in his voice. Like Lifa on screen, she had waited too long to acknowledge her feelings; she'd waited too long, denying they existed. And the result was not, as in Lifa's case, death. It was much, much worse—it was this air of indifference. After twenty-six years of adoring her from afar, he had stopped caring entirely.

Oh Yasha, Yasha, she cried in her heart, *what have I done, in my stupidity?*

"Come," he was saying. "I'll buy you a hamburger."

* * *

The commissary was an enormous, unadorned, cavernous room, bustling with activity. Zica felt out of place in her silk suit and pearl earrings, and alligator shoes. This was a no-nonsense sort of place where working film people ate their lunch. Extras in costume and full regalia plunked their trays down beside members of the crew.

Zica thought, How impersonal this place is . . . *He does not want to face me alone.*

The lithe, quick man beside her was not the man she'd married in Moscow fourteen years previously. Or was he . . . ? In many respects, he had always been this way, she reflected, thinking back to their youth. He had always planned to improve his station in life; he had always soaked up knowledge like a sponge. Nothing had ever stood in Yakov's way—except, perhaps, Zica herself.

Zica looked at Yakov cautiously as she set down her tray opposite his at a small table far from the studio crowd.

"Well," he said to her as he sat down, "now you've seen what I do for a living. It's not exactly refined, is it? A lot of it's drudgery and repetition—not as people imagine. And Harry's always yelling at *someone* about *something*—"

"It's thrilling," she remarked. "I'm really proud of you, Yasha."

"You are?" He regarded her quizzically, with a touch of irony. Then he bit hungrily into a ham sandwich. "See?" he laughed. "I've left the Pale far behind me, *dorogaya*. What my old *reb* would say if he could see me eating pork flesh . . ."

Zica twisted the pearl ring on her finger as he talked, observing the animation in his expressive face and dark, twinkling eyes. And, watching him, she recalled how Natasha Khazina had loved him dearly, during their youth on the Tverskaya. But she, Zica, had seen only an eager *shtetl* boy who was devoted to her.

Now she was just a woman in the presence of a marvelous, vibrant man. Maybe it was the films he had created—each one a gem of pure brilliance and humor. Maybe it was just that she had grown up! Her opinion and her focus had changed. But the young man who had seemed merely quick and eager now had a radiance so strong that it filled her with a tremendous sense of well-being, just having him close to her.

A young girl with tight auburn curls approached their table, did a double-take, and peered at Yakov with coy amusement. "Poker Jack," she exclaimed. "Why are you sitting here in the dark? We've got a table full of your greatest fans in the center of the room! Listen," she added, her green eyes covertly examining Zica, "my mother's having a barbecue on Saturday. I know it's not exactly exciting, but we could hang out and go for a drive afterwards. That is, if you'd like—" she taked on, shrugging lightly to offset her own embarrassment.

Yakov had risen courteously during this little speech, and he appeared to be blushing. He looked from one woman to the other.

"India, meet Zeinab Poliakov. Zica, this is India Granger. She works in the makeup department. We're good friends."

"How do you do?" Zica said, extending her hand. The other woman shook it and murmured a greeting. They remained staring at each other, each somewhat discomfited.

It was Yakov who broke the tension. "It sounds very nice," he said, a shy smile illuminating his face. "About that barbecue—Yes, I think I will go. Thanks for inviting me."

The woman with the curls smiled radiantly. "Wait till I tell the girls!" she cried, her eyes shining. "My folks'll be tickled pink! Mom's seen *Turntables* three times!"

"Aw, shucks," Yakov murmured, in make-believe bashfulness. "What can I say. . . ?"

"I'll see you later." India waltzed away, humming a little tune to herself.

When Yakov sat down again, there was silence. He stared at his food, while Zica seemed lost in thought. At length she asked: "Is this a girl you're dating?"

He shrugged. "Not really . . . dating. But she's a sweet kid. You can see—she's still awed by all this. Sometimes I take her to a ball game, or out for a quick meal somewhere. I feel like I've sort of adopted her."

Neither spoke for a moment. Yakov set down his sandwich and wiped his lips. "Tell me," he asked, "why you've come here, Zica. Is anything wrong with Vickie?"

She shook her head. "Not at all. She's fine. She's vice-president of the seventh grade. Oh, and she just got honorable mention in the debate competition." Zica could not think of anything else to tell him. Yakov and Vickie spoke so often on the phone that he knew practically everything she was doing.

His eyes were upon her, not willing to let her off the hook. Zica looked down, examining a pinpoint of dust to the right of her plate. She felt herself begin to blush.

"I'm sorry for the way I've treated you," she whispered. "I was young and foolish. I'm sorry that it's taken me so long to realize what I had when we were married. I guess...I guess *Deception* really is my story after all. I had a good life with the best of men, and I threw it away on an impulse...to run after a shooting star."

She looked up, encountering his dark eyes fixed intently on her face. It was impossible to decipher his reaction.

"Look," she said, stumbling over the words, "I did love Kyril Ostrov an awful lot. But that was back when we were all kids! And so I was unfair to you. I didn't give our marriage a chance. I thought...I thought I still loved him. I thought the past could be brought back, only without the pain and bad times."

"What are you trying to say, Zica?"

She gazed at him, eyes filling with tears. "You were always there for me, Yasha, and so I took your devotion for granted. I passed you by because you were so good and so decent. I thought that love, real love, was stormy weather, a turbulent sea—not the day-to-day business of two people learning to open up and trust each other. I was wrong."

He nodded, absorbed in her words. "Yasha," she continued, "when you left New York to come out here and try your luck in the movies, I felt abandoned. I felt as if I'd lost my best friend. And I had, you know. You were always my best friend, ever since you first came to work in my father's house. Like a fool, I thought friendship was no basis for a love affair. So I never thought to look at you, to see what kind of man you really were."

"I'm glad you told me this," Yakov said. "You know, I could never really understand why you left me. I mean, I *knew* I'd been wrong to keep you at home—and our life in Brooklyn was a hard one, a boring one. It wasn't the life you'd had on the Tverskaya. But I loved you so very much, Zica! Even if everything else about our lives was just poverty and dirty laundry and grime—" He gestured toward the Hester Street set. "Even with all that, I thought you would understand how much I loved you."

"I know it now," she said softly, "but it's too late, isn't it?"

He sighed. "Oh, Zica..." he murmured. "Do you think I've changed? I haven't changed at all! The only difference is that I don't love any more. I've killed the instinct inside me. I'm the same man, the same friend, the same father...but I don't have love affairs with women, because the last one cost me too damn much. That part of me is gone—I wouldn't want to find it again. I don't want the pain!"

"I hurt you that badly?"

"Or did I hurt *you* that badly?" he rejoined quickly. "Remember, Zica, you married me because there was no choice. You had to do *something* to escape being killed. I had no right to hope that a forced marriage could become a love match. But still, I couldn't *help* hoping. I wanted your love more than I've ever wanted anything in the world!"

"And . . . now?"

He stared at her, shaking his head. "Now, *what?*"

She sucked in her lower lip. "Yasha," she said, "I've changed a lot. I've learned to run a business, to take care of other people. I'm not the same dreamy young girl who lived on the Tverskaya and chatted with you behind the staircase. And you've changed. And you don't need me for anything anymore, because you've got all that you wished for! But you're still alone. You haven't found a woman to replace me in your heart."

"I don't choose to look for one," he repeated.

"And I've never found a man to replace what you brought into my life."

Zica reached out and picked up his hand. She turned it over, caressing the lines on his palm. "Yasha," she said, in a very small voice, "I've missed you. Isn't it strange—All along, it was *you* that I longed for . . . you that I was missing. Only I didn't understand. It was so simple that I didn't get it."

Slowly Yakov rose, his face tortured with bewilderment. "I don't know," he whispered. "I don't know, Zica. . . . It's been years, *years,* since I asked myself how I felt about you. I didn't want to hear the answer!"

She stood up too, facing him. She was weeping. "Please, please don't throw me away! Please think about it. . . . Please think of it now!

"Zeinab Lazarevna," he said to her. "You want me to believe you love me . . . ?"

She nodded. Then she came to his side and clasped his hands, looking up into his eyes. "I *do* love you." She touched his cheek, his lips. Her fingers stroked his smooth, trim beard. "Believe me," she repeated, "I do love you! Only I'm so afraid, so terribly afraid, that I'm Lifa—is it too late for me . . . ?"

He studied her face as if searching for the least sign of wavering. She returned his gaze steadily. "What about the gallery? Could Lena and Bruno Lesschi manage without you? What would you do here, with no friends, no life?"

Placing her arms around his neck, she said, tremulously: "I'd open a West Coast branch of the Poliakov Gallery. And I'd make friends. Vickie would love it here!"

"And what about you?" he asked her. "Would *you* love it here?"

"Of course I would, you goofy man," she answered, kissing him. "I'd be married to *you,* wouldn't I? I'd give you all the love you ever wished for! And we would have another child, maybe a boy, this time, if I'm not too old . . ."

He scooped her chin between his fingers. Then, lightly, he pressed his lips into the fragrance of her shining hair.

Zica could hear the din of voices all around her, in the commissary. She was aware that she was standing absurdly snuggled against the chest of Poker Jack, the funniest man in the Star Partners stable. But it did not matter they weren't alone; it only mattered that she had come back, at long last, into his arms.

"Let's get out of here," Yakov said suddenly, taking her by the hand. As they left the commissary, she was acutely conscious of the voices raised in greeting. He was popular; he belonged there; it was his own world, just as the distant rooms of statues, canvasses, and gilded frames were *her* special world.

"What if your producers tell you it's no good, your marrying me again?" she asked as they were leaving.

He glanced at her, reading the past in her eyes. "No one dictates to Poker Jack," he told her, shaking his head. "No one tells me what to do with my life."

She shivered, remembering the pot of white poinsettias resting in their marble niche at Forest Lawn Cemetery. A man had died because he'd given his life to the Hollywood machine, to Star Partners and its founders. Once, she had loved this man. But that had been in another world—a world of glittering, false images.

And Lifa, too, would die on the set of *Deception*. But Zica had been granted a reprieve—to embrace the love that had always been near at hand, ready to cherish, too often unrecognized.

"Let's go call Vickie," she said happily, squeezing his hand as they walked out into the winter sunlight. "It isn't every child who gets to toss rose petals down the aisle at her own parents' wedding! And *this* time," she told him, "it's going to be a *real* wedding, with all the trimmings! A nice winter wedding with music and dancing, and with all our friends around us to wish us well."

"That's a splendid idea," Yakov declared, grinning. "I'll order the champagne tonight."